COLLEGE SERIES OF LATIN AUTHORS

EDITED BY

CLEMENT LAWRENCE SMITH AND TRACY PECK

ODES AND EPODES OF HORACE

C. L. SMITH.

COLLEGE SERIES OF LATIN AUTHORS

THE

ODES AND EPODES

OF

HORACE

Edited, with Introduction and Notes,

BY

CLEMENT LAWRENCE SMITH
PROFESSOR OF LATIN IN HARVARD UNIVERSITY

———•———

Boston, U.S.A., and London
GINN & COMPANY, PUBLISHERS
1899

PREFACE.

In preparing this edition of the Odes and Epodes I have borne in mind the fact that the reading of these poems presents, at least to the American student, the first, as well as the best, opportunity for the discriminating study of Latin poetic usage in syntax and diction. Vergil and Ovid regularly precede Horace in our Latin course, but they come at a stage at which the pupil's faculties are so fully occupied in following the verses intelligently, that although these poets are undoubtedly read with pleasure by many pupils, anything beyond a rather dim appreciation of the quality and flavor of their poetry is hardly to be expected. With Horace the case is quite different. Horace is reserved for the college course, often for the second year of the course ; and at that stage the student should have acquired by practice in reading and writing such mastery of Latin prose idiom that the peculiarities of poetic language ought to arouse attention and interest. It has been usual for editors of Horace to notice the more striking of these peculiarities in the places where they occur. It has seemed to me better to treat the whole subject together in the Introduction, so that the various usages may be seen in their relations to one another, while their exemplification in any particular passage can be pointed out by a simple reference in the notes. I have desired, in presenting the matter in this form, to leave the teacher free to use it in whatever way he deems best, and according to his estimate of its importance. In my own judgment it is of vital importance ; for although the appreciation of poetry must in the last resort be a matter of taste and feeling, beyond the reach of categorical statement, yet an intelligent study of the poet's language and literary method is the only adequate basis for such appreciation.

In preparing this exposition I have had the benefit of a number of monographs in which certain parts of the subject are treated in a more or less thorough manner, but no previous work dealing with the whole subject is known to me. I am sensible of the imperfections which are inevitable in a first attempt of this kind, and shall welcome friendly suggestions from any quarter for its improvement. Two things ought perhaps to be said : While much, if not most, of my statement applies to other poets of the Augustan and subsequent periods, I have made it with sole reference to Horace ; and in the absence of any sharp line of division between the usage of prose and of poetry I have in some cases purposely included a recognized prose construction in order to set the poetic usage in a clearer light. For constructions not explained in the Introduction occasional reference is made in the notes to grammars in current use, chiefly to Madvig's, Roby's, and Allen and Greenough's. For the last named the abbreviation 'Gr.' is used.

The text of Horace is open in a number of places to the grave suspicion, which sometimes approaches certainty, of interpolation. In the absence, however, of any general agreement among scholars in condemning definite passages, I have not thought it desirable, in an edition of this kind, to bracket verses or strophes which appear to me suspicious or spurious, or to vex college students with critical discussions where they could be avoided. The text has been constituted in accordance with the principles stated in § 39 of the Introduction. A list of the most important variants has been given in an appendix, where I have adopted, with some modifications, the convenient method of indicating the comparative weight of MS. authority used by Professor Arthur Palmer in his edition of the Satires.

In printing the poems I have adhered to the traditional arrangement, which (not without some reason) has relegated the Epodes to the position of a sort of appendix to the Odes; but I cannot do so without advising every one who wishes to become acquainted with Horace, as well as with his poetry, to follow the chronological order and read the Epodes first.

For the interpretation and illustration of the poems I have availed myself freely of the resources which have been accumulated by many generations of Horatian scholars and are accessible in the larger editions and elsewhere. This general acknowledgment covers a great number of suggestions adopted from various sources, for which particular credit could not well be given, even when the author could be determined, in a book of this kind. Especial mention ought to be made, however, of the editions of Orelli (ed.[4] by Hirschfelder) and Wickham, and particularly of the stimulating and suggestive commentary of Kiessling, from all of which I have derived much assistance. In preparing the life of the poet, I have found, next to the material collected in the Prolegomena of the Orelli edition, Sellar's *Horace and the Elegiac Poets* the most useful of the works I have consulted.

I take this opportunity also to express my obligations to my friends and colleagues: to Professors Lane, Greenough, and Morgan, from each of whom I have received useful advice and criticism in preparing the Introduction; and especially to Professor Allen, who has kindly read a large part of both Introduction and Commentary, as they were passing through the press, and aided me with many valuable suggestions.

C. L. S.

CAMBRIDGE, MASSACHUSETTS,
September 15, 1894.

INTRODUCTION.

I. LIFE AND WRITINGS.

1. Our knowledge of the facts of Horace's life is derived in part from a biography, appended to certain manuscripts of his poems, which has been shown by conclusive evidence to be, in substance, the life of the poet which Suetonius wrote in his encyclopedic work, *De Viris Illustribus*. There are briefer lives in some of the other manuscripts, and scattered notices in the scholia. But all these sources afford — beyond a few dates and facts — little information that we do not already possess, in fuller and more authentic form, in the poet's own writings. To these we must go for an adequate understanding of his mind and character. In the Satires and Epistles, and to a less degree in the Epodes, Horace takes the reader into his confidence and speaks of his circumstances and feelings with singular frankness. The Odes, too, contain much biographical material, but it is of a kind that must be used with caution. As a poet Horace claims the freedom of his craft and frequently puts himself, for poetical effect, in situations which may perhaps reflect his mode of thought and feeling and even shadow forth his personal experiences, but must not be taken literally as autobiography.

Birth and Early Training.

2. Quintus Horatius Flaccus was born on the 8th of December, B.C. 65, and died on the 27th of November, B.C. 8.

It is important to observe the significance of these dates. Horace's life began when the Romans were still living under the forms of the Republic; when it closed, the Empire was fully established. When our poet first saw the light, Cicero was planning his canvass for the consulship. His boyhood fell in the stormy decade of the 'First Triumvirate' (B.C. 60–50), which formed the prelude of the Civil War. Horace was old enough to be interested in the later victories of Caesar in Gaul, and the destruction of Crassus with his army at Carrhae in 53 may well have made a deep impression on a lad of twelve. The two decades of civil strife which followed were experiences of his youth and early manhood, and when peace came with the deaths of Antony and Cleopatra in B.C. 30, Horace was thirty-five years old. The remaining twenty-two years of his life belong to the first half of the principate of Augustus, the period of the growth and consolidation of his power under the guidance of his two great ministers, Agrippa and Maecenas, whose deaths, B.C. 12 and 8, were closely followed by that of Horace.

3. Horace's birthplace was Venusia, a colony planted for military purposes in the Samnite wars, high up on the northern slope of the Apennine range, in Apulia, near the Lucanian border. It stood on a branch of the Aufidus, in that region a swift mountain stream, among the wooded hills which culminate in the lofty peak of Mt. Voltur. There the poet's father by shrewdness and thrift had not only secured his own freedom — for he was born a slave — but had acquired a modest farm and an income which enabled him to educate his son. His occupation was that of a *coactor*, that is, a collector of money — whether of money due for taxes or for goods sold at auction, the corrupt text of the Suetonian biography leaves us in doubt. It is supposed by some that he had acted in this capacity

as a public slave, and on his manumission took the name of Horatius because Venusia belonged to the Horatian tribe. But we do not know that freedmen were ever so named ; from the ordinary practice in such cases we should assume that he had belonged to a master named Horatius.

4. Horace himself was born free, that is, he was born after his father's manumission. His mother is nowhere mentioned. It may well be that he inherited from her his poetic nature ; but whether because she died in his infancy — which is probable — or from lack of personal force, she appears to have had little or no influence in moulding his character. His father's influence, on the other hand, was of the utmost importance and value, as the poet himself acknowledges with warm gratitude. The elder Flaccus was a shrewd observer of men and manners. Horace was, it seems, his only son, and the child of his later years, when he had accumulated a fund of experience and practical wisdom, and when he was, moreover, in possession of a competence which enabled him to lay aside his business and give his whole attention to the training of his boy. He naturally knew nothing of ethical theories, and he relied little on precept alone. He sought to awaken his son's moral perception by teaching him to observe good and bad in the world about him, to note the consequences of virtue and of vice in the actual lives of men, and to take to heart these examples and warnings in guiding his own life and guarding his reputation. The ethical code of the Venusian freedman was of a rough-hewn sort. It was a coarse sieve, and allowed some things to pass which do not meet the test of our finer standards. He claimed, in fact, no more for his moral teaching than that it would keep his son from falling into ruinous courses during that critical period when he was not yet able to 'swim without cork.' But so far as it went it was sound and wholesome. And it was effective :

Horace's habitual self-control during the period of his life
when we know him best, his dislike of passionate excess
either of desire or fear, his temperance in conduct and
language, his aversion to the grosser forms of vice, — these
were the fruit of inherited traits, fostered and strengthened
by wise training. To the same training Horace attributes
his habit of critical observation of social phenomena, which
led him to write satire.

SCHOOL DAYS AT ROME.

5. Horace's mental development received no less careful
attention. There was a school at Venusia, kept by one
Flavius and resorted to by the sons of the local aristocracy,
— 'great lads, from great centurions sprung.' But Horace's
father had higher views for his son, who had already, we
may suppose, given promise of exceptional ability. Anxious
to provide him with the best advantages, he determined to
send him to Rome, 'to receive the education which a knight
or a senator gives to his sons.' But unlike a knight or a
senator, the obscure freedman had no social connections
which would enable him to place his son under the charge
of some family or friend ; and rather than entrust him to
strangers or slaves, he determined to leave his farm and
accompany the boy in person to the city. Here, too, he
was unremitting in his watchful care. Horace has left us a
pleasing picture of the devoted father, going round to all
the lessons with his boy, whom he had fitted out with suitable dress and attendant slaves, so that he might hold up
his head with the best of his school-fellows.

6. Horace was taken to Rome perhaps in his ninth or
tenth year, and remained there possibly until he was twenty;
the precise dates are not recorded. Of his teachers only
one is known to us, Orbilius Pupillus, of Beneventum, an
old cavalry soldier who had resumed his books when his

campaigns were over, and at the age of fifty had set up a school in the capital in the year when Cicero was consul. He was a gruff old fellow, with a caustic tongue, and his ready resort to the rod Horace remembered many years after. The course of study which Horace pursued was presumably the ordinary course of the 'grammatical' and 'rhetorical' schools of the day, which aimed, first, at a mastery of the Latin tongue, and, secondly, at the cultivation of eloquence. With these ends in view the training, — after the elements of reading, writing, and reckoning were acquired, — was largely literary, and consisted mainly in a thorough study of Latin and Greek literature. Horace read Livius Andronicus — probably his version of the Odyssey — under the rod of Orbilius, and became familiar with the other old Roman poets, for whom he did not conceive, or did not retain, a very high admiration. He also read the Iliad, as he informs us, and no doubt other Greek classics in prose and verse ; and these kindled in him a genuine enthusiasm, which kept him a devoted student of Greek letters, particularly of Greek poetry, all his life.

ATHENS.

7. With this taste developed by his studies in Rome, it was natural that Horace should be drawn into the current which at that day carried the more ambitious students to Athens, in quest of what we may call their university training in the schools of philosophy there. Horace attended the lectures of the Academic school, and the acquaintance which he shows with the doctrines of the other sects must have been acquired at this time. For speculative philosophy and the subtleties of dialectics he had little taste. The Roman, as a rule, felt the strongest attraction to philosophy on its ethical side, where it came nearest to the practical problems of life ; and in Horace this ethical tendency was ingrained and was peculiarly strong. It was fostered by his father's training ; it no doubt added zest, at this time, to his study of the various ethical systems of the Greeks ; it was confirmed as his mind and character matured, and impressed itself strongly on all his writings, even his lyrics. In his later years he protested that his chief desire was to put aside poetry and devote the rest of his days to the study of the philosophy of life.

8. In his philosophical views Horace was, like most of his countrymen who interested themselves in the subject at all, eclectic ; he found something to his taste in this creed and in that, but declined to enroll himself as the disciple of any school. Of his religious belief it is not possible to speak definitely,— probably it never crystallized into definite shape in his own mind. For a time he was a convert to the doctrine of Epicurus,— probably from reading Lucretius, whose poem was published in his boyhood,— and believed that there were gods, but that their serene existence was never troubled by any concern for the affairs of men. In one of his odes he professes to have been startled out of this 'crazy' creed by the actual occurrence of what the Epicureans averred to be a physical impossibility,— a clap of thunder in a clear sky. It is not likely that this experience had the importance in actual fact which it appears to have in its lyrical setting ; Horace's change of view was a matter of growth. But it was real. Otherwise he would surely not have published this poem ; and there is, besides, plenty of evidence elsewhere in his works that in his maturer years he recognized a divine providence and control in human affairs. Horace's ethical views, too, were strongly tinged with Epicureanism, but here, as everywhere, he went to no extreme ; and, although he combats the Stoic theory and mocks at their ideal sage, he was at heart in sympathy with Stoic principles in their substance and practical application to life, and he more than once holds up their ideal of virtue for its own sake, — though even virtue itself he will not exempt from his maxim 'nil admirari'.

9. How far Horace pursued his study of the Greek poets along with his philosophy at Athens, we are not informed ; we may be sure that he gave them a large share of his attention. The broad and intimate acquaintance with Greek poetry, which is the very life-blood of his own poetic achievement, was not the acquisition of a few years ; but his sojourn was long enough for the influences of the place to give a permanent bent to his literary taste. One of Horace's marked characteristics as a poet is his freedom from Alexandrinism, which dominated Roman education and Roman poetry in his youth. Alexandrine learning, filtered through his Roman teachers, furnished him with his technical outfit as a poet, with a knowledge of the forms and categories and of the history of his art, and with the common stock of illustrative material, mythological, astrological, and other. There is evidence also of his diligent study of some of the Alexandrine poets : he is indebted to them for many phrases and figures and turns of thought. This is especially apparent in his love poetry. But the same evidence shows that the Alexandrine poets who exerted this influence on his style were precisely those who, like Callimachus and Theocritus, were freest from the peculiar weakness of their school, — the sacrifice of freshness and good taste to formality and erudition. In the spirit and form of his verse Horace took as his models the older Greek poets ; and his loving study of these masters we may confidently date from his residence at Athens, where the older traditions still maintained themselves.

10. The fashion of sending young men to get the finishing touches of their education at Athens had grown up with the generation into which Horace was born. Cicero, who in his

youth was eager to grasp every opportunity for the best
training, did not visit Greece at all until after he had
entered on the practice of his profession : Cicero's son, who
was just of Horace's age, was now at Athens studying
rhetoric and philosophy. There, too, Horace found a number of other young men of distinguished families, among
them Valerius Messala, who traced his descent from the
Valerius Poplicola who held with Brutus the first consulship
of the Republic. On what terms Horace stood with these
fellow-students we are left to conjecture ; but his genial
nature and conversational gifts, combined with tact and
good sense, must have drawn many to him. His friendship
with Messala and many closer intimacies, to which his poems
bear witness, date no doubt from this period. There was
nothing out of the way in this association of the freedman's
son with the young nobles in common studies and literary
interests. Aristocracy of birth has never aspired to monopo-
lize the brain-work of the world, and youth and good fellow-
ship are not strenuous about social distinctions. In the
next stage of Horace's career he found his position very
different.

In the Army of Brutus.

11. In September, 44 B.C., six months after the assassi-
nation of Julius Caesar, Marcus Brutus came to Athens, and
for some months, while waiting for the turn of political
events, devoted himself to the schools of philosophy. His
appearance created no little sensation. The Athenians, who
lived largely in the traditions of their past, welcomed 'the
liberator' with enthusiasm, and voted to set up his statue
beside those of their own tyrannicides, Harmodius and
Aristogeiton. The young Romans were flattered by the
accession of so illustrious a fellow-student, whose real interest
in philosophy was well known ; and before the winter was

over Brutus had enlisted a number of them in his service for the coming struggle with the triumvirs. Among these recruits was the young Cicero, who had already seen some service under Pompey. The most distinguished adherent was Messala, and the least distinguished, certainly, was Horace. It argues a high estimate on Brutus' part of Horace's intelligence and capacity, that he appointed this youth of one and twenty, with neither military experience nor family influence to recommend him, to a place among his officers, and eventually gave him, as tribune, the command of a Roman legion. It was high promotion for the freedman's son, and envious tongues were not slow to direct attention to the fact.

12. Horace was in Brutus' army the greater part of two years (B.C. 43 and 42). He is almost entirely silent about this experience, but from our knowledge of the movements of Brutus in those two campaigns we may gather that it gave him the opportunity to visit various places in Thessaly, Macedonia, and Thrace, and many famous cities of Asia Minor, which he mentions in his poems in a way that implies personal acquaintance. He remained with Brutus to the end, and shared the victory and subsequent rout at Philippi. The suicide of his chief at once absolved him from further allegiance and was a confession that the cause for which they had fought was irretrievably lost. Horace was fain to accept the result, and while some of his friends held out and joined the standard of Sextus Pompeius, he followed the example and advice of Messala and made his submission to the victors, who pardoned, or at least did not molest him.

RETURN TO ROME.

13. It was not improbably on his homeward voyage from Greece after Philippi that Horace came near being shipwrecked on the dangerous promontory of Palinurus, on the

Lucanian coast; the critical condition of the times may have been his motive for preferring that roundabout way to the ordinary route. He returned to Rome in a depressed and bitter mood. His father was dead. His estate had been swept away in the confiscation of the territory of Venusia. The outlook was gloomy. He seems, however, to have saved some money from his two campaigns, and with this he purchased a clerkship in the Quaestors' office, which yielded him a small income and, apparently, a good deal of leisure. Under these circumstances, poor in purse and still poorer in favor, Horace began life again at the age of twenty-three. He was thoroughly cured of his aspirations for a public career. His short, but severe experience had taught him that, however strong his interest in his country's welfare, he had no taste for the practical business of war and politics; and he had had enough of running counter to the popular prejudice against humble birth in high station. On the other hand his training and his knowledge of his own powers alike pointed to literature as the career most suitable and promising for him.

Choice of a Career.

14. That Horace had practiced verse-writing in the course of his literary studies might be taken for granted. He confesses that at one time, — it was probably while he was at Athens, — he undertook to write poetry in Greek ; and these essays were not, it should seem, in the nature of school exercises, but serious efforts. This was by no means a new thing in Roman literature. The earliest Roman annals were written in Greek, and the same phenomenon had reappeared in the highly Hellenized culture of the Ciceronian period, when Roman writers occasionally used Greek for prose or verse, partly for the pleasure of handling a language of so much richer capacity than their own, partly to reach a wider circle of appreciative readers. But Horace did not persist in an undertaking which his good sense presently convinced him was as futile as it was unpatriotic.

15. At the time when Horace began his literary career, Vergil, who was five years his senior, had published some youthful verses and was beginning to be known as a sweet singer of pastoral scenes by the publication of his earliest Eclogues. The epic poet of the day was Varius Rufus, who won credit and favor by his poem on the death of Julius Caesar. He was a few years older than Vergil, who lived to rival him in epos ; but that was many years later. Asinius Pollio, who as governor of Cisalpine Gaul had recently won Vergil's gratitude by timely assistance, and who was afterwards eminent as an orator and a critic and patron of literature, had at this time attained some distinction as a writer of tragedy. Various other fields were diligently cultivated by writers of less note, or less known to us. Looking over the ground Horace thought he saw a field suited to his powers in Lucilian satire, which Varro Atacinus and some others had undertaken to revive, but in Horace's opinion without success.

The Satires.

16. The word *satura* appears to have meant originally a medley. It was used as the name of a variety performance on the rude stage of early times, consisting of comic songs and stories, with dance and gesticulation, to the accompaniment of the pipe. It found its way into literature as the title of a collection of what we should call 'miscellanies in verse:' Ennius (B.C. 239–169) employed it for this purpose, and his example was followed by Lucilius. The *Saturae* of Lucilius, who had been dead about sixty years when Horace began to write satire, were a series of tracts on every topic that it came into his head to discuss, — personal, social, political, philosophical, literary, philological. In form they were equally varied, — sometimes didactic, sometimes narrative, or dramatic, or epistolary ; and they were written in a variety of metres. More than two thirds, however, of the thirty books were in dactylic hexameters, which Lucilius appears to have finally settled upon as most suitable for his purpose ; and this metre was used exclusively by his successors. And in spite of its heterogeneous variety of subjects, there were two features which gave distinctive character to Lucilius' work. One of these was the footing of personal and familiar intercourse on which he placed himself with his reader ; his tone was the tone of conversation and his words the utterance of his own mind and heart, as if on the impulse of the moment. The other was that he entered on a field which Roman literature had not yet ventured to tread, but which thenceforth became the peculiar province of *satura*, as it had been of the Old Comedy of the Greeks, — the criticism of contemporary manners and men.

17. By inheritance and training a critical observer of the life about him, Horace justly deemed himself fitted to take up the task of Lucilius, whom he greatly admired in everything but the roughness of his literary workmanship. The unreserved personalities in which Lucilius indulged were no longer permissible in Horace's day, and he avoided them except in a few of his earlier satires. Politics, too, were forbidden ground. In other respects he adopted the method of his master, but in a kindlier spirit and rarely with any exhibition of personal feeling. His manner is that of the accomplished man of the world in familiar conversation, easy and self-possessed, witty but never flippant, discussing with keen insight and a quick sense of humor, but with the abundant charity of a man who knows his own shortcomings, and with a ground-tone of moral earnestness, the various

phases of every-day life. He laughs at vice and folly ;
but satire is essentially didactic, and ridicule is the weapon
of a serious purpose. Horace never speaks from the platform, or with any assumption of superior virtue ; he talks as
one of the crowd who has stopped to reflect on their common
weaknesses, and he disarms resentment by sometimes turning the laugh against himself. There are some who esteem
these 'talks' (*sermones*), as he himself preferred to call them,
the greatest of Horace's achievements. Certainly there are
few works of classical antiquity in which literary art has
brought us so near to ancient life. The satires were written
from time to time in the decade following Horace's return
to Rome (B.C. 41–31), and became more or less widely
known before they were issued in collected form. The
collection consisted of two books, of which the first was
published about 35 or 34, and the second about 30, B.C.

The Epodes.

18. Horace constructed the hexameter of his satires with
some care, and succeeded in reconciling with the easy conversational tone a smoothness of rhythm which marked a
great advance on the strong but rugged verses of his model
Lucilius. But he hardly cared to claim for his satires the
dignity of poetry. They are in their nature, he protests,
and except for a certain recurrence of rhythm, mere prose
discourse. And meanwhile he was trying his hand at poetry
based on Greek models, and was in fact touched with the
ambition to strike out a new path for Latin literature in this
field. His first effort was to reproduce in Latin the iambic
rhythm which tradition said had been forged, as a weapon
of wrath, by Archilochus of Paros, — the fact being that
Archilochus, who lived in the seventh century B.C., had
developed and perfected the rhythm which had existed long

before him. The form which Horace adopted was a couplet, the second verse of which, as a sort of refrain, was called by metrical writers *epōdus* (ἐπῳδός, adjective ; cf. ἐπᾴδειν). This term was later extended in meaning, so that Horace's collection of seventeen poems, all but one composed of epodic couplets, has come down to us under the title of Epodes (*Epodon liber*). Horace himself called them only *Iambi*, which expresses their prevailing character and is sufficiently accurate, although other metres are combined with the iambic in some instances.

19. The composition of the Epodes probably began as early as that of the Satires, possibly earlier, and was continued through the same period. The sixteenth of the series, which displays at once remarkable mastery of form and immaturity of thought, was written in the first years after the poet's return from Philippi ; the ninth celebrates the victory at Actium. The book was published about the same time as the second book of the Satires, B.C. 30.

20. Horace says truly that he reproduced the spirit as well as the rhythms of Archilochus ; in some of his epodes he has certainly used the iambus as 'a weapon of wrath.' In others again he has descended to a depth of coarseness from which his later lyrics are, for the most part, happily free. These, the survivors perhaps of a larger number of their kind, belong, we must suppose, to his earliest efforts, and tell of a dark period in his mental history, — the first years after his return from Philippi, — when life went hard with him, and he was embittered and demoralized by associations which later, under more congenial influences, he was able to throw off. The most fortunate of these influences was his acquaintance with Varius and Vergil, who inspired him with warm admiration and regard ; and it was these friends who performed for him the inestimable service of introducing him to Maecenas.

MAECENAS.

21. Gaius Maecenas came of noble Etruscan stock. The Cilnii, once a powerful family of Arretium, were the most distinguished of his ancestors, and Tacitus (*Ann.* VI. 11) calls him Cilnius Maecenas ; but there is reason to believe that this was not his gentile name. He was born on the 13th of April in some year not far from 70 B.C., so that he was Horace's senior by a few years. From our earliest knowledge of him he appears as the trusted friend and confidential minister of the triumvir Octavian, who sent him on several occasions to negotiate with Antony, — at Brundisium in B.C. 40, at Athens in 38, at Tarentum in 37. In B.C. 36, during his absence in the war with Sextus Pompeius, and again in 31, on setting out for the final struggle with Antony, Octavian left Maecenas behind to watch over Rome and Italy with the power, if not the name, of the city prefect of regal times. This was as near as Maecenas ever came to holding public office. He studiously refrained from seeking or accepting political preferment, which would have raised him to the senatorial order, and remained all his life an untitled 'knight.' He was a man in whom the most opposite qualities appeared to be reconciled. His capacity was unquestioned, and on occasion he could display all necessary industry and vigor ; but ordinarily he lived a life of almost ostentatious indolence, and was self-indulgent to the point of effeminacy. Devoid of personal ambition and apparently indifferent to politics, he was yet public-spirited and patriotic, and by sheer force of sagacity and tact he exercised for many years a powerful and a wholesome influence in shaping the policy of the government. His self-indulgence appears to have been due to his health, which was always delicate. He was subject to fever and sleeplessness, which increased as he grew older ; we have

the elder Pliny's word for it that in the last three years of
his life he did not sleep at all. Maecenas married Terentia,
a sister (by adoption) of Licinius Murena, who was executed
for conspiracy against the emperor in B.C. 23. She was a
beautiful woman, who counted, the gossips said, Augustus
himself among her lovers ; and her husband oscillated
between furious jealousy and complete subjection to her
fascination. He incurred the emperor's displeasure, when
her brother's conspiracy was detected, by letting her draw
the secret from him. These jars produced no permanent
estrangement between Augustus and his minister, but there
were other circumstances which inevitably caused Maecenas'
influence to wane. When the rule of Augustus had become
firmly established and began to take on the character of an
hereditary monarchy, the members of his own family
naturally came into greater prominence in his councils.
Among these was Agrippa, who had married his daughter
Julia. Maecenas was outside the circle and his relation with
his chief could not be the same as before.

22. Maecenas was a man of cultivated mind and taste,
with a genuine appreciation of literature and enjoyment of
the conversation of men of letters. He even wrote indifferent verses himself. But he showed his love of literature in
a much better way by bestowing upon it a liberal, and what
was more to the purpose, a discriminating patronage. He
did this in part as a measure of policy ; he saw that literature
might serve a useful purpose in reconciling the nation to the
new order of things. It was rare good fortune for Octavian
to have a minister who not only saw the wisdom of this
policy, but had the taste and the tact to carry it out with
success ; it was something more than good fortune for
Maecenas that he won the gratitude and admiration of the
two greatest poets of the age, and that his name from that
day to this has been a synonym for patron of letters.

23. Horace was introduced to Maecenas apparently in B.C. 39 ; but it was not till nine months after the first meeting that he was definitely admitted to his circle. It was probably in B.C. 37 that Maecenas invited him, with Vergil and Varius, to accompany him on the journey to Brundisium, which he has humorously described in the fifth Satire. The acquaintance between the two men ripened gradually into a warm attachment. Maecenas found in Horace a man after his own heart, whose society gave him great content, and whose good sense and sound moral fibre were proof alike against servility and presumption. He won Horace's gratitude by very substantial favors ; he won his affection by the tact and sincerity which made it plain that these favors were the gifts of a friend and not of a mere patron, and that only friendship was exacted in return. Others were quick enough to point out the social inequality of the two men, and Horace was once more forced to hear ill-natured remarks about 'the freedman's son'; but he comforted himself with the knowledge that however it might have been on the former occasion, when he was tribune in the army of Brutus, humble birth was not a matter to be considered against personal qualities in the choice of a friend, and that the distinguished favor which he enjoyed was not purchased by any unworthy compliances on his part. The balance of obligation, in a material point of view, was enormously against him ; but he was ready, and frankly avowed his readiness, to resign all these advantages rather than surrender his own independence. And Maecenas accepted him on these terms.

THE SABINE FARM.

24. Chief of all the benefits that came to Horace from this friendship was the gift of a farm in the Sabine hills, which he received from Maecenas about 33 B.C., not long after the publication of the first book of Satires. The

precise situation of this estate has not been determined;
but it lay on the banks of the Digentia (now Licenza), a
cold mountain stream that flows directly south and joins the
Anio about eight miles above Tibur (Tivoli).   Near by was
a shrine of the Sabine divinity Vacuna, which archeologists
have located with considerable probability at the village
of Roccagiovane, about three miles up the valley on
its western slope.   Behind this point, within a distance
of two or three miles, there are mountain peaks rising to
a height of more than 3000 feet above the sea, one of
which may have been Lucretilis ; though that name is more
commonly supposed to have designated the whole mountain
mass lying between the Digentia and the more westerly
tributaries of the Anio, the highest point of which, Monte
Gennaro (or Zappi) rises above 4000 feet.   At the junction
of the valleys, on the Anio, was the market town of Varia
(Vicovaro) where Horace's five tenant-farmers carried their
produce to sell.   In the country-house, which Horace himself appears to have built or remodeled for his own use, he
maintained an establishment of eight slaves, including presumably the *vilicus*, who had charge of the whole estate.
The environment of beautiful scenery, with abundance of
shade, cool streams, and pure air, — it was about 2000
feet above the sea-level — made the place exceedingly
attractive to a man like Horace, who was strongly suscepti-
ble to the impressions of Nature in her various aspects.
He came into possession of his Sabine villa when he was
a little over thirty years old, and from that time on he spent
much of his life there, glad to escape from the feverish
bustle of the city to his mountain retreat, not thirty miles
away, but completely secluded and restful to both mind and
body.   To Maecenas' generous gift he was indebted for
a good deal more than the mere provision of an income
which secured him against want for the rest of his days,

though that too was all-important for a man of letters in that age.

POLITICAL VIEWS.

25. Through his intimacy with Maecenas Horace came to the acquaintance and notice of Octavian, towards whom his feelings, in the course of this decade, underwent a complete change. Like many of the followers of Brutus and Cassius, who had remained quiescent or hostile during the harmonious supremacy of the triumvirs, Horace saw that when it became necessary to choose between Octavian and Antony, the best hopes of the country were bound up with the success of the former. His change of heart was no doubt hastened by the influence of Maecenas, and in fact the prevailing influences at Rome set in that direction. When the contest reached its crisis at Actium, Horace's conversion was complete. He celebrated the victory and the death of Cleopatra, — with true Roman spirit he was silent about Antony, — with odes of triumph, and cordially accepted the result which placed the sole supremacy in the hands of the one man who could command peace. Towards Augustus personally, however, Horace was not inspired at this time, and probably not any time, with any warmer feeling than patriotic admiration and gratitude.

THE ODES.

26. When Octavian returned to Rome and celebrated his triple triumph in 29 B.C., — the year after Vergil completed his seven years' labor on the Georgics, — Horace had published his two books of Satires and the Epodes. In each of these the opening poem was addressed to Maecenas, which was equivalent to a dedication. Horace's work in satire was not pursued further, at least in the same form. He had become deeply interested in lyrical composition, and

his success in the Epodes had encouraged him to try his hand at more complicated lyrical metres. He made careful studies in early Greek lyric, taking as his especial models and guides the two great poets of Lesbos, Alcaeus and Sappho (about 600 B.C.) Just when Horace began to write what we call the Odes, but which he called simply poems (*carmina*), it is not possible to say. In fact, the line of division between the Epodes and the Odes is a somewhat arbitrary one, and a few poems are found under each head that might equally well have been placed under the other. The earliest of the odes to which a date can be assigned with certainty is I. 37, written on receiving the news of the death of Cleopatra in B.C. 30. Possibly some were written before this, but probably not many. From this time on, for about seven years, Horace devoted himself with great zeal and industry, and almost to the exclusion of every other kind of literary work, to lyrical composition. His mastery of form and fine rhythmical sense had here their highest opportunity, and the result was a body of lyric which in volume and variety and in perfection of finish was never equaled in Latin literature before or after. Catullus, a generation earlier, had written lyrics which in freshness and spontaneity, and as direct and unaffected expressions of the poet's personality, Horace himself could not equal. But Catullus had written chiefly in the easier lyrical metres, — iambics, Glyconics, and particularly the Phalaecean, his favorite rhythm. He tried the Sapphic strophe in only two poems, — one of these a translation, — and the Alcaic not at all. These two, with three Asclepiad strophes which Catullus did not touch, were the rhythms that Horace developed most successfully, and, after many experiments with other forms, came to use almost exclusively. He also worked in accordance with strict metrical theories, formulated probably by the Roman philologians of the time, and not by

Horace himself, whereas Catullus had allowed himself the full liberty of his Greek models as he found them, so that his verses sometimes, to the ears of later critics, had a touch of harshness. It was not unnatural that Horace should regard his own achievement, wrought out with much study and labor, as the first adequate and successful adaptation of the Lesbian rhythms to the Latin language, in comparison with which the slighter efforts of Catullus might be deemed to have gone, in point of artistic workmanship, little beyond the point he had himself reached in his Epodes. And his claim, in this limited sense, must be allowed. But it is to be wished that he had accorded to the genius of his predecessor in lyric the same generous recognition which he gave to that of Lucilius in satire.

27. Horace's Odes, many of which are addressed to one or another of his friends, were privately read and circulated long before they were published in collected form. The first publication, which embraced three books, dedicated in a fitting introductory ode to Maecenas, took place, according to almost conclusive internal evidence, in B.C. 23, when Horace had reached the age of forty-two. It was the gathered fruits of the best years of his life, when his mind had attained its full maturity and his spirit had not yet lost its freshness. The collection is arranged with some reference to the chronological order of composition, but with more to variety of subject and pleasing sequence of rhythms. The odes range in quality from mere studies or versions from the Greek to products of the poet's matured skill and poems in which motive and thought are wholly Roman. Horace gave his work to the world with the undisguised assurance of its immortality and his own. It did not immediately silence his detractors; but it won its way surely, and he did not have to wait many years for a general verdict of approval from the reading public.

THE FIRST BOOK OF EPISTLES.

28. With this achievement Horace's ambition to make for himself a unique place in Roman literature was satisfied, or his lyric impulse was spent; at any rate he wrote no more odes for some years. His old · propensity for the study of life reasserted itself and found expression in a new series of *sermones*, as he calls them, indicating their close resemblance in subject and method, as they were identical in metre, with the Satires. In form they were Epistles, and this is the title under which they have come down to us. Some are letters in fact as well as in form, relating to personal matters, — one is a letter of introduction. Others contain some admixture of personal communication, while in many the insertion of a name is no more than a compliment or serves only to lend a certain personal interest to the discourse. It was a practice to which he had become habituated in the Odes, the influence of which on the Epistles is further apparent in a more finished rhythm and a more compact and sententious style than he had attained in the Satires. The first series of Epistles was written in the years immediately following the publication of the Odes, and was published in B.C. 20 or 19. The book, like its predecessors, was dedicated to Maecenas.

PERSONAL TRAITS.

29. In the epilogue of this first book of Epistles Horace has left a brief sketch of his own person and temper at the age of forty-four: 'short of stature, prematurely gray, quick to take offense, but quickly appeased.' He was stout as well as short; but in his younger days, with black hair and the low forehead which the Romans admired, and an agreeable voice and smile, he was personally far from unattractive. He enjoyed good health in his youth except that he was troubled with an affection of the eyes. But as he grew older his health began to fail, and he found it necessary to guard it carefully. In spite of the friendly reproaches of Maecenas, he spent a good part of the year away from the city, among the hills at his villa or at Tibur or Praeneste, or on the seashore at Baiae or Tarentum.

30. Horace never married, nor was he ever taken possession of by an overmastering passion, like his friend Tibullus and the other elegiac poets. Among all the feminine names that occur in his lighter odes only one appears to be real, — that of Cinara, of whom he speaks only after her early death. The Lydias and Lalages, and all the rest of the Greek ladies who figure in his love poems are creatures of his fancy, or of the fancy of some Greek poet before him ; and if, as is no doubt to some extent true, the poems reflect the poet's own experiences, they also show how lightly these experiences touched him. Horace was not of a temperament to make a serious business of love ; and his artistic delineations of it are pretty, but they have not the ring of genuineness and true passion. Something of the same sort must be said of his convivial odes. They must be taken as artistic productions, not as self-portraiture. Horace enjoyed good wine and was very sociable by disposition, and he no doubt often found himself, especially in his younger days, in boisterous company ; but by his whole nature and training excess of all kinds was distasteful to him, and it is impossible not to believe that his strong self-control rarely failed to assert itself here. The odes in which he enjoins moderation in the use of wine reflect not only his rule but, we may confidently believe, his habitual practice.

THE *CARMEN SAECULARE* AND THE FOURTH BOOK OF ODES.

31. In the year 17 B.C. Horace's eminence as a poet received the stamp of official recognition in his appointment to write a hymn to be sung at the Secular Games which Augustus celebrated in that year. His services as poet laureate were further called upon a few years later to celebrate in two odes the exploits of the Emperor's stepsons, Tiberius and Drusus Nero, who had gained important successes against some of the Alpine tribes. In the meantime his reawakened lyrical activity had produced other odes, and in B.C. 13, or perhaps a little later, he gathered these together and added a fourth book to the three already published. This was done, Suetonius tells us, to gratify the emperor, who wished the odes in honor of his stepsons to have a permanent place in Horace's works. The *Carmen Saeculare* was not included in this book, but has been preserved separately.

RELATIONS WITH THE COURT.

32. The fourth book of the Odes, unlike all of the poet's previous publications, was not dedicated to Maecenas, and this circumstance has given rise to the suspicion that Horace was guilty of neglecting his old friend, now that he had himself come into the sunshine of court favor, while his benefactor had withdrawn into the background, or was even under a cloud. But there is no sufficient ground for such an aspersion, and it is contradicted by what we know of Horace's character and his ideals of life. Horace had long before this time come into entire sympathy, politically, with the government of Augustus. The emperor was fully alive to the value of such an ally, and was ready to bestow upon him social favors and rewards of a more substantial sort. Both the one and the other were no doubt agreeable enough to the poet, and Horace was not the man to withhold the one favor he could bestow in return, — the service of his muse. There is nothing to show that his relations with the court went beyond this interchange of civilities. Horace had already won the prizes of life that he most valued, and court favor could add nothing that he really cared for. Nor is there any evidence of a close friendship between the poet and the emperor. The warmest expression of Horace's feeling towards Augustus is in the fifth ode of the fourth book ; but it is the warmth of loyal gratitude to the author of his country's peace, and not at all of personal affection. On the other hand we are told that the emperor's advances towards a closer relation, in inviting the poet to become his private secretary, were coldly received and the appointment was declined. As to the new book of lyrics, Horace's unerring tact would forbid him to dedicate to Maecenas a work that he had published at the request of the emperor ; the significant fact is that it is not dedicated to Augustus. Of his loyalty to Maecenas, which we should otherwise have no right to question, he reminds us in the eleventh ode ; and of Maecenas' undiminished affection for the poet we have striking evidence in his dying message to the emperor, recorded by Suetonius : ' Horati Flacci ut mei esto memor.'

THE LITERARY EPISTLES.

33. Suetonius further tells us that Augustus reproached Horace not only for slighting his friendly advances, but for having left him, among so many friends addressed in his ' sermones,' conspicuous by his absence ; and that Horace absolved himself from this reproach by composing the poem which now stands at the head of the second book of Epistles. It is, in form, an epistle to the emperor ; in substance, a review of Latin poetry, with a defense of the modern school, of which Varius and Vergil and Horace himself were the foremost representatives, and with which the name of Augustus was destined to be permanently associated, against the disparagement of conservative critics and their indiscriminate veneration of the old Roman poets. The second

poem of this collection, an epistle to a young friend and man
of letters, Julius Florus, is also mainly devoted to literary
matters, and is especially interesting for its many allusions
to Horace's own literary career.   Its general purport is that
he has now come to a time of life when he must put aside
poetry with other amusements of youth, and address himself to the ' rhythms and harmonies of real life.'   For this
reason its composition is assigned with great probability to
the period immediately following the publication of the first
book of the Epistles, when Horace's lyrical muse was still
silent, — say B.C. 19 or 18.   The epistle to Augustus, on the
other hand, was probably written at least as late as B.C. 14.

34. These two epistles are followed in modern editions
by the longest of Horace's poems (476 hexameters) and
the one that approaches nearest to the character of a
formal treatise.   It is largely didactic, setting forth with
much detail of precept and illustration, the correct principles
of poetry as an art ; and as early as the first century it was
known under the title of *Ars Poetica* (or *De Arte Poetica
liber*).   It is, nevertheless, written in the form, and to a
considerable extent preserves the character and tone, of an
epistle, being addressed to three friends, a father and two
sons, of the Piso family, and ostensibly designed for the
special benefit of the elder of the two young men, who had
literary aspirations.   It is, moreover, for a formal treatise,
very incomplete ; it deals with only one branch of poetry,—
the drama, — with any degree of thoroughness, touching on
the rest lightly or not at all.   It seems probable, therefore,
that the somewhat pretentious title *Ars Poetica* did not
originate with Horace himself, but was given to the poem
later, when it was issued separately, either for educational
purposes or as material for learned commentary.   The
date of its composition is in dispute.   Some place it as
early as the first book of the Epistles, but the better view

appears to be that it was written in the last years of the poet's life.

DEATH AND PERMANENT FAME.

35. Of Horace's personal history in these last years we have no record. His health, as we have seen, had long been precarious, and he had not yet completed his fifty-seventh year when he died, in the latter part of November, B.C. 8. He was buried on the Esquiline, not far from the tomb of Maecenas, who had passed away only a few months before him.

36. The favor which Horace had won from the best minds of his own time has been confirmed by the permanent verdict of posterity. His works at once took their place among the classics of Latin literature. By the beginning of the second century, as we know definitely from Juvenal, and undoubtedly long before (see Quint. I. 8. 6), they were used as school-books, and thus became a part of the literary outfit of the educated Roman. They continued to be read to some extent through the middle ages, and since the revival of letters their popularity has been steadily maintained. Perhaps no ancient writer has won a warmer place in the personal regard of modern men, — and not only men of books, but men of affairs ; for the secret of his power is not merely, or perhaps so much, in the unrivaled mastery of language and rhythm which lends such charm to his lyric poems, — still less in the force of poetical genius, in which his greatness does not pass unchallenged, but rather in the character which shines through his verses, of the keen but kindly, urbane, wise, genial observer of life.

SCHOLIA AND MANUSCRIPTS.

37. Horace's poems became early the subject of learned criticism and interpretation. The oldest commentary that has come down to us is that of Pomponius PORPHYRIO, who is supposed to have written in the fourth century, perhaps earlier. At any rate he lived at a time when the old Roman pagan customs had not yet died out, and he had access to still older authorities which are now lost ; so that his work is of great value to us. We also have a collection of scholia under the name of Helenius ACRO, a distinguished grammarian who lived perhaps a century before Porphyrio ; but although Acro unquestionably wrote a commentary on Horace, the one which now bears his name is a composite production, made up at a much later date by one or more unknown writers, who quote liberally from Porphyrio.

38. If we may take the word of Jacques de Crusque (better known by his Latinized name, Cruquius), professor at Bruges in the latter part of the sixteenth century, the oldest manuscript of Horace known to exist in modern times was preserved in the monastery of St. Peter at Blankenberg (Mons Blandinius), near Ghent, and presumably perished in the fire which consumed that institution in 1566. It was one of four codices which Cruquius had borrowed from the monastery and collated for his edition of Horace, which he first published in complete form in 1578. Although, there-fore, these Blandinian manuscripts are themselves lost, we have in the edition of Cruquius a considerable number of readings from them ; and some of these are of a very strik-ing character. Cruquius regarded the manuscripts as of great value ; three of them he assigned to the ninth century while the other, which he called 'vetustissimus' he thought might possibly date from the seventh. We have no means of revising this estimate. Keller and Holder, to whom we are indebted for the fullest existing critical apparatus of Horace, question the accuracy and even the good faith of Cruquius, and set little value on his manuscripts. The majority of Horatian scholars, however, dissent from this view and acquit Cruquius of any worse offense than carelessness, while the 'Blandinius Vetustissimus' is justly held to be of exceptional importance both on account of the excellence of some of its peculiar readings and because it represents a tradition in large measure independent of the great mass of Horatian manuscripts. Cruquius also published in his edition a collection of scholia from his Blandinian manuscripts, the unknown writer or writers of which are commonly quoted as 'Commentator Cruquianus.' They are of no great value, being evidently derived, for the most part, from Acro and Porphyrio.

39. The extant manuscripts of Horace, about two hundred and fifty in number, range in date from the eighth or ninth to the fifteenth century. The oldest is one now in the public library at Berne, written by a Scotch or Irish monk in the latter part of the eighth or early in the ninth century. We have nearly twenty in all which appear to have been written before the end of the tenth century. All of the manuscripts (except one at Gotha, which appears to be derived from the Blandinian recension) come from a common archetype, which Keller thinks may have been written as early as the first or second century. No satisfactory classification has yet been discovered, which shall enable us to decide on disputed readings by the weight of manuscript testimony ; nor is it probable that the relations of the manuscripts to one another can ever be sufficiently made out to establish such a classification. Owing to the practice in which copyists and revisers often indulged, of comparing their codex with one or more others, and borrowing readings from these at their discretion, the lines of tradition have become so confused that it is probably no longer possible to separate them. This appears in Keller's attempted classification, in which an important manuscript will be found now in one class, now in another. Keller sets up three classes, and in general accepts the united testimony of two against the remaining one. His Classes II. and III. may be said to be fairly made out, though their value is much impaired by the vacillation of individual manuscripts. The case for his Class I. is by no means so clear. The serious problems of Horatian textual criticism involve, as a rule, the choice between two (seldom three) variants, each resting on good, but not conclusive, manuscript support ; and the decision cannot be reached by any balancing of authorities, but calls for the exercise of sound judgment, trained by careful study of the poet's mode of thought and habit of expression.

II. LANGUAGE AND STYLE.

40. Saturated as Horace was with Greek literature, it was inevitable that his language and style should bear the impress of a strong Greek influence. But to this influence he by no means surrendered himself unreservedly. His sturdy Roman character stamped itself upon his writings as upon his life, and he was no more spoiled as a literary artist by Greek culture than he was as a man by aristocratic society. He was strong enough to absorb the spirit of Greek art, and make it his own. The task he set himself was not to imitate the Greek poets, but to achieve with his own language what they had achieved with theirs. He understood well the genius of his native tongue, its capacities and its limitations; and his good sense and good taste saved him from attempting to do with it some of the things which the older poets had tried, — such as the formation of unwieldy compounds, — just as he refrained from their sonorous rhetoric and extravagant use of assonance and alliteration, and from the studied prettiness of Catullus and his school. While his syntax often has a strong Greek flavor, he rarely uses a construction of which we cannot find at least the germ in the Latin idiom. If we bear in mind that Latin was a spoken language, in process of growth and decay, not hardened into the forms in which the grammarians have systematized it for us, we may well hesitate to assert that Latin idiom was ever consciously violated by Horace. His language is, in the main, the every-day language of cultivated Romans, but free from the sprinkling of Greek words and phrases with which polite conversation covered up its own poverty, and which he expressly condemns in Lucilius. Horace uses Greek words sparingly, and as a rule only of Greek things. His diction betrays no striving to avoid the commonplace. His power and charm lie rather in the skill with which he moulds common materials into exquisite forms, and in that perfect adaptation of word to thought which invests his carefully wrought phrase with all the appearance and the freshness of a happy inspiration. This 'Horati curiosa felicitas,' as Petronius has so aptly characterized it, is his supreme merit ; and it is all his own.

The exposition which follows is designed to help the student to a better understanding of the poet by pointing out the most salient characteristics of his syntax, — chiefly those in which he goes beyond the limits of literary prose usage, — and to set forth some of the more striking features of his use and arrangement of words. This will serve, it is hoped, to show the student what to look for, but the largest part must still be done by himself. There are innumerable subtleties of form and setting which are beyond the reach of description. To grasp the full beauty and charm of Horace's style, we must read and read over again, read many times and learn by heart, till the poet's thought and his verse are inseparably blended in our memory.

(A) SYNTAX.

The Accusative.

41. The passive voice is sometimes used with its original middle force and takes an object accusative ; as

S. II. 7. 38 **nasum supinor,** *I lay back my nose; Ep.* II. 3. 302 **purgor bilem;** *Ep.* I. 1. 50 **coronari Olympia** (after the Greek στεφανοῦσθαι, *to win a crown for oneself*); *Ep.* I. 17. 28 **quidlibet indutus.**

42. In descriptions of dress or personal adornment the perfect participle, with an instrumental ablative, is frequently used in the middle sense, and takes an accusative of the part of the body affected ; as

C. I. 2. 31 **nube candentis umeros amictus,** *having thy bright shoulders wrapt in cloud; C.* II. 11. 15 **rosa odorati capillos;** *Ep.* II. 1. 110 **fronde comas vincti.**

43. The accusative of the 'part affected' is sometimes used with the passive voice in its proper sense, thus becoming practically an accusative of specification ; as

S. I. 8. 37 **caput inquiner,** *I get my head befouled; S.* I. 1. 5 **iam fractus membra labore,** *with his frame all shattered by toil and hardship; S.* II. 3. 295 **mentem concussa.**

44. The accusative specifying the 'part affected' occurs once in Horace with an active verb : *S.* II. 7. 57 **tremis ossa pavore** (cf. *C.* I. 23. 8 et corde et genibus tremit). Its occurrence with an adjective is doubtful, the *MSS.* in *C.* III. 10. 18 being divided between *animum mitior* and *animo mitior. Cetera* with an adjective occurs thrice : *C.* IV. 2. 60 **cetera fulvus;** *Ep.* I. 10. 3, 50. Cf. § 45 *b*.

45. (*a*) The character of the action may be expressed by an adjective with a cognate accusative ; as

C. III. 29. 50 **ludum insolentem ludere;** *C.* II. 17. 26 **laetum crepuit sonum.**

(*b*) The neuter plural of an adjective in this construction is equivalent to an adverb ; as

S. I. 8. 40 **alterna loquentes** (*alternately*) ; *S.* I. 4. 44 **os magna sonaturum** (*in lofty strain*) ; *Ep.* I. 1. 101 **insanire sollemnia** (*in the ordinary way*) ; *S.* I. 10. 37 **haec ego ludo.**

46. The action of a verb may be characterized by an adjective or participle in apposition with the verb itself, or with the whole predicate; as *S*. I. 4. 10 in **hora saepe ducentos, ut magnum, versus dictabat** (*as a great feat*); *S*. II. 1. 53 **dente lupus, cornu taurus petit,** — **unde nisi intus monstratum?** *S*. II. 2. 19 **cum sale panis latrantem stomachum bene leniet,** — **unde putas aut qui partum?**

47. The accusative singular neuter of pronouns and of *nihil* is freely used as a cognate object with adverbial force; as

C. I. 32. 1 **si quid lusimus;** *S*. II. 1. 78 **nisi quid tu dissentis;** *Ep*. II. 3. 354 **si peccat idem;** *C*. I. 14. 14 **nil pictis puppibus fidit;** *S*. II. 8. 41 **nihilum nocuere lagenis.** In one instance *nihil* is modified by an adjective: *Ep*. I. 12. 15 **nil parvum sapias** (*in no small way*).

48. The accusative singular neuter of many adjectives is attached to verbs, both transitive and intransitive, with adverbial force; as

C. I. 22. 23 **dulce ridentem;** *S*. I. 3. 26 **cernis acutum;** *Ep*. II. 2. 9 **canet indoctum sed dulce bibenti;** *C*. II. 12. 14 **lucidum fulgentis;** *S*. I. 8. 41 **resonarint triste et acutum.**

49. The accusative singular neuter of adjectives of quantity is used adverbially with adjectives and participles; as

C. I. 25. 5 **multum facilis;** *Epod*. 15. 11 **dolitura multum;** *Epod*. 17. 20 **amata multum;** *S*. II. 5. 80 **nec tantum Veneris quantum studiosa culinae.** So *nihilum: S*. II. 3. 54 **nihilum metuenda.**

50. Horace uses **insuesco** with two accusatives (on the analogy of *doceo*) in *S*. I. 4. 105 **insuevit pater hoc me.** The use of **decipior** with an accusative in *C*. II. 13. 38 **dulci laborem decipitur sono** is to be explained on the analogy of *celor* (cf. the use of *fallo* with an accusative of the thing disguised, e. g. *S*. II. 2. 12 **studio fallente laborem,** from which *fallor laborem* would be a natural development); but see § 67. In the expression, *Ep*. II. 3. 383 **census equestrem summam,** borrowed from legal phraseology (cf. Cic. *Flacc.* 80), **censeo** is likewise treated as a verb that takes two accusatives.

51. The tendency of verbs originally intransitive to acquire a transitive use appears at a more advanced stage in poetry than in prose. The following verbs, used transitively by Horace, had a very restricted transitive use, or were not so used at all, in prose before his day:

(*a*) Verbs denoting emotion or the expression of emotion: **erubesco, fleo, gemo, ploro, pallesco, expallesco, paveo, expavesco, tremo, contremisco, horresco, fastidio, gravor**; as, *Epod.* 14. 11 **cava testudine flevit amorem**; *C.* IV. 12. 5 **Ityn flebiliter gemens**; *C.* III. 27. 27 **pontum palluit** (*turned pale at the sight of*) ; *C.* IV. 11. 27 **Pegasus terrenum equitem gravatus.**

(*b*) Verbs expressing haste, strife : **propero, depropero, festino, certo, pugno, milito** ; as *Ep.* I. 2. 61 **poenas festinat**; *S.* II. 5. 27 **foro si res certabitur** ; *Epod.* 1. 23 **libenter hoc et omne militabitur bellum.**

(*c*) Verbs of vocal expression : (1) with object denoting the form or content of the expression: **sono, crepo, balbutio, elatro**; as *C.* II. 13. 26 **sonantem plectro dura navis, dura fugae mala**; *Ep.* I. 7. 84 **sulcos et vineta crepat** ; (2) with external object: **iurgo, sibilo, latro**; as *S.* II. 2. 100 **Trausius iurgatur** ; *S.* I. 1. 66 **populus me sibilat**; *Epod.* 5. 57 **senem latrent canes.**

(*d*) Verbs expressing some physical act or state : (1) in a literal sense: **ceno, stillo** ; *Ep.* II. 2. 168 **emptum cenat holus**; *Ep.* II. 3. 429 **stillabit ex oculis rorem** ; (2) in a figurative sense : **mano, spiro**; *Ep.* I. 19. 44 **fidis manare poetica mella te solum**; *C.* IV. 13. 19 **spirabat amores** ; (3) of dramatic action, the accusative denoting the character represented : **salto, moveor, edormio** ; *S.* I. 5. 63 **pastorem saltaret uti Cyclopa rogabat**; *Ep.* II. 2. 125 **nunc Satyrum, nunc agrestem Cyclopa movetur** (i. e. saltat ; cf. *Ep.* II. 3. 232) ; *S.* II. 3. 61 **Fufius ebrius Ilionam edormit**, '*slept off*' *Iliona*, i. e. actually went to sleep in his part, instead of simulating it (with the additional idea, however, that he was sleeping off a debauch, from the phrase *edormire crapulam*, which occurs in prose).

(*e*) **invideo, impero, regno** (see also § 68), **triumpho,** and **iuro** are used in the passive with a subject-nominative ; as *Ep.* II. 3. 56 **ego cur invideor?** *Ep.* I. 5. 21 **haec ego procurare imperor**; *C.* III. 29. 27 **regnata Cyro Bactra** ; *C.* III. 3. 43 **triumphatis Medis** ; *Ep.* II. 1. 16 **iurandas aras.** In *C.* IV. 6. 14 **mentior** is used for *simulo*.

(*f*) Many intransitive verbs acquire a transitive use in composition. Such are : **adnuo** (= *concedo*), as *S.* I. 10. 45 **molle atque facetum Vergilio adnuerunt Camenae** ; **adsuesco,** *S.* II. 2. 109 **pluribus adsuerit mentem** (*adsuetus* is common in prose) ; **circumgemo, circumtono, circumvolo, circumvolito** ; **exsudo,** *S.* I, 10. 28 **cum Pedius causas exsudet** (= sudans peragat) ; **evagor, insisto, intono, perambulo, pererro, praefluo, remeo, subrepo, supervenio.**

52. There are a few instances in the Satires and Epistles of a colloquial form of expression in which an object accusative depends on a verbal idea vaguely implied in the phrase itself ; as *S.* II. 7. 116 **unde mihi lapidem?** unde sagittas, *where shall I get,* etc.? *Ep.* I. 5. 12 **quo mihi fortunam, si non conceditur uti?** Here mihi is added to

quo (= *quorsum*) to mean 'What object can it be to me?' (as in *S.* I.
6. 24 ; see § 94 *p*), and **fortunam** depends on the vaguely implied idea
of having or obtaining.

The Dative.

53. The person towards whom motion is directed is
sometimes expressed, as 'the person for whom' action is
performed, by the dative ; and this usage is extended, by
a more or less conscious personification, to places and
things ; as

C. I. 28. 10 **habentque Tartara Panthoiden, iterum Orco demis-
sum** (i. e. to Orcus as a *person*, the *place* being already expressed by
Tartara ; cf. *Il.* I. 3 ψυχὰς "Αιδι προίαψεν) ; *C.* IV. 4. 69 **Carthagini
iam non ego nuntios mittam superbos**; *C.* I. 24. 15 **num vanae
redeat sanguis imagini,** *would the blood return* (i. e. be restored) *to
the empty form ? C.* III. 23. 1. **caelo si tuleris manus** (cf. Verg. *Aen.*
V. 451 it clamor caelo).

54. The dative is used with verbs (chiefly in the perfect
participle) of perception and emotion ; as

C. II. 1. 31 **auditum Medis sonitum** (i. e. audible to them ; cf. the
usual construction with *videor*); *C.* I. 1. 24 **bella matribus detestata**
(*hateful to*); I. 21. 4 **Latonam dilectam Iovi** (=dear to); *Ep.* II. 1. 256
formidatam Parthis Romam; *C.* III. 25. 3 **quibus antris audiar?**

55. The dative of the agent, which had its origin perhaps
in these and similar uses (notably its use in the gerundive
construction), is also found ; as

C. I. 32. 5 **(barbite) Lesbio modulate civi**; *Ep.* II. 3. 427 **versus
tibi factos.**

56. The dative is used with verbs signifying to *unite,
mix, compare;* such are

**iungo, figo, socio, continuo, gemino, coeo; misceo, confundo; confero,
comparo, contendo** ; as *Ep.* II. 3. 1 **humano capiti cervicem equi-
nam iungere** ; *Ep.* II. 3. 13 **ut serpentes avibus geminentur, tigri-
bus agni** ; *C.* I. 1. 30 **me dis miscent superis** (i. e. set me among
them ; cf. **stellis inserere,** *C.* III. 25. 6) ; *S.* I. 10. 20 **verbis Graeca
Latinis miscuit** (Latin being his vernacular) ; *S.* I. 1. 111 **neque se
maiori turbae comparet.**

57. The dative is used with verbs signifying *difference, disagreement, contention;* such are

differo, disto, discrepo, dissentio, dissideo, disconvenio, discordo, pugno, certo, decerto, luctor, altercor; as *C.* IV. 9. 29 distat inertiae virtus; *S.* I. 4. 48 differt sermoni; *C.* II. 2. 18 dissidens plebi; *S.* I. 2. 73 pugnantia istis.

58. The dative is used with adjectives, —

(*a*) Depending on a verbal idea contained in the adjective; as *C.* I. 11. 8 credula postero; *C.* III. 26. 8 foribus minacis; *C.* II. 15. 8 fertilibus domino priori (i. e. quae ferebant; cf. *C.* III. 24. 12) ; *S.* II. 2. 6 acclinis falsis animus; *S.* II. 7. 83 sibi imperiosus.

(*b*) With adjectives conveying the notion of fitness or likeness, or the reverse ; as *C.* I. 23. 12 tempestiva viro (*of fit age for*) ; *C.* III. 11. 12 cruda marito; *S.* II. 2. 101 divitias tribus amplas regibus; *Ep.* I. 18. 5 huic diversum vitio. So with idem: *Ep.* II. 3. 467 invitum qui servat, idem facit occidenti.

(*c*) To express purpose or use after adjectives of capacity, skill, incapacity; as *C.* I. 12. 42 utilem bello; *Ep.* II. 3. 82 natum rebus agendis; *Ep.* II. 2. 21 talibus officiis prope mancum; *C.* III. 27. 61 acuta leto saxa (i. e. sharp enough to kill).

59. The dative is rarely appended to a substantive to denote purpose, service, or destiny; as

Epod. 2. 33 tendit retia, turdis dolos; *S.* II. 5. 16 ne illi comes exterior ire recuses; *C.* II. 1. 13 insigne maestis praesidium reis et consulenti, Pollio, curiae; *S.* II. 2. 107 o magnus posthac inimicis risus!

60. In the predicate after *licet esse* and the like, Horace always uses the dative; as *Ep.* I. 16. 61 da mihi fallere, da iusto sanctoque videri; *Ep.* II. 3. 372 mediocribus esse poetis non homines, non di, non concessere columnae.

The Genitive.

61. The genitive of quality may be attached directly to the name of a definite individual or class; as

S. I. 1. 33 magni formica laboris (for 'formica, animal magni laboris') ; *C.* I. 36. 13 multi Damalis meri. Similarly, where the omitted appellative would be in the predicate; as *S.* I. 4. 17 di bene fecerunt, inopis me quodque pusilli finxerunt animi; *S.* II. 8. 84 Nasidiene, redis mutatae frontis. Sometimes coupled with an adjective; as *S.* II. 7. 52 ditior aut formae melioris.

62. The possessive genitive in the predicate is used with greater freedom than in prose, often differing little from a partitive genitive ; as

S. I. 7. 35 operum hoc tuorum est ; *C.* III. 13. 13 fies nobilium tu quoque fontium ; *Ep.* I. 9. 13 scribe tui gregis hunc.

63. The partitive genitive is often used with adjectives where in prose the substantive and adjective would stand in agreement ; as

C. IV. 6. 31 virginum primae ; *C.* I. 10. 19 superis deorum et imis ; *S.* II. 2. 60 natalis aliosve dierum festos ; *C.* I. 9. 14 quem fors dierum cumque dabit. Sometimes with an adjective and pronoun ; as *C.* I. 29. 5 quae tibi virginum barbara serviet? Or a pronoun and substantive, as *S.* II. 1. 61 maiorum ne quis amicus frigore te feriat. With unus (= solus) : *S.* I. 10. 42 unus vivorum (cf. *S.* II. 6. 57 unum mortalem). The genitive is also used with unus, *one, S.* I. 9. 72 unus multorum ; elsewhere the ablative with *de* or *ex.*

64. The genitive (partitive or possessive), used in this way with the neuter plural of an adjective in an abstract sense, gives the latter greater prominence than if it were merely expressed as an attribute of the substantive; thus in

C. IV. 12. 20 amara curarum, there is more stress on the *bitterness* than there would be in 'amaras curas' ; *C.* II. 1. 23 cuncta terrarum ; *C.* IV. 4. 76 acuta belli ; *S.* II. 2. 125 contractae seria frontis. The colorless genitive rerum especially is used in the Satires and Epistles to round out a phrase ; as *Ep.* I. 17. 21 vilia rerum ; *S.* II. 2. 25 vanis rerum ; *S.* II. 8. 83 fictis rerum. In one instance rerum is used in the same way with a masculine superlative : *S.* I. 9. 4 dulcissime rerum.

65. A geographical proper name is occasionally put in the genitive (instead of in apposition) with its generic noun ; as *C.* II. 6. 10 Galaesi flumen, *the river Galaesus ; C.* IV. 14. 50 tellus Hiberiae. Sometimes it is treated as an adjective : *C.* IV. 4. 38 Metaurum flumen ; *Ep.* II. 3. 18 flumen Rhenum. This adjective use of substantives is sometimes extended to personal names ; as *C.* I. 15. 10 Dardanae genti, *the race of Dardanus ; C.* IV. 5. 1 Romulae gentis ; and even to an appellative ; as *C.* III. 12. 1 patruae linguae. In the same way Horace is fond of using the shorter forms of adjectives of nationality, which are commonly used as substantives in prose ; as Marsus, Afer, Medus, Colchus, for *Marsicus, Africus,* etc.

66. The wide development and vague limits of the use of the objective genitive with adjectives (and participles with adjective meaning) gave the poets freer scope in this than in most other constructions. The examples in Horace comprise —

(*a*) The objective genitive proper, depending on adjectives implying the action of a transitive verb, or their opposites ; such are

tenax, ferax, fertilis, fecundus, prosperus, prodigus, benignus, parcus, fastidiosus, bibulus, avarus, metuens, timidus, securus, incautus ; as *Epod*. 5. 22 Hiberia venenorum ferax ; *C. S*. 29 fertilis frugum pecorisque tellus ; *Ep*. II. 3. 164 iuvenis prodigus aeris ; *S*. II. 3. 3 vini somnique benignus (cf. our expression, 'a generous liver') ; *S*. II. 5. 79 donandi parca iuventus ; *Ep*. II. 3. 28 timidus procellae ; *Ep*. II. 2. 17 poenae securus.

(*b*) The genitive of reference, with adjectives denoting mastery, knowledge, skill, and their opposites ; such are

potens, prudens, sciens, sollers, consultus, divinus (*prophetic*), sagax, docilis, indoctus, nescius, inscius ; as *C*. I. 3. 1 diva potens Cypri ; *Ep*. II. 3. 407 musa lyrae sollers ; *C*. I. 34. 2 insanientis sapientiae consultus (after the analogy of *iuris consultus*) ; *C*. III. 27. 10 imbrium divina avis ; *Ep*. II. 3. 218 utilium sagax rerum ; *C*. IV. 6. 43 docilis modorum ; *Ep*. II. 3. 380 indoctus pilae discive trochive.

(*c*) The genitive of reference, with adjectives of plenty and want ; such are

dives, opulentus, satur, lassus, inanis, egens (cf. § 67), pauper, exsors, liber, vacuus, purus, abstinens ; as *Ep*. II. 2. 31 multarum divite rerum ; *Ep*. I. 7. 35 satur altilium ; *C*. II. 6. 7 lasso maris et viarum militiaeque (cf. Verg. *Aen*. I. 178 fessi rerum) ; *C*. III. 11. 26 inane lymphae dolium ; *Ep*. I. 17. 22 nullius egentem ; *C*. III. 30. 11 pauper aquae ; *Ep*. II. 3. 212 liber laborum rusticus ; *S*. II. 2. 119 operum vacuo ; *C*. I. 22. 1 sceleris purus.

NOTE. — Of these adjectives, dives, vacuus, and purus are also used by Horace with the ablative ; as *Ep*. II. 3. 421 dives agris, dives positis in faenore nummis ; *C*. IV. 15. 8 vacuum duellis Ianum ; *S*. II. 3. 213 purum est vitio tibi cor ? With nudus, orbus, and viduus Horace uses the ablative only ; *C*. I. 14. 4 nudum remigio latus ; *C*. IV. 2. 44 forum litibus orbum ; *C*. I. 10. 11 viduus pharetra Apollo.

(*d*) The genitive of reference (specification), with other adjectives :

S. II. 3. 65 **integer mentis** (cf. Plaut. *Trin.* 454 satin tu sanu's mentis aut animi tui ?) ; *S.* I. 9. 11 **cerebri felicem** ; *C.* II. 2. 6 **notus animi paterni** ; *S.* I. 10. 21 **seri studiorum** ; *S.* II. 2. 66 **cultūs miser** ; *C.* III. 5. 42 **capitis minor** (for the technical *capite deminutus*).

67. The analogy of adjectives of plenty and want is extended in a few cases to verbs. Horace has the genitive with

egeo, solvo, purgo, abstineo, desino, invideo ; as *S.* I. 4. 118 **dum custodis eges** (cf. *egens* § 66 *c*) ; *C.* III. 17. 16 **famulis operum solutis** (cf. *operum vacuo* § 66 *c*) ; *S.* II. 3. 27 **miror morbi purgatum te** (cf. *liber, purus* § 66 *c*) ; *C.* III. 27. 69 **abstineto irarum** (cf. *abstinens* § 66 *c*) ; *C.* II. 9. 18 **desine querellarum** ; *S.* II. 6. 84 **neque ille sepositi ciceris nec longae invidit avenae** (cited by Quintilian IX. 3. 17 to illustrate Horace's fondness for Greek idioms). Here also belongs *C.* II. 13. 38 **laborum decipitur,** if that reading, given in some good *MSS.*, be correct ; but see § 50. Horace also uses the more common prose constructions, — the ablative with **egeo, solvo, abstineo,** and the accusative and dative with **invideo.**

68. For a supposed instance of the genitive with **regno** see note on *C.* III. 30. 12.

The Ablative.

69. The ablative is often used without a preposition to denote the ' place where ' ; as

C. I. 9. 10 **ventos aequore fervido deproeliantis** ; *C.* II. 9. 24 **exiguis equitare campis.** Often without an adjective, as *S.* I. 5. 87 **mansuri oppidulo.**

70. With verbs denoting separation or motion from a place, the ablative is often used without a preposition ; as

C. I. 1. 32 **me secernunt populo** ; *S.* II. 3. 203 **abstinuit vim uxore** ; *Ep.* II. 3. 379 **abstinet armis** ; ib. 370 **actor causarum mediocris abest virtute diserti Messalae** ; *C.* II. 20. 21 **absint funere neniae** ; *C.* III. 1. 39 **decedit aerata triremi** ; *Ep.* II. 3. 53 **si Graeco fonte cadent.**

71. The ablative is used with **haereo, religo, suspendo** ; as *C.* I. 2. 9 **summa haesit ulmo** ; *C.* I. 32. 8 **religarat litore navim** ; *S.* I. 6. 74 **suspensi loculoş tabulamque lacerto.** The ablative may be that of 'place where' (cf. *S.* I. 3. 32 in pede calceus haeret), but with *religo* and *suspendo*, at least, the feeling is probably that of (prevented) separation, as in Verg. *Aen*. VII. 106 gramineo ripae religavit *ab aggere* classem; Lucan, VII. 860 nullus *ab Emathio* religasset *litore* funem navita. With *haereo* Horace also uses the dative; as *C*. I. 32. 9 illi semper haerentem. (Cf. the opposite points of view that find expression in *proximus alicui* and *proximus ab aliquo*.)

72. The ablative of cause is used with certain verbs denoting passion or mental disturbance ; such are

ardeo, caleo, uro, pecco; furo, insanio; langueo, stupeo, torpeo; as *C*. II. 4. 8 arsit virgine rapta ; *C*. I. 27. 16 ingenuo semper amore peccas ; *S*. I. 4. 28 stupet Albius aere. Horace has the ablative with *in*, once each, with uro, laboro, and stupeo : *Epod*. 11. 4 ; *C*. I. 17. 19 ; *S*. I. 6. 17 ; and ardeo once, perhaps, with the accusative : *C*. IV. 9. 13 comptos arsit adulteri crinis (cf. Verg. *Ecl*. 2. 1 Corydon ardebat Alexin) ; but see note on the passage.

73. An instrumental ablative with a verbal substantive in *-tor* occurs *C*. III. 4. 55 truncis iaculator ; with a verbal adjective, *C*. IV. 6. 8.

74. The ablative of price, added to the accusative after muto may denote either the thing given or the thing received in exchange ; as *Ep*. I. 7. 36 nec otia divitiis muto, i. e. give up my leisure (acc.) for wealth (abl.) ; *C*. I. 17. 2 Lucretilem mutat Lycaeo Faunus, i. e. gives up Lycaeus (abl.) for Lucretilis (acc.). (Cf. the double use of ἀλλάσσω τί τινος.) Similarly with verto the ablative is twice used to denote that into which the object is transformed : *C*. I. 35. 4 vertere funeribus triumphos ; *Ep*. II. 3. 226 vertere seria ludo ; (cf. Ovid *M*. X. 157 nulla alite verti dignatur). The accusative with *in* is commonly used.

75. The ablative after comparatives is frequent, instead of the more logical expression with *quam ;* as

C. I. 8. 9 olivum sanguine viperino cautius vitat (for *quam sanguinem*) ; *C*. III. 1. 9 viro vir latius ordinet (for *quam vir*). So with *alius*: *Ep*. II. 1. 240 alius Lysippo (for *quam Lysippus*). The ablative is rarely used when the first member of the comparison is not in the nominative or the accusative ; as *Ep*. I. 10. 11 pane egeo, iam mellitis potiore placentis.

The Construction ἀπὸ κοινοῦ.

76. An inflected word is sometimes placed in such relation to two other words that it may be governed by either of them, and is, in some cases, necessary to both to complete their meaning. By this arrangement, called by grammarians the σχῆμα ἀπὸ κοινοῦ, a repetition of the idea, by means of a pronoun or otherwise, is avoided ; as

C. II. 11. 11 quid aeternis minorem consiliis animum fatigas?
(= quid aeternis consiliis animum, illis minorem, fatigas ?) ; C. II. 14. 15
frustra per autumnos nocentem corporibus metuemus austrum
(where both nocentem corporibus and corporibus metuemus can hardly fail to convey to the reader the usual significance of such juxtaposition); Epod. 9. 9 vincla quae detraxerat servis amicus perfidis.

Number and Tense of the Verb.

77. Horace is noticeably fond of using a singular verb where there are two or more subjects ; as

C. II. 13. 38 quin et Prometheus et Pelopis parens dulci laborem decipitur sono ; C. II. 18. 26 pellitur paternos in sinu ferens deos et uxor et vir sordidosque natos; C. III. 16. 32 rivus aquae silvaque . . . et segetis certa fides . . . fallit sorte beatior.

78. The colloquial present with future meaning, common in old Latin, is occasionally used by Horace ; as

C. III. 9. 17 quid si prisca redit Venus, diductosque iugo cogit aeneo, si flava excutitur Chloe, reiectaeque patet ianua Lydiae ? Ep. I. 7. 34 hac ego si compellor imagine, cuncta resigno, . . . nec otia divitiis Arabum liberrima muto.

79. The future indicative is sometimes used with a concessive force, expressing, with indifference or acquiescence, the action of some other person or persons, with which that of the speaker, or of some one in whom he is more nearly interested, is brought into contrast ; as

C. I. 7. 1 laudabunt alii claram Rhodon aut Mytilenen, . . . me nec tam, etc. ; C. II. 12. 10 tuque pedestribus dices historiis proelia Caesaris, . . . me dulcis dominae musa Licymniae cantus, me voluit dicere (Cf. Verg. Aen. VI. 847 excudent alii spirantia mollius aera, | credo equidem, vivos ducent de marmore voltus, | orabunt causas melius, . . . | tu regere imperio populos, Romane, memento.)

80. The perfect indicative is used by the Augustan poets, like the Greek 'gnomic' aorist, to express a general truth or a customary action, — the statement that such and such a thing has proved true in the past conveying the implication that it is always true (cf. *invictus*, 'unconquered,' hence by implication, *unconquerable*) ; as

> *Ep.* I. 17. 37 **sedit qui timuit ne non succederet,** *he sits still who fears he may fail ; C.* I. 28. 20 **nullum saeva caput Proserpina fūgit ;** *Ep.* I. 7. 21 **haec seges ingratos tulit et feret omnibus annis** (i. e. produces and always will produce).

81. (*a*) The archaic use of the perfect infinitive with *volo, nolo,* etc. (see § 94) was adopted by the poets, partly for metrical convenience, often merely to give variety to their diction. Horace in particular uses this construction with great freedom, the tense being often quite without significance ; as

> *S.* I. 2. 28 **sunt qui nolint tetigisse ;** *S.* II. 3. 187 **ne quis humasse velit Aiacem vetas** (an intentional imitation of the archaic legal form); *Ep.* II. 3. 455 **tetigisse timent fugiuntque poetam.**

(*b*) It may be doubted, however, whether the consciousness of the tense was ever entirely lost, and in many cases the idea to be expressed is distinctly that of completed action ; as

> *C.* III. 4. 51 **tendentes Pelion imposuisse Olympo** (i. e. aiming at the achievement of that feat) ; *S.* II. 8. 79 **nullos his mallem ludos spectasse** (*prefer to have seen*) ; *Ep.* I. 17. 5 **si quid et nos quod cures proprium fecisse loquamur ;** *Ep.* II. 3. 168 **commisisse cavet quod mox mutare laboret.**

Conditional and Concessive Clauses.

82. By a rhetorical exaggeration the pluperfect indicative is occasionally used in apodosis, instead of the pluperfect subjunctive, to indicate that the result of a condition contrary to fact was partly accomplished, or to give a vivid impression of the imminence of its accomplishment ; as

> *C.* III. 16. 3 **inclusam Danaen turris aenea robustaeque fores et vigilum canum tristes excubiae munierant satis, si non Acrisium Iuppiter et Venus risissent** (they had proved sufficient up to that point) ; *C.* II. 17. 28 **me truncus inlapsus cerebro sustulerat, nisi Faunus ictum levasset.**

83. In concessive clauses with *quamvis*, Horace, like the early Latin writers, uses both the indicative and the subjunctive, more commonly the former. The indicative usually expresses a conceded fact, the subjunctive an assumption ; but there are some exceptions ; as

C. III. 11. 18 cessit . . . Cerberus, quamvis furiale centum muniant angues caput . . . saniesque manet ore (fact) ; *C.* IV. 6. 7 tibi miles impar, filius quamvis Thetidis marinae Dardanas turris quateret (fact) ; *S.* II. 5. 15 qui quamvis periurus erit (assumption), . . . ne tamen illi tu comes exterior . . . ire recuses.

Relative Clauses.

84. In relative clauses of characteristic after *sunt qui* and the like, Horace more commonly uses the indicative (a construction frequent in comedy), but also the subjunctive, with no apparent distinction of meaning ; as

C. I. 7. 5 sunt quibus unum opus est; *Ep.* II. 1. 63 interdum volgus rectum videt, est ubi peccat; *Ep.* I. 1. 78 sunt qui viduas venentur avaras excipiantque senes ; *Ep.* II. 2. 182 sunt qui non habeant, est qui non curat habere (where the more definite implication of the second relative clause is due to the number, not to the mood).

85. In a relative clause of characteristic with causal or concessive implication, Horace commonly uses the subjunctive, but sometimes the indicative ; as

Ep. II. 3. 302 o ego laevus, qui purgor bilem sub verni temporis horam ! *C.* II. 13. 34 quid mirum, ubi illis carminibus stupens demittit atras belua centiceps auris et intorti capillis Eumenidum recreantur angues ?

86. In temporal clauses of repeated action after a past tense, Horace has the subjunctive once (two verbs):

S. I. 4. 107 cum me hortaretur parce frugaliter atque viverem uti contentus eo quod mi ipse parasset, . . . a turpi meretricis amore cum deterreret, . . . aiebat.

Elsewhere he uses the pluperfect indicative ; as

S. II. 1. 71 quin ubi se a volgo et scaena in secreta remorant, . . . nugari et ludere soliti (sc. *sunt*) ; *Ep.* I. 15. 34 hic ubi fautoribus nil aut paulum abstulerat, patinas cenabat omasi ; ib. 39 ubi omne verterat in fumum et cinerem, . . . aiebat; *Epod.* 11. 13 *sqq.*

Commands and Prohibitions.

87. In commands and prohibitions, Horace uses the hortatory subjunctive in the second person singular as well as in the third, and whether the injunction is addressed to a definite person or to the general reader ; as

C. I. 11. 6 (to Leuconoe) **sapias, vina liques, et spatio brevi spem longam reseces;** *C.* II. 11. 3 **quid bellicosus Cantaber et Scythes, Hirpine Quincti, cogitet, . . . remittas quaerere, nec trepides;** *S.* I. 1. 93 **cum habeas plus, pauperiem metuas minus, et finire laborem incipias;** *S.* II. 3. 88 **ne sis patruus mihi.**

88. In prohibition, besides the customary forms, — *ne feceris, cave* (or *cave ne*) *facias,* and *noli facere* with its various equivalents (see § 94 β) — Horace uses very rarely the imperative itself ; as

C. I. 28. 23 **ne parce;** *C.* II. 7. 20 **nec parce cadis;** *C.* III. 7. 30 **neque in vias despice.**

89. An emphatic *non,* standing at the head of a sentence and belonging rather to the whole sentence than to the verb, — as *C.* II. 10. 17 **non, si male nunc, et olim sic erit ;** *Ep.* I. 3 21 **non tibi parvum ingenium, non incultum est,** — is sometimes used even with a hortatory subjunctive in prohibition ; as

Ep. I. 18. 72 **non ancilla tuum iecur ulceret ulla puerve ;** *S.* II. 5. 91 **cautus adito, neu desis operae neve immoderatus abundes. . . . non etiam sileas ; Davus sis comicus,** etc.

NOTE. — *Nec* (*neque*), for *neve* (*neu*), is very common.

90. A command or prohibition is often expressed by the future indicative ; as

Ep. I. 1. 87 **cras ferramenta Teanum tolletis, fabri;** *Ep.* I. 13. 2 **ut docui te saepe diuque, Augusto reddes signata volumina, Vini ;** *Ep.* I. 18. 37 **arcanum neque tu scrutaberis illius umquam, commissumque teges . . . ; nec tua laudabis studia aut aliena reprendes.** (Cf. the form of modern military orders : ' You will proceed with your command to such and such a place, etc.')

The Infinitive.

91. The so-called '*Historical Infinitive*' occurs nowhere in the Odes and only once in the Epodes (5. 84 lenire). In the Satires it is not infrequent, and three instances of its use are found in the Epistles.

92. The *Infinitive in Exclamation* is used twice in the Epodes (8. 1 rogare ; 11. 11 valere), and four times in the Satires (I. 9. 73 surrexe ; II. 4. 83 *sq.* radere, dare ; II. 8. 67 torquerier). In all these examples except the first it is introduced by -*ne*. It does not occur in the Odes or Epistles.

93. The *Infinitive of Purpose* was an old colloquial construction, used especially after verbs of movement ; as Ter. *Hec.* 345 intro iit videre, *he has gone in to see.* It is frequent in comedy, but except in the phrase *do* (or, once, *ministro*) *bibere* is not found in classical prose writers ; nor did it, like most poetical constructions, obtain a footing in later prose. The Augustan poets took it up, under Greek influence, but used it sparingly. The examples in Horace are as follows :

After verbs of movement : *C.* I. 2. 8 pecus egit altos visere montis ; *C.* I. 23. 10 non te frangere persequor ; *C.* III. 8. 11 amphorae fumum bibere institutae. With trado : *C.* I. 26. 3 tristitiam et metus tradam protervis in mare Creticum portare ventis. With sumo, *to take* or *choose* (as a subject) : *C.* I. 12. 2 quem sumis celebrare ? *Ep.* I. 3. 7 quis sibi res gestas Augusti scribere sumit ? With other verbs ; *Ep.* I. 2. 27 fruges consumere nati ; *Epod.* 16. 16 (see note).

94. The *Complementary Infinitive.* For the colorless expression of will, desire, intention, effort, power, capacity, and the like, by such verbs as *volo, nolo, cupio, possum, cogito, conor*, which take a simple infinitive to denote the action (of the same subject) to which they point, it is natural in animated discourse to substitute words more vividly expressive of the feeling or power to be indicated. Some of these found their way into classical prose. Thus Cicero, to ex-

press desire, frequently uses *studeo, aveo, concupisco, gestio,*
and (once each) *praegestio* and *expeto,* with a complementary
infinitive ; for unwillingness through indifference he has
non curo, non laboro, non induco animum ; for unwillingness
due to fear, *vereor* and *timeo* (not *metuo*) ; for anxious effort
quaero, laboro. The poets, as was to be expected, carried
this process much further, and permitted themselves great
freedom, especially to give livelier expression to the feeling
which prompts or accompanies an action. The verbs used
by Horace in this construction (with the exception of those
very common in prose) are as follows :

(I.) Expressions of *will, desire, intention, effort.*

(**α**) POSITIVE.

(*a*) Mere *willingness* or *approval :* patior, dignor, probo ; as *C.* III.
9. 15 bis patiar mori ; *Ep.* I. 19. 40 non ego grammaticas ambire
tribus et pulpita dignor ; *C. S.* 15 Lucina probas vocari.

(*b*) *Concern, interest :* curo, laboro ; as *C.* II. 7. 25 quis deproperare
coronas curat ? (but *curo* is more commonly negative or with negative implication ; see (*i*), below) ; *Ep.* I. 3. 2 scire laboro (see also
under (*h*), below).

(*c*) *Preference, desire, passion :* praefero, amo, studeo, quaero, iuvat,
aveo, gestio, praegestio, furo ; as *Ep.* II. 2. 184 cessare et ludere et
ungui praeferat ; *C.* I. 2. 50 hic ames dici pater atque princeps ;
C. I. 16. 26 mitibus mutare quaero tristia ; *Epod.* 9. 37 capaciores
adfer huc, puer scyphos, . . . curam metumque iuvat dulci Lyaeo
solvere (i.e. I feel a desire to) ; *C.* I. 15. 27 furit te reperire.

(*d*) *Delight :* gaudeo, delector, glorior, renideo ; as *C.* III. 6. 21
motus doceri gaudet Ionicos ; *Ep.* I. 16. 32 vir bonus et prudens
dici delector ; *Epod.* 11. 23 gloriantis vincere ; *C.* III. 6. 12 adiecisse praedam torquibus exiguis renidet.

(*e*) *Demand, claim :* posco, flagito ; as *Ep.* II. 3. 339 ne poscat
sibi fabula credi ; *S.* II. 4. 61 flagitat refici.

(*f*) *Purpose, resolve :* meditor, coniuro ; as *C.* III. 8. 23 meditantur
cedere campis ; *C.* I. 15. 7 coniurata tuas rumpere nuptias.

(*g*) *Eagerness, haste :* propero, festino, occupo, urgeo, trepido ; as
C. II. 12. 28 (oscula) rapere occupet ; *C.* II. 18. 20 urges submovere litora ; *C.* II. 4. 23 octavum trepidavit aetas claudere lustrum.

(*h*) *Effort, struggle:* **peto, expeto, tendo, laboro, enitor, certo**; as
Ep. I. 11. 29 **navibus atque quadrigis petimus bene vivere**; *Epod.*
11. 3 **me expetit urere**; *Ep.* I. 10. 20 **aqua tendit rumpere plumbum**; *Ep.* I. 20. 16 **quis invitum servare laboret?** (No clear line
can be drawn between this use of **laboro,** 'anxiously try,' and that
under (*b*) above, 'anxiously wish.') ; *Ep.* II. 3. 236 **nec sic enitar tra-
gico differre colori**; *C.* I. 1. 8 **certat tollere honoribus.**

(β) NEGATIVE.

(*i*) *Unconcern, reluctance:* **non curo, non magni pendo, contemno,
sperno, non induco animum, indignor, invideo**; as *C.* II. 13. 39 **nec
curat Orion leones agitare**; *S.* II. 4. 92 **quem tu vidisse non
magni pendes**; *Ep.* I. 1. 50 **quis coronari contemnat Olympia?**
S. I. 3. 2 **ut numquam inducant animum cantare**; *Ep.* II. 3. 90 **in-
dignatur privatis ac prope socco dignis carminibus narrari cena
Thyestae**; *C.* I. 37. 30 **saevis Liburnis invidens deduci triumpho.**

(*j*) *Neglect, inaction:* **mitto, omitto, remitto, cesso, moror, differo**;
as *Epod.* 13. 7 **cetera mitte loqui**; *C.* II. 11. 3 **remittas quaerere**;
C. IV. 4. 21 **quaerere distuli.**

(*k*) *Refusal, avoidance:* **recuso, denego, vito, fugio, refugio, aufero,
caveo, parco**; as *Ep.* II. 3. 39 **quid ferre recusent, quid valeant
umeri**; *C.* III. 16. 38 **nec si plura vclim tu dare deneges**; *Ep.*
I. 3. 16 **ut tangere vitet**; *C.* I. 9. 13 **fuge quaerere**; *S.* II. 7. 43 **au-
fer me voltu terrere** (= **noli terrere**) ; *Ep.* II. 3. 168 **commisisse
cavet quod mox mutare laboret.**

(*l*) *Fear, hatred:* **vereor, timeo, metuo, formido, perhorresco, odi**;
as *C.* III. 9. 11 **non metuam mori**; *Ep.* I. 19. 46 **naribus uti formido**; *C.* III. 16. 18 **iure perhorrui late conspicuum tollere verticem**; *Ep.* I. 16. 52 **oderunt peccare boni.**

(*m*) *Pain, regret:* **doleo, ploro**: *C.* IV. 4. 62 **non Hydra secto corpore firmior vinci dolentem crevit in Herculem**; *C.* III. 10. 4 **me
obicere plorares Aquilonibus.**

(II.) Expressions of *power* or *capacity*.

(*n*) *Power:* **valeo, evalesco, habeo, est** (= ἔξεστι, *it is possible*) ; as *C.*
I. 34. 12 **valet ima summis mutare**; *Ep.* II. 1. 201 **quae pervincere
voces evaluere sonum, referunt quem nostra theatra?** *Epod.* 16.
23 **sic placet, an melius quis habet suadere?** *S.* II. 5. 103 **est
gaudia prodentem voltum celare.**

(*o*) *Capacity, skill, incapacity:* **scio, calleo, novi, nescio, ignoro**; as
Ep. I. 17. 14 **si sciret regibus uti** (*knew how*) ; *C.* IV. 9. 49 **callet
pauperiem pati**; *S.* II. 3. 24 **hortos egregiasque domos mercarier**

unus cum lucro noram; *Ep.* II. 3. 87 descriptas servare vices operumque colores cur ego si nequeo ignoroque poeta salutor?

(III.) Expressions of *propriety* or *necessity.*

(*p*) *Propriety, fitness, obligation :* **vincit** (= *praestat*), **quo tibi ?, restat ;** as *S.* II. 5. 73 sed **vincit** longe prius ipsum expugnare caput; *S.* I. 6. 24 quo tibi, Tilli, sumere depositum clavum fierique tribuno? (cf. § 52) ; *Ep.* I. 6. 27 ire tamen **restat** Numa quo devenit (i. e. that destiny is in store for you).

95. The complementary infinitive is often hardly distinguishable from a substantive object of the verb ; but in some cases the distinction is important ; as

C. I. 28. 31 neglegis fraudem **committere** ? *do you treat lightly the commission of a wrong?* *C.* III. 14. 15 nec **mori** per vim metuam, *nor shall I be in fear of a violent death* (in contrast with *C.* III. 9. 11 non metuam mori, = 'I shall be willing to die') ; *Ep.* I. 7. 4 quam mihi das aegro, dabis **aegrotare** timenti (*fear I am going to be ill*) ; *Ep.* I. 16. 60 labra movet, metuens **audiri.**

96. In one instance Horace uses the infinitive after a preposition : *S.* II. 5. 69 inveniet nil sibi legatum praeter **plorare.** But here the infinitive really depends on **legatum** ; cf. the example with **damnatus,** § 97 *b.*

97. The infinitive is used by Horace with the following verbs (after the analogy of *iubeo, cogo, doceo, sino, prohibeo*), denoting influence of the subject on the action of other persons :

(*a*) Verbs signifying to *ask, encourage, advise, bid :* **rogo, voco, hortor, moneo, admoneo, censeo, refero ;** as *S.* I. 3. 2 cantare rogati; *C.* II. 18. 40 levare pauperem vocatus; *Ep.* I. 1. 69 Fortunae te responsare superbae . . . hortatur et aptat; *S.* I. 6. 126 me fessum sol acrior ire lavatum admonuit; *Ep.* I. 2. 9 Antenor censet belli praecidere causam; *Ep.* I. 8. 1 Celso gaudere et bene rem gerere, Musa, rogata refer (i. e. 'tell him to' or 'tell him I bid him').

(*b*) Verbs signifying to *urge, command, require* (mostly passive) : **impello, impero, damno, auctoro, addico ;** as *C.* III. 7. 14 ut Proetum mulier perfida impulerit Bellerophontae maturare necem ; *Ep.* I. 5. 21 haec ego procurare imperor; *S.* II. 3. 86 gladiatorum dare centum damnati paria (by the terms of a will) ; *S.* II. 7. 59 uri virgis ferroque necari auctoratus (bound by the terms of enlistment as a gladiator) ; *Ep.* I. 1. 14 nullius addictus iurare in verba magistri.

(*c*) Verbs signifying to *show*, *teach* : **monstro, fingo, apto** ; as *S.* II. 8. 52 inulas ego primus monstravi incoquere ; *Ep.* I. 2. 64 fingit equum magister ire viam ; see also third example under (*a*), above.

(*d*) Verbs signifying to *permit* : **do, dono, reddo, permitto, concedo, relinquo, fero** ; as *S.* II. 3. 191 di tibi dent classem reducere ; *S.* II. 5. 60 divinare mihi donat Apollo ; *Ep.* I. 7. 27 reddes forte latus, . . . reddes dulce loqui, reddes ridere decorum, et inter vina fugam Cinarae maerere protervae ; *S.* II. 3. 190 dicere permitto (with dative) ; *Ep.* I. 5. 12 quo mihi fortunam, si non conceditur uti ? *S.* I. 1. 52 dum nobis tantundem haurire relinquas ; *Epod.* 15. 13 non feret potiori te dare noctes.

(*e*) Verbs signifying to *prevent* : **invideo, adimo, interpello** ; *S.* I. 2. 100 quae invideant apparere tibi rem ; *Ep.* I. 19. 9 adimam cantare severis ; *S.* I. 6. 127 pransus non avide, quantum interpellet inani ventre diem durare (*prevent me from passing*).

98. The infinitive of indirect discourse, with or without a subject accusative, is used after the following verbs :

induco (of dramatic representation), **vinco** and **evinco** (*maintain, triumphantly prove*), **contendo** (*assert*), **fido, do** (*admit, grant*) ; as *S.* I. 2. 21 pater ille Terenti fabula quem miserum vixisse inducit ; *S.* II. 3. 225 vincet enim stultos ratio insanire nepotes ; ib. 250 puerilius his ratio esse evincet amare ; *Ep.* 1. 16. 37 si clamet furem, neget esse pudicum, contendat laqueo collum pressisse paternum ; *Ep.* I. 19. 44 fidis manare poetica mella te solum ; *S.* I. 4. 39 dederim quibus esse poetas.

99. (*a*) In indirect discourse the subject of the infinitive is sometimes omitted if it is the same as the subject of the leading verb or is readily understood from the context ; as

Ep. I. 2. 11 quid Paris ? . . . cogi posse negat ; *Ep.* I. 9. 5 cum rogat et prece cogit, scilicet ut tibi se laudare et tradere coner, . . . munere cum fungi propioris censet amici, quid possim videt ac novit me valdius ipso. Sometimes both subject and verb (*esse*) are omitted ; as *Ep.* I. 18. 2 metues scurrantis speciem praebere, professus amicum.

(*b*) In two instances, where the subject is identical with that of the leading verb, the predicate is attracted, after the Greek manner, into the nominative :

C. III. 27. 73 uxor invicti Iovis esse nescis ; *Ep.* I. 7. 22 vir bonus et sapiens dignis ait esse paratus.

100. The infinitive of indirect discourse is used with the following, as verbs of feeling :

gestio, gemo, ploro, lamentor, indignor ; as *S.* I. 4. 37 quodcumque chartis inleverit omnis gestiet scire; *Ep.* I. 20. 4 paucis ostendi gemis (see § 99 *a*) ; *Ep.* II. 1. 9 ploravere suis non respondere favorem speratum meritis; ib. 76 indignor quicquam reprehendi; ib. 224 lamentamur non apparere labores.

101. *The Infinitive with Adjectives.* This construction is confined in classical prose to a few adjectives of verbal origin, like *paratus*, and is rare in poetry before the Augustan age. In the hands of Vergil and Horace it received a rich development and was thenceforth an established feature of poetic diction. The infinitive is usually complementary in character. It is attached to participles (used adjectively) of verbs which take an infinitive, as *sciens* (cf. § 94 *o*), *doctus* and *doctior, meritus ;* to adjectives of similar origin, as *nescius, indoctus, indocilis, audax, callidus, timidus;* finally, to a great number of adjectives expressing in various phases the power, will, capacity, fitness (or the reverse) to do something. The adjectives so used in Horace are as follows :

(*a*) Expressing *disposition :* praesens (of a goddess, implying power and readiness), lenis (also of a divinity, *indulgent, gracious*), saevus (*ruthless*), impotens (*wild, undisciplined*) ; audax, fortis, contentus, cautus, timidus ; as *C.* I. 35. 2 o diva . . . , praesens vel imo tollere de gradu mortale corpus ; *C.* I. 24. 17 (Mercurius) non lenis precibus fata recludere ; *Ep.* I. 15. 30 opprobria fingere saevus ; *C.* I. 37. 10 quidlibet impotens sperare ; *C.* I. 3. 25 audax omnia perpeti ; *C.* I. 37. 26 fortis et asperas tractare serpentes ; *S.* I. 10. 59 pedibus quid claudere senis, hoc tantum contentus ; *S.* I. 6. 51 cautum dignos (amicos) adsumere ; *C.* III. 19. 2 non timidus mori.

(*b*) Expressing *capacity, energy,* or their opposites : efficax, pertinax, celer, pernix, largus (*liberal, generous*), firmus (*to be depended upon*), impiger ; piger, segnis (*slow, reluctant*), dolosus (*not to be trusted, too fickle*) ; as *C.* IV. 12. 20 (cadus) spes donare novas largus amaraque curarum eluere efficax ; *C.* III. 29. 50 (Fortuna) ludum insolentem ludere pertinax ; *C.* I. 15. 18 celerem sequi ; *Ep.* II. 3. 165 amata relinquere pernix ; *Ep.* I. 17. 47 fundus nec vendibilis nec pascere firmus ; *C.* IV. 14. 22 impiger hostium vexare turmas ;

S. I. 4. 12 **piger scribendi ferre laborem**; *C.* III. 21. 22 **segnes nodum solvere Gratiae**; *C.* I. 35. 28 **amici ferre iugum pariter dolosi.**

(*c*) Expressing *knowledge, skill*, or the reverse : **sciens, doctus, doctior, callidus, catus, sollers, prudens, blandus** (*with charm*), **nobilis ; nescius, indoctus, indocilis, durus, minor**; as *C.* III. 7. 25 **flectere equum sciens**; *C.* III. 24. 56 **ludere doctior**; *C.* I. 10. 7 **callidum quicquid placuit iocoso condere furto**; *C.* III. 12. 4 **catus cervos iaculari**; *C.* IV. 8. 9 **hic saxo, ille coloribus sollers nunc hominem ponere, nunc deum**; *Epod.* 17. 47 **in sepulcris prudens anus dissipare pulveres**; *C.* I. 12. 11 **(Orphea) blandum et auritas fidibus canoris ducere quercus**; ib. 26 **[Pollucem] superare pugnis nobilem** (the infinitive here may possibly be attributed to the idea of *nosco* contained in the adjective, like that of *doceo* in *indocilis ;* cf. Sil. Ital. XII. 331 Troianos notus semper minuisse labores ; but it is much more probable that *nobilem* is intended to express preëminent skill, and that the infinitive is complementary; cf. Verg. *Ecl.* 5. 2. boni calamos inflare ; Lucan III. 697 eximius animam servare ; and the use of *minor*, below ; see also § 102) ; *C.* IV. 6. 18 **nescios fari** (= infantes) **pueros** ; *C.* I. 1. 18 **indocilis pauperiem pati**; *S.* I. 4. 8 **durus componere versus** (implying lack of capacity ; but see § 102) ; *S.* II. 3. 313 **certare minorem** (cf. Verg. *Ecl.* 7. 5 cantare pares.)

(*d*) Expressing *fitness, merit*, or the opposite : **idoneus, utilis, dignus, meritus, indignus, immeritus**: as *Ep.* I. 16. 12 **fons rivo dare nomen idoneus**; *Ep.* II. 3. 204 **(tibia) adspirare et adesse choris erat utilis**; *Ep.* I. 10. 48 **tortum digna sequi potius quam ducere funem** (see also (*e*), below) ; *Ep.* I. 3. 35 **indigni fraternum rumpere foedus** (i. e. men for whom such conduct is unbecoming) ; *C.* III. 2. 21 **immeritis mori.**   Cf. the dative with adjectives of this class, § 58 *b* and *c*.

(*e*) With **dignus** the passive infinitive is more frequent ; as *S.* I. 3. 24 **dignus notari**; and it is also found with **levis** and **cereus**; *C.* II. 4. 11 **leviora tolli Pergama** (*easier*) ; *Ep.* II. 3. 163 **(iuvenis) cereus in vitium flecti** (*like wax, as easy as wax*).

102. As the quality which fits one for an action is likely to be displayed in the action itself, — e.g. 'swift to pursue' passes into 'swift in pursuit,' — the infinitive with an adjective readily acquires the force of an ablative of respect. This is manifest in many of the examples given above, such as those with *saevus, cautus, pertinax, celer, impiger, nobilis, durus.*   In the following examples it is the prevailing signification, the infinitive, if it is passive, being equivalent to a verbal noun in *-u.*

C. S. 25 **veraces cecinisse,** where the perfect (found only here in this construction) has its proper force; *S.* II. 8. 24 **ridiculus totas simul absorbere placentas;** *C.* I. 19. 8 **voltus nimium lubricus adspici** (= adspectu) ; *C.* IV. 2. 59 **niveus videri** (= visu).

The Participle.

103. The participle is used, more freely than in prose, as a substantive or adjective, often retaining its verbal force ; as

Ep. I. 17. 43 **coram rege sua de paupertate tacentes plus poscente ferent;** *C.* II. 16. 1 **otium divos rogat in patenti prensus Aegaeo;** *C.* III. 7. 19 **peccare docentis historias.**

104. The future participle often fulfils the function of a clause appended to its subject, with various shades of meaning : —

(*a*) Simple future fact or intention; as *C.* I. 35. 29 **serves iturum Caesarem in ultimos orbis Britannos** (i. e. qui iturus est).

(*b*) With prophetic force, — 'sure to,' 'doomed to' ; as *Epod.* 15. 11 **o dolitura multum Neaera;** *C.* II. 3. 27 **versatur urna serius ocius sors exitura et nos in aeternum exsilium impositura cumbae.**

(*c*) Equivalent to a relative clause of characteristic ; as *Epod.* 6. 4 **quin me remorsurum petis ?** (*a dog that will bite back*) ; *S.* II. 8. 85 **Nasidiene, redis mutatae frontis, ut arte emendaturus fortunam** (*as one resolved,* etc.) ; *Epod.* 15. 3 **cum tū, magnorum numen laesura deorum, in verba iurabas mea** (with concessive implication).

(*d*) Conditional statement : *S.* II. 8. 44 **haec gravida capta est, deterior post partum carne futura** (i. e. quae quidem carne deterior esset, si post partum capta esset) ; *Epod.* I. 22 **non, ut adsit, auxili latura plus** (i. e. etsi non plus auxilii ferat, si adsit) ; *S.* I. 10. 89 **doliturus si placeant spe deterius** (*and I should be sorry if,* etc.).— Hence

(*e*) With a vague condition, like *si libeat, si opus sit,* expressed or understood, giving it the force of 'ready to,' 'able to'; as *C.* IV. 3. 20 **o mutis quoque piscibus donatura cycni, si libeat, sonum** (= 'able to give') ; *C.* II. 6. 1 **Septimi, Gadis aditure mecum** (*ready to go*).

105. (*a*) The combination of a substantive with a participle, an adjective, or another substantive to express an

abstract idea, — familiar in prose in the gerundive construction, in the ablative absolute, and in the similar use, to a
limited extent, of the accusative (as *ante me consulem* =
ante meum consulatum) — was given a much wider range by
the poets ; as

C. II. 4. 10 postquam ademptus Hector tradidit leviora tolli Pergama Grais (*the taking-off of Hector*) ; *C.* III. 6. 29 non sine conscio
marito (*with the connivance of her husband*) ; *Epod.* 9. 2 victore laetus
Caesare (*glad of Caesar's victory*).

(*b*) The ablative of this construction is sometimes equivalent to an ablative of manner or means ; as

S. II. 1. 84 iudice laudatus Caesare, *commended by the verdict of
Caesar ; Ep.* I. 1. 94 curatus inaequali tonsore capillos, *my hair
trimmed with a lopsided cut ; Ep.* I. 16. 42 quo multae magnaeque
secantur iudice lites, quo res sponsore, et quo causae teste tenen-
tur (*by whose verdict, credit, testimony*).

(B) ORDER AND USE OF WORDS.

106. In reading Latin prose the feature of the language
which is at once the most difficult and the most important
for us to master, is the freedom which inflexion gives of
separating in expression ideas closely connected in sense,
and the consequent demand that is made upon us to hold
in suspense, as we proceed, a partially expressed thought,
and to grasp at once the meaning of a whole group of
words. For us, who speak an uninflected language, this
must be an acquired habit ; but it is quite indispensable :
he who has not cultivated it cannot read Latin, though he
may be able to translate it. For reading Latin poetry we
have to carry this cultivation still farther ; but it is only a
higher degree of the same capacity that is required, not a
new kind of capacity.

107. There is, in fact, no clear line of distinction between
prose and verse, in respect to the order of words, although

their general characteristics are plainly marked. In prose the greatest freedom of movement is accorded to the verb, which may be placed, with little reference to the position of its subject or object, wherever emphasis or the order of thought or rhetorical form may suggest. On the other hand a modifier of any kind must keep reasonably near its noun or verb, and the least liberty of all is allowed to an attribute and its substantive. These as a rule are not separated except by unemphatic words, — pronouns, particles, and the like, — as 'magna ex parte,' 'angustos se fines (habere),' 'quanto id cum periculo (fieret).' Yet Roman prose writers permit themselves occasionally a compact group like 'eodem usi consilio,' '(de) ea quam habeat gratia'; or even a longer group, especially where the inserted words themselves constitute a modifier, as 'tua in me vel nota omnibus vel ipsa novitate meorum temporum clarissima et maxima beneficia,' 'meam tuorum erga me meritorum memoriam.' But such combinations have a rhetorical flavor in prose, and are in fact sparingly used. In verse, on the other hand, they are rather the rule than the exception; the poets have studiously wrought out artistic groupings and sequences which the reader must train himself to grasp and follow, if he would appreciate the beauty of poetical expression. The forms are too varied and complex to be set forth fully, but the following examples, chiefly from Horace's lyric poems, may serve to indicate their character and point out the way to study them.

Grouping of Connected Words.

108. The following are examples of simple groups :

(*a*) Groups of three words (very common) :

C. I. 3. 8	animae dimidium meae
C. I. 27. 11	quo beatus volnere
C. II. 13. 29	sacro digna silentio

C. I. 35. 12　　　　　purpurei metuunt tyranni
C. I. 5. 4　　　　　　flavam religas comam
C. III. 17. 5　　　　　　auctore ab illo

　　(*b*) Groups of four words :

C. S. 29　　　　　fertilis frugum pecorisque tellus
C. III. 16. 17　　crescentem sequitur cura pecuniam
C. I. 7. 23　　　　populea fertur vinxisse corona
C. IV. 2. 3　　　　　vitreo daturus nomina ponto

　　(*c*) Groups of five words :

C. I. 27. 1　　　　　natis in usum laetitiae scyphis
C. I. 3. 30　　　　nova febrium terris incubuit cohors
C. III. 1. 10　　generosior descendat in campum petitor
C. I. 4. 15　　　　spem nos vetat incohare longam
C. I. 4. 9　　　viridi nitidum caput impedire myrto

　　(*d*) Longer groups :

C. III. 29. 11　beatae | fumum et opes strepitumque Romae
Ep. I. 10. 48　tortum digna sequi potius quam ducere funem
C. I. 27. 9　(voltis) severi me quoque sumere | partem Falerni?

　　109.　The arrangement within these groups presents great
variety.　(The arrow-head in the following examples indicates the governing word.)

C. I. 1. 22　　　　　aquae lene caput sacrae

C. IV. 1. 4　　　　　dulcium | mater saeva Cupidinum

C. III. 13. 9　　　　flagrantis atrox hora Caniculae

C. III. 8. 13　　　cyathos amici sospitis centum
　(a rare form)

C. III. 1. 16　　　omne capax movit urna nomen

C. III. 13. 6　gelidos inficiet tibi | rubro sanguine rivos

C. II. 3. 11　obliquo laborat | lympha fugax trepidare rivo

110. When a word within a group is closely connected in sense with a word preceding or following the group, there results an alternating or interlocked order, which occurs in great variety ; as,

C. II. 12. 1   longa ferae bella Numantiae

C. III. 3. 5   dux inquieti turbidus Hadriae

C. III. 5. 22   retorta tergo bracchia libero

A remarkable example is *C*. I. 9. 21 :

latentis proditor intimo | gratus puellae risus (ab) angulo

where the three ideas shadowed forth in the first verse, — some one hiding, a betrayer, a hiding-place — are filled out one after another to complete a charming picture.

111. Two groups are sometimes linked together by the connection of their interior words ; as

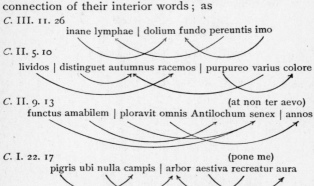

C. III. 11. 26
                    inane lymphae | dolium fundo pereuntis imo

C. II. 5. 10
          lividos | distinguet autumnus racemos | purpureo varius colore

C. II. 9. 13   (at non ter aevo)
          functus amabilem | ploravit omnis Antilochum senex | annos

C. I. 22. 17   (pone me)
          pigris ubi nulla campis | arbor aestiva recreatur aura

112. The reader who has trained himself to recognize coherent groups of words, will be able to keep his hold on the connection even when their continuity is interrupted ; as

C. III. 20. 3   *dura* post paulo fugies *inaudax*
                              proelia raptor

C. IV. 7. 27   nec *Lethaea* valet Theseus abrumpere *caro*
                              vincula Pirithoo

C. I. 2. 39   *acer* et Marsi peditis *cruentum*
                              voltus in hostem

C. III. 4. 9   *me fabulosae* Volture in Apulo
                              nutricis extra limen Apuliae
                              ludo fatigatumque somno
                                  fronde nova *puerum palumbes*
                              texere

where *puerum*, reviving the idea of *me*, supplies the necessary link between *fabulosae* and *palumbes*.   Similarly in

C. I. 22. 9   namque *me* silva *lupus* in Sabina,
                              dum meam canto Lalagen et ultra
                              terminum curis vagor expeditis,
                                  fugit inermem

fugit recalls *me* through its subject *lupus*.

113. The poet often uses the metre to suggest the connection of separated words, by placing them at the beginning and end of a verse or other definite portion of the
rhythm ; as

C. I. 1 14   *Myrtoum* pavidus nauta secet *mare*

C. II. 3. 1   *aequam* memento rebus in arduis
                              servare *mentem* ‖

C. II. 6. 15   ‖ *viridi*que certat
                              baca *Venafro*

C. III. 18. 11   *festus* in pratis vacat otioso
                              cum bove *pagus*

or one at the end of each half of a verse (especially in the
Sapphic verse, and in the Asclepiad, where a rhyme is often
produced) ; as

C. I. 22. 17   pone me *pigris* ‖ ubi nulla *campis*
                              arbor *aestiva* ‖ recreatur *aura*

C. I. 1. 9   illum si *proprio* ‖ condidit *horreo*
                              quicquid de *Libycis* ‖ verritur *areis*

or by giving them corresponding positions in different verses
or hemistichs ; as

C. II. 6. 13   *ille* terrarum mihi praeter omnis
                    angulus ridet

C. I. 26. 2   tradam *protervis* ‖ in mare Creticum
                    portare *ventis* ‖

C. I. 20. 6   simul et *iocosa*
                    redderet laudes tibi Vaticani
                        montis *imago*

C. II. 2. 23   quisquis *ingentis* ‖ oculo inretorto
                        spectat *acervos*

C. IV. 4. 69   Carthagini iam non ego *nuntios*
                    mittam *superbos* ‖

This is especially common at the close of an Alcaic or
Sapphic strophe ; as

C. I. 16. 11   nec *tremendo*
                    Iuppiter ipse ruens *tumultu*

C. I. 12. 7   unde vocalem temere *insecutae*
                    Orphea *silvae*

114. A relative or interrogative pronoun or a particle
which regularly stands at the head of a clause or phrase is
often taken within the group, giving place to a more important word ; as

C. I. 25. 17 laeta *quod* pubes hedera virenti gaudeat ; C. I. 2. 7 omne
cum Proteus pecus egit ; C. I. 2. 18 vagus *et* sinistra labitur ripa ;
C. I. 37. 20 daret *ut* catenis fatale monstrum.

Sometimes two or more words precede ; as

C. I. 18. 3 siccis omnia *nam* dura deus proposuit ; C. III. 1. 17 destrictus ensis *cui* super impia cervice pendet ; *Epod*. 16. 40 Etrusca
praeter *et* volate litora ; C. IV. 4. 42 dirus per urbis Afer *ut* Italas . . .
equitavit.

Prepositions.

115. (*a*) A preposition placed between a substantive and
its modifier, often follows the substantive ; as

mensis per omnis ; tempus in ultimum ; collibus in suis.

(*b*) Dissyllabic prepositions still in use as adverbs, — *circa, circum, citra, supra, prope,* — with *inter, praeter, sine,* are used with great freedom of position, often separated from their object, whether preceding or following it ; as

haec inter ; quos inter ; aequalis inter ; *C.* III. 27. 31 nihil astra praeter vidit et undas ; *S.* I. 10. 31 natus mare citra ; *S.* I. 3. 60 genus hoc inter vitae ; *S.* II. 3. 40 insanos qui inter vereare insanus haberi ; *C.* III. 19. 15 tris prohibet supra ; *S.* I. 10. 91 discipularum inter iubeo plorare cathedras.

(*c*) In such cases Horace is fond of placing the preposition before the verb of the sentence, as if it were an unattached prefix ; as

C. II. 16. 33	te greges centum Siculaeque *circum mugiunt* vaccae
C. III. 3. 37	dum longus *inter* ‖ *saeviat* Ilion Romamque pontus
C. III. 27. 51	utinam *inter errem* | nuda leones
Ep. I. 3. 4	freta vicinas *inter currentia* turris
Ep. II. 1. 43	veteres *inter ponetur*

(*d*) Conversely the prefix of a compound verb is treated as detachable in some cases :

S. I. 1. 86	cum tu argento *post* omnia *ponas*
Ep. II. 2. 93	quanto molimine *circum spectemus*
Ep. II. 3. 424	si sciet *inter noscere* mendacem verumque beatus amicum

(*e*) The caesura of the verse is sometimes allowed to fall between a monosyllabic prepositional prefix and the following syllable of a compound word ; as

C. I. 37. 5	antehac nefas de‖promere Caecubum
C. II. 12. 25	cum flagrantia de‖torquet ad oscula
C. I. 16. 21	hostile aratrum ex‖ercitus insolens

Emphasis.

116. Emphasis is secured (besides the methods usual in prose) —

(*a*) By placing in juxtaposition the two words of a group which express contrasted ideas ; as

C. I. 3. 10   qui *fragilem truci* | commisit *pelago ratem*
C. IV. 4. 31   neque *imbellem feroces* | progenerant *aquilae columbam*

(*b*) By rhythmical position. The places best adapted for this purpose are the beginning of a strophe or verse (especially when the word is held in reserve and stands at the end of its sentence in this position) and the end of a verse or hemistich ; as

C. III. 18. 2   per meos finis et aprica rura
                  lenis incedas, abeasque parvis
                       aequus alumnis

C. IV. 9. 25   vixere fortes ante Agamemnona
                  multi

C. II. 10. 9   *saepius* ventis agitatur *ingens*
                  pinus, et *celsae* ‖ *graviore* casu
                  decidunt turres, feriuntque *summos*
                       fulgura montis

In C. II. 9 observe the emphasis on *non semper, tu semper, at non,* vss. 1, 9, 13 (under the first ictus), *usque* 4, *omnis* 6, *omnis* 14, *semper* 17, *minores* 22.

(*c*) By giving related or contrasted words prominent rhythmical positions ; as

C. III. 2. 17   virtus *repulsae* ‖ nescia *sordidae*
C. III. 11. 31   impiae sponsos potuere *duro*
                       perdere *ferro*
C. II. 10. 13   s p e r a t *infestis*, ‖ m e t u i t *secundis*

(See also the examples under § 113.)

(*d*) By repetition, — either immediately, in the same clause (Epizeuxis, especially common in the Epodes) ; as

Epod. 4. 20 *hoc hoc* tribuno militum ; ib. 14. 6 *deus deus* nam me vetat ; C. II. 17. 10 *ibimus ibimus,* utcumque praecedes ;

(*e*) or immediately, at the beginning of a new clause, sometimes with some variation of form (Anadiplosis) ; as

C. III. 5. 21   'arma
militibus sine caede' dixit
'derepta *vidi ; vidi* ego civium
retorta tergo bracchia libero'

C. III. 16. 15   subruit aemulos
reges *muneribus ; munera* navium
saevos inlaqueant duces

(*f*) or, after intervening words, at the beginning of a new clause or of successive clauses (Anaphora) ; as

C. III. 3. 65   *ter* si resurgat murus aeneus
auctore Phoebo, *ter* pereat meis
excisus Argivis, *ter* uxor
capta virum puerosque ploret

(*g*) The emphasis of Anaphora is usually enhanced by rhythmical position ; as

C. II. 4. 4   serva Briseis niveo colore
movit Achillem
movit Aiacem . . .

C. II. 8. 13   *ridet* hoc, inquam, Venus ipsa, *rident*
simplices Nymphae

(*h*) Anaphora, however, is sometimes used without special emphasis, merely serving the purpose of a connective ; as

Epod. 5. 17   *iubet* sepulcris caprificos erutas,
iubet cupressos funebris . . .
flammis aduri Colchicis

117. (*a*) The poet, whose appeal is to the imagination rather than to the intellect, seeks to make a more vivid impression by presenting a picture in preference to an abstract conception, and by putting forward a particular person, object, or action to represent a whole class ; as

C. I. 1. 9 proprio condidit horreo (for amassing wealth in general) ; 11 findere sarculo (i. e. to till). Cf., further, 3 pulverem *Olympicum ;* 10 *Libycis* areis ; 13 trabe *Cypria ;* 14 *Myrtoum* mare ; 15 *Icariis* fluctibus *Africum ; C.* II. 18. 3 non trabes *Hymettiae* premunt columnas ultima recisas *Africa,* neque *Attali* ignotus heres regiam occupavi, nec *Laconicas* mihi trahunt honestae purpuras clientae. So the wind is *Eurus, Notus, Aquilo ;* wine is *Falernum, Caecubum, Sabinum ;* the

Roman legionary *Marsus* et *Apulus;* the outside barbarian *Dacus* et *Aethiops;* and so on in endless variety.

(*b*) In the same way a part may produce a more distinct impression than the whole (Synecdoche); as

C. I. 1. 13 *trabe* Cypria (i. e. ship); I. 8. 7 Gallica *ora* (i. e. horse); C. III. 2. 16 nec parcit (mors) imbellis iuventae *poplitibus* timidove *tergo*; *Epod.* 16. 59 *Sidonii* (i. e. Phoenicians).

Ellipsis.

118. The common substantive of the antecedent and relative clauses is sometimes expressed only in the clause that comes second ; as

Epod. 2. 37 malarum quas amor habet curas (in prose, malarum cura-rum quas amor habet) ; *S.* I. 4. 2 alii quorum comoedia prisca virorum est ; *S.* II. 2. 59 vinum et cuius odorem olei nequeas perferre (i. e. et oleum cuius odorem nequeas perferre).

119. (*a*) A word or phrase belonging to two words, phrases, or clauses in common is sometimes expressed with the second only ; as

Epod. 7. 13 furorne caecus an *rapit* vis acrior? *C.* III. 25. 2 quae nemora aut quos *agor in* specus.

(*b*) It is a favorite device of Horace to indicate this ellip-sis by attaching an enclitic *-que* or *-ve* to the word, which then, as nothing precedes to which the conjunction can join it, suggests *itself* as the word to fill the omission ; as

C. III. 1. 12 moribus hic meliorque fama (= melior moribus melior-que fama) ; *S.* II. 3. 139 non Pyladen ferro violare aususve sororem (= non Pyladen violare ausus aususve sororem) ; *C.* I. 30. 6 solutis Gratiae zonis properentque Nymphae (= properent Gratiae properent-que Nymphae) ;

(*c*) So *sive* (*seu*) often implies a preceding *si* or *sive;* as

S. II. 5. 11 turdus sive aliud privum (= si(ve) turdus sive aliud) ; *C.* I. 3. 16 quo non arbiter Hadriae maior, tollere seu ponere volt freta (= sive tollere seu ponere).

(*d*) But *sive* (*seu*) in such a position more frequently fol-lows an absolute statement or injunction or a description,

to which it adds an alternative with a condition attached, —
to be translated *or, if;* as

> *C.* I. 15. 25 Sthenelus sciens pugnae, sive (= vel, si) opus est impe-
> ritare equis, non auriga piger; *S.* II. 6. 20 Matutine pater, seu Iane
> libentius audis (= vel Iane, si 'Iane' libentius audis).

120. A group of words which belongs to two or more
members of a sentence in common is sometimes distributed
among them, each part serving to suggest the rest; as

> *Ep.* I. 3. 29 si patriae *volumus,* si nobis *vivere cari; C.* III. 21.
> 2 seu *tu* querellas sive *geris* iocos; *C.* II. 13. 39 nec *curat Orion*
> leones aut timidos *agitare* lyncas · *C.* I. 27. 11 quo *beatus* volnere,
> qua *pereat* sagitta.

121. *Suggestion by similarity.* Where two or more qualities
belong to a series of objects, the poet is sometimes content
to express one with each, leaving the rest to suggestion; as

> *Ep.* I. 16. 50 cautus enim metuit foveam lupus, accipiterque suspectos
> laqueos, et opertum miluus hamum, — where the cautiousness of the
> animal (*cautus*) and his distrust (*suspectos*) of a masked danger (*opertum*)
> are to be understood of all three instances; *Epod.* 5. 37 exsecta uti
> medulla et aridum iecur (*the dry marrow and liver, cut out*).

122. *Suggestion by contrast.* Where a twofold contrast
exists between two objects, it may be indicated by attribut-
ing to them single qualities which *do not match.* Each quality expressed will then suggest its opposite in the other
object; as

> *C.* III. 13. 6 *gelidos* inficiet tibi *rubro* sanguine rivos, — where the
> *clear, cold* water is contrasted with the *warm, red* blood; *C.* II. 3. 9
> quo pinus *ingens albaque* populus umbram hospitalem consociare amant,
> — i. e. the *tall, dark* pine and the *shorter, white* poplar.

123. In illustrative comparisons Horace is fond of giving
greater vividness to the figure by identifying the subject
with it completely (with or without omission of the particle
of comparison); as

> *Ep.* II. 2. 97 caedimur et totidem plagis consumimus hostem, lento
> Samnites ad lumina prima duello (i. e. velut Samnites, etc.); *Ep.*. II.
> 3. 475 quem vero arripuit [poeta] tenet occiditque legendo, non missura

cutem nisi plena cruoris hirudo ; *C.* I. 15. 29 quem *tu,* cervus uti vallis in altera visum parte lupum *graminis immemor, sublimi fugies mollis anhelitu.*

Attributes.

124. In poetical language a quality of a person or thing is often attributed to some part of it, or to some object which from close association is felt to partake of the quality, or to some action which manifests it ; as

C. III. 1. 17 destrictus ensis cui super *impia cervice* pendet ; *C.* I. 3. 40 neque patimur *iracunda* Iovem ponere *fulmina ; Epod.* 10. 14 *impiam* Aiacis *ratem ; C.* I. 37. 6 dum Capitolio regina *dementis ruinas* . . . parabat ; *C.* III. 1. 42 purpurarum *sidere clarior usus.* In this way a quality is often suggested without being expressly attributed ; as *C.* IV. 4. 57 ut ilex tonsa bipennibus nigrae feraci frondis in Algido, — where the dark foliage is that of the ilex itself.

125. A quality is often attributed to an object which it does not itself possess, but which is reflected upon it, as it were, from the effect it produces in others ; as

C. I. 5. 7 *nigris* ventis (i. e. those that darken the sky) ; so I. 7. 15 *albus* Notus ; *C.* II. 7. 21, *oblivioso* Massico (that induces forgetfulness) ; *C.* II. 10. 15 *informis* hiemes (marring the face of nature).

126. An attribute may be brought into greater prominence — (*a*) By Hendiadys ; as

Epod. 5. 54 iram atque numen, *all-powerful wrath ;*

(*b*) By means of an abstract substantive, with the person who possesses the quality and is the logical subject of the sentence appended in the form of a limiting genitive or an adjective (a Homeric device) ; as

S. II. 1. 72 ubi se a volgo et scaena in secreta remorant *virtus Scipiadae* et *mitis sapientia Laeli ; C.* III. 21. 11 narratur et prisci *Catonis* saepe mero caluisse *virtus ; Ep.* II. 1. 191 trahitur *regum fortuna ; C.* I. 3. 36 perrupit Acheronta *Herculeus* labor ;

(*c*) By a substantive in apposition ; as

C. I. 1. 1 atavis edite *regibus* (= *regiis*); *C.* I. 4. 16 iam te premet nox *fabulae*que manes. The appositive may itself have a modifier ; as *C.* I. 3. 20 *infamis scopulos* Acroceraunia.

Enallage.

127. The singular is occasionally used for the plural, either collectively (especially with an adjective of number or quantity) or putting one object to represent its class ; as

Epod. 2. 31 *multa cane; Ep.* II. 3. 203 (tibia) *foramine pauco; Epod.* 3. 14 (Medea) *serpente* fugit *alite; C.* I. 37. 3 ornare *pulvinar* deorum.

128. The poets use the plural not only of abstracts and of names of things reckoned in bulk (*amores, irae, calores, acumina; cruores, vina, Caecuba,* and the like), expressing occurrences of a quality, kinds of a substance, etc., as in prose, but even of substantives which designate only a single object or action ; as

C. I. 2. 15 *monumenta* regis *templa*que Vestae (each a single structure) ; *C.* III. 27. 75 *tua* sectus orbis *nomina* ducet ; *C.* III. 5. 52 populum *reditus* (sc. of Regulus to Carthage) morantem ; *Epod.* 17. 3 Dianae non movenda *numina.*

129. The poet often uses an archaic simple verb in place of the more exact compound form in current use ; as

C. III. 25. 16 manibus *vertere* fraxinos (for *evertere*) ; *C.* III. 27. 74 *mitte* singultus (for *omitte*) ; *C.* III. 24. 32 virtutem incolumem odimus, sublatam ex oculis *quaerimus* invidi (for *requirimus*).

Metonymy.

130. The name of a divinity standing for his special province is particularly common ; as

Epod. 7. 3 campis atque *Neptuno* super (i. e. on land and sea) ; *C.* III. 24. 13 iugera liberas fruges et *Cererem* ferunt ; *C.* III. 16. 34 *Bacchus* in amphora languescit. (See Lucr. II. 652 *sqq.*)

Alliteration and Assonance.

131. Alliteration and assonance hold a very subordinate place in the structure of Horace's poetry, but he employs them to a limited extent. Alliterative sequences that bear the stamp of conscious effort, such as

S. I. 6. 57   *p*udor *p*rohibebat *p*lura *p*rofari

are extremely rare, except where correspondence of sound
with sense is aimed at, as

S. II. 8. 78   videre*s*
                     *s*tridere *s*ecreta divi*s*os aure *s*u*s*urros
C. I. 4. 13   *p*allida mors aequo *p*ulsat *p*ede *p*au*p*erum tabernas
C. III. 5. 49   quae sibi *b*a*r*ba*r*us
                     *tor*tor pa*rar*et

  Alliterative or assonant pairs, like

              dulce decus,   Pontica pinus,   vera virtus,
              maius meliusve,   arcis attigit,   obruit otio,

come in from time to time in a natural way; sometimes
two pairs in succession, as

C. I. 1. 16   *m*ercator *m*etuens, *o*tium et *o*ppidi
C. II. 1. 1   *m*otum ex *M*etello *c*onsule *c*ivicum
C. III. 2. 1   *a*ngustam *a*mice *p*auperiem *p*ati

But in general Horace avoids mere iteration by alternating the recurring sounds with one another or judiciously
distributing them, often with reference to metrical or
syntactical connection, so that the reader feels the pleasing effect with little or no consciousness of the manner
in which it is produced.   The following examples will
illustrate his method :

C. I. 29. 11   *p*ronos *r*elabi *p*osse *r*ivos
C. IV. 5. 24   *c*ulpam *p*oena *p*remit *c*omes
C. III. 17. 8   *li*to*r*ibus *t*enui*ss*e *Lir*im | *la*te *t*yrannu*s*
C. IV. 2. 3   *n*ititur *p*ennis, vitreo daturus
                     *n*omina *p*onto
C. II. 8. 15   semper *a*rdentis *a*cuens *s*agittas
                     *c*ote *c*ruenta
C. II. 6. 15   *vi*ridique certat | baca *V*enafro
C. II. 1. 36   quae *c*a*r*et *or*a cru*or*e n*os*tr*o* ?
Epod. 16. 47   *mel*la cava *m*anant ex *il*ice, *m*ontibus *al*tis
                     *l*evis cre*p*ante *l*ym*p*ha desi*li*t *p*ede

III. VERSIFICATION AND PROSODY
OF THE LYRIC POEMS.

(A) VERSIFICATION.

NOTE. — In all the rhythms used by Horace the last syllable of the verse is *syllaba anceps*, i. e., its quantity is not considered. This is to be understood in all cases, though, for the sake of greater simplicity, it has not been indicated in the metrical schemes here given, being common to all. The sign ‿ is used to indicate two short syllables which are to be pronounced in the time of one short. In other respects the metrical notation is that adopted in the grammars in current use. 'Caesura' (‖) is used to denote the regular pause in the verse, whether it falls within a measure (caesura in the stricter sense) or between two measures (diaeresis).

Dactylic Verses.

132. The *Hexameter* (dactylic hexameter catalectic):

$$\_\smile\smile \mid \_\smile\smile \mid \_\Vert\smile\smile \mid \_\smile\smile \mid \_(\smile\smile) \mid \_\smile \wedge$$

Caesura in the second and fourth feet instead of the third, and 'feminine' caesura (*i. e.* between the short syllables of the dactyl) in the third are occasionally found, as *Epod.* 16. 31, *C.* I. 28. 15. A spondee in the fifth foot occurs four times, always in proper names: *C.* I. 28. 21 *Ōri|ōnis; Epod.* 13. 9 *Cyllē|neā;* 16. 17 *Phōcāe|ōrum;* 16. 29 *Āppēn|nīnus.* (There is only one spondiac verse in the Satires and Epistles, — *Ep.* II. 3. 467.)

133. The *Dactylic Tetrameter* (catalectic):

$$\_\smile\smile \mid \_\smile\smile \mid \_(\smile\smile) \mid \_\smile \wedge$$

A spondee in the third foot occurs once (*C.* I. 28. 2).

134. The *Lesser Archilochian* verse (dactylic trimeter catalectic):

$$\_\smile\smile \mid \_\smile\smile \mid \_\overline{\wedge}$$

Iambic and Trochaic Verses.

135. The *Iambic Trimeter :* *

$$\breve{\smallfrown} \;\; \bar{} \;\; \smile \;\; \bar{} \;\; | \;\; \breve{\smallfrown} \; \| \;\; \bar{} \;\; \smile \;\; \bar{} \;\; | \;\; \breve{\smallfrown} \; \bar{} \;\; \smile \; \bar{}$$

$$\smile \; \breve{\smile}\breve{\smile} \;\; \smile \;\; \breve{\smile}\breve{\smile} \;\; | \;\; \smile \; \| \; \breve{\smile}\breve{\smile} \;\; \smile \;\; \breve{\smile}\breve{\smile} \;\; |$$

$$> \; \breve{\smile}\breve{\smile} \qquad\qquad | \; > \; \| \; \breve{\smile}\breve{\smile} \qquad\qquad |$$

$$(\smallsmile \; \bar{}) ? \qquad\qquad\qquad | \qquad\qquad\qquad | \; (\smallsmile \; \bar{}) ?$$

The caesura is occasionally hepthemimeral (as *Epod.* 1. 15 ;
4. 3 ; 5. 3, etc.) ; in two verses it falls after the prefix of
a compound word : *Epod.* 1. 19 *im ‖ plumibus ;* 11. 15
in ‖ aestuet (cf. 149, 150, 155, and see 115 *e*).   Resolution
is sparingly used.   The apparent dactyl occurs chiefly in
the first foot, seldom in the third ; the tribrach oftenest
in the second and third, rarely in the first or fourth ; and
both of these substitutions are always so made that the
ictus coincides with a word-accent (in two cases with a
secondary accent only : *Epod.* 17. 12 *hómicidam ;* 74 *ínimi-
cis*), usually falling on the antepenult of a trisyllabic word.
The anapaest occurs in the first foot only twice : *Epod.* 2.
35 *pavidum*, 65 *positos* (which are perhaps to be read by
syncope as spondees ; see 183) ; and apparently three
times in the fifth : *Epod.* 2. 35 *laqueo*, 5. 79 *inferius*, 11. 23
mulierculam ; but see 180, 181.

136. The *Pure Iambic Trimeter :*

$$\smile \; \bar{} \; \smile \; \bar{} \; | \; \smile \; \| \; \bar{} \; \smile \; \bar{} \; | \; \smile \; \bar{} \; \smile \; \bar{}$$

A hepthemimeral caesura occurs once (*Epod.* 16. 4).

137. The *Iambic Dimeter :*

$$\breve{\smallfrown} \;\; \bar{} \;\; \smile \;\; \bar{} \; | \; \breve{\smallfrown} \; \bar{} \;\; \smile \; \bar{}$$

$$> \; \breve{\smile}\breve{\smile} \;\; \smile \; \breve{\smile}\breve{\smile} \; |$$

---

* The metrical scheme is here given, to avoid confusion, in the form
presented in the Greek and Latin grammars in common use.   Iambic
rhythm may also be represented, in accordance with our modern system
of musical notation, thus : $\breve{\smallfrown}$: ͜ $\smile$ ͜ $\breve{\smallfrown}$ | ͜ $\smile$ etc. ; and it will be
necessary to adopt this method for those rhythms which are used in
composite and logaoedic verse, where, though technically iambic, they
are essentially trochaic in character.

Resolution occurs in only four verses (*Epod.* 2. 62 ; 3. 8 ; 5. 48 ; 15. 24) and under the same restrictions as in the trimeter (135). The scheme may also be written thus :

$$\breve{\supset} \vdots \; \angle \; \cup \; \angle \; \breve{\supset} \; | \; \angle \; \cup \; \angle \; \wedge$$

138. The *Iambic Trimeter Catalectic:*

$$\breve{\supset} \vdots \; \angle \; \cup \; \angle \; \breve{\supset} \; \| \; \angle \; \cup \; \angle \; \cup \; | \; \underline{\cup} \; \angle \; \wedge$$
$$(\cup\cup)?$$

Resolution occurs once, — *C.* II. 18. 34 *regumque pueris,* — unless we are to read by synizesis, *pùeris* (see 180).

139. The *Nine-Syllable Alcaic* (two trochaic dipodies, with anacrusis) : $\breve{\supset} \vdots \; \angle \; \cup \; | \; \angle \; > \; | \; \angle \; \cup \; | \; \angle \; \cup$

The second trochee is always irrational.

140. The *Euripidean* verse (pure trochaic dimeter catalectic) : $\angle \; \cup \; \angle \; \cup \; | \; \angle \; \cup \; \angle \; \wedge$

Composite Verses.

141. In several of the epodic distichs used by Horace, one of the verses is made up of two distinct *cola*, one dactylic and the other iambic or trochaic. Such a verse is usually 'asynartete,' that is, its two *cola* are not welded together (as, for example, the two halves of a hexameter are), but the end of the first *colon* is treated in all respects as the end of a verse, having *syllaba anceps*, and admitting hiatus before a following vowel. Whether the dactyl was read in trochaic time (cyclic dactyl) is uncertain. It is not improbable that there was a change of time in the middle of the verse.

142. The *Greater Archilochian* verse, composed of a dactylic tetrameter acatalectic and a trochaic tripody :

$$\angle \; \overline{\cup\cup} \; | \; \angle \; \overline{\cup\cup} \; | \; \angle \; \| \; \overline{\cup\cup} \; | \; \angle \; \cup\cup \; | \; \angle \; \cup \; | \; \angle \; \cup \; | \; \angle \; \cup$$

In the ten verses which Horace has left us in this measure

(*C.* I. 4) there is always caesura after the third ictus, and the first *colon* ends with a short final syllable, without hiatus.

143. The *Elegiambus*, composed of a lesser Archilochian (134) — which is identical with the second *colon* of the elegiac pentameter — and an iambic dimeter (137) :

$$\_\cup\cup \mid \_\cup\cup \mid \_\wedge \mid \stackrel{\smile}{\cup} \vdots \_\cup\_\stackrel{\smile}{\cup} \mid \_\cup\_\wedge$$

144. The *Iambelegus*, composed of the same *cola* as 143, but in reverse order :

$$\stackrel{\smile}{\cup} \vdots \_\cup\_\stackrel{\smile}{\cup} \mid \_\cup\_\wedge \mid \_\cup\cup \mid \_\cup\cup \mid \_\bar{\wedge}$$

No resolution occurs in the iambic *cola*, and no substitution in the dactylic, of either 143 or 144.

Logaoedic Verses.

145. Most of the Odes are composed in logaoedic rhythms, made up of trochaic, with an admixture of dactylic, elements. The combination of dactyl and trochee produces a succession of syllables identical with the *choriamb* (— ∪ ∪ —), especially where the trochee is syncopated ($\stackrel{\smile}{\cup}\cup \mid \stackrel{\smile}{\cup}$) and the measure thus formed is repeated (as in 149 and 150, below). For this reason the rhythms were regarded by late Roman metrical writers as choriambic, and some of the verses (147–150, and sometimes 152) are still so called. Their choriambic character is only apparent ; but it is nevertheless important to observe this measure, — which may, for convenience be called the 'choriambic measure' — as its repetition constitutes the characteristic feature of some of the verses now to be explained. Thus, in 149 the rhythm proceeds through the choriambic measure (‾∪ ∪ ∣ ∟) precisely as in 148 ; it then goes back, as it were, to the beginning of that measure and repeats it, but without syncopation (‾∪ ∪ ∣ ∟ ∥ ‾∪ ∪ ∣ — ∪), and continues with trochaic movement to the close of the verse, as in 147. In the same way, 150 is developed from 149, and 152 from 151.

146. In his logaoedics Horace observes the following rules, prescribed in the metrical theories of his time, but unknown to the Greek lyric poets and to Catullus :

(*a*). Two choriambic measures in the same verse are separated by caesura.

(*b*). An irrational spondee takes the place of a trochee before the first dactyl ; thus, $-\; > \;|\; \overset{\smile}{-}\; \smile\; |$, not $-\; \smile\; |\; \overset{\smile}{-}\; \smile\; |$.

Horace's logaoedic verses are as follows :

147. The *Glyconic* (second Glyconic catalectic) :

$$\overset{\prime}{-}\; > \;|\; \overset{\prime}{-}\; \smile\; |\; \overset{\prime}{-}\; \smile\; |\; \overset{\prime}{-}\; \wedge$$

Horace appears to have admitted a trochee before the first dactyl (cf. 146 *b*) in *C.* I. 15. 36 ; but see note.

148. The *Pherecratic* (second Pherecratic, to be read as a doubly catalectic tetrapody) :

$$\overset{\prime}{-}\; > \;|\; \overset{\prime}{-}\; \smile\; |\; \overset{\prime}{-}\; |\; \overset{\prime}{-}\; \wedge$$

149. The *Lesser Asclepiad :*

$$\overset{\prime}{-}\; > \;|\; \overset{\prime}{-}\; \smile\; |\; \overset{\prime}{-}\; \|\; \overset{\prime}{-}\; \smile\; |\; \overset{\prime}{-}\; \smile\; |\; \overset{\prime}{-}\; \wedge$$

Caesura is neglected in *C.* IV. 8. 17 ; but the text here is in doubt. Caesura falls after the prefix of a compound word in II. 12. 25 *de*‖*torquet* (cf. 135, 150, 155, and see 115 *e*).

150. The *Greater Asclepiad :*

$$\overset{\prime}{-}\; > \;|\; \overset{\prime}{-}\; \smile\; |\; \overset{\prime}{-}\; \|\; \overset{\prime}{-}\; \smile\; |\; \overset{\prime}{-}\; \|\; \overset{\prime}{-}\; \smile\; |\; \overset{\prime}{-}\; \smile\; |\; \overset{\prime}{-}\; \wedge$$

Caesura falls after a prefix in *C.* I. 18. 16 *per*‖*lucidior* (cf. 135, 149, 155, and see 115 *e*).

151. The *Lesser Sapphic :*

$$\overset{\prime}{-}\; \smile\; |\; \overset{\prime}{-}\; > \;|\; \overset{\prime}{-}\; \|\; \smile\smile\; |\; \overset{\prime}{-}\; \smile\; |\; \overset{\prime}{-}\; \smile$$

In the hands of Sappho and Alcaeus, and of Catullus, this verse had a much freer movement. The quantity of the fourth syllable was not fixed, and there was no regular caesura. In Horace the fourth syllable is invariably long (see 146 *b*) and caesura in the dactyl is strictly observed, usually falling after the long syllable; 'feminine' caesura (⏜‖⏑) is frequent in the *Carmen Saeculare* and in Book IV., rare in the earlier books.

152. The *Greater Sapphic :*

$$\underline{} \smile \mid \underline{} > \mid \underline{} \parallel \smile\smile \mid \underline{} \parallel \underline{}\smile \smile \mid \underline{} \smile \mid \underline{} \smile$$
(or, perhaps, $\parallel \underline{}\smile \smile \mid \underline{} \smile \mid \underline{} \mid \underline{} \wedge$)

153. The *Adonic :*

$$\underline{}\smile \smile \mid \underline{} \smile \text{ (or, perhaps, } \underline{}\smile \smile \mid \underline{} \mid \underline{} \wedge)$$

154. The *Aristophanic :*

$$\underline{}\smile \smile \mid \underline{} \smile \mid \underline{} \smile \text{ (or, perhaps, } \underline{}\smile \smile \mid \underline{} \smile \mid \underline{} \mid \underline{} \wedge)$$

155. The *Greater (eleven-syllable) Alcaic :*

$$\breve{\smile} \vdots \underline{} \smile \mid \underline{} > \parallel \underline{}\smile \smile \mid \underline{} \smile \mid \underline{} \wedge$$

In Alcaeus the fifth syllable, like the anacrusis, is of variable quantity, and there is no fixed caesura. In Horace the anacrusis is usually, and in Book IV. always, long; caesura is neglected in only two instances (*C.* I. 37. 14, IV. 14. 17); in three it falls after a prefix, — *C.* I. 16. 21 *ex‖ercitus;* 37. 5 *de‖promere;* II. 17. 21 *in‖credibili* (cf. 135, 149, 150, and see 115 *e*).

156. The *Lesser (ten-syllable) Alcaic :*

$$\underline{}\smile \smile \mid \underline{}\smile \smile \mid \underline{} \smile \mid \underline{} \smile$$

Strophes and Systems.

157. In the Epodes, with the exception of the seventeenth, which consists of 81 iambic trimeters, every poem has an even number of verses, the unit of versification being a strophe of two verses, — the epodic distich from which the book derives its name (§ 18). In the Odes the number of verses is in all cases a multiple of four, with the exception of *C.* IV. 8, which contains 34 verses. In view of this striking fact, and in spite of *C.* IV. 8, — the text of which is open to grave suspicion on grounds quite independent of its metrical structure, — Meineke laid down the canon that Horace's odes were composed in tetrastichs, or strophes of four verses, and that accordingly where an ode is apparently written in distichs or monostichs, these were designed to be grouped together to form tetrastichs. This theory rests on a much narrower basis of induction than appears at first sight ; for of Horace's 104 odes only 18 are written in distichs, and in monostichs only 7. Horace may have desired to make these few odes conform to the rule imposed on the great majority by their metrical structure, but that is a different thing from saying that the unit of versification was the tetrastich. In a number of the odes the distichs are of the same character, — in two odes identical (see 162), — with those used in the Epodes, where they cannot be grouped in twos. It is true that the text of *C.* IV. 8 is probably corrupt, but it is by no means clear that a reduction to 32 or to 28 verses is the way to heal it. It is true, further, that in *C.* III. 9, which is a dialogue, two distichs at a time are assigned to each speaker, — one would be rather short for the purpose ; but in *C.* I. 1, on the other hand, a division into tetrastichs is curiously at cross purposes with the course of thought, while the significant manner in which the first two and the last two verses are set off by their content from the rest of the poem points to a probable grouping of such monostichs in twos, if they have any strophic character at all. In the remaining monostichic odes (I. 11, 18, III. 30, IV. 10) — leaving out of account III. 12 which has only four verses — the connection of thought gives no suggestion of an arrangement by strophes.

The lyric metres used by Horace are as follows :

158. The *Iambic Trimeter* (see 135).   *Epode* 17.

159. The *Iambic Strophe:* an iambic trimeter (135) coupled with an iambic dimeter (137) : —

$$\overline{\smile} \; \acute{\smile} \cup \acute{\smile} \mid \overline{\smile} \; \| \; \acute{\smile} \cup \acute{\smile} \mid \overline{\smile} \; \acute{\smile} \cup \acute{\smile}$$
$$\overline{\smile} \; \acute{\smile} \cup \acute{\smile} \mid \overline{\smile} \; \; \acute{\smile} \cup \acute{\smile}$$

For substitutions see 135, 137.   *Epodes* 1–10.

160. The *First Pythiambic Strophe:* a dactylic hexameter (132) coupled with an iambic dimeter (137) : —

$$\acute{\smile} \; \overline{\cup\cup} \mid \acute{\smile} \; \overline{\cup\cup} \mid \acute{\smile} \; \| \; \overline{\cup\cup} \mid \acute{\smile} \; \overline{\cup\cup} \mid \acute{\smile} \; \cup\cup \mid \acute{\smile} \cup \wedge$$
$$\overline{\smile} \; \acute{\smile} \cup \acute{\smile} \mid \overline{\smile} \; \acute{\smile} \cup \acute{\smile}$$

Epodes 14, 15.

161. The *Second Pythiambic Strophe :* a dactylic hexameter (132) coupled with a pure iambic trimeter (136) : —

$$\acute{\smile} \; \overline{\cup\cup} \mid \acute{\smile} \; \overline{\cup\cup} \mid \acute{\smile} \; \| \; \overline{\cup\cup} \mid \acute{\smile} \; \overline{\cup\cup} \mid \acute{\smile} \; {}^{(\overline{\cup\cup})} \mid \_ \cup \wedge$$
$$\cup \acute{\smile} \cup \acute{\smile} \mid \cup \; \| \; \acute{\smile} \cup \acute{\smile} \mid \cup \acute{\smile} \cup \acute{\smile}$$

Epode 16.

162. The *Alcmanian Strophe;* a dactylic hexameter (132) coupled with a dactylic tetrameter (133) : —

$$\acute{\smile} \; \overline{\cup\cup} \mid \acute{\smile} \; \overline{\cup\cup} \mid \acute{\smile} \; \| \; \overline{\cup\cup} \mid \acute{\smile} \; \overline{\cup\cup} \mid \acute{\smile} \; {}^{(\overline{\cup\cup})} \mid \acute{\smile} \cup \wedge$$
$$\acute{\smile} \; \overline{\cup\cup} \mid \acute{\smile} \; \overline{\cup\cup} \mid \acute{\smile} \; {}^{(\overline{\cup\cup})} \mid \acute{\smile} \cup \wedge$$

C. I. 7, 28 ; *Epod.* 12.

163. The *First Archilochian Strophe:* a dactylic hexameter (132) coupled with a lesser Archilochian verse (134):—

$$\acute{\smile} \; \overline{\cup\cup} \mid \acute{\smile} \; \overline{\cup\cup} \mid \acute{\smile} \; \| \; \overline{\cup\cup} \mid \acute{\smile} \; \overline{\cup\cup} \mid \acute{\smile} \; \cup\cup \mid \acute{\smile} \cup \wedge$$
$$\acute{\smile} \; \cup\cup \mid \acute{\smile} \; \cup\cup \mid \acute{\smile} \overline{\wedge}$$

C. IV. 7.

164. The *Second Archilochian Strophe:* a dactylic hexameter (132) coupled with an iambelegus (144) : —

$$\_\,\smile\smile \mid \_\,\smile\smile \mid \_\,\| \smile\smile \mid \_\,\smile\smile \mid \_\,\smile\smile \mid \_\,\smile \wedge$$
$$\smile : \_\,\smile \_\,\smile \mid \_\,\smile \_\,\wedge \mid \_\,\smile\smile \mid \_\,\smile\smile \mid \_\,\overline{\wedge}$$

Epod. 13.

165. The *Third Archilochian Strophe:* an iambic trimeter (135) coupled with an elegiambus (143) : —

$$\smile \_\,\smile \_\, \mid \smile \| \_\,\smile \_\, \mid \smile \_\,\smile \_\,$$
$$\_\,\smile\smile \mid \_\,\smile\smile \mid \_\,\wedge \mid \smile : \_\,\smile \_\,\smile \mid \_\,\smile \_\,\wedge$$

Epod. 11. (For vs. 23, see, 135, 181.)

166. The *Fourth Archilochian Strophe:* a greater Archilochian verse (142) coupled with an iambic trimeter catalectic (138) : —

$$\_\,\smile\smile \mid \_\,\smile\smile \mid \_\,\| \smile\smile \mid \_\,\ \smile\smile \mid \_\,\smile \mid \_\,\smile \mid \_\,\smile$$
$$\smile : \_\,\smile \_\,\smile \| \_\,\smile \_\,\smile \mid \llcorner\,\_\,\wedge$$

C. I. 4.

167. The *Trochaic Strophe:* a Euripidean verse (140) coupled with an iambic trimeter catalectic (138) : —

$$\_\,\smile \_\,\smile \mid \_\,\smile \_\,\wedge$$
$$\smile : \_\,\smile \_\,\smile \| \_\,\smile \_\,\smile \mid \llcorner\,\_\,\wedge$$

C. II. 18. (For vs. 34, see 138).

168. The *Ionic System,* consisting of pure *Ionici a minore* ($\smile\smile \_\,\_\,$) in series of ten. There is usually diaeresis at the end of each foot.

$$\smile\smile \_\,\_\, \mid \smile\smile \_\,\_\, \mid \smile\smile \_\,\_\, \mid \smile\smile \_\,\_\, \mid$$
$$\smile\smile \_\,\_\, \mid \smile\smile \_\,\_\, \mid \smile\smile \_\,\_\, \mid \smile\smile \_\,\_\, \mid$$
$$\smile\smile \_\,\_\, \mid \smile\smile \_\,\_\,$$

C. III. 12.

169. The *Lesser Asclepiad Metre:* a series of lesser Asclepiad verses (149 ; see also 157) : —

$$\_\,> \mid \smile\smile \mid \llcorner\,\| \smile\smile \mid \_\,\smile \mid \_\,\wedge$$

C. I. 1 ; III. 30 ; IV. 8.

170. The *Greater Asclepiad Metre:* a series of greater Asclepiad verses (150; see also 157) :—

$$\underline{\angle} > \mid \underline{-} \cup \mid \underline{\angle} \parallel \underline{-} \cup \mid \underline{\angle} \parallel \underline{-} \cup \mid \underline{\angle} \cup \mid \underline{\angle} \wedge$$

C. I. 11, 18; IV. 10.

171. The *First Asclepiad Strophe:* a Glyconic (147) coupled with a lesser Asclepiad (149) :—

$$\underline{\angle} > \mid \underline{-} \cup \mid \underline{\angle} \cup \mid \underline{\angle} \wedge$$
$$\underline{\angle} > \mid \underline{-} \cup \mid \quad \underline{\angle} \parallel \underline{-} \cup \mid \underline{\angle} \cup \mid \underline{\angle} \wedge$$

C. I. 3, 13, 19, 36; III. 9, 15, 19, 24, 25, 28; IV. 1, 3. Elision at the end of the Glyconic occurs *C.* IV. 1. 35.

172. The *Second Asclepiad Strophe:* three lesser Asclepiads (149) and a Glyconic (147) :—

$$\underline{\angle} > \mid \underline{-} \cup \mid \underline{\angle} \parallel \underline{-} \cup \mid \underline{\angle} \cup \mid \underline{\angle} \wedge$$
$$\underline{\angle} > \mid \underline{-} \cup \mid \underline{\angle} \parallel \underline{-} \cup \mid \underline{\angle} \cup \mid \underline{\angle} \wedge$$
$$\underline{\angle} > \mid \underline{-} \cup \mid \underline{\angle} \parallel \underline{-} \cup \mid \underline{\angle} \cup \mid \underline{\angle} \wedge$$
$$\underline{\angle} > \mid \underline{-} \cup \mid \underline{\angle} \cup \mid \underline{\angle} \wedge$$

C. I. 6, 15, 24, 33; II. 12; III. 10, 16; IV. 5, 12.

173. The *Third Asclepiad Strophe:* two lesser Asclepiads (149), a Pherecratic (148), and a Glyconic (147) :—

$$\underline{\angle} > \mid \underline{-} \cup \mid \underline{\angle} \parallel \underline{-} \cup \mid \underline{\angle} \cup \mid \underline{\angle} \wedge$$
$$\underline{\angle} > \mid \underline{-} \cup \mid \underline{\angle} \parallel \underline{-} \cup \mid \underline{\angle} \cup \mid \underline{\angle} \wedge$$
$$\underline{\angle} > \mid \underline{-} \cup \mid \underline{\angle} \mid \underline{\angle} \wedge$$
$$\underline{\angle} > \mid \underline{-} \cup \mid \underline{\angle} \cup \mid \underline{\angle} \wedge$$

C. I. 5, 14, 21, 23; III. 7, 13; IV. 13.

174 (*a*). The *Sapphic Strophe:* three lesser Sapphic verses (151) and an Adonic (153) :—

$$\underline{\angle} \cup \mid \underline{\angle} > \mid \underline{\angle} \parallel \sim \mid \underline{\angle} \cup \mid \underline{\angle} \cup$$
$$\underline{\angle} \cup \mid \underline{\angle} > \mid \underline{\angle} \parallel \sim \mid \underline{\angle} \cup \mid \underline{\angle} \cup$$
$$\underline{\angle} \cup \mid \underline{\angle} > \mid \underline{\angle} \parallel \sim \mid \underline{\angle} \cup \mid \underline{\angle} >$$
$$\underline{-} \cup \mid \underline{\angle} \cup$$

Next to the Alcaic (176) the metre most used by Horace :
C. I. 2, 10, 12, 20, 22, 25, 30, 32, 38 ; II. 2, 4, 6, 8, 10, 16 ;
III. 8, 11, 14, 18, 20, 22, 27 ; IV. 2, 6, 11 ; *C. S.*

(*b*). For the 'feminine' caesura, see 151. Sappho appears to have treated the third Sapphic and the Adonic as
one continuous verse. Horace does not follow this practice
absolutely, but he has hiatus between the two verses in only
four cases (*C.* I. 2. 47 ; 12. 7, 31 ; 22. 15) in a total of 206
strophes ; and in all but 12 instances a spondee (by synapheia) precedes the dactyl of the Adonic. He makes the
two verses continuous in *C.* I. 2. 19, 25. 11, II. 16. 7 ; and
he allows elision at the end of the third verse in IV. 2. 23
and *C. S.* 47. Elision at the end of the second verse occurs
in II. 2. 18, 16. 34, IV. 2. 22.

175. The *Greater Sapphic Strophe:* an Aristophanic verse
(154) coupled with a greater Sapphic (152) : —

$$-\smile\smile \mid -\smile \mid -\smile$$
$$-\smile \mid -> \mid - \parallel \smile\smile \mid \smile \parallel -\smile\smile \mid -\smile \mid -\smile$$
C. I. 8.

176 (*a*). The *Alcaic Strophe:* two greater Alcaic verses
(155), a nine-syllable Alcaic (139), and a lesser Alcaic
(156) : —

$$\breve{\circ} : -\smile \mid -> \parallel -\smile\smile \mid -\smile \mid -\wedge$$
$$\breve{\circ} : -\smile \mid -> \parallel -\smile\smile \mid -\smile \mid -\wedge$$
$$\breve{\circ} : -\smile \mid -> \mid -\smile \mid -\smile$$
$$-\smile\smile \mid -\smile\smile \mid -\smile \mid -\smile$$

The metre most frequently used by Horace : *C.* I. 9, 16,
17, 26, 27, 29, 31, 34, 35, 37 ; II. 1, 3, 5, 7, 9, 11, 13, 14,
15, 17, 19, 20 ; III. 1–6, 17, 21, 23, 26, 29 ; IV. 4, 9, 14, 15.

(*b*). Elision at the end of the third verse occurs II. 3. 27 ;
III. 29. 35.

(B) PROSODY.

177. A final syllable ending in a short vowel is not length-ened in Horace before a word beginning with two conso-nants.

178. The prosody of certain proper names is unsettled :
C. III. 30. 13 *Ītalos*, but II. 7. 4 *Ĭtalo ;* I. 28. 20 *Prōser-pina*, II. 13. 21 *Prŏserpinae ;* I. 28. 21 *Ōrionis, Epod.* 15. 7
Ŏrion ; C. S. 1 *Dĭana*, ib. 70 *Dīana.* Cf. also *Epod.* 2. 42
Apŭli, 3. 16 *Apūliae.*

Horace has *-ĕrunt* in the third person plural of the perfect
indicative active, *Epod.* 9. 17 *vertĕrunt.* It occurs also
S. I. 10. 45 *adnuĕrunt* and *Ep.* I. 4. 7 *dedĕrunt* (cf. *C.* III.
6. 7 *dedērunt*); but nowhere in the Odes.

179. The final syllable of the third person singular,
present or perfect, indicative is long in a few instances
under the ictus, as in old Latin (see Allen's *Remnants of
Early Latin, Introd.* 52 ff.) :

C. I. 3. 36	pérrupít Acherónta Hérculeús labór
C. I. 13. 6	cérta séde manét ‖ úmor et ín genás
C. II. 6. 14	ángulús ridét ‖ ubi nón Hymétto
C. II. 13. 16	caéca timét aliúnde fáta
C. III. 16. 26	quám si quícquid arát ‖ ímpiger Ápulús
C. III. 24. 5	sí figít adamántinós

Once in arsis, before the caesura :

C. III. 5. 17   si nón perírēt ‖ immiserabilis

Horace practiced this license in the Satires also, but in
his latest writings, the Epistles and the fourth book of the
Odes, he abstained from it altogether.

180. SYNIZESIS : *C.* II. 7. 5 *Pompei ;* apparently also, *Epod.*
2. 35 *laqueo* (see 135) ; and perhaps *C.* II. 18. 34 *pueris* (see
138). Under this head also are usually classed *C.* I. 35. 17
anteit and 37. 5 *antehac ;* but the *e* of *ante* was probably elided,
and the words pronounced *ant'it, ant'hac.*

181. SYNAERESIS : *C.* III. 4. 41 *consilium ;* III. 6. 6 *prin-cipium* (in both cases the consonantal *i* lengthens the preceding syllable, and its own syllable is elided at the caesura); *Epod.* 12. 7 *vietis ;* perhaps also *Epod.* 5. 79 *inferius*, and 11. 23 *mulierculam* (see 135).

182. DIALYSIS : *C.* I. 23. 4, *Epod.* 13. 2 *siluae.*

183. SYNCOPE : *C.* I. 36. 8 *puertiae ;* II. 2. 2 *lamnae ;* III. 20. 1 *periclo ;* IV. 13. 20 *surpuerat ; Epod.* 9. 1 *repostum ;* 9. 9, 17. 72 *vincla ;* perhaps also *Epod.* 2. 35 *pav(i)dum*, 65 *pos(i)tum* (see 135). Syncopated verb forms like *natarunt, complesti, intrarit, promorat* are of frequent occurrence.

184. ELISION. In his earliest Epodes Horace appears to have studiously avoided elision. In Epode 16 the hexameters are altogether free from it, and it occurs but three times in the iambics. There is no case in Epode 13, and only one in Epode 12. Later he was less strict, but confined it chiefly to short final syllables, and avoided harsh combinations. Monosyllables are never elided, except the pronouns *me* and *te*, and (once) the adverb *iam* (*Epod.* 17. 1).

185. HIATUS occurs after the interjections *a* and *o*, which, for obvious reasons, are never elided, and in the following undisputed cases : *Epod.* 5. 100 *Esquilinae alites ;* 13. 3 *Threicio Aquilone : C.* I. 28. 24 *capiti inhumato.* The following are doubtful : *C.* II. 20. 13 *Daedaleo ‖ ocior* ; III. 14. 11 *male ominatis* (see notes). For hiatus between the *cola* of ' asynartete ' verses, see 141.

Q. HORATI FLACCI

CARMINA

LIBER PRIMVS

I.

Maecenas atavis edite regibus,
o et praesidium et dulce decus meum :

I. This is Horace's prologue, as III. 30 is his epilogue, to the first edition of his Odes (Intr. 27); and the two poems thus set apart from the rest are written in a metre reserved for them alone. In addressing the prologue to Maecenas the poet dedicates the volume to him. After a brief tribute to his patron he puts forward a modest assertion of the claim of literature, and of lyric poetry in particular, to a place among the varied objects of human pursuit and ambition, which, after all, he implies, have no defense, as against one another, but the overmastering force of individual bent and taste ; and he closes with an expression of his own aspiration to win for himself a place among the poets of the lyre. — Metre, 169 (page lxxxiii).

1. **Maecenas :** Intr. 21 ff. — **atavis :** here used, like *avus*, in a general sense, but indicating re-

moter ancestors, — *forefathers.* — **regibus :** in apposition with **atavis ;** Intr. 126 *c.* The compliment is not an extravagant one, as *rex* suggested to a Roman a much less exalted monarch than 'king' does to us. For similar allusions to Maecenas' ancestry, cf. III. 29. 1, *S.* I. 6. 1 *sqq.*, Prop. IV. 8. 1 *Maecenas eques Etrusco de sanguine regum.*

2. **o et :** for the hiatus, see Intr. 185. — **praesidium, decus :** cf. II. 17. 4 *mearum grande decus columenque rerum.* In each of these places the poet acknowledges both sides of his obligation to his patron, for substantial support and protection, and for the distinction which the friendship of so eminent a man confers. Horace elsewhere (*S.* II. 6. 32) confesses how sweet this distinction was to him ; but **dulce** here, with double application, expresses also his affection for Maecenas ; cf. *dulcis amice, Ep.* I. 7. 12.

Sunt quos curriculo pulverem Olympicum
collegisse iuvat metaque fervidis
5   evitata rotis palmaque nobilis
terrarum dominos evehit ad deos ;
hunc, si mobilium turba Quiritium
certat tergeminis tollere honoribus ;
illum, si proprio condidit horreo

3–6. The ruling passion of the Greek is athletic contests, and a victory at the national games is the summit of his aspirations. For Horace's method in this and the following descriptions, see Intr. 117.

3. sunt quos . . . iuvat, *some men delight.* For the mood, see Intr. 84. — curriculo (from *curriculus*), *with the chariot.* — Olympicum : *i.e.* at Olympia, in the great national games held there every four years.

4. collegisse, *to whirl;* lit., 'to gather' (in a cloud); cf. *pulvis collectus turbine, S.* I. 4. 31. For the tense, see Intr. 81. The meaning is, to be in the chariot race in full career. To make the picture more telling, the two most critical points of the race, the turning-post and the finish, are included (vss. 4, 5).— meta evitata (sc. *iuvat*), *to clear the goal:* Intr. 105. The Greek *hippodromos,* like the Roman circus, was divided longitudinally by a low wall, round which the racing chariots were driven several times. At each end of this wall was a column or turning-post (meta). To turn this as closely as possible, without striking either it or other chariots, called for the utmost skill and, being attended with considerable danger, was the most exhilarating part of the race.

5. palmaque : for *quosque palma ;* cf. *C. S.* 26. The victor at

Olympia was crowned with olive, and a palm branch was placed in his hand (Paus. VIII. 48. 2). The latter practice was borrowed by the Romans (Liv. X. 47. 3), and hence the palm became to them the especial symbol of victory.

6. dominos : in apposition with deos. — evehit ad deos, *exalts them to gods ;* expressing the pride and exultation of victory; cf. IV. 2. 17 ; Cic. *Flacc.* 31 *hoc* (to win at Olympia) *est apud Graecos prope maius et gloriosius quam Romae triumphasse.*

7–10. The highest objects of Roman endeavor, political preferment and wealth. Cf. *Ep.* I. 1. 42 *quae maxima credis esse mala, exiguum censum turpemque repulsam.*

7. hunc : sc. *iuvat,* the force of which, from vs. 4, is still felt, *evehit ad deos* 6 being only a more specific expression of the same idea. — mobilium : in disparagement ; Horace had no respect for office-seeking for the mere purpose of self-advancement. Cf. *S.* I. 6.

8. tergeminis honoribus : instrumental abl. The reference is to the three curule offices, the curule aedileship, praetorship, and consulship. — tollere : Intr. 94 *h.*

9. illum : see vs. 7 n. The great landowner is put forward as a type of successful but unsatisfied craving for wealth. — proprio : *i.e.* not acting merely as agent for

10   quicquid de Libycis verritur areis.
      Gaudentem patrios findere sarculo
      agros Attalicis condicionibus
      numquam demoveas, ut trabe Cypria
      Myrtoum pavidus nauta secet mare ;
15   luctantem Icariis fluctibus Africum
      mercator metuens otium et oppidi

another or for the government. —
horreo : Intr. 69.

10. **quicquid,** *all the grain that,*
suggesting unbounded desire ; cf.
III. 16. 26. — **Libycis** : before the
conquest of Egypt Africa was the
largest source of the city's grain
supply, and expressions like this
appear to have become proverbial ;
cf. *S.* II. 3. 87. — **verritur areis** :
the *area* was a circular space, en-
closed with a low wall and paved
with concrete, on which the heads
of grain, usually without the straw,
were trampled out by cattle (*tri-
tura*). A common way of winnow-
ing was by tossing in the wind with
a shovel (*ventilatio*) till the chaff
was blown away. The grain was
then swept together and removed.

11. **gaudentem,** etc.: from national characteristics the poet proceeds to individual tastes, which he
presents in a series of contrasted
sketches ; and first the rustic who
finds his happiness in keeping up
the old farm. — **patrios** : indicating his lack of enterprise ; he has
added nothing to the fields his
fathers tilled before him. Cf. 12.
43, and the picture of contentment
in *Epod.* 2. 3 ; for the opposite
spirit, II. 18. 23, *S.* II. 6. 8, Juv.
14. 140 *sqq.* — **findere** : Intr. 94 *d.*
— **sarculo** : suggesting the small
scale on which he farms ; he works
with his own hands. The *sarcu-
lum* was a hoe used for loosening

the soil between the rows of growing grain (*sarritio*).

12. **Attalicis condicionibus,**
terms that an Attalus might offer.
The Attali, kings of Pergamon, in
Asia Minor, were famous for their
patronage of literature and for
the munificence with which they
adorned their capital with works
of art. The Romans received a
vivid and lasting impression of
their splendor when the treasures
of Attalus III., the last of the
line, who died B.C. 133, bequeath-
ing his kingdom to the Roman
people, were brought to Rome.

13. **demoveas ut,** *tempt away
to.* — **Cypria** : Cyprus produced
within its own borders all kinds of
material required for shipbuilding
(Am. Marc. XIV. 8. 14). For the
epithets **Cypria, Myrtoum,** etc.,
see Intr. 117, and cf. 35. 7 *sq.*

15. **luctantem,** etc.: in contrast
with the farmer, the restless trader
cannot endure the dullness of
country life, though in the storm
he may sigh for peace and long
for the quiet rural scenes of his
childhood. — **fluctibus** : dative;
Intr. 57.— **Africum,** *the Sou'wester*
(blowing from Africa).

16. **mercator** : not 'merchant'
in our sense, but *trader*, who sails
with his wares in his own ship. —
metuens : with an accusative, because the fear is temporary; with
the genitive it would express a per-

laudat rura sui : mox reficit ratis
quassas, indocilis pauperiem pati.
Est qui nec veteris pocula Massici
20   nec partem solido demere de die
spernit, nunc viridi membra sub arbuto
stratus, nunc ad aquae lene caput sacrae.
Multos castra iuvant et lituo tubae
permixtus sonitus bellaque matribus

manent trait, as *S.* II. 2. 110.—
otium, *peace and quiet;* cf. II. 16.
1 *sqq.*— **oppidi rura :** every town
had its *ager,* or adjacent country
district under its jurisdiction (cf.
ager Romanus, ager Tusculanus,
etc.).

17. **laudat :** *sc.* as happy or conferring happiness (εὐδαιμονίζει), a
sense in which Horace often uses
the word ; cf. *S.* I. 1 9, *Ep.* I. 11.
6. — **sui,** *his native.* — **mox :** the
asyndeton suggests the promptness
with which his natural disposition
asserts itself when the danger is
past.

18. **pauperiem :** *i.e.* moderate
circumstances, such as those of
the farmer, not actual want (*inopia,
egestas*). Horace calls his father,
who was a man of some means,
macro pauper agello (*S.* I. 6. 71).
— **pati :** Intr. 101 *c.*

19–22. Between the restless
enterprise of the trader and the
excitement of war and the chase,
the poet sets a quiet picture of
leisurely enjoyment.

19. **est qui:** the singular suggests
that this character is met with only
now and then. — **Massici** (*sc.
vini*): a much esteemed wine produced on the slopes of Mt. Massicus, on the border between Latium
and Campania. See Intr. 117.

20. **solido die :** *i.e.* one (that
would otherwise be) devoted whol-

ly to business or serious work (cf.
Sen. *Ep.* 83. 3 *hodiernus dies soli-
dus est ; nemo ex illo quicquam
mihi eripuit*). The Roman 'day,'
in this sense, lasted from early
dawn to about the middle of the
afternoon, *octavam circiter horam*
(*Ep.* I. 7. 47).— **demere :** see Intr.
94 *i.*

21. **(nec) spernit :** *i.e.* does
not deem it beneath his dignity,
as, according to the old Roman
notions, it was. For the mood,
see Intr. 84. — **membra :** Intr. 41.
— **arbuto :** a handsome flowering
shrub or tree, common in Greece
and Italy, with evergreen leaves
something like those of our laurel,
and fruit resembling the straw-
berry, — hence called the 'straw-
berry tree.' See Sibthorp's *Flora
Graeca,* tab. 373.

22. **ad aquae caput :** *i.e.* by
the side of some spring.— **lene,
sacrae :** the epithets are inter-
changed : the stream is gentle, and
the spring is sacred (as the haunt
of a naiad). Cf. Intr. 124.

23. **lituo :** for *litui sonitu,* an
economy of phrase common in
prose and verse. The *lituus* was
a long, straight brass trumpet,
curved slightly at the larger end ;
it was used by the cavalry. —
tubae : the trumpet of the in-
fantry, straight throughout.

24. **matribus :** Intr. 54.

25   detestata.   Manet sub Iove frigido
     venator tenerae coniugis immemor,
     seu visa est catulis cerva fidelibus,
     seu rupit teretis Marsus aper plagas.
     Me doctarum hederae praemia frontium
30   dis miscent superis; me gelidum nemus
     Nympharumque leves cum Satyris chori
     secernunt populo, si neque tibias

25. manet, *spends the night,* as in *S.* I. 5. 37; cf. *S.* II. 3. 234. — **Iove,** *the open sky.* The poets use the name of *Iuppiter*, with certain cognate forms from the root *DI, DIV* (cf. *sub divo*, III. 2. 5, *sub divum*, I. 18. 13, *sub diu*, Lucr. IV. 211), for the sky or the air, in which the god of heaven manifests his presence and power in the various phases of sunshine and rain, heat and cold, storm and lightning. Cf. Ennius *ap.* Varr. *L. L.* V. 65 *istic est is Iúpiter quem díco, quem Graecí vocant | áerem, qui véntus est et núbes, imber póstea, | átque ex imbre frígus, ventus póst fit, aer dénuo.*

26. tenerae coniugis : *i.e.* of her anxiety for his safety, the contrast, as in *matribus detestata* 24, bringing out in stronger relief the hardihood of the man.

27. seu . . . seu : in either case the game will be lost unless pursued at once.

28. Marsus : Intr. 117. — **plagas :** used to bar the openings in the thicket (cf. *Epod.* 2. 31 *sq.*). The boar has escaped into the open country.

29. me : the emphatic position (Intr. 116 *b*) marks the transition to his own taste and ambition. In contrast with such pursuits as those last described, Horace finds his own greatest happiness far away

from the busy world, in the presence of nature, where his poetic fancy sees the light-footed denizens of the woods and hears strains of divine music. — **doctarum :** *of men of letters. Doctus* denotes accomplishment in any art (cf. *docte Trebati, S.* II. 1. 78 ; *docte Cati, S.* II. 4. 88). In literature it is a connoisseur as well as a writer (*e.g.*; *S.* I. 10. 87). Here its meaning is limited by **hederae,** the ivy wreath which was the especial prerogative (**praemia**) of the poet, as being sacred to Bacchus, who was one of the patron gods of poets (cf. *Ep.* II. 2. 78, I. 19. 4). — **praemia :** here rather the emblem (cf. *S.* I. 5. 35, Verg. *E.* 7. 25) of the recognized poet than a prize of victory.   For the plurals, see Intr. 128.

30. dis miscent superis : cf. vs. 6 ; but here the feeling expressed is ecstatic delight.

32. si neque, etc.: the favor of the muse is an essential condition. — **tibias,** *pipes.* The *tibia* (αυλός) was a straight, flute-like instrument, but with mouth-piece at the end, like the clarinet ; in some varieties the outer end was curved and flaring. The plural is used because two were commonly played together. (See Howard, *Harv. Studies* IV. p. 1.) The *tibia* as well as the lyre was associated with lyric

Euterpe cohibet nec Polyhymnia
Lesboum refugit tendere barbiton.
35   Quod si me lyricis vatibus inseris,
       sublimi feriam sidera vertice.

II.

Iam satis terris nivis atque dirae
grandinis misit pater, et rubente

poetry; cf. I. 12. 1 *sq.* III. 4. 1.—
neque cohibet : *i.e.* plays freely.

33. Euterpe, Polyhymnia: see
note on *Clio*, 12. 2.

34. Lesboum tendere barbi-
ton : *i.e.* to inspire him as she had
inspired Alcaeus and Sappho ; see
Intr. 26. — tendere, *to tune ;* lit.,
to stretch or tighten (the chords).
For the mood see Intr. 94 *k.*

35. quod si, *and if.* The ode
closes as it began, with two verses
of personal address to Maecenas.
These two couplets are rather
sharply divided from the rest of
the poem, giving the impression
that the intervening verses may
have been originally written without reference to their present purpose, though they are admirably
adapted to it. — lyricis vatibus :
i.e. those of Greece, of whom
there were nine recognized by the
critics as classic. Horace's hope
is that his achievement in Latin
lyric may be regarded by his patron
as making him worthy to be added
to this noble company. — inseris :
cf. II. 5. 21. For the tense, see
Intr. 78 ; for its use with a future
in the apodosis, cf. III. 24. 5.

36. sublimi : proleptic. — feriam sidera : expressing pride of
achievement, like vs. 6. The extravagant phrase is legitimate enough,
involving, as it does, a compliment
to Maecenas' literary judgment,
and there is a touch of humor in it.

II. The first place in the volume
after the dedication is very properly given to an ode in honor of the
emperor. It is the poet's declaration of allegiance to the second
Caesar. There are no certain indications of its date ; the two
great inundations of the Tiber in
B.C. 27 and 22 (Dio Cassius LIII.
20. 1 ; LIV. 1. 1) were too late to
be treated by Horace as visitations
of divine wrath for the killing of
Julius Caesar (B.C. 44). But as an
appeal to rescue the country from
ruin (vs. 25), the ode could not
have been composed after the
settlement of January 27, when
Octavian as first citizen (*princeps*)
received, with the new title *Augustus*, a renewal of the *imperium*
for ten years, and his friends, at
least, regarded the fortunes of the
state as established on a firm
basis. It was probably written in
the period of uncertainty which
preceded this settlement, *i.e.* between the return and triumph of
Octavian in August, 29, and the
end of 28. The portents which
form the subject of the opening
strophes need not be supposed to
have all occurred at one time ;
they may have extended through a
number of years. Beginning with
an impressive account of these
signs of the wrath of heaven at
the Romans for shedding the
blood of their countrymen, the

dexterā sacrās iaculātus arcis
  terruit urbem,

5 terruit gentīs, grave nē redīret
  saeculum Pyrrhae nova monstra questae,
  omne cum Prōteus pecus ēgit altōs
    vīsere montīs,

  piscium et summā genus haesit ulmō,
10 nōta quae sēdes fuerat columbīs,

poet points out the need of a divine mediator, and then leads on
skilfully to the suggestion that the
messenger of heaven is already
among them, fulfilling his appointed task. — Metre, 174.

1. satis, etc.: for the repetition
of the *is* sound, see Intr. 131. It
suggests to the ear the fierce persistency of the storm. — terris :
dative ; Intr. 53. — dirae, *portentous*, applying to nivis as well as
to grandinis ; Intr. 119 *a*. A
heavy fall of snow or a severe
hail-storm was rare enough at
Rome to be accounted a *monstrum*,
or sign of divine displeasure.

2. pater, *the Father* (of gods
and men ; cf. 12. 13 *sqq.*), Jupiter ;
here as the god who wields the
elements ; cf. 1. 25 n. — rubente :
from the glow of the red-hot
thunderbolt.

3. iaculatus : here with an accusative of the thing aimed at ;
cf. *cervos iaculari*, III. 12. 4. —
arcis : the twin summits of the
Capitoline hill, on one of which
was the *Capitolium*, the great temple of Jupiter, Juno, and Minerva
(hence sacras), while the other
was the *Arx* proper.

5. terruit : Intr. 116 *g*. — gentis
(sc. *humanas*), *all mankind ;* cf.
3. 28, II. 13. 20. — ne : after the
idea of fear implied in terruit.
For its position and that of cum,

et, and quae, below, see Intr.
114.

6. saeculum Pyrrhae : *i.e.* the
Deluge (Ovid, *M.* I. 260 *sqq.*).
Pyrrha, daughter of Epimetheus
and Pandora, was the wife of
Deucalion, the Noah of Greek
mythology. Many people believed
that the earth would one day be
overwhelmed in a second flood (cf.
Sen. *N. Q.* III. 27. 1 *cum fatalis
dies diluvii venerit*) ; and the
dreadful prodigy of Jove hurling
his bolts at his own greatest
temple was to the superstitious a
warning that the time was at
hand.— nova, *strange*.— monstra,
marvels ; lit., 'signs' (cf. *moneo*) ;
see note on *dirae* 1.

7. omne cum, etc. : it is a
favorite device of Horace to break
the continuity of an enumeration
of persons or events by dwelling on
some subject in the series and letting the reader's mind rest for a
moment on a picture. Better examples than this are 12. 27 *sqq.*,
III. 4 60 *sqq.* — Proteus: the
keeper of Neptune's sea-calves
(seals), endowed with the gift of
prophecy and the power of assuming various forms (hence our word
'protean') ; cf. *Odys.* IV. 455 *sqq.*,
Verg. *G.* IV. 405 *sqq.*— egit, *drove.*

8. visere : see Intr. 93.

9. piscium genus, *the finny
tribe.* — ulmo : Intr. 71.

et superiecto pavidae natarunt
   aequore dammae.

Vidimus flavum Tiberim retortis
litore Etrusco violenter undis
15 ire deiectum monumenta regis
   templaque Vestae,

Iliae dum se nimium querenti
iactat ultorem, vagus et sinistra

11. **superiecto,** *the overwhelming.*

12. **aequore** : Intr. 69.

13. **vidimus** : the poet returns from his digression to the prodigies which his own generation has witnessed. — **flavum** : a standing epithet of the Tiber, owing to its permanent muddy color ; cf. 8. 8, II. 3. 18 Verg. *A.* VII. 31 (*Tiberinus*) *multa flavus harena.* — **retortis** : as the river falls only fifteen feet between Rome and Ostia, an unusually high tide would cause a stagnation or even a reversal of the current and inundate the lower parts of the city (*nusquam magis aquis quam in urbe stagnantibus*, Plin. *N. H.* III. 55). But the description here of what was evidently an extraordinary inundation implies a stronger current (**violenter**) than we can suppose to have come from the mouth of the river ; it suggests rather a great flood, due to heavy rains and melting snows in the mountains, pouring down the stream and overflowing the banks. The sharp bend which the river makes to the right just below the Island would send the water with some force over the low ground between the Palatine and the Capitoline, with the appearance of being 'hurled away' from the opposite shore.

14. **litore Etrusco** : ordinarily

designating the Italian coast from the mouth of the Tiber northward; but *litus* is also used of the bank of a river (*e.g.* Verg. *A.* VIII. 83), as *ripa* is for the seashore (cf. II. 18. 22, III. 27. 24).

15. **deiectum** : supine. The river is here the river-god, coming in wrath to destroy; cf. *sub Iove,* 1. 25 n. — **monumenta regis** : the Regia, or 'palace' of Numa, used under the Commonwealth as the official residence of the pontifex maximus. *Monumentum* ('memorial'; cf. *moneo*) is often used of a building.

16. **templa Vestae** : adjoining the Regia, so that the latter was sometimes called 'Atrium Vestae,' being used in part as a dwelling for the Vestal virgins. The buildings were situated on the south side of the lower end of the Forum, at the foot of the Palatine. The flood is represented as threatening the most venerable monuments of the city and its holiest shrine. The visitation of divine wrath on a holy place was the punishment for its desecration (cf. 12. 59), — in this case by the murder of the pontifex maximus, Caesar. For the plurals **monumenta, templa,** see Intr. 128.

17. **Iliae** : mother of Romulus and Remus. According to the older tradition, which Horace fol-

labitur ripa Iove non probante u-
20   xorius amnis.

Audiet civis acuisse ferrum,
quo graves Persae melius perirent,
audiet pugnas vitio parentum
    rara iuventus.

25   Quem vocet divum populus ruentis
imperi rebus ?   Prece qua fatigent

lows, she was the daughter of
Aeneas and therefore sister of
Iulus, the mythical ancestor of the
Julian family. After the birth of
the twins she was thrown into the
Tiber, but received by the river-
god as his wife. He is here represented as enraged at the wrong
done her family in the murder of
Julius Caesar.—**dum:** introducing,
as mere attendant circumstance,
the cause or occasion of the main
action ; cf. 6. 9 and see Roby 1665.

18. **sinistra:** *i.e.* the eastern.
The banks of a river are designated as 'right' or 'left' in reference to the personified river himself as he moves in his course.

19. **ripa:** here *over* the bank, in
contrast with *Epod.* 2. 25. The
ablative in both places is that of
'the way by which.' — **non probante:** *i.e.* he had not appointed
the river to this office nor ordained
such extreme retribution. — **u-xo-
rius:** see Intr. 174 *b.*

21. **audiet,** etc. : after setting
forth the signs of divine wrath the
poet proceeds to the cause of it,
— unnatural civil strife ; and this
he presents more effectively by
carrying his reader forward to a
time when it will be dispassionately judged by a generation which
feels only its disastrous effects. —
civis: the emphasis (Intr. 116 *b*)

and the usual meaning of 'fellow-
citizens' attaching to the word
indicate that they are preparing for
a struggle against one another,
as if we should speak, *e.g.*, of
'*brothers* drawing their daggers.'

22. **Persae:** *i.e.* the oriental
peoples, called by Horace indif-
ferently *Medi, Persae,* and *Parthi,*
at this time under the sway of the
Parthian kings, but formerly subject to the Medes and Persians successively, whose names were thus
permanently impressed upon them.
— **perirent:** imperfect subjunctive
of softened assertion in past time,
with apodosis implied in **melius ;**
cf. *falleret,* IV. 6. 16 n ; Gr. 311 *a.*

23. **pugnas:** not only of
preparations for war (**acuisse
ferrum**) but of actual conflict.

24. **rara,** *thinned.* — **iuventus:**
i.e. a younger generation.

25. **divum:** implying that no
mere human help would avail. —
ruentis: the figure is taken from
a building ; cf. II. 1. 32 *Hesperiae
sonitum ruinae.*

26. **rebus:** dative, because **vocet,** with **divum,** expresses a call
for favor or help. — **prece qua,**
with what (new) *prayer,* in contrast with the ordinary ritual (**carmina**). — **prece:** the singular is
rare, and is used by Horace only in
the ablative. — **qua:** Intr. 114.

virgines sanctae minus audientem
    carmina Vestam ?

Cui dabit partis scelus expiandi
30 Iuppiter ?   Tandem venias precamur,
nube candentis umeros amictus,
    augur Apollo ;

sive tu mavis, Erycina ridens,
quam Iocus circum volat et Cupido ;
35 sive neglectum genus et nepotes
    respicis, auctor,

27. **virgines sanctae :** the Vestals. — **minus :** here merely a softened negative (like *parum*) with
no definite comparative force ; cf.
Plaut. *Cas.* 998 *monebo, si quidem
meministi minus.* According to
Ovid (*F.* III. 699 *sqq.*) Vesta was
offended by the wrong done her in
the murder of her priest, Caesar.

28. **carmina,** *their litanies.*
These were old formulas (the
proper meaning of *carmen*) cast
in rythmical form in order to be
better held in memory at a time
when the art of writing was not in
common use.

29. **partis,** *office;* properly 'rôle.'
— **scelus expiandi,** *of purging
away our sin,* sc. by casting out the
spirit of strife and leading the people to worthy achievements. For
scelus, cf. 35. 33. For answer to
his question the poet appeals in
succession to three divinities who
might be supposed to have a
special interest in the welfare of
Rome : Apollo, who had recently
rendered such signal assistance in
the critical struggle at Actium (cf.
Verg. *A.* VIII. 704, Prop. V. 6. 27.)
and was adopted by the emperor as
his patron god ; Venus, as mother
of Aeneas, the divine ancestress

of the race (*Aeneadum genetrix,*
Lucr. I. 1) and of the Julian family in particular ; and Mars, the
father of Romulus, and hence
auctor generis (36).

30. **tandem :** implying that our
prayers have long been in vain. —
venias : Intr. 87.

31. **umeros :** Intr. 42.

32. **augur :** as the god of prophecy ; cf. Verg. *A.* IV. 376.

33. **sive tu mavis** = *vel tu
(venias) si mavis;* Intr. 119 *d.* —
Erycina, *Lady of Eryx, i.e.* Venus. The epithet is appropriate
here, as her temple at Eryx, in
Sicily, was ascribed to Aeneas
(Verg. *A.* V. 759).   There was
also a temple of Venus Erycina
in Rome near the Colline gate. —
ridens : after the Homeric φιλομ-
μειδής ; with **Iocus** (*Mirth*) and
Cupido it makes up a picture in
bright contrast to the grim scene
next presented.

34. **circum :** see Intr. 115 *c.*

35. **sive respicis :** see 33 n. —
neglectum : cf. *tandem,* 30 n. —
genus et nepotes : expressing
the same idea in two aspects, —
collectively and individually.

36. **auctor :** Mars is appealed
to, not as the god of war, as the

> heu nimis longo satiate ludo,
> quem iuvat clamor galeaeque leves
> acer et Marsi peditis cruentum
> 40   voltus in hostem ;
>
> sive mutata iuvenem figura
> ales in terris imitaris almae
> filius Maiae, patiens vocari
>   Caesaris ultor,
>
> 45   serus in caelum redeas diuque
> laetus intersis populo Quirini,
> neve te nostris vitiis iniquum
>   ocior aura

next strophe shows, but as the father of the race.

37. ludo : the nature of the sport is explained in the picture that follows, which, as a specimen of Horace's skill in graphic portrayal may be compared with II. I. 17 *sqq.* See also note on vs. 7.

38. leves : notice the quantity of the penult.

39. acer voltus, *the fierce look* — **Marsi :** see Intr. 117. The Marsian troops were among the bravest in the Roman army ; cf. II. 20. 18, Verg. *G.* II. 167, and the proverb 'No triumph over the Marsi, nor without them' (Appian *B. C.* I. 46). If the reading **Mauri** be adopted, **peditis** will mean 'unhorsed.' — **cruentum :** the epithet places the scene in the midst of a hot fight at close quarters.

41. sive : see 33 n ; the apodosis begins with **serus** 45 and extends to the close of the ode. — **mutata :** *sc.* from that of a god ; cf. **ales.** — **iuvenem :** here the poet gives the first intimation of the thought to which he has been gradually leading us. He indicates

who the *iuvenis* is in vs. 44, but reserves the full revelation of his personality to the very end of the poem. Octavian was at this time about thirty-five years old.

42. ales filius : in agreement with the subject of **imitaris.** — **in terris imitaris,** *dwellest on earth under the form of.*

43. Maiae : daughter of the titan Atlas, and mother of Mercury. — **vocari :** Intr. 94 *a.*

44. Caesaris ultor : the punishment of his uncle's assassins was avowed by Octavian as one of the chief objects of his career.

47. iniquum, *estranged. Aequus* and *iniquus* are regular expressions for the favorable or adverse disposition of a divinity towards men ; cf. 28. 28, II. 4. 15.

48. ocior aura : keeping in mind the character of the god as *ales* (42). Observe how, while the language of the last two strophes applies equally well to the god and the man, the human side is gradually brought out more distinctly till fully revealed in the name itself at the end.

tollat ; hic magnos potius triumphos,
50 hic ames dici pater atque princeps,
neu sinas Medos equitare inultos
te duce, Caesar.

III.

Sic te diva potens Cypri,
sic fratres Helenae, lucida sidera,

49. **triumphos**: in allusion probably to the three triumphs which Octavian celebrated on his return from the East in August, B.C. 29.

50. **ames** : see Intr. 94 c and 119 a. For the combination of an object accusative with a complementary infinitive, cf. 1. 19 sqq. — **pater** : here a general expression of reverence, habitually applied to a god (as *Bacche pater*, 18. 6, *Iane pater*, *Ep.* I. 16. 59), and often to a man, as in the phrases *pater patriae*, *pater senatus*, *pater urbis*, etc., and also absolutely (cf. *S.* II. 1. 12, *Ep.* I. 6. 54, 7. 37). The formal title of *pater patriae* was not conferred upon Augustus till many years later, B.C. 2. — **princeps** : apparently abbreviated originally from *princeps senatus* (the title given to the senator of highest dignity, who was placed first on the roll by the censors), and used even under the Republic in the sense of *princeps civitatis*, since the 'first senator' would usually be in fact 'first citizen.' Octavian became *princeps senatus* in B.C. 28, and from that time on he cherished the title in its shorter form and wider signification as best expressing the character in which he wished to appear to his fellow-citizens. It thus came to be the usual term to designate the civil power of the ruler, *imperator* expressing his military power ; cf. Tac. *Ann.* I. 1. 3 *cuncta discordiis civilibus fessa nomine principis sub imperium accepit.*

51. **Medos** : see 22 n. — **equitare**, *to ride on their raids*.

52. **te duce**, *so long as thou art*, etc. — **Caesar** : the name by which Octavian (as we call him, to avoid ambiguity) was known to his contemporaries from the time of his adoption by Julius Caesar (in his will, B.C. 44), his full name being C. Julius Caesar Octavianus. In B.C. 27 the title *Augustus* was added, but he was still usually called simply *Caesar*, as in III. 14.3, *Ep.* II. 1. 4 etc.; and this name is used by Horace for Julius Caesar in only two places, vs. 44, above, and *S.* I. 9. 18.

III. The third place in the series of odes is given to Vergil, and bears witness to Horace's warm regard for the friend to whom he owed his introduction to Maecenas (*S.* I. 5. 40 sqq., I. 6. 55 ; Intr. 20). The occasion is a proposed visit of Vergil to Athens, and in wishing him a safe voyage Horace indulges in some rather extravagant reflections on the temerity of man in braving the dangers of the sea, which is only an instance of the daring

ventorumque regat pater,
    obstrictis aliis praeter Iapyga,
5   navis, quae tibi creditum
        debes Vergilium, finibus Atticis

spirit with which in all things he overleaps the bounds that Providence has established. The poem bears the marks of an early effort and, like many of the odes of this book, was probably worked out on a Greek model. Of the voyage referred to nothing further is known. It could not have been the voyage of B.C. 19, on the return from which Vergil died, as there is convincing evidence that these books were published before that time. — Metre, 171.

1. **sic**, *so ; i.e.* on condition that (you grant my prayer) ; cf. *Ep.* I. 7. 69 *sic ignovisse putato me tibi, si cenas hodie mecum.* The prayer begins in vs. 6, and the words **sic . . . Iapyga** are parenthetical, introducing the prayer by an expression of good will to the ship, which is here the power appealed to ; cf. *S.* II. 3. 300 ; Verg. *E.* 9. 30 *sic tua Cyrneas fugiant examina taxos, | sic cytiso pastae distendant ubera vaccae, | incipe* ; Prop. V. 3. 67. The clause with *sic* sometimes follows the prayer, as I. 28. 23 *sqq.* In the present instance the appeal is not quite logical, since the fortunes of the ship and the voyager are bound up together. — **diva potens Cypri**: *i.e.* Venus, Ἀφροδίτη πελαγία or ποντία (*Venus marina ;* cf. III. 26. 5 and 9 ; IV. 11. 15), whose worship, as a protectress of seafaring men, was widely disseminated by the Phoenician traders. — **Cypri** : objective gen. after **potens** (Intr. 66 *b*), expressing here the worshippers over whom the goddess' control

is exercised. The phrase is sometimes used to denote the special province of the divinity, as 5. 15 *potenti maris deo (i.e.* Neptune); 6. 10 *imbellis lyrae musa potens ; C. S.* 1 *silvarum potens Diana.*

2. **fratres Helenae :** Castor and Pollux, whose constellation (Gemini) was believed to have a quieting influence on the sea ; cf. 12. 27 *sqq.*, IV. 8. 31 *sq.* Sailors also told of twin lights, which they attributed to these gods, appearing on the yards of their ships in the darkness of the storm, heralds of good weather (Plin. *N. H.* II. 101).

3. **ventorum pater :** Aeolus. — **regat,** *guide.*

4. **obstrictis aliis** : cf. Verg. *A.* I. 52 *sqq.* — **Iapyga** : so named by the Greeks as blowing from the southeastern extremity of Italy, which they called Iapygia, across the Ionian sea ; hence favorable in the present instance. It is the same as the Latin Favonius.

5. **creditum debes** : a figure borrowed from commercial life : the ship has received Vergil as a *depositum,* and accordingly is bound to give him up (**reddas**) in unimpaired condition, at the time and place stipulated. **Vergilium,** standing in the accusative with **reddas,** in the place where the amount of the *depositum* is usually put, and before the caesura of the verse (Intr. 116 *b*) expresses emphatically the greatness of the ship's responsibility.

6. **finibus** : best taken as dative, but with **reddas** only, and not ἀπὸ κοινοῦ, see last note.

reddas incolumem precor
    et serves animae dimidium meae.

Illi robur et aes triplex
10   circa pectus erat, qui fragilem truci
commisit pelago ratem
    primus, nec timuit praecipitem Africum
decertantem Aquilonibus
    nec tristis Hyadas nec rabiem Noti,
15 quo non arbiter Hadriae
    maior, tollere seu ponere volt freta.

Quem mortis timuit gradum,
    qui siccis oculis monstra natantia, ·

7. **reddas**, *deliver him*. The prefix *red-* denotes the reversal of the operation of giving, so far as it affects the recipient, — the *giving up* of what was received, not necessarily restoring it to the first giver; so here and *Ep.* I. 13. 2 *Augusto reddes volumina ;* cf. also the regular expression for delivering a letter, *epistulam reddere.* From this it is a short step to the meaning ' to pay' *sc.* what is due (*debitum* = ' withheld ').

8. **animae dimidium** : cf. II. 17. 5. The conception is borrowed from an old Greek defini-nition of friendship, μία ψυχή δύο σώματα ἐνοικοῦσα (Diog. Laert. V. 1. 20); cf. Cic. *Lael.*92 *cum amicitiae vis sit in eo ut unus quasi animus fiat ex pluribus.*

9. **illi**, etc., *his heart was cased in*, etc., *i.e.* was impenetrable to all impressions of fear. The figure is taken from the heavy armor of the soldier, but it is only a figure, and **pectus** is the heart ; cf. IV. 4. 34.

10. **erat** : Intr. 77. — **fragilem truci** : Intr. 116 *a.*

12. **primus** : Intr. 116 *b.* —

praecipitem : as coming in sudden squalls (*creber procellis,* Verg. *A.* I. 85 ; *protervus, Epod.* 16. 22). — **Africum** : see 1. 15 n.

13. **Aquilonibus**, *with the blasts of Boreas ;* see Intr. 57. Aquilo blew from between north and north-east, and his name was derived by some from the resemblance of his violent onset to the swoop of an eagle (Fest. *ap.* Paul. p. 22).

14. **tristis** : as bringing wet and gloomy weather ; cf. *tristis Orion, Epod,* 10. 10 ; *pluvias Hyadas,* Verg. *A.* III. 516. — **Noti** : the Greek name corresponding to Auster, the South Wind.

15. **quo non arbiter maior** (sc. *est*), *than whom no mightier master sways ;* cf. III. 3. 4.

16. **seu** : see Intr. 119 *c.* — **ponere**, *to allay ;* cf. 40 n.

17. **quem** (= *qualem ;* cf. *Ep.* I. 15. 1 *sq.*) **mortis gradum**, *what form of death's approach.* For this conception of death cf. vs. 33 and III. 2. 14; Tib. I. 10. 4.

18. **siccis oculis** : *i.e.* without being moved to tears. The argument is *a fortiori:* the man who

　　　qui vidit mare turbidum et
20　　　　infamis scopulos Acroceraunia?
　　　Nequiquam deus abscidit
　　　　prudens Oceano dissociabili
　　　terras, si tamen impiae
　　　　non tangenda rates transiliunt vada.
25　　Audax omnia perpeti
　　　　gens humana ruit per vetitum nefas.

could contemplate these things without profound emotion would of course not be daunted by mere physical danger. The thought in this strophe is not, as in the preceding, of the storm with its perils, which might attract a man of adventurous spirit, but of the awful grandeur of the sea itself, the tremendous force of its waves, and the portentous shapes that people its waters. The man who gazes with indifference on these manifestations of a power immeasurably above all human strength is lacking, not in fear, but in reverence (*pietas*), and will brave the displeasure of Heaven in other ways. This thought is developed in the remainder of the ode.

20. infamis : from the frequency of shipwrecks there. — scopulos : Intr. 126 *c*.— Acroceraunia : a long narrow promontory forming the northwestern extremity of Epirus and enclosing the gulf of Oricum. It had to be passed on the voyage to Athens.

21. deus prudens, *divine providence*. The divine power that rules the world is often expressed by the word *deus* without further definition (cf. 18. 3, 34. 13, III. 16. 43, 29. 30, *Epod.* 13. 7, *Ep.* I. 11. 22, 16. 78), giving evidence of the persistence of a dim conception of

a supreme being through the multifarious development of Roman polytheism. See Preller-Jordan, *Röm. Myth.*, I. 48. As a personality, however, this supreme ruler was no other than Jupiter ; incomparably more powerful than all other beings in the universe (cf. 12. 13 *sqq.*) but not the one God. — abscidit, *set apart . . . from ;* cf. Ov. *M.* I. 22 *nam caelo terras et terris abscidit undas.*

22. prudens : *sc.* for man's best good. — Oceano : Intr. 70. — dissociabili, *incompatible ;* cf. Tac. *Agr.* 3 *res olim dissociabiles, principatum ac libertatem.* The separation of land and water was necessary to make human life possible.

23. impiae : Intr. 124.

24. non tangenda, *which they ought not to touch.* — transiliunt, *course over ;* suggesting entire freedom from scruple or caution.

25. audax perpeti : Intr. 101 *a.* — omnia : 'everything' (without exception), hence *anything ;* more forcible than *quidlibet* (cf. *Ep.* II. 3. 10 *quidlibet audendi*) or *quidvis* (III. 24. 43, *Ep.* I. 15. 17) ; cf. *holus omne, Ep.* I. 5. 2.

26. ruit : cf. *transiliunt* 24 n. — per vetitum nefas : *i.e.* not only through sin, but in the face of an express prohibition.

Audax Iapeti genus
    ignem fraude mala gentibus intulit.
Post ignem aetheria domo
30   subductum macies et nova febrium
terris incubuit cohors,
    semotique prius tarda necessitas
leti corripuit gradum.
    Expertus vacuum Daedalus aera
35 pennis non homini datis ;
    perrupit Acheronta Herculeus labor.
Nil mortalibus ardui est ;
    caelum ipsum petimus stultitia, neque

27. **audax** : the anaphora (Intr.
116 *f*) indicates that the cases
now cited are instances of the impious audacity just described. —
Iapeti genus : Prometheus.

28. **ignem**, etc.: in the separation of the four elements from
chaos (cf. 21 n), fire, the subtlest
of all, rose to the highest place, in
the ethereal spaces (**aetheria
domo** 29) above the air (Ov. *M.* I.
26 *sq.*) From there it was obtained for man surreptitiously and
in defiance of the will of Zeus by
Prometheus, who brought down a
portion concealed in a reed (Hes.
Op. 50.) — **mala**, *wicked ;* cf. *malos
fures*, *S.* I. 1. 77 and the legal
form *dolus malus*. — **gentibus** :
cf. *gentis*, 2. 5 n.

29. **post ignem subductum** :
Intr. 105 *a.*

30. **macies**, etc. : according to
the same myth (Hes. *l.l.*) disease
came among mankind with the
first woman, Pandora, whom Zeus
sent with her fatal box (or vase) in
resentment for the theft of fire.
— **nova** : cf. ᴖ. 6 n.

31. **incubuit**, *settled upon ;* cf.
Verg, *A.* I. 89 *ponto nox incubat*

atra ; Lucr. VI. 1143 (*mortifer
aestus*) *incubuit populo.* — **cohors,**
troop ; properly 'retinue.'

32. **semotique**, etc.: *i.e.* death
formerly, though inevitable (**necessitas**), was far off and came with
slow pace ; cf. Tib. II. 3. 38 *hinc
cruor, hinc caedes, mors propiorque
venit.* **prius** modifies the whole
description, more particularly **se-
moṭi** and **tarda** (Intr. 76).

34. Daedalus invaded still another element not designed for
such use.   For the story, see
Verg. *A.* VI. 14, Ov. *M.* VIII.
183. — **vacuum**, *unsubstantial.*

35. **non datis** : *i.e.* designedly
withheld (litotes).

36. Hercules invaded even the
realms of death. — **perrupit**, *broke
into.* For the prosody, see Intr.
179. — **Herculeus labor** : Intr.
126 *b.*

37. **nil ardui est** (to be pronounced *arduist*), *no path is steep.*
Strictly, however, **est** is predica-
tive ('there is'). — **mortalibus** :
dat. of reference.

38. **stultitia** : in attempting the
impossible ; **scelus** : in transgress-
ing the bounds set by divine will.

per nostrum patimur scelus
40   iracunda Iovem ponere fulmina.

IV.

Solvitur acris hiems grata vice veris et Favoni,
    trahuntque siccas machinae carinas,
ac neque iam stabulis gaudet pecus aut arator igni,
    nec prata canis albicant pruinis.

40. **iracunda** : Intr. 124. —
ponere : equivalent to *deponere*,
as often in prose and poetry ; cf.
Intr. 129.

IV. L. Sestius, who is thought
to have been a son of the P.
Sestius defended by Cicero in a
speech now extant, had been an
enthusiastic partisan of Brutus,
under whom he served as quaes-
tor. Horace's acquaintance with
him very likely dated from that
time. On his return to Rome,
Sestius was wealthy enough to be
independent, but in spite of his
undisguised fidelity to the memory
of his former chief, he accepted
the new order of things, and in
B.C. 23 became consul (suffectus)
on the retirement of Augustus
from the consulship in July, — a
fact that may have determined the
place of this ode in the collection,
which was probably published in
that year.

The ode is a highly artistic production, with an elaborate metre
and a carefully balanced strophic
symmetry. The main motive,
expressed in the two middle
couplets (vss. 9–12) grows naturally out of the description of
spring which precedes (vss. 1–8)
and is again enforced by the
thought presented in the conclud-

ing verses (13–20). ' The cramp-
ing fetters of winter are bursting
under the warm breath of spring,
and man and nature are full of
fresh, glad life. The season invites to enjoyment ; and life is too
short and death too sure for us to
count on many such opportuni-
ties.' The poem is similar in construction to I. 7 ; in sentiment, to
IV. 7. — Metre, 166.

1. **solvitur**, *is breaking up*. The
hard and fast condition of the
ground produced by winter is attributed to the season itself, just
as death is 'pale' (vs. 13 n) etc.
For the literal application of the
word, see vs. 10. — **Favoni** : the
West Wind (Ζέφυρος), which began
to blow, according to the Italian
Farmer's Almanac, about February 10, and was accounted a
harbinger of spring (*veris prae-
nuntius*, *Zephyrus*, Lucr. V. 737).
The season for navigation opened
about a month later. Notice the
alliteration in this verse (Intr. 131).

2. **trahunt** : the technical term
is *deducere ;* here the direction in
which the ships are drawn is indicated by **siccas**. — **machinae** :
simply rope and tackle and rollers
(*phalangae*); cf. Caes. *B.C.* II. 10. 7.

3. **neque iam gaudet** : marking the contrast between winter,
which made the warm stable and

5   Iam Cytherea choros ducit Venus imminente luna,
        iunctaeque Nymphis Gratiae decentes
    alterno terram quatiunt pede, dum gravis Cyclopum
        Volcanus ardens visit officinas.
    Nunc decet aut viridi nitidum caput impedire myrto,
10   aut flore terrae quem ferunt solutae ;
    nunc et in umbrosis Fauno decet immolare lucis,
        seu poscat agna sive malit haedo.

the cosy fireside so attractive, and
the spring, which has robbed them
of their charm.

5. The awakening of the regen-
erative power of nature and the
renewal of life and beauty in the
spring of the year are typified in
mythology by the renewed activity
of Venus. Cf. the fine invocation
to Venus in Lucr. I. 6, *te, dea, te
fugiunt venti, te nubila caeli | ad-
ventumque tuum, tibi suavis dae-
dala tellus | summittit flores, tibi
rident aequora ponti, | placatumque
nitet diffuso lumine caelum ; | nam
simul ac species patefactast verna
diei*, etc.; and the picture in V. 737
sqq. — **Cytherea** : *i.e.* in Cythera ;
cf. *Delius et Patareus Apollo*, III.
4. 64 n. — **choros ducit**, etc.: cf.
the picture in the Homeric hymn
to Apollo 194, αὐτὰρ ἐυπλόκαμοι
Χάριτες καὶ εὔφρονες Ὧραι | Ἁρμονίη
θ' Ἥβη τε Διὸς θυγάτηρ τ' Ἀφροδίτη |
ὀρχεῦντ' ἀλλήλων ἐπὶ καρπῷ χεῖρας
ἔχουσαι. — **imminente luna** : the
scene is laid in the solitude of the
night, when the gods love best
to visit the earth (*sub nocte silenti,
cum superis terrena placent*, Stat.
Silv. I. 1. 94).

6. **iunctae** : *sc.* with their arms,
forming a row or ring (ἐπὶ καρπῷ
χεῖρας ἔχουσαι).—**decentes**, *comely*.

7. **alterno terram** : the spondees imitate the measured tread of
the dance. — **dum gravis**, etc.;

a contrasted picture with heavy
strokes, to set off the lighter lines
of the preceding picture. — **gravis**, *ponderous*. — **Cyclopum offi-
cinas** : popularly located under
the 'Volcanic' islands north of
Sicily ; cf. Verg. *A*. VIII. 416.
The Cyclopes were three sons of
Uranus and Gaea, who forged the
thunderbolts of Zeus (Hes. *Theog.*
139), a conception of them quite
distinct from that of the Odyssey,
where they are represented as living the peaceful life of shepherds.

8. **ardens** : as the god of fire,
working assiduously at the forge.—
visit : cf. the description in Verg.
A. VIII. 423 *sqq.* The conception
of the gods visiting from time to
time their favorite haunts or the
scenes of their activity is a familiar
one in classical mythology ; cf.
17. 1 *sqq.*, III. 28. 14 *sq.*, Verg. *A*.
IV. 144. (According to many
MSS. the verb here is **urit**, *fires*.)

9. **nitidum** : *sc.* with ointment.
— **impedire** : poetical for *cingere*.
Perfumes and garlands were regular concomitants of a feast ; cf. II.
3. 13 n. — **myrto** : *i.e.* with a garland of its leaves ; see II. 15. 6 n.

10. **flore** : the singular is used
collectively ; Intr. 127. — **solutae** :
cf. *solvitur*, 1 n.

11. **nunc et** (*too*) etc.: another
form of feasting ; the victim will
furnish forth the banquet.

Pallida mors aequo pulsat pede pauperum tabernas
    regumque turris. O beate Sesti,
15 vitae summa brevis spem nos vetat incohare longam.
    Iam te premet nox fabulaeque manes
    et domus exilis Plutonia ; quo simul mearis,
        nec regna vini sortiere talis
    nec tenerum Lycidan mirabere, quo calet iuventus
20   nunc omnis et mox virgines tepebunt.

12. **seu poscat,** etc.: economy
of phrase for *vel agnā, si (agnā
immolari) poscat, vel haedo, si malit,*
or the like ; cf. 2. 33 n. For the
ablatives, which are instrumental,
cf. Cic. *Leg.* II. 29 *quibus hostiis
immolandum cuique deo.*

13. **pallida** : the paleness which
accompanies death is ascribed as
a physical characteristic to the
personified figure of the destroyer;
Intr. 125. — **aequo,** *impartial ;*
Intr. 124.— **pulsat pede** : for the
practice cf. Plaut. *Most.* 453 *pul-
tando pedibus paene confregi hasce
foris.* For the repetition of the
p-sound, see Intr. 131.

14. **regum,** *princes.* The word
is constantly used for a man of
wealth, and particularly for the
patron of a person in humble circumstances ; cf. *Ep.* I. 7. 37. —
turris : *i.e.* lofty houses. — **beate,**
favored; usually referring to riches.

15. **summa,** *span ;* properly
the 'sum' of the days (or whatever portion of time we may take
as a unit) allotted to us ; cf. IV.
7. 17. — **brevis, longam** : the
contrast is enhanced by rhythmical position ; Intr. 116 c.

16. **te premet,** *will close round
you ;* cf. Verg. *A.* VI. 827 *con-
cordes animae dum nocte premun-
tur.* — **fabulae** (in apposition with
manes; Intr. 126 c), *phantom ;* lit.
talk, mere talk, empty names. Cf.

Epod. 11. 8. *per urbem fabula
quanta fui ;* Pers. 5. 152 *cinis et
manes et fabula fies.*

17. **domus Plutonia** : here the
whole lower world. — **exilis** : in
contrast with the comforts with
which Sestius is now surrounded.
— **simul** : without *ac*, as often.

18. **regna vini** : at a drinking
bout (*comissatio*) it was usual to
select by lot a *magister convivii,*
who presided with arbitrary power
over the festivities, regulating the
strength of the wine, the amount
drunk, etc., in accordance with
certain stringent rules. For the
manner of choosing this *arbiter
bibendi,* see II. 7. 25 n. For the
plural **regna,** see Intr. 128.—**talis** :
like dice, except that two sides were
rounded, leaving only four num-
bered sides (1, 3, 4, 6) on which
they could fall.

19. **Lycidan** : the name, like
all of Horace's Greek names, is
fictitious, and stands for any handsome lad ; Intr. 117 a.— **mirabere,**
feast your eyes upon.   Miror
expresses a fascinated gaze, as
III. 25. 14, 29. 11 ; *Ep.* I. 6. 18
Tyrios mirare colores. — **quo** :
Intr. 72. — **calet,** *are enamoured.*

20. **mox** : *i.e.* when he is a little
older — **tepebunt** : denoting a
milder degree of warmth than
calet,—the first step from indifference to interest.

V.

Quis multa gracilis te puer in rosa
perfusus liquidis urget odoribus
　　grato, Pyrrha, sub antro ?
　　Cui flavam religas comam,
5　simplex munditiis ?　Heu quotiens fidem
mutatosque deos flebit et aspera
　　nigris aequora ventis
　　emirabitur insolens,

V. To a coquette. The poet writes in the character of one who has himself been led on to shipwreck under her spell, and retains a lively recollection of her wiles. — Metre, 173.

1. **multa rosa** : Intr. 127. The singular here suggests quantity rather than number. — **in** : *i.e.* wearing them ; cf. *Ep.* II. 3. 228 *regali conspectus in auro nuper et ostro ;* Cic. *Fin.* II. 65 *potantem in rosa.* The roses were worn in a great garland round the head and shoulders. — **gracilis puer**, *slip of a boy ;* in disparagement, as *S.* I. 5. 69 *gracili sic tamque pusillo.* There is nothing disparaging in **puer** itself ; see 9. 16 n.

2. **perfusus liquidis odoribus**, *bathed in perfume.*— **urget**, *courts.*

3. **Pyrrha** : Πυρρά (cf. πῦρ), maid with the auburn hair (**flavam comam** 4), much admired by the Romans ; cf. II. 4. 14, III. 9. 19, IV. 4. 4 ; Verg. *A.* IV. 698 (of Dido).— **sub** : for *in,* but directing the thought more specifically to the shelter afforded by the grotto ; cf. II. 1. 39, III. 29. 14 *sub lare, Epod.* 9. 3 *sub alta domo.*— **antro** : such grottos or bowers, natural or artificial, were common in Roman country places, serving the pur-

pose of our summer-house. The youth and maid are making holiday together in the manner suggested in 1. 19 *sqq.* Hence the roses and perfume (see 4. 9 n).

4. **cui**, *for whose eyes ?*—**religas** : *i.e.* in a knot at the back of the head, the simplest mode of wearing the hair ; cf. II. 11. 23 ; Ov. *M.* VIII. 319 *crinis erat simplex, nodum collectus in unum.*

5. **simplex munditiis**, *in unadorned neatness.* The girl adopts a very effective simplicity of dress. — **fidem** : here broken faith, as the context shows. *Fides* is sufficiently elastic to take on this meaning ; cf. 18. 16 *arcani fides prodiga,* III. 24. 59 *periura fides.*

6. **mutatos deos** : *sc.* in their disposition towards him, — the loss of their favor ; see Intr. 105 *a.* — **flebit** : Intr. 51 *a.* — **aspera** etc.: *i.e.* when she is tired of him and seeks a quarrel to get rid of him. The metaphor prepares the way for the figure with which the ode closes.

7. **nigris** : Intr. 125 ; cf. *Epod.* 10. 5 *niger Eurus.*

8. **emirabitur** : the e- is intensive, as in *ediscere, elaborare, edurus,* etc. The word first occurs in Horace. — **insolens,** *innocent soul.*

qui nunc te fruitur credulus aurea,

10   qui semper vacuam, semper amabilem

sperat, nescius aurae

fallacis.   Miseri quibus

intemptata nites: me tabula sacer

votiva paries indicat uvida

15   suspendisse potenti

vestimenta maris deo.

The word is here used in its primitive sense of 'unaccustomed to,' 'unfamiliar with' something. Horace also uses it objectively, as II. 3. 3 *insolenti laetitia, unusual* or *excessive joy;* and in this sense it was sometimes applied to a person, as Ter. *And.* 907 *quid tu Athenas insolens,* (*i.e.* seldom seen, 'a stranger')? Finally it is used of a person who holds himself aloof, is reserved, unsympathetic, haughty, arrogant, — its commonest meaning, as 16. 21, II. 4. 2, etc.

9. **credulus aurea** : the juxta-position of the two epithets (Intr. 116 *a*) is as expressive as a separate clause (*credens te auream esse*). — **aurea,** *all gold ;* denoting supreme excellence ; cf. IV. 2. 23 *mores aureos,* II. 10. 5 *auream mediocritatem,* Verg. *A.* X. 16 *Venus aurea* (χρυσέης Ἀφροδίτης, *Il.* III. 64), and our 'golden rule,' 'silence is golden,' etc.

10. **vacuam,** *fancy-free ;* cf. 6. 19.

11. **nescius aurae** : returning to the figure introduced in vs. 6 ; but *aura* in the sense of fickle

favor had almost ceased to be figurative ; cf. *popularis aurae,* III. 2. 20.

13. **nites** : of outward beauty ; cf. *S.* II. 1. 64 *nitidus per ora* (*i.e.* in public) *cederet, introrsum turpis.* — **tabula sacer,** etc.: alluding to the custom, not yet extinct, by which the shipwrecked mariner commemorated his escape and his gratitude by depositing in the temple of the divinity to whom he attributed his safety a picture (**tabula**) of the occurrence, together with his clothes, the sole possessions which he saved with his life. Cf. Vergil's description of the sacred olive-tree of Faunus at Laurentum (*A.* XII. 766), *nautis olim venerabile lignum,* | *servati ex undis ubi figere dona solebant* | *Laurenti divo et votas suspendere vestes.*

14. **votiva** : the sailor in his peril would vow the offering ; cf. *votas vestes,* Verg. *l.l.,* — **paries** : that of the temple, on which the picture was hung.

16. **maris** : with **potenti** ; cf. *Cypri,* 3. 1 n. — **deo** : Neptune.

VI.

Scriberis Vario fortis et hostium
victor Maeonii carminis alite,
quam rem cumque ferox navibus aut equis
miles te duce gesserit.

VI. To Marcus Agrippa; an apology. It would seem that Agrippa had intimated a desire that Horace should write an ode in his honor. Horace protests in half playful strain that the subject is beyond his humble powers, a theme fit for epic verse, and by weaving in a good deal of complimentary allusion really grants the favor he professes to withhold. For similar instances of his skill in declining such requests, cf. *S.* II. 1. 12 *sqq.*, *Ep.* II. 1. 250 *sqq.*—Metre, 172.

1. **scribēris**: the emphasis (Intr. 116 *b*) is that of assurance, and the ground of the assurance naturally follows at once, — 'Your achievements will not lack a historian; there's Varius, etc.,' — drawing **Vario** away from its syntactical connection. *Scribere* with a personal object (cf. vs. 13 *quis Martem scripserit*) or with a personal subject in the passive is rare; and the real subject here is not merely *tu*, understood, but *tu* **fortis et hostium victor**, *i.e.* your prowess and success; see Intr. 105 *a*.— **Vario . . . alite**: ablative absolute, but with a force approaching that of the examples in Intr. 105 *b*. The thought is, 'Your fame is safe in the fact that Varius is an epic poet.' (Some editors change unnecessarily to *aliti*, making **Vario** dat. of the agent.)

2. **Maeonii**: *i.e.* Homeric. According to one of many conflicting traditions Homer was born at

Smyrna in Lydia (Maeonia). When this ode was written Varius was looked upon as the epic poet of the age, and even after• the publication of the Aeneid in B.C. 19 Horace couples his name with that of Vergil on equal terms (*Ep.* II. 1. 247, 3. 55); see Intr. 15.— **alite**: for poet or 'singer'; cf. IV. 2. 25 *Dircaeum cycnum* (of Pindar), and II. 20.

3. **quam rem cumque,** etc.: *i.e.* whatever exploit the army or navy has achieved under your command will be an occasion for Varius to record your praises in his expected epic. The construction is similar to our own use of the general relative clause, when it is equivalent to a general condition, summing up all cases that may have occurred : 'If in any case the soldier, etc. (*i.e.* in every case where the soldier, etc.), your prowess will be recorded.' Cf. *Ep.* I. 2. 14 *quicquid delirant reges, plectuntur Achivi.* — **cumque** : treated by Horace as a detachable suffix ; cf. 7. 25, 9. 14, 16. 2, etc. — **navibus** : alluding especially to the naval victories of Naulochus, B.C. 36, and Actium, B.C. 31. — **equis** : *i.e.* (in contrast with **navibus**), on land. Agrippa commanded in Gaul in B.C. 39 and 38, and gained some successes on the Rhine and elsewhere.

5. **nos** : Intr. 116 *b.* — **neque haec dicere nec** : *i.e.* I no more attempt these themes than I

5　Nos, Agrippa, neque haec dicere nec gravem
　　Pelidae stomachum cedere nescii
　　nec cursus duplicis per mare Vlixei
　　　nec saevam Pelopis domum

　　conamur, tenues grandia, dum pudor
10　imbellisque lyrae musa potens vetat
　　laudes egregii Caesaris et tuas
　　　culpa deterere ingeni.

should, etc. ; cf. III. 5. 27 *sqq.*
By classing Agrippa's exploits with
those of the heroes of Greek epos
and tragedy, ostensibly to excuse
himself, he pays the highest possible compliment to the Roman
general. — **gravem Pelidae stomachum :** the subject of the
Iliad, — μῆνιν . . . Πηληιάδεω Ἀχι-
λῆος οὐλομένην, *Il.* I. 1. — **dicere,**
to sing; a common use of the
word, especially where the theme
of song is given ; cf. 12. 25, 21. 1
sq., II. 13. 30, I. 32. 3, III. 4. 1,
IV. 12. 9, etc.

6. **stomachum,** *spleen ;* cf. *S.*
II. 7. 44. The word has a colloquial flavor, and is used in playful
irony of so dignified a subject ;
so also **duplex** (7), *wily,* for the
Homeric πολύτροπος, πολύμητις. —
cedere : see Intr. 101 *c.*

7. **cursus,** etc.: the theme of
the Odyssey. — **Vlixei :** genitive ;
cf. *Achillei,* 15. 34, *Epod.* 17. 14.
The name of Ὀδυσσεύς invariably
used by Latin writers is *Vlixes,*
from a dialectic (Doric) form,
Οὐλίξης. The genitive *Vlixei,*
from a parallel form *Vlixeus,*
which however does not occur
(cf. *Perses* and *Perseus*), is quad-
risyllabic here and *Epod.* 16. 60,
17. 16 ; but necessarily trisyllabic in hexameter (*Ep.* I. 6. 63,
7. 40).

8. **saevam Pelopis domum,**
Pelops' savage line, — the subject
of many of the most famous Greek
tragedies, among them the *Agamemnon* of Aeschylus, the *Electra*
of Sophocles, and the *Orestes, Electra,* and *Iphigenia* of Euripides,
still extant. Varius himself had
written a *Thyestes.* The story of
the family was a series of murders,
from Pelops himself, who slew his
father-in-law Oenomaus, to Orestes, who killed his mother Clytem-
nestra.

9. **tenues grandia** (agreeing
with **nos** and **haec** respectively),
grand themes for slender powers ;
Intr. 116 *a.* — **dum :** see 2. 17 n.

10. **imbellis :** indicating the
nature of his unfitness to deal with
Agrippa's exploits. — **lyrae :** cf.
Cypri, 3. 1 n. — **musa :** see note
on *Clio,* 12. 2. — **vetat :** Intr. 77.

11. **egregii Caesaris :** cf. III.
25. 4, and see 2. 52 n. The poet
dexterously introduces the fact
that Agrippa was associated with
Augustus in his greatest achievements.

12. **culpa ingeni :** cf. *Ep.* II.
1. 229 *sqq.,* where Horace expresses
himself at length on this subject.
— **deterere,** *to belittle.* — **ingeni :**
substantives with stems in *-io-* have
only the shorter form of the genitive in Horace.

Quis Martem tunica tectum adamantina
digne scripserit aut pulvere Troico
15 *nigrum Merionen aut ope Palladis
Tydiden superis parem ?

Nos convivia, nos proelia virginum
sectis in iuvenes unguibus acrium
cantamus vacui, sive quid urimur,
20   non praeter solitum leves.

VII.

Laudabunt alii claram Rhodon aut Mytilenen
aut Epheson bimarisve Corinthi

13–16. Scenes from the Iliad. It is implied, of course, that Agrippa's prowess is to be ranked with that of the god and the heroes mentioned.

13. **tunica tectum adaman-tina**: a paraphrase of χαλκοχίτων, a stock epithet of the Homeric warrior. *Adamas* (ἀδάμας, *unyielding;* cf. δαμάω) is not a specific metal, but a poetic term for the hardest iron or brass.

14. **digne scripserit**: the more accurate Latin use of the future perfect, the question having reference not so much to the action itself as to its quality, which can be submitted to judgment only after the action is completed.

15. **Merionen**: charioteer of Idomeneus of Crete (*Il.* XIII. 528); cf. 15. 26, IV. 9. 20 n.— **ope Palladis** etc.: alluding to the combat (*Il.* V. 334 *sqq.*) in which Diomed, with the aid of Athena, wounds Venus and Mars and drives them from the field.

18. **sectis**, *but . . . pared;* not really dangerous.— **in iuvenes acrium**: cf. *acer in hostem*, 2. 39.

19. **vacui**: see 5. 10 n.— **sive**: Intr. 119 *d.* — quid, *at all*.

20. **non praeter solitum**, *as usual*.

VII. This ode is similar in plan to Ode 4, the main motive being an exhortation to forget the troubles and enjoy the pleasures of life, with an introduction and a conclusion designed to enforce this counsel. The introduction commends the beauty of a place (as in Ode 4 of a season) that invites to enjoyment, and the conclusion supports the counsel given by an example. The parts are not so skilfully fitted together, however, as in Ode 4, so that some critics, as early as the second century, have thought that we really have here two odes (vss. 1–14 and 15–32) ; and this division appears in some manuscripts. It is possible that vss. 1–14 were originally written independently, but there is no sufficient reason to doubt that Horace finally composed the ode in its present form, on the plan indicated above.

moenia vel Baccho Thebas vel Apolline Delphos
    insignis aut Thessala Tempe.
5 Sunt quibus unum opus est intactae Palladis urbem
    carmine perpetuo celebrare et
undique decerptam fronti praeponere olivam ;

L. Munatius Plancus, to whom
the ode is addressed, was a man of
advanced years and great prominence in the state. He had been
one of Caesar's lieutenants in Gaul
and in B.C. 43, while holding the chief
command in that country, founded
the colony of Lugdunum (Lyons).
He was consul in 42, and for many
years after that was the trusted
friend and agent of Antony in the
East. The latter's relations with
Cleopatra however, finally drove
him (or gave him an excuse) to go
over to Octavian just before the
decisive struggle at Actium. His
course made him, justly or unjustly,
many bitter enemies, who have
painted him as an unscrupulous
trimmer. If so, it was a master
stroke to make in the senate
in B.C. 27 the proposal by which
the title of Augustus was conferred upon Octavian ; and for
this he received his reward in the
censorship in B.C. 22. Horace's
tribute implies nothing as to his
character, being little more than a
formal compliment. — Metre, 162.

1. **laudabunt** : Intr. 79. For
the meaning, see 1. 17 n. — **claram**, *renowned* (cf. *Rhodum nobilem*, Cat. 4. 8), applying to the
first three cities named (connected
by **aut . . . aut**). All three were
noted for beauty of situation and
delightful climate. Rhodes was
also famous for its commerce and
for its school of rhetoric which exerted no small influence on Roman
oratory, counting Cicero among its
pupils. Mytilene was the capital

of Lesbos, the city of Alcaeus and
Sappho. Ephesus was the capital
of the province of Asia.

2. **bimaris** : from its position
on the Isthmus. The word, formed
on the model of the Greek διθά-
λασσος, occurs first here, but was
afterwards much used by Ovid. —
Corinthi moenia : at this time in
ruins. The city was destroyed by
the Romans in B.C. 146, and the
colony of freedmen established
there by Julius Caesar had not
as yet attained any great degree
of prosperity.

3. **Baccho, Apolline** : abl. of
cause, with **insignis**.

4. **Tempe** (Τέμπη, acc. pl. neut.,
like γένη) : the beautiful defile
through which the Peneus makes
its way between Olympus and
Ossa to the sea.

5. **quibus unum opus est** : *i.e.*
who devote themselves wholly to
this one theme. — **intactae**, *the
Virgin*, Ἀθήνη Παρθένος. —**urbem**:
Athens.

7. **undique decerptam** etc.:
i.e. to seek distinction by writing
on every possible topic in Attic
history and legend. The same
figure is used by Lucretius, I. 928:
iuvatque novos decerpere flores |
*insignemque meo capiti petere inde
coronam,* | *unde prius nulli velarint
tempora musae.* — **fronti praeponere** : *i.e.* in a garland. — **olivam**,
an olive twig. The olive, the gift of
Athena to Athens, grew in great
abundance in Attica and was
closely associated with the fame
of that country.

plurimus in Iunonis honorem
aptum dicet equis Argos ditisque Mycenas.
10   Me nec tam patiens Lacedaemon
nec tam Larisae percussit campus opimae
quam domus Albuneae resonantis
et praeceps Anio ac Tiburni lucus et uda
mobilibus pomaria rivis.
15 Albus ut obscuro deterget nubila caelo

8. **plurimus,** *a great many;* cf. Verg. *A.* II. 369 *plurima mortis imago;* Juv. 3. 232 *plurimus hic aeger moritur vigilando;* Lucan III. 707 *multus sua volnera puppi adfixit moriens.* — in Iunonis honorem, etc : cf. *Il.* IV. 51, where Hera says : ἦ τοι ἐμοὶ τρεῖς μὲν πολὺ φίλταταί εἰσι πολῆες, | Ἄργος τε Σπάρτη τε καὶ εὐρυάγυια Μυκήνη.

9. **aptum equis Argos**=Ἄργος ἱππόβοτον (*Il.* II. 287). — dicet : cf. 6. 5 n. — ditis Mycenas : cf. πολυχρύσοιο Μυκήνης, *Il.* VII. 180. The city was already in ruins in Horace's time.

10. **me:** cf. 1. 29 n. The enumeration of Greek cities is continued into this sentence, and makes the connection with what follows. — **patiens,** *hardy.* — Lacedaemon : the third of the favorite cities of Juno. Cf. vs. 8 n. All these were insignificant at this time, and interesting to Horace and his readers, as they are to us, from their historical or traditional associations.

11. **Larisae :** in Thessaly, in the fertile valley of the Peneus. — **percussit** : *sc.* with admiration. — **opimae** : cf. Λάρισαν ἐριβώλακα, *Il.* II. 841.

12. **domus,** etc : *i.e.* Tibur (Tivoli) and its beautiful surroundings. — domus Albuneae : *i.e.* the grotto sacred to this sibyl, which

was resorted to as an oracle in early times from all parts of Italy. See Verg. *A.* VII. 82 *sqq.* — **resonantis,** from the neighboring cataract.

13. **praeceps Anio** : after passing through the town, which stands on the edge of the Sabine hills, commanding a fine view of the Campagna, the river descends to the plain in a series of beautiful waterfalls. — **Tiburni** : the mythical eponymous founder of Tibur. Tradition made him a grandson of the Argive prophet Amphiaraus, banished with his brothers Catillus and Coras ; cf. II. 6. 5 *Tibur Argeo positum colono,* I. 18. 2, where the town is called *moenia Catili,* and Verg. *A.* VII. 670 *sqq.* — **lucus,** *the sacred grove;* the regular meaning of *lucus* in distinction from *nemus.* Cf. *Ep.* I. 6. 32. — **uda:** *i.e.* irrigated ; cf. III. 29. 6.

14. **mobilibus rivis:** the streams that flow into the Anio, with their frequent waterfalls. — **pomaria :** cf. Propert. V. 7. 81 *pomosis Anio incubat arvis.*

15. Here begins the second and main part of the ode, for which the preceding praise of Tibur paves the way. — **albus,** *bright ;* cf. III. 27. 19; Intr. 125. It belongs with **saepe** and the predicate : *as the South Wind is often bright and wipes away,* etc. Notus was ordinarily

saepe Notus neque parturit imbris
perpetuos, sic tu sapiens finire memento
tristitiam vitaeque labores
molli, Plance, mero, seu te fulgentia signis
20   castra tenent seu densa tenebit
Tiburis umbra tui.   Teucer Salamina patremque
cum fugeret, tamen uda Lyaeo

a stormy wind (cf. 3. 14 *rabiem*
Noti), but sometimes brought clear
weather, in which case he was
called by the Greeks Λευκόνοτος.

16. **parturit**, *is pregnant with*,
breeds.

17. **perpetuos** : cf. *primus*, 3.
12 n. — **sapiens** : equivalent to an
adverb with finire. — **finire**, *to
seek relief from ;* lit. to set limits
to, so that they shall not be *per-
petua.* Cf. III. 4. 39 ; *Ep.* II. 3.
406 *ludusque repertus et longorum
operum finis.* — **memento** : a common form of command or advice,
softening the direct injunction ; cf.
II. 3. 1, III. 29. 32, *S.* II. 5. 52,
Ep. I. 8. 16, etc.

18. **labores**, *troubles*.

19. **molli** : referring at once to
the mellowness of the wine (from
age) and to its soothing influence.
—**fulgentia** : the eagle of the
legion and the silver disks on the
standards of the cohorts were
kept highly polished.

20. **tenent . . . tenebit** : the
natural inference from this change
of tense,— that Plancus was at the
time in camp,— places the date of
the ode at least as early as B.C. 30,
as there is no evidence and no
probability that Plancus was
engaged in military operations
after that year.

21. **tui** : according to Porphyrio
Plancus was a native of Tibur.
He must at least have had a villa
there. — **Teucer** : the example

which the poet quotes to enforce
his counsel is that of a man who,
with hardships and struggles star-
ing him in the face, refused to let
them gain complete possession of
his mind, and devoted to enjoyment the few hours that were left
before the inevitable time of their
coming. It is idle to search for
any special resemblance to his
case in that of Plancus. Teucer,
the son of Telamon and brother
of Ajax, on returning home to
Salamis after the Trojan war, was
repulsed and driven into banish-
ment by his father, who had sent
the brothers to the war with the
strict injunction that neither
should return without the other.
Teucer sailed with his companions
to Cyprus and there founded a
city, to which he gave the name of
his native Salamis ; cf. Verg. *A.*
I. 619. The story was familiar to
Horace's contemporaries from a
popular play of Pacuvius.

22. **cum fugeret**, *when going into
exile from ;* cf. *S.* I. 6. 13 *Tarquinius regno pulsus fugit*, and the
Greek φεύγειν. The time indicated
is apparently the night before he
sailed away from Salamis. — **uda
Lyaeo**, *moist from wine, i.e.* from
drinking ; cf. Tibul. I. 2. 3 *multo
perfusum tempora Baccho.* Lyaeus
('the Releaser'; as if from λύω), a
surname of Bacchus, stands here
for his province, as *Baccho* in the
example quoted ; Intr. 130.

tempora populea fertur vinxisse corona,
    sic tristis adfatus amicos :
25 'Quo nos cumque feret melior fortuna parente,
    ibimus, o socii comitesque !
Nil desperandum Teucro duce et auspice Teucro ;
    certus enim promisit Apollo
ambiguam tellure nova Salamina futuram.
30   O fortes peioraque passi
mecum saepe viri, nunc vino pellite curas ;
    cras ingens iterabimus aequor.'

23. pōpulea : the poplar was
sacred to Hercules, the great
traveller of heroic times (*vagus
Hercules*, III. 3. 9), under whose
protection Teucer at this juncture
would naturally place himself. —
corona : cf. 4. 9 n.
    25. cumque : cf. 6. 3 n.— melior,
kinder. — parente : represented,
in the tragedy of Pacuvius, as
harsh and stern (Cic. *de Or.* II.
193).
    27. Teucro : the use of his own
name instead of *me*, — the name
by which he is known to them,
with the associations attached to
it in their minds, — is an appeal
to their confidence in him. — duce
et auspice : an expression borrowed from the institutions of the
Commonwealth, under which all
military operations in the province
of a consul were done under his
auspicia, though not necessarily
under his immediate personal direction (*ductus*). Cf. Suet. *Aug.* 21
*domuit autem partim ductu partim
auspiciis suis Cantabriam*, etc. The
phrase here, however, expresses
something more than complete
leadership, auspice being used
with reference to the prophecy
which he proceeds to quote.
    28. certus, *unerring*.

29. ambiguam : *i.e.* one that
will rival the original Salamis so
that the name will no longer serve,
without further definition, to indicate which of the two is meant. —
futuram : *sc. esse*.
    30. o fortes peioraque passi :
cf. Verg. *A.* I. 198 *o passi gravi-
ora*.
    31. nunc : *i.e.* while you may ;
in contrast with cras ; cf. 9. 18
and 21.
    32. iterabimus : having just
completed one voyage (from Troy);
cf. *Odys.* XII. 293 ἠῶθεν δ' ἀναβάντες
ἐνήσομεν εὑρέι πόντῳ.

VIII. A spirited sketch of a
young athlete in love. The name
Lydia, sometimes Lyde (Λύδη), as
III. 11 and 28, occurs frequently
in amatory poetry, and is here
appropriate with its suggestion of
oriental effeminacy. Sybaris, after the name of a town in Magna
Graecia proverbial for its luxury,
is equally suitable for the lover in
his present state. The poet expresses his amazement at the
transformation which has been
wrought, in a volley of questions
which do not wait for an answer,
adjuring Lydia to tell how she has
worked such a spell upon the

VIII.

Lydia, dic, per omnis
    te deos oro, Sybarin cur properes amando
perdere, cur apricum
    oderit campum, patiens pulveris atque solis.
5 Cur neque militaris
    inter aequalis equitat, Gallica nec lupatis
temperat ora frenis?
    Cur timet flavum Tiberim tangere? Cur olivum

youth. The questions are at first indirect, depending on *dic*, but afterwards proceed more quietly in the direct form. The ode is no doubt formed on a Greek model, — Horace's only experiment in this difficult metre, — but is worked out as usual with Roman details. — Metre, 175.

1. **per omnes te deos oro**: this interlocked order (Intr. 110) is a favorite one in adjurations; cf. Ter. *And.* 538 *per te deos oro;* 834 *per ego te deos oro.* Here **te** brings out the emphasis on **omnes** and **deos** by separating them.

2. **cur properes amando**: *i.e.* why he is hastening to his ruin under her spell; not asking why she does so, but adjuring her to explain the marvelous result. What has she done to him to change him so utterly? — **amando**: used in a neutral sense, neither active nor passive, like an abstract noun; cf. Verg. *E.* 8. 71 *cantando rumpitur anguis;* Lucr. I. 312 *anulus in digito subter tenuatur habendo.*

4. **campum**: *sc. Martium,* a portion of which, on the bank of the river, was set apart for athletic exercises. The usual time was early in the afternoon, before the hottest part of the day. See *S.* I.

6. 125 *sqq.* — **patiens**, *he who can bear;* cf. *metuens,* 1. 16 n.

5. **neque . . . nec**: *i.e.* neither in the common exercises nor alone. — **militaris aequalis**, *the soldierly young fellows of his own age.*

6. **equitat**: an exercise which Augustus made more fashionable by the institution (or restoration) of the Game of Troy (*lusus Troiae,* Suet *Aug.* 43; Verg. *A.* V. 545); cf. III. 7. 25 *sq.,* 12. 3, 24. 54 *sq.* — **Gallica**: *i.e.* of the Gallic steed. Gaul supplied the Romans with their best horses. — **lupatis**: cf. Verg. *G.* III. 208.

7. **temperat**, *govern.*

8. **timet tangere**: humorous exaggeration to express the extreme distaste which the youth has conceived for what was once his favorite exercise. For the infinitive see Intr. 94 *l.* — **flavum**: see 2. 13 n. — **Tiberim**: swimming in the warm climate of Rome was naturally a very attractive form of exercise. Cf. III. 7. 27 ; 12. 3 ; *S.* II. 1. 8 ; Cic. *Cael.* 36 *ad Tiberim, eo loco quo omnis iuventus natandi causa venit.* — **olivum**: with which the body was anointed before swimming (cf. III. 12. 3) and the exercises of the palaestra, such as those that follow. Cf. Sat. I. 6. 123.

sanguine viperino
10   cautius vitat neque iam livida gestat armis
bracchia, saepe disco,
    saepe trans finem iaculo nobilis expedito?
Quid latet, ut marinae
    filium dicunt Thetidis sub lacrimosa Troiae
15 funera, ne virilis
    cultus in caedem et Lycias proriperet catervas?

9. **sanguine viperino**: regarded as poisonous; cf. *Epod.* 3. 6. For the abl. see Intr. 75.

10. **cautius vitat**: cf. *timet tangere*, 8 n. — **neque iam**, *and no longer.* — **livida**: *e.g.* from carrying the discus, from occasional bruises, perhaps from blows with the boxing glove (*caestus*, called *arma* Verg. *A.* V. 412). — **gestat**: seldom used except of things separate from the body, but cf. *non obtusa pectora gestamus*, Verg. *A.* I. 567. — **armis**: *sc. campestribus* (*Ep.* II. 3. 379); *i.e.* the discus, javelin, and other implements used in the sports on the Campus.

11. **disco**: a heavy disc of stone or metal. The exercise was similar to our 'throwing the hammer' and 'putting the shot.' See the cut of Myron's famous *discobolus* in Baumeister II., p. 1003. Apparently the javelin was also used in this way, among others.

12. **trans finem expedito**, *for having put . . . clear beyond the farthest mark* ('broken the record'), like Ulysses among the Phaeacians, *Od.* VIII. 192: ὁ δ (λᾶας) ὑπέρπτατο σήματα πάντων. For the construction see Intr. 105 *a.* — **nobilis**, *he who is famous;* concessive, like *patiens* 4 n.

13. **ut dicunt**: the story that Thetis, foreseeing the fate of her son if he should join the expe-

dition against Troy, placed him, disguised in girl's clothes at the court of Lycomedes, king of Scyros, where he was discovered by the shrewdness of Ulysses, is not alluded to in Homer, but occurs in later Greek literature. Cf. Ovid *M.* XIII. 162, and Stat. *Achil.* I. 207 *sqq.*, where it is worked out in detail.

14. **filium**: Achilles. — **sub**, *on the eve of;* see III. 7. 30 n.

16. **cultus**, *dress.* — **Lycias catervas**: the most important allies of the Trojans.

IX. In contrast with Ode 4, the scene is here laid in mid-winter, when the forbidding aspect of nature invests the warm fireside with a special charm. The ode is modeled upon a drinking song of Alcaeus, a part of which is preserved (*Fr.* 34):

"Ὕει μὲν ὁ Ζεύς, ἐκ δ' ὀράνω μέγας
χείμων, πεπάγασιν δ' ὑδάτων ῥόαι.

   . . . .

κάββαλλε τὸν χείμων', ἐπὶ μὲν τίθεις
πῦρ, ἐν δὲ κίρναις οἶνον ἀφειδέως
μέλιχρον, αὐτὰρ ἀμφὶ κόρσᾳ
μάλθακον ἀμφι⟨τίθη⟩ γνόφαλλον·

but the details of the picture are, as in the preceding ode, Italian. 'Thaliarchus' (θαλίαρχος = *magister convivii;* cf. 4. 18 n) is in all probability not an assumed name

IX.

Vides ut alta stet nive candidum
Soracte, nec iam sustineant onus
silvae laborantes, geluque
flumina constiterint acuto.

5   Dissolve frigus ligna super foco
large reponens, atque benignius
deprome quadrimum Sabina,
o Thaliarche, merum diota.

for one of Horace's friends, but with the whole setting of the ode existed only in the poet's fancy. The poem is one of Horace's early studies of his Greek masters, and may be counted among the most successful. — Metre, 176.

1. **ut**, *how.* — **stet** : of the mountain towering up against the sky; more picturesque than *sit.* Cf. Verg. *A.* VI. 471 *stet Marpesia cautes.*

2. **Soracte** : on the western side of the Tiber valley, rising to a height of about 2000 feet. It was in sight from the city, about 25 miles to the north, but the scene, so far as it is definitely conceived at all, must here be imagined at some country place.

3. **laborantes**, *struggling, sc.* to hold their own against the weight of snow.

4. **constiterint** : *i.e.* are frozen entirely over: cf. Ov. *Tr.* V. 10. 1 *ut sumus in Ponto, ter frigore constitit Hister.* Such extreme cold and heavy snow as here described did not occur in middle Italy once in a lifetime. The picture is borrowed from the Greek original; cf. πεπάγασιν δ' ὑδάτων ῥόαι in the fragment quoted above.

5. **dissolve** : cf. *solvitur*, 4. 1 n. — **super**, *upon ;* cf. *super Pindo*, 12. 6. In this sense *super* usually takes the accusative in prose, and with the ablative is more commonly equivalent to *de*, as III. 8. 17, *C. S.* 18. — **foco** : in country houses a low square platform of stone or brick in the middle of the atrium. The fire of logs was built on the top of it, and the smoke made its way out through the roof. On one side was the altar of the Lares. It was the centre of household worship and work, and around it the family would gather evenings, with such guests as they had with them ; cf. *Epod.* 2. 65 *sq.*, *S.* II. 6. 65 *sqq.*

6. **reponens**, *replenishing.* The word properly means to make good the loss of what has been consumed, which carries with it, however, the notion of an adequate supply. Cf. *epulae repostae*, Verg. *G.* III. 527. — **benignius**, *more generously.*

7. **deprome**, *draw.* — **Sabina** : *i.e.* containing Sabine wine (Intr. 124). It was a plain wine (cf. 20. 1), but in this case somewhat mellowed by age (**quadrimum**).

8. **Thaliarche** : see intr. note. — **diota**, *flagon ;* the amphora or

Permitte divis cetera ; qui simul
10   stravere ventos aequore fervido
       deproeliantis, nec cupressi
          nec veteres agitantur orni.

Quid sit futurum cras fuge quaerere, et
   quem fors dierum cumque dabit lucro
15   adpone, nec dulcis amores
          sperne puer neque tu choreas,

donec virenti canities abest
   morosa.   Nunc et campus et areae

two-handled (lit. 'two-eared') jar
in which the wine was kept in
the *cella vinaria,* and from which
it was poured (**deprome**) into the
mixing-bowl (*cratera*) on the table.

9. **cetera,** *all else, sc.* than enjoyment of· the present moment ;
cf. III. 29. 33 *sq.* — **qui simul,** *the
moment they.* See 4. 17 n.

10. **stravere,** *have laid.* —
aequore : Intr. 69.

11. **deproeliantis :** *sc.* with one
another ; cf. 3. 12 *sq.* The prefix
is intensive, as in *deamo, demiror,
depereo,* etc. — **nec cupressi :** *i.e.*
the warring winds give place to
absolute calm. The meaning of
the whole strophe is that the gods,
and they alone, can make the
storm cease ; we must bide their
time, and not waste such oppor-
tunities for enjoyment as the present affords in fretting over what
is beyond our control. This
thought Horace proceeds to work
out with details which are obviously his own, and not taken
from Alcaeus. For **cupressi** see
II. 14. 23 n.

13. **fuge quaerere :** Intr. 94 *k.*

14. **quem . . . cumque,** *each
day that.* — **fors :** here personified
and equivalent to *Fortuna.* The

goddess was worshipped under the
name of *Fors Fortuna ;* cf. Ter.
Phor. 841 ; Cic. *Leg.* II. 28. — **dierum :** Intr. 63. — **lucro adpone,**
set down as gain ; lit. insert it in
that category, on that side of the
balance-sheet.

15. **nec sperne :** see Intr. 88
and 89 note. — **amores :** the plural
of repeated instances ; see Intr. 128.

16. **puer,** *while you are young.*
The word is frequently used for
early manhood (cf. III. 2. 2, IV.
4. 28, *S.* II. 1. 60), as *puella* is often
a young woman. — **neque tu:** the
insertion of the pronoun with the
second verb points the exhortation
with special emphasis at the person
addressed, — 'However it may be
with others, don't *you,* at any rate,
etc.' Cf. *Ep.* I. 2. 63 *hunc frenis,
hunc tu compesce catena.*

17. **virenti :** *sc. tibi.*

18. **morosa,** *fretful,* easily irri-
tated, and hence incapable of enjoyment. — **nunc :** repeating with
emphasis the idea of **donec virenti,** etc. — **campus :** see 8. 4 n ;
areae, *the squares,* open spaces
about public buildings ; both especially attractive for saunterers in
a city where the streets were very
narrow.

lenesque sub noctem susurri
20   composita repetantur hora ;

nunc et latentis proditor intimo
gratus puellae risus ab angulo
pignusque dereptum lacertis
aut digito male pertinaci.

X.

Mercuri, facunde nepos Atlantis,
qui feros cultus hominum recentum

19. **sub noctem,** *at nightfall ;*
cf. 8. 14 n.

20. **composita,** *appointed* (by
agreement).—**repetantur,** *be claimed. Repetere,* ''to demand what is
due' (cf. **composita hora**), corresponds to *reddere* (3. 7 n.), as *petere*
to *dare ;* cf. the technical phrases
for demanding and making resti-
tution, *res repetere, res reddere.*

21. **nunc et:** the anaphora (Intr.
116 *h*) carries over from the preceding sentence (with a slight
zeugma) the idea of **repetantur.**
—**latentis,** etc.: the arrangement
is highly artistic, each word in
this verse expressing a partial
notion, to be completed by the
word holding the corresponding
position in the next verse ; see
Intr. 110.

23. **pignus :** *i.e.* a bracelet or a
ring, as the following words show.
—**lacertis :** dative.

24. **male pertinaci,** *not very
obstinate. Male,* like a negative
quantity in mathematics, dimin-
ishes the force of an adjective
which expresses a positive or desirable quality, as here and in *male
sanos, Ep.* I. 19. 3, *male parentem,
Ep.* I. 20. 15 ; but strengthens one
that expresses a negative quality

or a defect, as *male dispari,* 17. 25,
male laxus, S. I. 3. 31, *rauci male,
S.* I. 4. 66.

X. A hymn to Mercury, after
Alcaeus. The first lines of the
original were perhaps (*Fr.* 5) :—

Χαῖρε Κυλλάνας ὃ μέδεις, σὲ γάρ μοι
θῦμος ὕμνην, τὸν κορύφαις ἐν αὔταις
Μαῖα γέννατο Κρονίδᾳ μίγεισα.

Accordingly Mercury appears here
with the finer attributes of the
Greek Hermes, with whom he was
identified at a very early period,
rather than as the god of trade,
which was the character under
which he was most widely worshipped in the Roman world ; and
his attributes of cunning and decep-
tion, which he necessarily bore as
the patron of traders in an age
when trade had not even advanced
so far as to regard honesty as the
best policy, are lightly touched
upon and presented in the more
agreeable aspect of the harmless
practical joke.— Metre, 174.

1. **facunde :** as the *nuntius deorum* (vs. 5), Ἑρμῆς λόγιος.—**nepos
Atlantis :** as *filius Maiae* (2. 43 n).

2. **feros cultus,** etc., *the savage
life of early man.*

voce formasti catus et decorae
　　more palaestrae,

5　te canam, magni Iovis et deorum
　nuntium curvaeque lyrae parentem,
　callidum quicquid placuit iocoso
　　condere furto.

Te boves olim nisi reddidisses
10　per dolum amotas puerum minaci
　voce dum terret, viduus pharetra
　　risit Apollo.

3. **voce**, *by language*, *i.e.* by teaching them articulate speech, the first step in civilization which raised man above the level of the brute. Cf. *S.* I. 3. 99 *sqq.*, where the poet's Epicurean view of man's progress is the same, except that it excludes the intervention of any god. — **formasti**, *didst mould, i.e.* reduce to symmetry and order. — **catus** : *i.e.* in foreseeing the efficacy of such means. The word has an antique flavor, an instance of the rule which Horace lays down *Ep.* II. 2. 115.

4. **more**, *the practice ; i.e.* by the institution of it.—**palaestrae:** here the exercise, not the place ; hence **decorae.** Physical training was regarded by the Greeks as an essential factor of education.

6. **nuntium** : as Ἑρμῆς διάκτορος. In this capacity he appears frequently in Greek and Latin literature, *e.g.* Odys. V. 29, Verg. *A.* I. 297, IV. 222 *sqq.* — **lyrae parentem:** according to the myth, which is substantially the same as given in the Homeric *Hymn to Hermes* 22 *sqq.*, this feat and the one recounted in the next strophe occurred on the day the god was born. The lively infant caught a

tortoise and with the shell constructed the first tetrachord.

7. **iocoso** : *i.e.* in fun, with no malice.

8. **condere**, *to hide*. For the mood see Intr. 101 *c*.

9. **te** : cf. vss. 5, 13, and 17. The emphatic repetition of the personal pronoun of the second person (Intr. 116 *f*) is particularly characteristic of hymns and eulogies ; cf. 35. 5–21, IV. 14. 33–51. — **nisi reddidisses** : the apodosis is implied in **minaci voce,** which must have stated what would happen if the cattle were not brought back. The pluperf. subj. is here used in indirect discourse to represent the future perf. indic. used by Apollo : *nisi boves reddideris.*

10. **puerum minaci:** Intr. 116 *a*.

11. **dum terret** : *i.e.* before the threat was out of his mouth he found his quiver gone.

12. **risit:** emphatic (Intr. 116 *b*), indicating the complete success of his joke : even his victim was left in good humor and joined in the laugh. The two brothers at once became fast friends ; Mercury gave Apollo his lyre, and received from the latter the magic rod (*virga* 18 n.).

Quin et Atridas duce te superbos
Ilio dives Priamus relicto
15   Thessalosque ignis et iniqua Troiae
'castra fefellit.

Tu pias laetis animas reponis
sedibus virgaque levem coerces
aurea turbam, superis deorum
20   gratus et imis.

13–20. The poet now returns to
Mercury's office as *nuntius deorum*
in their dealings with men, recalling a signal example of his success
in that capacity and closing with
a reference to his high function
of conductor of the shades of
the righteous to Elysium (Ἑρμῆς
ψυχοπομπός).

13. **quin et** : the story is introduced as merely a more marked
example of the god's success in
concealment, and hence suggested
by the preceding. But it serves to
make the transition to the subject of his beneficent activity in
behalf of mankind, and to the
more serious thought with which
the ode very properly closes. The
story is from *Il.* XXIV. 159 *sqq.*

14. **Ilio** : here and elsewhere in
Horace (III. 19. 4, IV. 4. 53, *Epod.*
10. 13), neuter in the ablative. He
uses a feminine nominative and
accusative, *Ilios, Ilion* (IV. 9. 18,
Epod. 14. 14). — **Ilio relicto** : and
so placing himself at the mercy of
his enemies. — **dives** : and hence
a prize they would have been most
eager to capture, had they known
of his presence.

15. **Thessalos** : *i.e.* those of
Achilles' men, the Myrmidons,
from Phthia, in Thessaly. Cf. II.
4. 10. — **ignis** : suggesting the
danger of detection. — **Troiae** :
dative.

16. **fefellit,** *passed unobserved.*

17. **tu** : cf. *te* 9 n. — **laetis . . .
reponis sedibus,** *dost bring safely
to the homes of bliss.* *Re-ponere,* in
the sense of 'put away' (cf. *tellure
repostos,* Verg. *A.* VI. 655) gives to
sedes here the meaning of *permanent* abode. For the case of **sedibus** see Intr. 69.

18. **virga aurea** : cf. *Hymn to
Herm.* 529: ὄλβου καὶ πλούτου δώσω
περικαλλέα ῥάβδον, | χρυσείην,
τριπέτηλον, ἀκήριον ἥ σε φυλάξει, |
πάντας ἐπικραίνουσ' οἴμους ἐπέων τε
καὶ ἔργων | τῶν ἀγαθῶν. The *cadu-
ceus,* with its two intertwining serpents, symbolical of peace and
commerce, was of later origin. —
levem coerces turbam, *keepest
together the unsubstantial throng,*
as a shepherd his flock ; cf. 24. 16
sqq.; Odys. XXIV. 1 *sqq.*

19. **deorum** : Intr. 63.

20. **imis** : for the more usual
inferis.

XI.

Tu ne quaesieris (scire nefas) quem mihi, quem tibi
finem di dederint, Leuconoe, nec Babylonios
temptaris numeros.   Vt melius quicquid erit pati,
seu pluris hiemes seu tribuit Iuppiter ultimam
5 · quae nunc oppositis debilitat pumicibus mare
Tyrrhenum.   Sapias, vina liques, et spatio brevi
spem longam reseces.   Dum loquimur fugerit invida
aetas·; carpe diem, quam minimum credula postero.

XI. The superstition of the
Romans made them an easy prey
to the soothsayers and astrologers
(cf. *S.* I. 6. 114) who flocked to
the city after the conquest of the
East. Leuconoe,— a name chosen
apparently for its pleasing sound
and its metrical value,— represents
in the poet's fancy a young person
whose attachment to him leads
her to resort to the fortune-tellers,
to learn what she can of his future
and of her own. Horace meets
this folly with his usual Epicurean
maxims,— a repetition, substantially, of 9. 13 *sqq.* The ode is no
doubt, like the two others written
in this metre (I. 18., IV. 10), a
free imitation or paraphrase of a
Greek original. — Metre, 170.

  1. **scire nefas,** *it is not vouchsafed us to know.* Cf. III. 29. 29 *sq.*
— **quem finem** etc.: *i.e.* when is
our appointed time to die.

  2. **nec:** for *neve* (Intr. 89 note).
The clause defines more particularly the kind of inquiry against
which his warning (**ne quaesieris**)
is directed. — **Babylonios numeros :** the calculations of the Chaldean astrologers.

  3. **temptaris,** *meddle with.* —
ut, *how much.*

  4. **hiemes :** *i.e.* years, but used

as in modern poetry, to give
the desired color to the thought,
— the same background as in Ode .
9. — **tribuit,** *has assigned, i.e.* at
our birth, the question which the
astrologers professed to solve.
For its position see Intr. 119 *a.*
— **ultimam :** agreeing with the
antecedent of **quae** (*sc. hanc*), *as
the last.*

  5. **debilitat,** *breaks;* lit. 'crip-
ples.' — **pumicibus :** instrumental
abl. The word is here used of
the rocks eaten away and hollowed
out by the action of the waves ;
cf. Plin. *N. H.* XXXVI. 154 *appel-
lantur quidem ita* (*sc. pumices*)
erosa saxa ; Verg. *A.* V. 213
*columba | cui domus et dulces late-
broso in pumice nidi.*

  6. **Tyrrhenum :** see Intr. 117.
— **sapias,** etc.: Intr. 87. — **liques,**
strain. The wine as it came from
the amphora contained a good
deal of sediment, which was removed by pouring it through a
coarse linen *saccus* or a colander
(*colum*). — **spatio brevi** (abl. abs.),
since our time is short, sc. for the
realization of far-reaching plans
and hopes.

  7. **spem longam :** cf. 4. 15. —
reseces, *prune down.* — **fugerit,**
will be gone. — **invida :** personify-

XII.

Quem virum aut heroa lyra vel acri
tibia sumis celebrare, Clio,

ing **aetas**, to express more vividly
the inexorable promptness of its
departure.

8. **diem**, *the passing day*, **carpe**
implying a transitory character in
its object ; cf. Mart. VII. 47. 11
fugitiva gaudia carpe. — **credula** :
cf. 5. 9 ; it expresses more than
credens (= *fidens*), and alludes to
her foolish faith in the astrologers. — **postero** (*sc. diei*) : Intr.
58 *a*.

XII. This ode, like Ode 2, was
written to glorify the mission of
Caesar Augustus, as the heaven-
sent ruler of the world. For the
form, Horace has worked upon a
suggestion which he found in
Pindar's second Olympian ode, the
opening verses of which he has
closely imitated : —

Ἀναξιφόρμιγγες ὕμνοι,
τίνα θεὸν, τίν' ἥρωα, τίνα δ' ἄνδρα
κελαδήσομεν ;

As in this ode Pindar approaches
the praise of the victor Thero
through the long story of the
fortunes and sorrows of his ancestors, so Horace presents Augustus as the culmination of the long
line of benefactors,— gods, heroes,
and men,— to whose activity or
suffering mankind is most indebted
for its progress. The tone of the
ode, in keeping with Augustus'
professed view of his mission, is
serious and free from any note of
triumph. It presents him as the
bearer of a great responsibility,
the successor, not of the great
warriors and powerful monarchs of
the past, but of the men who died

for their country or who served
her without exalting themselves.
See notes on vss. 35 and 41–44.

The allusion to Marcellus (vs. 45
sq.) shows that the ode could not
have been written much before his
marriage with Julia, the daughter
of Augustus (B.C. 25), nor later
than 23, the date of his death. —
Metre, 174.

1. **quem virum . . . heroa
. . . deum** : these three classes are
taken up in reverse order,— *dei*
in vss. 13–24, *heroes* in vss. 25–33,
viri in 34–48.— **heroa**, *demigod*.—
lyra vel tibia : cf. III. 4. 1–4.
Either instrument from its traditional use would be suitable for
the present purpose : the Greek
rhapsodist sang the exploits of his
heroes to the notes of the lyre ;
the tibia was said to have been
used to accompany the songs
which the Romans in early times,
according to Cato (Cic. *Tusc.* IV.
3), sang at banquets in praise of
their ancestors. — **acri**, *shrill*, a
highly appropriate and expressive
epithet according to Quintilian
(VIII. 2. 9).

2. **sumis**, *dost thou take, i.e.* as
a subject. Cf. *Ep.* II. 3. 38 *sumi-
te materiam vestris, qui scribitis,
aequam | viribus.* The present im-
plies that the muse has already
determined to sing ; the poet feels
her inspiration, and asks what is
the theme. The future, which is
found in a few MSS., would be
suitable if it were an invitation to
sing. — **celebrare** : Intr. 93. —
Clio : possibly addressed here in
the character, which she gradually
acquired, of muse of history. But

quem deum ?   Cuius recinet iocosa
    nomen imago

5   aut in umbrosis Heliconis oris
aut super Pindo gelidove in Haemo ?
Vnde vocalem temere insecutae
    Orphea silvae,

arte materna rapidos morantem
10 fluminum lapsus celerisque ventos,
blandum et auritas fidibus canoris
    ducere quercus.

the special attributes of the muses
which have come down to us are
not sharply defined in Horace,
whose muse is sometimes Euterpe
or Polyhymnia (1. 33), or Clio, as
here, or Melpomene (cf. 24. 3, III.
30. 16, IV. 3. 1), or Calliope (III.
4. 2) ; often simply *musa*, as II. 1.
37, 12. 13, III. 3. 70, etc.; or *mea
musa*, 17. 14 ; sometimes with a
qualifying phrase, as 6. 10 *imbellis
lyrae musa potens ; S.* II. 6. 17
musa pedestris ; Ep. II. 3. 407 *musa
lyrae sollers ;* cf. II. 1. 9 *musa tragoediae.*

3. iocosa, *merry,* personifying
Echo, as if she mocked people in
jest.   Cf. Ov. *M.* III. 356 *sqq.,*
where Echo is represented as a
nymph.

4. imago : used in prose also
for the Greek ἠχώ ; cf. Varro,
R. R. III. 16. 12 *ubi non resonent
imagines.*

5. Heliconis : a mountain in
Boeotia, on the borders of which,
at Ascra, there existed from very
early times a μουσεῖον, devoted to
the worship of the muses, and
under their protection to the promotion of literature.   Hesiod was
the most famous leader of this
school or guild, and ancient copies

of his works with the Homeric
and doubtless other poems were
preserved there.   The mountain in
consequence, and particularly the
springs of Aganippe and Hippocrene, had come to be regarded as
a favorite haunt of the muses.

6. super : cf. 9. 5 n. — Pindo :
the mountain range between Thessaly and Epirus, also regarded as
a seat of the muses ; cf. Verg. *E.*
10. 11. — Haemo : tradition made
the Heliconian school of song an
offshoot from an older school
which had been established at
Libethrum, in Pieria, on the
slopes of Olympus, by a tribe or
guild of Thracians whose leader,
Orpheus, was the son of the muse
Calliope and the Thracian king
Oeagrus.   Hence the name *Pieris*
for muse.

7. unde : *i.e.* from Haemus. —
temere : *i.e.* spell-bound, not of
their own will and intent ; they
could not choose but follow.

9. arte materna : *i.e.* music.
See note on *Haemo,* 8.

11. blandum, *with charm.* — et:
Intr. 114. — auritas (proleptic),
to lend ears to . . . and.

12. ducere : for the mood see
Intr. 101 *c.*

Quid prius dicam solitis parentis
laudibus, qui res hominum ac deorum,
15 qui mare et terras variisque mundum
temperat horis?

Vnde nil maius generatur ipso,
nec viget quicquam simile aut secundum ;
proximos illi tamen occupavit
20 Pallas honores.

13. **quid prius**, etc.: it being
prescribed by ancient tradition to
begin heroic songs with the glory
of Jove (**solitis laudibus**). Cf.
Pind. *Nem.* 2. 1 ὅθέν περ καὶ Ὁμη-
ρίδαι ῥαπτῶν ἐπέων τὰ πόλλ᾽ ἀοιδοὶ
ἄρχονται, Διὸς ἐκ προοιμίου. The
form ἐκ Διὸς ἀρχώμεσθα is found in
Aratus (*Phaen.* 1) and Theocritus
(17. 1) ; cf. Verg. *E.* 3. 60 *ab Iove
principium.* — **parentis** : *sc.* of
gods and men, as is indicated in
the following clause ; cf. II. 19. 21,
and see I. 2. 2 n.

14. **laudibus** : Intr. 75.

15. **mundum**, *the firmament.*
Mundus strictly includes the earth
(**mare ac terras**), but as we naturally think of the latter more in
its connection with our own lives
than its place in the universe,
mundus comes to mean the sky
and the heavenly bodies.

16. **temperat**, *governs.* — **horis**,
seasons; cf. *hora Caniculae,* III.
13. 9 ; *sub verni temporis horam,*
Ep. II. 3. 302.

17. **unde** = *ex quo,* referring to
parentis 13 ; cf. *S.* I. 6. 12. *Valeri
genus, unde superbus Tarquinius
regno pulsus fugit.* The use of
unde with a personal antecedent
is not infrequent in prose, as Sal.
Iug. 14. 22 *tibi, unde minime de-
cuit, vita erepta est.* — **nil**, *no one ;*
but stronger than *nemo* ; cf. *S.* I.

3. 18. — **generatur** : the present
expresses what is true at all
times, so that the meaning is that
Jove is eternally supreme. The
statement includes all gods and
men, Jove being here thought of
as the parent of all (cf. *parentis,*
13 n.)

18. **nec viget**, etc.: *i.e.* no living
being can compare with Jove in
power and glory (**viget**). The
relative construction is abandoned,
and *ei* must be supplied with
simile. — **quicquam**: cf. *nil,* 17 n.
— **aut secundum ; proximos
tamen** : *i.e.* though Pallas, as
compared with the common throng
of gods, is *nearest* to Jove, she
cannot be called *next* to him : she
is separated from him by a long
interval. Cf. Cic. *Brut.* 173 *duo-
bus summis, Crasso et Antonio, L.
Philippus proximus accedebat, sed
longo tamen intervallo proximus ;
itaque eum . . . neque secundum
neque tertium dixerim ; neque enim
in quadrigis eum secundum nomi-
naverim . . . qui vix e carceribus
exierit cum palmam iam primus
acceperit ;* Verg. *A.* V. 320.

19. **occupavit**, *holds.*

20. **Pallas** : as goddess of wisdom exalted above all other gods
but Jove himself. Cf. Hesiod,
Theog. 896 ἴσον ἔχουσαν πατρὶ μένος
καὶ ἐπίφρονα βουλήν.

Proeliis audax neque te silebo
Liber, et saevis inimica virgo
beluis, nec te, metuende certa
    Phoebe sagitta.

25 Dicam et Alciden puerosque Ledae,
hunc equis, illum superare pugnis
nobilem ; quorum simul alba nautis
    stella refulsit,

defluit saxis agitatus umor,

21. **proeliis audax** : Horace
not infrequently begins an address
with a descriptive phrase in agreement with the name of the person
addressed, which is inserted in the
sentence later, as II. 7. 1, *Ep.* I.
1. 1. Bacchus was endowed with
a greater variety of attributes and
epithets (cf. Ov. *M.* IV. 11 *sqq.*)
than any other god. His prowess in
war was displayed in the battle of
the Giants (II. 19. 21 *sqq.*), and his
triumphal Indian journey, according to one form of the myth, was
a military expedition. The poet
naturally mentions this, one of his
nobler qualities, in a list of gods
and heroes who have contributed
to the welfare of mankind. So
Diana is here not simply the goddess of the chase, but the destroyer
of monsters (**saevis beluis**), and
Apollo is joined with her as the
god of the bow ; see vs. 23 n.
Hercules and the Dioscuri are well
known benefactors of the race.

22. **et** : connecting the description of Diana with **proeliis audax
Liber.** The idea of **neque te
silebo** (= *te quoque memorabo ;
non silere* being a mere rhetorical
variation (litotes) for *dicere* or
memorare ; cf. IV. 9. 31) is repeated with **virgo**, which is voca-
tive.

23. **metuende sagitta** : see vs.
21 n. The allusion is to Apollo's
destruction of the python (Ov. *M.*
I. 438 *sqq*). — **certa**, *unerring.*

25. **dicam** : see 6. 5 n. — **et**, *too.*
— **Alciden** : Hercules, whose reputed father, Amphitryon, was the
son of Alceus. His services, like
those of the Roman heroes who
follow, are not enlarged upon,
being well known. — **pueros Ledae** : Castor and Pollux.

26. **hunc**, etc.: cf. *S.* II. 1. 26
*Castor gaudet equis, ovo prognatus
eodem | pugnis ; Il.* III. 237 Κά-
στορα θ' ἱππόδαμον καὶ πὺξ ἀγαθὸν
Πολυδεύκεα. — **superare nobilem** :
see Intr. 101 *c.* — **pugnis** : from
pugnus.

27. **quorum simul** : cf. *qui
simul,* 9. 9 n, and the whole description there. — **alba**, *bright.*

28. **stella** : cf. 3. 2 n. — **refulsit,**
has flashed (out of the darkness)
upon.

29. **defluit**, etc.: Horace here
introduces one of his graphic
pictures (cf. 2. 7 n), to break the
monotony of his long catalogue
of benefactors. In this passage
and in IV. 8. 31 he reproduces a
description of Theocritus, 22. 17
ἀλλ' ἔμπας ὑμεῖς (*sc.* Διόσκουροι) γε
καὶ ἐκ βυθοῦ ἕλκετε νᾶας | αὐτοῖσιν
ναύταισιν ὀιομένοις θανέεσθαι · | αἶψα

30   concidunt venti fugiuntque nubes,
        et minax, quod sic voluere, ponto
            unda recumbit.

        Romulum post hos prius an quietum
        Pompili regnum memorem an superbos
35   Tarquini fascis dubito, an Catonis
            nobile letum.

δ' ἀπολήγοντ' ἄνεμοι, λιπαρὰ δὲ
γαλήνα | ἀμ' πέλαγος· νεφέλαι δὲ
διέδραμον ἄλλυδις ἄλλαι.

31. voluere, *have willed.* Such
parenthetical clauses, referring the
events described to the will of
some deity, are not uncommon;
cf. *Il.* I. 5 Διὸς δ' ἐτελείετο βουλή.

32. recumbit, *subsides;* lit. 'lies
down,' having been **minax,** *i.e.*
towering aloft as it approached.

33. Romulum, etc.: from the
demigods who have befriended
mankind, Horace proceeds to
the founders and builders of the
great empire which is destined to
bring the whole earth under its
beneficent sway. The number of
these is so large as to be embar-
rassing, and the poet is in doubt
where to begin.

34. Pompili : *sc. Numae.*
Roman tradition assigned almost
equal merit to Romulus and
Numa for their very different
services in establishing the state.
Cf. Liv. I. 21. 6 *duo deinceps reges,
alius alia via, ille bello hic pace,
civitatem auxerunt.* — **superbos
Tarquini fascis,** *the haughty
power of the Tarquin.* The
epithet belongs logically to **Tarquini** (Intr. 124), and hence the
reference must be to Tarquin the
Proud, whose contributions to
Rome's greatness, through the
subjection of neighboring tribes,
were very considerable, and whose

memory, in spite of the bitter
hatred which he incurred in his
struggle with the people, was at
least respected. Cf. Cic. *Phil.* 3, 9
*Tarquinius . . . non crudelis, non
impius, sed superbus habitus est :
. . . nihil humile de Tarquinio,
nihil sordidum accepimus.*

35. Catonis, etc. : it is noteworthy that Horace, coming now
to the time of the Commonwealth,
passes over the greatest warriors
and statesmen, and selects only
typical instances of the Roman
virtus which courted poverty or
death for the public good.

36. nobile letum : Cato's contemporaries were entirely convinced of his disinterestedness and
his sincerity in carrying his Stoic
principles into political life, and
his dramatic suicide at Utica, after
Caesar's victory at Thapsus, in
B.C. 46, invested him with something of the halo of a saint, whose
lofty character and motives were
a safe subject of eulogy even in
an ode in honor of the heir and
successor of Caesar. Horace's
admiration for him, which appears
here and in II. 1. 24, dated no
doubt from the time when he
joined the army of Brutus. Vergil's tribute is still higher : he
makes Cato another Minos, judg-
ing the dead (*secretosque pios, his
dantem iura Catonem, A.* VIII.
670).

Regulum et Scauros animaeque magnae
prodigum Paullum superante Poeno
gratus insigni referam camena
40   Fabriciumque.

37. Regulum: the poet's second
example of a *nobile letum*. M.
Atilius Regulus, in his second
consulship, B.C. 256, during the
first Punic war, successfully invaded Africa, but the next year he
was defeated and captured by the
Carthaginians. The story of his
mission to Rome with a Cartha-
ginian embassy to arrange ransom
for the prisoners, his advice to the
senate to leave the latter to their
fate, and his voluntary return to
captivity and death, is told in III.
5. 13 *sqq.* — **Scauros:** M. Aemilius
Scaurus and his son. The latter
was involved in the panic of the
Roman cavalry under Catulus in
the disastrous battle on the Adige
(B.C. 101), when they were so
effectively routed by the Cimbri
that they abandoned their general
and fled incontinently to the city.
Young Scaurus was met by a
stern message from his father that
his dead body brought home from
the battle-field would have been
more welcome than his return
alive after so disgraceful a repulse,
and thereupon put an end to his
own life. Val. Max. V. 8. 4.

38. prodigum, *that squanderer*.
The touch of censure implied in
the word only heightens the effect
of the eulogy. L. Aemilius Paullus,
consul in B.C. 216 with Terentius
Varro, fell in the battle of Cannae,
which his colleague had brought
on against his advice. As the story
is told by Livy (XXII. 49. 6) Paullus could have escaped without
personal dishonor, but chose to die
with his men rather than return
from such a disastrous defeat.

39. gratus : *i.e.* for the sacrifice
which such splendid devotion to
duty and country has cost. — **insigni camena,** *with no ordinary
song.* The Camenae (earlier form,
Casmenae ; cf. *carmen = casmen*),
originally nymphs in whose songs
the magical or prophetic knowledge
of the spirits of the woods found
expression, enjoy a wider province in the Augustan and later
poets, who identify them with the
Greek muses (cf. II. 16. 38 *Graiae
Camenae ; C. S.* 62), and use the
singular, as here, concretely for
'song' (cf. *Ep.* I. 1. 1).

40. Fabriciumque : by including one of the group of great men
next described in his *grata relatio*
Horace virtually includes them all.

41–44. The three worthies
named in this strophe too are
selected not so much for the greatness of their achievements as for
the lesson which their example
conveys. They stand for the
highest type of citizenship in the
best days of the Commonwealth,—
men whose training for public
service was hard work at home,
and whose eminence in the state
did not affect the simplicity of
their lives and their indifference
to riches. C. Fabricius Luscinus
and M'. Curius Dentatus were
prominent in the wars against the
Samnites and Pyrrhus, and tradition loved to tell of the futile
efforts of the latter to move them
either with flattery or with gold
(Val. Max. IV. 3. 5 *sq.,* Cic. *C.
M.* 55, *Rep.* III. 6). M. Furius
Camillus, the conqueror of Veii
(B.C. 396) and deliverer of Rome

Hunc et intonsis Curium capillis
utilem bello tulit et Camillum
saeva paupertas et avitus apto
    cum lare fundus.

45 Crescit occulto velut arbor aevo
fama Marcelli ; micat inter omnis

from the Gauls (390), was the most
eminent Roman of his time.

41. **intonsis capillis:** this characteristic of earlier and simpler times
was made familiar to every Roman
by the public statues. Cf. Varro *R.
R.* II. 11. 10 *olim tonsores non fuisse
adsignificant antiquorum statuae,
quod pleraeque habent capillum et
barbam magnam.* There were no
barbers in Rome, according to Varro (cf. Plin. *N. H.* VII. 211), till B.C.
300, which was in the lifetime of
Curius, and it was a long time after
that date that the fashion of trim-
ming the hair short and shaving off
the beard became general. Hence
intonsus, barbatus, etc., are used to
connote ancient times and simple
manners. Cf. *intonsi Catonis;* II. 15.
11 ; *barbato regi,* Juv. 4. 103.

42. **utilem:** applying to all three
men. — **bello :** dative ; Intr. 58 *c.*

43. **saeva paupertas :** cf. III.
6. 33–44, where the poet points
more sharply the contrast between
the severe training which made
the sturdy manhood of early times,
and the degeneracy of his own day
when poverty was a reproach (III.
24. 42). — **avitus :** *i.e.* not purchased or enlarged by him, implying his abstinence from the pursuit of wealth ; cf. *patrios agros*
I. 11 n. — **apto,** *to match ;* not a
great country-house such as a man
of his station would now have.

44. **lare,** *a dwelling.* The word
itself excludes the idea of a large
house.

45. **crescit,** *is growing.* The
present prepares the reader for
the transition which the poet now
makes to his own times. This he
does by selecting as his last
example of the great men of old,
M. Claudius Marcellus, the con-
querer of Syracuse (B.C. 212) and
the first Roman general who
fought Hannibal with success. He
was killed in a skirmish in his 5th
consulship, B.C. 208. The mention
of this famous warrior could not
fail to carry with it to Horace's
readers an allusion to Marcellus,
the nephew and son-in-law of
Augustus, whose untimely death
Vergil commemorates in the
Aeneid (VI. 860) ; and the poet
manages, without expressly naming this young man, who had performed no achievement as yet
worth mentioning, to intimate that
he has a great career before him.
— **occulto aevo,** *which does not
show its age ;* descriptive ablative.
Since the time of the great Marcellus no member of that family
had attained any special eminence;
his fame, which would have been
enhanced by distinguished descendants, appeared to be at a stand-
still ; but like a tree, which
appears the same from year to
year, it is really growing. The
compliment to the young Marcellus is obvious.

46. **inter omnis :** sc. *duces,* or
the like ; 'in the whole galaxy,'
as we should say, of great men.

Iulium sidus velut inter ignis
    luna minores.

Gentis humanae pater atque custos,
50 orte Saturno, tibi cura magni
    Caesaris fatis data : tu secundo
        Caesare regnes.

Ille seu Parthos Latio imminentis
    egerit iusto domitos triumpho
55 sive subiectos Orientis orae
        Seras et Indos,

te minor latum reget aequus orbem ;
    tu gravi curru quaties Olympum,
    tu parum castis inimica mittes
60   fulmina lucis.

47. **Iulium sidus** : *i.e.* the
Julian house. The figure was
possibly suggested by the comet
which appeared after the death of
Julius Caesar (Suet. *Iul.* 88., Verg.
E. 9. 47), but more probably was
chosen simply with a view to the
comparison that follows. The
poet wishes us to think of Augustus and not of Julius Caesar. —
inter ignis, etc.: cf. *Epod.* 15. 2.

49. **gentis humanae**, etc.: the
ode closes with a solemn appeal to
Jupiter, the father of all mankind,
to accept the predestined ruler of
the race as his vicegerent on earth.

51. **secundo Caesare**, *with
Caesar next to thee.* There is no
allusion to verse 18, the point of
view here being entirely different.
The other gods have their special
provinces and do not come under
consideration at all here, where
the government of the earth is
the topic in mind.

53. **ille seu**, etc.: *i.e.* he, on his
part, whatever triumphs may be in

store for him, will ever own his
dependence on thee. — **Parthos** :
see 2. 22 n. — **Latio** : used like
Roma for the Roman state ; cf.
35. 10 with III. 3. 44.

54. **egerit**, *shall lead ;* lit. ' shall
have driven,' a more exact expression than *ducere* (which is also
used), since the prisoners preceded
the victor's car in the triumphal
procession. — **iusto**, *well earned.*
Iustus triumphus is a technical
phrase, expressing compliance with
certain well understood conditions
relating to the rank of the general
and the extent and importance of
his victory.

55. **subiectos Orientis orae,**
*who dwell beneath the borders of the
eastern sky.* **Orientis** is a substantive, like *Occidentis*, *Epod.* 1. 13.

56. **Sĕrăs** (Σῆρας) **et Indos** :
vague names to convey the impression of unlimited future conquests ; cf. IV. 15. 21 *sqq.*, *C. S.*
53 *sqq.*

57. **te minor,** *as subordinate to*

XIII.

Cum tu, Lydia, Telephi
  cervicem roseam, cerea Telephi
laudas bracchia, vae meum
  fervens difficili bile tumet iecur.

5 Tum nec mens mihi nec color
  certa sede manet, umor et in genas
furtim labitur, arguens
  quam lentis penitus macerer ignibus.

Vror, seu tibi candidos
10 turparunt umeros immodicae mero

thee ; cf. III. 6. 5 *dis te minorem quod geris, imperas.* For **te, tu, tu,** see 10. 9 n ; Intr. 116 *f.* — **aequus,** *with justice.*

58. **tu gravi,** etc.: *i.e.* thou wilt maintain thy supreme authority by the usual manifestations of thy power and of thy wrath.

59. **parum castis,** *polluted.* — **inimica fulmina :** cf. 3. 40 n, and see Intr. 124.

60. **lucis :** dat.; cf. *terris,* 2. 1 ; Intr. 53. Lightning as a sign of the divine will held a prominent place in Roman divination, and it was regarded as of momentous significance if a sacred grove or temple (cf. 2. 16 n.) was struck. Preller-Jordan *Röm. Myth.* I. 192.

XIII. The jealous lover's appeal. — Metre, 171.

2. **cerea :** *i.e.* smooth and free from blemishes, like a waxen image. — **Telephi :** repeated with bitterness, in imitation of her maddening iteration of the name. Cf. *S.* I. 6. 45 *sq.*

3. **vae,** *ugh !*

4. **difficili,** *uncomfortable.* —

iecur : regarded as the seat of the passions, especially of anger (cf. *S.* I. 9. 66 *meum iecur urere bilis*) and love (cf. IV. 1. 12).

5. **nec mens,** etc.: *i.e.* I lose control of my feelings and my color comes and goes. For this use of *mens* cf. Cat. 61. 33 *mentem amore revinciens.*

6. **manēt :** Intr. 179. — **umor,** *the tear.*

7. **furtim,** etc.: *i.e.* to my surprise, making me aware of the depth of my feeling.

8. **quam :** with **penitus.** — **lentis,** *persistent, lingering.* — **macerer,** *I am wasting away.*

9. **uror,** etc.: *i.e.* I am enraged by the sight of these unseemly marks of the intimacy which you have allowed him.

10. **turparunt :** *i.e.* have left them 'black and blue.' Cf. 17. 25 *sqq.;* Prop. III. 7. 19 *quin etiam, si me ulterius provexerit ira,* | *ostendes matri bracchia laesa tuae.* — **immodicae,** (*carried to excess*), *indecent.* — **mero,** *over your cups.* The abl. expresses the cause of **immodicae.**

rixae, sive puer furens
    impressit memorem dente labris notam.
Non, si me satis audias,
    speres perpetuum dulcia barbare
15 laedentem oscula, quae Venus
    quinta parte sui nectaris imbuit.
Felices ter et amplius,
    quos inrupta tenet copula nec malis
divolsus querimoniis
20   suprema citius solvet amor die.

11. **sive**, etc.: the passionate youth has been as violent in his caresses as in his anger.

14. **perpetuum**, *constant*.

16. **quinta parte**: *i.e.* a generous share. Others explain the phrase as indicating the degree of sweetness, referring to a fancy found in the Greek lyric poets that honey was ἔνατον μέρος τῆς ἀμβροσίας or τῆς ἀθανασίας δέκατον μέρος (Athen. II. 8, Schol. on Pind. *Pyth.* 9. 16); but this would imply that the substance with which Venus bathed Lydia's lips was something else than nectar. It has also been conjectured that *quinta pars* was used, like *quinta essentia* in mediaeval Latin, *for ἡ πέμπτη οὐσία*, the name given by the Pythagorean philosophers to the ether, the subtlest of the five elements. This would be very appropriate here (*quintessence*), but there is no evidence and little probability that the phrase was used in this sense. — **sui**, *her own*.

17. **ter et amplius**: cf. Verg. *A.* I. 94 *terque quaterque beati*.

18. **inrupta**, *that nothing can sever*. The word is found only here and is used, like *invictus*, *indomitus*, etc., with the force of an adjective in *-ilis*. — **nec malis**,

etc., *and whom no estrangement, begotten of hateful reproaches*, etc.; an amplification of the preceding clause.

19. **divolsus amor**: see Intr. 105 *a*.

20. **suprema**, *the last* (*sc.* of life). — **solvet**: with reference to *copula*, 18. — **die**: Intr. 75.

XIV. Quintilian (VIII. 6. 44) cites this ode as an example of that species of allegory (*inversio*) which *aliud verbis aliud sensu ostendit*, and adds this explanation: *navem pro re publica, fluctus et tempestates pro bellis civilibus, portum pro pace atque concordia dicit*. The figure of the 'ship of state' Horace found already employed by Greek writers (as Theognis 671, Plato *Rep.* VI. 4), and among others by Alcaeus in an ode (*Fr.* 18) beginning

Ἀσυνέτημι τῶν ἀνέμων στάσιν·
τὸ μὲν γὰρ ἔνθεν κῦμα κυλίνδεται,
    τὸ δ' ἔνθεν· ἄμμες δ' ἀν τὸ μέσσον
ναῒ φορήμεθα σὺν μελαίνᾳ,
χείμωνι μοχθεῦντες μεγάλῳ μάλα·
πὲρ μὲν γὰρ ἄντλος ἰστοπέδαν ἔχει,
    λαῖφος δὲ πᾶν ζάδηλον ἤδη
    καὶ λάκιδες μέγαλαι κὰτ' αὖτο·
χόλαισι δ' ἄγκυραι.

XIV.

O navis, referent in mare te novi
fluctus !   O quid agis ?   Fortiter occupa·
portum !   Nonne vides ut
nudum remigio latus

5   et malus celeri saucius Africo
antemnaeque gemant ac sine funibus
vix durare carinae
possint imperiosius

Horace's treatment, however, is essentially different. In the Greek poet the ship is merely the metaphor under which he pictures to his fellow-citizens their political situation ; in the present ode, as in Longfellow's famous poem, she is the personified Commonwealth, the ideal object of patriotic devotion which we usually express by 'our country.' There is no direct evidence to show when the ode was written, but it probably belongs to the period of uncertainty between the battle of Actium and the settlement of the year 27. The ship is still at sea, sailing now in the quieter waters near the shore, but so shattered and torn that she cannot possibly live through another storm. Her only safety lies in making without delay a secure harbor. The plain meaning of this is that the state is in too exhausted a condition to endure another civil contest ; what is needed above all else is peace, — the very sentiment to which Octavian appealed and on which he established his power. — Metre, 173.

1. **in mare**, *out to sea*. The ship is imagined as sailing along, according to the ancient practice, within a safe distance of the shore; cf. II. 10. 1–4. — **novi fluctus :** *i.e.* another storm coming up, (another civil conflict).

2. **fortiter. occupa,** *be active now, and gain.*

3. **nonne vides,** *seest thou not ?* But **vides** is vague enough in its meaning to express the perception of sounds (**gemant,** 6); cf. *S.* II. 8. 77 *videres stridere susurros ;* Verg. *A.* IV. 490 *mugire videbis | sub pedibus terram et descendere montibus ornos.* — **ut:** cf. 9. 1 n.

4. **nudum remigio** (*sc. sit*), *is stripped of its oars* (broken off by the violence of the storm). See Intr. 66 *c*, note.

5. **mālus :** to be taken with **gemant.**

6. **gemant,** *creak*, — not by rubbing against one another, but each for itself ; they have all been strained by the force of the storm. — **funibus:** used for undergirding the ship (cf. *N. T. Acts* 27. 17), to keep the planks from springing apart under the strain of a rough sea.

7. **durare,** *hold out against.* — **carinae,** *the hull.* For the plural see Intr. 128.

8. **imperiosius,** *in his sterner mood*, personifying **aequor.**

aequor ?   Non tibi sunt integra lintea,
10   non di, quos iterum pressa voces malo.
      Quamvis Pontica pinus,
          silvae filia nobilis,

      iactes et genus et nomen inutile,
      nil pictis timidus navita puppibus
15   fidit.   Tu nisi ventis
          debes ludibrium, cave.

      Nuper sollicitum quae mihi taedium,
      nunc desiderium curaque non levis,
          interfusa nitentis
20   vites aequora Cycladas.

10. **non di** : *i.e.* the images
of gods, which were carried
in the stern (cf. Verg. *A.* X. 171
aurato fulgebat Apolline puppis ;
Pers. 6. 30), have been dashed
overboard in the storm. —**iterum
pressa malo,** *when again in distress.*

11. **Pontica:** the woods of Pontus and Bithynia were famous for
their excellent ship-timber. Cf. Cat.
4. 9 *Ponticum sinum,* | *ubi iste post
phaselus antea fuit* | *comata silva.*

12. **silvae filia :** cf. Mart. XIV.
90. 1 *silvae filia Maurae* (of a
table).

13. **iactes :** observe that this is
the emphatic word of the verse,
and **inutile** is only thrown in incidentally : *boast as thou wilt of
thy worthless pedigree and name.* —
genus et nomen : carrying out
the fancy expressed in filia.

14. **pictis :** the after part of a
ship was often richly decorated;
cf. Seneca, *Ep.* 76. 13.

15. **tu :** cf. 9. 16 n, 11. 1.

16. **debes,** *art bound to furnish*
(*sc.* by fate), *art doomed to be* (so
that no effort can save thee). —

ludibrium, *food for laughter.* —
cave : used absolutely (as in *Epod.*
6. 11), but the caution is expressed
more fully below (vss. 19, 20).

17. **nuper sollicitum,** etc.,
*whom I but lately looked upon
with apprehension and disgust ;*
i.e. disgust at the turn things had
taken, and apprehension of worse
results that might ensue.   The
allusion is to the time following
the defeat of the republican army
at Philippi, when Horace, whose
whole heart was in the lost cause,
could see in the triumph of its
enemies nothing but the utter
rottenness of politics; cf. *Epodes*
7 and 16. — **quae** : *sc. eras.*

18. **nunc desiderium,** etc., *now
my heart's desire and deep solici-
tude.* Cf. Cic. *Fam.* XIV. 2. 2 (to
Terentia) *mea lux, meum desiderium ;* Cat. 2. 5 ; Verg. *A.* I. 678
puer, mea maxima cura.

19. **nitentis,** *glistening ;* alluding
to their marble-quarries. Cf. III.
28. 14 *fulgentis Cycladas ;* Verg.
A. III. 126 *niveam Parum.*

20. **Cycladas** : object of **inter-
fusa.** The sea in the neighbor-

XV.

Pastor cum traheret per freta navibus
Idaeis Helenen perfidus hospitam,
ingrato celeres obruit otio
    ventos ut caneret fera

5 Nereus fata : ' Mala ducis avi domum
quam multo repetet Graecia milite,
coniurata tuas rumpere nuptias
    et regnum Priami vetus.

hood of these islands, like the rest of the Aegean (cf. II. 16. 2, III. 29. 63, etc.), was subject to sudden and dangerous storms. The mention of these particular waters has no significance in the allegory (Intr. 117 a).

XV. The motive of this ode, according to Porphyrio, was borrowed from an ode of Bacchylides, in which Cassandra was represented as foretelling the events of the Trojan war. If so, Horace has improved upon his model by transferring the scene to the ship of Paris on his homeward voyage with Helen, and substituting for the Trojan prophetess the sea-god Nereus; for Paris is thus confronted with the disastrous consequences of his crime in the very hour of his triumph. — Metre, 172.

1. pastor : Paris, who was exposed in his infancy and brought up among the shepherds on Mt. Ida. So *Phrygius pastor*, Verg. *A.* VII. 363. — traheret, *was carrying off*.

2. Idaeis : *i.e.* built of wood from Mt. Ida. — perfidus hospitam : Intr. 116 a. No treachery could be more heinous than that of the man who used the sacred rights of hospitality to plot against his host.

3. ingrato, *unwelcome* (*sc.* to the winds). — obruit, *smothered*.

4. caneret, *foretell;* frequently used in this sense, oracles and prophecies being in metrical form. Cf. *C. S.* 25 ; Verg. *A.* II. 124.

5. Nereus : eldest of the sons of Pontus, father of Thetis and the other Nereids; always called in Homer the 'old man of the sea' (*e.g. Il.* I. 556 ἁλίοιο γέροντος), and never by name. Cf. Hes. *Theog.* 233 Νηρέα δ' ἀψευδέα καὶ ἀληθέα . . . καλέουσι γέροντα | οὕνεκα νημερτής τε καὶ ἤπιος. — malā avi: for *malis auspiciis;* cf. *mala alite, Epod.* 10. 1 ; *bona alite,* Cat. 61. 20. — dūcis (sc. *eam*) domum, *thou art bringing home a bride.*

6. multo milite : Intr. 127.

7. coniurata : referring probably not to the oath by which Tyndareus bound the suitors of Helen before her marriage, but to the league of the assembled chiefs at Aulis, alluded to in Verg. *A.* IV. 425 *non ego cum Danais Troianam exscindere gentem* | *Aulide iuravi.* — rumpere, *to break up.* For the mood, see Intr. 94 *f.*

Heu heu, quantus equis, quantus adest viris
10   sudor !   Quanta moves funera Dardanae
     genti !   Iam galeam Pallas et aegida
        currusque et rabiem parat.

     Nequiquam Veneris praesidio ferox
     pectes caesariem grataque feminis
15   imbelli cithara carmina divides ;
        nequiquam thalamo gravis

     hastas et calami spicula Cnosii
     vitabis strepitumque et celerem sequi

9. **heu heu,** *ah me!* The sympathy of the god is called forth by
the actual vision which he has as
a seer of the events foretold. The
following scenes are all taken from
the Iliad. — **quantus equis,** etc.:
cf. *Il.* II. 388 ἱδρώσει μέν τευ
τελαμών . . . ἱδρώσει δέ τευ ἵππος.
10. **quanta moves funera,**
*what a train of disaster . . . thou
art starting.* For the plural, see
Intr. 128 and cf. 8. 15. — **Dardanae :** Intr. 65.
11. **iam,** *even now.* — **Pallas,**
etc.: cf. *Il.* V. 719 *sqq.* — **aegida :**
sometimes represented as the
shield of Zeus, more commonly as
the corselet of Athena (*Il.* V. 738).
As such it appears in numerous
statues of that goddess, — a coat
of mail, with the head of the gor-
gon Medusa in the middle, as described by Verg. *A.* VIII. 435 :
*aegidaque horriferam, turbatae
Palladis arma,* | *certatim squa-
mis serpentum auroque polibant* |
*conexosque anguis, ipsamque in
pectore divae* | *Gorgona, desecto ver-
tentem lumina collo.*
12. **currus :** Intr. 128. — **et
rabiem :** added with powerful
effect to complete the inventory of
her outfit for battle ; cf. *Il.* IV. 447

σύν ῥ᾽ ἔβαλον ῥινούς σὺν δ᾽ ἔγχεα καὶ
μένε᾽ ἀνδρῶν.
13. **nequiquam** etc.: cf. the
taunt of Hector, *Il.* III. 54 οὐκ ἄν
τοι χραίσμῃ κίθαρις τά τε δῶρ᾽ Ἀφρο-
δίτης | ἥ τε κόμη τό τε εἶδος, ὅτ᾽ ἐν
κονίῃσι μιγείης. — **ferox,** *embolden-
ed.* The phrase suggests a scornful
contrast with genuine courage.
14. **grata feminis :** contempt-
uous, like **imbelli cithara** and
thalamo, below.
15. **imbelli cithara :** cf. *imbellis
lyrae,* 6. 10. — **divides,** *wilt sing
to the accompaniment of.* The
word, which is nowhere else used
in this sense, is apparently intended to express the effect of the
instrumental accompaniment in
marking the parts or measures of
the air. Others, however, suppose
that Horace had in mind the
division into strophes by inter-
ludes on the lute.
16. **thalamo :** see Intr. 69. and
cf. *Il.* III. 380 τὸν δ᾽ (*sc.* Paris)
ἐξήρπαξ᾽ Ἀφροδίτη | κὰδ᾽ δ᾽ εἶσ᾽ ἐν
θαλάμῳ εὐώδεϊ, κηώεντι.
17. **Cnosii :** Intr. 117 *a.* The
Cretans were famous archers, and
Cnosus was one of their principal towns ; cf. Verg. *A.* V. 306
Cnosia spicula.

Aiacem : tamen, heu, serus adulteros
20   crinis pulvere collines.

Non Laertiaden, exitium tuae
gentis, non Pylium Nestora respicis ?
Vrgent impavidi te Salaminius
    Teucer, te Sthenelus sciens

25   pugnae, sive opus est imperitare equis,
non auriga piger.   Merionen quoque
nosces.   Ecce furit te reperire atrox
    Tydides, melior patre,

quem tu, cervus uti vallis in altera
30   visum parte lupum graminis immemor
sublimi fugies mollis anhelitu,
    non hoc pollicitus tuae.

18. **vitabis,** *wilt thou stay . . . out of the way of.*— **sequi** : Intr. 101 *b*.

19. **Aiacem** : the son of Oileus ('Οιλῆος ταχὺς Αἴας, *Il.* II. 527).— **serus,** *though long deferred the day will come when.* Cf. III. 11. 28 *sera fata.* For the adjective used to express time, cf. 2. 45, *Ep.* II. 1. 161.— **adulteros crinis**: Intr. 124.

21. **Laertiaden** : Ulysses. — **exitium tuae gentis** : to the shrewdness of Ulysses, culminating in the seizure of the Palladium, the success of the Greeks was held to be chiefly due. Cf. *Ep.* I. 2. 18 *Vlixen, qui, domitor Troiae,* etc., a free translation of the opening lines of the Odyssey.

22. **non respicis,** *seest thou not behind thee?* cf. Verg. *A.* VIII. 697 *necdum geminos a tergo respicit anguis.* The god in his vision sees the dangers of the battle-field already close upon the unconscious Paris.

24. **Teucer** : see 7. 21 n. — **Sthenelus** : charioteer of Diomed.

25. **sive** : Intr. 119 *d*.

26. **Merionen** : see 6. 15 n.

27. **reperire** : Intr. 94 *c.*

28. **Tydides** : cf. 6. 15 n. — **melior patre** : *i.e.* as a warrior ; suggested by the saying of Sthenelus, *Il.* IV. 405 ἡμεῖς τοι πατέρων μέγ᾽ ἀμείνονες εὐχόμεθ᾽ εἶναι.

29. **cervus uti,** etc.: *sc. fugit,* of which **lupum** is the object. — **in altera parte,** (on the other side of), *across ; i.e.* without waiting for him to come near.

30. **visum,** *at the sight of.*— **graminis immemor** : a further touch to indicate the fright of the stag.

31. **sublimi anhelitu,** *panting with head high in air.* This description properly belongs to the stag : the comparison and its subject are purposely confused ; Intr. 123. — **mollis,** *faint heart.*

32. **non hoc,** etc.: *i.e.* something very different from this (litotes). With this final touch of scorn the god dismisses Paris, and closes his prophecy with the fate of Troy itself. — **tuae**: cf. *tuo,* 25. 7.

Iracunda diem proferet Ilio
matronisque Phrygum classis Achillei:
35   post certas hiemes uret Achaicus
ignis Iliacas domos.'

XVI.

O matre pulchra filia pulchrior,
quem criminosis cumque voles modum

33. **iracunda classis**: see Intr.
105 *a*. The followers of Achilles,
who shared the inactivity of their
chief, are regarded as sharing the
wrath to which it was due. — **diem
proferet**, *will put off the day*, *i.e.*
the day of doom, already foreshad-
owed in vss. 8 and 21.

34. **matronisque Phrygum** :
not strictly necessary after the
comprehensive **Ilio**, but added to
lend a touch of pathos to the
otherwise colorless statement, by
recalling the class of persons on
whom the calamity will bring the
most intense suffering ; cf. 1. 24,
35. 11 n.— **Phrygum**: for Trojan,
as in II. 9. 16 ; cf. Verg. *A*. I. 182,
etc. — **Achillei** : for the form, cf.
Vlixei, 6. 7 n.

35. **post certas hiemes,** *when
the predestined number of winters
is past*, *i.e.* in the fullness of time.
Observe the asyndeton and the
emphatic position of these words.
The preceding sentence is not concessive, but the two together sum
up, in its successive stages, the
course of the war which is to come.
Translated into prose the thought
is: For a time internal dissension
will paralyze the Greek and the
doom of Troy will be withheld ;
when the appointed hour is come,
he will burn the city. For **hiemes**
cf 11. 4 n.

36. **Iliacas :** this reading of all
the MSS. has been questioned with
good reason, (1) because of **Ilio**
in 33, and (2) on account of the
trochee **īgnis**, which violates a
rule elsewhere strictly observed by
Horace (see Intr. 146 *b*, 147). The
second objection may be explained
on the supposition that in this,
which is probably one of his early
odes, Horace followed his Greek
models, and allowed himself a
liberty which he subsequently
refrained from using. The first
objection has some weight, but no
substitute for **Iliacas** is offered by
any authority. Conjectures such
as *Pergameas, Dardanias, barbaricas* have been adopted by various
editors.

XVI. The inscription in the
manuscripts, *Palinodia*, indicates
the nature of this ode, in which
the poet represents himself as
having given vent to his anger
against his mistress in some verses
which he now begs her to destroy
and forget. The fact that he calls
the offending verses *iambi*, his
own name for the Epodes (*Ep*. I.
19. 23, II. 2. 59), gives some color
to the supposition that here for
once Horace is dealing with a
definite experience of his own.
But the humorous extravagance

pones iambis, sive flamma
  sive mari libet Hadriano.
5   Non Dindymene, non adytis quatit
  mentem sacerdotum incola Pythius,
    non Liber aeque, non acuta
      sic geminant Corybantes aera

with which he urges the lady to calm her mind and dilates on the dreadful effects of anger is hardly to be taken as the expression of genuine repentance. In any case the ode cannot be connected with any of the extant Epodes.— Metre, 176.

2. **criminosis**, *abusive.* — **cumque** : cf. 6. 3 n. — **modum pones,** *you shall put an end to.* The context gives the future a half-concessive, half-hortatory force ; Intr. 79, 90.

3. **iambis** : a rapid rhythm (cf. vs. 24 and *Ep.* II. 3. 251 *iambus, pes citus*) well adapted for invective, a use to which it was said to have been turned by its reputed inventor Archilochus (*Ep.* II. 3. 79 *Archilochum proprio rabies armavit iambo ;* see Intr. 18).

4. **mari Hadriano** : Intr. 117 *a.* The language is purposely exaggerated, as if we should say, 'You may fling them into the middle of the Atlantic.'

5. **non**, etc.: the poet proceeds to discourse with humorous irony on the overmastering force of anger, which unbalances the intellect of man and drives him irresistibly upon a course of slaughter and destruction. It is first compared with the religious frenzy exhibited in the worship of certain divinities. — **Dindymene :** *i.e.* Cybele, identified with Rhea, the mother of Zeus. Dindymus was a mountain in Phrygia, near Pessinus, one of the principal seats of the worship of Cybele, whose rites were celebrated with the wildest orgies, the priests in their frenzy often slashing themselves with knives. Cf. Catullus 63.— **adytis,** *in the sanctuary,* in contrast with the mountains and woods where Cybele and Bacchus exercise their power. For the abl. see Intr. 69.

6. **incola Pythius,** *he that dwelleth in Pytho, i.e.* Apollo, Pytho being the ancient name of Delphi. The frenzy of the priestess of Apollo (the Cumaean sibyl), when possessed by the oracular spirit of the god, is described by Vergil, *A.* VI. 77 *sqq.*

7. **Liber :** alluding to the orgiastic rites practiced by the bacchanals, under the overpowering inspiration, as they claimed, of the god. Cf. II. 19. 5 *sqq.* — **aeque,** *as much,* completing the predicate, **non aeque mentem sacerdotum quatit,** which is distributed, in Horace's favorite manner, among the three subjects ; Intr. 120. The place of *ac,* which would naturally follow **aeque,** is supplied by **ut,** vs. 9, the change being due to the intervening **sic,** vs. 8. — **acuta,** *shrill.*

8. **sic,** *with such effect, sc.* in exciting the mind. — **geminant,** *clash together ;* lit. put together in pairs. Cf. Stat. *Theb.* VIII. 221 *gemina aera sonant.* — **Corybantes :** priests of Cybele. — **aera :** *i.e.* cymbals, used by the Corybantes in their rites.

tristes ut irae, quas neque Noricus
10   deterret ensis nec mare naufragum
nec saevus ignis nec tremendo
Iuppiter ipse ruens tumultu.

Fertur Prometheus, addere principi
limo coactus particulam undique
15   desectam, et insani leonis
vim stomacho adposuisse nostro.

9. **tristes ut irae,** *as unhappy anger has.* The predicate to be supplied, however, is *mentem quatiunt* or the like, expressing the general sense of the preceding strophe, which is implied even in **sic,** on which **ut** grammatically depends. — **irae :** Intr. 128. — **Noricus :** Intr. 117. The iron foundries in Noricum are alluded to by Ovid, *M.* XIV. 712 *durior et ferro quod Noricus excoquit ignis.*

10. **deterret :** *i.e.* from pursuing its course of vengeance. — **ensis, mare, ignis :** stock examples of obstacles ; cf. *S.* I. 1. 38 : *cum te neque fervidus aestus | demoveat lucro, neque hiems ignis mare ferrum, | nil obstet tibi.*

12. **Iuppiter :** cf. *Iove,* 1. 25 n. — **ruens,** *descending. i.e.* in thunder and lightning.

13. **fertur,** *we are told that.* — **Prometheus :** the myth of the creation of man and the other animals from clay and water by Prometheus, though unknown to Homer and Hesiod, was very old (cf. Plato, *Protag.* 11). In its present form, however, it is not found in any other author now extant, though the notion of man being endowed with the qualities of various other animals, — the cunning of the fox, the timidity of the hare, etc., — occurs very early. — **principi,** *first, original,* that of which the first man was created.

14. **particulam :** that a material portion is meant, and not a portion of the soul (as *S.* II. 2. 79), is shown by **desectam.** The idea seems to be that each of the animals had been created by mixing with the clay out of which it was shaped a certain material which gave it its peculiar disposition, but that when he came to the creation of man, Prometheus was obliged, in order to obtain the requisite amount, to take from each of the animals which he had already created (**undique**) a portion of its predisposing substance.

16. **stomacho :** *i.e.* to the organ which is the seat of our passion (cf. 6. 6 n) was added, among other elements (**et**), a particle taken from the lion, bringing with it the violence of his rage.

17. **irae :** repeated from vs. 9. — **Thyesten :** son of Pelops and brother of Atreus, whose vengeance took the monstrous form of a supper at which Thyestes was induced to eat unawares the flesh of his own son. — **exitio,** etc.: this part of the myth has not come down to us. It was probably familiar to Horace and his readers from the *Thyestes* of Varius, recently published.

Irae Thyesten exitio gravi
stravere et altis urbibus ultimae
stetere causae cur perirent
20   funditus imprimeretque muris

hostile aratrum exercitus insolens.
Compesce mentem !   Me quoque pectoris
temptavit in dulci iuventa
fervor et in celeres iambos

25   misit furentem : nunc ego mitibus
mutare quaero tristia, dum mihi
fias recantatis amica
opprobriis animumque reddas.

18. **altis** : a frequent poetical epithet of cities, denoting lofty walls and buildings, and hence implying power and splendor ; cf. IV. 6. 3 ; Verg. *A.* I. 7 *altae moenia Romae.* — **urbibus** : virtually dative of possessor (see note on **stetere**), anticipating the subject of the interrogative clause. — **ultimae**, *primary*, the last reached in tracing backwards the series of results ; cf. Cat. 4. 15 *ultima ex origine.*

19. **stetere** : more expressive than *fuere*, implying the persistent efficacy of the cause.

20. **imprimeretque muris**, etc.: amplification of **funditus**, to illustrate how far the victor is carried in his rage.   To drive a plow over the ruins of a city as the Romans did in the case of Carthage (Mommsen *Hist.* III. p. 54), was to proclaim its absolute and final effacement.

21. **hostile aratrum** : Intr. 124. — **insolens** : cf. 5. 8 n.   For the caesura of this verse, see Intr. 155.

22. **compesce mentem** : the moral of his discourse, which was therefore meant as a warning to the lady, and not an apology for his own indulgence in anger.   That, he goes on to say (**me quoque**, etc.), is a thing of the past.

23. **temptavit**, *attacked* (as a disease); cf. *Ep.* I. 6. 28 *si latus aut renes morbo temptantur acuto.* — **dulci** : not an idle epithet.   The **fervor pectoris** was one phase of the strong passions and quick impulses that made life so sweet at that time.

24. **celeres iambos**: see vs. 3 n.

25. **mitibus** . . . **tristia**, *kind feelings . . . bitterness.*   For the use of the neuter plural cf. *ima summis,* 34. 12 n ; for the construction see Intr. 74, and cf. 17. 1 *sq.*

26. **mutare** : Intr. 94 *c.*

27. **recantatis**, *now that I have retracted ;* the verb being here used as a translation of παλινῳδεῖν. — **amica**, *friendly.*

28. **animum reddas**, *give me back your heart.*

XVII.

Velox amoenum saepe Lucretilem
mutat Lycaeo Faunus et igneam
defendit aestatem capellis
usque meis pluviosque ventos.

5   Impune tutum per nemus arbutos
quaerunt latentis et thyma deviae
olentis uxores mariti,
nec viridis metuunt colubras

XVII. On the attractions of his Sabine farm, with an invitation to a fair friend, whom he calls Tyndaris, to visit him there and enjoy with him the quiet country pleasures which it affords. — Metre, 176.

1. **Lucretilem** : Intr. 24.

2. **mutat** : see Intr. 74 and cf. 16. 25. — **Lycaeo** : the mountain range on the eastern border of Arcadia. — **Faunus** : an old Italian divinity, still worshipped in the country, sometimes as a benevolent god of woods and pastures (cf. III. 18), sometimes as a prophetic spirit who secluded himself in the forest, from which his loud voice occasionally resounded, filling all who heard it with terror and foreboding (Cic. *Div.* I. 101., *D. N.* II. 6, III. 15 ; cf. Liv. II. 7. 2). The Arcadian Pan, the son of Hermes, with whom Faunus was identified in literature, was also a spirit of the hills and woods, who punished men that disturbed his midday sleep (Theocr. 1. 15) by frightening them out of their senses with demoniacal cries (hence the expression ' panic fear ') ; but in general he was a merry spirit, always accompanied by

dancing and singing nymphs, to whom he played on his marvelous pipe, while the shepherds down in the valley listened in spell-bound silence or terror (Mart. IX. 61. 12).

3. **defendit,** *wards off.* — **aestatem** : *i.e.* heat. — **capellis** : dative ; cf. Verg. *E.* 7. 47 *solstitium pecori defendite.* Gr. 229 *c.*

5. **impune,** *with impunity;* referring to **deviae,** which implies a neglect of the precautions ordinarily necessary to keep them from harm. — **arbutos** : see 1. 21 n.

6. **quaerunt deviae,** *stray . . . in search of.* — **latentis** : *i.e.* easily escaping notice among the other trees and bushes.

7. **olentis uxores mariti,** *the wives of the unfragrant spouse.* — **mariti** : *sc. gregis ;* a common way of designating the male animal. Cf. Verg. *E.* 7. 7 *vir gregis ipse caper ;* Theocr. 8. 49 ὦ τράγε, τᾶν λευκᾶν αἰγῶν ἄνερ.

9. **Martialis** : *i.e.* sacred to Mars ; cf. *Martius lupus,* Verg. *Aen.* IX. 566, and the story of the birth of Romulus and Remus. — **haediliae** (*sc. metuunt*), *the kids.* The word does not occur elsewhere, but this interpretation of it as a diminutive form from *haedus*

nec Martialis haediliae lupos,
10   utcumque dulci, Tyndari, fistula
    valles et Vsticae cubantis
      levia personuere saxa.

Di me tuentur, dis pietas mea
  et musa cordi est. Hic tibi copia
15   manabit ad plenum benigno
     ruris honorum opulenta cornu ;

hic in reducta valle Caniculae
  vitabis aestus et fide Teia

is supported by the parallel form *porcilia*, from *porcus*. The old hypothesis, that *Haedilia* was the name of a place in the neighborhood, rejected by Bentley, is still maintained by some editors.

10. **utcumque**: always temporal in Horace. With the perfect definite, here and IV. 4. 35, it introduces a determining circumstance, like *simul* (*e.g.* 9. 9). — **fistula,** *with his pipe. Fistula* is the Latin name for the Greek σύριγξ, Pan's pipe. Cf. Tib. II. 5. 31 *fistula, cui semper decrescit harundinis ordo ;* | *nam calamus cera iungitur usque minor;* and Verg. *E.* 3. 25.

11. **Vsticae** : said by Porphyrio to be a hill or mountain of gentle slope (**cubantis**) in the neighborhood of the Sabine farm.

12. **personuere,** *have rung ;* perfect, because the strains of the *fistula,* once heard, are an assurance of the presence of the god, inspiring the animals with the feeling of security described. The music is not thought of as continuing.

14. **musa** : see note on *Clio,* 12. 2. — **copia** : not personified as in *C. S.* 60 and *Ep.* I. 12. 29,

where *Plenty* is the goddess who showers blessings from her overflowing horn. Here, as in the oldest Greek conception of the 'horn of plenty' (the horn of Amalthea, the nurse of Zeus, taken by Hercules from the river-god Acheloos), **copia** is the contents of the horn, which was represented as in the possession of various divinities, Demeter, Dionysus, Fortuna (Tyche), Autumnus, etc.

15. **benigno** : cf. 9. 6 n.

16. **honorum,** *the glories, i.e.* fruits, vegetables, flowers ; cf. *S.* II. 5. 12 *dulcia poma* | *et quoscumque feret cultus tibi fundus honores.* For the case, see Intr. 66 *c.*

17. **Caniculae,** *the Dog-star ;* properly the constellation of the Lesser Dog, which the Greeks called Προκύων (cf. III. 29. 17 n) as rising before the (Greater) Dog; but the name was popularly applied to Sirius, the chief star of the Greater Dog, whose rising, July 26, heralded the hot season. Cf. III. 13. 9, *S.* II. 5. 39.

18. **aestus** : Intr. 128. — **fide Teia** : *i.e.* in love songs, such as those of Anacreon, who was a

dices laborantis in uno
20   Penelopen vitreamque Circen :

hic innocentis pocula Lesbii
duces sub umbra, nec Semeleius
cum Marte confundet Thyoneus
proelia, nec metues protervum

25   suspecta Cyrum, ne male dispari
incontinentis iniciat manus
et scindat haerentem coronam
crinibus immeritamque vestem.

native of Teos (*Epod.* 14. 10); cf. *Lesboum barbiton*, 1. 34 n. The ablative is instrumental and means 'to the accompaniment of.'

19. dices : cf. *dicere*, 6. 5 n. — laborantis (*sc. amore*), *heartsick;* cf. *ambitione laborat*, S. I. 4. 26. — in : an extension of its use in the sense of 'in the case of'; see Intr. 72 and cf. Verg. *A.* II. 540 *at non Achilles | talis in hoste fuit Priamo ; Epod.* 11. 4 ; Cat. 64. 98 *in flavo hospite suspirantem ;* translate *for.* — uno : Ulysses.

20. vitream, *crystal,* suggesting a brilliant, dazzling beauty ; cf. 19. 5 *Glycerae nitor splendentis Pario marmore purius* and III. 13. 1 *splendidior vitro.* The Romans, though they used glass very little for their windows, on account of its expensiveness, were very skilful in working it for artistic purposes — vases, ornaments, imitations of precious stones, etc. The epithet is perhaps applied to her as a sea-goddess ; cf. IV. 2. 3 *vitreo ponto* and *Epod.* 13. 16 *mater caerula* (Thetis). — Circen: *Odys.* X. 274 *sqq.*

21. innocentis : *i.e.* not intoxi-

cating, as explained in the next clause. — Lesbii : one of the sweeter Greek wines.

22. duces, *you shall quaff.* For the tense, cf. 16. 3 n. — nec Semeleius, etc.: *i.e.* nor will there be any quarrelling over the cups, as there is in the companies where she meets his rival. — Semeleius, *the son of Semele ;* cf. Cat. 61. 225 *Telemacho Penelopeo.*

23. confundet proelia : a variation of the ordinary *committere proelia,* to express a disorderly squabble. — Thyoneus : a name of Bacchus meaning 'son of the raving one,' (Θυώνη ; cf. θύω). The latter name was very early applied to Semele ; cf. Hom. *Hym. to Dionys.* (34) 21 σύν μητρὶ Σεμέλῃ ἥνπερ καλέουσι Θυώνην.

25. suspecta : because of his jealousy.— male, *very ;* see 9. 24 n.

26. incontinentis manus : cf. 13. 9 n, and see Intr. 124.

27. coronam : cf. 4. 10 n.

28. crinibus : probably dative, as *S.* I. 10. 49 *haerentem capiti multa cum laude coronam ;* but see Intr. 71. — immeritam: *i.e.* having done nothing to deserve such treatment.

XVIII.

Nullam, Vare, sacra vite prius severis arborem
circa mite solum Tiburis et moenia Catili.
Siccis omnia nam dura deus proposuit neque
mordaces aliter diffugiunt sollicitudines.
5 Quis post vina gravem militiam aut pauperiem crepat?

XVIII. On the blessings of
wine when used with moderation,
and the folly and sin of intem-
perance. The ode appears to be
a translation, with a few touches
to give it a local setting, of a poem
of Alcaeus, in the same metre, of
which the first verse is preserved
(*Fr.* 44):

Μηδὲν ἄλλο φυτεύσῃς πρότερον δέν-
  δριον ἀμπέλω.

The Varus addressed is probably
the literary critic, Quintilius Varus,
whose death is mourned in Ode
24. — Metre, 170.

1. **sacra** : *sc.* to Bacchus. The
word sets the tone of the ode at
the outset : wine is not for the
mere pleasure of our palate ; it is
a divine gift, the abuse of which
will be punished as sin. — **severis**,
plant ; cf. Caecilius *ap.* Cic. *C.
M.* 24 *serit arbores quae alteri
saeclo prosint.* — **arborem** : cf. δέν-
δριον, intr. note, and Plin. *N. H.*
XIV. 9 *vites iure apud priscos
magnitudine quoque inter arbores
numerabantur.*

2. **circa**, *about ;* used in different senses, as the English word
may be, with its two objects :
with **solum**, equivalent to 'here
and there in,' with **moenia**, 'in
the neighborhood of.' — **mite**,
mellow, i.e. light and crumbling,
yielding readily to the plough.
Such soil was suitable for the vine

(Verg. *G.* II. *226 sqq.*). — **Tiburis** :
it would seem that Varus had a
country place there. — **moenia
Catili** : see 7. 13 n. With the
name of Catillus (Verg. *A.* VII.
672) Horace has allowed himself a
Homeric license ; cf. Ἀχιλλεύς,
Ἀχιλεύς, *e.g. Il.* I. 148, 199.

3. **siccis** : *i.e.* those who abstain ; cf. IV. 5. 39, *Ep.* I. 19. 9.
— **omnia dura**, *only the hard side
of life ;* **dura** has a predicate force,
expressing the aspect under which
everything is presented. — **nam** :
Intr. 114. — **deus** : cf. 3. 21 n.

4. **aliter**, *in any other way,*
used illogically, as if the preceding
statement had been put in the
converse form : all things are softened to those who drink wine.

5. **gravem militiam**, *the hardships of a soldier's life.* This topic
would hardly have occurred to
Horace, who had seen nothing of
war for a dozen years ; it is no
doubt taken from the ode of
Alcaeus ; cf. 32. 5 *sqq.* — **crepat**,
prattles ; cf. *Ep.* I. 7. 84 *sulcos
et vineta crepat mera.* The word
simply means rattling on, as men
do when their tongue is loosened
by wine, about subjects fit or
unfit (*Ep.* I. 7. 72), and is to be
understood in this sense in the
next verse. The censure is directed against the depressing topics
of conversation, and not specially
against the manner of talking.

Quis non te potius, Bacche pater, teque, decens Venus?
Ac ne quis modici transiliat munera Liberi,
Centaurea monet cum Lapithis rixa super mero
debellata, monet Sithoniis non levis Euhius,
10   cum fas atque nefas exiguo fine libidinum
discernunt avidi.   Non ego te, candide Bassareu,
invitum quatiam nec variis obsita frondibus

6. **te potius**, etc. : *i.e.* of the
brighter side of life, — its joys and
solaces, rather than of its troubles.
— **Bacche, Venus** : cf. 19. 2 n,
32. 9. — **pater** : a title of reverence (cf. 2. 50 n) suited to the character of benefactor, in which Bacchus is here invoked; cf. III. 3. 13,
Ep. II. 1. 5 *Liber pater.* — **decens** :
cf. 4. 6 n.

7. **ac**, *and yet*, qualifying the preceding recommendation of wine.
For this use of *ac* cf. *S.* II. 2. 118,
Ep. II. 1. 208. — **ne quis transiliat**, *against a reckless use of.* —
munera Liberi : not simply wine,
but wine as Liber designed it, for
the good of mankind. The condition imposed in his design is expressed in **modici**. With **munera**
thus limited the poet uses **transiliat**, *go beyond*, with the implication
of recklessness, as in 3. 42.

8. **Centaurea**, *of the Centaurs.*
At the wedding of Pirithous, king
of the Lapithae, with Hippodamia, Eurytion, one of the Centaurs, who were present as guests,
attempted in his drunkenness to
carry off the bride. The battle that
ensued became a famous subject
in literature (cf. *Odys.* XXI. 295,
Ov. *M.* XII. 210) and in art (as
in the metopes of the Parthenon
and in the pediment of the temple
at Olympia). — **monet**, *there is
warning in.* — **super** : cf. 9. 5 n.

9. **debellata** : the contest ended
in the extirpation of the Centaurs

(*Il.* I. 267), a result which, in the
form of the myth which Horace
follows, took place then and there
(**super mero**). — **Sithoniis** ; a
Thracian tribe, used here for the
Thracians in general. — **non levis**,
the severity of ; Intr. 105 *a*. The
allusion is to the bloody quarrels
over their wine for which they were
notorious (cf. I. 27. 1 *sq.*), and which
are here represented as punish-
ments inflicted by the god. —
Euhius : a name of Bacchus,
formed from εὐοῖ (cf. II. 19. 5),
the cry of the bacchantes.

10. **exiguo**, *faint*, scarcely per-
ceptible, instead of the broad and
distinct line that separates right
and wrong in the mind of one
whose moral perceptions are unclouded.— **fine libidinum**, *the line
which appetite draws;* cf. III. 24. 44
virtutis viam (the path that virtue
prescribes) ; *S.* I. 1. 50 *naturae
finis* (the limits that nature sets).

11. **avidi**, *in their strong craving*.
— **non ego te** : this is the usual
order where *non* and *ego* are both
emphatic ; cf. 23. 9, II. 7. 26,
17. 9, *S.* I. 1. 103, etc. — **candide**,
radiant ; of the ever youthful
beauty of the god (cf. *candide
Bacche*, Ov. *F.* III. 772 ; *candida
Dido*, Verg. *A.* V. 571), in accordance with the ordinary Greek conception, yet not inconsistent with
the more serious character attributed to him here. — **Bassareu** :
a name of Bacchus said to be de-

sub divum rapiam.   Saeva tene cum Berecyntio
cornu tympana, quae subsequitur caecus amor sui
15 et tollens vacuum plus nimio gloria verticem
arcanique fides prodiga, perlucidior vitro.

XIX.

Mater saeva Cupidinum
Thebanaeque iubet me Semeles puer

rived from βασσάρα, a fox-skin,
worn by the Thracian bacchantes,
hence called Βασσαρίδες. Under
this name he was represented with
a beard and the features of mature
age (Macrob. *Sat.* I. 18. 9).

12. **quatiam**, *rouse.* — **variis
obsita frondibus,** *the mysteries
enveloped in divers leaves* (especially grape and ivy); alluding to
the caskets containing mysterious
symbols carried in bacchanalian
processions. See the vivid description in Catullus, 64. 254 *sqq.*
Under the figure of respect for
these mysteries the poet professes
his own resolution to conform to
the will of the god, and again
deprecates intemperate indulgence.

13. **sub divum,** *to light;* cf. *sub
Iove* 1. 25 n. — **saeva,** *barbarous.* —
Berecyntio cornu: named from
Berecyntus, one of the mountains
in Phrygia on which the orgies of
Cybele were celebrated, and therefore belonging, like the **tympana**
(vs. 14), *tambourines* (cf. Cat. 63. 21),
to the worship of that goddess; but
the orgies of the two divinities
were always more or less confused
with one another. See III. 19. 19 n.

14. **quae subsequitur:** keeping up the figure, the qualities that
follow being personified in the
bacchanals who march behind this
wild music.

15. **tollens verticem:** cf. 1. 36.
— **plus nimio,** *all too high;* a
colloquial expression (cf. Cic. *Att.*
X. 8 A. 1 *quia te nimio plus diligo*),
in Horace always used of censurable excess (33. 1, *Ep.* I. 10. 30). —
gloria, *vainglory, vanity,* as in
Ep. I. 18. 22 *gloria quem supra
viris et vestit et ungit.*

16. **arcanique fides prodiga:**
see 5. 5 n. — **perlucidior:** *i.e.* with
no more power of concealment,
a familiar result of intoxication;
cf. the practice of the Germans
described by Tacitus, *Ger.* 22. For
the peculiar caesura of this verse,
see Intr. 150. — **vitro:** see note
on *vitream,* 17. 20.

XIX. The poet will have us
believe that he has once again had
to surrender to the charms of a
fair girl, when he thought his days
of love were over long ago. —
Metre, 171.

1. **Cupidinum:** the original
conception of Eros as the one son
of Aphrodite was later enlarged
by poets and artists, who represented numberless Loves, all in
the shape of pretty winged boys,
in attendance on Aphrodite, and
sometimes on Bacchus. See Preller-Plew, *Gr. Myth.* I. p. 417.

2. **Semeles puer:** cf. *Semeleius,* 17. 22. Here, in contrast

et lasciva Licentia
　　finitis animum reddere amoribus.
5　Vrit me Glycerae nitor
　　splendentis Pario marmore purius;
urit grata protervitas
　　et voltus nimium lubricus adspici.
In me tota ruens Venus
10　　Cyprum deseruit, nec patitur Scythas
et versis animosum equis
　　Parthum dicere nec quae nihil attinent.
Hic vivum mihi caespitem, hic
　　verbenas, pueri, ponite turaque
15　bimi cum patera meri:
　　mactata veniet lenior hostia.

with the last ode, he is the youthful Bacchus (**puer**), the companion of Venus. Cf. 32. 9.

4. **animum reddere**: cf. 16. 28 n.

5. **nitor**, *the beauty.* Cf. *nites*,
5. 13.

6. **splendentis purius**, *who
shines with purer lustre.* — **Pario**:
from Paros, one of the *nitentes
Cyclades* (14. 20), preferred for
sculpture on account of its fineness
and purity.

8. **et voltus**, etc., *and her too
dazzling face.*— **lubricus adspici**:
i.e. on which one's glance can no
more rest steadily than one's foot
upon a slippery surface. For the
infinitive, see Intr. 102.

9. **tota**, *with all her force.* —
ruens: cf. 16. 12.

10. **Cyprum**: cf. 3. 1, 30. 2.—
Scythas, Parthum: subjects of
national importance that engage
the public attention. Cf. 26. 5 n.

11. **animosum**: in contrast with
versis equis (Intr. 116 *a*), which
ordinarily indicates fear or coward-

ice. The allusion is to the favorite
stratagem of the Parthian cavalry,
of turning suddenly while in full
retreat and sending a shower of
arrows in the face of the pursuing
enemy ; cf. Verg. *G.* III. 31.

12. **quae nihil attinent**, *any
such irrelevant subject;* a delicious
touch of feminine assumption.

13. **hic . . . hic**: Intr. 116 *g*.
The case calls for immediate attention ; a sacrifice must be instituted on the spot. — **vivum caespitem**: often used for a temporary altar ; cf. III. 8. 4.

14. **verbenas**, *green sprigs* (of
certain sacred trees and plants,
here probably myrtle). — **pueri** :
i.e. slaves (not necessarily young);
the usual term in addressing them ;
cf. 38. 1.

15. **patera** : a saucer-shaped
vessel with a handle, used especially
for libations. — **meri** : in its literal
sense, only unmixed wine being
permitted for this purpose.

16. **veniet lenior** : in contrast

XX.

Vile potabis modicis Sabinum
cantharis, Graeca quod ego ipse testa
conditum levi, datus in theatro
  cum tibi plausus,

5 care Maecenas eques, ut paterni
fluminis ripae simul et iocosa

with *tota ruens,* 9. — **hostia** : victims were sometimes sacrificed to Venus (Plaut. *Poen.* 449 *sqq.*, Tac. *H.* II. 3), but her sacrifices were commonly bloodless.

XX. To Maecenas, in anticipation of a visit from him, perhaps at the poet's country place (Intr. 24). The ode lacks the usual finish of Horace's lyric works, and if genuine, — which some even of the more conservative editors doubt, — must be regarded as a hasty and informal production, preserved only for the sake of the allusion in vss. 3 *sqq.* The abrupt beginning may be explained on the supposition that the poem is an answer to a note from Maecenas, announcing his intended visit. — Metre, 174.

1. **vile,** *plain,* in contrast with the fine and costly brands mentioned in the last strophe. — **modicis,** *modest,* referring not so much to the size of the cups as to the quality of their contents. Cf. *S.* II. 6. 70 *modicis* (sc. *poculis*) *uvescit laetius,* where it is contrasted with *acria pocula; S.* I. 5. 2 *hospitio modico; Ep.* I. 5. 2 *modica cenare patella.* — **Sabinum** (sc. *vinum*): the wine of the district; cf. 9. 7 n. According to *Ep.* I. 14. 23, it could not have been produced on his own place.

2. **cantharis,** *bowls.* The *cantharus* was a large cup with handles, said to have been named for its inventor. — **Graeca testa** : *i.e.* a jar which, having contained Greek wine, would improve the flavor of the Sabine put into it. For the case of **testa** see Intr. 69. — **ipse,** *with my own hands.*

3. **conditum levi,** *stored and sealed.* The cork of the amphora was smeared with pitch to make it air-tight ; cf. III. 8. 10. — **datus** : sc. *est.* — **theatro:** probably that of Pompey, the only permanent theatre existing in Rome at the time. It stood in the Campus Martius, about a thousand feet from the river.

4. **cum,** *at the time when.* See Intr. 114.—**plausus:** the occasion, as appears from II. 17. 22 *sqq.,* was the first public appearance of Maecenas after a serious illness, probably in B.C. 30. The date of this ode must be set some years later.

5. **care** : cf. *dilecte Maecenas,* II. 20. 7. — **eques** : Intr. 21. — **paterni fluminis** : the Tiber, as rising in Etruria (*amnis Tuscus, S.* II. 2. 32), the home of Maecenas' ancestors.

6. **ripae** : the plural for one side of the river only, as *Aen.* VI. 305. See Intr. 128. — **iocosa imago** : cf. 12. 3 n.

redderet laudes tibi Vaticani
·montis imago.

Caecubum et prelo domitam Caleno
10   tu bibes uvam: mea nec Falernae
temperant vites neque Formiani
pocula colles.

XXI.

Dianam tenerae dicite virgines,
intonsum, pueri, dicite Cynthium,
Latonamque supremo
dilectam penitus Iovi.

7. **redderet,** *repeated.* — **Vaticani montis :** here used for the whole range of hills along the west bank of the Tiber, rising to a height of over 250 feet above the river. The part opposite the theatre of Pompey was called *Ianiculum.* Echoes from the steep slopes of this hill were no doubt familiar to the Romans, but Horace's introduction of them here is purely ornamental. The applause in the theatre, could not possibly have been so reëchoed. The short *i* of *Vaticanus* is peculiar to Horace.

9. **Caecubum,** etc.: fine wines of Latium and Campania respectively, standing for rich wines in general (Intr. 117 *a*). — **domitam,** *crushed.*

10. **tu bibes :** *sc.* at home ; not the simple future, like *potabis,* vs. 1, but with a concessive-hortatory force, brought out by the antithesis of **tu** and **mea** ; see Intr. 79. — **Falernae . . . Formiani :** again a choice Campanian and a choice Latin wine, from the same districts respectively as the Calenian

and the Caecuban. They therefore repeat, with variation of form, the same general idea.

11. **temperant,** *flavor;* lit. 'mix' (in due proportion), as *Epod.* 17. 80; hence ' determine the quality of.' Observe that the subject is not the wine but the vines and the hills.

XXI. An ode in honor of Apollo and Diana, — especially the former as the patron god of Augustus, — in the form of an address to a chorus of boys and girls employed in some festival of these divinities. It may be compared with the latter part of IV. 6 (vss. 31 *sqq.*) addressed to the chorus that sang the *Carmen Saeculare,* and with Catullus 34. — Metre, 173.

1. **Dīanam :** Intr. 178. — **dicite :** cf. 6. 5 n.

2. **intonsum :** as possessed of eternal youth, Apollo was represented with a beardless face (*lēvis,* IV. 6. 28) and long golden locks (ἀκερσεκόμης, *Il.* XX. 39 ; ὁ χρυσοκόμας, Pind. *Ol.* 7. 58). Cf. Tib. I. 4. 37 *solis aeterna est Phoebo Bacchoque iuventa,* | *nam decet in-*

5 Vos laetam fluviis et nemorum coma
    quaecumque aut gelido prominet Algido
      nigris aut Erymanthi
        silvis aut viridis Gragi;

    vos Tempe totidem tollite laudibus
10 natalemque, mares, Delon Apollinis
      insignemque pharetra
        fraternaque umerum lyra.

tonsus crinis utrumque deum, and II. 5. 121. — **Cynthium** : Apollo ; so named from the hill Cynthus, in Delos, where Apollo and Diana were born. The latter is for the same reason often called *Cynthia*, as III. 28. 12.

3. **Latonam** : to be included in the hymn as the mother of the twin deities.

5. **vos** : sc. *dicite;* addressed to the girls, as *mares*, 10, shows. — **fluviis**, etc.: cf. Verg. *A.* I. 498 *qualis in Eurotae ripis aut per iuga Cynthi | exercet Diana choros*, etc. — **coma**, *the tresses, i.e.* the foliage, as in IV. 7. 2.

6. **prominet**, *tower aloft*. — **Algido** : the range of hills between Tusculum and the Via Latina, north of the Alban mount, being the northern member of the semi-circular range that encloses that extinct volcano. The whole range, which was thickly wooded and cool in comparison with the surrounding plain (hence the name *Algidus* and the epithet **gelido** ; cf. *nivali* III. 23. 9), was regarded as a favorite haunt of Diana (*quae tenet Algidum*, *C. S.* 69), and at its southern extremity, near Aricia, there was a famous grove and altar of the goddess (*Diana Nemorensis;* cf. *Ep.* II. 3. 16). For the case see Intr. 69.

7. **nigris** : referring rather to the color of the leaves than to the thickness of the foliage. See note on **viridis**, 8. — **aut** : Intr. 114.— **Erymanthi** : a mountain on the north-western borders of Arcadia, a famous hunting ground of Artemis (*Odys.* VI. 103).

8. **silvis**, *in the forests*, of which the *nemora* (open woods and glades) are a part. — **viridis** : the lighter color of deciduous trees in contrast with the dark evergreens (**nigris**) of Erymanthus ; cf. IV. 12. 11 *nigri colles Arcadiae ;* though not belonging grammatically to **silvis**, it supplants the epithet **nigris**, and *silvis* alone is understood with **Gragi**.— **Gragi** : a mountain range (Κράγος; cf. *Agrigentum* for Ακράγας) on the western coast of Lycia, the seat of some of the oldest legends of Latona and her children.

9. **Tempe** : see 7. 4 n. Here Apollo was purified after slaying the Python, and here an altar marked the spot where he plucked the laurel branch with which he returned to establish his oracle at Delphi.

10. **natalem Delon** : see note on *Cynthium*, 2.

12. **fraterna** : as a present from Mercury; cf. 10. 12 n.— **umerum** : object of **tollite** ; cf. III. 28. 9 *cantabimus Neptunum et Nereidum comas*. Some editors take it as

Hic bellum lacrimosum, hic miseram famem
pestemque a populo et principe Caesare in
15   Persas atque Britannos
vestra motus aget prece.

XXII.

Integer vitae scelerisque purus
non eget Mauris iaculis neque arcu
nec venenatis gravida sagittis,
Fusce, pharetra,

5   sive per Syrtis iter aestuosas
sive facturus per inhospitalem
Caucasum vel quae loca fabulosus
lambit Hydaspes.

an accusative of specification with
insignem, which would then stand
for *eum qui insignis est* (cf. *laetam*,
5) ; but it is very doubtful
whether Horace ever used a masculine accusative, in this construction, with an *adjective;* see Intr. 44.
13. **hic,** etc.: an extension of
his functions as ἀλεξίκακος, or de-
fender against plague ; cf. Preller-
Robert, *Gr. Mythol.* I., p. 276.
14. **principe:** see 2. 50 n.
15. **Persas :** see 2. 22 n. —
Britannos : cf. III. 5. 3, where
they are coupled, as here, with the
Parthians as not yet vanquished
foes of Rome.

XXII. Aristius Fuscus, to whom
this ode is addressed, was a man
who dearly loved his joke, as appears from the part he took in
Horace's famous encounter with
the bore, *S.* I. 9. 61 *sqq.;* and
Horace was in thorough sympathy
with him (*paene gemelli, fraternis*

animis, Ep. I. 10. 1 *sqq.;* cf. also
S. I. 10. 83). Fuscus therefore
could not have been misled by
the high moral tone in which this
ode opens, only to be puzzled by
the somewhat flippant anticlimax
at the end. No one who has
learned to know Horace in the
Satires could for a moment suppose that he would seriously pro-
pound the extravagant sentiment
in the first two strophes, much
less that he would seriously point
to himself as an example of such
lofty virtue. The incident of the
third strophe was probably real,
and our ode has no higher purpose than to tell his friend the
story with a mock-serious moral
attached. — Metre, 174.
1. **vitae:** Intr. 66 *d.* — **sceleris:**
Intr. 66 *c.*
2. **Mauris:** Intr. 117 *a.*
3. **gravida,** *stuffed.*
5. **Syrtis :** here not (as in
Epod. 9. 31) the dangerous waters

Namque me silva lupus in Sabina,
10 dum meam canto Lalagen et ultra
terminum curis vagor expeditis,
    fugit inermem,

quale portentum neque militaris
Daunias latis alit aesculetis
15 nec Iubae tellus generat, leonum
    arida nutrix.

Pone me pigris ubi nulla campis
arbor aestiva recreatur aura,

of that name, but the adjacent
coast of Libya, east of the province
of Africa ; a district infested with
wild beasts and poisonous serpents
(Plin. *N. H.* V. 26.) — **iter facturus** (sc. *est*): Intr. 120. — **aestuosas**, *sweltering ;* cf. *aestuosae
Calabriae*, 31. 5.

7. **fabulosus**, *storied, i.e.* rich in
legends.

9. **me silva lupus :** observe
the skilful arrangement. The first
three words set before us the
scene and the two characters in
the little drama ; then follow, in
their actual order, the poet's light-
hearted unconcern before the encounter, the quick *dénoûment*, and
the impression left behind by the
retreating monster. See, further,
Intr. 112.

10. **Lalagen :** the name (Λα-
λαγή, 'prattle') is paraphrased in
dulce loquentem, vs. 24. The accusative of the theme of song is
usual after *cantare ;* cf. 6. 17 *sqq.*

11. **terminum :** apparently that
of his own farm. He had strolled
away deeper into the forest. —
curis expeditis : for the usual
curis expeditus, as if the cares were
fettered to the man instead of the
man by the cares. Cf. *Epod.* 13. 5
obducta solvatur fronte senectus ;

Cat. 31. 7 *o quid solutis est bea-
tius curis?*

12. **fugit inermem:** Intr. 116 *a.*

13. **quale portentum :** *i.e. tale
portentum* (nom., in apposition
with **lupus**) *quale* (acc.). — **militaris:** *i.e.* producing good soldiers ;
cf. III. 5. 9.

14. **Daunias :** Apulia, so named
from a mythical king Daunus (III.
30. 11 n, IV. 14. 26), who ruled
over the northern part of the country. In the Aeneid he is the father
of Turnus (X. 616); elsewhere the
father-in-law of the exiled Diomed.
In form the word is a Greek feminine adjective, like Ἰλιάς, Ἀμβρα-
κιάς, etc. That Apulia was infested
with wolves appears also from 33.
7 *sq.*

15. **Iubae tellus :** Mauritania.
Iuba may be either the elder king
of that name, who lost his kingdom in consequence of his defeat
at Thapsus, or his son, who was
educated at Rome and restored to
his throne by Augustus in B.C. 25.

16. **arida**, *parched.*

17. **pone :** equivalent to a condition. — **pigris**, *sluggish*, with no
quickening power for vegetation.—
nulla arbor recreatur : *i.e.* there
is no summer breeze and hence
no tree or shrub (cf. 18. 1 n).

quod latus mundi nebulae malusque
20   Iuppiter urget;

pone sub curru nimium propinqui
solis, in terra domibus negata:
dulce ridentem Lalagen amabo,
dulce loquentem.

XXIII.

Vitas inuleo me similis, Chloe,
quaerenti pavidam montibus aviis
matrem non sine vano
aurarum et siluae metu;

5   nam seu mobilibus vepris inhorruit
ad ventum foliis, seu virides rubum
dimovere lacertae,
et corde et genibus tremit.

19. **quod latus**, etc.: cf. *quale portentum*, 13 n. — **latus mundi**: in accordance with the Roman conception of the earth as a flat surface; cf. Tac. *Agr.* 12. The far North is the 'side' referred to. — **malus**, *unkind*.

20. **Iuppiter**: cf. 1. 25 n. — **urget**, *broods over*.

21. **sub curru**, etc.: *i.e.* in the far South. — **nimium propinqui** *where he is all too near*.

23. **dulce**: Intr. 48.

XXIII. The comparison which forms the substance of this pretty ode is found in a fragment of Anacreon (52):

Ἀγανῶς οἷά τε νεβρὸν νεοθηλέα
γαλαθηνόν, ὅστ᾽ ἐν ὕλῃ κεροέσσης
ἀπολειφθεὶς ὑπὸ μητρὸς ἐπτοήθη·

and we probably have here another of Horace's early studies. The

name Chloe (χλόη, 'a young shoot') is perhaps chosen to suit the character portrayed. — Metre, 173.

2. **quaerenti**: *i.e.* having strayed away or been left behind, and suddenly found herself alone. — **pavidam**, *timid*, enhancing the impression of the timorous nature of the fawn. — **aviis**, *lonely*.

3. **non sine**: a favorite litotes with Horace; cf. 25. 16, III. 4. 20, etc.

4. **siluae**: see Intr. 182.

5. **seu**, *if.* — **vepris . . . ad ventum**: Bentley's conjecture for *veris . . . adventus* of the MSS., which is interpreted by those who retain it to mean the blowing of Favonius (see 4. 1 n). — **inhorruit**, *rustles*.

6. **ad ventum**, *in the wind;* lit., when the wind blows, **ad** denoting the occasion of the action, as in *ad haec, ad famam*, etc.

Atqui non ego te tigris ut aspera
10   Gaetulusve leo frangere persequor ;
    tandem desine matrem
    tempestiva sequi viro.

XXIV.

Quis desiderio sit pudor aut modus
tam cari capitis ? Praecipe lugubris
cantus, Melpomene, cui liquidam pater
vocem cum cithara dedit.

7. **dimovere :** *i.e.* in gliding through it.

10. **Gaetulus :** cf. III. 20. 2 and see Intr. 117 *a*. — **frangere,** *to crush you ;* suggested, perhaps, by the Homeric simile, *Il.* XI. 113 ὡς δὲ λέων ἐλάφοιο ταχείης νήπια τέκνα | ῥηιδίως συνέαξε λαβὼν κρατεροῖσιν ὀδοῦσιν. For the infinitive see Intr. 93.

12. **tempestiva viro :** cf. Verg. *A.* VII. 53 *iam matura viro, iam plenis nubilis annis.* Intr. 58 *b*.

XXIV. To Vergil, on the death of their common friend, Quintilius Varus, in B.C. 24. Quintilius, so far as we know, was not an author himself ; but as an accomplished critic he ·had a high reputation among the writers of the day, who often submitted their compositions to his friendly judgment. (*Ep.* II. 3. 438.) Vergil's affection for him is sufficiently attested by the present ode. He was the friend of the poet's maturer years — he is not mentioned in the Eclogues — and his death was at once a personal bereavement and the loss of an invaluable literary adviser. Horace apparently stood on no such intimate terms with him ; otherwise he could hardly have failed to mention him among the literary friends whose good opinion he valued, in *S.* I. 10. 81 *sqq.* But Horace's relations with him were nevertheless, — perhaps not till later than the period of the Satires, — so friendly that he addressed to him the eighteenth ode of this book. — Metre, 172.

1. **quis desiderio,** etc.: *i.e.* who can feel ashamed of mourning, or can control his grief. The case of **desiderio** is determined by **modus ;** the dative would hardly be used with **pudor** alone.

2. **tam cari capitis,** *for one so dear.* For this use of *caput,* in the sense of 'person,' cf. *Epod.* 5. 74 ; Verg. *A.* IV. 354 *puer Ascanius capitisque iniuria cari.* — **praecipe :** *i.e.* start the strain, so that the poet may sing with her voice to guide and sustain him.

3. **Melpomene :** the muse of tragedy ; but see 12. 2 n. — **liquidam :** *i.e.* clear and smoothly flowing.— **pater :** *i.e.* Jupiter. The muses were daughters of Zeus and Mnemosyne (Hes. *Theog.* 52).

5   Ergo Quintilium perpetuus sopor
     urget! Cui Pudor et Iustitiae soror,
     incorrupta Fides, nudaque Veritas
        quando ullum inveniet parem ?

     Multis ille bonis flebilis occidit,
10 nulli flebilior quam tibi, Vergili,
     tu frustra pius heu non ita creditum
        poscis Quintilium deos.

     Quid si Threicio blandius Orpheo
     auditam moderere arboribus fidem ?
15 Num vanae redeat sanguis imagini,
        quam virga semel horrida,

5. **ergo,** *and so ;* an expression of reluctant conviction and resignation ; cf. *S.* II. 5. 101 *ergo nunc Dama sodalis nusquam est.*

6. **urget,** *holds in its embrace ;* cf. *premet,* 4. 16 n. — **cui :** dative with **parem,** vs. 8. — **Pudor,** etc.: personified not simply as qualities of the man, but in the abstract, as in *C. S.* 57 *sq.* Judged by the standard of these personified virtues Quintilius was a rare type of man, — unassuming, absolutely just, sincere, and candid. — **soror :** *i.e.* the constant companion, implying that *Iustitia* also dwelt with Quintilius. Cf. Cic. *Off.* I. 23 *fundamentum autem iustitiae est fides, id est dictorum conventorumque constantia et veritas.*

7. **incorrupta Fides ;** the epithet is included in the personification. See note on *fidem* 5. 5, and cf. *rara Fides,* 35. 21, *vitiosa Cura,* II. 16. 21, *Pudor priscus, C. S.* 57.

9. **ille flebilis occidit,** *his death was cause for tears.* See II. 14. 6 n.

11. **frustra pius,** *with vain piety ;* cf. Cat. 76. 26 *o di reddite mi hoc pro pietate mea,* and see note on *poscit,* 31. 1. — **non ita creditum :** sc. *illis a te.* The meaning is that Vergil, in his anxiety for his sick friend, had piously commended him to the keeping of the gods, but **non ita,** — not that they should never give him back.

13. **quid si,** etc.: the thought gently suggested in *frustra,* vs. 11, is now further developed, and forms the transition from the sympathetic tone with which the poem opens to the exhortation to firmness with which it closes. — **Threicio,** etc.: see 12. 7 *sqq.* — **blandius :** cf. 12. 11 n.

14. **arboribus :** Intr. 54.

15. **vanae imagini,** *to the empty form.* The ancient conception of the dead in the underworld was very similar to the modern idea of ghosts, — not disembodied spirits, but disembodied forms, which were intangible, but retained, along with the spirit, enough of their material quality to be seen and heard, — *tenuis sine corpore vitas, cava sub imagine formae* (Verg. *A.* VI. 292 *sq.*) For the dative see Intr. 53. —

non lenis precibus fata recludere,
nigro compulerit Mercurius gregi?
Durum: sed levius fit patientia
20   quicquid corrigere est nefas.

XXV.

Parcius iunctas quatiunt fenestras
iactibus crebris iuvenes protervi,
nec tibi somnos adimunt, amatque
ianua limen,
5   quae prius multum facilis movebat

sanguis : cf. *Odys.* XI. 98, 153,
etc., where the dead are revived
by drinking blood.

16. virga : cf. 10. 18 n.— semel,
once (for all) ; implying, as often,
that the act is decisive and final.

17. precibus : with recludere,
better taken as ablative of cause :
because of (*i.e.* in answer to) our
prayers. *Recludere* with the dative
means to open to those who are
to enter, as II. 18, 33, III. 2. 21.
— fata recludere, *to open the doors
of fate, i.e.* the doors of the tomb,
which fate has closed forever on
the departed; cf. Prop. V. 11. 2 *pan-
ditur ad nullas ianua nigra preces.*
For the infinitive see Intr. 101 *a.*

18. nigro gregi: *i.e.* the endless
procession passing into the darkness of the underworld. *Niger*
is sometimes used like *ater* (see
28. 13 n) as an epithet of death and
of things connected with death ;
cf. IV. 2. 23, IV. 12. 26 ; Tib. I.
3. 4 *abstineas avidas, mors modo
nigra manus* ; | *abstineas mors
atra, precor.*— compulerit, *has
gathered to.*

19. levius fit patientia : cf. 11.
3. According to Donatus, Vergil
himself was in the habit of com-

mending patience as the most useful of human virtues.

20. est nefas, *Heaven forbids us.*

XXV. In this ode Horace portrays, with his usual light touch
but with powerful effect, the career
of a courtesan, — her short-lived
triumph, her waning power, and
her inevitable doom of a despised
and neglected old age, in which
the passions she has fostered remain to torture her. — Metre, 174.

1. iunctas, *closed ;* cf. the phrase
iungere flumen (*e.g.* Liv. XXI.
47. 2) for bridging a river. The
word is here used with reference
to the two wooden shutters with
which alone the window-aperture
was closed (cf. *bifores fenestras*, Ov.
Pont. III. 3. 5).

2. iactibus : *i.e.* of stones and
the like, the windows being as a
rule above the ground floor, which
was occupied by shops. Cf. III.
7. 29 *domum claude, neque in vias
despice.*

3. amat : *i.e.* cleaves to, seldom
parts from ; cf. Verg. *A.* V. 163
*litus ama et laeva stringat sine
palmula cautes.* — -que: cf. 27.16 n.

5. multum : Intr. 48.

cardines; audis minus et minus iam
‘Me tuo longas pereunte noctis,
  Lydia, dormis?’

Invicem moechos anus arrogantis
10 flebis in solo levis angiportu,
Thracio bacchante magis sub inter-
  lunia vento,

cum tibi flagrans amor et libido,
quae solet matres furiare equorum,
15 saeviet circa iecur ulcerosum,
  non sine questu,

laeta quod pubes hedera virenti
gaudeat pulla magis atque myrto,
aridas frondis hiemis sodali
20 dedicet Euro.

7. **me tuo**, etc.: words of a serenade. Hence the plural **noctis**:
the lover complains of her persistent indifference. — **tuo**, *your
lover;* cf. *tuae*, 15. 32.— **pereunte**,
languishing.

9. **invicem**, *your turn will come,
and;* the arrogance will be on
the other side. — **moechos**: no
longer the *protervi iuvenes* (vs. 2),
the bold admirers and the sighing
lovers of the days of your pride;
even the most vulgar sort of game
will be beyond your reach.

10. **in solo levis angiportu**,
neglected in your lonely alley. The
window and door mentioned above
open on an alley which runs along
the side and rear of the tenement
(*insula*), separating it from other
buildings (whence its name). For
levis cf. *Ep.* II. 3. 423 *levi pro
paupere.*

11. **Thracio vento**: Boreas
(Aquilo) whose home was in

Thrace; cf. *Threicio Aquilone,
Epod.* 13. 3.— **bacchante magis**,
pursues his wilder revels. The
expression accords with his character as *Thracius;* cf. 18. 9 n.—
sub: cf. 8. 14. The cold and
darkness out of doors enhance the
impression of the loneliness of the
wretched creature waiting within.
— **inter-lunia**: Intr. 174 *b.*

14. **matres equorum**: a paraphrase similar to that of 17. 7.
For the force of the comparison
cf. Verg. *G.* III. 266.

15. **circa**, *through;* cf. 18. 2 n.—
iecur: cf. 13. 4 n. Here it is the seat
of sensual passion. — **ulcerosum**,
inflamed; cf. *Ep.* I. 18. 72.

16. **non sine**: cf. 23. 3 n.

17. **virenti . . . pulla**, *fresh . . .
dark green;* both epithets applying to each of the two substantives (Intr. 121), and contrasted
with **aridas**.

18. **magis** (sc. *quam aridis fron-*

XXVI.

Musis amicus tristitiam et metus
tradam protervis in mare Creticum
    portare ventis, quis sub Arcto
        rex gelidae metuatur orae,

5   quid Tiridaten terreat, unice

dibus) : see Intr. 119 *a*. — **atque** :
Intr. 114.

19. **hiemis sodali** : cf. Verg.
G. II. 339 *hibernis parcebant flati-
bus Euri*, and, for the expression,
28. 21 and IV. 12. 1.

20. **dedicet**, *consigns.* Cf. 26. 2.

XXVI. In honor of L. Aelius
Lamia, one of the two sons of the
intimate friend and devoted adherent of Cicero of the same name.
(See Cic. *Fam*. XI. 16. 2, *Sest*. 29.)
Horace enjoyed the friendship of
both brothers. He alludes to the
death of one, Quintus, in *Ep*. I. 14. 6.
Lucius, whose name is 'enshrined'
in this ode, and in 36. 7 and III.
17, is described by Velleius (II.
116. 3) as *vir antiquissimi moris,
et priscam gravitatem semper huma-
nitate temperans.* He was consul A.D.
3, and his death *vivida senectute* in
A.D. 33 is recorded by Tacitus (*Ann.*
VI. 27. 2). He must therefore have
been much younger than Horace.

The date of this ode is fixed
with considerable certainty by the
allusions in vss. 3 *sqq.*, as B.C. 30 ;
that it was one of the earliest odes
is implied in *fidibus novis,* vs. 10.
— Metre, 176.

1. **amicus** : here used in the
sense of *gratus* or *acceptus* (*C.S.* 62),
as in *dis amicum carmen*, IV. 6. 41.
Cf. II. 17. 2, III. 4. 25 n, and, for
the opposite, *dis inimice senex*, S.
II. 3. 123.

2. **in mare Creticum**: see Intr.
117 *a* and cf. 16. 4.

3. **portare** : Intr. 93. — **quis
metuatur**, etc.: depending on **securus**, 9. **quis** is better taken as
nominative singular; cf. *quis pudor*,
24. 1. The form *quis* (= *quibus*)
occurs in the Satires and Epodes,
but in the Odes this would be the
only instance. — **sub Arcto** : *i.e.*
in the far north ; cf. *subiectos Orientis orae*, 12. 55 n.

4. **rex** : apparently Cotiso, king
of the Dacians, whose threatened
incursion alarmed the Romans
about the time of the war of Actium. He was finally defeated by
Crassus; cf. III. 8. 18 n.

5. **Tiridaten** : king of Parthia
at the time of the battle of Actium,
having headed a successful revolt
against Phraates a few years before. In the next year (B.C. 30) the
contest was renewed and Tiridates
was forced to take refuge in Syria.
These verses must have been
written before January, B.C. 29,
when the news of his flight reached
Rome. Subsequently Tiridates
succeeded in regaining the throne,
and held it till about B.C. 27, when
Phraates, with the aid of the
Asiatic Scythians, among whom
he had taken refuge, finally defeated him and drove him into
permanent exile under the protection of Augustus. — **unice securus**, *perfectly unconcerned.*

　　　securus.　O quae fontibus integris
　　　　　gaudes, apricos necte flores,
　　　　　　　necte meo Lamiae coronam,

　　　Pimplei dulcis.　Nil sine te mei
10　　prosunt honores.　Hunc fidibus novis,
　　　　　hunc Lesbio sacrare plectro
　　　　　　　teque tuasque decet sorores.

XXVII.

　　Natis in usum laetitiae scyphis
　　　pugnare Thracum est: tollite barbarum
　　　　morem, verecundumque Bacchum
　　　　　sanguineis prohibete rixis.

6. **fontibus integris :** such as Aganippe, Hippocrene, and others less famous ; cf. note on *Heliconis*, 12. 5. There is reason to believe that in the oldest Greek conception of them the muses were inspired, spring-haunting nymphs (Preller-Plew, *Gr. Mythol.* I. 401). **integris**, however, is no doubt intended, like *novis* 9, to convey the idea of fresh, unhackneyed poetry, and is perhaps a reminiscence of Lucr. I. 927.

7. **apricos,** *sunny; i.e.* the bright, gaily-colored ones which seem to carry with them the sunshine in which they bloom ; cf. Intr. 124. — **necte flores, necte,** etc.: a graceful way of saying *necte floribus coronam.* The meaning is not 'make Lamia a poet,' but 'distinguish him in song.' Of course, the ode itself, commending him to the muses as worthy, serves that end.

9. **Pimplei,** *nymph of Pimplea.* The latter was a spring in Pieria, on the slope of Olympus, sacred to the muses ; see note on *Haemo*

12. 6. — **mei :** *i.e.* those that I confer, the possessive pronoun here representing the subjective genitive. More commonly it retains its possessive force, as 6. 11 *laudes tuas.*

10. **fidibus novis :** *i.e.* in a new kind of poetry, explained by **Lesbio plectro** in the next verse ; cf. *Lesboum barbiton*, 1. 34 n.

11. **sacrare,** *to enshrine, to immortalize ;* to set his name in verse, as an offering is placed in a temple to be preserved forever. — **plectro :** a small stick of ivory or other substance for striking the strings of the lyre ($\pi\lambda\hat{\eta}\kappa\tau\rho o\nu$; cf. $\pi\lambda\acute{\eta}\sigma\sigma\omega$). The player held it in one hand, playing with the fingers of the other.

XXVII. A convivial scene, dramatically portrayed, though there is but one speaker. The poet finds his friends in hot dispute over their wine ; offense has been given, and from angry words they have come to the verge of blows,

5   Vino et lucernis Medus acinaces
    immane quantum discrepat: impium
       lenite clamorem, sodales,
          et cubito remanete presso.

    Voltis severi me quoque sumere
10   partem Falerni?   Dicat Opuntiae

when he checks them with the
sharp rebuke with which the poem
opens. They laugh, and for answer
put a goblet into his hand. Having
thus secured their attention, he
proceeds to play a little comedy
before them with one of the
younger members of the party, in
watching which they forget at once
their quarrel and his reproof.

Though the wine is Falernian,
the Greek origin of the sketch is
hardly disguised. Porphyrio says
that the poem was taken in substance from Anacreon, referring
perhaps to this fragment (63):

Ἄγε δηῦτε μηκέθ' οὕτω
πατάγῳ τε κἀλαλήτῳ
Σκυθικὴν πόσιν παρ' οἴνῳ
μελετῶμεν, ἀλλὰ καλοῖς
ὑποπίνοντες ἐν ὕμνοις.

—Metre, 176.

1. natis : i.e. designed from the
very beginning of their existence.
— in usum laetitiae, to promote
joy and gladness—scyphis: a large,
two-handled cup of wood, earthenware, or metal. Its size would
make it a very effective weapon.

2. Thracum est : Thracian
drunkenness was proverbial ; cf.
18. 9 n. — tollite, away with !

3. verecundum, modest. The
epithet (cf. modici, 18. 7 n.) is used
to indicate the quality which the
god approves in his worshippers.

4. prohibete, keep . . . free from;
cf. Ep. I. 1. 31 corpus prohibere che-
ragra. For the sense cf. 17. 22 sqq.

5. vino et lucernis : Intr. 57.
— Medus : cf. 2. 22 n. — acinaces : a short sword or dagger
worn at the belt in front of the
right thigh. Such a weapon would
never be seen at a Roman convivium. Horace found it no doubt
in his Greek original, and retained
it to continue the idea of barbarum morem, 2.

6. immane quantum discre-
pat, is a monstrous anomaly amid,
etc. The phrase immane quantum (like nescio quis = aliquis)
has lost its interrogative character,
and hence takes the indicative ;
cf. Liv. II. 1. 11 id mirum quantum profuit ad concordiam. — im-
pium renewing the thought
already suggested in verecundum
Bacchum, 3.

8. cubito presso : i.e. on the
cushions of the couches. The
Greeks as well as the Romans re-
clined at table.

9. severi, strong. There were
two kinds of Falernian wine, one
harsh and tart (austerum, αὐστηρός),
the other sweet (γλυκάζων); Athen.
I. 26 c.

10. Falerni : the only strictly
Italian feature which Horace has
added to the poem. — dicat, must
tell us ; i.e. that we may drink her
health. There was nothing extraordinary in the demand : on being
asked to take a cup with the rest,
he calls for a toast. — Opuntiae :
from Opus in Locris, near the
Euboean gulf.

frater Megillae quo beatus
volnere, qua pereat sagitta.

Cessat voluntas ?   Non alia bibam
mercede.   Quae te cumque domat Venus,
15   non erubescendis adurit
ignibus, ingenuoque semper

amore peccas.   Quicquid habes, age
depone tutis auribus. — A miser,
quanta laborabas Charybdi,
20   digne puer meliore flamma!

11. **frater Megillae** : a humorous variation on such honorary
designations as *filius Thetidis*,
8. 14, *nepos Veneris*, Verg. *A*. IV.
163, etc.; substituted for the lad's
own name, it implies, of course,
that his chief recommendation to
the present company is his handsome sister. — **beatus pereat** :
Intr. 120.

12. **pereat** : of love, as in 25. 7,
and frequently in the poets.

13. **cessat voluntas,** *does inclination falter ?*

14. **mercede,** *terms.*—**cumque**:
cf. 6. 3 n. — **Venus,** *love,* in a personal sense ; cf. Verg. *E*. 3. 68 *parta
meae Veneri sunt munera.*

15. **non** : with **erubescendis,**
for which see Intr. 51 *a.*

16. **ingenuo semper**, etc., *your
weakness is never for a lowborn
love.* — **-que** : Horace often uses
-que or *et* after a clause containing a negative, when the latter
is closely connected with a particular word, so that the clause as
a whole is felt to be affirmative ;
cf. 28. 34, II. 20. 4, III. 30. 6,
Epod. 15. 14.

17. **amore** : used of a person,
like *Venus*, 14. For the case, see
Intr. 72. — **quicquid habes,** etc.:

he urges the lad to whisper the
name in his ear, if he will not tell
it to all.

18. **auribus** : Intr. 69. — **a
miser** : his exclamation on hearing (or pretending to hear) the
name. His expectation of an *ingenuus amor* is disappointed.

19. **laborabas,** *you are struggling ;* cf. 9. 3 n. The imperfect
is in keeping with the humorous
outburst of horror and pity. It
refers to the time, just before,
when he was urging the lad to
confess, all unconscious of the
dreadful fact now revealed ; cf.
Ter. *Phor.* 857 *oh, tu quoque
aderas ?* — **Charybdi** : expressing
the insatiable rapacity of the
woman ; cf. Cic. *Phil.* 2. 67 *quae
Charybdis tam vorax ?* The comparison of this class of persons to
all sorts of monsters, Chimaeras,
Hydras, Scylla, Sphinx, etc., appears to have been not uncommon
(Athenaeus, XIII. 558 a).

20. **flamma** : returning to the
figure of vss. 15 *sq.*

21. **solvere . . . poterit** : cf.
beatus pereat, 11 n. — **Thessalis** :
Thessaly was notorious for magic
and necromancy ; cf. *Epod.* 5. 45,
Ep. II. 2. 209.

Quae saga, quis te solvere Thessalis
magus venenis, quis poterit deus?
  Vix inligatum te triformi
    Pegasus expediet Chimaera.

XXVIII.

Te maris et terrae numeroque carentis harenae
  mensorem cohibent, Archyta,

22. **venenis**, *drugs*, used to produce magical influences on the
mind; cf. *S.* I. 8. 19 *carminibus quae
versant atque venenis | humanos
animos; Epod.* 5. 87. — **deus**: observe the climax, **saga, magus,
deus.**

23. **inligatum**: *i.e.* in the coils
and limbs of the monster. — **triformi**: in front a lion, behind a
dragon, in the middle a goat; cf.
Lucr. V. 905; *Il.* VI. 181.

24. **Pegasus**: the meaning is:
even with the aid of the winged
horse on which Bellerophon rode
when he destroyed the original
Chimaera you will not escape. —
Chimaera: cf. *Charybdi,* 19 n.

XXVIII. This ode, like the
last, is a dramatic presentation,
the details of which, however, are
obscure. Whether the poem is a
dialogue or a monologue; if the
former, how it is to be divided;
who the speaker or speakers are,
— these are questions which have
always puzzled scholars and on
which they are not yet agreed.
The effort, however, to arrange
the ode as a dialogue may be said
to have failed. According to Porphyrio, the ode is a monologue in
the mouth of Archytas, whose
shipwrecked body lies on the seashore. In the opening verses he

apostrophizes himself, contrasting
his former world-embracing range
of thought with his present low
estate, and reflecting on the vanity
of all human achievement in the
presence of the universal destroyer.
He then appeals to a passing sailor
for the three handfuls of dust
which constituted due burial. The
first part of this interpretation is
difficult to accept. The language
of vss. 1–20 is hardly natural in
the mouth of Archytas, and the
view is much more probable which
attributes the monologue to a
shipwrecked man whose body
has been cast ashore close to
the tomb of Archytas, the sight
of which suggests the reflections
of the opening lines. — Metre,
162.

1. **numero carentis**, *countless*.
— **harenae**: referring perhaps to
a discussion of the subject in the
lost works of Archytas.

2. **cohibent**, *holds, confines*. —
Archyta: a statesman and general of Tarentum (about 400–360
B.C.), and a philosopher of such
eminence that his instruction and
friendship were sought by Plato.
As a Pythagorean, Archytas directed his studies to the solu-
tion, by mathematical methods,
of the problems of the physical
universe.

> pulveris exigui prope litus parva Matinum
>   munera, nec quicquam tibi prodest
> 5 aerias temptasse domos animoque rotundum
>   percurrisse polum morituro.
> Occidit et Pelopis genitor, conviva deorum,
>   Tithonusque remotus in auras,
> et Iovis arcanis Minos admissus, habentque

3. **pulveris exigui parva munera,** *the poor boon of a handful
of dust; i.e.* the 'few feet of earth'
which enclose his bones, called
munera, the last offering of affection or pity, to enhance the idea
of his present helpless dependence.
We have here the familiar contrast between man's unbounded
ambition and the 'narrow house'
to which death consigns him. Cf.
Juvenal 10. 168 *sqq.* For the plural
munera see Intr. 128. (Those
who accept Porphyrio's interpretation of the ode are obliged to
assume that the body of Archytas
lies unburied on the shore (see
vss. 23 *sqq.*), and to take **munera
... cohibent** as meaning 'the gift,
etc., holds you here,' *i.e.* is all that
prevents you from entering the
lower world.) — **litus Matinum** :
the shore of the Adriatic near Mati-
nus, which was apparently a mountain (cf. *Matina cacumina, Epod.*
16. 28), and has been placed by
geographers on the southern side
of the promontory of Garganus,
where there is a modern village
named Matinata. We are safe in
supposing that it was within the
region familiar to Horace in his
boyhood, and that he had seen the
tomb or mound near the shore
which tradition assigned to Archytas. For the form **Matinum** see
Intr. 65.

5. **aerias domos,** *the mansions
of the air,* the spaces where the
heavenly bodies (which the Py-
thagoreans regarded as divinities)
dwell. — **temptasse,** *to have ex-
plored,* with the idea of boldness
in venturing into the region ; cf.
III. 4. 30 *insanientem navita Bos-
porum* | *temptabo.* — **animoque** :
Intr. 119 *a.*

6. **morituro** : expressing in a
word the reason of **nec quicquam
prodest.** For the meaning see
Intr. 104 *b.*

7. **occidit et,** *fallen too is.* The
main thought is presented first ;
cf. III. 8. 18, 21. — **Pelopis geni-
tor** : Tantalus, a favorite of Jove
until his head was turned by the
honor, and his impiety consigned
him to the punishment which made
his name proverbial. — **conviva
deorum,** *though he was a guest,* etc.
In like manner **remotus in auras**
and **Iovis arcanis admissus** are
concessive.

8. **Tithonus** : brother of Priam
and husband of Aurora, at whose
request he was endowed with immortality, but not with eternal
youth (*Hom. Hymn in Ven.* 218
sqq). He consequently shrunk away
(*longa minuit senectus,* II. 16. 30)
until he became a mere voice, like
a cicada. — **remotus,** *translated.* —
in auras : *i.e.* to heaven ; cf. *aerias
domos,* 5 n.

9. **Iovis arcanis** : the famous
laws of Minos were represented
by tradition as a revelation from
his father, Zeus.

10   Tartara Panthoiden iterum Orco
      demissum, quamvis clipeo Troiana refixo
          tempora testatus nihil ultra
      nervos atque cutem morti concesserat atrae,
          iudice te non sordidus auctor
15   naturae verique.   Sed omnis una manet nox
          et calcanda semel via leti.
      Dant alios Furiae torvo spectacula Marti,
          exitio est avidum mare nautis;
      mixta senum ac iuvenum densentur funera; nullum
20   saeva caput Proserpina fugit.

10. **Tartara** : for the lower world in general. — **Panthoiden** : properly Euphorbus (Πανθοίδης Εὔφορβος, *Il.* XVI. 808), a Trojan hero, killed in battle by Menelaus (*Il.* XVII. 9 *sqq.*); but the patronymic is here used ironically for Pythagoras. The story was told that the latter, in accordance with his doctrine of metempsychosis, asserted that his own soul had previously inhabited, among others, the body of Euphorbus, and to prove his assertion offered to identify the shield he had carried, which was dedicated among many others in the temple of Hera at Argos. The shield he pointed out, on being taken down (**clipeo refixo**), was found to be inscribed with the name of Euphorbus. — **Orco** : Intr. 53.

11. **quamvis**, etc.: *i.e.* although, since he proved his previous existence in Trojan times, he had in fact given up nothing, etc.

13. **concesserat** : Intr. 83. — **atrae**, *sable;* a standing epithet of death and of things associated with death ; cf. *S.* II. 1. 58 *mors atris circumvolat alis;* II. 3. 16, 13. 34, 14. 17, etc.

14. **auctor**, *interpreter, expounder*.

15. **sed omnis** : cutting short the list of examples with a comprehensive statement. — **una** : *i.e.* the same for all.

16. **semel** : *i.e.* there is no return ; cf. 24. 16 n. — **via leti** : *i.e.* the one that death opens to man (cf. *fine libidinum* 18. 10 n); a different conception from that of 3. 17, where see note.

17. **alios**, *some*, although there is no second *alius*, a special class of persons (*nautae*) being substituted. — **Furiae** : as inflaming the passions which lead men to fight with one another. — **torvo**, *grim ;* his expression as he watches the show. — **spectacula** : a striking comparison, representing war as a sort of gladiatorial contest for the entertainment of Mars; cf. 2. 37 *sqq.*

18. **exitio est** : Gr. 233 *a.*

19. **mixta**, *without distinction.* — **funera**, *the funeral trains.* — **nullum** : emphatic (Intr. 116 *b*), summing up (like *sed omnis*, 15) the fact which the foregoing examples illustrate.

20. **caput**: alluding to the fancy that Proserpina doomed her vic-

Me quoque devexi rapidus comes Orionis
    Illyricis Notus obruit undis.
At tu, nauta, vagae ne parce malignus harenae
    ossibus et capiti inhumato
25 particulam dare: sic, quodcumque minabitur Eurus
    fluctibus Hesperiis, Venusinae
plectantur silvae te sospite, multaque merces
    unde potest tibi defluat aequo
ab Iove Neptunoque sacri custode Tarenti.
30   Neglegis immeritis nocituram

tim to death by clipping a lock of
hair, as the priest did from the
head of the victim before the altar;
cf. Eurip. *Alc.* 74 ; Verg. *A.* IV. 698
nondum illi flavom Proserpina
vertice crinem | abstulerat Stygio-
que caput damnaverat Orco. —
Prōserpina : see Intr. 178. —
fūgit, *shuns, i.e.* omits, in performing the function referred to. For
the tense see Intr. 80.

21. **devexi**, *setting.* The time
was early in November, a season
of storms, which were attributed
as usual to the influence of the
constellation ; cf. III. 27. 17; *Epod.*
15. 7; Verg. *A.* VII. 719.— **comes** :
cf. *veris comites animae,* IV. 12. 1.
— **Orionis** : for the prosody and
rhythm see Intr. 178, 132.

22. **Illyricis undis** : *i.e.* in the
Adriatic. See Intr. 117.— **Notus** :
cf. 3. 14 n.

23. **at tu**, etc.: see intr. note.
— **vagae** : *i.e.* of no value, and
hence a thing it would be niggardly
(**malignus**) to withhold. — **ne**
parce : Intr. 88.

24. **capiti inhumato** : for the
hiatus see Intr. 185.

25. **dare** : Intr. 94 *k.* — **sic** : cf.
3. 1 n.— **quodcumque**, etc. : for
the construction cf. *quam rem*
cumque 6. 3 n.

26. **fluctibus Hesperiis** : that
wash the shores of Italy (*Hesperia,*
III. 6. 8 n); here those of the
Adriatic (cf. vs. 22).— **Venusinae**
silvae : about forty miles inland,
but exposed by their elevated situation on the spurs of the Apennines
to the fury of the eastern winds.

27. **plectantur**, *suffer the loss.*
— **multa merces**, *abundant rec-*
ompense.

28. **unde potest** (sc. *defluere*):
anticipating **ab Iove Neptunoque.**
He can offer no reward from any
earthly source. For *unde* with a
personal antecedent cf. 12. 17 n.—
aequo, *approving;* cf. 2. 47 n. Jove
would reward him as the god of
hospitality and the protector of
strangers.

29. **sacri** : *sc.* to Neptune as its
patron divinity (**custode**). The
mythical founder of Tarentum was
Taras (gen. *Tarantos*), a son of Neptune. The sailor is thought of as
belonging to Tarentum, and therefore as an object of Neptune's care.

30. **neglegis**, *will you lightly*
. . . ? cf. Cat. 30. 5 *facta impia . . .*
quae tu neglegis, and see Intr. 95.
The sailor has turned away as if
not disposed to grant the request.
For the tense see Intr. 78.— **noci-**
turam : Intr. 104 *b.*

postmodo te natis fraudem committere?   Fors et
    debita iura vicesque superbae
te maneant ipsum: precibus non linquar inultis,
    teque piacula nulla resolvent.
35 Quamquam festinas, non est mora longa: licebit
    iniecto ter pulvere curras.

XXIX.

Icci, beatis nunc Arabum invides

31. **postmodo**: with **nocituram.** — **te natis,** *your children.*—
fraudem, *a wrong.*   To refuse
burial was to rob the dead of his
just due (cf. *debita iura,* 32). —
fors et, *may be, as likely as not;*
a phrase used where the speaker
regards his conjecture as altogether
probable, and not a mere guess;
cf. Verg. *A.* II. 139, XI. 50, Prop.
II. 9. 1, where it is used with the
indicative.

32. **debita iura,** etc.: *i.e.* your
turn may come to need the service
which you now withhold, and to
have your righteous demand refused with the same scornful indifference. — **debita iura,** *rights withheld,* referring to the right of the
dead to burial. — **vices superbae,**
pitiless retribution.   For the epithet see Intr. 124.

33. **precibus inultis** : *i.e.* without being avenged for the wrong
you do me in denying my prayer.
— **linquar** (sc. *a te*) : *i.e.* in the
predicament I am now in ; cf. *S.*
I. 9. 73 *me sub cultro linquit,* and
see Intr. 129.

35. **quamquam festinas,** *you
are in haste, I know, but.* — **non
est mora longa** : the indicative
is similar to that in the phrase
longum est ('it would be tedious');
Gr. 311 *c.*

36. **iniecto ter pulvere:** to meet
the requirements of the gods of the
dead, the solemn form of burial in
accordance with certain prescribed
rules was sufficient ; cf. Antigone's
burial of her brother, Soph. *Ant.*
429 *sqq.*   The number *three* constantly occurs in solemn rites; cf. *C.
S.* 23, *Ep.* I. 1. 37; Verg. *A.* VI. 229.

XXIX. Iccius, to whom this
ode and *Ep.* I. 12 are addressed,
was a man in whom a taste for
philosophy was combined with a
restless and discontented spirit,
which led him to join, with a view
to bettering his circumstances, the
expedition of Aelius Gallus into
Arabia in B.C. 24.   Horace banters
his friend good-humoredly on his
high hopes, and his desertion of
philosophy for the pursuit of
wealth.   The expedition was a
disastrous failure, and Iccius was
disappointed. In *Ep.* I. 12 (written
B.C. 20) we find him in Sicily, the
agent in charge of Agrippa's estates
there, — a sufficiently good place,
it would seem, — but still discontented with his condition. — Metre,
176.

1. **Icci,** *What, Iccius!* — **nunc** :
in contrast with his former devotion to philosophy and high thinking. — **invides,** *you are coveting?*

gazis et acrem militiam paras
　　non ante devictis Sabaeae
　　　　regibus horribilique Medo
5　nectis catenas?　Quae tibi virginum
　　sponso necato barbara serviet?
　　　Puer quis ex aula capillis
　　　　ad cyathum statuetur unctis,
　　doctus sagittas tendere Sericas
10　arcu paterno?　Quis neget arduis
　　pronos relabi posse rivos
　　　montibus et Tiberim reverti,

2. **gazis** : appropriate here, as an oriental (Persian) word. — **acrem militiam**, *a vigorous campaign.*

3. **Sabaeae,** *of Sheba,* the western portion of southern Arabia, famous for its wealth in spices and gold and precious stones (Plin. *N. H.* VI. 161; *O. T. Kings* I. 10.

4. **Medo** : see 2. 22 n. There is no probability that any operations against the Parthians were actually contemplated in connection with this expedition, but no doubt at Rome the most extravagant expectations were entertained in regard to it.

5. **nectis catenas**: implying full assurance of victory. — **quae virginum** : Intr. 63.

6. **sponso necato**: *sc.* by Iccius, who thereby obtains the *sponsa* as his prize ; cf. the picture of the young Roman warrior in battle, III. 2. 6 *sqq.*

7. **puer ex aula,** *royal page ;* see Madv. 298. 2.

8. **ad cyathum statuetur** : *i.e.* will be appointed to serve you and your guests with wine, dipping it from the *cratera* with the ladle-like *cyathus* and pouring it into the goblets.

9. **doctus,** etc.: the lad whom Iccius is to bring home from the palace of some Arab king, is a captive from the far East, where he had been trained for no such menial service.　The possession of such a rare slave as a cup-bearer was a fashionable luxury of the day (*S.* II. 8. 14 *sq.;* cf. Juv. 5. 56), but naturally a very costly one, and marks Iccius as a great nabob. — **tendere,** *to speed ;* lit. to direct towards a goal ; cf. Verg. *A.* V. 508 *pariterque oculos telumque tetendit ;* IX. 606 *spicula tendere cornu ;* V. 489. For the mood see Intr. 101 *c.* — **Sericas** : see 12. 56 n.　This epithet, in connection with **paterno,** serves to indicate the nationality of the boy (Intr. 124).

11. **pronos** : *i.e.* according to their nature, to which the supposed reversal of their course would do violence ; and this is the point of the comparison.

12. **montibus,** *up the mountains;* abl. of the way by which.　Others regard it as dat. (Intr. 53); but in that case **arduis** would be an idle epithet. — **reverti,** *reverse his course.*

cum tu coemptos undique nobilis
libros Panaeti Socraticam et domum
15   mutare loricis Hiberis,
          pollicitus meliora, tendis?

XXX.

O Venus, regina Cnidi Paphique,
sperne dilectam Cypron et vocantis
ture te multo Glycerae decoram
          transfer in aedem.
5   Fervidus tecum puer et solutis

13. **coemptos undique,** *after buying up from every quarter,* indicating the zeal with which Iccius had pursued the studies he now abandons. — **nobilis** : better taken as accusative plural; that he could sacrifice such books shows the completeness of his apostasy.

14. **Panaeti** : a Stoic philosopher of Rhodes, who came to Rome about 156 B.C. and lived for many years on terms of great intimacy with Scipio Aemilianus and Laelius. — **domum,** *school* (cf. *lare, Ep.* I. 1. 13); *i.e.* the disciples of Socrates who recorded the teachings of their master, especially Plato, Xenophon and Aeschines. The authors here, of course, by a familiar figure of speech, stand for their works.

15. **mutare** : *i.e.* to sell; Intr. 74. — **Hiberis** : Intr. 65. Spanish steel was famous in ancient as in modern times (Plin. *N.H.* XXXIV. 144, 149).

16. **tendis,** *are bent upon.*

XXX. A hymn to Venus, imploring the goddess to bestow her favor on Glycera. In all probability a study from the Greek. — Metre, 174.

1. **regina Cnidi Paphique** : cf. 3. 1; Pind. *Fr.* 99 δέσποινα Κύπρου. Cnidus was a city in Caria, where Venus had three temples. In one of these was the famous statue of the goddess by Praxiteles, of which the Medicean Venus is a copy. Paphos, in Cyprus, was a very old seat of the worship of Venus (*Odys.* VIII. 363) at the spot where she was said to have come ashore on rising out of the sea ; cf. Verg. *A.* I. 415. Her rites are described by Tac. *Hist.* II. 3.

2. **sperne,** *slight, forsake ;* cf. *deseruit,* 19. 10.

4. **aedem** : here a private chapel (*sacrarium*) in the girl's own lodgings. The meaning is 'Be ever present to answer her prayers,' which of course were for the enhancement and perpetuation of her own charms.

5. **puer** : Cupid.—**solutis zonis** : cf. Sen. *Ben.* I. 3. 2 *tres Gratiae, sorores, manibus implexis, ridentes et virgines, solutaque ac pellucida veste.*

Gratiae zonis properentque Nymphae
et parum comis sine te Iuventas
     Mercuriusque.

XXXI.

Quid dedicatum poscit Apollinem
vates ? Quid orat de patera novum
     fundens liquorem ?   Non opimae
          Sardiniae segetes feracis,

5   non aestuosae grata Calabriae

6. **Gratiae, Nymphae**: cf. 4. 6.
— **properentque** : Intr. 119 *b*.
7. **parum comis** : *i.e.* headstrong and impatient, the unsoft-
ened temper that belongs to the
confidence of youth. The description is no doubt Horace's
own ; only a Roman could treat
Iuventas in the retinue of Venus
as a personified abstraction. —
Iuventas : "Ηβη ; cf. *Hom. Hymn.
in Apol.* quoted at 4. 5 n.
8. **Mercurius** : the worship of
Hermes was associated, in many
places in Greece, with that of Aphrodite (Preller-Robert, *Gr. Myth*. I.
387). In Horace's mind, however,
it is perhaps as the *facundus deus*
(cf. 10. 1) that he has a place in
her retinue.

XXXI. The poet's prayer. The
dedication of the temple of Apollo
on the Palatine, October 9, B.C.
28, was an event of great interest
in Roman literary circles; for with
the temple was united a public
library (cf. *Ep.* I. 3. 17, II. 1.
216 *sq*.). Horace records his reflections on the occasion in this
fine ode, in which, against a background of the various forms of
wealth which the multitude crave,

he formulates his own simple prayer for the few needs of a happy life.
The closing verses of Epode 1
were written in a somewhat similar
strain. — Metre, 176.
1. **dedicatum**, *enshrined*. For
this use of the word, applied to
the divinity instead of the shrine,
cf. Cic. *N. D.* II. 61, Ov. *F.* VI.
637. — **poscit** : notice the tense,
which is to be taken strictly: 'what
does (not what *shall*) he demand.'
As to the word itself, we must re-
member that the Roman idea of
the relation between gods and men
was that of mutual obligation. On
the erection of a splendid temple
the people would feel that they
could *claim* some boon of the god
in return ; cf. 24. 12, III. 29. 59 n.
2. **patera** : see 19. 15 n. —
novum liquorem : *i.e.* wine of
the vintage just gathered. The
time was late autumn.
4. **Sardiniae** : one of the great
sources of the grain supply of
Rome. — **segetes**, *grain lands*.
For this use of *seges*, cf. *Ep.* II. 2.
161, Verg. *G.* I. 47.
5. **aestuosae**: cf. 22. 5 n.—**grata**:
i.e. a pleasing sight. — **Calabriae**:
an excellent grazing country, except in the hot season when the

armenta, non aurum aut ebur Indicum,
　　non rura quae Liris quieta
　　　　mordet aqua taciturnus amnis.

　　Premant Calena falce quibus dedit
10　Fortuna vitem, dives et aureis
　　　mercator exsiccet culullis
　　　　vina Syra reparata merce,

　　dis carus ipsis, quippe ter et quater
　　anno revisens aequor Atlanticum
15　　impune: me pascunt olivae,
　　　　me cichorea levesque malvae.

flocks were driven over into the mountains of Lucania and Sabinum; cf. *Epod.* 1. 27 *sq.*

6. ebur : very costly ; cf. Plin. *N. H.* VIII. 31 *dentibus* (tusks) *ingens pretium.* It was used for household decorations.

8. mordet : cf. *lambit,* 22. 8. — **taciturnus** : cf. *loquaces lymphae,* III. 13. 15.

9. premant Calena, etc.: with a change of form the poet continues the catalogue of objects of desire which he does not covet.—**premant,** *prune;* lit. keep back, check luxuriant growth ; cf. Verg. *G.* I. 157 *ruris opaci falce premes umbras.* — **Calena falce** : cf. 20. 9 n ; Intr. 124.— **quibus dedit** : sc. *eam premere* (Intr. 97 *d*); *i.e.* 'to whom Fortune has given the control of rich vineyards,' which those of Cales here typify (Intr. 117 *a*).

11. mercator : see 1. 16 n.— **exsiccet,** *drain.*— **culullis** : properly a kind of earthenware cup used by the pontifices and vestals in religious rites. Here and *Ep.* II. 3. 434 the name is used for drinking cups of a richer sort.

12. Syrā : *i.e.* brought from the ports of Syria, especially Antioch,

which had become the chief emporium for the merchandise of Arabia and the far East. — **reparata,** *purchased.* From its meaning, 'to get' (cf. 17 n.) *parare* with the prefix *re-* (see 3. 7 n.) denotes 'to get *back*' in return for something given. The construction is similar to that of *mutare* in 17. 2. The two pictures of this strophe are designed to go together, — the vine grower living quietly at home in oriental luxury, the more restless trader roving the seas according to his bent (cf. 1. 17) and enjoying the best that life affords. The impression of such enviable happiness is further heightened by the exclamation that follows, in order to point the contrast with the poet's own simple fare and simple wants.

13. quippe revisens : equivalent to *quippe qui revisat,* the reason for saying **dis carus.**

14. anno : *i.e.* between the opening of navigation in the spring (cf. 4. 2) and its close at the approach of winter.

15. impune : Intr. 116 *b.* — **me pascunt,** *my fare is ;* cf. 1. 29 n.

16. leves : *i.e.* easily digested; cf.

Frui paratis et valido mihi,
Latoe, dones et, precor, integra
    cum mente nec turpem senectam
20   degere nec cithara carentem.

XXXII.

Poscimur. Si quid vacui sub umbra
lusimus tecum, quod et hunc in annum
    vivat et pluris, age dic Latinum,
        barbite, carmen,

Epod. 2. 57 *gravi malvae salubres
corpori.*

17. **paratis,** *what I possess ;* cf.
Ep. II. 2. 196 *plura parare labores.*
— **et valido,** etc.: the construction
is as follows : **et . . . et** connect
the two infinitives **frui, degere,**
which depend upon **dones** (Intr.
97 *d*), while **nec . . . nec,** which
are subordinate to the second **et,**
connect **turpem** and **cithara carentem ; precor** is parenthetical.
For this use of **et . . . nec . . .
nec** cf. Cic. *C. M.* 7 *moderati et
nec difficiles nec inhumani senes.*
For the purport of the prayer
cf. Juv. 10. 356 *orandum est ut
sit mens sana in corpore sano.*
— **valido mihi,** *that I in good
health may.*

18. **Latoe :** formed after the
Greek Λατῷος, from Λάτω (Attic
Λήτω), Latona ; cf. 21. 3. For
the form cf. *Semeleius,* 17. 22 n. —
integra cum mente : thought of
in closer connection with old age,
as **valido** with bodily comfort
(**frui paratis**); health and strength
may fail with years, but the failure
of the mental faculties makes a
turpem senectam.

20. **cithara carentem :** *i.e.*
robbed of the poetic gift.

XXXII. The poet to his lyre.
The ode appears to be a prelude
to another or to other compositions (as IV. 6 is to the *Carmen
Saeculare*), but to which, it would
be fruitless to inquire. The lyre
is addressed as the lyre of Alcaeus,
on which the poet has already
played lighter strains (*lusimus sub
umbra*) not without success. As
the song he now calls for is characterized in no other way than as
Latinum carmen, it is probable
that the 'lighter strains' are his
studies from the Greek, many of
which are preserved, especially in
this book, and this ode preludes
his undertaking in compliance
with the demand of his friends
(*poscimur*), more serious and original lyric composition on strictly
Roman subjects, — such odes as
I. 2, etc., and the majority of
those in the following books. —
Metre, 174.

1. **poscimur** (sc. *carmen*): the
construction is the passive of that
of 24. 12 and 31. 1 ; cf. Ov. *M.*
V. 333 *poscimur, Aonides ; F.*
IV. 721 *Parilia poscor.* — **si quid,**
etc., *if ever . . . I have sung with
thee in lighter mood some strain
that,* etc.; cf. IV. 9. 9 ; *S.* I. 10. 37

XXXI. 17–XXXII. 16.]   HORATI CARMINA.   87

5   Lesbio primum modulate civi,
     qui ferox bello tamen inter arma,
     sive iactatam religarat udo
          litore navim,

     Liberum et Musas Veneremque et illi
10   semper haerentem puerum canebat
     et Lycum nigris oculis nigroque
          crine decorum.

     O decus Phoebi et dapibus supremi
     grata testudo Iovis, o laborum
15   dulce lenimen, mihi cumque salve
          rite vocanti !

haec ego ludo. — sub umbra : cf.
5. 3 n.
   2. hunc in annum, *this year ;*
cf. such phrases as *in praesens, in
tempus,* etc.
   3. dic : see 6. 5 n.
   5. Lesbio civi : Alcaeus (Intr.
26) ; civi, to recall his prominence
in the political struggles of his
time ; cf. 2. 21 n. For the case
see Intr. 55. — primum modulate : *i.e.* not the lyre in general,
but as used by Alcaeus, the great
master of the type of lyric poetry
which Horace aspired to write.
   6. inter arma, sive, etc.: *i.e.* in
the midst of war or in exile (danger
and excitement or adversity and
discouragement).
   7. sive : Intr. 119 *d.*
   8. litore : Intr. 71.
   10. puerum : cf. 30. 5 n.
   11. Lycum : a favorite boy. —
nigris . . . nigro : notice the
variation of prosody. The same
description occurs *Ep.* II. 3. 37.
   13. dapibus : probably dative,
though we say *at.*—supremi Iovis :
cf. 21. 3.

   14. testudo : see 10. 6 n. —
laborum, *in trouble.*
   15. mihi salve, *accept my
greeting, i.e.* hear my call. — mihi
is ethical dat. with salve (which
in form is a command ; cf. *iubeo
te salvere,* etc.), expressing technically the person who is interested in having the command ful-
filled, *i.e.* the person from whom
the greeting proceeds ; cf. Verg.
A. XI. 97 *salve aeternum mihi,
maxime Palla, aeternumque vale.*
— cumque vocanti, *whenever I
call. Cumque* does not occur elsewhere except as a suffix to a relative pronoun or adverb. It is
supposed by some to be an archaic
form, corresponding to *quandoque*
= *quandocumque* (IV. 1. 17 n),
quique = *quicumque* (*e.g.* Plaut.
Men. 571) ; or it may be a bold
use of the detachable suffix *cumque*
(=‘ever’), the relative notion to
which it belongs being implied in
the participle, so that mihi cumque vocanti=*mihi quandocumque
vocabo;* cf. *quippe revisens* = *quippe
qui revisat,* 31. 13 n.

XXXIII.

Albi, ne doleas plus nimio memor
immitis Glycerae, neu miserabilis
decantes elegos, cur tibi iunior
    laesa praeniteat fide.

5   Insignem tenui fronte Lycorida
Cyri torret amor, Cyrus in asperam
declinat Pholoen ; sed prius Apulis
    iungentur capreae lupis

quam turpi Pholoe peccet adultero.

XXXIII. To the elegiac poet Albius Tibullus, who, at least in his later years (he died in the same year with Vergil, B.C. 19), was on friendly terms with Horace. The latter does not mention him in the Satires, but *Ep.* I. 4 is addressed to him, and shows, as does the present ode, a certain degree of intimacy between the two men. The character of Tibullus here represented is quite in keeping with his portrayal of himself in his elegies, but the name Glycera does not occur in any of his extant poems. — Metre, 172.

1. ne doleas : Intr. 87. — plus nimio, *overmuch ;* see 18. 15 n ; to be taken with doleas.

3. decantes, *keep droning ;* cf. *Ep.* I. 1. 62 *puerorum nenia Curiis et decantata Camillis.* — elegos : poems in elegiac verse, the unit of which is a couplet consisting of a dactylic hexameter and a 'pentameter' (*versibus impariter iunctis, Ep.* II. 3. 75). It became in the Alexandrine period the verse of sentimental love, and in this use was successfully cultivated by Tibullus and other Augustan poets. — cur, etc.: cf. *Ep.* I. 8. 9 *irascar*

amicis, cur me funesto properent arcere veterno ; Cic. *Att.* III. 13. 2 *me saepe accusas cur hunc meum casum tam graviter feram.* This use of *cur (quor, qua re)* is probably a survival of an original relative use after *causa* and the like ; cf. 16. 19 *causae cur perirent* and our 'the reason why.' — iunior : Tibullus was born about 55 B.C., and may have been 30 when this ode was written.

4. laesa fide, *her plighted faith is broken and.* — praeniteat, *outshines* (sc. *ei,* 'in her eyes'; cf. 5. 13 *quibus nites*).

5. tenui fronte : a low forehead was greatly admired by the Romans ; cf. *Ep.* I. 7. 26 ; Mart. IV. 42. 9. — Lycorida, Cyri : these and the following are probably fictitious persons as well as names.

6. Cyri (objective gen.) torret amor : cf. III. 19. 28.—asperam, *waspish.*

7. declinat : *sc.* from Lycoris.

8. lupis : Intr. 56.

9. turpi, *ugly,* in contrast with the pretty Lycoris ; cf. *imparis formas,* 10. — peccet, cf. 27. 16 n ; Intr. 72. — adultero, *paramour.*

10   Sic visum Veneri, cui placet imparis
       formas atque animos sub iuga aenea
       saevo mittere cum ioco.

       Ipsum me melior cum peteret Venus,
       grata detinuit compede Myrtale
15   libertina, fretis acrior Hadriae
       curvantis Calabros sinus.

XXXIV.

       Parcus deorum cultor et infrequens,
       insanientis dum sapientiae
          consultus erro, nunc retrorsum
          vela dare atque iterare cursus

10. **sic visum,** *such is the will of.*
Cf. 12. 31 n; Verg. *A.* II. 428 *dis
aliter visum.*

11. **aenea :** *i.e.* that cannot be
broken ; there is no escape for her
victims. Cf. III. 9. 18.

12. **saevo ioco,** *with grim
humor.*

13. **melior Venus:** *i.e.* a woman
of higher social position than a
libertina. For *Venus* cf. 27. 14 n.

14. **grata detinuit compede,** *I
lingered, a willing captive, in the fetters of ;* cf. IV. 11. 23 *sq. Compede*
also occurs *Epod.* 4. 4, *Ep.* I. 3. 3;
the plural *compedibus* only *Ep.* I. 16.
77. The singular is not found in
any author before Horace. — **Myr-
tale:** a common name of *libertinae.*

15. **fretis acrior Hadriae:** concessive ; a further reason why he
should have followed the dictates
of his good sense. Cf. III. 9. 23.

16. **curvantis,** *when it hollows
out ; i.e.* in time of storm, the
force of which changes the outline
of a sandy shore like that of Calabria ; cf. Verg. *A.* III. 533 *portus
ab Euroo fluctu curvatus in arcum.*

— **sinus,** *bays.* The acc. expresses
the effect of the action (Goodwin's
Gk. Gr. 1055).

XXXIV. For the occasion and
subject of this ode see Intr. 8, and
cf. *S.* I. 5. 101 *sqq.;* Lucr. VI. 400
*denique cur numquam caelo iacit
undique puro | Iuppiter in terras
fulmen sonitusque profundit?* The
place of the ode in the collection
was no doubt determined by the
closing sentence, which prepares
the reader for the more elaborate
portrayal of the attributes of Fortuna in the next ode. — Metre, 176.

1. **parcus et infrequens :** *i.e.*
coming seldom to the altar and
bringing scanty offerings, at that.
The time referred to is past (*I who
was*, etc.), as is indicated by the
contrasted *nunc*, 3.

2. **insanientis sapientiae:** oxymoron.

3. **consultus,** *an adept in ;* see
Intr. 66 *b.* — **erro,** *I strayed from
the truth.* Gr. 276 *e.*

4. **iterare,** *to traverse again ;* cf.
7. 32. — **cursus :** see Intr. 128.

5   cogor relictos.   Namque Diespiter,
     igni corusco nubila dividens
          plerumque, per purum tonantis
             egit equos volucremque currum,

        quo bruta tellus et vaga flumina,
10   quo Styx et invisi horrida Taenari
        sedes Atlanteusque finis
          concutitur.   Valet ima summis

5. **Diespiter :** see 1. 25 n.
6. **nubila dividens plerumque,**
who commonly cleaves the clouds.
For the emphasis on **plerumque**
see Intr. 116 *b*, and cf. 3. 12, 31. 2.
7. **per purum,** *across the clear
sky.* — **tonantis egit equos,** etc.:
the phenomenon described is that
of thunder rumbling overhead and
passing away in the distance. The
two epithets are not to be taken
strictly with their substantives, but
are designed to give an impression
of the whole phenomenon, — the
god in his car, with flying steeds,
thundering across the sky ; see
Intr. 121.
9. **quo,** *that car by which ;* passing from the special incident to a
general description.—**bruta,** *heavy,
sluggish* (cf. *terram inertem,* III.
4. 45) ; in contrast with **vaga.**
10. **invisi,** *repulsive;* a frequent
epithet of things connected with
death ; cf. II. 14. 23 *invisas
cupressos ;* Verg. *A.* VIII. 245
regna pallida, dis invisa; Sen.
Herc. Fur. 664 *Ditis invisi domus.*
— **Taenari :** the southern point
of the Peloponnesus (Cape Mata-
pan), where, under a temple of
Poseidon, tradition placed one of
the entrances of the lower world
(cf. Verg. *G.* IV. 467 *Taenarias
fauces, alta ostia Ditis*); here used,
like *Avernus,* for the lower world
itself. For the case see Intr. 65.

11. **Atlanteus finis :** the end
of the earth, where Atlas supports the sky on his shoulders ;
cf. τερμόνων Ἀτλαντικῶν εἴσω, Eurip.
Hippol. 3.
12. **valet,** etc.: the power of the
supreme god is also manifested in
the astonishing vicissitudes of fortune in human experience. — **ima
summis mutare,** *to reverse high
and low.* The neuter of the adjectives is used abstractly, compre-
hending both persons and things
(cf. *Ep.* I. 9. 4 *legentis honesta Ne-
ronis ;* II. 2. 178 *metit Orcus grandia cum parvis*). The plural is that
of repeated occurrence. The ambiguity in the construction of the
cases with *mutare* (Intr. 74) here
has its natural application, both
objects having the same relation to
the subject, who neither gives nor
receives, but puts each in place
of the other. For the mood see
Intr. 94 *n.*
13. **insignem,** etc.: repeating in
detail the idea just expressed collectively, by indicating the visible
effect on each of the two classes
mentioned. The presentation is
also made more vivid by **insignem,** which brings a person before
us, though the abstract recurs in
obscura. Horace had in mind
Hes. *Op.* 6 ῥεῖα δ᾽ ἀρίζηλον μινύθει
καὶ ἄδηλον ἀέξει . . . Ζεὺς ὑψιβρεμέ-
της. — **deus :** see 3. 21 n.

mutare et insignem attenuat deus,
obscura promens ; hinc apicem rapax
15   Fortuna cum stridore acuto
sustulit, hic posuisse gaudet.

XXXV.

O diva, gratum quae regis Antium,
praesens vel imo tollere de gradu

14. hinc apicem, etc.: in a moment Fortuna makes or unmakes kings. Fortuna is here obviously the minister of Jove, the μοῖρα Διός of Homer (*Il.* XV. 117); cf. Pind. *Ol.* 12. 1 παῖ Ζηνὸς, Τύχα, and Paus. VII. 26. 8 ἐγὼ μὲν οὖν Πινδάρου πείθομαι τῇ ᾠδῇ, Μοιρῶν τε εἶναι μίαν τὴν Τύχην καὶ ὑπὲρ τὰς ἀδελφάς τι ἰσχύειν. — apicem, *the crown, i.e.* kingly power. — rapax : not an epithet of Fortuna, but expressing, in place of an adverb, the zest with which she performs this part of her function. The same idea is expressed in the other case by gaudet, 16.

15. stridore : *sc.* of her wings ; cf. III. 29. 53, and Vergil's *stridentibus alis* (*A.* I. 397).

16. sustulit : the perfect here expresses the quick completion of the action, and in posuisse also the tense appears to retain its proper force ; but see Intr. 80, 81.

XXXV. A hymn to Fortuna. The powerful goddess, whose sway is owned alike on sea and land, in every nation and in every calling, whose favor is sought by peasant and king, is implored to preserve Caesar in his contemplated expedition to far-off Britain, and the throng of young Romans who were preparing to invade the

East. These allusions show that the ode was written B.C. 27, when Augustus set out from the city ὡς καὶ ἐς τὴν Βρεττανίαν στρατεύσων, or in 26, when, though detained in Spain, he still cherished the project until diverted from it by risings there and in the Alps (Dio Cass. LIII. 22. 5, 25. 2). The expedition of Aelius Gallus into Arabia (see intr. note to Ode 29) was in preparation at this time. — Metre, 176.

1. diva quae regis : cf. *diva potens Cypri*, 3. 1 ; *Venus, regina Cnidi Paphique*, 30. 1. The designation of a divinity by a favorite haunt or a famous sanctuary, either with or (as here) instead of the proper name, is common in Greek hymns. — gratum : cf. Cic. *Att.* IV. 8ª. 1 (speaking of Antium) *nihil quietius, nihil alsius, nihil amoenius.* — Antium : the seat of a renowned temple and oracle, which continued to exist to the latest pagan times. There were here two images, *Fortunae Antiates* (see Baumeister, fig. 606 f.), regarded as sisters (*veridicae sorores*, Mart. V. 1. 3), by certain motions of which oracular responses were conveyed. See Preller-Jordan, *Röm. Myth.* II. 192. They were probably consulted in regard to the military expeditions now on foot.

2. praesens : equivalent to *po-*

mortale corpus vel superbos
vertere funeribus triumphos :

5   te pauper ambit sollicita prece
ruris colonus, te dominam aequoris
quicumque Bithyna lacessit
Carpathium pelagus carina ;

te Dacus asper, te profugi Scythae
10   urbesque gentesque et Latium ferox
regumque matres barbarorum et
purpurei metuunt tyranni,

iens, because by the 'presence' of a divinity we mean only the manifestation of his power. — **imo gradu :** cf. our 'lowest round of the ladder.'

3. **mortale corpus,** *our perishable clay ;* i.e. man in his most helpless state, stripped of all outward show and resources ; cf. Liv. XXII. 22. 7 *transfugam nihil aliud quam unum vile atque infame corpus esse ratus.*

4. **vertere,** *to turn . . . into.* It has here the meaning and construction of *mutare* (Intr. 74). — **funeribus triumphos :** both in a literal sense, — the conqueror's march to the Capitol and the march to the grave. The Romans could recall in their own history at least one conspicuous example of each of these vicissitudes of fortune, — the rise of Servius Tullius from slavery to the throne, and the pathetic case of Aemilius Paullus, the conqueror of Macedonia, who lost his two sons at the very time of his triumph (Liv. XLV. 41).

5. **te :** see 10. 9 n. — **ambit,** *courts,* as the Roman candidate courted the favor of the voter (hence *ambitio, ambitus*). — **sollicita :** Intr. 124.

6. **colonus :** a type of humble circumstances, as in II. 14. 12. But the farmer was regarded as especially dependent on the favor of Fortuna (cf. III. 1. 29 *sqq.*); like the mariner, he was at the mercy of the elements. In certain figures of Fortuna (see Baumeister, fig. 605) the goddess is represented with a rudder in one hand (**dominam aequoris**), and in the other a horn of plenty (cf. 17. 14 n). — **te :** sc. *ambit,* the subject of which is the antecedent implied in **quicumque.**

7. **quicumque,** etc.: *i.e.* any mariner ; see Intr. 117 *a*, and cf. 1. 13 *sq.* — **Bithyna :** cf. *Pontica,* 14. 11 n. — **lacessit,** *braves ;* lit. challenges.

9. **te Dacus,** etc.: **te** carries with it the idea of **ambit** 5, but the strict meaning of the word is lost, as the reader proceeds, in the vaguer notion of a helpless dependence ; and without distinctly marking the transition, the poet introduces the idea of fear (**metuunt**), which is only another aspect of the same feeling. — **Dacus :** cf. 26. 4 n. — **profugi,** *nomad ;* cf. III. 24. 10.

10. **urbesque,** etc.: *i.e.* collectively, as organized bodies, the cases hitherto presented being those of individual men ; the

iniurioso ne pede proruas
    stantem columnam, neu populus frequens
15   ad arma cessantis ad arma
       concitet imperiumque frangat.

Te semper anteit saeva Necessitas,
    clavos trabalis et cuneos manu
      gestans aena, nec severus
20   uncus abest liquidumque plumbum.

strongest community is helpless against the power of the goddess. — **Latium** : the Roman state, as in 12. 53.—**ferox**, *dauntless* (against all other adversaries) ; cf. *Roma ferox*, III. 3. 44.

11. regumque matres : the introduction of the more poignant anxieties of woman adds a touch of pathos, as in III. 2. 7; cf. 15. 34 n. — **barbarorum** : *i.e.* in the East. Under the system of polygamy which prevailed there, the succession of a prince to the throne was often due to the influence or intrigues of his mother, who therefore obtained an importance which she did not ordinarily have elsewhere. The nearest approach to it in Roman history was the case of Livia, the mother of Tiberius.

12. purpurei (for *purpurati*), *in scarlet robes.*—**tyranni** : in the proper sense of the word, men who have seized the supreme power (**imperium**), and whose position is therefore the more precarious. This thought is developed in the next strophe into a picture in which the portrayal of the goddess's power is brought to a climax. See also 2. 7 n.

13. iniurioso, *irreverent* (from the point of view of the *tyrannus*), not respecting his just rights (*iura*); cf. *Epod.* 17. 34 n; Intr. 124.

14. stantem columnam : figu-

rative, meaning their established power and dignity.

15. ad arma : the repetition has the effect of introducing the actual cry into the verse. Cf. Liv. XXI. 49. 10 n. — **cessantis** : *i.e.* the cooler heads, whose adhesion to the rebellion would mean the fall of the monarch.

17. anteit: Intr. 180. Necessity walking before Fortuna with the symbols of her power, as the lictors with the fasces before the Roman magistrate, declares the fixedness of her decrees.

18. clavos trabalis, etc.: devices employed in building to secure firmness and durability, here symbols of immutability. *Clavus* in this figurative sense was not uncommon ; cf. Cic. *Verr.* II. 5. 53 *ut hoc beneficium, quemadmodum dicitur, trabali clavo figeret.* — **cuneos** : used to tighten imperfect joints. — **manu aena** : cf. our 'iron grasp.' The characteristic of Necessitas is transferred to her hand. Intr. 124.

19. severus, *rigid, unyielding.*

20. uncus, plumbum: the iron clamp by which two blocks of stone were held together, and the lead, poured in hot, by which the iron was firmly fixed in the stone (Vitruv. II. 8). Such clamps may be seen in the walls of the Parthenon to this day.

Te Spes et albo rara Fides colit
velata panno, nec comitem abnegat,
utcumque mutata potentis
veste domos inimica linquis ;
25   at volgus infidum et meretrix retro
periura cedit, diffugiunt cadis
cum faece siccatis amici
ferre iugum pariter dolosi.

21. **te Spes et . . . Fides** : in
this and the following strophe we
have a different conception of
Fortuna from the one portrayed
above, illustrating the confusion
which existed in the Roman mind
on the subject. Except in the
single word **inimica**, 24, we have
no longer the inexorable goddess,
dealing out good and evil to men,
which was perhaps the character
of the Fortunae Antiates, but a
more abstract conception of a
changeable divinity, a sort of genius (cf. *Ep.* II. 2. 187 *sqq.*), attending as well as determining
the lives of men, — of a state
or city, of a class, or even of a
family or an individual. Such a
conception was *Fortuna Populi
Romani, Fortuna Muliebris,
Fortuna Caesaris,* etc. (Preller-
Jordan *Röm. Myth.* II. 182). This
divinity typifies misfortune as well
as good fortune, — wears white or
black (**mutata veste**); and to her
cling Hope and Fidelity, — the
hope that never dies in the heart,
and the rare fidelity that can stand
the test of adversity. — **albo** :
typical of purity ; cf. 'unsullied
faith.'—**rara**, *rare ;* with the same
accessory notion of excellence as
in English. For the neutral meaning of *fides*, see 5. 5 n, and for the
personification, 24.·7 n.

22. **velata panno** : from the
custom of the priests in the worship of Fides, as instituted by
Numa, who (Liv. I. 21. 4) '*ad id
sacrarium flamines bigis curru
arcuato vehi iussit, manuque ad
digitos usque involuta rem
divinam facere, significantes fidem
tutandam, sedemque eius etiam in
dextris sacratam esse.*' The cloth
by which the priest veils his hand
is here transferred to the figure of
the goddess. — **comitem** (sc. *se*),
her companionship ; cf. Ovid. *A.
A.* I. 127 *siqua comitem negabat ;
S.* II. 8. 2 *quaerenti convivam* (sc.
te).—**abnegat** : with **Spes** as well
as **Fides** as its subject.

23. **mutata veste** : *i.e.* putting
on mourning. — **potentis domos,**
the home of power (Intr. 124). This
home the once prosperous man
must now leave and go out into
the world with his changed fortune ; but hope still attends him,
and a few faithful friends.

24. **linquis** : Intr. 129.

25. **at volgus,** etc.: but the
great majority of those who were
the devoted friends of his prosperity will not share with him the
burden of adversity.— **retro cedit,**
fall back, refuse to follow.

27. **cum faece,** *dregs and all.*

28. **ferre iugum pariter :** to
bear, as in true friendship. an
equal share of the hardships, as
well as the pleasures, of life ; cf.

Serves iturum Caesarem in ultimos
30   orbis Britannos et iuvenum recens
     examen Eois timendum
      partibus oceanoque rubro.

Eheu cicatricum et sceleris pudet
  fratrumque.   Quid nos dura refugimus
35   aetas? Quid intactum nefasti
     liquimus? Vnde manum iuventus

metu deorum continuit? Quibus
  pepercit aris? O utinam nova
   incude diffingas retusum in
40   Massagetas Arabasque ferrum.

Theocr. 12. 15 ἀλλήλους δ' ἐφίλησαν
ἴσῳ ζυγῷ. For the construction
of **ferre** see Intr. 101 *b*.

29. serves : the poet returns to
the first conception of Fortuna. —
ultimos orbis, *at the ends of the
earth.*

30. recens : *i.e.* newly recruited.

31. Eois partibus : a general
designation prefixed to the more
definite one, — *the parts of the East
towards*, etc.; cf. Verg. *A.* VIII.
686 *victor ab Aurorae populis et
litore rubro*.

32. oceano rubro : for *mare
Erythraeum*, the part of the Indian
ocean adjoining Arabia. **partibus** and **oceano** are dative with
timendum, the places standing
for their inhabitants.

33. eheu, *ah me.*— **cicatricum**,
etc.: each cause of shame suggests
and explains the next : we are
ashamed of our scars, — they remind us of our guilt, — guilt
against our brothers. — **sceleris** :
see 2. 29 n.

34. dura, *hardened.* — **refūgi-
mus**, *shrunk from, i.e.* not dared
to do.

35. intactum, *untried, unat-
tempted ;* cf. *S.* I. 10. 66, and Sall.
Iug. 66. 1 *nihil intactum pati.* —
nefasti : better taken as genitive.

36. unde, *from what.*

38. o : Intr. 185. — **nova** : because of the feeling that things
were doomed to a certain career in
the making, as men at their birth ;
cf. 27. 1. The sword is to be broken
up and forged anew (**diffingas**)
under altogether new influences.

39. in (with **diffingas**): *i.e.* for
use against.   The desire to wash
out the stain of civil war in the
blood of the enemy was no doubt
a genuine feeling on the part of
Horace's contemporaries, and not
merely a happy fancy of the poet ;
cf. the feeling of the soldiers of
Germanicus after their mutiny in
A.D. 14 (Tac. *Ann.* I. 49. 5) : *truces
etiam tum animos cupido involat
eundi in hostem, piaculum furoris ;
nec aliter posse placari commilito-
num manes quam si pectoribus impiis honesta volnera accepissent.*

40. Massagetas : a powerful
Scythian people, east of the Caspian sea.

XXXVI.

Et ture et fidibus iuvat
    placare et vituli sanguine debito
custodes Numidae deos,
    qui nunc Hesperia sospes ab ultima
5 caris multa sodalibus,
    nulli plura tamen dividit oscula
quam dulci Lamiae, memor
    actae non alio rege puertiae
mutataeque simul togae.

XXXVI. A welcome to Numida on his safe return from the 'far West,'— possibly as one of the *iuvenes nuper sospites* (III. 14. 9) in the train of Augustus, B.C. 24. Numida, whose *nomen* is variously given as Plotius or Pomponius, was a much younger man than Horace, being of the same age with their common friend Lamia (see intr. note to Ode 26); and we may therefore suppose that the sacrifice and banquet with which his return was celebrated were instituted by Lamia, at whose request Horace wrote this ode for the occasion. — Metre, 171.

1. **et ture et fidibus:** both indispensable accompaniments of a sacrifice. During the progress of the rites, amid the absolute silence of the spectators, a *fidicen* (or more commonly a *tibicen*) played a solemn strain to make more sure that no ill-omened sound should reach the ears of the priest; and no sacrifice was acceptable unless the smoke of the victim was fragrant with incense. — **iuvat,** *we will gladly;* expressing here, as in *Epod.* 9. 37, disposition to do the thing rather than,

as more commonly, satisfaction or pleasure in doing it; see Intr. 94 *c.*

2. **placare,** *gratify.*—**sanguine:** *i.e.* the life. Only the entrails of the victim were consumed on the altar ; the flesh furnished forth the banquet which followed. — **debito :** because the sacrifice had been vowed on Numida's departure, probably by Lamia ; cf. *obligatam dapem,* II. 7. 17.

3. **custodes deos :** cf. 28. 29, and see Intr. 126 *c.*

4. **Hesperia ultima :** probably Spain is meant.

6. **plura,** *a larger share.*— **dividit,** *bestows.*

8. **non alio,** *under the very same* (litotes).— **rege,** *leader* (in games); *i.e.* they had been playmates; cf. *Ep.* I. 1. 59; Allen's *Early Latin Remn.* 213 n. Others conjecture that *rex* here is equivalent to *rector* in *rectores imperatoriae iuventae* (Burrus and Seneca), Tac. *Ann.* XIII. 2. 2, which would make the sentence mean they had been schoolfellows. — **puertiae :** Intr. 183.

9. **mutatae togae :** from the *toga praetexta* of boyhood to the *toga virilis.* The change was made at about the age of sixteen and

10   Cressa ne careat pulchra dies nota,
     neu promptae modus amphorae
          neu morem in Salium sit requies pedum,
     neu multi Damalis meri
          Bassum Threicia vincat amystide,
15   neu desint epulis rosae
          neu vivax apium neu breve lilium.
     Omnes in Damalin putris
          deponent oculos, nec Damalis novo

was of course a memorable event in a man's life.

10. **Cressa** : *i.e.* white, made with *creta*, which was commonly supposed to stand for *Creta* (= *Cressa*) *terra*, though in fact no chalk was obtained from Crete. The meaning is, 'that the day may be a bright one in our memory'; from the practice of recording especially happy days with a white mark, and unhappy with black; cf. Cat. 107. 6 *o lucem candidiore nota.* Another method, which Pliny (*N. H.* VII. 131) attributes to the Thracians, of determining the color of one's life by depositing in an urn at the end of each day a stone, white or black as the day had been happy or the reverse, had also passed into a proverb; cf. Cat. 68. 148 *quem lapide illa diem candidiore notat;* Pers. 2. 1 *hunc, Macrine, diem numera meliore lapillo;* cf. also *S.* II. 3. 246.— **ne careat** : better taken as a final clause, expressing the purpose of the action urged in the following verses.

11. **promptae** (proleptic), *broached;* lit. 'brought out,' *sc.* from the *apotheca;* cf. III. 21. 8.— **amphorae** : dative; cf. 24. 1.— The repetition of **neu** in the following verses, answering to that of *et* in vss. 1, 2, gives the impression of lively anticipation and thoughts crowding for utterance.

12. **Salium** : for the usual *Saliarem ;* cf. Intr. 65. The Salii were a college of twelve priests, instituted by Numa to keep the sacred shield (*ancile*) which he received from heaven. To baffle any attempt to steal it, he caused eleven others to be made exactly like it, and with these twelve the Salii, at their annual festival in March, dressed in a motley costume, half military and half sacerdotal, moved through the streets and about the altars of the gods, singing and dancing.

13. **neu**, etc.: *i.e.* Bassus, who it would seem was ordinarily a moderate drinker, must on this occasion keep it up with the best of them. — **multi meri** : *i.e.* a generous drinker. For the construction see Intr. 61.

14. **Bassum** : otherwise unknown. — **Threicia** : cf. 27. 2 n. — **amystide**, *bumper ;* from ἄμυστιν (or ἀμυστὶ) πίνειν, to drink without closing the lips (μύω).

15. **rosae**, etc.: for the use of flowers at feasts, see II. 3. 13 n.

16. **breve**, *short-lived* (as in II. 3. 13); in contrast with **vivax**.

17. **putris**, *languishing.*

18. **deponent**, *will rest.* — **nec**, *but . . , not,*

divelletur adultero,
20   lascivis hederis ambitiosior.

XXXVII.

Nunc est bibendum, nunc pede libero
pulsanda tellus, nunc Saliaribus
    ornare pulvinar deorum
        tempus erat dapibus, sodales.

19. **adultero** : see 33. 9 n.
20. **lascivis**: a part of the comparison : twining (her arms) round him with no more restraint than the ivy round the tree. — **ambitiosior** : in a literal sense ; cf. *Epod.* 15. 5 *artius atque hedera procera adstringitur ilex lentis adhaerens bracchiis;* Cat. 61. 33, 106.

XXXVII. On the good news from Egypt, September, B.C. 30. A year had elapsed since the victory at Actium, when Marcus Cicero, son of the orator, consul suffectus, published at Rome the glad tidings that Alexandria had fallen on the first of August, Antony and Cleopatra were dead, and the war was over. Of Antony the poet is silent, conforming in this to the national feeling, which never permitted a triumph to be celebrated except over a foreign foe. The ode is devoted wholly to Cleopatra, who is presented in two strikingly dissimilar scenes. The burst of exultant joy with which the poem opens is modeled upon an ode of Alcaeus on the death of the Lesbian tyrant Myrsilus, beginning (*Fr.* 20):

Νῦν χρῆ μεθύσθην καί τινα πρὸς βίαν
πώνην, ἐπειδὴ κάτθανε Μύρσιλος.

In this strain the poet portrays the Egyptian queen in her furious onslaught on Italy and her ignominious flight. Then with sudden transition (vs. 21), his aversion and abhorrence give place to admiration as he contemplates the last scene, where she resolutely carries out her determination to die rather than be taken captive to Rome ; and the ode, which began as a song of triumph over the fallen foe, fittingly closes with a warm tribute to her courage and lofty spirit. — Metre, 176.

1. **libero,** *unshackled ; i.e.* no longer restrained by anxieties for the danger which had threatened the state ; Intr. 124.

2. **Saliaribus :** *i.e.* such as are provided for the Salii (see 36. 12 n), who, with the pontifices (cf. II. 14. 28), were proverbial for the sumptuousness of their banquets ; cf. Cic. *Att.* V. 9. 1 *cum epulati essemus Saliarem in modum.*

3. **ornare pulvinar**, etc.: *i.e.* to celebrate a *lectisternium,* in which the images of the gods were placed in pairs on rich couches, and banquets served to them for several days in succession ; cf. Liv. V. 13. 6, XXII. 10. 9. A banquet for the priests was, as usual, an appendage of the ceremony. For the number of **pulvinar** see Intr. 127.

4. **tempus erat,** *would be the*

5   Antehac nefas depromere Caecubum
        cellis avitis, dum Capitolio
            regina dementis ruinas
                funus et imperio parabat

        contaminato cum grege turpium
10   morbo virorum, quidlibet impotens
            sperare fortunaque dulci
                ebria.   Sed minuit furorem

        vix una sospes navis ab ignibus,
        mentemque lymphatam Mareotico

time, sc. for the priests ; Gr. 311 *c*, with Rem.

5. **antehac** : Intr. 180. — **Caecubum** : see 20. 9 n. The Caecuban was a wine of the richer sort, which would be especially reserved for such occasions as this ; cf. *Epod.* 9. 1 *repostum Caecubum ad festas dapes ;* III. 28. 2 *sq.*

6. **cellis avitis** : *i.e.* made in our fathers' time. The wine was not brought directly from the *cella vinaria,* where it was fermented in large *dolia,* but from the *apotheca* in the upper part of the house (hence **de-promere** ; cf. *descende,* III. 21. 7), where it was kept in sealed *amphorae ;* cf. III. 8. 10 *sqq.* — **Capitolio** : see III. 30. 8 n.

7. **regina,** *a queen ;* suggesting a worse prospect than the traditional *bête noire* of the Romans, subjection to a king ; cf. Prop. IV. 11. 47 *quid nunc Tarquinii fractas iuvat esse secures, | si mulier patienda fuit ? —* **dementis ruinas** : Intr. 124. The most extravagant reports of the designs of Cleopatra were believed at Rome, and her absolute power over Antony, as well as her previous influence over Julius Caesar, gave real cause for anxiety.

8. **funus et :** Intr. 114.— **parabat :** the imperfect gives **dum** the sense of 'so long as'; Gr. 276 *e,* N.

9. **contaminato grege :** *i. e.* eunuchs (cf. *Epod.* 9. 13), a class of persons who often rose to high positions under oriental kings.

10. **morbo :** *i.e.* unnatural lust. — **virorum :** used (rather than *hominum*) with a touch of irony, to enhance the force of **turpium;** they have debased their *manhood.* — **impotens** (sc. *sui*), *wild enough to.* See Intr. 101 *a.*

12. **minuit :** sc. *ei.*

13. **vix una sospes,** *the bare escape of a single ;* Intr. 105 *a.* So it was probably reported at Rome in the first news of the battle, and Horace had not yet learned the actual fact, that she took all of her sixty ships safely out of the fight. It was Antony's fleet that was burned.

14. **lymphatam,** *unbalanced,* rendered 'flighty'; the word is apparently derived from *Lymphae,* water-nymphs (see *S.* I. 5. 97 n), at the sight of whom in the water, according to the popular belief, the unfortunate beholder was bereft of his senses (νυμφόληπτος).

15   redegit in veros timores
                Caesar, ab Italia volantem
        remis adurgens, accipiter velut
        mollis columbas aut leporem citus
                venator in campis nivalis
20   Haemoniae, daret ut catenis
        fatale monstrum.   Quae generosius
        perire quaerens nec muliebriter
                expavit ensem nec latentis
                classe cita reparavit oras ;

See Preller-Jordan, *Röm. Myth.*,
II. 127, and cf. 'panic fear' (see
17. 2 n) and 'lunatic.' — **Mareo-
tico**: sc. *vino:* a sweet, fragrant
wine produced at Marea, near
Alexandria.

15. **veros timores**: in contrast
with the fanciful hopes with which
she had come to the conflict.

16. **ab Italia**, *away from Italy;*
having been turned back from her
journey thither. — **volantem** : sc.
eam.

17. **remis adurgens**, etc.: a poetical exaggeration, based perhaps
on misinformation (see vs. 13 n).
Cleopatra was pursued by nothing
more than the fear of Octavian,
who did not go to Egypt till the
next year. — **accipiter velut**, etc.:
cf. *Il.* XXII. 138 ἠύτε κίρκος ὄρε-
σφιν, ἐλαφρότατος πετεηνῶν, | ῥηι-
δίως οἴμησε μετὰ τρήρωνα πέλειαν ;
Verg. *A.* XI. 721 ; Ov. *M.* V.
605 *sq.*

19. **nivalis** : *i.e.* in winter, the
time for hunting hares ; cf. *S.* I.
2. 105 *sq.*

20. **Haemoniae** : poetic name
for Thessaly.— **daret ut**: Intr. 114.
The clause depends on **adurgens**
17, which takes its time from
redegit 15.

21. **fatale**, *deadly.*—**monstrum**:
as a strange being in woman's
shape. — **quae** : a construction according to the sense, which would
not permit *quod ;* cf. Cic. *Fam.* I.
9. 15 *illa furia* (*i.e.* Clodius) *muli-
ebrium religionum, qui non pluris
fecerat Bonam Deam quam tres
sorores, impunitatem est adsecu-
tus.* The idea of the frantic queen,
which dominates in the preceding
sentence at the expense of the
strict grammatical construction, is
understood here as there. See
notes on *minuit* 12 and *volantem* 16.
From this point she is consistently
treated as the grammatical subject
to the end. — **generosius**, *a nobler
death, sc.* than that of a captive in
chains, which would be the death
of a slave.

22. **perire** : Intr. 94 *c.* — **nec
muliebriter expavit**, *showed no
womanish terror of ;* alluding perhaps to the story (Plut. *Ant* 79)
that Cleopatra at the sight of Proculeius, whom Octavian had sent
to take her prisoner, seized a dagger and was barely prevented from
stabbing herself. For **expavit** see
Intr. 51 *a.*

23. **nec latentis**, etc.: *i.e.* she
did not seek safety in flight and

25   ausa et iacentem visere regiam
     voltu sereno, fortis et asperas
        tractare serpentes, ut atrum
           corpore combiberet venenum,

     deliberata morte ferocior,
30   saevis Liburnis scilicet invidens
        privata deduci superbo
           non humilis mulier triumpho.

concealment. There can be here
no allusion to the story (Plut. *Ant.*
69) that Cleopatra attempted to
have her fleet transported across
the isthmus of Suez with a view
to escape to some place on the
coast of the Red Sea. Horace
wrote in the belief that this fleet
had been all but annihilated at
Actium (see vs. 13 n), and the
fleet he has in mind is one that
might have been prepared, in the
year that had since intervened,
especially for flight. — **latentis**,
some unknown.

24. **reparavit**, *gained ;* lit. got as
a recompense for (the loss of her
own); cf. *reparata* 31. 12 n.

25. **et**, *even.* So in the next
verse. — **iacentem**, *prostrate, i.e.*
humbled, stripped of its splendor
and prestige as a *domus potens* (35.
23); cf. Cic. *Or.* 224 *depressam,
caecam, iacentem domum pluris
quam te et fortunas tuas aestimasti.*
— **visere**, *to gaze upon.*

26. **asperas**, *irritable*, violent
if touched ; cf. III. 2. 10.

27. **tractare**, *to handle.* For the
mood see Intr. 101 *a*. — **atrum** :
i.e. deadly ; see 28. 13 n.

28. **corpore**, *into* (lit. *with*) her
body. — **combiberet**, *absorb.* The

manner of Cleopatra's death is
not free from doubt (Dio Cass.
LI. 14. 1); the report which
Horace follows, that she died from
the bite of an asp, was the one
generally believed at Rome ; cf.
Verg. *A.* VIII. 697, Prop. IV. 11.
53.

29. **deliberata morte ferocior,**
*her courage rising with her resolu-
tion to die.*

30. **Liburnis** : fast-sailing craft,
small and low-built, modeled on
those of the Liburnian pirates.
They had won great renown at
Actium (cf. *Epod.* 1. 1) where they
proved more than a match for
Antony's immense, but unwieldy
ships. — **invidens** : personifying
Liburnis (cf. also **saevis**). She
begrudged them the honor of
bringing her to Rome in triumph.
It is said that Cleopatra repeatedly
expressed her determination not
to be led in triumph (οὐ θριαμβεύ-
σομαι).

31. **privata** : *i.e.* no longer a
queen. — **deduci** : Intr. 94 *i*. —
superbo : cf. 35. 3.

32. **triumpho** : ablative. The
triumph is thought of as proceed-
ing all the way from Alexandria
to the Capitol.

XXXVIII.

Persicos odi, puer, apparatus ;
displicent nexae philyra coronae ;
mitte sectari rosa quo locorum
　　　sera moretur.

5　Simplici myrto nihil adlabores
sedulus curo; neque te ministrum
dedecet myrtus neque me sub arta
　　　vite bibentem.

XXXVIII. The first book closes in a quiet tone with an ode which is singularly simple in form as it is in spirit. The poet in the country, reclining under the deep shade of his vine, with a single slave to fill his cup, each of the two wearing a simple wreath of myrtle, — such is the picture with which Horace has chosen to leave his readers at the close of the first book. — Metre, 174.

1. **Persicos odi**, etc.: a general expression of dislike for all such elaborate furnishings of a feast, called out by seeing the garland which the slave in his zeal is constructing for him. — **Persicos**: the Persians were proverbial among the Greeks for their luxury and the splendor of their banquets. — **puer** : cf. *pueri*, 19, 14 n.

2. **nexae philyra** : *i.e.* elaborately constructed of choice flowers, which the *philyra* served to hold together (*coronae sutiles*). — **coronae** : cf. 4. 9.

3. **sectari** : Intr. 94 *j.* — **quo locorum** : Intr. 63.

4. **moretur**, *lingers ;* as if the rest had in reality gone away.

5. **myrto** : see II. 15. 6 n. A simple chaplet would be made by twining the sprigs together (*corona plectilis*).—**nihil**, *not . . . at all*, the negative belonging with **curo**, as in the familiar idiom with *nego, nolo*, etc. — **adlabores**, *try to embellish. Adlaborare* (= *cum labore addere*) is found only in Horace.

6. **sedulus** : with **adlabores**.— **ministrum**, *as you wait ;* corresponding to **bibentem** 12.

7. **arta** : of the foliage.

LIBER SECVNDVS

I.

Motum ex Metello consule civicum
bellique causas et vitia et modos

I. C. Asinius Pollio, who holds
the place of honor in this book,
was a man whose prominence in
the community and services to
literature fully entitled him to that
distinction. Eleven years older
than Horace, Pollio had been a
friend and correspondent of Cicero,
had fought under Caesar at Pharsalus, and had subsequently held
important commands, first under
the Dictator and then under Antony. He was governor of Trans-
padane Gaul in B.C. 43-41, and consul, B.C. 40. The next year he won
a triumph over the Parthini, a Dalmatian tribe. With these laurels
he withdrew from politics and his
public life thenceforth was confined
to the senate and the courts, in
which he was accounted one of the
foremost orators of the day. He
declined to accompany Octavian
to Actium, pleading his friendship
for Antony. By his great ability
and energy and a courage of opinion that was tempered with excellent discretion, he maintained
a position of independence which
Augustus found it prudent to respect. In literature Pollio already
had a recognized position both as
an author and as a friend of authors. He had written tragedies
(*S. I.* 10. 42) and other poetry.
Vergil was indebted to him for substantial aid at a very critical time.
From the spoils of his Dalmatian

campaign he established a library
of Greek and Latin works, with
busts of authors, and threw it
open to the people, — the first
public library in Rome.

It is not certain when he undertook the history of the civil war
which Horace heralds in the present
ode, nor how far down he actually
brought his account; but it certainly
included Pharsalus and Thapsus,
and probably Philippi. As it was
Pollio who introduced the practice
of reading new compositions to
a company of friends invited for
the purpose (*recitatio*), — a practice which thenceforth became a
marked feature of literary life at
Rome, — we may infer that Horace
had heard portions of the work
which he so enthusiastically extols.
— Metre, 176.

1. **motum :** more comprehensive than *bellum*, and embracing
the whole disturbance of the normal order of the state. The actual war did not begin for ten
years after the date named. — **ex
Metello consule :** *i.e.* beginning
with the year 60 B.C., when Q.
Caecilius Metellus and L. Afranius
were consuls. For the construction see Intr. 105 *a*. — **civicum:** an
archaic form for *civile*, preserved in
the technical phrase *civica corona*,
but otherwise only in poetry. So
hosticus for *hostilis*, III. 2. 6.

2. **belli :** limiting the three fol-

ludumque Fortunae gravisque
principum amicitias et arma
5   nondum expiatis uncta cruoribus,
periculosae plenum opus aleae,
tractas et incedis per ignis
suppositos cineri doloso.

Paulum severae musa tragoediae
10   desit theatris; mox ubi publicas
res ordinaris, grande munus
Cecropio repétes coturno,

lowing nouns (connected by et).
— **vitia** : faults committed in con-
ducting the war, *blunders;* **modos** : methods of carrying it on,
measures.

3. **ludum** : Fortuna is here
thought of, not as the stern goddess of fate of I. 35, but as de-
lighting, like Mars in I. 2. 37,
28. 17, in the exercise of her
power; cf. III. 29. 49 *sq.* No
vicissitudes of fortune could be
more striking than those of the
three great political leaders, who
for a time had the Roman world
at their feet, and then one after
another came to a violent end.
— **gravis,** *momentous (sc.* to the
state).

4. **principum,** *leaders; i.e.* Caesar, Pompey, and Crassus. The
genitive limits both of the following substantives. — **amicitias:** *i.e.*
the so-called ' first triumvirate,'
which (unlike the second) was
merely a personal alliance of the
three political chiefs, invested with
no legal authority. — **arma** : *i.e.*
those which they (in this case
only Caesar and Pompey) took up
against one another.

5. **nondum expiatis:** cf. I. 2. 29.
— **uncta,** *smeared ;* stronger than

the more usual *tincta.* — **cruoribus** : Intr. 128.

6. **plenum aleae** : because so
many persons still living are affected by the story of events in
which either they themselves or
their kinsmen took part. — **opus** :
in apposition with the whole sentence (**tractas** with its objects) ;
cf. *grande certamen,* III. 20. 7.

7. **per,** *over ;* cf. *per mare,* I.
6. 7. — **ignis,** etc.: *i.e.* the smoul-
dering passions of the civil war,
which burned for a long period
after peace was restored on the
surface.

9. **paulum,** etc.: *i.e.* the theatre
must do without tragedy for a
time ; an extravagant compliment
to Pollio, whose tragedies, however, it would appear from this,
were actually performed on the
stage, and not written merely for
the *recitatio.*— **musa tragoediae** :
equivalent in effect to Tragedy
(personified) ; see note on *Clio,* I.
12. 2.

10. **desit** : denoting a lack of
something needed ; stronger than
absit, which would denote mere
absence ; cf. Cic. *Brut.* 276 *hoc
unum illi, si nihil utilitatis habebat,
afuit; si opus erat, defuit.* — **pub-**

insigne maestis praesidium reis
et consulenti, Pollio, curiae,

15   cui laurus aeternos honores
Delmatico peperit triumpho.

Iam nunc minaci murmure cornuum
perstringis auris, iam litui strepunt,
iam fulgor armorum fugacis

20   terret equos equitumque voltus.

licas res (with emphasis on publicas), *public events, the history of
the state;* in contrast with the
remoter interests that form the
ordinary subjects of tragedy.

11. ordinaris, *have set in order,*
brought out of the confusion of
inaccurate and contradictory reports. The expression is a somewhat extravagant substitute for
ordine narraveris, the usual phrase
for giving a complete and connected account of an occurrence.
— munus, *calling, function.*

12. Cecropio: *i.e.* Attic; cf. IV.
12. 6. The greatest writers and,
according to tradition, the inventor
(cf. *Ep.* II. 3. 275 *sqq.*) of tragedy,
were Athenians. — repetes, *return
to.* — coturno, *with the buskin, i.e.*
wearing it. The high shoe worn
by the tragic actor to give him a
more imposing appearance, and
used by the poets as the symbol
of tragedy (*e.g. Ep.* II. 3. 80), is
here assigned to the author, as
the *soccus* of comedy to Plautus in
Ep. II. 1. 174; cf. Milton *L'Allegro*
132 'If Jonson's learnèd sock be
on.'

13. insigne, etc.: with the exception of the political prosecution
of one C. Cato with which Pollio,
after the usual manner of aspiring
politicians at Rome, began his
career, all his orations of which
we have any notice were for the

defense.— praesidium, *safeguard,
reliance;* cf. I. 1. 2 n.

14. curiae: for the senate itself,
as we say 'the House.' For its
case and that of reis, see Intr. 59.

17. iam nunc : *i.e.* in lively
anticipation. Although Horace
had probably heard portions of the
work, he here makes himself the
spokesman of the general public, to
express the great expectations with
which they awaited its appearance.
The scene in this strophe is the
cavalry fight in the battle of
Pharsalus. For the word-painting
cf. Intr. 131.— cornuum . . . litui:
both used by cavalry. The *cornu*
had the shape of a semicircle or
even a larger arc. For the *lituus,*
see I. 1. 23 n.

19. fugacis : proleptic.

20. equitumque voltus : *i.e.*
'and paints terror on the faces of
the riders.' The vivid picture
instead of the plain fact (*equites
terret*) is quite in Horace's manner;
but it was no doubt suggested by
the actual circumstances. The
battle was decided by the rout of
Pompey's inexperienced cavalry,
who were terrified by the blows
which the Gallic and German
troopers, by Caesar's order, *aimed
at their faces;* cf. Plut. *Caes.* 45,
Florus IV. 2. 50 (*vox Caesaris*)
*cruenta, sed docta et ad victoriam
efficax, 'miles, faciem feri!'*

Audire magnos iam videor duces
non indecoro pulvere sordidos
    et cuncta terrarum subacta
        praeter atrocem animum Catonis.

25 Iuno et deorum quisquis amicior
Afris inulta cesserat impotens
    tellure victorum nepotes
        rettulit inferias Iugurthae.

21. audire : to hear with my own ears, not merely read. The word is placed first for emphasis and to continue the thought of the preceding strophe: I am transported to the presence of the events themselves instead of reading of them as cold facts. This distinction, with disregard of the precise meaning of *audire* (as in III, 10. 5; cf. *vides* I. 14. 3), is carried on to the second half of the strophe : I learn of the subjection of the world as a living fact accomplished before my eyes. — **magnos duces :** *i.e.* their voices (in battle, as the next verse shows). He means Caesar and Pompey themselves.

23. cuncta terrarum: Intr. 64.
24. atrocem, *stern.*— **Catonis:** see I. 12. 36 n.
25–40. The mention of Cato suggests the battle of Thapsus, in which the poet sees the impressive fact that just there, on the very soil where Rome had gained her most signal victories, she was doomed to witness a costly sacrifice of her own sons. This leads him on to some general reflections on the enormous outpouring of Roman blood in the civil war, till he suddenly checks himself and recalls his muse from the pursuit of so mournful a theme to her own proper sphere of love and mirth.

25. Iuno : the patron-goddess of Carthage ; cf. Verg. *A.* I. 15 *sqq.* — **et deorum quisquis,** etc., *and every* (*other*) *divinity who, though disposed to be friendly to the Africans, had retired from the land, powerless to avenge it.* It was the common belief that the gods of a doomed city abandoned it before its fall ; cf. Verg. *A.* II. 351 *excessere omnes adytis arisque relictis | di ;* Silius Ital. II. 365 *et iam damnata cessit Karthagine Mavors.* It is said that in the third Punic war Scipio instituted certain rites to transfer Juno from Carthage to Rome (Serv. on Verg. *A.* XII. 841). — **deorum :** Intr. 63. — **quisquis,** *whoever else. Alius* is usually omitted in such phrases ; cf. Liv. IX. 18. 13 *mirabiliores quam Alexander aut quisquam rex.*

26. impotens : here in its literal sense, which is unusual ; cf. I. 37. 10. The helplessness is of course not general, but only relates to one object, implied in **inulta.**

27. victorum : *sc.* in the Jugurthine war. That this war was more prominent in Horace's mind than the greater, though more remote, Punic wars, was perhaps due to the recent publication of Sallust's monograph on the subject.— **nepotes :** among the slain at Thapsus there may well have been actual grandsons of those

Quis non Latino sanguine pinguior
30   campus sepulcris impia proelia
        testatur auditumque Medis
            Hesperiae sonitum ruinae?

Qui gurges aut quae flumina lugubris
    ignara belli?   Quod mare Dauniae
35   non decoloravere caedes?
            Quae caret ora cruore nostro?

Sed ne relictis, musa procax, iocis
    Ceae retractes munera neniae;

who fought in the Jugurthine war; the Pompeian commander himself, Metellus Scipio, was the grandson of Metellus Numidicus, who had earned his surname by victory over Jugurtha.

28. rettulit, *have offered up* (by way of atonement); see I. 3. 7 n. For the number, see Intr. 77.

29. quis non, etc.: two questions compressed into one : What plain is not more fertile, and does not bear witness, etc.?— pinguior: cf. Verg. *G.* I. 491 *nec fuit indignum superis bis sanguine nostro | Emathiam et latos Haemi pinguescere campos.*

30. impia : as fought by 'brothers' (cf. I. 35. 34) against one another.

31. Medis : see I. 2. 22 n ; for the case, Intr. 54. It was a sore aggravation of the calamity to think of the glee with which the great enemy of the empire watched the Romans cutting one another's throats. Cf. *Il.* I. 255 *sqq.*

32. Hesperiae : here an adjective (= *Italae*); see III. 6. 8 n.— ruinae, *the downfall;* cf. I. 2. 25 n.

33. gurges, *flood*, open waters, in contrast with running streams. In the following questions we

have another contrasted pair, sea and shore.   It is noteworthy how skilfully the poet, without monotony, keeps the reader's attention fixed through two strophes on the one thought that holds for the moment his own fancy,—the battle ground of the civil war, stretching from one end of the empire to the other. Allowing for poetic license, the picture is a true one ; cf. Flor. IV. 2. 3 *sqq.*

34. Dauniae : see I. 22. 14 n ; here used as a special type to represent the Roman soldier in general; cf. III. 5. 9 and see Intr. 117 *a.*

35. decoloravere, *deeply dyed.* The de- is here intensive as in *dealbare, denigrare ;* cf. I. 9. 11 n.

36. For the assonance see Intr. 131.

37. sed ne, etc.: cf. I. 6. 10 and 17 *sqq.* (with intr. note); III. 3. 69.

38. Ceae retractes, etc., *take up again the function of the Cean dirge, i.e.* undertake the service in poetry once performed by Simonides of Ceos, whose elegies (θρῆνοι; cf. *lacrimis Simonideis,* Cat. 38. 8 ; here *neniae*), — for example those in honor of the warriors who fell at Marathon and at Thermopylae, — were the best of their class.

mecum Dionaeo sub antro
40   quaere modos leviore plectro.

II.

Nullus argento color est avaris
abdito terris, inimice lamnae
Crispe Sallusti, nisi temperato
splendeat usu.

39. **Dionaeo :** *i.e.* of Venus, daughter of Dione. Venus herself was sometimes called Dione ; cf. *Dionaei Caesaris* (as descendant of Venus), Verg. *E.* 9. 47 ; Ov. *F.* II. 461. — **sub antro** : cf. I. 5. 3 n.

40. **leviore plectro :** *i.e.* of a lighter strain (descriptive abl.); cf. IV. 2. 33 n ; Ov. *M.* X. 150 *cecini plectro graviore gigantas* \ *... nunc opus est leviore lyra.* For the *plectrum* see I. 26. 11 n.

II. C. Sallustius Crispus was the grandnephew and adopted son of the historian Sallust, and at the death of the latter, B.C. 34, inherited his enormous wealth. Like Maecenas, he abstained from the usual pursuit of political honors, but under the affectation of indolence and lack of ambition exercised an influence beyond that of the most powerful senators; and by his intelligence and sagacity he won a place in the secret counsels of Augustus second only to that of Maecenas himself. He maintained his influence to the end of Augustus' life and through the first years of Tiberius, and died at an advanced age A.D. 20 (Tac. *Ann.* III. 30). In regard to his style of living Tacitus calls him *diversus a veterum instituto per cultum et munditias, copiaque et adfluentia luxu*

propior. Horace's testimony in this ode, on the contrary, distinctly credits Sallustius with moderation and liberality in the use of his wealth. The poem was probably written in B.C. 29, when the restoration of Phraates was still fresh in the public mind. — Metre, 174.

1. **color,** *lustre ;* cf. Plin. *N. H.* XXXIII. 58 *color in argento clarior est* (sc. *quam in auro*), *magisque diei similis.* — **avaris** : the disposition of the miser is attributed to the earth, in which he hoards his money; Intr. 124.

2. **abdito terris** : cf. *S.* I. 1. 41 *quid iuvat immensum te argenti pondus et auri* \ *furtim defossa timidum deponere terra ?* **terris** may be either abl. (Intr. 69) or dative (Intr. 53; cf. Verg. *A.* II. 553 *lateri abdidit ensem*). — **inimice** : apodosis to the condition **nisi temperato,** etc., — (who wouldst be) *a foe . . . unless,* etc.—**lamnae:** probably a colloquial expression, used here in disparagement for money as mere metal, — *bullion.* For the form see Intr. 183.

3. **Crispe Sallusti** : such inversion of the *nomen* and *cognomen* (with omission of the *praenomen*) appears to have been common in colloquial language from early times. It is frequent in Cicero's letters, and is much affected by Tacitus.

5   Vivet extento Proculeius aevo,
     notus in fratres animi paterni ;
     illum aget penna metuente solvi
       fama superstes.

     Latius regnes avidum domando
10   spiritum quam si Libyam remotis
     Gadibus iungas et uterque Poenus
       serviat uni.

     Crescit indulgens sibi dirus hydrops,
     nec sitim pellit, nisi causa morbi

5. **vivet** : *i.e.* in fame, as indicated in the following verses. — **extento aevo**, *a prolonged life* (*sc.* beyond its natural limits). — **Proculeius** : C. Proculeius Varro Murena, brother of Terentia, the wife of Maecenas. Like Maecenas and Sallustius he remained in the equestrian order, but Augustus held him in such high esteem and confidence (see I. 37. 22 n) that he at one time thought of him as a husband for his daughter Julia (Tac. *Ann.* IV. 40. 8).

6. **in**, *towards*.— **animi paterni** : he divided his own property in equal shares with his two brothers, who had lost theirs in the civil war. For the case see Intr. 66 *d*.

7. **aget**, *will waft.* — **penna**, *wing;* cf. Verg. *A.* IX. 473 *pinnata Fama*.— **metuente** : *i.e.* that refuses (Intr. 94 *l*); not implying that there is any danger of it (cf. Intr. 95).

9. **regnes** : the indefinite second person subjunctive in apodosis, the protasis being expressed in **domando**. For the thought cf. *O. T. Prov.* 16. 32 'He that ruleth his spirit (is better) than he that taketh a city.'

11. **iungas** : *i.e.* under your sway, as explained by the following clause, which repeats the same idea in another form. — **uterque Poenus** : *i.e.* the Carthaginians of Africa and those of Spain, where there was a *Carthago nova* with other Punic colonies.

12. **uni** : sc. *tibi* (implied in **iungas**).

13. **crescit**, *is aggravated;* Intr. 116 *b*. The subject is still, in thought, the *avidus spiritus*, but it is merged, in Horace's favorite manner, in the figure which he employs to describe its nature ; cf. *Ep.* II. 2. 28 *sqq.*, and see Intr. 123. — **indulgens sibi**, *by self-indulgence;* joined loosely to **hydrops**, which is in a manner personified and confused with the *hydropicus*, the disease with the patient.

14. **nec sitim pellit**, etc.: *i.e.* covetousness is not cured by gratifying it, but rather increased ; the only cure is to root out the desire. The patient is sick ; if you give him to drink he will only want more ; you must make him well, and then his thirst will cease. The comparison was not uncommon ; cf. Polyb. XIII. 2. 2, Ov. *F.* 1. 215, Stob. *Flor.* X. 46; Cic. *Cat.* 1. 31.

15   fugerit venis et aquosus albo
         corpore languor.

      Redditum Cyri solio Phraaten
      dissidens plebi numero beatorum
      eximit Virtus populumque falsis
20   dedocet uti

      vocibus, regnum et diadema tutum
      deferens uni propriamque laurum,
      quisquis ingentis oculo inretorto
         spectat acervos.

15. venis, corpore : Intr. 70. —
aquosus : *i.e.* due to the water
settling under the skin. — albo :
the unhealthy whiteness of disease.
17–24. This subjection of the
desires, and not the gratification
even of the very highest of human
wishes, constitutes true happiness
and true power ; cf. IV. 9. 45
sqq.

17. Cyri solio : the throne of
Parthia is properly so called, because the Arsacidae succeeded to
the power of the Persian kings
(see I. 2. 22 n), which in the popular estimate was the summit of
earthly happiness ; cf. III. 9. 4. —
Phraaten : see I. 26. 5 n.

18. plebi : *i.e.* from the popular
judgment ; cf. III. 14. 1 n. For
the case see Intr. 57. — beatorum :
for the synapheia see Intr. 174 *b.*

19. Virtus, etc.: cf. *S.* I. 3. 41
*vellem . . . isti | errori nomen Vir-
tus posuisset honestum.* He means
virtue as set forth by its expound-
ers, the philosophers, especially the
Stoics, whose doctrine on the present subject falls in with Horace's
own views, so that he even employs, though only in a figurative

sense, their favorite paradox that
the wise man alone is king, in
which elsewhere (*S.* I. 3. 124 *sqq.*)
he finds rich material for his satire.
See Intr. 8 (end).— falsis, *wrong;*
the opposite of *vera vocabula rerum,* Sal. *Cat.* 52. 11.

21. tutum : intimating the defect in the earthly crown, as exemplified in the recent experience of
Phraates.

22. propriam, *which shall not
be taken away from him ;* cf. *Ep.*
II. 2. 171 *sqq.; S.* II. 6. 4 *nil
amplius oro, | Maia nate, nisi ut
propria haec mihi munera faxis;*
Lucil. XXVII. 6 M *cum sciam nihil
esse in vita próprium mortali datum ;* and see note on *tutum,*
above.

23. quisquis, *whoever he be,
that,* — whether peasant or king.
— oculo inretorto spectat : *i.e.*
merely glances at them as he
passes by, but does not keep rolling his eyes back to see them as
long as possible ; gives them no
further thought ; cf. *respicio* and
'regard.'

24. acervos : *sc.* of money; cf.
S. I. 1. 44.

III.

Aequam memento rebus in arduis
servare mentem, non secus in bonis
  ab insolenti temperatam
    laetitia, moriture Delli,

5   seu maestus omni tempore vixeris,
    seu te in remoto gramine per dies

III. Although Horace puts at
the head of this ode his favorite
maxim of the golden mean (II. 10,
S. I. 1. 106 *sqq.*), he devotes the
main part of it to only one side
of that doctrine. The warning
against over-confident joy in prosperity is left as a mere parenthetical remark in the first strophe,
and the poet proceeds to teach at
length the maxim, *sapiens finire
memento tristitiam vitaeque labores*
(1. 7. 17). 'There is nothing to
be gained by brooding over the
troubles of life ; death will come
all the same, and the brief time
given us for enjoyment will be
irrecoverably spent.' Q. Dellius,
to whom the ode is addressed,
had attained a questionable reputation in the recent political
struggles, and had been wittily
dubbed by Messala *desultor bello-
rum civilium* from the happy
faculty he had displayed of jump-
ing at the right moment and
always lighting on his feet in the
successful party (Sen. *Suas.* 1. 7).
He was now among the more
intimate friends of Augustus, and
being a man of literary tastes and
a writer, — he prepared a history
of Antony's Parthian campaign,
in which he had himself commanded part of the forces, — he
was no doubt brought into more

or less familiar relations with
Horace in the circle of Maecenas.
— Metre, 176.

1. **aequam,** *unruffled.*— **arduis:**
in prose, *adversis* (cf. 10. 13 n) ;
'when the way is steep.'

2. **servare :** (not *parare,* as in
Ep. I. 18. 112) implying that he
has the *aequus animus* now, and
putting the *res arduae* into the
future, — 'when hardship comes.'
— **non secus :** sc. *memento servare.*

3. **insolenti,** *extravagant ;* see
I. 5. 8 n.

4. **moriture :** Intr. 104 *b.* It is
the apodosis of the two conditional clauses which follow: 'since
you will die just the same whether
. . . or . . .' It expresses the reason
for the preceding injunction (cf. I.
28. 6 n), but has more special
reference to the first part, which
continues to be the text through
the rest of the ode ; see intr.
note.

6. **remoto gramine,** *some grassy
nook ;* cf. I. 1. 21 *sq.*, *Epod.* II. 23
sq. — **per dies festos :** in contrast
with **omni tempore.** The alternative is '*always* melancholy, or
sometimes (on proper occasions)
seeking relaxation.' **per** is distributive : on those days as they
come round ; cf. *per autumnos,*
14. 15.

festos reclinatum bearis
interiore nota Falerni.

Quo pinus ingens albaque populus
10   umbram hospitalem consociare amant
ramis?   Quid obliquo laborat
lympha fugax trepidare rivo?

Huc vina et unguenta et nimium brevis
flores amoenae ferre iube rosae,
15   dum res et aetas et sororum
fila trium patiuntur atra.

Cedes coemptis saltibus et domo

8. **interiore**: *i.e.* older. The
jars farther back in the *apotheca*
would be those which had been
left undisturbed the longest. —
nota, *brand;* properly the stamp
or inscription on the amphora, or
on a tag attached to it, recording
the name and date (consuls of the
year) of the vintage; hence used
in general for quality of wine;
cf. *S.* I. 10. 24. — **Falerni**: cf. I.
20. 10 n.

9. **quo**, *what does it mean that;*
lit. *what* (is all this beauty) *for?* —
ingens albaque: Intr. 122.

10. **hospitalem**, *inviting.*—**consociare**: Intr. 94 *c.* The object
umbram expresses the result of
the action, as if it were *consociando
facere;* cf. *sinus*, I. 33. 16 n.

11. **quid**, *why*, in the same sense
as *quo* 9. — **obliquo**, *zigzag, wind-
ing*, always oblique in reference
to the direct course. — **laborat
trepidare**, *struggle and bustle;* cf.
Ep. I. 10. 21 (*aqua*) *per pronum
trepidat cum murmure rivum.* For
the construction see Intr. 94 *h.*

12. **rivo**: ablative of the 'way
by which.'

13. **huc**, etc.: the poet proceeds

as if the answer to the preceding
question were obvious.— **vina . . .
unguenta . . . flores**: the three
essentials of a Roman *convivium.*
The ointment was for the hair,
the flowers for garlands; cf. 7. 21
sqq., I. 4. 9. — **et . . . et**: repeated
in vs. 15.— **brevis**: cf. *breve lilium*,
I. 36. 16 n.

15. **res**, *circumstances.*— **aetas**:
cf. I. 9. 16 *sq.*—**sororum**: the Fates,
Clotho, Lachesis and Atropos, of
whom the first spun (κλώθω) the
thread of life, the second determined (λαγχάνω) its length, the
third, 'the Inexorable' (ἀ+τρέπω)
cut it off.

16. **atra**: cf. I. 28. 13 n. Although the thread is the symbol
of life, the whole conception relates to death; the purpose of the
allegory is to represent not the
giving of life, but the ending of
it.

17. **coemptis saltibus**: extensive mountain pastures, formed by
buying up (**co-**) a number of con-
tiguous tracts from small owners.
Great incomes were derived from
the flocks and herds raised on
such pastures. — **domo**: in the

villaque flavus quam Tiberis lavit,
   cedes et exstructis in altum
20   divitiis potietur heres.

Divesne prisco natus ab Inacho
   nil interest an pauper et infima
     de gente sub divo moreris,
       victima nil miserantis Orci.

25 Omnes eodem cogimur, omnium
   versatur urna serius ocius
     sors exitura et nos in aeternum
       exsilium impositura cumbae.

city; cf. Mart. IV. 64. 25 *hoc rus, seu potius domus vocanda est.*

18. villa, *country-seat.* A villa on the Tiber was especially desirable, and the banks of the river were thronged with them (Plin. *N. H.* III. 54).— **flavus :** see I. 2. 13 n.— **lavit :** in the Odes and Epodes Horace uses the forms of *lavere* only; in the Satires and Epistles those of *lavare* as well.

19. cedes : Intr. 116 *f.*— **exstructis in altum :** cf. *ingentis acervos,* 2. 23.

21. dives natus ab, *a wealthy descendant of.* — **Inacho :** first (mythical) king of Argos, here typical of very ancient as well as illustrious ancestry; Intr. 117 *a.*

23. sub divo moreris, *you linger in the light of day, i.e.* live, but suggesting that our life is but a brief sojourn on earth. For **divo** cf. I. 18. 13 n. The subject is no longer Dellius, but the indefinite 'you.'

24. victima, etc.: *i.e.* 'since you are a victim (all the same),' etc.; cf. *moriture,* 4 n.—**nil miserantis,** *pitiless ;* cf. 14. 6.

25. omnes ... omnium : Intr.

116 *g.* **omnium** (limiting **sors**) would more naturally have been *cuiusque.*

26. urna : another conception of the allotment of death to the individual. Necessity (cf. III. 1. 14 *sqq.*) holds in her capacious urn a **sors** (a small piece of wood or similar material, with distinguishing marks) for every man ; the urn is continually shaken (**versatur**), and when a lot flies out the man is doomed to die. For this method of determining by lot cf. *Il.* VII. 175 *sqq.* — **serius ocius :** between two words or phrases which are opposite in meaning and together form a complete idea the conjunction is commonly omitted, as *comminus eminus, a tergo a fronte, velit nolit,* etc.

27. exitura, impositura : Intr. 104 *b.* — **in,** *for ;* cf. I. 7. 8. — **aeternum :** Intr. 176 *b.*

28. exsilium : the suggestion in *moreris,* that life is only a temporary sojourn and not a home, is abandoned again, and the poet recurs to the thought of the preceding strophe, *cedes,* etc. — **cumbae :** Charon's.

IV.

Ne sit ancillae tibi amor pudori,
Xanthia Phoceu, prius insolentem
serva Briseis niveo colore
    movit Achillem ;

5   movit Aiacem Telamone natum
forma captivae dominum Tecmessae ;
arsit Atrides medio in triumpho
    virgine rapta,

IV. To 'Xanthias of Phocis,' on his having fallen in love with his maid-servant. Whether Xanthias here stands for a real person or is a mere creature of fancy it is impossible to say with certainty, in spite of the allusion to the poet's own age at the close. The air of reality that pervades the poem and the quality of the humor certainly give the impression that Horace is here chaffing, under an assumed name, one of his own acquaintances; but it is quite possible that his only aim was to give an impression of reality to a situation wholly fictitious. He points out with mock gravity that there is illustrious precedent for being enamoured of a slave girl, and further comforts his friend with the assurance that one so noble and so disinterested must be a princess in disguise at least. — Metre, 174.

1. **ne sit tibi pudori,** *you needn't be ashamed of.* The clause is perhaps best taken as a parenthetical clause of purpose (Gr. 317 *c*), explaining the poet's motive in citing the following examples ; cf. IV. 9. 1 *sqq.* Others take it as hortatory.

2. **Xanthia Phoceu** : cf. *Opuntiae Megillae,* I. 27. 10. — **prius** : *i.e.* before you. — **insolentem,** *haughty* (see I. 5. 8 n), and hence likely to hold himself high above a **serva** ; see Intr. 116 *a*.

3. **Briseis** : see *Il.* I. 346 *sqq.*, IX. 342 *sq.* — **niveo colore** : cf. III. 27. 25 ; I. 19. 5 *Glycerae nitor, splendentis Pario purius marmore.* The ablative is instrumental.

4. **movit,** *touched.* For the anaphora, with change of rhythm, cf. I. 2. 5 ; Intr. 116 *g*.

6. **captivae dominum** : cf. *insolentem serva,* vs. 2 n. — **Tecmessae** : the daughter of a Phrygian king whom Ajax slew in single combat in one of his raids during the siege of Troy ; Soph. *Aiax* 210, 487 *sqq.*

7. **arsit** : *sc.* with love. — **Atrides** : Agamemnon. — **medio in triumpho** : with **arsit,** suggesting much the same contrast as *insolentem* 2.

8. **virgine** : Cassandra, who at the fall of Troy became the prize of Agamemnon. For the case see Intr. 72. — **rapta** : by Ajax, the son of Oileus, from the altar of Athena ; cf. Verg. *A.* II. 403 *sqq.*, I. 39 *sqq.*

barbarae postquam cecidere turmae
10 Thessalo victore et ademptus Hector
tradidit fessis leviora tolli
    Pergama Grais.

Nescias an te generum beati
Phyllidis flavae decorent parentes ;
15 regium certe genus et penatis
    maeret iniquos.

Crede non illam tibi de scelesta
plebe dilectam, neque sic fidelem,
sic lucro aversam potuisse nasci
20   matre pudenda.

9. **barbarae**, etc.: an amplification of **triumpho**, to relieve the monotony of the list of examples ; see I. 2. 7 n. — **barbarae** : (from the Greek point of view), those of the Trojans and their allies ; cf. *Ep.* I. 2. 7 *Graecia barbariae lento collisa duello.* — **cecidere turmae** : the allusion is probably to the time when Achilles came out to battle with his Myrmidons (**Thessalo**) after the death of Patroclus, routed the Trojans with great slaughter, and finally killed Hector (*Il.* XX.–XXII.).

10. **Thessalo** : used collectively; cf. *Poeno*, I. 12. 38. — **ademptus Hector**, *the loss of Hector ;* Intr. 105 *a.* Cf. *Il.* XXIV. 243 ῥηίτεροι γὰρ μᾶλλον Ἀχαιοῖσιν δὴ ἔσεσθε | κείνου τεθνηῶτος ἐναιρέμεν.

11. **tradidit**, *delivered . . . into the hands of ;* in what sense, is defined by **leviora tolli** (= 'an easier prey'). — **tolli** : for the infinitive see Intr. 101 *e.*

13. **nescias an**, etc.: continuing in the same vein, the poet plays on the well known fact that children of good families were some-

times kidnapped and sold into slavery. — **nescias an,** *very likely,* —*you can't tell ;* with the usual affirmative implication of *nescio an.* The meaning is : You must look up her parents, and no doubt it will turn out that you will make a distinguished match with your Phyllis.— **beati,** *rich, well to do ;* cf. I. 4. 14 n.

14. **flavae** : see note on *Pyrrha,* I. 5. 3.— **te decorent,** *will be an honor to you.*

15. **regium genus et penatis,** etc., *she mourns* (*the loss of*) *royal ancestry,* — *i.e.* she is no longer accounted their descendant, a slave being *filius nullius,* — *and the unkindness of household gods* (Intr. 105 *a*). The two objects of **maeret** correspond accurately to *fidem mutatosque deos*, objects of *flebit,* I. 5. 5.

17. **crede,** *rest assured.* — **non illam** : cf. *non ego,* I. 18. 11 n. — **tibi** : cf. *Iovi,* I. 21. 4 ; Intr. 54. — **de plebe** : sc. *esse.*

19. **aversam** : the strong expression betrays the irony. — **potuisse** : emphatic ; Intr. 116 *b.*

Bracchia et voltum teretisque suras
integer laudo: fuge suspicari
cuius octavum trepidavit aetas
    claudere lustrum.

V.

Nondum subacta ferre iugum valet
cervice, nondum munia comparis
    aequare, nec tauri ruentis
        in venerem tolerare pondus.

5   Circa virentis est animus tuae
campos iuvencae, nunc fluviis gravem
    solantis aestum, nunc in udo
        ludere cum vitulis salicto

21. **teretis**, *shapely, well turned.*
22. **integer**, *dispassionately;* cf.
III. 7. 22. — **suspicari** : sc. *eum
(one).* For the mood see Intr. 94 *k.*
23. **cuius**, etc.: Horace was 40
in B.C. 25. — **trepidavit claudere**,
has fluttered to the verge of; Intr.
94 *g.*

V. Counsel and encouragement
to an impatient lover. 'She is
too young still, — a frolicsome
heifer, an unripe grape. Wait
patiently : by and by she will come
to you of herself.' As it is Horace's practice to name the person
he addresses, the ode is regarded
by some as a soliloquy, like III. 12.
— Metre, 176.

1. **nondum valet** : the subject
(*iuvenca tua*) is postponed to the
beginning of the positive description, vs. 5, and there expressed in a
modified form, **animus tuae iuvencae ;** cf. I. 37. 14 *mentemque (eius)
. . . redegit, . . . ab Italia volantem*

remis adurgens. This vagueness
and the absence of any direct intimation in the whole description that
a young girl is the real subject, —
quite in contrast with III. 11. 9 *sqq.,*
— shows that though the offensive
form of the comparison was toler-
able to Roman taste, the poet is
not insensible to its grossness, and
uses some skill to keep it from
coming in too close contact with
the subject ; see vs. 9 n. — **ferre** :
Intr. 94 *n.*

2. **munia comparis aequare** :
equivalent to *ferre iugum pariter,*
I. 35. 28. Her strength (**valet**) 'is
not equal to' the task of a yoke-
fellow.

5. **circa** : cf. I. 18. 2 n.

8. **ludere** : Intr. 94 *c.* — **cum
vitulis** : *i.e.* (stripped of the image-
ry) she has still the feelings of
a child, and loves best to play
with other children.

9. **tolle** : cf. I. 27. 2 n. The
new figure enforces the exhortation

> 　　praegestientis.　Tolle cupidinem
> 10　immitis uvae ; iam tibi lividos
> 　　　distinguet autumnus racemos
> 　　　　purpureo varius colore.
>
> 　　Iam te sequetur ; currit enim ferox
> 　　aetas, et illi quos tibi dempserit
> 15　　adponet annos; iam proterva
> 　　　　fronte petet Lalage maritum,
>
> 　　dilecta quantum non Pholoe fugax,
> 　　non Chloris, albo sic umero nitens
> 　　　ut pura nocturno renidet
> 20　　　luna mari, Cnidiusve Gyges,
>
> 　　quem si puellarum insereres choro,

to patience, and serves the further purpose of throwing the former comparison somewhat into the background, as we approach the name and person of Lalage.

10. **lividos**: the color of the half-ripe grapes,—a leaden blue spreading over the green ; cf. Prop. V. 2. 13 *variat liventibus uva racemis.*

11. **distinguet,** *will tint.*

12. **purpureo colore** (with **distinguet**): denoting a further stage of ripening ; cf. Ov. *M.* III. 484 *ut variis solet uva racemis | ducere purpureum nondum matura colorem.* Apparently a deep wine color that precedes dead ripeness (which is expressed by *niger*) is intended.— **varius** : as clothing the face of nature in many hues. For the order of words in this sentence see Intr. 111.

13. **ferox,** *headstrong;* cf. *invida aetas,* I. 11. 7.

14. **quos tibi dempserit annos:** *i.e.* the time you 'lose' by waiting will bring her to maturity. **annos** is used in a pregnant sense, the

years of our life with all they bring or take away. In this sense the years that bring us to the prime of life are thought of as coming, those after our prime as passing away ; cf. *Ep.* II. 3. 175 *multa ferunt anni venientes commoda secum, | multa recedentes adimunt; Ep.* II. 2. 55 *singula de nobis anni praedantur euntes.*

16. **fronte** : index of the feelings, as the cheek with us ; cf. *frontis urbanae, Ep.* I. 9. 11.— **maritum,** *a mate.*

17. **dilecta quantum non,** *a greater favorite than.* **dilecta** takes its time from **petet.** — **fugax,** *capricious.*

18. **albo,** etc.: descriptive of Chloris.

19. **pura,** *unclouded;* cf. I. 34. 7.

20. **mari** : Intr. 69.— **Cnidius Gyges**: cf. *Xanthia Phoceu,* 4. 2 n.

21. **quem si,** etc.: cf. I. 2. 7 n. The poet has in mind here the story of Achilles at the court of Lycomedes ; see I. 8. 13 n.— **choro,** *a bevy.*

mire sagacis falleret hospites
discrimen obscurum solutis
crinibus ambiguoque voltu.

VI.

Septimi, Gadis aditure mecum et
Cantabrum indoctum iuga ferre nostra et
barbaras Syrtis, ubi Maura semper
aestuat unda:

22. mire, etc., *it's astonishing how keen-sighted strangers would fail to detect.* For **falleret** cf. I. 10. 16.

23. obscurum, *disguised (as it is).*—**solutis,** *flowing;* cf. III. 4. 62.

VI. Of the trusty friend to whom the poet here confides his longings for a quiet old age nothing further is known with certainty. It is probable, however, that he is the same Septimius to whom Horace gave a letter of introduction to Tiberius (*Ep.* I. 9), in which he commends him as '*fortem bonumque,*' and also identical with the friend mentioned by Augustus in a letter to the poet which Suetonius has preserved: '*tui qualem habeam memoriam poteris ex Septimio quoque nostro audire.*' The ode was probably written in B.C. 27 or 26, when the recently conquered Cantabrians rebelled, and Augustus went to Spain to conduct the war against them in person. That it was not among the earliest odes is shown by the last verse: Horace would not have called himself *vates* unless he had felt sure that his friends at least already recognized his success in lyric poetry. Some years

later he expresses (*Ep.* I. 7. 44) the same preference for the two resorts whose attractiveness he here extols. — Metre, 174.

1. Gadis: *i.e.* to the end of the world; cf. 2. 11. — **aditure:** see Intr. 104 *e.* — **et . . . et:** the conjunctions serve to bridge over the pauses between the verses, with an effect similar to that of elision (Intr. 174 *b*).

2. Cantabrum: cf. *Thessalo,* 4. 10 n. The Cantabrians were first reduced by Statilius Taurus B.C. 29, and after successive rebellions finally subdued by Agrippa B.C. 19. — **iuga:** Intr. 128. — **ferre:** Intr. 101 *c.*

3. barbaras, *wild.* The epithet shows that by **Syrtis** is probably meant here, as in I. 22. 5 and Verg. *A.* IV. 41 *inhospita Syrtis,* the coast rather than the adjacent waters. The thought, however, is not of travelling there but of the dangerous voyage thither. The three objects of **aditure** indicate by special examples the fatigues and dangers expressed in general terms by *maris et viarum militiaeque,* 7 *sq.* — **Maura:** most of the Roman poets betray a certain vagueness in their geographical notions; cf. Verg. *G.* I. 490 *sqq.*

5   Tibur Argeo positum colono
sit meae sedes utinam senectae,
sit modus lasso maris et viarum
      militiaeque.

Vnde si Parcae prohibent iniquae
10 dulce pellitis ovibus Galaesi
flumen et regnata petam Laconi
      rura Phalantho.

Ille terrarum mihi praeter omnis
angulus ridet, ubi non Hymetto
15 mella decedunt viridique certat
      baca Venafro ;

5. **Argeo** (=Ἀργείῳ): in prose,
Argivo.—**positum** : for *conditum ;*
cf. Verg. *A.* IV. 212 *urbem posuit.*
—**colono**, *settler*, as in Verg. *A.*
I. 12 *Tyrii tenuere coloni.* For the
story see I. 7. 13 n ; for the case,
Intr. 55.

6. **senectae** : better taken as
dative ; see note on *lasso,* 7.

7. **modus** : equivalent to *finis ;*
cf. Tac. *Ann.* II. 14. 6 *si taedio viarum ac maris finem cupiant, hac acie
parari* (an imitation apparently of
this passage).—**lasso**, *when I am
weary* (future); agreeing in case
with *mihi (seni),* implied in *meae
senectae,* 6.—**maris et viarum** :
i.e. travelling by sea and land. For
the case see Intr. 66 *c.*

9. **unde si**, *and if from there ;*
cf. I. 12. 7.—**prohibent**, *exclude ;*
cf. I. 27. 4.—**iniquae**, *unkind ;*
cf. 4. 16, I. 2. 47 n.

10. **pellitis**, *skin-clad,* covered
with skins to protect the fine wool ;
cf. Varro *R. R.* II. 2. 18 *ovibus
pellitis, quae propter lanae boni-
tatem, ut sunt Tarentinae et
Atticae, pellibus integuntur.* — **Galaesi** : a few miles from Taren-

tum ; cf. Verg. *G.* IV. 125 *sub
Oebaliae (i.e. Tarentinae) memini
me turribus arcis | qua niger umec-
tat flaventia culta Galaesus,* etc.
For the case see Intr. 65.

11. **regnata** : Intr. 51 *e.*

12. **Phalantho** : the leader of a
body of Lacedaemonian immigrants
who colonized Tarentum after the
second Messenian war, about 700
B.C. For the case see Intr. 55.

13. **omnis**: sc. *(alios) angulos terrarum.* See note on *quisquis,* I. 25.

14. **angulus**, *corner ;* of a re-
tired spot, out of the current ; cf.
angulus iste (the poet's farm), *Ep.*
I. 14. 23 ; *angulus hic mundi,*
Prop. V. 9. 65.—**ridet**, *has a
charm.* For the prosody see Intr.
179.—**Hymetto** : for *Hymettio
(melli)*; cf. *Venafro,* 16, *Aulon,* 18,
Formiani colles, I. 20. 11. Hymet-
tus is a mountain near Athens,
famous for its honey.

15. **decedunt**, *yield precedence.*
The *mella* and *baca* are personified, like *Aulon* in the next strophe.
—**viridi** : as being filled with olive
groves.

16. **baca** : *i.e.* the olive, with

ver ubi longum tepidasque praebet
Iuppiter brumas et amicus Aulon
fertili Baccho minimum Falernis
20   invidet uvis.

Ille te mecum locus et beatae
postulant arces, ibi tu calentem
debita sparges lacrima favillam
vatis amici.

reference, however, to the quality of the oil it yields ; cf. *S.* II. 4. 69 *pressa Venafranae quod baca remisit olivae.*—**Venafro** : an old Samnite town on the eastern slope of the hills between the lower Liris and the upper Volturnus, now Venafro; famous for the excellence of its olive oil ; cf. *S.* II. 8. 45 ; Varro *R. R.* I. 2. 6 *quod vinum (conferam) Falerno, quod oleum Venafro?* For the case see Intr. 57.

18. **amicus,** *favored of ;* cf. *dilectus* in the quotation from Statius below, and see I. 26. 1 n.—**Aulon** : '*locus contra Tarentinam regionem*' (Porphyrio) ; whether a mountain (as Acro says) or not is uncertain. Cf. Mart. XIII. 125 *nobilis et lanis et felix vitibus Aulon | det pretiosa tibi vellera, vina mihi.*

19. **fertili:** the quality conferred by the god is attributed to him ; cf. *modici Liberi,* I. 18. 7, and Intr. 125. — **Falernis uvis** : cf. I. 20. 10 n, and Varro's words, 17 n.

20. **invidet** : see note on *decedunt* 15. This passage has been imitated by Statius *Silv.* II. 2. 4 *qua Bromio dilectus ager collesque per altos | uritur et prelis non invidet uva Falernis.*

21. **et beatae arces,** *those favored heights ;* nearer definition of **locus.** For **arces** cf. I. 2. 3.

22. **postulant,** *call for ;* a sort of personification, as in our expression ' an *inviting* place.' — **ibi tu,** etc. : *i.e.* there we will live till death shall part us, taking *me* away, — a delicate expression of the sincerity of his affection : he wishes to be spared the pain of losing his friend. — **calentem favillam** : *i.e.* my ashes, when you gather them warm from the pyre and put them in the urn.

23. **debita** : *sc.* to me as your friend.

VII. The poet's greeting to his old friend and comrade in arms, Pompeius Varus, on his return to Rome after long years of absence. Of Pompeius nothing is known beyond what is indicated in the ode itself,— that he had made the campaign of Philippi with Horace, and afterwards persisted in the struggle against the triumvirs, serving presumably under Sex. Pompeius (Intr. 12). The mention of *ciboria* (vs. 22 n) has been conjectured to be an allusion to his having served also under Antony, but that point as well as the time of his return must remain undetermined, except that the latter, on the general evidence of the date of the odes, must be placed after the end of the war of Actium. — Metre, 176.

VII.

O saepe mecum tempus in ultimum
deducte Bruto militiae duce,
  quis te redonavit Quiritem
  dis patriis Italoque caelo,

5 Pompei, meorum prime sodalium,
cum quo morantem saepe diem mero
  fregi coronatus nitentis
  malobathro Syrio capillos?

1. **saepe :** Horace's service under Brutus extended through the
greater part of the two years 43
and 42, B.C. — **tempus ultimum,**
extreme peril ; lit. 'the last extremity,' like *extremae res (e.g.*
Caes. *B. G.* II. 25. 5); cf. Cat. 64.
150 *potius quam tibi supremo in
tempore deessem.*

2. **deducte . . . duce:** regarded
by some as a reflection on Brutus ;
but the play on words is probably
not intentional; cf. *fregi . . . fracta,*
vss. 7, 11; *adduxere . . . ducere,*
IV. 12. 13 *sq.*

3. **quis :** not necessarily implying that Pompeius owed his restoration to the favor or mediation of
any particular person. The question refers not to permission to
come home, which Pompeius had
under the general amnesty after
Actium, but to the circumstances
which brought him or enabled him
to come. The question is an expression of surprise, and **quis** may
have for answer a god as well as a
man ; cf. vss. 13 and 17. — **redonavit :** stronger than *reddidit.*
The word is found only in Horace.
— **Quiritem,** *a citizen,* in double
contrast with his former condition ; no longer a soldier nor an
outlaw and exile. The singular

is archaic and is used only by the
poets.

4. **dis patriis :** *i.e.* to the home
of your fathers ; cf. III. 27. 49
liqui patrios penatis. — **Italo :** for
the prosody see Intr. 178.

5. **Pompei :** dissyllabic ; Intr.
180. — **prime,** *first ;* probably in
the sense of *earliest.*

7. **fregi :** with reference to
morantem, which indicates a persistent monotony that yields to
the treatment named ; the monot-
onous day is '*broken*' as we speak
of 'breaking up' a cold or 'killing' time. The idea is not of
'making shorter,' but of destroy-
ing ; cf. Cic. *de Or.* I. 265 *nunc et
Scaevola paulum requiescet dum se
calor frangat;* Verg. *A.* IV. 569
rumpe moras; Lucan, I. 204 *moras solvit belli.* — **coronatus :** see
3. 13 n.

8. **malobathro :** a Greek word
corrupted from the Indian name,
tamalapattram (= 'leaf of the
tamala'), — of the fragrant leaf of
the laurus cassia ; here used for
the *oil* of cassia. — **Syrio :** cf.
Syra merce, I. 31. 12 n.— **capillos :**
Intr. 42. With the whole description cf. Tib. III. 6. 63 *iam dudum
Syrio madefactus tempora nardo |
debueram sertis implicuisse comas.*

Tecum Philippos et celerem fugam
10   sensi, relicta non bene parmula,
        cum fracta virtus et minaces
            turpe solum tetigere mento.

Sed me per hostis Mercurius celer
        denso paventem sustulit aere ;
15   te rursus in bellum resorbens
            unda fretis tulit aestuosis.

9. **Philippos,** etc.: *i.e.* the battle and the flight ; not a case of hendiadys.

10. **sensi,** *I experienced.* — **relicta parmula :** whether Horace is here recalling a literal fact or merely employs the familiar Greek phrase in a figurative sense, it is difficult to say; but the latter is much more probable. The Greek ideal of 'returning with one's shield or on it' was foreign to the more business-like Roman, and belonged to war on a smaller scale, with simpler organization, and where personal prowess counted for more. It is true that as tribune Horace would have immediate charge of his men in battle, and might have occasion to use a shield (cf. Ennius *Ann.* 450 *sqq.* M), but it was no part of his duty to expose himself to personal danger. That, however, would not prevent him from using the stock phrase, — which is at least as near the reality as vss. 13 *sq.*, — especially as he found in each of his great models in Greek lyric, Archilochus, (*Fr.* 6), Alcaeus (Herod. V. 95), and apparently Anacreon (*Fr.* 28), a similar confession of the loss of his shield in battle. — **non bene :** not a confession of cowardice, as some too seriously take it ; the phrase is entirely colorless and not only says nothing that is not

already implied in **relicta parmula,** but rather breaks the force of that confession, as a man disarms criticism by anticipating it with a frank avowal that he does not defend his conduct. The diminutive **parmula** is in keeping with this deprecatory tone.

11. **fracta** (sc. *est*) **virtus,** etc.: *i.e.* when brave men went down in the crash, and braggarts (**minaces**) were humbled to the dust.

12. **turpe :** Intr. 125. — **solum tetigere mento :** *i.e.* in prostrating themselves before the victors ; cf. Caesar's description of his prisoners at Pharsalus, *B. C.* III. 98. 2 *passis palmis proiecti ad terram flentes ab eo salutem petiverunt.*

13. **sed me,** etc., *but* (at this point we were separated ;) *I,* etc.— **Mercurius :** Horace in effect calls his safe escape to Italy, through what were doubtless very real dangers (cf. **paventem**), 'providential'; cf. III. 4. 26, 28 ; Intr. 13. Mercury as διάκτορος conducted him as he did Priam unseen through the Greek camp (I. 10. 13 *sqq*). See, however, 17. 29 n.

14. **denso aere :** ἠέρι πολλῇ, as Aphrodite rescued Paris, *Il.* III. 381. The device occurs frequently in Homer, and was borrowed by the Latin poets, as Verg. *A.* I. 411, etc.

16. **unda :** the surging sea of

Ergo obligatam redde Iovi dapem,
longaque fessum militia latus
　　depone sub lauru mea, nec
20　　　parce cadis tibi destinatis.

Oblivioso levia Massico
ciboria exple, funde capacibus
　　unguenta de conchis.　Quis udo
　　deproperare apio coronas
25　curatve myrto ?　Quem Venus arbitrum

public life (cf. *mersor civilibus undis, Ep.* I. 1. 16).　When Pompeius seemed to be so near the shore (of peaceful private life) that like Horace he would actually gain a footing, the receding wave drew him back (**resorbens**) and carried him once more out to sea. — **fretis** : instrumental ablative.

17. **ergo** : *i.e.* since in spite of all this you are safely home at last ; referring back to vs. 3. — **obligatam** (sc. *votis ;* cf. 8. 5), *pledged ;* cf. *debito,* I. 36. 2 n. — **Iovi** : as the universal source of help and blessing (*Iuppiter Opitulus, Conservator, Custos*), and particularly as protector of strangers ; cf. I. 28. 28 n. — **dapem** : here in its proper sense of a sacrificial feast ; see, further, note on *sanguine,* I. 36. 2.

18. **latus** : often used, as here, in a wider sense, for the whole body or person, or for any part of it, in reference to external contact or influence ; cf. III. 10. 20; 27. 26; *S.* I. 3. 59 *nulli malo latus obdit apertum ;* II. 6. 34 *aliena negotia centum circa saliunt latus ;* Mart. VI. 76. 1 *sacri lateris custos* (*i.e.* the emperor's body-guard).

19. **lauru** : a favorite shade-tree on account of its thick foliage ; cf. I 5. 9 n.—**nec parce:** Intr. 88, 89 N.

20. **cadis :** Intr. 128. — **tibi destinatis :** *i.e.* as the event has proved ; the wine was set apart for keeping high holiday (cf. *Epod.* 9. 1) and Pompeius' unexpected return has brought the fitting occasion.

21. **oblivioso :** cf. Tib. II. 1. 46 *securo mero ;* Intr. 125. — **Massico** : see I. 1. 19 n.

22. **ciboria :** cups of polished metal (**levia**) shaped, according to Porphyrio, like the leaves of the Egyptian bean after which they were named.—**exple,** *fill high.* The chiastic asyndeton (**exple, funde**) marks the poet's eagerness, as he hastens forward, in imagination, to the enjoyment of the feast.

23. **conchis :** shell-shaped vessels for ointment.— **quis:** sc. *puer;* cf. 11. 18, I. 38. 1.

24. **deproperare:** a compressed expression for *propere conficere* or the like ; cf. III. 24. 62.　For the prefix **de-** see 1. 35 n, I. 9. 11 n. For the infinitive see Intr. 94 *b.* — **apio** : cf. I. 36. 16.

25. **curat,** *will see to.* — **-ve :** Intr. 119 *b.* — **Venus :** *i.e.* the *iactus Veneris,* the highest throw of the *tali,* in which the numbers turned up were all different. — **arbitrum bibendi :** see I. 4. 18 n.

dicet bibendi?   Non ego sanius
bacchabor Edonis ; recepto
dulce mihi furere est amico.

VIII.

Vlla si iuris tibi peierati
poena, Barine, nocuisset umquam,
dente si nigro fieres vel uno
turpior ungui,

5   crederem; sed tu simul obligasti
perfidum votis caput, enitescis
pulchrior multo, iuvenumque prodis
publica cura.

---

27. **Edonis**: a Thracian tribe ;
cf. I. 27. 2 n.—**recepto,** *found again.*

VIII. Barine, 'the Maid of Ba-
rium,' is a heartless coquette. The
poet declines her professions of
devotion with ironical compli-
ments on the impunity and success
with which she plays her perfidious
game. — Metre, 174.

1. **ulla . . . umquam, uno . . .
ungui**: the alliteration (Intr. 131)
aids the emphasis. — **iuris peierati** : formed from *peierare* after
the analogy of *ius iurandum* from
iurare, the perfect being naturally
used, especially with **poena**, to express the accomplished fact to which
the punishment should follow.
The phrase is not found elsewhere.

2. **poena nocuisset** : strictly
either *poena fuisset* or *ius peieratum
nocuisset* would have expressed the
idea sufficiently.   The more pregnant expression marks the poet's
earnestness, which takes two points
for the emphasis to rest on.

3. **dente, ungui**: abl. of measure

of difference.   The predicate **fieres
turpior** is divided (Intr. 120), and
with it the two adjectives **uno
nigro**, both of which belong with
each substantive (Intr. 121). — **si
fieres** : *i.e.* if ever.

5. **simul** : see I. 4. 17 n. — **obligasti** : cf. 7. 17 n.   There the
victim (implied in *dapem*) was
pledged, to be forfeited in case
the prayer for a safe return was
granted ; here the **caput** is put in
pawn, to be offered up to the vengeance of the gods if Barine should
break her oath.

6. **perfidum** : Intr. 124.   The
perjury was committed in the very
act of swearing. — **votis,** *imprecations,* prayers to the gods to
shower curses on her head should
she prove false ; cf. Hannibal's
oath, Liv. XXI. 45. 8.

7. **prodis** : *sc.* into the streets.

8. **cura** : cf. I. 14. 18 n.

9. **expedit,** *it pays* (with emphasis). — **opertos,** *buried.*

10. **fallere** : by swearing falsely
by them ; cf. Prop. II. 20. 15 *ossa*

Expedit matris cineres opertos
10   fallere et toto taciturna noctis
    signa cum caelo gelidaque divos
        morte carentis.

Ridet hoc, inquam, Venus ipsa, rident
simplices Nymphae ferus et Cupido,
15   semper ardentis acuens sagittas
        cote cruenta.

Adde quod pubes tibi crescit omnis,
servitus crescit nova, nec priores
impiae tectum dominae relinquunt,
20   saepe minati.

Te suis matres metuunt iuvencis,
te senes parci miseraeque nuper
virgines nuptae, tua ne retardet
    aura maritos.

tibi iuro per matris et ossa parentis;
| si fallo cinis heu sit mihi uterque
gravis. For the assonance of this
verse and the next see Intr. 131.

13. **ridet . . . rident**: Intr. 116 *g*.
—**Venus ipsa**: who has lovers
especially under her protection.

14. **Nymphae**: to whose nature
(**simplices**) such duplicity is utterly foreign. They are in the
retinue of Venus here as in I. 4. 6,
30. 6. — **Cupido**: with his arrow
fresh from the bleeding hearts.
All the powers of love feel Barine's
fascination, and can only smile
when she defies their authority.

15. **ardentis**, *burning*. The attribute properly belongs to Cupid
(Intr. 124).

16. **cruenta**: from the arrow-
tip. Observe how, by a skilful
disposition of epithets (**ferus, cruenta, ardentis**), the picture (cf. I. 2.
7 n) is made more full and graphic.

17. **adde quod**, etc.: further
reason for *expedit* 9.

18. **servitus crescit nova**: explaining the somewhat vague **tibi
crescit**. **servitus nova** is used
concretely : *a new set of slaves.*

19. **impiae**: recalling the main
theme, her ready perjury, and indicating the reason of **minati**.

21. **te . . . te . . . tua** : in mock
eulogy; cf. I. 10. 9 n.— **iuvencis** :
i.e. their sons ; cf. 5. 6.

22. **parci** : such a person would
be *impotens, procax, magnifica,
sumptuosa, nobilis* (Ter. *Heaut.* 227)
at the expense of her lovers.

23. **virgines**: used by the poets,
like *puella,* of young wives.

24. **aura** : see I. 5. 11 n. The
metaphor is here used more consciously, — 'the breeze that draws
to you'; cf. Cic. *Sest.* 101 *quem
neque honoris aura potuit umquam
de suo cursu demovere.*

IX.

Non semper imbres nubibus hispidos
manant in agros aut mare Caspium
vexant inaequales procellae
usque, nec Armeniis in oris,

5   amice Valgi, stat glacies iners
mensis per omnis aut Aquilonibus
querceta Gargani laborant
et foliis viduantur orni:

IX. To C. Valgius Rufus, beg-
ging him to dry his tears for the
loss of his favorite slave-boy Mystes, and turn from his incessant
elegies to sing the triumphs of
Augustus. Valgius was one of the
group of Horace's literary friends
named in *S*. I. 10. 81 *sqq.*, a writer of
elegies and epigrams and perhaps
of epic (*Paneg. Messal.* 180), as
well as of works in prose. He was
consul B.C. 12, and therefore probably considerably younger than
Horace. The ode was written
between B.C. 27, when Octavian
received the title of Augustus (cf.
vs. 19), and 23, the year of publication of these books. The allusions in vss. 20 *sqq.* do not fix the
date more definitely. They refer
to triumphs of diplomacy only,
brought about by internal dissen-
sions in oriental monarchies, especially Armenia and Parthia, which
led one or other of the rival princes
to appeal to Rome (cf. I. 26. 5 n);
but of the details we are not accurately informed. The allusion in
vs. 23 may be to a Scythian embassy which came to Augustus
when he was in Tarraco, B.C. 26 or
25. — Metre, 176.
1. **non semper**, etc.: for the
arrangement of words in this ode

see Intr. 116 *b*.— **imbres, procellae, glacies, Aquilonibus**: the
gloomy aspects of nature, types of
human tears and grief, do not last
always. The examples are grouped
by **non** . . . **nec** in two pairs, each
connected by **aut**: brief showers or
squalls, protracted cold or storm.
In the last example **et** merely
connects the two kinds of trees
named, and is subordinate to **aut**.
— **nubibus** : Intr. 70.— **hispidos**,
squalid, as they appear at the
end of the winter, after long neglect and exposure to the rain ;
in contrast with their trim and
cheerful aspect when under cultivation. The epithet is therefore necessary for the present
comparison.
2. **Caspium** : Intr. 117 *a*. The
Caspian was described as *atrox*,
saevum, *sine portibus*, *procellis
undique expositum* (Mela III. 38).
3. **inaequales**, *fitful*.
4. **Armeniis** : cf. *Caspium*, 2 n.
It is clear that Armenia was much
in the thoughts of the Romans
when Horace wrote this ode. See
also vs. 20 n.
5. **stat** : more expressive than
(*e.g.*) *manet ;* cf. I. 9. 1 n.
7. **Gargani** : exposed by its
situation, with the sea on three

tu semper urges flebilibus modis
10   Mysten ademptum, nec tibi Vespero
          surgente decedunt amores
             nec rapidum fugiente solem.

At non ter aevo functus amabilem
      ploravit omnis Antilochum senex
15   annos, nec impubem parentes
          Troilon aut Phrygiae sorores

flevere semper: desine mollium
      tandem querellarum, et potius nova
          cantemus Augusti tropaea
20   Caesaris et rigidum Niphaten

sides of it, to the fury of the
winds.— **laborant** : see I. 9. 3 n.
   9. **urges**, *pursue, dwell upon.*
   10. **Mysten ademptum** : Intr.
105 *a.* — **Vespero** : the planet
Venus.
   11. **surgente** : *i.e.* in the evening. The planet was said to 'rise'
when it began to be visible as
evening star. — **decedunt**, *abate.*
— **amores** : the plural (Intr. 128)
is used with reference to the repeated expression of his love.
   12. **rapidum**: apparently a standing epithet of the sun (cf. Verg.
G. I. 92, 424), which appears to
have been used originally of his
fierce, consuming heat (*rapio*);. cf.
Verg. *G.* IV. 263 *rapidus ignis,*
425 *rapidus Sirius, E.* 2. 10 *rapido
aestu ;* but here it perhaps refers to
the rapidity with which he seems
to move at his rising. — **fugiente
solem** : *i.e.* at dawn, when Venus
is morning star (Lucifer) ; rising
before the sun, she is visible while
he is still below the horizon, but
vanishes as he advances.
   13. **ter aevo functus senex** :
i.e. Nestor ; *aevum* here, like *aetas*

hominum in Cic. *C. M.* 31 (*tertiam
iam aetatem hominum vivebat*) is
the ordinary or average life of
man ; cf. 2. 5. The phrase is a
reproduction of the familiar description, *Il.* I. 250 τῷ δ' ἤδη δύο μὲν
γενεαὶ μερόπων ἀνθρώπων | ἐφθίαθ'
. . . μετὰ δὲ τριτάτοισιν ἄνασσεν ·
cf. *Odys.* III. 245.
   14. **Antilochum**: son of Nestor,
one of the most charming characters in the Iliad. He was killed in
battle, while defending his father,
by Memnon.
   16. **Troilon** : a stock instance
of premature death ; cf. Cic. *Tusc.*
I. 93. He was slain by Achilles ;
cf. Verg. *A.* I. 474 *sqq.* The examples of Antilochus and Troilus,
both cut off in their youth, are
cited as parallel to that of Mystes.
— **Phrygiae** : cf. *Phrygum,* I. 15.
34 n.
   17. **desine querellarum** : see
Intr. 67. — **mollium**, *tender*, with
a suggestion of unmanliness.
   19. **tropaea**: probably referring
to the Roman victories in Spain
in 26 or 25 ; see Ode 6, intr. note.
   20. **rigidum** : *sc.* with snow and

Medumque flumen gentibus additum
victis minores volvere vertices,
    intraque praescriptum Gelonos
        exiguis equitare campis.

X.

Rectius vives, Licini, neque altum
semper urgendo neque, dum procellas
    cautus horrescis, nimium premendo
        litus iniquum.

ice. — **Niphaten** : a mountain in the interior of Armenia, mentioned also by Vergil, *G.* III. 30. Later poets supposed it to be a river (Luc. III. 245, Sil. XIII. 765, Juv. 6. 409, etc.).

21. **Medum flumen** : the Euphrates ; cf. *Scythicum amnem* (the Tanais), III. 4. 36 ; *amnis Tusci* (the Tiber) *S.* II. 2. 32. For the form of the adjective see Intr. 65.

22. **minores** : indicating humbled pride; cf. Verg. *A.* VIII. 726 *Euphrates ibat iam mollior undis.* — **volvere** : for the acc. with inf. joined with the simple acc. of the object cf. Prop. IV. 2. 7 *et cecini Curios fratres et Horatia pila* | . . . *Hannibalemque lares Romana sede fugantes,* | *anseris et tutum voce fuisse Iovem.*

23. **praescriptum** : *sc.* by conditions of peace imposed upon them. — **Gelonos** : a Scythian tribe ; here used for the Scythians in general ; cf. *Sithoniis,* I. 18. 9 n.

24. **equitare** : cf. I. 2. 51 n. — **campis** : Intr. 69.

X. Licinius Murena, to whom this ode is addressed, was probably the son of Cicero's client of that name, but was adopted by

Terentius Varro, the father of Proculeius and Terentia (see 2. 5 n). He reduced the Salassi in 25 B.C., and established in their territory the colony now called Aosta. In 23 he was the colleague of Augustus in the consulship, an evidence of high esteem on the part of the emperor ; but in the same year he was convicted of complicity in the conspiracy of Fannius Caepio and executed. The present ode is one of the most finished of Horace's poems, and consists, like much of his best work, of a chain of pithy epigrammatic *sententiae* on the conduct of life, presenting in various forms and under various figures his favorite doctrine of the golden mean, with its corollary, μηδὲν ἄγαν, or, as he expresses it in *Ep.* I. 6, *nil admirari,* — the *aequam memento servare mentem* of Ode 3. — Metre, 174.

1. **rectius** : not used in a moral sense, but with reference to the practical ordering of one's life. — **altum urgendo**, *by pressing out to sea.* The 'voyage of life' is a favorite figure with Horace; cf. vs. 23 *sq.,* I. 34. 3 *sq.,* III. 29. 57 *sqq.,* *Ep.* II. 2. 200 *sqq.,* etc.

3. **premendo**, *hugging.*

5   Auream quisquis mediocritatem
    diligit, tutus caret obsoleti
    sordibus tecti, caret invidenda
       sobrius aula.

    Saepius ventis agitatur ingens
10   pinus et celsae graviore casu
    decidunt turres feriuntque summos
       fulgura montis.

    Sperat infestis, metuit secundis
    alteram sortem bene praeparatum
15   pectus. Informis hiemes reducit
       Iuppiter, idem

    submovet ; non, si male nunc, et olim

4. **iniquum**, *unfriendly*, on account of its rocks and shoals.

5. **auream** : see I. 5. 9 n. — **mediocritatem** : a translation of ἡ μεσότης. Cf. Cic. *de Off.* I. 89 *mediocritatem illam quae est inter nimium et parum.*

6. **diligit**, *cherishes.*— **tutus caret**, *is secure from.* — **obsoleti**, etc.: *i.e.* not merely poverty, but the slovenly poverty of the sluggard. The man who aims at *mediocritas* is *sure* to rise above this low state, because his aim is not too high to attain, nor will he be in danger of falling down to it, because he does not climb so high as to risk a fall. On the other hand, his temperateness (**sobrius**) will save him from ever becoming the mark of envy as the lord of a palace.

7. **caret** : Intr. 116 *h.*

9–12. The suggestion in **invidenda** is developed in three striking illustrations of the danger of rising too high. For the position of the emphatic words see Intr. 116 *b.*

13. **sperat**, etc.: the wise man will observe the same moderation in dealing with the conditions of his life which are beyond his control, refraining from both extremes of despair in adversity and overconfidence in prosperity.—**infestis** (for the more commonplace *adversis*), **secundis** : neut. pl., with abstract force ; cf. I. 34. 12 n. They are best taken as dative ; cf. Sal. *Cat.* 40. 2 *requirere coepit quem exitum tantis malis sperarent ; ib.* 2 (*illos videt*) *miseriis remedium mortem exspectare.*

14. **alteram**, *a reversal of ;* lit. ‘the other’ (not ‘another,’ *aliam*).

15. **informis** : Intr. 125 ; cf. Verg. *G.* III. 354 *sed iacet aggeribus niveis informis et alto | terra gelu late.*— **reducit**, *brings round.* Compounds of *re-* are frequently used in this sense of the movement of the heavenly bodies and the seasons ; cf. III. 8. 9, IV. 2. 58.

17. **non si**, etc.: the position of **non** shows that it belongs to the whole sentence, and denies not

sic erit ; quondam cithara tacentem
suscitat musam neque semper arcum
20   tendit Apollo.

Rebus angustis animosus atque
fortis appare ; sapienter idem
contrahes vento nimium secundo
    turgida vela.

XI.

Quid bellicosus Cantaber et Scythes,
Hirpine Quincti, cogitet Hadria
   divisus obiecto, remittas
    quaerere nec trepides in usum

the apodosis, — which may perhaps prove to be true, — but the
validity of the inference ; equivalent to 'it doesn't follow that, if,
etc.' — **male** (sc. *est*), *things go ill.*
— **et,** *also.* — **olim,** *by and by ;*
see IV. 4. 5 n.

18. **quondam** : usually restricted to the past or (rarely) to the
future ; here general, *sometimes.*—
tacentem : music is silent in times
of pestilence, which Apollo sends
with his arrows ; cf. *Il.* I. 44 *sqq.*
The same god who brings disease
and suffering brings songs and
gladness.

22. **sapienter,** *if you are wise.*
— **idem,** *yet you.*

23. **contrahes,** etc.: closing with
the metaphor with which he began.
— **nimium** : with **secundo.**

XI. Of Quinctius Hirpinus nothing is definitely known, not even
whether he is the 'optimus Quinctius' to whom *Ep.* I. 16 was
written. In the present verses the
poet represents himself as talking
to his friend on one of his favorite

themes, the folly of taking too
much thought for the morrow.
We may suppose the two to be
walking together in the country
or in a park, with the streets not
far away. The allusions in the
first strophe assign the ode to the
years 27–25 B.C. — Metre, 176.

1. **Cantaber** : see 6. 2 n. —
Scythes : the allusion is probably
to some disturbance that occa-
sioned the Scythian embassy to
Augustus at Tarraco ; see Ode 9,
intr. note (end).

2. **Hirpine Quincti** : see 2. 3 n.
— **Hadria divisus** : a ground for
security, added only in the case of
the Scythians, because there was
nothing to be feared from the
Cantabrians but stubborn resistance. On the other hand, a successful incursion of a barbarian
horde into Moesia or Pannonia
would expose Italy itself to the
danger of invasion.

3. **obiecto,** *the barrier of.*— **remittas quaerere** : Intr. 87, 94 *j.*

4. **nec** : Intr. 89 N.— **trepides,**
fret yourself ; cf. III. 29. 32. — **in,**

5 poscentis aevi pauca. Fugit retro
levis iuventas et decor, arida
pellente lascivos amores
canitie facilemque somnum.

Non semper idem floribus est honor
10 vernis, neque uno luna rubens nitet
voltu. Quid aeternis minorem
consiliis animum fatigas?

Cur non sub alta vel platano vel hac
pinu iacentes sic temere et rosa
15 canos odorati capillos,
dum licet, Assyriaque nardo

('in reference to'), *about.* — usum **aevi**, *the use of a life, i.e.* the way to live it. For the thought cf. I. 9. 13 *sqq.*, II. 1 *sqq.*

5. **pauca:** Intr. 116 *b.* — **fugit,** etc.: reason for the advice just given; cf. I. 11. 7.

6. **lēvis,** *smooth-cheeked,* as in IV. 6. 28 (of Apollo).

8. **facilem:** *i.e.* that comes readily; cf. III. 21. 4 and III. 1. 21 n.

9. **non semper,** etc.: reminders that everything is transitory are all about us; cf. IV. 7. 7 *sqq.* — **semper idem:** *i.e.* changeless, imperishable; it fades away. — **honor,** *beauty.*

10. **neque uno,** etc.: *i.e.* it waxes or wanes and changes its hue (**rubens**).

11. **aeternis:** *i.e.* reaching out into the unlimited future: cf. *spem longam,* I. 4. 15, II. 7. — **minorem,** *which is unequal to them,* unable to cope with them.

12. **consiliis:** with both **minorem** and **fatigas;** Intr. 76.

13. **alta, hac:** to be taken together with each substantive; Intr. 121. — **platano:** the oriental

plane tree (sycamore), with leaves more jagged and of a darker green, but otherwise closely resembling our occidental species (buttonwood). Its stately form and heavy foliage made it a favorite shade tree; cf. 15. 4.

14. **sic temere,** *just as we are, offhand;* the Homeric μὰψ οὔτω (*e.g. Il.* II. 120); cf. Verg. *A.* IX. 329 *tris iuxta famulos temere inter tela iacentis.* **temere** has its proper meaning of *sine consilio,* without premeditation. — **rosa, nardo:** see 3. 13 n. For the singular **rosa** see Intr. 127.

15. **canos:** Horace at least began to grow gray early (Intr. 29). The word adds significance to **dum licet.** — **odorati:** *i.e.* 'wreathed with fragrant,' etc. — **capillos:** Intr. 42.

16. **dum licet:** cf. 3. 15 *sq.* — **Assyria:** really Arabian or Indian, but imported from Syria, with which Assyria is often confused by the poets; cf. 7. 8, I. 31. 12 n; Tib. I. 3. 7 *Assyrios odores.* — **nardo:** here fem.; elsewhere in Horace (*Epod.* 5. 59, 13. 9) neuter.

potamus uncti ?   Dissipat Euhius
curas edacis.   Quis puer ocius
   restinguet ardentis Falerni
20   pocula praetereunte lympha ?

Quis devium scortum eliciet domo
Lyden ?   Eburna dic age cum lyra
   maturet, in comptum Lacaenae
      more comam religata nodum.

XII.

Nolis longa ferae bella Numantiae
  nec durum Hannibalem nec Siculum mare

17. **potamus** : the present in a
hortatory question, common in
colloquial language, especially with
quin (as Liv. I. 57. 7 *quin con-
scendimus equos*), and frequent in
comedy. See Intr. 78.— **Euhius** :
see I. 18. 9 n.

18. **edacis** : cf. *mordaces sollicitudines*, I. 18. 4.— **quis puer** : cf.
7. 23.— **ocius**, *quickly*.

19. **restinguet** : *i.e.* dilute its
strength. The word is chosen
with reference to **ardentis** (*fiery*),
for which cf. Juv. 10. 27 *lato Seti-
num ardebit in auro.*— **Falerni** :
cf. I. 27. 9 n.

21. **devium** : *i.e.* living apart,
not consorting with the common
herd ; cf. I. 17. 6, III. 25. 12.

22. **eburna** : *i.e.* decorated with
ivory, as in *S.* II. 6. 103 *eburnos
lectos.*— **age** : with **dic**, as III.
4. 1, *S.* II. 7. 92.

23. **maturet** : sc. *venire ;* cf. *deproperare*, 7. 24 n. — in **comptum nodum** : cf. Ov. *M.* VIII.
319 *crinis erat simplex, nodum
collectus in unum.* The toilet of
the music girl was to be neat but
simple, in keeping with the whole

spirit of the occasion, which was
a protest against elaborate preparation for enjoyment ; and she was
not to keep them waiting. — **Lacaenae more** : cf. Prop. IV. 14. 28
(of the Spartan women) *est neque
odoratae cura molesta comae.*

24. **comam religata** : Intr. 41.

XII. In this ode, as in I. 6,
Horace declines to undertake epic
themes with his *imbellis lyra*, and
tells Maecenas that his own prose
will serve better to record the
achievements of Augustus. He
then turns to a fit subject for his
lyre, the beauty and accomplishments of Licymnia, who is undoubtedly Terentia, Maecenas'
wife (Intr. 21). From the last
strophes it would appear that the
ode was written during their honey-
moon. In the assumed name
Horace has followed the usual
practice of the Latin poets, selecting a Greek name metrically equiv-
alent ($\smile \_ \smile \smile$) to Terentia, as Catullus' Lesbia (for Clodia), Tibullus'
Delia (for Plania), etc. (Apuleius,
Apol. 10). — Metre, 172.

Poeno purpureum sanguine mollibus
  aptari citharae modis,
5 nec saevos Lapithas et nimium mero
  Hylaeum domitosque Herculea manu
  Telluris iuvenes, unde periculum
    fulgens contremuit domus

  Saturni veteris ; tuque pedestribus
10 dices historiis proelia Caesaris,

1. **nolis** (standing emphatically at the head of the sentence), *you surely would not have*, etc.—**longa**: the siege of Numantia lasted from 141 to 133 B.C.—**ferae**: the Numantines after their long and stubborn resistance finally set fire to their city, and in large numbers put themselves to death rather than surrender.

2. **nec**: carrying on the negative in **nolis**; see Madv. 458 *c*, Obs. 2. — **Siculum mare**: the scene of the most important battles of the first Punic war.

3. **mollibus**, etc.: *i.e.* to have such themes presented in a form so unsuitable and inadequate; cf. I. 6. 9 *sqq.*

5. **nec saevos**, etc.: the same objection applies to mythological subjects. These are grouped together by **et** and **-que,** subordinate to **nec**; cf. *et*, 9. 8, and note on 9. 1.—**Lapithas**: see I. 18. 8 n.— **nimium**, *elated, insolent ;* cf. Tac. *Hist.* IV. 23 *rebus secundis nimii.*

6. **Hylaeum**: one of the Centaurs ; cf. Verg. *G.* II. 457 *et magno Hylaeum Lapithis cratere minantem.* — **domitosque**, etc.: in their battle with the Giants (**Telluris iuvenes**, γηγενεῖς) the gods were assisted by Hercules. Gaea had made her sons proof against the weapons of the gods, so that they could be conquered only with

mortal aid ; see Preller-Robert, *Gr. Myth.* I. p. 73. — **Herculea manu**: cf. I. 3. 36.

7. **unde** (for *a quibus ;* cf. I. 12. 17 n) **periculum**: cf. *aliunde fata,* 13. 16; *metu insidiarum a meis*, Cic. *Rep.* VI. 14 ; Madv. 298 *b.* 2. Usually a participle, *ortum*, or the like, would be inserted.

8. **fulgens domus**: cf. III. 3. 33 *lucidae sedes* (sc. *deorum*). — **contremuit**: Intr. 51 *a.*

9. **Saturni**: *i.e.* of the gods, who were Saturn's descendants.— **tuque**: a third subject, which was more than once suggested to him (see *S.* II. 1. 10 *sqq.*), Horace puts away with a compliment to Maecenas. Hence the change to an affirmative conjunction, and the emphasis on **tu**. — **pedestribus**, *prose*. The word, so far as appears, was first used by Horace in this sense (*S.* II. 6. 17 *musa pedestri*) in imitation of the Greek πεζὸς λόγος. With a similar figure he calls his hexameters *sermones repentis per humum* in contrast with the lofty style in which the exploits of Augustus should be sung (*Ep.* II. 1. 250 *sq.*). Whether Maecenas actually wrote or proposed to write such a work as is here suggested we do not know. See Plin. *N. H.* VII. 148.

10. **dices**: for the force of the future see Intr. 79.

Maecenas, melius ductaque per vias
   regum colla minacium.

Me dulcis dominae Musa Licymniae
cantus, me voluit dicere lucidum
15 fulgentis oculos, et bene mutuis
   fidum pectus amoribus ;

quam nec ferre pedem dedecuit choris
nec certare ioco nec dare bracchia
ludentem nitidis virginibus sacro
20   Dianae celebris die.

Num tu quae tenuit dives Achaemenes

11. **per vias** : *sc.* of Rome, in the triumphal procession.

12. **regum colla** : instead of *reges*, because they were led by the neck ; cf. Prop. II. 1. 33 (*canerem*) *regum auratis circumdata colla catenis* (also referring to the triumphs of Augustus).—**minacium** : cf. 7. 11 n, IV. 3. 8. The epithet sets off by contrast their present humbled state ; cf. *Ep.* II. 1. 191 *mox trahitur manibus regum fortuna retortis.*

13. **dulcis**: accusative.—**dominae**, *my lady*. Married ladies were regularly addressed by this title.

14. **lucidum fulgentis**: Intr. 48.

15. **bene fidum** : like 'bien fidèle'; cf. *bene sano, S.* I. 3. 61, *bene firmum*, Enn. *Ann.* I. 105 M; and the opposite, *male fida*, Verg. *A.* II. 23. Cf. I. 9. 24 n.

17. **quam nec dedecuit**, *who could with perfect grace, i.e.* keeping within the bounds of what was becoming and womanly.— **ferre**, *to move ;* cf. Verg. *G.* I. 11 *ferte simul Faunique pedem Dryadesque puellae.*—**dedecuit** : cf. I. 38. 7. The perfect has its proper force, referring to the time when Mae-

cenas became fascinated with her charms.— **choris** : dances at home or in private companies, which at this time were permissible for women within certain limits ; cf. III. 6. 21.

18. **certare ioco** : *i.e.* in conversation ; cf. Sall. *Cat.* 25. 5 (of Sempronia) *posse versus facere, iocum movere, sermone uti vel modesto vel molli vel procaci.* — **dare bracchia** : graceful movements of the arms were carefully studied in training for the dance.

19. **ludentem** : *i.e.* dancing, as in Verg. *E.* 6. 27 *tum vero in numerum Faunosque ferasque videres | ludere.*—**nitidis**, *spruce*, in holiday attire. — **virginibus** : dative with **dare**.

20. **Dianae celebris die** : for *die quo Diana celebris est, i.e.* when her temple is thronged (August 13); cf. Tib. IV. 4. 23 *Phoebe fave, . . . iam celeber, iam laetus eris.* Terentia as *virgo ingenua* could take part in this public religious dance.

21. **Achaemenes** : mythical founder of the Persian dynasty (Herod. I. 125, VII. 11); cf. III. 9. 4.

aut pinguis Phrygiae Mygdonias opes
permutare velis crine Licymniae,
   plenas aut Arabum domos,

25   cum flagrantia detorquet ad oscula
cervicem, aut facili saevitia negat
quae poscente magis gaudeat eripi,
   interdum rapere occupet ?

XIII.

Ille et nefasto te posuit die,

22. Mygdonias : *i.e.* of Midas, the mythical Phrygian king, whose touch turned all things to gold. Mygdonia was a district of Macedonia, which was associated with the legends of Midas and the Bryges, who were supposed to have migrated from that region into Asia Minor (Herod. VIII. 138, VII. 73). Another legend, however, told of a Phrygian king Mygdon (*Il.* III. 186).

23. permutare : see Intr. 74.

24. Arabum : see I. 29. 3 n.

25. flagrantia, *passionate.* — **detorquet cervicem** : *i.e.* turns away (de-) so as to expose her neck to the kiss. For the caesura of this verse see Intr. 149.

26. negat : sc. *ea* (*oscula*), the antecedent of **quae.**

27. quae gaudeat, occupet : subjunctive to express the reason for calling her *saevitia* '*facilis.*' — **poscente** : see Intr. 75, 103.

28. rapere occupet, *snatches them first herself ;* cf. Liv. I. 30. 8 *cum bellum utrimque summa ope pararent, occupat Tullus in agrum Sabinum transire.* Intr. 94 *g.*

XIII. On the first of March B.C. 30 Horace had a narrow escape from the fall of a tree on his farm, an incident which he mentions repeatedly (17. 27, III. 4. 27, III. 8. 7) and makes the subject of the present ode. After roundly abusing the tree for so nearly causing his death, he proceeds to reflect on man's incapacity to foresee the fate which is closest at hand, and then on the great dead whom he would have met in the lower world, — a thought suggested perhaps by the famous passage in Plato's Apology of Socrates, but worked out in the form of a tribute to the power of lyric song. For the date of the accident see III. 8, intr. note. — Metre, 176.

1. ille : repeated with savage emphasis in the poet's outburst of wrath, which softens into reproach in **te . . . te,** vs. 11; cf. Tennyson's *The Fleet* 1 'You, you, if you should fail to understand, What England is and what her all-in-all, On you will come the curse of all the land.' — **nefasto die** : properly a day on which *nefas est praetori, apud quem lege agitur, fari tria verba '*do dico addico*' (Fest. p. 165). There was the same superstition about beginning anything

   quicumque primum, et sacrilega manu
      produxit, arbos, in nepotum
         perniciem opprobriumque pagi ;

5   illum et parentis crediderim sui
      fregisse cervicem et penetralia
         sparsisse nocturno cruore
            hospitis ; ille venena Colcha

   et quicquid usquam concipitur nefas
10   tractavit, agro qui statuit meo
      te triste lignum, te caducum
         in domini caput immerentis.

Quid quisque vitet, numquam homini satis
   cautum est in horas.   Navita Bosporum

on such a day that many people
nowadays feel in regard to Friday.
— posuit, *planted.*

2. **quicumque** : sc. *posuit.* —
primum : belonging in sense with
posuit, although placed in the
relative clause. Translate, *whoever it was in the first place.*

3. **produxit,** *reared.*—in, *to the;*
expressing the purpose or destiny
of both acts.— **nepotum,** *posterity.*

4. **pagi,** *the countryside.*

5. **et . . . et,** *both . . . and,* corresponding to et . . . et in the first
strophe. 'He was capable of both
of the two heinous forms of *impietas* named.'— **sui** : emphatic.

6. **fregisse cervicem** (sc. *laqueo*), *strangled;* cf. *Epod.* 3. 2, Sall.
Cat. 55. 5 *laqueo gulam fregere.* —
penetralia, *his very hearthstone ;*
properly the shrine of the household gods, under whose protection
the life of the guest was sacred.

7. **nocturno,** *at dead of night.*

8. **Colcha** : *i.e.* such as Medea
concocted ; cf. *Epod.* 17. 35. For
the form, see Intr. 65.

9. **quicquid** : here used adjectively as in *S.* II. 1. 60 *quisquis
color ;* cf. Verg. *A.* X. 493 *quisquis
honos tumuli, quicquid solamen
humandi est.*

10. **tractavit,** *dabbled in.* There
is at most a very slight zeugma,
nefas being the class of things to
which **venena** are assigned.

11. **te . . . te** : cf. *ille,* vs. 1 n. —
triste lignum, *dismal log.*— **cadu-
cum,** *ready to fall;* to be taken with
statuit, as if this result was contemplated in 'setting up' the tree.

13. **quid vitet** : representing
the 'question of doubt' (*quid
vitem ?*) of the man who is on the
lookout for danger. — **homini,**
man (in the abstract) ; the fact is
stated as characteristic of the race.

14. **cautum est,** *is . . . on his
guard.* Grammatically the subject
is the clause quid vitet, and the
perfect has its proper force ('has
been provided against'). **homini**
is ethical dative ; cf. *tibi cautum
volo* Plaut. *Pers.* 369. — **in horas** :
formed after the analogy of *in dies.*

15   Poenus perhorrescit neque ultra
            caeca timet aliunde fata ;

        miles sagittas et celerem fugam
        Parthi, catenas Parthus et Italum
            robur: sed improvisa leti
20   vis rapuit rapietque gentis.

        Quam paene furvae regna Proserpinae
        et iudicantem vidimus Aeacum
            sedesque discriptas piorum et
            Aeoliis fidibus querentem

25   Sappho puellis de popularibus,
        et te sonantem plenius aureo,
            Alcaee, plectro dura navis,
            dura fugae mala, dura belli.

—**Bosporum Poenus**: Intr. 117 a.
The Thracian Bosporus is meant ;
cf. III. 4. 30.

15. **perhorrescit**: transitive, as
often in Cicero. — **ultra** : with
timet; when the danger of the sea
is past, he *feels no further fear*.

16. **caeca** : here in a passive
sense, *hidden*, — **timet** : for the
prosody, see Intr. 179. — **aliunde
fata** : cf. *unde periculum*, 12. 7 n.

17. **miles**: the Roman legionary,
whose massive array (cf. *robur*, 19)
was ill adapted to meet the stratagem referred to. — **sagittas**,
etc.: *i.e.* the arrows of the Parthian
in full flight ; see I. 19. 11 n.

18. **catenas et Italum robur** :
he is afraid to face *the solid
strength of Italy*, and runs away to
save himself from *chains*.

21. **furvae**, *dusky*, as queen of
the lower world. The word was
originally used (Gell. I. 18. 4) in
the sense of *ater*, on which see I.
28. 13 n. — **regna** : Intr. 128. —
Prŏserpinae : Intr. 178.

22. **iudicantem**, *sitting in judgment*. — **Aeacum** : son of Zeus
and Aegina, and grandfather of
Achilles ; in his lifetime renowned
for his righteousness, and after
his death made a judge in the
lower world.

23. **discriptas**, *allotted*.

24. **Aeoliis** : the dialect of
Lesbos.—**querentem** : because of
their coldness.

25. **Sappho** : Greek accusative
(Σαπφώ). See Intr. 26.

26. **sonantem** : Intr. 51 c. —
plenius, *in richer strain*, *sc.* than
the love songs of Sappho. —
aureo : implying his preëminence
in song ; cf. I. 5. 9 n, II. 1. 40 ;
Quintil. X. 1. 63 *Alcaeus in parte
operis aureo plectro merito donatur,
qua tyrannos insectatus multum
etiam moribus confert.*

27. **plectro** : see I. 26. 11 n. —
dura, etc.: cf. I. 32. 6 *sqq.* Intr.
116 g. — **navis**, *of the sea*.

28. **fugae**, *of exile;* cf. *fugeret,*
I. 7. 22 n.

Vtrumque sacro digna silentio
30   mirantur umbrae dicere ; sed magis
pugnas et exactos tyrannos
densum umeris bibit aure volgus.

Quid mirum, ubi illis carminibus stupens
demittit atras belua centiceps
35   auris et intorti capillis
Eumenidum recreantur angues ?
Quin et Prometheus et Pelopis parens

29. **utrumque :** emphatic ; in contrast with **sed magis**, etc. — **sacro silentio :** *i.e.* profound silence, such as was enjoined during the performance of a religious ceremony. See I. 36. 1 n ; III. 1. 2. For the ablative, which influences both **digna** and **mirantur**, see Intr. 76.

30. **mirantur**, *listen in wonder*. — **dicere :** depending on the notion of *hearing* contained in **mirantur**. The present infinitive here, as often, expresses a direct perception of the words spoken (not indirect through report) ; cf. Cic. *Mur.* 58 *saepe hoc maiores natu dicere audivi* ('I have heard them say,' not 'that they said '). For the meaning see I. 6. 5 n.

31. **pugnas**, etc.: the themes sung by Alcaeus.—**exactos tyrannos :** Intr. 105 *a.*

32. **densum** (= *stipatum*) **umeris :** in their eagerness to get near the singer.—**bibit aure :** cf. Prop. IV. 6. 8 *suspensis auribus ista bibam ;* Verg. *A.* IV. 359 *vocemque his auribus hausi.*

33. **quid mirum :** *sc.* that the happy shades in Elysium should be entranced, when (ubi) even the monsters of the lower world are charmed, and the wicked in Tar-

tarus forget their torments. For the construction of the verbs see Intr. 85.

34. **demittit :** as a watch-dog he keeps his ears usually pricked up. — **atras:** see I. 28. 13 n.—**belua:** Cerberus. — **centiceps :** like the Hydra, Cerberus was pictured with an indefinite number of heads. Hesiod (*Theog.* 312) describes him as κύνα πεντηκοντακάρηνον. In the Latin poets he usually has three, as in 19. 31; cf. Verg. *A.* VI. 417.

36. **recreantur**, *are relieved* (as in III. 24. 16), *i.e.* by the softening influence of the music on the temper of the Furies. — **angues:** masculine, as it more commonly is in prose ; in poetry the feminine is more frequent.

37. **quin et**, *nay even ;* passing to the stronger case of the soothing of pain. For similar descriptions of the power of music in the lower world ; cf. III. 11. 15 *sqq.*, Verg. *G.* IV. 481.— **Prometheus :** usually represented as having been released from the under-world. Horace alone of extant authors (here, 18. 35, and *Epod.* 17. 67) represents him as still suffering in Tartarus. — **Pelopis parens :** see I. 28. 7 n, and cf. *Epod.* 17. 65.

dulci laborem decipitur sono,
    nec curat Orion leones
40   aut timidos agitare lyncas.

XIV.

Eheu fugaces, Postume, Postume,
    labuntur anni, nec pietas moram
        rugis et instanti senectae
            adferet indomitaeque morti ;
5   non si trecenis quotquot eunt dies,

38. **laborem,** *suffering.* For the case see Intr. 50. (For the genitive *laborum*, which has the support of some good manuscripts, and is perhaps right, see Intr. 67.) — **decipitur :** *i.e.* loses the sense of it, under the spell of the music ; cf. *S.* II. 2. 12 *molliter austerum studio fallente laborem.*

39. **curat agitare :** Intr. 120. For the construction, see Intr. 94 *i.* — **Orion :** a mighty hunter, killed by Diana. He is devoted to his favorite pursuit even in Hades. (*Odys.* XI. 572); cf. Verg. *A.* VI. 653 *quae gratia currum | armorumque fuit vivis, quae cura nitentis | pascere equos, eadem sequitur tellure repostos.*

40. **lyncas :** more commonly feminine.

XIV. Whether the Postumus of this ode is a friend of the poet or merely a convenient name we can only guess. In him Horace addresses a man of wealth, surrounded by all the comforts that can contribute to the enjoyment of life, but perhaps a trifle over-careful in the use of his means.

Horace preaches to him on one of his favorite themes, the swift flight of time and the inevitable approach of death, but the moral which he is fond of drawing, that not possession, but enjoyment, is the end to be sought, is here rather implied than distinctly expressed. — Metre, 176.

2. **labuntur,** *glide by.*

3. **rugis, senectae, morti :** notice the climax.

4. **indomitae,** *inexorable.* Death is here personified, the Ἀΐδης ἀμείλιχος ἠδ᾽ ἀδάμαστος of *Il.* IX. 158.

5. **non si,** *no, not if.* The apodosis is contained in **non,** which repeats **nec adferet.** — **trecenis tauris :** three hecatombs ; an intentional hyperbole to make the assertion as strong as possible ; cf. vs. 26. Such enormous sacrifices, however, were not unknown, as, for example, after the battle of Lake Trasimenus ; see Liv. XXII. 10. 7. — **quotquot eunt dies,** *every day that goes by ;* a paraphrase for *quotidie.* For **eunt** (more expressive than *sunt*) cf. IV. 5. 7 *gratior it dies ; Ep.* II. 2. 55 *anni euntes.*

amice, places inlacrimabilem
Plutona tauris, qui ter amplum
Geryonen Tityonque tristi

compescit unda, scilicet omnibus,
10   quicumque terrae munere vescimur,
enaviganda, sive reges
sive inopes erimus coloni.

Frustra cruento Marte carebimus
fractisque rauci fluctibus Hadriae,
15   frustra per autumnos nocentem
corporibus metuemus Austrum.

6. **plăces** : conative. — **inlacri-mabilem** : 'inaccessible to tears,'
either in an active sense, 'incapa-ble of weeping,' *tearless*, as here,
or passively, 'incapable of being wept for,' as IV. 9. 26; cf. *flebi-lis*, IV. 2. 21 (active) and I. 24. 9 (passive).

7. **ter amplum**, *threefold huge;*
referring both to his triple form (*forma tricorporis umbrae*, Verg.
VI. 289) and supernatural size.

8. **Geryonen** : a gigantic mon-ster of the island of Erythia, in
the far West, killed by Hercules, who had been sent to take his
cattle ; Verg. *A*. VIII. 201 *sqq*. — **Tityon** : a giant, son of Gaea,
killed by Apollo and Diana for insulting Latona. His body lay
in the underworld *porrectus novem per iugera terrae* (Tib. I. 3. 75),
with a vulture ever feeding on his liver; cf. Verg. *A*. VI. 595 *sqq*.

9. **compescit**, *confines.*—**unda**:
the Styx. — **scilicet omnibus**, *yes, all of us ;* passing from the
particular examples of the irresist-ible power of Hades to the general
fact; cf. *sed omnis*, I. 28. 15,

10. **quicumque**, etc.: a para-phrase for 'all mankind,' formed

after the Homeric οἳ ἀρούρης καρ-πὸν ἔδουσιν, *Il*. VI. 142. — **munere,**
bounty. The plural is more usual; cf. IV. 9. 48, 10. 1, 15. 26.

11. **enaviganda** : not found in this sense before Horace. *Enavi-gare* (= *traicere navigando*) is like
evadere (= *traicere vadendo*), *e.g.*
angustias evadit, Liv. XXI. 32. 13. — **reges** : see I. 4. 14 n.

12. **inopes coloni** : cf. I. 35. 6 n. — **erimus** : *i.e.* when our time
shall have come.

13. **frustra**, etc.: no precautions are of any use ; cf. 13. 13 *sqq*. — **carebimus**, *keep away from ;* cf.
10. 6.

14. **fractis**, *breaking;* *sc*. on the rocks or the beach, (breakers). — **Hadriae** : Intr. 117 *a*.

15. **frustra** : Intr. 116 *g*. — **per autumnos** : a very hot and un-healthy season at Rome ; cf. III.
23. 8 ; *S*. II. 6. 18 *plumbeus Auster autumnusque gravis; Ep*. I. 7. 1
sqq.

16. **corporibus** : Intr. 76. — **Austrum** : the hot south wind
(Sirocco) prevailing especially in August and September.

17. **ater** : see I. 28. 13 n. — **flumine**, *current.*— **languido** : cf.

Visendus ater flumine languido
Cocytos errans et Danai genus
    infame damnatusque longi
20   Sisyphus Aeolides laboris.

Linquenda tellus et domus et placens
uxor, neque harum quas colis arborum
    te praeter invisas cupressos
        ulla brevem dominum sequetur.

25   Absumet heres Caecuba dignior
    servata centum clavibus et mero
        tinguet pavimentum superbo,
            pontificum potiore cenis.

Verg. *G.* IV. 478 *limus niger et deformis harundo* | *Cocyti tarda- que palus inamabilis unda.*

18. **errans**, *meandering.* — **Danai genus** : see III. 11. 25 n.

20. **Sisyphus**: mythical founder of Corinth, of extraordinary cunning and wickedness ; killed by Theseus and condemned to roll to the top of a hill a stone, which always slipped from his hands and rolled down again ; *Odys.* XI. 593 *sqq.* — **laboris** : Gr. 220.

21. **linquenda**, etc.: for a similar picture cf. Lucr. III. 894 *iam iam non domus accipiet te laeta, neque uxor* | *optima nec dulces oc- current oscula nati* | *praeripere et tacita pectus dulcedine tangent.* — **placens**, *sweet ;* cf. III. 7. 23.

23. **invisas**, *detested ;* see I. 34. 10 n. — **cupressos** : a tall ever- green common in southern Europe, in growth like a cedar, in shape not unlike a Lombardy poplar. Cypress was associated with death from the custom of placing it before the house of mourning and around the funeral pyre, and was regarded as sacred to Pluto.

24. **brevem**, *short-lived*, like *breve lilium*, I. 36. 16 ; but here, with **dominum**, contrasting his brief ownership with the longer lives of the trees.

25. **Caecuba** : see I. 20. 9 n ; for the number, Intr. 128. — **dig- nior** : because knowing better how to use the wine. In this single ironical expression is contained the only intimation of the moral which Horace usually draws from his discourses on the shortness of life and the gloominess of death, — that we must make the most of the brief space that is given us for enjoyment ; cf. I. 4, I. 9. 13 *sqq.*, I. 11, II. 3, II. 11.

26. **centum**: cf. *trecenis*, vs. 5 n.

27. **tinguet**, etc.: implying reck- less extravagance ; cf. Cic. *Phil.* 2. 105 *natabant pavimenta vino, madebant parietes.* — **superbo** : at- tributing to the wine a conscious- ness of its excellence and a feeling of humiliation under such un- worthy treatment.

28. **pontificum cenis** : see I. 37. 2 n. For the case of **cenis** see Intr. 75.

XV.

Iam pauca aratro iugera regiae
moles relinquent ; undique latius
    extenta visentur Lucrino
        stagna lacu, platanusque caelebs
5   evincet ulmos ; tum violaria et
    myrtus et omnis copia narium
        spargent olivetis odorem
            fertilibus domino priori ;

XV. A protest against the growing extravagance of the day, which
spends immense sums in building
luxurious palaces and turns useful
land into pleasure grounds, in contrast with the spirit of the fathers,
who were poor for themselves and
rich only for the state. The ode
is singular in containing no personal allusion whatever. — Metre,
176.

1. **iam**, *soon.* — **regiae** (here for
regales), *regal.*

2. **moles**, *piles ;* cf. III. 29. 10.

3. **visentur**, *will meet our gaze ;*
cf. I. 37. 25. — **Lucrino lacu** : a
sheet of salt water near Baiae,
separated from the gulf of Pozzuoli by a natural dike about a mile
long. By strengthening this dike
and opening a passage through it
into Lucrinus and thence into
Lake Avernus, Agrippa formed
the Portus Iulius (cf. *Ep.* II. 3. 63)
in 37 B.C.

4. **stagna**, *ponds,* artificially constructed both for ornament and
as fish preserves. — **platanus** : cf.
11. 13 n. ← **caelebs** : the familiar
figure of the vine 'wedded' to the
tree on which it twines ; cf. *Epod.*
2. 9 *adulta vitium propagine | altas
maritat populos ;* Cat. 62. 54 (*vitis*)

ulmo   coniuncta   marito.   The
denser shade of the platanus
unfits it for this service. The
meaning is that shady lawns will
take the place of vineyards.

5. **evincet,** *will crowd out ;* cf.
Plin. *N. H.* XVIII. 185 *faba evin-
cit herbas.* — **ulmos** : the unex-
pressed epithet, *maritatas* or the
like, is suggested by **caelebs ;** cf.
Intr. 122. Elms and poplars were
the trees chiefly used for training
vines upon. — **tum** : *i.e.* when the
state of things prophesied in the
preceding lines has come to pass.
— **violaria,** etc.: *i.e.* flower beds
and ornamental shrubs will supplant the olive orchards.

6. **myrtus** : a bushy shrub, with
small, lustrous, dark-green leaves,
and pinkish white flowers, not unlike the apple blossom. — **omnis
copia narium,** *all the wealth of
the nostrils,* a somewhat contempt-
uous expression for 'every variety
of fragrant flower.'

7. **olivetis** : ablative; Intr. 69.

8. **fertilibus,** *which bore fruit.*
— **domino** : Intr. 58 *a.*—With this
whole passage cf. Quint. VIII.
3. 8 *sterilem platanum tonsasque
myrtos quam maritam ulmum et
uberes oleas praeoptaverim ?*

tum spissa ramis laurea fervidos
10 excludet ictus.   Non ita Romuli
praescriptum et intonsi Catonis
auspiciis veterumque norma.

Privatus illis census erat brevis,
commune magnum ; nulla decempedis
15   metata privatis opacam
porticus excipiebat Arcton,

nec fortuitum spernere caespitem
leges sinebant, oppida publico

9. **laurea** (sc. *arbor*): for *laurus;* the bay, an evergreen, bush-like tree, growing often to a height of sixty feet, with rich, dark-green foliage, small yellowish blossoms, and a dark-purple berry.

10. **ictus** (sc. *solis*, suggested by **fervidos**), *rays;* cf. Lucr. I. 147 *lucida tela diei*, and our word 'sun-stroke.'

11. **praescriptum** : sc. *est.* — **intonsi**: see I. 12. 41 n.—**Catonis**: the Censor, prominent in his day for his uncompromising hostility to all corrupting innovations, and to posterity a typical Roman of the olden time.

12. **auspiciis** : *i.e.* while those men guided the state. The *auspicia* could be taken only by those highest in authority; cf. I. 7. 27 n.— **veterum norma** : the old Roman maxims on the requirements of good citizenship, which he proceeds to set forth.

13. **census** : properly the man's list of possessions returned to the Censor ; hence **brevis.**

14. **commune**: neuter used substantively, equivalent to *res publica, the common wealth.* — **nulla decempedis**, etc. : *i.e.* no private portico on a great scale, the latter

being indicated by the unit of measurement (**decempedis**). For the indirect use of the epithet **privatis**, cf. Intr. 124.

15. **opacam** : as the side on which the shadows fall. Strictly the epithet belongs to the portico itself.

16. **excipiebat**, *lay open to ;* cf. Juv. 7. 183 *algentem rapiat cenatio solem*, of a winter dining-room. — **Arcton**, *the North.*

17. **fortuitum**, *the chance,* i.e. the first that presented itself; in contrast with **novo.**— **caespitem**: for building private altars (cf. I. 19. 13 n), where marble and other costly material had now begun to be used.

18. **leges** : probably referring to the rules of Roman ritual, which strictly prescribed the use of certain traditional forms and materials. What Horace points out is that under those old laws even the sod under our feet had its honorable use, for which no man could reject it as common and cheap. — **oppida** : *sc.* with public buildings, etc.— **publico,** *of the people in common,* who spent their means for this end instead of for their personal luxury.

sumptu iubentes et deorum
20   templa novo decorare saxo.

XVI.

Otium divos rogat in patenti
prensus Aegaeo, simul atra nubes
condidit lunam neque certa fulgent
sidera nautis ;

5   otium bello furiosa Thrace,
otium Medi pharetra decori,

19. iubentes decorare: divided between the two objects, and so uniting **publico sumptu** and **novo saxo**, both of which belong to **oppida** as well as to **templa**; Intr. 120, 121.

20. **novo**: see I. 2. 6 n.— **saxo**: *i.e.* marble, which in Horace's day was brought in great variety from different parts of the empire for the decoration of private houses as well as of public buildings ; cf. 18. 3 *sq.*

XVI. To Pompeius Grosphus, a Roman knight, the owner of extensive estates in Sicily, in the neighborhood of those which Iccius managed for Agrippa. See I. 29 (intr. note) and *Ep.* I. 12. 22 *sq.*, where Grosphus is recommended to Iccius as a man who would not take advantage of his friendship to ask improper favors. The subject of the ode is peace of mind, which is never overtaken by those who restlessly pursue it, but dwells with those who take home to themselves the truth that no man's lot can be entirely perfect, and who find their happiness in the contented enjoyment of the blessings they have. — Metre, 174.

1. **otium**, *peace*, in its widest sense, freedom from care, anxiety and passion. The subjects of **rogat** are types of men restless by nature and fond of excitement : even they pray for peace. For the first instance cf. I. 1. 15.— **patenti**, *open*, *i.e.* not near any island where he could take refuge in a harbor.

2. **prensus**: *sc.* by a storm. The nautical term was *deprensus* (Schol. on Verg. *G.* IV. 421); see Intr. 129. For the use of the participle see Intr. 103. — **Aegaeo**: Intr. 117 *a.* — **simul**: see I. 4. 17 n. — **atra**, etc.: see I. 2. 7 n. The picture is of the inky darkness of a stormy night, when the mariner without a compass was peculiarly helpless.

3. **certa**, *sure* (*sc.* as guides to the mariner), such as the Great and Little Bear (Cic. *Arat.* 37 *sqq.*); cf. Tib. I. 9. 10 *ducunt instabiles sidera certa rates.*

5. **otium**: Intr. 116 *g.* — **bello furiosa** : concessive; they are warriors at heart, and love fighting with a passion that amounts to frenzy.— **Thrace** : the country for the people; cf. IV. 14. 49.

6. **Medi** : see I. 2. 22 n.— **pharetra** : associated in the Roman

Grosphe, non gemmis neque purpura ve-
nale neque auro.

Non enim gazae neque consularis
10 submovet lictor miseros tumultus
mentis et curas laqueata circum
tecta volantis.

Vivitur parvo bene cui paternum
splendet in mensa tenui salinum
15 nec levis somnos timor aut cupido
sordidus aufert.

mind with their dashing cavalry
(cf. I. 19. 11 n, II. 13. 17), and suggesting the restless and adventurous spirit of the raider (I. 2. 51).

7. **non**, etc., *peace, which no . . .
can buy.* — **purpura** : used (as in
English) for purple robes, tapestries, etc., which are named with
precious stones and gold as the
costliest things that a man could
offer. — **ve-nale** : Intr. 174 *b.*

8. **neque** : the only instance in
which Horace has admitted elision
in the Adonic verse.

9. **non gazae neque . . . lictor** :
i.e. no wealth nor power.

10. **submovet tumultus** : a
figure borrowed from the progress
of the magistrate through the
streets, the lictors making the
disorderly crowd give way to let
him pass undisturbed. **submovet** is the technical term for this,
and there is a zeugma with **gazae.**

11. **curas . . . volantis** : included in the figure : another annoy-
ing crowd against which the consul's power is helpless. — **laqueata
tecta**, *panelled ceilings, i.e.* those
of rich and splendid houses. Such
a ceiling in its simplest form was
made by inserting cross-pieces between the joists which supported

the floor above, thus dividing the
whole space into square or oblong
panels (*lacunaria*), which could be
decorated at pleasure. This simple
device was imitated in stucco and
elaborated with panels of divers
shapes, richly ornamented with
gold and ivory (cf. 18. 1 *sq.*) and
various tints.

13. **vivitur** : sc. *ab eo*, the antecedent of **cui.** — **parvo** : abl. neut.,
as in *S.* II. 2. 1. — **cui**, etc., *on
whose modest board*, etc.; *i.e.* who
lives in the *aurea mediocritas* of
10. 5, above the slovenly neglect
of indigence, but free from the
worry of wealth. For the suggestion of contentment in **paternum** see I. 1. 11 n.

14. **splendet**, etc.: in his plain
table service only one vessel, and
that the smallest, is of silver ; but
it is an heirloom, ever kept bright,
and it gives a certain tone of elegance to his humble board. —
salinum : cf. Plin. *N. H.* XXXIII.
153 (*Fabricius*) *bellicosos imperato-
res plus quam pateram et salinum
habere ex argento vetabat.*

15. **nec**, *and whose . . . no.* **cui**
is understood here in substantially
the same construction as above.—
timor aut cupido : accompani-

Quid brevi fortes iaculamur aevo
multa ?　Quid terras alio calentis
sole mutamus ?　Patriae quis exsul
20　　se quoque fugit ?

Scandit aeratas vitiosa navis
Cura nec turmas equitum relinquit,
ocior cervis et agente nimbos
ocior Euro.

25　Laetus in praesens animus quod ultra est
oderit curare, et amara lento
temperet risu : nihil est ab omni
parte beatum.

ments of wealth, fear of losing what
one has, and greed for more. *Cupido*, always masculine in Horace, is
usually feminine in other authors,
except as the name of the god.

17. **brevi aevo** : to be taken
with **iaculamur**, but **brevi**, contrasted by its position with **fortes**,
suggests the folly of our confident
projects ; cf. I. 4. 15.

18. **multa** : the emphatic word
of the sentence (Intr. 116 *b*); cf. 11.
5 *poscentis aevi pauca*. — **terras
alio calentis sole** : *i.e.* foreign
countries ; cf. Verg. *G.* II. 512
*alio patriam quaerunt sub sole
iacentem*. The omitted ablative
after **mutamus** (*patriā* or *nostrā*)
is implied in this description, and
the next sentence assumes that it
is already understood. For the
construction see Intr. 74.

19. **patriae**, *from his country ;*
cf. *exsul mundi*, Ov. *M.* VI. 189.

20. **se quoque fugit** : cf. Sen.
Ep. 28. 2 *quaeris quare te fuga ista
non adiuvet ?　Tecum fugis ;*
Lucr. III. 1053 *sqq.* For the tense
of **fugit** see Intr. 80.

21. **scandit**, etc.: amplification

of the preceding : a man **cannot**
run away from his own discontent,
though he take the swiftest ship
or the fastest horse ; cf. III. 1.
37 *sqq.*; *Ep.* I. 11. 27 *sqq.;* Lucr.
II. 48 *sqq.* That Horace himself
had his periods of restless discontent, he confesses *S.* II. 7. 111 *sqq.*,
Ep. I. 8. 3 *sqq.* — **aeratas**, *brass-
bound.*—**vitiosa**, *morbid ;* included
in the personification ; cf. I. 24. 7 n.

22. **relinquit**, *falls behind ;* cf.
deseruit, III. 2. 32.

23. **ocior** : Intr. 116 *b.*

25. **laetus in praesens** : to be
taken with the predicate, in the
same sense as III. 8. 27 *dona praesentis cape laetus horae.* — **quod
ultra est**: *i.e.* the future; cf. I. 9. 13.

26. **oderit**: stronger than *nolit;*
Intr. 94 *l.* — **lento risu**, *with a
quiet smile.*

27. **nihil**, etc.: reason for the
preceding ; the wise man will
cheerfully accept the disagreeable
along with the good, and not run
away from it in a futile chase after
unalloyed happiness.

29. **abstulit**, etc.: two contrasted examples of the drawbacks

Abstulit clarum cita mors Achillem,
30 longa Tithonum minuit senectus,
et mihi forsan tibi quod negarit
porriget hora.

Te greges centum Siculaeque circum
mugiunt vaccae, tibi tollit hinnitum
35 apta quadrigis equa, te bis Afro
murice tinctae

vestiunt lanae : mihi parva rura et
spiritum Graiae tenuem Camenae
Parca non mendax dedit et malignum
40 spernere volgus.

attending the most coveted blessings: a brilliant career, cut short by
an untimely death; eternal life, an
infinitely prolonged bodily decay.

30. **Tithonum** : see I. 28. 8 n.
— **minuit** : perfect.

31. **et mihi**, etc.: a slight shifting of the point of view, suggested
by the two examples just cited,
each of whom possessed what the
other lacked. But the underlying
thought remains unaltered. On
the basis of the truth '*nihil ab
omni parte beatum*' the poet boldly
compares his own humble lot with
that of his wealthy friend, and
points out that he may perhaps be
more happy in some respects than
one who, according to ordinary
standards, was in every way more
fortunate.

32. **hora**, *the hour ; i.e.* any
given hour in which our fortunes
may be compared.

33. **greges Siculaeque vaccae**:
equivalent to *greges Sicularum
vaccarum* (hendiadys).— **centum**:
for an indefinitely large number ;
cf. 14. 26, III. 11. 17.— **circum** :
Intr. 115 c.

34. **tollit** : cf. *risum tollant, Ep.*
II. 3. 381, and our phrase '*lift up*
their voice.'— **hinnitum** : for the
synapheia, see Intr. 174 *b*.

35. **apta**, *fit for;* implying a fine
breed and a high market value. —
quadrigis: *i.e.* for the chariot race.
— **equa** : mares were preferred for
this purpose; cf. Verg. *G.* I. 59. —
bis tinctae : a translation of the
technical term *dibapha* (δι-βαφα,
'twice dipped'); cf. Plin. *N. H.* IX.
137.— **Afro** : *i.e.* from the island
of Girba, in the Syrtis Minor.

37. **mihi parva rura**, etc.: cf.
18. 1 *sqq.* and Bacchylides *Fr.* 28
οὐ βοῶν πάρεστι σώματ', οὔτε χρυσός,
οὔτε πορφύρεοι τάπητες, ἀλλὰ θυμὸς
εὐμενής, | μοῦσά τε γλυκεῖα καὶ Βοιω-
τίοισιν ἐν σκύφοισιν οἶνος ἡδύς.

38. **spiritum**, *inspiration*, as in
IV. 6. 29 ; cf. *spiro*, IV. 3. 24. —
Graiae Camenae: cf. I. 12. 39 n
and note on *lyricis vatibus*, I. 1.
35. — **tenuem**, *fine, delicate.*

39. **Parca** : Intr. 127. — **non
mendax** : a permanent attribute ;
cf. *C. S.* 25 ; Pers. 5. 48 *Parca
tenax veri.*

40. **spernere**, *a contempt for*

XVII.

Cur me querellis exanimas tuis?
Nec dis amicum est nec mihi te prius
    obire, Maecenas, mearum
        grande decus columenque rerum.

5   A, te meae si partem animae rapit
maturior vis, quid moror altera,
    nec carus aeque nec superstes
        integer?   Ille dies utramque

(Intr. 97 *d*); *i.e.* a capacity to hold himself above their envy (*invidia maior*, 20. 4). — **volgus** : the unrefined 'rabble' of readers and critics who were incapable of appreciating the finer spirit of Greek poetry (cf. III. 1. 1), and pursued Horace with ridicule and detraction (*S.* I. 10. 78 *sqq.*), due partly to envy of his social advancement, until his success was established beyond cavil (IV. 3. 16).

XVII. Maecenas was a confirmed invalid, suffering constantly from fever and insomnia (Intr. 21 ; Plin. *N. H.* VII. 172); and at the same time he had a passionate attachment to life (Sen. *Ep.* 101. 10) which made his frequent sicknesses occasions of gloomy forebodings. Horace here consoles him with the assurance of his devotion, which will not permit death to separate them, with appeals to astrology (to which Maecenas was addicted), and by recalling their common escape from imminent death, for which thank-offerings were still due. This allusion shows that the ode was written not long after B.C. 30 (see Ode 13, intr. note). — Metre, 176.

1. **exanimas**, *kill ; i.e.* torment, by suggesting such distressing thoughts ; cf. *Epod.* 14. 5 *occidis saepe rogando ;* Ter. *Andr.* 660 *quor me enicas?*

2. **amicum est** (equivalent to *placet*), *it is the pleasure of;* cf. *Il.* IX. 23 οὕτω που Διὶ μέλλει ὑπερμενέι φίλον εἶναι. In point of fact Horace survived his patron only a few months (Intr. 35).

4. **decus columenque** : see I. 1. 2 n.

5. **partem animae** : cf. I. 3. 8 n. — **rapit . . . moror** : for the tense see Intr. 78.

6. **vis** : used properly of premature death ; cf. 13. 20 (where it is joined, as here, with *rapere*) and Cic. *C. M.* 71 *vitam adulescentibus vis aufert, senibus maturitas.* — **altera** : sc. *pars.*

7. **carus** : sc. *mihi*, as the context implies ; cf. *Ep.* I. 3. 29 *si patriae volumus, si nobis vivere cari.* — **aeque** : *sc.* as before.— — **superstes** : to be taken with **carus** as well as with **integer**; Intr. 119 *a.*

8. **integer** : repeating the thought of *te meae partem animae* 5.—**utramque** (sc. *nostrum ;* cf. vs. 21 n), *of both of us. Vtriusque*

ducet ruinam.   Non ego perfidum
10   dixi sacramentum : ibimus, ibimus,
        utcumque praecedes, supremum
         carpere iter comites parati.

Me nec Chimaerae spiritus igneae
nec, si resurgat, centimanus Gyas
15   divellet umquam ; sic potenti
        Iustitiae placitumque Parcis.

Seu Libra seu me Scorpios adspicit

nostrum would be more usual, but **utramque** is quite in accord with the Latin mode of thought, which conceives of two *ruinae* in this case : cf. IV. 14. 19.

9. **ducet ruinam** : a phrase suggested in its literal use by the appearance of a falling building, where one part gives way and 'draws' the rest after it ; cf. Verg. *A.* II. 465 *elapsa repente* (*turris*) *r u i n a m   c u m   s o n i t u   t r a h i t.* — **non ego** : see I. 18. 11 n. **non** qualifies **perfidum** only, on which cf. 8. 6 n.

10. **dixi,** *pronounced;* the technical term ; cf. Caes. *B. C.* I. 86. 3 *neu quis invitus sacramentum dicere cogatur.* — **sacramentum**: the soldier's oath, by which he bound himself to follow wherever his general might lead : cf. Liv. XXII. 38. 3. — **ibimus, ibimus** : Intr. 116 *d.*

11. **utcumque** : cf. I. 17. 10 n.

13. **Chimaerae** : see I. 27. 23 n. — **igneae** : properly an attribute of **spiritus** ; Intr. 124.

14. **si resurgat** : *i.e.* from Tartarus. — **Gyas** : son of Uranus and Gaea, brother of Briareus (Hes. *Theog.* 149).

15. **sic,** etc.: *i.e.* such is the just and immutable decree of heaven.

16. **Iustitiae** : here not the per-

sonified virtue of I. 24. 6, but the powerful goddess Δίκη, daughter of Themis and sister of the Fates (Hes. *Theog.* 902), whose authority she shares. — **placitumque** : Intr. 119 *b.*

17. **seu ... seu,** *if ... or if ;* cf. I. 23. 5 *sq.* The meaning is : If our destinies are governed by the stars, there is a marvelous agreement in the influences that rule our two lives. Horace had no faith in astrology (see I. 11), but he adopts its language to express more emphatically to his patron, who did believe in it, his confidence that their friendship was not to be severed by death.— **adspicit** : cf. IV. 3. 1. *sqq.* The astrologers held that a man's destiny was determined by the constellations and planets which looked down upon him at his birth. These constituted, grouped as they were at that moment, his 'nativity' (**natalis hora**), each member (**pars**) of which exerted its own influence, good or ill, but only so far as it was not counteracted by some other member. Libra and Jupiter were held to be salutary in their influence ; the others here mentioned, baleful. The present **adspicit** expresses the continuing influence of the constellation.

formidulosus, pars violentior
   natalis horae, seu tyrannus
20   Hesperiae Capricornus undae,

utrumque nostrum incredibili modo
consentit astrum : te Iovis impio
   tutela Saturno refulgens
     eripuit volucrisque fati

25 tardavit alas, cum populus frequens
laetum theatris ter crepuit sonum ;
   me truncus inlapsus cerebro
     sustulerat, nisi Faunus ictum

18. **pars violentior :** referring to any of the three constellations. It means the influence which tends to bring violence and danger into his life.

19. **tyrannus,** etc.: cf. I. 3. 15 n. Certain constellations were held to have a dominant influence in certain parts of the earth ; cf. Manil. IV. 791 *tu, Capricorne, regis quidquid sub sole cadente | est positum gelidamque Helicen quod tangit ab illo, | Hispanas gentes et quot fert Gallia dives.*

21. **nostrum :** gen. pl., substantive ; cf. note on *utramque,* 8. For the caesura of the verse see Intr. 155.

22. **consentit :** *i.e.* (as appears from what follows) the *pars violentior* has in both cases been thwarted just before the fulfilment of its fatal influence. This whole passage has been imitated by Persius, 5. 45 *sqq.*—**Iovis tutela :** Intr. 126 *b.* — **impio :** the character of the Kronos of Greek mythology, with whom Saturn was identified.

23. **refulgens :** cf. I. 12. 28 n.

24. **volucris :** better taken with **alas ;** cf. III. 29. 53 *si celeris*

quatit pennas (of Fortuna). — **fati :** *i.e.* of death. This conception of the approach of death is similar to that of I. 3. 32.

25. **cum populus,** etc.: see I. 20. 4 n.

26. **theatris :** Intr. 69, 128. — **ter :** apparently the usual number, like our three cheers ; cf. Prop. IV. 10. 4 *Camenae . . . manibus faustos ter crepuere sonos ;* cf. also I. 28. 36 n. — **sonum :** see Intr. 45 *a,* and cf. Prop. *l. c.*

27. **truncus,** etc.: see Ode 13, intr. note. — **inlapsus cerebro sustulerat :** Intr. 82.

28. **Faunus :** as the accident took place on his farm, he naturally attributes his escape to the god of the woods and fields (cf. I. 17. 1 *sqq.,* III. 18) who had moreover a natural interest in poets, as the *protégés* of his father Mercury (see vs. 29 n). Cf., however, III. 8. 7.

29. **levasset,** *had averted.* — **Mercurialium virorum :** Horace here appropriates the name familiarly applied to successful business men (cf. *S.* II. 3. 25) for poets, who also stand under the protection of Mercury as the god of

dextra levasset, Mercurialium
30   custos virorum.   Reddere victimas
aedemque votivam memento ;
nos humilem feriemus agnam.

XVIII.

Non ebur neque aureum
mea renidet in domo lacunar,
non trabes Hymettiae
premunt columnas ultima recisas
5   Africa, neque Attali
ignotus heres regiam occupavi,

eloquence and the inventor of the lyre (I. 10. 1, 6).   Cf. 7. 13 *sq.*

30. **reddere,** *pay* (see I. 3. 7 n), *sc.* to Jove.

XVIII. The poet illustrates his favorite maxim of the *aurea medi-ocritas* by contrasting his own happy lot, in which small means are united with character, talent, and a contented spirit, with the folly and blindness of those whose grasping ambition and love of show set at defiance the bounds of nature and of right. He gives the ode a slightly dramatic character by singling out one of this class for reproach, but he names no name, and probably had no particular person in mind. The reference to his own position in life will remind the reader of I. 31 and II. 16. 33 *sqq.*, and is similar to the fragment of Bacchylides quoted at 16. 37 n. Cf. also Tib. I. 1, Prop. IV. 2. 9 *sqq.* — Metre, 167.

1. **ebur** : used, like the gold, in decorating the ceiling. In prose it would be *neque eburneum neque,* etc.

2. **lacunar:** cf. *laqueata tecta,* 16. 11 n.

3. **trabes Hymettiae:** *i.e.* archi-traves of marble from Mt. Hymet-tus in Attica (6. 14 n), which was of a light bluish tint.

4. **premunt,** *rest upon.* — **co-lumnas :** the reference is to the atrium, which being the public room of the house, was decorated with the greatest splendor ; cf. III. 1. 45 *sq.* The columns supported the roof, around the *impluvium.* — **ultima,** *far ;* cf. 20. 18. — **reci-sas,** *quarried.*

5. **Africa :** the yellow Numidian marble (*giallo antico*) is meant. The Romans were fond of combining marbles of various colors in their buildings, and the innumerable fragments of these dug up at the present day bear striking testimony to the former magnificence of the city. — **neque,** etc.: *i.e.* nor have I unexpectedly come into posses-sion of enormous wealth, — a pro-verbial result of which is extrava-gant expenditure. — **Attali,** *of an Attalus.* See I. 1. 12 n.

6. **ignotus heres :** the inherit-

nec Laconicas mihi
　　trahunt honestae purpuras clientae ;
at fides et ingeni
10　　benigna vena est, pauperemque dives
me petit : nihil supra
　　deos lacesso nec potentem amicum
largiora flagito,
　　satis beatus unicis Sabinis.
15　Truditur dies die
　　novaeque pergunt interire lunae :

ance of great fortunes by insignificant persons unconnected by
kindred with the testator, — often
adventurers who had ingratiated
themselves by flattery and baser
means, — was a familiar feature of
Roman life in Horace's day. See
S. II. 5, intr. note.

7. Laconicas: the purple-fish
(*murex*) was found especially at
Gythium on the Sinus Laconicus
and on the coast of Cythera.

8. trahunt, *spin;* standing here,
however, for the whole process
of manufacture. — **honestae,** *re-
spectable, well-born.* Horace says,
in effect, that he is not a powerful
patron whose dependents are not
merely slaves and freedmen, but
well-to-do families, who court his
favor with rich presents; cf. Cic.
Verr. II. 4. 59. — **purpuras,** *purple stuffs ;* cf. III. 1. 42.

10. benigna, *generous.* — **vena:**
cf. *divite vena, Ep.* II. 3. 409. The
figure is probably taken from the
underground water-course (*vena
aquae ;* cf. Hirt. *B. G.* VIII. 43. 4,
venae fontis intercisae sunt)
rather than veins of metal ; cf.
Ovid, *Tr.* III. 14. 33 *ingenium
fregere meum mala, cuius et ante |
fons infecundus parvaque
vena fuit.* — **est:** sc. *mihi.* —

pauperemque dives, *poor as I
am, the rich man ;* Intr. 116 *a.*
dives is used collectively (Intr.
127). A number of rich men were
among Horace's friends.

11. me petit: *i.e.* is attracted
to me, seeks my society.

12. lacesso, *I importune,* with
two accusatives, as a verb of asking. — **amicum :** Maecenas, as
vs. 14 shows.

14. beatus: in its participial
sense, *made rich ;* cf. *Epod.* I. 31
*satis superque me benignitas tua |
ditavit.* — **unicis,** *my one,* the only
one I possess; cf. *unicus filius.* —
Sabinis, *Sabine farm ;* Intr. 24.
An estate in a given territory is
sometimes designated by the plural
of the name of the people, —
Sabini for *fundus Sabinus ;* cf. III.
4. 22 ; Plin. *Ep.* V. 6. 1 *Tuscos meos.*

15. truditur dies die, *day
crowds upon day ;* cf. *Epod.* 17. 25.

16. novae lunae: not in the
narrower technical sense, but as
new phenomena coming with each
successive month ; cf. Cat. 5. 4
soles occidere et redire possunt. —
pergunt: *sc.* as they always have
done ; the order of nature goes on,
keeping the lesson ever before us.
Cf. IV. 7. 7 *sqq.* — **interire:** *i.e.* to
wane.

tu secanda marmora
　　locas sub ipsum funus, et sepulcri
immemor struis domos,
20　　marisque Bais obstrepentis urges
submovere litora,
　　parum locuples continente ripa.
Quid quod usque proximos
　　revellis agri terminos et ultra
25　limites clientium
　　salis avarus? Pellitur paternos

17. **secanda marmora**: *sc.* into slabs for pavements and walls; Plin. *N. H.* XXXVI. 50.

18. **locas**, *are giving contracts for;* the technical term. The corresponding word for the contractor's part was *redimere* (cf. III. 1. 35). The work to be done is expressed by the gerundive construction with either verb. — **sub**: see I. 8. 14 n. — **sepulcri**: the 'house' to which you must soon inevitably remove, in contrast with earthly houses (**domos**); see 29 n.

20. **Bais**: the favorite watering-place of Rome at this time (*Ep.* I. 1. 83, 15. 2 *sqq.*), situated on the gulf of Pozzuoli, about ten miles west of Naples. The word is dative after **ob-strepentis**. — **urges submovere litora**, *you press on the work of pushing out the shore*, for the purpose of building a house close upon the water; cf. III. 1. 33 *sqq.*, and Martial's description (X. 30) of the country-house of Apollinaris at Formiae. Horace, however, represents the rich builder as fretting within the narrow bounds of the shore, which he pushes away (**submovere**) as an obstacle in his path.

22. **continente ripa**, *while the shore confines you;* cf. Caes. *B. G.*

I. 2. 3 *undique loci natura Helvetii continentur.* For **ripa** see I. 2. 14 n.

23. **quid quod**: a phrase frequently used by the orators in passing to a stronger point; in this case it is from the folly to the wickedness of the rich man. **quid**, without suggesting any particular verb, calls attention to the fact expressed by the *quod*-clause. — **usque**, *one after another.* **usque proximos** is equivalent to *proximum quemque*, the one which on each occasion is nearest.

24. **revellis**: stronger than the usual term *exarare* or *movere*, expressing, like *salis* 26, the man's unscrupulous violence. — **agri terminos**, *landmarks, boundary stones.* Such a stone was sacred, and a curse was pronounced on one who should remove it.

25. **clientium**: the wickedness was aggravated when the man he wronged was his own client, whom it was his sacred duty to protect against aggression. The laws of the Twelve Tables took cognizance of this crime in the clause: PATRONVS SI CLIENTI FRAVDEM FECERIT, SACER ESTO.

26. **salis**, *stride;* see note on *revellis*, 24, and on *transiliunt*, I. 3. 24.— **pellitur**: Intr. 77.— **pater-**

in sinu ferens deos
    et uxor et vir sordidosque natos.
Nulla certior tamen
30   rapacis Orci fine destinata
aula divitem manet
    erum.   Quid ultra tendis ?   Aequa tellus
pauperi recluditur
    regumque pueris, nec satelles Orci
35   callidum Promethea
    revexit auro captus.   Hic superbum

nos deos : *i.e.* the little images of
their household gods, their only
remaining possessions ; cf. Juv.
8. 110. The acquisition of the
*angulus proximus qui nunc denor-
mat agellum* (*S.* II. 6. 8) was usually a slower and safer process
than in the poet's graphic picture,
but was effected no less surely
by gradually involving the poor
neighbor in debts which in the end
drove him from his farm utterly
impoverished.

28. **sordidos,** *ragged;* indicating
the poverty of the parents.

29. **nulla,** etc.: a fuller expression of the suggestion in vs. 18 :
the rich lord builds palace upon
palace, but there is none he can
count on so surely as the palace of
Death. The construction is: *nulla
aula divitem erum certior manet
(aulā) rapacis Orci fine destinatā*
(for *quam aula r. O. f. destinata ;*
Intr. 75).

30. **Orci fine :** the limit which
Orcus (Pluto) sets, *i.e.* death, the
limit of life (*mors ultima linea
rerum est, Ep.* I. 16. 79); cf. *fine
libidinum,* I. 18. 10 n. The ablative
is instrumental. Some editors take
fine as feminine (as in *Epod.* 17.
36; elsewhere in Horace it is masculine), **and** (with **destinata**) as

ablative after **certior.** In either
case **fine** is similar to *modus,* 6. 7.
— **destinata :** sc. *ei.*

32. **ultra :** *i.e.* beyond the *finis
Orci ;* why do you make plans
that reach far out beyond your
brief span of life ? cf. I. 4. 15, 11.
7, II. 11. 11 *sq.,* 16. 17. — **aequa
tellus :** cf. *aequo pede* and the
whole passage, I. 4. 13 n.

34. **pueris :** for the prosody
see Intr. 138. — **satelles Orci :**
Charon.

36. **revexit captus,** *was enticed
. . . to ferry back ;* cf. *hunc capit
argenti splendor, S.* I. 4. 28. The
story of such an attempt does not
occur elsewhere ; see 13. 37 n. —
hic : Orcus. The meaning is :
Death, the great leveler, comes to
all alike, — tears the rich man in-
exorably away from his luxurious
life, and relieves the poor man of
his heavy burden.

37. **Tantalum :** see I. 28. 7 n.
— **Tantali genus :** Pelops and
his powerful line; see I. 6. 8 n.

38. **levare :** depending both on
vocatus (see Intr. 97 *a* and cf.
Lucr. V. 945 *at sedare sitim fluvii
fontesque vocabant*), and on **audit,**
which from the context acquires
the meaning of *exoratur ;* Intr. 76.
— **functum laboribus :** equivalent

Tantalum atque Tantali
    genus coercet, hic levare functum
pauperem laboribus
40   vocatus atque non vocatus audit.

XIX.

Bacchum in remotis carmina rupibus
    vidi docentem (credite posteri)
Nymphasque discentis et auris
    capripedum Satyrorum acutas.

to *defunctum laboribus*, III. 24. 15 (cf. Intr. 129); but the phrase is used here, on the analogy of (*de*)*functus vita* (cf. 9. 13), to denote the close of a life that is all toil, and is equivalent to *functum vita laboriosa* ; cf. IV. 15. 29.

40. **non vocatus audit**: oxymoron. — **audit**, *gives ear*.

XIX. A hymn to Bacchus. The main part of the poem, which is devoted, like I. 10, to the attributes and achievements of the god, is introduced by two strophes in the spirit of the dithyramb (cf. IV. 2. 10 n). The poet represents himself as having come unexpectedly, while strolling in the woods, upon the god himself, in whose overpowering presence he feels a touch of the frenzy of the bacchanal; and when the first tumultuous emotions have subsided his mind is left in a fit state of exaltation to sing the praises of the god. — Metre, 176.

1. **in remotis rupibus**: the gods when they visited the earth always sought solitary places, far away from the paths of men; cf. note on *imminente luna*, I. 4. 5. The haunts of Bacchus were in the hills and woods, hence the epithets ὄρειος, ὀρειφοίτης frequently applied to him. — **carmina docentem**: the dithyrambic hymns were attributed to the inspiration of Bacchus himself (cf. III. 25), who is here represented as training the nymphs and satyrs, as Apollo inspires and trains the muses (cf. 10. 18).

2. **credite posteri**: parenthetical, asserting the truth of the story against its inherent improbability, which will tell against it with greater force when the narrator's personal authority is no longer felt; cf. *Epod.* 9. 11. The appeal shows that the poet is not here telling of a vision, but represents himself as having actually seen the god.

3. **Nymphas ... Satyrorum**: both always represented as musical; cf. I. 1. 31; Lucr. IV. 580 *sqq.* — **auris Satyrorum**: a poetical variation of *Satyros audientis* (parallel to **nymphas discentis**); cf. *umerum*, I. 21. 12 n, and Intr. 126 *b*.

4. **capripedum**: so also in Lucretius (*l. c.*) and in some of the later Greek poets. The attribute is borrowed from Pan and the Panisci. The Satyr was generally

5   Euhoe, recenti mens trepidat metu
    plenoque Bacchi pectore turbidum
       laetatur ; euhoe, parce Liber,
          parce gravi metuende thyrso !

    Fas pervicacis est mihi Thyiadas
10 vinique fontem lactis et uberes
       cantare rivos atque truncis
          lapsa cavis iterare mella ;

    fas et beatae coniugis additum
    stellis honorem tectaque Penthei

represented with pointed ears, conspicuous against his bald head, a tuft of hair on his neck, and a tail; in other respects his figure was human.

5. euhoe: the cry of the bacchantes (εὐοῖ) in their orgies (cf. I. 18. 9); here interjected and repeated to express vividly the poet's complete possession by the divine enthusiasm. — **recenti**: *i.e.* not yet quieted. — **metu**: the sight of a god was always a strain on human nerves (χαλεποὶ δὲ θεοὶ φαίνεσθαι ἐναργεῖς, *Il.* XX. 131); cf. Verg. *A.* IV. 279 *sqq.*

6. pleno Bacchi: cf. III. 25. 1 sq. — **turbidum**: Intr. 48.

7. parce: *sc.* from the full force of his inspiration, which would drive the poet to frenzy; cf. Verg. *A.* VI. 77 *sqq.*

8. gravi, *dread*, because its touch brought on madness.—**metuende**: cf. I. 12. 23.

9. fas, *vouchsafed ;* cf. I. 24. 20. He feels the assurance of this in the revelation with which the god has favored him. — **pervicacis**, *untiring, persevering, i.e.* in their fanatical orgies, which were kept up day and night. — **Thyiadas**: θυιάδες (cf. θύω, 'rave') was

another name for the maenads (μαινάδες; cf. μαίνομαι) or Bacchae (βάκχαι), the women who took part in the orgies of the god.

10. vini fontem, etc. : these miracles, effected by the stroke of the thyrsus, are described in Eurip. *Bacch.* 704 *sqq. ;* cf. also 141 ὁ δ' ἔξαρχος Βρόμιος εὐοῖ. ῥεῖ δὲ γάλακτι πέδον, ῥεῖ δ' οἴνῳ, ῥεῖ δὲ μελισσᾶν νέκταρι. — et : Intr. 114.

11. truncis lapsa: Intr. 70. Cf. *Epod.* 16. 47 ; Verg. *E.* 4. 30.

12. iterare : to go over in words, equivalent to *narrare ;* cf. Plaut. *As.* 567 *tua malefacta iterari multa et vero possunt.*

13. fas: Intr. 116 *h.* — **et**, *too.* —**beatae**, *blessed, i.e.* by being received into heaven.— **coniugis** : Ariadne.

14. honorem : *i.e.* the golden crown, her wedding present from Bacchus, which the god, on receiving her into heaven, placed among the stars (the 'Northern Crown') ; cf. Ov. *M.* VIII. 176 *sqq., F.* III. 459 *sqq.* For the form of expression cf. *umerum,* I. 21. 12 n. — **Penthei** : grandson of Cadmus and his successor as king of Thebes. For resist-

15   disiecta non leni ruina
            Thracis et exitium Lycurgi.

        Tu flectis amnis, tu mare barbarum,
        tu separatis uvidus in iugis
            nodo coerces viperino
20   Bistonidum sine fraude crinis.

        Tu, cum parentis regna per arduum
        cohors Gigantum scanderet impia,
            Rhoetum retorsisti leonis
                unguibus horribilique mala,

ing the worship of Bacchus he was torn to pieces by his own mother Agave and other women, who in their frenzy mistook him for a wild beast, and his house was destroyed; Ov. *M.* III. 513 *sqq.* For the form cf. *Vlixei*, I. 6. 7 n.

16. Lycurgi: a king of the Edoni (7. 27 n) who attempted to suppress the bacchanalian orgies and the cultivation of the vine. He was driven mad by Bacchus, and after killing his own wife and son was himself devoured by panthers (Hygin. *Fab.* 132). There are, however, other versions of his punishment, as *Il.* VI. 130 *sqq.;* and later writers (as Nonnus, *Dionys.* XX. 149 *sqq.*) make him an Arab prince.

17. tu: see I. 10. 9 n. — **flectis,** *dost subdue to thy will* (cf. IV. 1. 6); alluding to the miracles of his Indian expedition, and particularly to his crossing the Hydaspes without wetting the feet of his panthers, and reducing the rebellious river to obedience (Nonn. *Dionys.* XXIII. 125 *sqq.,* XXIV. 7 *sqq.*). That he exercised a similar power over the waters of the Indian ocean (**mare barbarum**) is implied by Seneca, who calls him *Lycurgi domitor et rubri maris* (*Herc. Fur.* 903).

18. separatis: cf. *remotis,* 1 n. — **uvidus:** sc. *vino;* see IV. 5. 39 n.

19. nodo viperino: *i.e.* with a snake instead of a ribbon; cf. Cat. 64. 258 (*bacchantes*) *pars sese tortis serpentibus incingebant.*

20. Bistonidum: *i.e.* Thracian bacchantes, the Bistones being a Thracian tribe; cf. *Sithoniis,* I. 18. 9 n. — **fraude,** *harm* (*sc.* to them); an archaic use of the word, borrowed from certain legal formulas; cf. Liv. I. 24. 5 *rex respondit: quod sine fraude mea populique Romani Quiritium fiat, facio.*

21. tu, cum, etc.: according to one form of the tradition, Bacchus as well as Hercules was summoned to the aid of the gods in their battle with the giants; see 12. 6 n. — **parentis,** *thy father* (Jove). — **regna:** Intr. 128. — **per arduum,** *up the steep path to.*

22. impia: as attacking the gods.

23. Rhoetum: one of the Giants; cf. III. 4. 55. — **leonis,** etc.: this feature of the story is not found elsewhere, but in his adventure with the pirates Bacchus turned himself into a lion to frighten his captors; *Hom. Hymn. in Dionys.* (7). 44.

25   quamquam choreis aptior et iocis
        ludoque dictus non sat idoneus
            pugnae ferebaris ; sed idem
                pacis eras mediusque belli.

        Te vidit insons Cerberus aureo
30   cornu decorum, leniter atterens
            caudam, et recedentis trilingui
                ore pedes tetigitque crura.

26. **dictus**: a present passive participle, if the language possessed one, would here be in place, to express what was true up to and during the time of **ferebaris**. The perfect, however, is in keeping with the feeling of the language, which tends to express the cause as preceding the effect in time as well as logically.

27. **idem**, etc.: *i.e.* thou wast (as the event proved) quite as well qualified for war as for peace. **idem** is predicate; (medius) **pacis** and **medius belli** belong to the subject. For the position of -**que**, showing that **medius** is to be understood with **pacis**, and hence excluding the meaning 'half-way between peace and war,' see Intr. 119 *b*. The use of the genitive with **medius** for *in media pace*, etc., is poetical, and is not found elsewhere. It is used in a different sense in *Ep.* I. 18. 9.

29. **te vidit**, etc.: the hymn concludes, like I. 10, with the visit of the god to the lower world, where he went to bring away his mother Semele and take her to heaven. — **insons**: to be closely connected with **vidit**.

30. **cornu**: apparently not here attributed to Bacchus as the sym-

bol of strength and courage (cf. III. 21. 18 n), as it often is (*e.g.* Tib. II. 1. 3, Prop. IV. 17. 19), but the drinking horn with which he is sometimes represented in vase-paintings, the κέρας, βεβυσμένον ἡδέος οἴνου, χρύσεον εὐποίητον, which he carried in his left hand (the thyrsus in his right) as he marched at the head of his army to India (Nonn. XIV. 240). With the wine from this he quiets Cerberus. — **atterens**, *wagging*.

31. **recedentis**: genitive. The first part of the strophe referred to the *entrance* of Bacchus into Hades. — **trilingui ore**: equivalent to *linguis triplicis oris*. There is no good reason to suppose that Horace intended to present a conception of Cerberus different from the prevailing one; it was necessary to mention the tongue, and it was obviously desirable here to keep the number of heads so far as possible in the background, as the picture of a fawning dog with three heads is at best a difficult one to manage. Where it suits his purpose (13. 34) he makes the monster hundred-headed.

32. **tetigit**: *i.e.* licked. — -**que**: see Intr. 119 *b*.

XX.

Non usitata nec tenui ferar
penna biformis per liquidum aethera
   vates, neque in terris morabor
     longius, invidiaque maior

5 urbis relinquam.   Non ego pauperum
sanguis parentum, non ego quem vocas,
   dilecte Maecenas, obibo,
     nec Stygia cohibebor unda.

XX. The poet foretells his own immortality in the form of an allegory based on the familiar fancy of the Greeks that the souls of poets after death passed into swans and in this form continued to exercise their gift of song (Plat. *Rep.* X. 620 a). Such outspoken appreciation of his own merits, though foreign to our habits, was not offensive to Roman taste, and perhaps the same is true of the extremely realistic description of the transformation, though some editors have doubted this and would strike out the third strophe as at least unworthy of a man of Horace's taste. Its realism certainly goes beyond the passage of Euripides (*Fr.* 903) by which perhaps it was suggested:

Χρύσεαι δή μοι πτέρυγες περὶ νώτῳ
καὶ τὰ Σειρήνων πτερόεντα πέδιλ᾽
   ἁρμόζεται,
βάσομαί τ᾽ εἰς αἰθέρα πολὺν ἀερθεὶς,
Ζηνὶ προσμίξων.

The ode is not improbably the result of Horace's first attempt to write an epilogue for the three books, and was relegated to its present subordinate position when he had composed the much supe-

rior poem which now worthily fills that place. — Metre, 176.

1. non usitata : signifying that his fame rests on a new kind of poetry (cf. III. 30. 13); nec tenui : *i.e.* strong, signifying that his fame is secure.

2. biformis : *i.e.* first a man and then a bird. Others, however, following Porphyrio, understand it to refer to Horace's achievements in two departments of poetry (*quod et lyrica scribat et hexametros*).

4. -que : see I. 27. 16 n ; the negatives in vs. 1. belong to the adjectives, and neque morabor conveys an affirmative idea (= *discedam*). — maior, *raised above, superior to ;* the result of success which can no longer be questioned.

5. urbis : more picturesque than *terram ;* cf. I. 35. 10, III. 4. 46.— non ego: cf. I. 18. 11 n; Intr. 116 *g.* —pauperum sanguis parentum: a fact of which Horace was never ashamed even in his younger days (cf. *S.* I. 6. 71 *sqq.*), and which he brings into prominence here as adding lustre to his fame, because it shows that he owed his success solely to his own merits.

6. quem vocas (sc. *ad te*), *whom you invite, i.e.* admit to your

Iam iam residunt cruribus asperae
10   pelles et album mutor in alitem
        superne nascunturque leves
            per digitos umerosque plumae.

Iam Daedaleo notior Icaro
visam gementis litora Bospori
15   Syrtisque Gaetulas canorus
        ales Hyperboreosque campos.

society; the converse of *me petit*,
18. 11 n; cf. *revocas*, S. I. 6.
61. The present expresses customary action. This appears to be
the most probable explanation, but
the expression is vague, and the
suggestion of Bücheler (Rhein.
Mus. XXXVII. p. 238) that *vocare*
is the technical word for the relation of patron to client (*is qui
cluet*) is plausible. In either case
Horace's clear purpose is to recall,
in contrast with his present position (**invidia maior**) and prospect-
ive immortality, his humble origin
and the envy and detraction to
which as the friend of Maecenas
he was subjected in the earlier
part of his career (Intr. 23).

9. **residunt**, *is settling*, owing
to the limbs growing slimmer. —
cruribus: Intr. 69. — **asperae**:
with **residunt**.

10. **pelles**: Intr. 128. — **album
alitem**: see intr. note.

11. **superně**: referring especially to **album**. The -*e* is short
also in Lucr. VI. 544 and 597. —
lēves: in contrast with **asperae**;
Intr. 116 *b*.

13. **Daedaleo Icaro**: cf. *Semeleius Thyoneus*, I. 17. 22 n. The
adjective here virtually includes
the father in the comparison, which
would have been a more fortunate
one if the mention of the son

could have been omitted altogether; the reader can hardly help
remembering the unhappy end of
his flight. — **notior**: for the reading *ocior*, which has the support
of some good manuscripts, see
Intr. 185.

14. **visam**, etc.: signifying that
his poems will be read and sung
in the remotest parts of the earth.
— **gementis Bospori**: cf. *rauci
Hadriae*, 14. 14.

15. **Gaetulas**: for 'African';
cf. Intr. 117 *b*.

16. **Hyperboreos   campos**:
originally a mythical happyland
situated 'beyond Boreas' (*ultra
Aquilonem gens felix, si credimus,
quos Hyperboreos appellavere*, Plin.
N. H. IV. 89), and hence not exposed to his cold blasts, a paradise
of innocence and peace. The myth
was variously located by different
authors, but mostly, in accordance
with the name, in the far North, so
that *hyperboreus* came to be a
poetical term for 'northern,' as
here; cf. Verg. *G.* IV. 517 *hyper-
boreas glacies;* III. 381.

17. **me Colchus**, etc.: the converse of the same idea: 'I shall
visit the remotest lands (13–16), and
their peoples shall learn to know
me (17–20).' Observe further
that the nations named represent
two classes, the barbarians beyond

Me Colchus et qui dissimulat metum
Marsae cohortis Dacus et ultimi
noscent Geloni, me peritus
20   discet Hiber Rhodanique potor.

Absint inani funere neniae
luctusque turpes et querimoniae ;
compesce clamorem ac sepulcri
mitte supervacuos honores.

the frontier and the peoples who
have already come under the
influence of Roman civilization ;
and the verbs (**noscent, discet**)
are chosen with reference to this
distinction.— **dissimulat metum** :
i.e. is afraid, in spite of his bold
front.

18. **Marsae** : cf. I. 2. 39 n. —
Dacus : see I. 26. 4 n. — **ultimi** :
see 18. 4 n.

19. **Geloni** : see 9. 23 n.— **peritus,** *accomplished*. That literature
was already cultivated at this time
in Spain is shown by the number
of poets and prose writers whom
that country began to produce in
the next generation. The Senecas,
Quintilian, Lucan, and Martial
were the most prominent.

20. **Rhodani potor** : the Gaul.
The importance of a great river
to the communities through which
it flows makes the phrase an appropriate one ; cf. 9. 21 *sq.*

21. **absint,** etc. : cf. the epitaph
of Ennius (Cic. *Tusc.* I. 34) :

*Nemo me lacrumis decoret nec fu-
nera fletu | faxit! Cur? Volito
vivus per ora virum.* — **inani** : because there will be no body to
burn.—**funere** : Intr. 70.—**neniae** :
formal *dirges*, chanted usually by
women hired for the purpose
(*praeficae*) ; cf. 1. 38.

22. **luctus** : plural, of various
forms of mourning.— **turpes,** *unseemly*, such as tearing the hair
or face, beating the breast, etc. ;
Intr. 125. This, too, was done by
hired mourners. — **querimoniae** :
of friends and relations.

23. **compesce** : addressed to
Maecenas, as the chief mourner. —
clamorem : the *clamor supremus*
(Ov. *Tr.* III. 3. 43) or wail of sor-
row raised by those present at a
deathbed when life was extinct.

24. **supervacuos** : because his
fame was secure without any material monument ; cf. III. 30. 1.
Horace always uses this form instead of the Ciceronian *supervaca-
neus.*

LIBER TERTIVS

I.

Odi profanum volgus et arceo.
Favete linguis ! Carmina non prius
audita Musarum sacerdos
virginibus puerisque canto.

The six odes with which this book opens are marked by certain characteristics which unite them together as a group and give them a unique and conspicuous place in the collection. In contrast with Horace's usual method of arrangement, they are all in the same metre ; they are addressed, not to any individual, but to all patriotic Romans ; they are furnished with a common introduction, which sets the key for a discourse of unusual dignity and earnestness ; and throughout them all, with whatever license of poetic digression and embellishment, the thought pursues one main theme, — the moral qualities that are indispensable alike to the happiness of the individual and to the strength of the state. For these reasons some critics, ancient and modern, have regarded them, not as separate odes, but as parts of a single poem, and have sought, with much ingenuity, to trace a connection of thought between the close of each and the opening of the next. In this, it must be said, they have not been completely successful : the odes bear the appearance of having been written separately; but they were probably all written about the same time,— the internal evidence points to the period immediately following the political settlement of B.C. 27, when Octavian, with the title of 'Augustus,' was definitely invested with the principate, and Horace's mind was full of visions of the coming regeneration of the state. And there can be no question that Horace designedly arranged the odes, as we find them, in a lyrical sequence, as poems with a common subject and purpose, and gave them here a position worthy of their dignity and importance. Not less certain is the design of the first strophe, in which, with almost startling impressiveness, he steps forward as the priest of the Muses, and, warning off the 'uninitiate herd,' makes his appeal, with solemn earnestness, to those who have ears to hear, and especially to the young, whose hearts are not yet hardened by the vices he is about to attack. Clearly, this is an introduction to the whole series, and does not belong to the first ode alone.

I. After the opening strophe, the poet sets forth the futility of seeking happiness in wealth and power. First, he raises his hearers to a higher point of view, from

5   Regum timendorum in prop os greges,
     reges in ipsos imperium est Iovis,
        clari Giganteo triumpho,
        cuncta supercilio moventis.
     Est ut viro vir latius ordinet

which the human distinctions we
make so much of are seen in truer
perspective: kings sink to the level of their meanest subjects before
the supreme might of Jove; riches,
high birth, fame, influence count
for nothing against the inexorable
allotment of death. Wealth cannot buy, nor power create, the
peace of mind which belongs to
him alone who has learned contentment.— Metre 176.

1. profanum volgus: *i.e.* all
the uninitiated, whose mere presence would defile the holy rite
which the bard is (figuratively)
about to perform (cf. Verg. *A.* VI.
258). They typify the ignorant
multitude, whose stolid minds are
incapable of receiving his teaching.

2. favete linguis: addressed
to those who remain. It means
properly 'Speak only words of
good omen' (cf. 14. 11), but practically (like εὐφημεῖτε) 'Keep reverent silence' (cf. *sacro silentio,* II.
13. 29 n), since laymen could not
be sure what words might have an
unlucky significance. Cf. Aristoph.
Thesmoph. 39 εὔφημος πᾶς ἔστω
λαός, στόμα συγκλήσας.— non
prius audita: the poems belong
to the class called gnomic, for
which the Greeks (*e.g.* Theognis)
commonly used the elegiac metre.
In his use of the Alcaic for this
purpose, as well as in his manner
of dealing with his subject, Horace
might fairly lay claim to originality.

3. Musarum sacerdos: *i.e.*
the inspired mouthpiece of their
teachings. For Horace's view of

the office of the poet as instructor
of youth (virginibus puerisque)
see *Ep.* II. 1. 126 *sqq.*

5. regum, etc.: sc. *imperium
est;* but timendorum is virtually
part of the predicate. The whole
clause is in the nature of a concession : 'Dreadful is the might
of kings to their own subjects,
who tremble as cattle before them;
but' etc. — in : with the accusative
expressing the object on which
power or influence is exercised;
cf. Plaut. *Men.* 1030 *si quid im-
perist in te mihi;* Tac. *Ann.* III.
24. 2 *valida divo Augusto in rem
publicam fortuna.* — greges : not
to be confused with the Homeric
figure of kings as 'shepherds of
the people'; the thought here is
quite the reverse, being complementary to that of timendorum.

7. Giganteo triumpho: cf. II.
1. 16. The unapproachable superiority of Jove's physical power is
summed up in this allusion: To
him whose arm has subdued the
portentous strength of the Giants,
what are the puny kings of men ?

8. cuncta, etc.: the figure is
Homeric (*Il.* I. 528 *sqq.*); cf. Cat.
64. 204 *sqq.*; Verg. *A.* IX. 106.

9. est, *it is true;* a meaning
given to it by its emphatic position, making the sentence concessive, — just as we say 'He *was*
(no doubt) at fault, but etc.,' and
the like. The apodosis begins
with *aequa lege,* 14. For the construction of est ut, see Gr. 332 *a* 3.
— viro vir : Intr. 75. The juxta-
position was a favorite one ; cf.

10   arbusta sulcis, hic generosior
            descendat in Campum petitor,
                moribus hic meliorque fama
        contendat, illi turba clientium
        sit maior : aequa lege Necessitas
15   sortitur insignis et imos,
                omne capax movet urna nomen.

        Destrictus ensis cui super impia
        cervice pendet, non Siculae dapes
            dulcem elaborabunt saporem,
20   non avium citharaeque cantus

Verg. *A.* XI. 632 *implicuere inter se acies legitque virum vir ;* Liv. XXII. 14. 14, etc.—latius ordinet, etc.: *i.e.* is a more extensive land-owner.

10. **arbusta** : *i.e.* vineyards, in which the vines were trained on trees planted at regular intervals (ordinet sulcis); cf. II. 15. 4 n.

11. **descendat** : *sc.* from the hills, where the houses of the better class were situated. — **Campum** : sc. *Martium*, where the elections were held. Observe that the thought here is concerned with the distinctions among men, and not with the political contest, which is introduced only as the scene in which these distinctions are conspicuously displayed.

12. **meliorque** : Intr. 119 *b.*

13. **turba clientium** : in his *atrium* at the *salutatio*, or morning reception, when the clients were expected to call and pay their respects to their patron, or in public, when they escorted him on his way to or from the Forum or the Campus.

14. **aequa** : see I. 4. 13 n, II. 18. 32 ; expressing the main point of contrast with what precedes, it

naturally comes to the front in its own clause. — **Necessitas** : personified, as in I. 35. 17, where she appears as the minister who executes the decrees of Destiny; here and in 24. 6, with special reference to the decree of death to man.

15. **sortitur,** *dooms.*—**insignis:** cf. I. 34. 13

16. **urna** : see II. 3. 26 n.

17. **destrictus ensis,** etc.: *i.e.* this ever-impending presence of death hangs over the godless man like the sword of Damocles, and robs him of all enjoyments in the midst of luxury. The well-known story of Damocles is told by Cicero, *Tusc.* V. 61. — **cui** : Intr. 114. — **super** : cf. I. 9. 5 n. — **impia** : Intr. 124.

18. **Siculae** : *i.e.* such as those served to Damocles. The high living of the Sicilian Greeks was proverbial.

19. **elaborabunt:** implying that his natural appetite is gone. For the prefix, cf. I. 5. 8 n.

20. **avium citharaeque :** artificial devices to induce sleep; cf. *Ep.* I. 2. 31. Aviaries were kept in many wealthy establishments.

> somnum reducent ; somnus agrestium
> lenis virorum non humilis domos
>   fastidit umbrosamque ripam,
>   non zephyris agitata tempe.
>
> 25 Desiderantem quod satis est neque
>   tumultuosum sollicitat mare
>   nec saevus Arcturi cadentis
>   impetus aut orientis Haedi,
>
>   non verberatae grandine vineae
> 30 fundusque mendax, arbore nunc aquas

Maecenas, who suffered from insomnia, resorted to the device of soft music played at a distance (Sen. *de Prov.* 3. 10).

21. reducent: implying that it has deserted him ; cf. *reponi*, 5. 30. Sleep is half personified here, as in the next sentence. — **agrestium virorum** : limiting **domos**, although felt also ἀπὸ κοινοῦ with **somnus** (Intr. 76). The words are drawn away from their grammatical connection towards the head of the sentence for more emphatic contrast with the preceding. Cf. *Epod.* 2. 25 *sqq.* This brings us to the other side of the poet's subject, the contented man, whose happier lot he sets forth in the next two strophes ; cf. Verg. *G.* II. 458 *sqq.*

24. tempe : see I. 7. 4 n ; here it is an appellative, as it had already come to be used by the Greeks (*e.g.* Theocr. I. 67); cf. Cic. *ad Att.* IV. 15. 5, Verg. *G.* II. 469.

25. desiderantem, etc.: cf. *Ep.* I. 2. 46 *sqq.* The man who bounds his desires by his wants is free from the harassing anxieties of avarice, as exemplified in the trader (25–28) and the great land-

owner (29–32). Vss. 27, 28 might also refer to the latter (see Verg. *G.* I. 204 *sq.*), but **non** (29) clearly divides the two instances.

27. Arcturi cadentis : near the end of October ; **cadentis** for *occidentis*, as in *Epod.* 10. 10; Intr. 129.

28. impetus : with reference to the violent storms which accompanied (and were supposed to be caused by) the setting of the constellation. — **orientis Haedi** : in the middle of October ; also regarded as a source of storms ; cf. *nimbosis Haedis*, Ov. *Tr.* I. 11. 13.

29. verberatae vineae : Intr. 105 *a.* Cf. *Ep.* I. 8. 4 *sq.*

30. fundusque mendax: the exasperated cry of the disappointed planter, whose abuse of the farm, as if it were a living thing, is thoroughly human. Cf. *Ep.* I. 7. 87. Personification of the farm, with which the farmer's life was so closely bound up, was very common, as it was very natural; cf. Cic. *de Sen.* 51.— **arbore**: the personification is still kept up: the tree, speaking for itself and its fellows, is always offering some excuse for their shortcomings. **arbore** may stand for the vine (see

culpante, nunc torrentia agros
    sidera, nunc hiemes iniquas.

Contracta pisces aequora sentiunt
    iactis in altum molibus ; huc frequens
35   caementa demittit redemptor
        cum famulis dominusque terrae

fastidiosus : sed timor et minae
    scandunt eodem quo dominus, neque
    decedit aerata triremi et
40   post equitem sedet atra Cura.

I. 18. 1 n), but as this has just been
mentioned, the poet no doubt
has in mind here simply fruit-
bearing trees, and in particular the
olive. — **aquas** : *i.e.* excess of wet
weather.

31. **torrentia**, etc.: *i.e.* drouth,
attributed, like all other meteor-
ological conditions, to the influence of certain constellations. Cf.
29. 17 *sqq.*

33. **contracta**, etc.: cf. II. 18.
20 *sqq.;* III. 24. 3 *sq.* — **pisces
sentiunt** : *i.e.* they find their realm
encroached upon by creatures of
another element. The hyperbole
has been condemned as extravagant by rod-and-line critics, but it
adds a telling stroke to the picture
of wealth making its elaborate
and costly provision for a life of
pleasure: even the bounds which
nature has set offer no check to
these ambitious projects.

34. **molibus** : of stone, to serve
as foundations for the house. —
huc : *i.e. in altum.* — **frequens** :
singular for plural ; cf. Plin. *N. H.*
IX. 180 *ibi frequens hic piscis,* and
the corresponding use of *rarus,*
IV. 1. 34. The use is similar to
that of *multus* (I. 5. 1), *plurimus*
(I. 7. 8 n), etc.

35. **caementa**: broken stones (cf.
caedo) of irregular size and shape,
used to fill the spaces between
the larger blocks. — **redemptor** :
here *builder ;* see II. 18. 18 n.

36. **famulis** : *i.e.* his workmen,
who would naturally be slaves. —
dominus : he too is present, hur-
rying on the work, — showing his
impatient eagerness to realize his
dream of pleasure. — **terrae**: with
fastidiosus ; Intr. 66 *a.*

37. **timor et minae** : hendiadys; the menaces are those which
he sees in the object of his fear.
The thought is the same as that
expressed by the sword of Damocles, above.

38. **scandunt eodem** : he cannot take refuge from them in his
lofty sea-castle.

39. **aerata**, etc.: see II. 16. 21 n,
where the whole thought is the
same as here. — **triremi** : usually
a war vessel, here the large private
yacht of the rich man ; cf. *Ep.* I.
1. 93 *quem ducit priva triremis.*
For the case, see Intr. 70.

40. **atra** : in II. 16. 21, *vitiosa ;*
but the uppermost thought here
is that of death (see I. 28. 13 n).

41. **quod si**, *now if ;* summing
up the preceding considerations ;

Quod si dolentem nec Phrygius lapis
     nec purpurarum sidere clarior
          delenit usus nec Falerna
               vitis Achaemeniumque costum,

45   cur invidendis postibus et novo
          sublime ritu moliar atrium?
               Cur valle permutem Sabina
                    divitias operosiores?

II.

Angustam amice pauperiem pati

cf. I. 1. 35.— dolentem : sc. *me.*
— Phrygius lapis : one of the
rich marbles (see II. 18. 5 n) used
by the Romans in their more
splendid edifices. It was mottled
with red. For this and the following epithets, see Intr. 117 *a.*

42. purpurarum : *i.e.* scarlet
robes and tapestries; cf. II. 18.
8 n.— clarior usus : Intr. 124.
Cf. Verg. *G.* II. 466 *nec casia
liquidi corrumpitur usus olivi.*

43. Falerna vitis : cf. I. 20. 10
and 11 nn.

44. Achaemenium : *i.e.* costly
oriental; cf. *Attalicis condicionibus*
I. 1. 12. For Achaemenes, see II. 12.
21 n.— costum : see II. 3. 13 n.

45. invidendis : cf. II. 10. 7.—
novo ritu, *in the modern style,*
some features of which are indicated, — the handsome marble
portal and the great height of the
atrium (sublime). With the establishment of peace and security under Augustus came a great flow of
capital to the city and a great impetus to the building of ornate private
houses as well as public edifices.
We have here grammatically an
ablative of manner combined with
one of characteristic; but novo

ritu is practically a qualifying ad-
junct of sublime, which is parallel
with invidendis postibus.

46. moliar, *build;* suggesting
a massive, laborious structure;
cf. II. 15. 2; III. 29. 10.— atrium:
see note on *columnas,* II. 18. 4.

47. valle Sabina: Intr. 24. For
the construction, see Intr. 74.

II. In the first ode, the poet's
aim was mainly negative, — to
strip of their glamour the two
most coveted objects of human
endeavor, honor and, more particularly, riches; to show that the
possession of them is but vanity
and vexation of spirit. In the
present ode, he assumes a positive
attitude and proposes a more excellent way. In the cultivation of
character and, in particular, of the
sterling Roman virtues of manli-
ness and loyalty (*virtus* and *fides*),
he points out to the young Roman
the worthy object of a nobler ambition, and one that brings its
own sure reward.— Metre, 176.

1. angustam, etc.: he takes
up the thought where he left it in
the preceding ode : For this life of
contented poverty, let the young

robustus acri militia puer
    condiscat, et Parthos ferocis
        vexet eques metuendus hasta,

5 vitamque sub divo et trepidis agat
    in rebus ; illum ex moenibus hosticis
        matrona bellantis tyranni
           prospiciens et adulta virgo

suspiret, eheu, ne rudis agminum
10 sponsus lacessat regius asperum
    tactu leonem, quem cruenta
        per medias rapit ira caedes.

Dulce et decorum est pro patria mori :

Roman train himself in the hard-ships and perils of warfare, where his ambition is to be a terror to our foes, and his glory to die, if need be, for his country. Cf. IV. 9. 49 *sqq.* — **amice**, *cheerfully, gladly*, as something to be wel-comed. Cf. *clementer ferre, molli-ter ferre* in Cicero, and our 'take kindly.' For the alliteration in this verse, see Intr. 131.

2. **robustus**, *grown sturdy, i.e.* through the sturdiness he has ac-quired. — **militia**: with **robustus**. — **puer**: see I. 9. 16 n.

3. **condiscat**: subjunctive of wish. — **ferocis**, *bold ;* said with a touch of depreciation : our lad shall humble their pride.

4. **eques**, *as a*, etc.

5. **sub divo**: see I. 1. 25 n.

6. **illum**: notice the emphasis, — 'my aspiration for *him* is,' etc. The scene which follows is mod-eled upon *Il.* XXII. 25 *sqq.*, where Priam and Hecuba, watching Achilles from the walls, entreat Hector not to expose himself to a combat with him. — **hosticis**: cf. *civicum*, II. 1. 1 n.

7. **tyranni**: the king whose city is besieged by the Romans. The queen and princess, like the women in the Iliad (III. 141 *sqq.*, XXII. 460 *sqq.*), watch the battle from the ramparts.

9. **eheu**: expressing the woman's sigh ; but what follows is not a quotation of her words.—**ne**, etc.: depending on the notion of fear conveyed by **suspiret**. — **agmi-num**, *of battalions, i.e.* of warfare in general.

10. **sponsus regius** : the son of some neighboring king, be-trothed to the princess. — **aspe-rum tactu** : see I. 37. 26 n.

11. **leonem**: the young Roman warrior. — **cruenta ira** : see Intr. 124.

13. **dulce**, etc.: the connection of thought is this : 'And if such heroic conduct should cost him his life, it is a joyful and glorious privilege; for death comes to every man, whether he face it or flee from it.' Cf. Cic. *Phil.* 14. 31 *o fortunata mors, quae naturae debita pro patria est potissimum reddita !*

mors et fugacem persequitur virum
15   nec parcit imbellis iuventae
            poplitibus timidoque tergo.

Virtus repulsae nescia sordidae
intaminatis fulget honoribus,
        nec sumit aut ponit securis
20   arbitrio popularis aurae ;

virtus recludens immeritis mori
caelum negata temptat iter via,
        coetusque volgaris et udam
            spernit humum fugiente penna.

14. **et,** *as well.* — **persequitur:** the prefix denotes the persistency of the pursuit, — death is ever at his heels, no matter how fast he may run away (cf. vs. 32), and despatches him at last with a wound in the back. Horace had doubtless read in his Simonides (*Fr.* 65) ὁ δ᾽ αὖ θάνατος κίχε καὶ τὸν φυγόμαχον.

15. **imbellis,** *faint-hearted.*

16. **poplitibus,** etc.: cf. Liv. XXII. 48. 4 *aversam adoriuntur Romanam aciem, tergaque ferientes ac poplites caedentes stragem ingentem . . . fecerunt.*

17. **virtus,** *true manhood,* the character of the ideal man (*vir*). The clauses that follow are not designed to describe the attitude of the man of character towards political honors, but to express the inherent nobility of character itself, and the figures borrowed from the political arena are used to mark the superiority of the power which character confers over the coveted prizes of political life : The success of character is sure, with no risk of humiliating defeat; its 'honors' are unsullied by any base practices used in win-

ning them; its power is permanent, and not held for a brief space by the favor of the fickle populace. The same figure is used still more boldly in IV. 9. 39. — **repulsae :** the technical term for defeat as a candidate for office.

18. **fulget :** cf. 16. 31 *fulgentem imperio.* — **honoribus :** cf. I. 1. 8 n.

20. **aurae :** see I. 5. 11 n.

21. **virtus :** Intr. 116 *g.* — **recludens,** etc.: it is manhood, in its highest development, that, at the end of his earthly career, exalts the hero to heaven and makes him a god. The third ode is an expansion and illustration of this text. — **mori :** Intr. 101 *d.*

22. **negata :** *sc.* as a rule, — not open to common men ; cf. *indocili collo,* 3. 14. — **temptat iter :** the conception is here shifted a little ; *virtus,* which in vs. 21 is the power that opens heaven to the hero, is now merged in the personality of the hero himself, as the immortal part of him which rises above earth and death, and finds a way to heaven.

23. **udam :** referring to the rain and fogs of the lower air, and sug-

25   Est et fideli tuta silentio
       merces. Vetabo qui Cereris sacrum
         volgarit arcanae sub isdem
           sit trabibus fragilemque mecum
       solvat phaselon : saepe Diespiter
30   neglectus incesto addidit integrum ;
         raro antecedentem scelestum
           deseruit pede Poena claudo.

gesting by contrast the fine, pure quality of the *aether* above, the abode of the gods.

25. est et, etc.: another maxim from Simonides (*Fr.* 66), ἔστι καὶ σιγᾶς ἀκίνδυνον γέρας, which is said to have been adopted by Augustus (Plutarch *Moral.* 207 D). The virtue of loyalty is coupled with *virtus*, as its complement in those whose lot or whose gifts do not call them to great achievement. There can be no doubt that Horace had Maecenas here chiefly in mind; cf. Prop. IV. 8. 33 *Caesaris et famae vestigia iuncta tenebis ; | Maecenatis erunt vera tropaea fides.* Being merely a negative virtue, the importance of loyalty is best appreciated by contemplating its opposite, the wicked betrayal of trust, on which the poet accordingly dwells, expressing in a vivid way his abhorrence of it, and the certainty that sooner or later it will be overtaken by the just retribution of heaven. Cf. I. 18. 11 *sqq.*

26. Cereris sacrum : *i.e.* the Eleusinian mysteries, used simply as an illustration; Intr. 117 *a*.

27. arcanae, *mystic.* Intr. 125.

28. sit : the subjunctive without *ne* after *veto* is suggested, perhaps, by the familiar form of prohibition, *cave sis.* — **trabibus** : *i.e.* roof. — **fragilem** : suggesting the

opportunity offered to the deity to inflict the merited punishment.

29. phaselon, *yacht,* as in Catullus 4 ; a long, narrow, fast-sailing craft of Egyptian origin, named from its resemblance in shape to the kidney bean (φάσηλος). — **Diespiter** : see I. 1. 25 n, 34. 5.

30. neglectus : cf. 6. 7. The neglect might consist either of failure to recognize his supremacy by due worship and sacrifice (cf. I. 34. 1) or of indifference to his commandments ; more commonly the two would go together. — **incesto**, *impure*, polluted by sin, and hence offensive to the god ; cf. I. 12. 59. — **addidit**, *involves . . . with ;* sc. in the same punishment, such as the fall of the building or the capsizing of the boat. For the tense, see Intr. 80. — **integrum,** *the holy man ;* in meaning (from *in* and root of *tango*) it is the opposite of **incesto.**

31. raro: with **deseruit.**—**antecedentem** : *i.e.* though punishment does not instantly follow the crime ; implying (with **pede claudo**) a feeling of security in the offender.

32. deseruit : *i.e.* is left behind and gives up the pursuit ; cf. II. 16. 22. — **pede claudo** : concessive, whether taken as ablative absolute or ablative of characteristic.

III.

Iustum et tenacem propositi virum
non civium ardor prava iubentium,
non voltus instantis tyranni
mente quatit solida, neque Auster,
5   dux inquieti turbidus Hadriae,
nec fulminantis magna manus Iovis :

III. The poet now reverts to the praise of strong manhood, and develops the thought embodied in the strophes on *virtus* in the preceding ode, the transition from which is so natural that the two odes have been regarded as one, and are so written in some good manuscripts. What was there said of manly character in the abstract is here restated with concrete illustrations. In the fine climax of the first two strophes we see the man of upright character and resolute will stemming the tide of popular passion, braving the threats of power, facing calmly the most violent convulsions of nature. This is the quality, the poet exclaims, which carried the great benefactors of our race through their trials and enabled them to attain heaven at last, — a Hercules, a Pollux, a Bacchus, a Romulus. The last illustration tempts him away from his subject, and he follows his fancy in describing the scene in heaven, when the gods in council consented to admit the founder of Rome to their company. This long description, which occupies the greater part of the ode, is at the end treated playfully by the poet as an unwarranted digression, for which he rebukes his muse ; but it is quite in keeping with the patriotic purpose of these odes, and it serves, like the episode of Regulus in the fifth, to break the monotony of his long moral discourse. The use of the title *Augustus* in vs. 11 shows that the poem was not written before B.C. 27. — Metre, 176.

1. **iustum et tenacem propositi,** *upright and steadfast, i.e.* steadfast in the right; for of course the *propositum* of a *iustus vir* must itself be *iustum.* The quality described (*hac arte,* 9) is *constantia,* one of the cardinal Roman virtues, based on rectitude,—the man who first makes sure the course of action he proposes is right, and then consistently adheres to it.

2. **civium ardor :** Horace may have had in mind the conduct of Socrates at the trial of the nine generals (Xen. *Mem.* I. 1. 18).

3. **tyranni :** the word implies irresponsible, and hence arbitrary power. It is possible that Socrates (under the Thirty Tyrants) was the model for this part of the picture also.

4. **mente :** ablative of respect. —**neque Auster,** etc.: *i.e.* if right impels him, he will go undaunted through storm and flood. What is *audacia* in I. 3. 9 *sqq.* is here *fortitudo.*

5. **dux Hadriae :** cf. I. 3. 15 *arbiter Hadriae;* II. 17. 19. —**turbidus,** *boisterous.*

si fractus inlabatur orbis,
      impavidum ferient ruinae.
    Hac arte Pollux et vagus Hercules
10   enisus arcis attigit igneas,
      quos inter Augustus recumbens
        purpureo bibet ore nectar ;
    hac te merentem, Bacche pater, tuae
      vexere tigres indocili iugum

7. **fractus,** *should break and.*— **orbis :** here used in a wider sense (= *mundus*), the sphere of the heavens ; cf. vs. 53, where *mundus* (like our 'world') is used for the earth only.

9. **hac arte:** see vs. 1 n.—**Pollux:** suggesting also his inseparable twin brother; cf. 29. 64; Verg. *G.* III. 89; Prop. IV. 22. 26.—**vagus:** in reference to the long journeys which his labors entailed.

10. **enisus :** in its literal sense of struggling out of difficulties and hindrances to a position where one is free from them. Cf. Tac. *Ann.* I. 70. 6 *Vitellius in editiora enisus eodem agmen subduxit.* — **arcis,** *heights ;* cf. *aetherias arcis,* Ov. *Tr.* V. 3. 19. — **igneas :** in reference to the stars (called *ignes,* I. 12. 47). Cf. Cic. *Somn. Scip.* 16 *sqq.* '*iustitiam cole et pietatem ...; ea vita via est in caelum et in hunc coetum eorum qui iam vixerunt et corpore relaxati illum incolunt locum quem vides*'—*erat autem is splendidissimo candore inter flammas circulus ...* '*Nonne aspicis quae in templa veneris ? Novem tibi orbibus vel potius globis conexa sunt omnia, quorum unus caelestis est extimus ... in quo sunt infixi illi qui volvuntur stellarum cursus sempiterni.*

11. **quos inter,** etc.: *i.e.* like Pollux and Hercules, the great benefactor of the world in our day will be received, when his work is done, among the gods. Cf. Verg. *G.* I. 24, 503 and *Ep.* II. 1. 5 *sqq.*, where Horace makes the same comparison, writing at a time when the worship of Augustus was already an accomplished fact. However extravagant the compliment may seem to us, and however perfunctory it may have been on Horace's part, there was nothing in it repugnant to Roman religious notions. See the curious discussion of the subject in Tacitus, *Ann.* IV. 38. 4 *sqq.*—**recumbens:** *i.e.* at a banquet: cf. *Ep.* I. 5. 1.

12. **purpureo ore,** *with rosy lips;* the hue of eternal youth, the *lumen iuventae purpureum* (Verg. *A.* I. 590) proper to a god. Cf. Verg. *A.* II. 593.

13. **hac ... hac :** ablatives of cause (unlike *hac arte,* 9), the first with **merentem,** the second with *merens* (with **Quirinus**), suggested by the anaphora: cf. I. 18. 6 n.—**Bacche pater:** cf. I. 18. 6 n.

14. **vexere :** *sc. in caelum,* as the anaphora and **merentem** sufficiently imply. — **tigres :** so, too, Vergil (*A.* VI. 805) and Ovid (*Ars Amat.* I. 550, *Am.* I. 2. 48) ; in Greek poetry and art Bacchus is drawn by panthers. His control of wild beasts typifies his civilizing influence. — **indocili :** cf. *negata,* 2. 22 n.

15   collo trahentes ; hac Quirinus
            Martis equis Acheronta fugit,

       gratum elocuta consiliantibus
       Iunone divis : ' Ilion, Ilion
            fatalis incestusque iudex
20   et mulier peregrina vertit

       in pulverem, ex quo destituit deos
       mercede pacta Laomedon mihi
            castaeque damnatum Minervae
            cum populo et duce fraudulento.

16. **equis :** *i.e.* in his chariot (though the abl. is instrumental); cf. *conscendit equos Gradivus,* Ov. *Met.* XII. 820, where the apotheosis of Romulus is described. See also Liv. I. 16.

17. **gratum** (with **divis**): implying that all the rest were ready to welcome the hero. The poet's object is obviously to show how Rome now enjoys the unanimous favor of the gods, divided as they had been in feeling towards Rome's mother city. Juno voices the sentiments of those who had hated the Trojans. Her speech is thoroughly natural : in yielding all that was desired, she is at great pains to show that she yields nothing at all. Her righteous enmity was against Troy and its perjured people, — her rekindled wrath breaks out in a savage repetition of the name, **Ilion, Ilion ;** but Troy has perished, and her vengeance is satisfied. Let the remnants of the accursed race live and prosper, — if only in exile ; let them extend their sway over the farthest lands and people, — but they must not rebuild Troy. That she dwells at such length and recurs again to this condition, which saves her dignity and her

consistency, is sufficiently explained by the poet's desire to make the scene true to life. Cf. her speech in Verg. *A.* XII. 823 *sqq.*

19. **fatalis :** *i.e.* an instrument in the hands of fate ; referring to iudex only.—**incestus :** cf. 2. 30 n. His sin was in giving his verdict for a bribe in dealing with the gods.— **iudex et mulier :** Paris and Helen. The goddess in her lofty scorn cannot take their names on her lips ; so again below, vss. 25 *sq.*

20. **vertit :** cf. Verg. *A.* I. 20 ; Intr. 129.

21. **ex quo,** *ever since ;* defining the time of **damnatum.** — **deos :** Poseidon and Apollo, who served him for a year, one building the walls of the city, the other keeping his flocks, according to *Il.* XXI. 446 *sqq.* According to another myth, which Horace appears to have in mind in vs. 66, Apollo built the wall ; cf. Verg. *G.* III. 36 *Troiae Cynthius auctor.*

23. **damnatum,** *forfeited,* given over to our vengeance. See Roby 1199.—**Minervae :** against whom, with Juno, the judgment of Paris had gone.

24. **duce :** Laomedon, at the time ; but the doom actually fell on his son Priam.

25   Iam nec Lacaenae splendet adulterae
        famosus hospes nec Priami domus
            periura pugnacis Achivos   •
                Hectoreis opibus refringit,

        nostrisque ductum seditionibus
30   bellum resedit : protinus et gravis
            iras et invisum nepotem,
                Troica quem peperit sacerdos,

        Marti redonabo ; illum ego lucidas
            inire sedes, discere nectaris
35   sucos et adscribi quietis
                ordinibus patiar deorum.

25. **adulterae** : dative ; cf. *quibus nites*, I. 5. 12.

26. **famosus**, *notorious* (*sc.* as a *hospes*). — **nec**, *no longer* (from the influence of **iam**, which belongs to both clauses).

28. **opibus** : here equivalent to *viribus;* cf. IV. 4. 60.— **refringit**, *shatters;* more commonly used in prose of breaking down an obstacle ; here, of presenting so firm a resistance that the assailing force is shattered upon it. Cf. the use of *debilitat*, I. 11. 5, and Prop. IV. 3. 44 *Teutonicas Roma refringit opes*.

29. **ductum**, *prolonged*.

30. **resedit** : a very expressive word : the 'storm of war' has given way to a calm. — **protinus** : rather logical than temporal in meaning,—she is completely satisfied and waits for nothing further.

31. **nepotem**: Romulus, as son of her son Mars ; **invisum**, for the reason given in the next verse; she will not make him suffer for the sins of his race, but she cannot love him.

32. **Troica** : see I. 2. 17 n. — **sacerdos** : as a Vestal.

33. **redonabo** : see II. 7. 3 n. The word is here employed, however, in the sense of 'giving up' rather than 'giving back' (cf. I. 3. 7 n), and is made to serve for both objects, **iras** and **nepotem** : she will give up, in favor of Mars, her displeasure, and she will give up to him her grandson, whom she might withhold.— **illum**: emphatic; against *him* she harbors no resentment. — **lucidas** : see vs. 10 n.

34. **discere**, *to taste ;* lit. to become acquainted with (an object previously unknown), as in II. 20. 20. — **nectaris** : genitive of nearer definition ; Gr. 214 *f*.

35. **sucos**: Intr. 128. — **et**: connecting the second and third infinitives, as expressing what took place after Romulus had entered heaven, more closely with one another than with the first, which expresses the entrance itself. Cf. *Ep.* I. 7. 53 and 55. — **adscribi ordinibus**: both words are borrowed from the Roman political and military systems. — **quietis** : their normal condition. In contrast with *seditionibus*, above, it expresses the

Dum longus inter saeviat Ilion
Romamque pontus, qualibet exsules
    in parte regnanto beati ;
40   dum Priami Paridisque busto

insultet armentum et catulos ferae
celent inultae, stet Capitolium
    fulgens triumphatisque possit
      Roma ferox dare iura Medis ;

45 horrenda late nomen in ultimas
extendat oras, qua medius liquor
    secernit Europen ab Afro,
      qua tumidus rigat arva Nilus.

goddess' desire for peace. The beautiful rhythm enhances the impression of serene existence which the words convey.

37. **inter saeviat** : Intr. 115 *c*.

38. **exsules**, *in exile ;* limiting the concession in **qualibet**.

39. **regnanto**: concessive ; cf. *occupato*, 29. 44 n.

40. **busto**: ablative of place (Intr. 69) with **insultet** (used absolutely; cf. Verg. *A.* XI. 599 *fremit aequore toto insultans*) and **celet**. When these lines were written, Vergil had not yet published the Aeneid and fixed for all time the legend of the death of Priam (*iacet ingens litore truncus | avolsumque umeris caput et sine nomine corpus, A.* II. 557); so that there was no preconceived notion in the minds of Horace's readers (as there is in ours) to deter him from introducing a crumbling tomb of the Trojan king to complete his picture of desolation and to make a more striking contrast with the splendor of the Capitol.

42. **stet Capitolium** : see 30. 8 n.

43. **fulgens**: in reference to its gilded roof ; cf. Verg. *A.* VIII. 347 *Capitolia . . . | aurea nunc, olim silvestribus horrida dumis.* — **triumphatis**, *to lead in triumph and ;* proleptic. — **possit**, *have the power to ;* the event had not yet justified prophecy in going any further than this.

44. **dare iura** : the act of an absolute sovereign ; cf. Liv. I. 8. 1 (of Romulus) *vocata ad concilium multitudine, quae coalescere in populi unius corpus nulla re praeterquam legibus poterat, iura dedit.* — **Medis** : see I. 2. 22 n.

45. **horrenda**, *spreading terror.* —**late**: with **horrenda**.—**nomen**: *i.e.* her political power; cf. *Latinum nomen,* IV. 15. 13.

46. **qua . . . qua**, *where, on the one side, . . . where, on the other ;* so *qua parte . . . qua,* below (55 *sq.*). — **medius liquor** : the straits of Gibraltar.

47. **Afro** : the name of the inhabitant standing for the country. The plural is more common in this use; cf. IV. 4. 63; Intr. 127.

48. **tumidus rigat** : referring

Aurum inrepertum et sic melius situm,
50   cum terra celat, spernere fortior
quam cogere humanos in usus
omne sacrum rapiente dextra,

quicumque mundo terminus obstitit,
hunc tanget armis, visere gestiens
55   qua parte debacchentur ignes,
qua nebulae pluviique rores.

Sed bellicosis fata Quiritibus
hac lege dico, ne nimium pii
rebusque fidentes avitae
60   tecta velint reparare Troiae.

to its annual inundation, on which
the fertility of Egypt depends.

49. **aurum**, etc.: at this point
the goddess, catching for a moment the inspiration of her theme,
changes from assent to prophecy
(*tanget*, 54, after *stet, possit, extendat;* cf. also *fata dico*, 57), and
she warms with admiration for the
moral fortitude of the Roman,
which will enable him to triumph
over all obstacles. As prophecy, this
refers to the best times of the commonwealth ; to Horace's readers it
was designed to convey a lesson, to
point out the condition of future
success. — **inrepertum** : *i.e.* not
sought for, though known to exist.

50. **spernere** : Intr. 101 *a*, 102.
— **fortior**, *showing her courage
more in.*

51. **cogere**, *gathering* (*it*). —
humanos in usus (with **rapiente**), etc.: describing the opposite
disposition, — one that shrinks
from nothing in the mad race for
riches. **humanos** is in contrast
with **sacrum**.

52. **omne**: *i.e.* all without distinction, any and every; cf. I. 3. 25 n.

53. **mundo** : see note on *orbis*,
7. — **obstitit** : perf. definite (from
obsisto) expressing a present state
(= *obstat*); cf. *constiterint*, I. 9. 4.

54. **visere**: cf. I. 37. 25 n, II. 15. 3.

55. **qua parte**, etc.: cf. I. 22. 17
sqq. nn.—**debacchentur**, *revel unrestrained, i.e.* have full sway, with
no counteracting forces to moderate them, as in the temperate zone.
For this intensive force of *de-*, cf.
I. 9. 11 n, and *Ep.* I. 3. 14 *desaevit.*
The subjunctive indicates that
these clauses are part of the wish
(**gestiens**).

56. **pluvii rores** : although *ros*
is used by the poets for water in
general (*e.g.* 4. 61), the phrase is
here a singularly happy one to express the persistent 'drizzle' which
is so prominent a feature of the
weather in some parts of northern
Europe during a considerable portion of the year.

57. **sed** : the goddess closes
with an emphatic reiteration of
the terms of her concession. —
fata : see vs. 49 n.

58. **hac lege dico** : implying
that she had some control over

Troiae renascens alite lugubri
    fortuna tristi clade iterabitur,
        ducente victricis catervas
            coniuge me Iovis et sorore.

65   Ter si resurgat murus aeneus
        auctore Phoebo, ter pereat meis
            excisus Argivis, ter uxor
                capta virum puerosque ploret.'

Non hoc iocosae conveniet lyrae :
70   quo, musa, tendis ?   Desine pervicax
        referre sermones deorum et
            magna modis tenuare parvis.

their destiny. *Fatum* (from *fari*)
is originally nothing but the expressed will (*quod semel dictum
est, C. S.* 26) of Jove or of some
other divinity; cf. *fato divom*, Verg.
A. VII. 50, and see Preller-Jordan,
Röm. Myth. II. 194. — ne . . .
velint : in apposition with lege.
— pii : here of devotion to ancestors (avitae).

59. fidentes : also modified by
nimium. The expression implies
that in entertaining such a desire
they would *consciously* incur danger
(cf. I. 3. 25), — that of undertaking
to undo what the gods had done.

61. Troiae : Intr. 116 *e.* — renascens, etc.: sc. *si renascetur.*
The protasis, already implied in
the preceding strophe, is again
suggested by renascens, which is
itself, however, a part of the conclusion. — alite lugubri : cf. *mala
avi*, I. 15. 5 n.

62. fortuna, *the career.*

64. coniuge et sorore : cf.
Verg. *A.* I. 47.   Intr. 116 *b.*

65. ter, etc.: cf. Verg. *G.* I. 281,
283.   Intr. 116 *b* and *f.* — aeneus
auctore Phoebo : of the very
strongest material and with a divine
architect. For Phoebus, see above,
21 n. — meis : see I. 7. 8 n.

67. Argivis : Intr. 55.

69. non hoc, etc.: the poet
breaks off as if suddenly conscious
that he is trespassing with his
playful lyre on epic ground.   Cf.
II. 1. 37 *sqq.*   The tone in which
he rebukes his headstrong muse
is hardly in keeping with his character as *Musarum sacerdos*, and
indicates that the ode was originally written independently.—conveniet : the future is natural, just
as we say ' this will never do,' and
the like.

72. tenuare : cf. I. 6. 12 n. —
parvis, *petty;* cf. 25. 17 ; IV. 2.
27 *sqq.*

IV.

Descende caelo et dic age tibia
regina longum Calliope melos,
    seu voce nunc mavis acuta,
        seu fidibus citharave Phoebi.

5 Auditis, an me ludit amabilis
    insania?   Audire et videor pios
        errare per lucos, amoenae
            quos et aquae subeunt et aurae.

IV. With a fresh invocation and a renewed declaration of his loyalty to the service of the Muses, the poet proceeds in this ode to inculcate the supremacy of mind over brute force, of strength tempered with wisdom over ungoverned violence. This gentle wisdom is the gift of the Muses to men. This is their gift to Caesar, — this, and not merely diversion and refreshment, — when he leads his veterans home from war. The victory of Jove over the Titans and Giants, which Horace cites as an illustration of his precepts, could not fail to be understood by his readers as typical of the victory of Augustus, the champion of order and culture, over the turbulent forces of anarchy and civil strife. — Metre, 176.

1. descende caelo: the Muses were conceived as dwelling in heaven ('Ολύμπια δώματ' ἔχουσαι, *Il.* II. 484), though having, like other divinities, their favorite haunts on earth. — caelo: Intr. 70. — dic age: cf. I. 32. 3, II. 11. 22. For the meaning of dic, see I. 6. 5 n. — tibia, etc.: see I. 1. 32, 34; 12. 1 n. For the case, see note on *fide Teia*, I. 17. 18.

2. regina: expressing the poet's homage; cf. III. 30. 14 *sqq.*, IV. 3.

The title, like ἄνασσα and δέσποινα in Greek, was a common form of honorary address to a goddess; cf. III. 26. 11. — longum: he prays for, not a brief or fitful, but a long-sustained inspiration. — Calliope: see note on *Clio*, I. 12. 2.

3. seu: see I. 4. 12 n. — voce: *i.e.* without instrumental accompaniment.

4. fidibus citharave: on a Greek vase preserved in Munich are figures of the nine muses, of whom two are playing on the *lyra* and the *cithara* respectively (Baumeister, p. 1544), and two on *tibiae*, while one is apparently singing (cf. voce) from a scroll. — Phoebi: as being its inventor. The lyre (fidibus) was invented by Mercury; cf. I. 10. 6.

5. auditis: sc. *melos;* the divine melody that fills his soul comes with such vividness that at first he doubts whether it is not real music.

6. audire et videor (sc. *mihi*): see Intr. 119 *a*, and cf. II. 1. 21.— pios, *holy;* hallowed by the presence of the Muses and undefiled by the contact of the crowd; cf. I. 1. 30 *sqq.*

7. amoenae: Intr. 114.

8. quos subeunt, '*neath which course.*

Me fabulosae Volture in Apulo
10   nutricis extra limen Apuliae
    ludo fatigatumque somno
        fronde nova puerum palumbes

    texere, mirum quod foret omnibus,
    quicumque celsae nidum Acherontiae
15   saltusque Bantinos et arvum
        pingue tenent humilis Forenti,

9. **me**: the emphasis here marks the connection with what precedes, not by way of contrast (as in I. 1. 29, 7. 10, etc.), but of explanation. That he could hear the divine strains, inaudible to others, was in keeping with his constant experience of the muses' favor. In recalling his marvelous preservation in childhood, — the incident may very well have been a real one, though given to us with poetical embellishment, — Horace had in mind, perhaps, the stories told of the infancy of some of the Greek poets, — as of Stesichorus, on whose lips a nightingale was said to have alighted and sung; of Pindar, whose lips, in his sleep, were bathed with honey by the bees. — **fabulosae**: with **palumbes**, a connection indicated by their being joined with **me** and **puerum** respectively (Intr. 112). For the meaning, cf. I. 22. 7 n; they are the doves 'of story,' the birds of Venus, which draw her car and carry ambrosia to Jove (*Odys.* XII. 63).

10. **Apuliae**: the text is almost certainly wrong here, and no satisfactory correction has been proposed. Apart from the improbability of the substantive following so closely upon its adjective, the double change of prosody from Ăpŭlo to Ăpūliae has a very suspicious look, and the second form finds poor support in the uncertain *Ăpūlicum* of 24. 4. Some other word, in all probability, originally stood at the end of verse 10, and has been displaced and lost by the blunder of a copyist whose eye was caught by the word **Apulo** above it. See Crit. App.

11. **fatigatum**, *overcome.* For the position of **-que**, see Intr. 119 *b.* For the *fatigatum* to be supplied with **ludo**, a somewhat different translation will be necessary.

12. **nova**, *fresh; i.e.* green, plucked for the purpose.

13. **mirum quod foret omnibus**, *a marvel to all;* characteristic relative clause; cf. *Epod.* 2. 28 n. The subject of **mirum foret** is (through **quod**) the preceding sentence, but it is expanded in the interrogative clauses which follow in the next strophe, *ut tuto*, etc.

14. **quicunque**, etc.: *i.e.* all within a range of a dozen or fifteen miles, — implying that many witnesses could be called to confirm the story. The places are briefly characterized, Acherontia as perched on a hill, Bantia among the mountain pastures, Forentum in fertile lowland. They have left their names to the modern Acerenza, Banzi, and Forenza.

ut tuto ab atris corpore viperis
    dormirem et ursis, ut premerer sacra
    lauroque conlataque myrto,

20   non sine dis animosus infans.

Vester, Camenae, vester in arduos
    tollor Sabinos, seu mihi frigidum
    Praeneste seu Tibur supinum

25   seu liquidae placuere Baiae.

Vestris amicum fontibus et choris
    non me Philippis versa acies retro,
    devota non exstinxit arbor,

          nec Sicula Palinurus unda.

17. **ut**: with *mirum*, 13; see
note above, and cf. *Epod.* 16. 53.
— **atris**, *deadly;* see I. 28. 13 n,
and cf. Verg. *G.* I. 129 *ille malum
virus serpentibus addidit atris.*

18. **premerer**, *I was covered
all over;* cf. *Epod.* 1. 33. — **sacra**:
to Phoebus, as the myrtle was to
Venus. Both **sacra** and **conlata**
are to be taken with each of the
substantives; see Intr. 121.

19. **-que . . . -que**: cf. I. 26.
12. — **conlata**: *i.e.* not at hap-
hazard, but showing design.

20. **non sine dis**: in reference
to **animosus**; the child's courage
came from no human inspiration.
Cf. *Il.* V. 185 οὐχ ὅ γ' ἄνευθε θεοῦ
τάδε μαίνεται, ἀλλά τις ἄγχι | ἕστηκ'
ἀθανάτων.

21. **vester . . . vester . . . tollor**,
yours I am, . . . yours, when I climb.
The emphatic **vester** expresses
both their choice of him and his
surrender to them. Theirs he is
always and everywhere; under
their protection he has escaped
from imminent peril in the past,
with them he will cheerfully face
any dangers in the future.

22. **Sabinos**: see II. 18. **14 n;**
it may mean here, however, merely
the country.— **frigidum**: from its
high situation (*altum Praeneste*,
Verg. *A.* VII. 682).

23. **supinum**: cf. Juv. 3. 192
proni Tiburis. Both Praeneste
and Tibur were favorite resorts of
Horace; cf. I. 7. 11 *sqq.*, II. 6.
5 *sqq.*, *Ep.* I. 2. 2, 7. 45.

24. **liquidae**: probably referring to the atmosphere. — **placuere**, *attract.* — **Baiae**: see II. 18.
20 n; for Horace's visits to it, cf.
Ep. I. 15. 2 *sqq.*

25. **vestris**: Intr. 116 *g.*— **amicum**, *welcome;* see I. 26. 1 n. —
fontibus: cf. I. 26. 6 n.

26. **Philippis**: cf. II. 7. 9; Intr.
12. — **versa acies**: Intr. 105 *a.*

27. **arbor**: cf. II. 13; 17. 27.

28. **Palinurus**: a promontory
of Lucania, named, according to
Vergil, after the pilot of Aeneas
(*A.* VI. 381). The natural inference from the allusion is, that
Horace had had a narrow escape
from shipwreck off this point; but
we know nothing of the circumstances. See, however, Intr. 13.

Vtcumque mecum vos eritis, libens

30   insanientem navita Bosporum

     temptabo et urentis harenas

       litoris Assyrii viator ;

visam Britannos hospitibus feros

et laetum equino sanguine Concanum,

35   visam pharetratos Gelonos

     et Scythicum inviolatus amnem.

Vos Caesarem altum, militia simul

fessas cohortis abdidit oppidis,

     finire quaerentem labores

40   Pierio recreatis antro.

---

29. **utcumque :** see I. 17. 10 n.

30. **Bosporum :** cf. II. 13. 14.

32. **litoris Assyrii :** used vaguely of the far East, — the shore of the Persian gulf or Indian ocean ; cf. II. 11. 16 n. — **viator,** *a wayfarer ;* in contrast with **navita.**

33. **hospitibus feros :** Horace probably means that they sacrificed them, as they did their captives (Tac. *Ann.* XIV. 30). Human sacrifices were a part of their druidical rites, according to Tacitus.

34. **Concanum:** one of the Cantabrian tribes (see II. 6. 2 n). The practice here attributed to them was a Scythian custom ; cf. Verg. *G.* III. 461 *Gelonus cum . . . lac concretum cum sanguine potat equino.*

35. **Gelonos :** see II. 9. 23 n.

36. **Scythicum amnem :** the Tanais (Don) ; cf. *Medum flumen,* II. 9. 21.

37. **vos :** continuing the emphasis in *vester* and *vestris,* above. The anaphora keeps prominent the main idea of the ode, the intellectual activity inspired and fostered by the Muses, — here as affording refreshment after the

physical fatigue of war ; in the next strophe as subduing the fierce passions engendered by strife, and restoring the calm control of reason. — **altum,** *august ;* cf. *S.* II. 5. 62 ; Verg. *A.* X. 875 *altus Apollo.*

38. **abdidit :** aptly expressing the disappearance from public view of the formidable army of 120,000 men which threatened the peace of Italy when the victor returned after Actium.

39. **finire quaerentem:** implying a distaste for war and a longing for peace. For the inf., see Intr. 94 *c.*

40. **Pierio antro:** *i.e.* by literary study or conversation in some quiet retreat. Grottos, however, were actually used for entertainments ; cf. Tac. *Ann.* IV. 59. Donatus (*Vita Verg.* 27) tells us that, on his way home from the East in B.C. 29, Octavian spent some time at Atella, in Campania, to recuperate, and there listened during four days to the Georgics, then just finished, which were read to him by Vergil and Maecenas. His taste for literature is attested by Suetonius (*Aug.* 84. 85). For

Vos lene consilium et datis et dato
  gaudetis, almae.   Scimus ut impios
    Titanas immanemque turbam
      fulmine sustulerit caduco

45   qui terram inertem, qui mare temperat
  ventosum et urbis regnaque tristia
    divosque mortalisque turmas
      imperio regit unus aequo.

Magnum illa terrorem intulerat Iovi
50   fidens iuventus horrida bracchiis,
    fratresque tendentes opaco
      Pelion imposuisse Olympo.

Pierio, see I. 12. 6 n. Cf. also
Dionaeo antro, II. 1. 39.

  41. **vos:** see 37 n. — **lene consilium :** in allusion to the moderate policy pursued by Augustus
after his victory. For the synaeresis in **consilium,** see Intr. 181.

  42. **gaudetis :** implying that
their teaching is accepted, with
beneficent results; otherwise they
would have no cause to rejoice.
This thinly veiled commendation
of Augustus continues to be the underlying thought of what follows,
where the poet cites in support of
his thesis a well-known (**scimus**)
example. — **ut :** cf. vs. 17.

  43. **Titanas,** etc. : Horace is
not careful to distinguish the
Titans from the Giants. — **imma-
nem :** alluding to the monstrous
shapes of the Giants.   On the
great altar at Pergamon, which
Horace possibly had seen (Intr.
12), they are represented in a variety of grotesque forms, in which
the human figure is combined with
that of other animals (Baumeister,
p. 1252). — **-que:** epexegetical, *and
all the.*

  44. **caduco,** *descending ;* καται-
βάτης κεραυνός, Aesch. *Prom.* 359.

  45. **qui,** etc.: the triple contrast,
suggesting the manifold variety of
detail in the universe which Jove
controls, conveys a livelier impression of his power ; **inertem** (cf.
II. 9. 5, and *bruta tellus et vaga
flumina,* I. 34. 9) is contrasted
with **ventosum; urbis** (where life
is fullest and richest) with **regna
tristia,** the abode of the dead ;
divos (the immortals) with **mortalis turmas** (the ranks of mortal
men).   The objects of **temperat**
are **terram** and **mare,** which stand
for inanimate nature ; with the
remaining objects, which represent
sentient beings, **regit** is used.

  49. **terrorem :** cf. II. 12. 7.

  50. **fidens :** best taken absolutely. — **iuventus :** the Hecaton-
cheires or hundred-handed (**horrida bracchiis**) sons of Uranus
and Gaea.   In the ordinary form
of the myth in Greek writers these
three brothers take the side of Zeus.

  51. **fratres :** the Aloidae, Otus
and Ephialtes ; *Odys.* XI. 308,
Verg. *A.* VI. 582.

Sed quid Typhoeus et validus Mimas,
aut quid minaci Porphyrion statu,
55   quid Rhoetus evolsisque truncis
Enceladus iaculator audax
contra sonantem Palladis aegida
possent ruentes?   Hinc avidus stetit
Volcanus, hinc matrona Iuno et
60   numquam umeris positurus arcum,
qui rore puro Castaliae lavit
crinis solutos, qui Lyciae tenet

52. Pelion, etc.: cf. *Odys.* XI.
315 "Οσσαν ἐπ' Οὐλύμπῳ μέμασαν
θέμεν, αὐτὰρ ἐπ' "Οσσῃ | Πήλιον
εἰνοσίφυλλον, ἵν' οὐρανὸς ἀμβατὸς εἴη·
Verg. *G.* I. 280; Prop. II. 1. 19.—
imposuisse: Intr. 81 *b*.

53. Typhoeus, etc.: Horace's
picture of the Gigantomachia is
conceived on a less portentous
scale than in some forms of the
myth, in which the combatants
hurl mountains and islands at one
another. Here, as in II. 19. 21 *sqq.*,
we must imagine an assault on
Olympus, and the gods fighting
side by side like Homeric warriors.
— **Typhoeus**: the youngest of
the sons of Gaea, and the strongest
and most terrible of them, sent by
his mother to take vengeance on
the gods for their destruction of
the Giants (or, in Hesiod, of the
Titans).   Here he is not distinguished from the rest of the
Giants. — **Mimas**: a Giant.

54. Porphyrion: βασιλεὺς Γι-
γάντων, Pind. *Pyth.* 8. 17.— **statu**,
posture.

55. Rhoetus: see II. 19. 23.—
truncis: instrumental abl. with the
verbal idea in **iaculator**; Intr. 73.

56. Enceladus: imprisoned under Etna; Verg. *A.* III. 578.

57. contra, etc.: to be taken
with **possent**, though understood
also with **ruentes**. — **sonantem**:
from being shaken by the goddess
herself, to inspire terror. In Homer
the crash of thunder is associated
with the shaking of the aegis by
Zeus (*Il.* XVII. 595).— **aegida**:
see I. 15. 11 n.

58. hinc . . . hinc: *i.e.* ranged
on either side of Pallas, who is the
central figure; the goddess of
wisdom is the foremost champion.
— **avidus**: sc. *pugnae;* so Tac.
Ann. I. 51. 1 *avidas legiones.*

60. numquam positurus: *i.e.*
forever armed and prepared; see
Intr. 104 *a*, and cf. *ponere*, I. 3. 40.
In the following strophe the poet
allows us to pause and contemplate the beautiful god, as a relief
from the stern conflict and the
grave thoughts it suggests. Cf. I.
12. 29 n.

61. Castaliae: a spring on Par-
nassus.— **lavit crinis**: cf. IV. 6. 26.
For **lavit**, see II. 3. 18 n.

62. solutos: cf. I. 21. 2 n.—
tenet: *sc.* under his sway; cf. 26. 9
(= I. 3. 1), *C. S.* 69; here, however,
used more with reference to the
abode of the god (cf. vs. 16).   Horace follows the legend which made

dumeta natalemque silvam,
Delius et Patareus Apollo.

65   Vis consili expers mole ruit sua :
vim temperatam di quoque provehunt
in maius ; idem odere viris
omne nefas animo moventis.

Testis mearum centimanus Gyas
70   sententiarum, notus et integrae
temptator Orion Dianae,
virginea domitus sagitta.

Iniecta monstris Terra dolet suis,
maeretque partus fulmine luridum
75   missos ad Orcum ; nec peredit
impositam celer ignis Aetnen,

Apollo spend the six winter months at Patara, in Lycia, where he had a famous temple and oracle, and the summer in Delos (Serv. on *Aen.* IV. 143). The reference to these two places is repeated chiastically in the epithets of vs. 64.

63. **natalem** : see I. 21. 2 n.

65. **vis**, etc.: this strophe at once sums up the moral of the story,—the ineffectiveness of force without intelligence, — and advances the thought a step farther : divine favor promotes force that is under control ; divine wrath overtakes the strength that pursues its selfish ends unrestrained by any controlling principle ; and with illustrations of this truth the poem closes.

68. **omne** : cf. 3. 52 n.

69. **testis** : sc. *est;* cf. *scimus*, 42. — **Gyas** : see II. 17. 14 n and vs. 50 n, above.

70. **notus** : another appeal to the reader's knowledge, as in 42.

— **integrae** : cf. *intactae Palladis*, I. 7. 5.

71. **temptator**, *assailant;* the word is found only here in classical literature. — **Orion** : here classed among the Giants; by others he is made a son of Poseidon. See II. 13. 39 n.

72. **virginea**: cf. *Hectoreis opibus*, 3. 28.

73. **monstris suis** : *i.e.* the Giants. — **Terra** : cf. *Telluris*, II. 12. 7 ; both for Γαῖα or Γῆ, who was the mother of both Titans and Giants. In some representations of the battle of the Giants she appears rising from the ground, pleading for her offspring ; see Baumeister, figg. 637, 1420. — **dolet, maeret** : the first of the pain of lying upon them (**iniecta**), the second of her grief for their calamity.

74. **partus** : more particularly the Titans, who were hurled into Tartarus (Verg. *A.* VI. 580), though Tityus, the example given

incontinentis nec Tityi iecur
reliquit ales, nequitiae additus
    custos ; amatorem trecentae
80   Pirithoum cohibent catenae.

V.

Caelo tonantem credidimus Iovem
regnare : praesens divus habebitur
    Augustus adiectis Britannis
        imperio gravibusque Persis.

below, was a Giant (*Odys.* XI. 576).
— **luridum Orcum** : cf. *furvae Proserpinae*, II. 13. 21.

75. **nec peredit** : *i.e.* the imprisoned Giant has found no release ; his punishment is eternal. For the tense, see Intr. 80.

76. **impositam** : *sc.* on one of the Giants. Enceladus, Typhoeus, and Briareus are consigned by various myths to this fate. — **celer**, *swift consuming.*

77. **incontinentis** : his offense was offering violence to Latona.— **nec** : Intr. 114.— **iecur** : the punishment was aimed at what was regarded as the seat of the passion; cf. IV. 1. 12.

78. **ales** : a vulture (Verg. *A.* VI. 597).— **additus custos**, *set to keep watch upon.*

79. **trecentae** : used simply to express a very large number ; cf. II. 14. 5, 26 ; *S.* I. 5. 12.

80. **Pirithoum** : king of the Lapithae and friend of Theseus, who accompanied him to the lower world on his impious enterprise of carrying off Proserpina. Both were chained to a rock there, and Hercules, who succeeded in releasing Theseus, was obliged to leave Pirithous to his doom. Cf. IV. 7. 27.

V. From the contemplation of Jove triumphantly maintaining his supremacy in heaven the poet leads our thoughts down to earth again, where Augustus has a divine mission to fulfill in restoring the old Roman valor and the glory of Roman arms. Courage and patriotism in the soldier have sunk to a low ebb, — the legitimate result of relaxation of the stern discipline of earlier times, which is finely portrayed in the story of Regulus. — Metre, 176.

1. **caelo** : with **regnare** ; Intr. 69.— **credidimus** : Intr. 80.

2. **praesens**, *on earth.* Augustus is placed in the same relation to Jove as in I. 12. 57 *sqq.*

3. **adiectis** : equivalent to *cum adiecerit.*—**Britannis** : see introd. note to I. 35.

4. **gravibus Persis** : see I. 2. 22 n. In passages like this Horace no doubt voiced the general feeling that Augustus should justify his leadership by completing the conquests of Julius Caesar, and, above all, should retrieve the repeated disasters which the Romans had suffered at the hands of the Parthians. The recollection of these disasters leads naturally to the reflections that follow.

5   Milesne Crassi coniuge barbara
    turpis maritus vixit et hostium
        (pro curia inversique mores !)
            consenuit socerorum in armis,

    sub rege Medo Marsus et Apulus,
10 anciliorum et nominis et togae
        oblitus aeternaeque Vestae,
            incolumi Iove et urbe Roma?

    Hoc caverat mens provida Reguli
    dissentientis condicionibus
15   foedis et exemplo trahenti
            perniciem veniens in aevum,

5. **milesne Crassi**: the defeat
at Carrhae, B.C. 53, left thousands
of Romans in the hands of the
Parthians, and subsequent events
brought them no prospect of release. They took service in the
Parthian armies and even fought
against the Romans. — **coniuge
barbara** : abl. of cause with **turpis** ; Intr. 105 *a*.

6. **vixit** : in close connection
with **turpis maritus** : 'Has he
consented to *live* at the cost of
such humiliation ? '

7. **curia**: the symbol of Roman
law and sovereignty. — **mores,**
discipline.

8. **socerorum,** *whose daughter
he has wedded ;* dwelling with
scorn on the odious relation already expressed in **coniuge barbara** and **maritus.**

9. **sub rege** : a hateful suggestion, even without **Medo.** —
Marsus et Apulus : the best
types of the Roman soldier ; cf.
I. 2. 39 n, II. 20. 18, I. 22. 13.

10. **anciliorum,** etc.: the twelve
sacred shields in the keeping of
the Salii (see I. 36. 12 n), closely

associated, therefore, with the
foundation of the city, and, like
the fire of Vesta, with its perma-
nence. — **nominis** : the evidence
of his birthright. — **togae** : the
badge of his citizenship.

12. **Iove** : *i.e.* his temple, the
Capitol.

13. **hoc** : emphatic : *It was just
this that.* — **Reguli** : consul B.C.
256, in the first Punic war.   In
that year the Romans successfully
invaded Africa, and in the following year Regulus, who was left in
command there, was defeated and
taken prisoner with a part of his
army.   According to the story
which Horace here follows, he
was subsequently sent by the Carthaginians to Rome to negotiate
for an exchange of prisoners, under
oath to return to Carthage if the
negotiations should fail.

14. **dissentientis,** *when he refused his assent.*   On reaching
Rome Regulus persuaded the
senate to reject the overtures
which he brought. — **condicionibus** : dative ; Intr. 57.

15. **exemplo,** *a precedent.* —

. si non periret immiserabilis
captiva pubes.   'Signa ego Punicis
    adfixa delubris et arma
20   militibus sine caede' dixit

'derepta vidi ; vidi ego civium
retorta tergo bracchia libero
    portasque non clausas et arva
      Marte coli populata nostro.

25 Auro repensus scilicet acrior
miles redibit.   Flagitio additis
    damnum.   Neque amissos colores
      lana refert medicata fuco,

nec vera virtus, cum semel excidit,

trahenti, *that would entail ;* equivalent to *quod traheret,* and containing the apodosis of the conditional clause of the next strophe.

17. **periret:** Intr. 179.

18. **ego . . . vidi; vidi ego:** Intr. 116 *e*. He urges his appeal with the force of personal experience; he has seen with his own eyes the humiliation of captivity.

19. **adfixa:** as thank offerings of victory. Cf. IV. 15. 6 *sq.*

20. **sine caede:** implying that they should have shed their blood rather than submit to the indignity.

21. **civium:** emphatic, to mark by contrast the depth of their degradation. It may be translated: *I have seen* CITIZENS, *with their arms pinioned,* etc.

22. **tergo:** Intr. 69. — **libero,** *their freeman's ;* repeating the thought of **civium.**

23. **portas** (sc. *Carthaginis*), etc.: *i.e.* as if there were no war; a humiliating proof of the complete failure of the Roman invasion.

24. **Marte:** Intr. 130.

25. **auro repensus:** instead of being left to the fate which his cowardice has brought upon him. The phrase, however, suggests more than this, — the degradation of the warrior who has had a price set upon him, like a slave, and has resorted to this base substitute for valor as a means of safety. — **scilicet:** indicating the irony of the sentence.

26. **flagitio:** the dishonor the state has suffered through the conduct of these prisoners ; **damnum:** the breaking down of discipline which will result from their ransom.

27. **neque . . . nec:** *i.e.* the second is no more possible than the first; cf. I. 6. 5 n. — **colores:** Intr. 128. The natural color of the wool is meant.

28. **refert,** *renews, shows again.*

29. **virtus:** cf. 2. 17 n.— **semel excidit:** the phrase itself suggests what is next explicitly stated,— cowardice is not a temporary weakness; the loss of courage is instant and final, as of a jewel. Cf. I.24.16 n.

30   curat reponi deterioribus.

    Si pugnat extricata densis
      cerva plagis, erit ille fortis

qui perfidis se credidit hostibus,
et Marte Poenos proteret altero

35   qui lora restrictis lacertis
      sensit iners timuitque mortem.

Hic, unde vitam sumeret inscius,
pacem duello miscuit.   O pudor !
    O magna Carthago, probrosis

40   altior Italiae ruinis ! '

    Fertur pudicae coniugis osculum
    parvosque natos ut capitis minor
    ab se removisse et virilem
      torvus humi posuisse voltum,

30. **reponi**: Intr. 94 *i*.— **deteri-oribus** : the same persons that are understood with **excidit**; the word characterizes them as they are left when this virtue of courage has gone out of them. For the case, see Intr. 53, and cf. Liv. II. 43. 8 *si animus hosti redisset.*

33. **perfidis** : in reference to the proverbial *Punica fides;* cf. IV. 4. 49 n.— **se credidit**: in contrast with **perfidis**; Intr. 116 *a*.

34. **Marte** : cf. 24 n.— **altero**, *some other;* the war in which they were taken prisoners being regarded as ended. *Alter* is used to denote any other person or thing that is brought into comparison with the one in hand, so that these two alone are for the time under consideration; cf. 24. 22 ; *S*. I. 1. 40 *ne sit te ditior alter* ('thy neighbor'); Madv. 496.

35. **restrictis** : cf. *retorta*, 22.

36. **iners**, *tamely.*

37. **unde sumeret**: representing a question of doubt, *unde sumam ?* The question is, in effect, ' to what he should owe his life,' *sc.* to his sword and his valor, and not to the compassion of the enemy.

38. **pacem**, etc.: *i.e.* confused the two, treated the enemy as if they were friends.

40. **ruinis** : instrumental abl. with the comparative,— higher by that much, *exalted upon*, etc.; cf. Liv. I. 30. 1 *Roma interim crescit Albae ruinis.*

41. **fertur**, *men say.* The word prepares us for something surprising; cf. I. 7. 23.

42. **capitis minor** : for *capite deminutus*. In the word *caput* were summed up a Roman's personal and political rights. As a prisoner, Regulus was technically a slave, and unfit, in his own eyes, for the caress of a Roman matron

45   donec labantis consilio patres
      firmaret auctor numquam alias dato,
        interque maerentis amicos
          egregius properaret exsul.

      Atqui sciebat quae sibi barbarus
50   tortor pararet : non aliter tamen
        dimovit obstantis propinquos
          et populum reditus morantem

      quam si clientum longa negotia
      diiudicata lite relinqueret,
55   tendens Venafranos in agros
          aut Lacedaemonium Tarentum.

or her children. This humility of
the man is the background against
which the poet paints in effective
contrast his moral heroism (**patres
firmaret**) and his splendid victory
of self-sacrifice (**egregius exsul**).
For the genitive see Intr. 66 *d*.

46. **auctor**, *by his influence.*—
alias, *before or since.*

48. **properaret** : his alacrity
(cf. also *dimovit obstantis*, 51) and
cheerfulness (53 *sqq*.), now that
his patriotic purpose is achieved,
are set forth in contrast with the
sternness of his attitude (43 *sq*.)
as long as there was any chance of
a dishonorable release from mar-
tyrdom.

49. **sciebat**: observe the tense;
he knew all the while.

50. **tortor** : Roman tradition
told of the most exquisite tortures
especially devised for Regulus by
the Carthaginians (cf. Cic. *Off.* I.
39, III. 100 ; Gell. VII. 4); but
they rest on no historical evidence.
Polybius, our oldest authority,
knows nothing of them, nor, in-
deed, of any embassy of Regulus.

52. **reditus** : Intr. 128 ; the
plural is here preferred for the
sake of euphony, as in *Epod*. 16.
35 for the metre.

54. **lite** : either one in which
he had acted as arbitrator between
his clients, or one in which some
of the latter were engaged in court,
where, as *patronus*, he was bound
to aid them with counsel and influence. — **relinqueret**: for purposes of comparison Regulus is
transported in imagination to the
present, — 'than (he would), if
(living in our day) he were leaving,
etc.' The places named as holiday
retreats had no such character in
the time of Regulus.

55. **Venafranos agros**: see II.
6. 16 n.

56. **Lacedaemonium Taren-
tum** : see II. 6. 12 n, 13 *sqq.; Ep*.
I. 7. 45. The quiet picture in this
closing strophe, softening without
weakening the tragic suggestion
of vs. 49, in which the stern moral
earnestness of the ode reaches its
climax, is one of Horace's happiest
touches.

VI.

Delicta maiorum immeritus lues,
Romane, donec templa refeceris
　　aedisque labentis deorum et
　　　foeda nigro simulacra fumo.

5 Dis te minorem quod geris, imperas :
hinc omne principium, huc refer exitum.
　　Di multa neglecti dederunt
　　　Hesperiae mala luctuosae.

VI. This ode, like the preceding, deals with the degeneracy of
the times, but in a broader way.
The decline of the old Roman
spirit is but part of a wide-spread
corruption which has contaminated
even the sanctity of family life
and thus poisoned the springs of
national strength. This corruption with its train of disasters has
come in through the neglect of
religion, and until religion is restored to its due honor, the sins of
the fathers must continue to be
visited on the children. But of
this restoration the poet is not
sanguine. From his own picture
of the simple life of Rome's heroic
age he turns away in despair, and
sees in the deterioration of each
succeeding generation an augury
of the same downward course in
the future. The ode is the least
cheerful of the six, and its pessi-
mistic close, so ill adapted to
conclude the series, is of itself
sufficient proof that the poems
were not written on a single plan,
but composed independently, and
afterwards arranged, perhaps with
some adaptations, in a group. The
present ode is assigned with much
probability to the year 28 B.C.,
when Augustus, in his sixth con-

sulship, instituted many vigorous
reforms, and began the restoration
of eighty-two temples which had
fallen into decay (*Mon. Ancyr.* 4.
17). — Metre, 176.

1. **immeritus**: in close connection with **lues,** not implying
innocence in general: 'Thou shalt
bear the guilt of sins thou hast not
committed.'

2. **Romane**: used collectively,
as in Verg. *A.* VI. 851 *tu regere
imperio populos, Romane, memento.*
Cf. *S.* I. 4. 85. — **templa, aedis**:
here used as practically synony-
mous.

4. **foeda fumo** : some of the
temples had suffered from fire.

5. **dis te minorem,** etc.: Horace here utters not a philosophical
principle, but what was in the profound conviction of probably the
great majority of his countrymen
a historical fact. Cf. Polyb. VI.
56. 7 καί μοι δοκεῖ τὸ παρὰ τοῖς ἄλλοις
ἀνθρώποις ὀνειδιζόμενον, τοῦτο συνέ-
χειν τὰ Ῥωμαίων πράγματα · λέγω
δὲ τὴν δεισιδαιμονίαν; Cic. *N. D.*
III. 5 *nostrae civitatis, quae numquam profecto sine summa placa-
tione deorum immortalium tanta
esse potuisset.*

6. **principium**: sc. *est ;* cf. *hinc
illae lacrimae, Ep.* I. 19. 41, and

Iam bis Monaeses et Pacori manus
10   non auspicatos contudit impetus
nostros et adiecisse praedam
torquibus exiguis renidet.

similar phrases. For the synaeresis
see Intr. 181.—**exitum** : sc. *omne.*

7. **di neglecti** : Intr. 105; but
here **di** is still consciously the
subject.

8. **Hesperiae** : *i.e.* Italy, ‘the
Land of the West,’ in contrast
with the countries he has in mind
and is about to name. Cf. II. 1.
32. In I. 36. 4 it is used apparently for Spain, of a man returning
thence to Italy.—**luctuosae** : proleptic.

9. **iam bis** : referring to the
invasion of Crassus in B.C. 53,
which ended in the memorable
disaster at Carrhae (cf. 5. 5 n),
and the expedition of Antony with
an army of 100,000 men into
Media Atropatene in B.C. 36, from
which he was forced to retreat
with ignominy, and at the cost of
enormous loss and suffering to his
troops (Merivale, Ch. XXVIII).
Some editors think the first of the
two disasters referred to was the
defeat of Decidius Saxa in B.C. 40
by the Parthians under the rene-
gade T. Labienus ; but the defeat
of Saxa, though severe, was only
a temporary reverse in a war in
which the Romans were, on the
whole, brilliantly successful, and
their general, Ventidius, earned a
triumph. It was a war, moreover,
in which the Romans were repel-
ling an invasion of the Parthians,
and cannot therefore be included
under *non auspicati impetus.* —
Monaeses : a powerful Parthian
noble who went over to the
Romans in B.C. 37 and was received with great honor by Antony, but subsequently became

reconciled with Phraates and returned to his allegiance. He is
not known to have commanded
the Parthians in any of the campaigns here referred to. — **Pacori
manus** : cf. *Porsenae manus, Epod.*
16. 4. Pacorus, son of the Parthian king Orodes, commanded his
father's troops in the invasion of
Syria and Asia Minor in B.C. 40,
and in the succeeding campaigns
until he was defeated and killed
by Ventidius, B.C. 38. Horace
uses the names of Monaeses and
Pacorus as conspicuous Parthian
leaders, with little thought, and very
likely with no accurate knowledge
of their individual achievements.

10. **non auspicatos** : the expedition of Crassus was notorious
in this respect ; cf. Cic. *Div.* I. 29,
II. 84 ; Val. Max. I. 6. 11; Merivale,
Ch. XI. No similar particulars
are recorded of Antony's expedition ; but Horace refers, in both
cases, rather to the wickedness
(*impietas*) of the Roman people as
a nation, in neglecting the gods and
fighting brother against brother
(cf. I. 35. 33 *sqq.*, and *impia proelia,*
II. 1. 30), thus inevitably incurring the displeasure of Heaven on
all their undertakings.— **contudit:**
Intr. 77.

11. **adiecisse** : Intr. 94 *d,* 81 *b.*

12. **torquibus** : used as decorations for bravery or distinguished
service. Among the Persians they
could only be worn by those on
whom the king had conferred them
(Xen. *Cyrop.* VIII. 2.8).—**exiguis:**
i.e. in comparison with the ample
booty obtained from the Romans.
— **renidet,** *beams with joy.*

Paene occupatam seditionibus
delevit urbem Dacus et Aethiops,
15   hic classe formidatus, ille
missilibus melior sagittis.

Fecunda culpae saecula nuptias
primum inquinavere et genus et domos;
hoc fonte derivata clades
20   in patriam populumque fluxit.

Motus doceri gaudet Ionicos
matura virgo et fingitur artibus,
iam nunc et incestos amores
de tenero meditatur ungui;

13. **paene** : with **delevit.** This strophe carries the thought a step farther : the Romans had not only failed in their aggressive enterprises, they were so carried away by the passions of civil strife that they almost put the city itself at the mercy of the barbarian.

14. **Dacus et Aethiops** : auxiliaries who fought at Actium, the former in the army of Antony (see also I. 26. 4 n), the latter in the fleet of Cleopatra. They stand for the barbarian allies of Antony, whose approach the citizens had regarded with genuine, though no doubt exaggerated, alarm. Cf. Verg. *G.* II. 497.

17. **fecunda,** etc.: the poet proceeds to show *how* the neglect of religion and consequent looseness of living saps the strength of the nation. — **culpae,** *vice;* here, as often, with special reference to unchastity.

18. **inquinavere** : cf. *Epod.* 16. 64. — **genus,** *the stock;* cf. IV. 4. 29 *sqq.* — **domos** : *i.e.* the sanctity of domestic life and discipline; cf. IV. 4. 25 *sqq.*

19. **hoc fonte,** etc.: *i.e.* corruption in the family makes the state unsound at the core, and so robs it of the strength to resist the forces that tend to destroy it. This thesis he illustrates by the contrasted pictures of the next six strophes.

21. **motus,** *dances,* especially of a mimetic character ; cf. *movetur,* *Ep.* II. 2. 125. The Ionic was a voluptuous kind of dance, which was often provided for the amusement of the guests at a dinner party (Athen. XIV. 27), the dancers being usually professionals; cf. *Anth. Pal.* V. 129 (quoted vs. 24 n).

22. **matura** : it would be innocent in a child. — **artibus** : instrumental abl. ; instead of developing in a healthy and natural way, she is trained to pose on all occasions and manage her personal charms as weapons of skill.

23. **iam nunc** : *i.e.* even before marriage ; in contrast with *mox,* 25. — **et** : Intr. 114.

24. **de tenero ungui,** *to her finger-tips ;* cf. Apul. *Met.* X. 22 *ex unguiculis perpruriscens mulier*

25   mox iuniores quaerit adulteros
     inter mariti vina, neque eligit
         cui donet impermissa raptim
         gaudia luminibus remotis,

     sed iussa coram non sine conscio
30   surgit marito, seu vocat institor
         seu navis Hispanae magister,
         dedecorum pretiosus emptor.

     Non his iuventus orta parentibus
     infecit aequor sanguine Punico,

(an imitation of Plaut. *Stich.* 761). The phrase is a translation of the Greek ἐξ (ἀπαλῶν) ὀνύχων, used to express intensity of feeling (*e.g.* of impassioned movements in dancing, τὴν ἀπὸ τῆς ᾿Ασίης ὀρχηστρίδα, τὴν κακοτέχνοις | σχήμασιν ἐξ ἀπαλῶν κινυμένην ὀνύχων, | αἰνέω, οὐχ ὅτι πάντα παθαίνεται, οὐδ᾽ ὅτι βάλλει | τὰς ἁπαλὰς ἁπαλῶς ὧδε καὶ ὧδε χέρας, *Anth. Pal.* V. 129; of a mother's love for her young children, ὡς ἂν ἔνδοθεν καὶ τὸ δὴ λεγόμενον ἐξ ὀνύχων ἀγαπῶσαι τὰ τέκνα, Plut. *Mor.* 3 c), apparently with reference to the extreme sensitiveness of the nerves under the finger-nails. It appears also to have been used in the sense of 'from earliest childhood,' and possibly that is the sense in which Cicero understood it, *ad. Fam.* I. 6. 2, *qui mihi a teneris, ut Graeci dicunt, unguiculis es cognitus.* This interpretation is excluded here by **matura**, above. — **meditatur**, *is filled with thoughts of.*

26. **inter mariti vina:** *i.e.* among the guests at his table. — **neque eligit**, etc.: *i.e.* it is not merely a case of censurable flirtation with some favored admirer, allowing him a stolen kiss or the like. —

impermissa, which occurs here for the first time, was coined or chosen to express a mild form of wrong-doing : the offense in the supposed case is purposely softened to set off the unspeakable baseness of her actual conduct. Observe the contrast in particulars: **eligit** with **vocat institor**, etc.; **donet** with **emptor**; **impermissa** with **dedecorum**; **raptim** with **iussa coram**; and **luminibus remotis** with **conscio marito**.

29. **coram**, *bluntly*, without any affectation of delicacy. — **conscio marito**: Intr. 105 *a.*

30. **institor**, *pedlar;* a despised class, but having plenty of ready money and access, in pursuit of their trade, to the women of the household. Cf. *Epod.* 17. 20.

31. **magister**, *the skipper:* another coarse character and, as a sailor, a great spendthrift on shore.

33. **non his**, etc.: from this climax of iniquity the poet turns to the Romans of earlier times, and draws a companion picture of wholesome discipline and pure living.

34. **infecit aequor**: in the first Punic war, which was waged mainly by sea.

35   Pyrrhumque et ingentem cecidit
            Antiochum Hannibalemque dirum,

      sed rusticorum mascula militum
      proles, Sabellis docta ligonibus
            versare glaebas et severae
40   matris ad arbitrium recisos

      portare fustis, sol ubi montium
      mutaret umbras et iuga demeret
            bobus fatigatis, amicum
                tempus agens abeunte curru.

45   Damnosa quid non imminuit dies?
      Aetas parentum, peior avis, tulit
            nos nequiores, mox daturos
                progeniem vitiosiorem.

35. **ingentem**: a poetical variation of his surname, *Magnus* (see Cic. *pro Deiot.* 36); cf. Verg. *A.* XI. 124 *fama ingens, ingentior armis vir.* The word in this sense is found also in Sallust and in later prose writers.—**cecidit**, *overthrew.*

36. **dirum**: cf. *dirus Afer*, IV. 4. 42.

38. **Sabellis**: Intr. 124. The epithet places the scene among the Sabines, who were proverbial for their strictness and purity of manners; *quo genere nullum quondam incorruptius fuit*, Liv. I. 18. 4.

41. **sol ubi**, etc.: even when the day's work was done, and the tired ox was allowed to rest, they must deny themselves the repose which the quiet evening hour made so tempting, and go forth again to cut and carry firewood for their mother. Horace dwells on the description of evening in his favorite way (cf. I. 12. 29 n, III. 4. 60 n), but here no stroke is superfluous.

42. **mutaret**: *i.e.* lengthened. As the sun descends lower, the change in the shadows becomes more rapid and hence more noticeable. Cf. Verg. *E.* 2. 67 *et sol crescentis decedens duplicat umbras.* The subjunctive looks like that of repeated action (**docta** = *adsueta*); but as Horace elsewhere uses the indicative with *ubi* in such clauses (see Intr. 86) it is probably to be explained as due to its close dependence on the infinitive (Gr. 342).

43. **amicum**, *welcome;* cf. I. 26. 1 n.

44. **agens**, *bringing on;* cf. Verg. *E.* 8. 17 *praeque diem veniens age, Lucifer, almum.*

45. **imminuit**: perfect. — **dies**, *time.*

46. **aetas**, etc.: the course of deterioration through four generations is skilfully expressed in three verses. — **peior avis**: Intr. 75.

47. **daturos**: Intr. 104 *b.*

VII.

Quid fles, Asterie, quem tibi candidi
  primo restituent vere Favonii
    Thyna merce beatum,
      constantis iuvenem fide,

5   Gygen?   Ille Notis actus ad Oricum
  post insana Caprae sidera frigidas
    noctis non sine multis
      insomnis lacrimis agit.

Atqui sollicitae nuntius hospitae,
10   suspirare Chloen et miseram tuis

VII. The unbroken vein of serious thought which runs through the preceding group of odes is fittingly relieved by a poem of more than usual lightness and grace, an idyl, as it has been called, of a young trader's love. He lies storm-bound in a foreign port, fretting at wind and wave, while the forlorn maid sits weeping at home, with no message to tell her why he tarries. The poet comforts her with the assurance that her lover is neither lost nor untrue; the spring winds will bring him back to her; meanwhile let her keep well her own troth. — Metre, 173.

1. **fles**: the object is *eum* (*one*) understood, with which **iuvenem** and **Gygen** are successively in apposition. — **Asterie** : Ἀστερίη, 'fair as a star'; cf. 9. 21, *sidere pulchrior.* — **candidi**, *fair;* cf. I. 5. 7 n, 7. 15 n.

2. **Favonii**: see I. 4. 1 n.

3. **Thyna merce**: cf. *Bithyna negotia, Ep.* I. 6. 33. *Thyni* and *Bithyni* were once separate peoples, but in Horace's day they had long ceased to be distinguished, and the

shorter adjective was used as a poetical substitute for the other. Cf. Cat. 31. 5 *Thyniam atque Bithynos.* — **beatum,** *enriched.*

4. **fide**: contracted form of the genitive, used also by Caesar and Sallust (Gell. IX. 14. 25); cf. *S.* I. 3. 95 *fide* (dative).

5. **Notis** : see I. 7. 15 n. — **Oricum** : on the coast of Epirus, sheltered by the Acroceraunian headland.

6. **post Caprae sidera** : *i.e.* after the setting of that constellation, which occurred about the middle of December and was a sign of storm. For the expression cf. *post vina,* I. 18. 5. — **insana** : *i.e.* causing furious storms; cf. *stella vesani leonis,* 29. 19 ; Intr. 124.

7. **non sine** : cf. I. 23. 3 n.

9. **atqui,** *and yet* (he could easily console himself). — **sollicitae** : cf. *amore sollicitus, S.* II. 3. 252.

10. **Chloen** : the *hospita* of vs. 9, the wife of his host. — **tuis ignibus** : *i.e.* with the passion which is rightfully yours, — the passion inspired by Gyges. The

dicens ignibus uri,
    temptat mille vafer modis.
Vt Proetum mulier perfida credulum
falsis impulerit criminibus nimis
15   casto Bellerophontae
    maturare necem refert ;
narrat paene datum Pelea Tartaro,
Magnessam Hippolyten dum fugit abstinens,
    et peccare docentis
20   fallax historias movet.

expression is the poet's and not that of the *nuntius.*

12. **temptat** : sc. *eum.* — **mille vafer modis**, *with a thousand wiles.*

13. **ut**, etc. : stock tales of the fury of a woman scorned, 'cum stimulos odio pudor admovet' (Juv. 10. 329). — **Proetum** : king of Tiryns. The story of Bellerophon is told *Il.* VI. 152 *sqq.* — **mulier** : Anteia, in the Homeric account ; according to others, Stheneboea, the name which Juvenal (*l. c.*) gives. — **perfida credulum** : Intr. 116 *a.*

15. **Bellerophontae** : Horace uses the Homeric form (Βελλεροφόντης) here and 12. 3, but has the accusative *Bellerophontem* IV. 11. 28.

16. **maturare necem** : *i.e.* to put him to death before his time. For the infinitive see Intr. 97 *b.* — **refert, narrat** : chiastic ; cf. Intr. 116 *e.*

17. **datum Tartaro** : cf. *morti dedit, S.* II. 3. 197 ; both are variations on the old formal phrase much affected by the poets, *leto dare:* cf. Enn. *Telephus* 289 (Ribb.) *quorum liberi leto dati sunt in bello;* Verg. *A.* V. 806 ; Juv. 10. 119. The construction of **paene datum Pe-**

lea is that of Intr. 105 *a* (= 'the narrow escape of Peleus '), not indirect discourse ; hence the indicative in vs. 18. The adventure is thought of as already well known to the reader. — **Pelea** : while a guest at the house of Acastus, king of Iolcus, Peleus, so the story ran, was obliged to repel the advances of his hostess, with the same result as in the case of Bellerophon. Acastus decoyed him into the wilderness and there left him alone unarmed, hoping the Centaurs would destroy him. The gods, however, protected him, and Hephaestus gave him a sword which was a sufficient defense against the Centaurs. According to another account he was found by Chiron, who received him kindly and sheltered him in his cave. Subsequently he made war on Acastus and captured Iolcus.

18. **Magnessam** : *i.e.* from the Thessalian Magnesia ; to distinguish her from the more famous Hippolyte, the Amazon wife of Theseus.

19. **docentis** : Intr. 103.

20. **movet**, *rehearses ;* lit. 'sets a-going' (cf. I. 15. 10 n). Vergil has *movere cantūs, A.* VII. 641.

Frustra : nam scopulis surdior Icari
voces audit adhuc integer.   At tibi
   ne vicinus Enipeus
     plus iusto placeat cave,

25   quamvis non alius flectere equum sciens
aeque conspicitur gramine Martio,
   nec quisquam citus aeque
     Tusco denatat alveo.

Prima nocte domum claude, neque in vias
30   sub cantu querulae despice tibiae,
   et te saepe vocanti
     duram difficilis mane.

21. **frustra**: cf. 13. 6, where *nam* follows, as here. — **scopulis surdior**: *i.e.* no more moved than they are by the waves that dash upon them ; cf. *Epod.* 17. 54. **surdior**, with audit, forms a very effective oxymoron. — **Icari** : the island; cf. I. 1. 15.

22. **integer** : cf. II. 4. 22.—**tibi**, *on your part.* See Intr. 116 *b.*

23. **Enipeus** : the name is borrowed from a river-god of Thessaly; cf. *Hebri*, 12. 2.

25. **quamvis** : Intr. 83. — **flectere equum** : cf. I. 8. 6 n, III. 12. 3. For the mood see Intr. 101 *c.*

26. **aeque . . . aeque** (with sciens and citus, respectively) : Intr. 116 *b.* — **gramine Martio** : Intr. 69. Cf. *per gramina Martii campi*, IV. 1. 39, and see I. 8. 4 n.

28. **Tusco alveo** : *i.e.* the Tiber; cf. I. 20. 5 n. — **denatat** : found only here.   For this form of exercise see I. 8. 8 n.   The poet dwells on the athletic prowess of the youth, knowing well its power to captivate a girl's heart. Cf. 12. 3 *sq.*

29. **neque** : Intr. 89 N.

30. **sub cantu**, *while he is playing,* *i.e.* serenading you. *Sub,* in this use, means, with the ablative, ' during (the continuance of) '; with the accusative, ' just before ' or ' just after.' Cf. *sub luce* and *sub lucem.* — **despice** : in a literal sense.

31. **vocanti** (sc. *illi*): equivalent to a concessive clause.

32. **duram**, *unfeeling:* **difficilis**, *stubborn.*

VIII.

Martiis caelebs quid agam Kalendis,
quid velint flores et acerra turis
plena miraris, positusque carbo in
    caespite vivo,
5   docte sermones utriusque linguae?
Voveram dulcis epulas et album

VIII. An ode for the anniversary of the poet's escape from
death by the fall of a tree, recorded
in II. 13. The form is dramatic.
The poet is busily engaged with
his servants in preparations for a
sacrifice, when Maecenas appears.
In answer to his expression of
surprise, Horace explains the
significance of the day to him, and
begs his friend to join him in his
quiet festival of thanksgiving.

The date of the ode, and consequently of the event in the poet's
life which it commemorates, is fixed
with great probability by the allusions of the last three strophes.
Maecenas, presumably in the absence of Octavian (Intr. 21), is in
charge of affairs. The campaigns
of M. Crassus against the Dacians
and other tribes of the Danube
frontier (vss. 18, 23) were fought
in the years immediately following
the battle of Actium, B.C. 30–28.
The news of the struggle between
Phraates and Tiridates in Parthia
reached Rome in January B.C. 29;
and in the summer of the same
year Octavian returned to Italy.
Our ode was therefore composed
in the spring of B.C. 29, and the
date of the fall of the tree is March
1, B.C. 30. For it is clear that it is
the *first* anniversary which is here
celebrated. — Metre, 174.

1. **Martiis Kalendis** : called by

Juvenal (9. 53) *femineae kalendae*,
being the day of the Matronalia,
when the married women of Rome
made their offerings to Juno Lucina on the Esquiline (Ov. *Fast.*
III. 245 *sqq.*). The day was also
kept as a family festival : the
mother received presents from her
husband and children, and like the
men at the Saturnalia waited on
her slaves at table; hence called
by Martial (V. 84. 10) the women's
Saturnalia. Why an unmarried
man should be found celebrating
that day, was a puzzle which Maecenas, with all his learning, as the
poet playfully says, could not solve.

2. **velint,** *mean.*— **flores** : these
were a part of the offering to Juno
(Ovid. *l. l.*).

4. **caespite** : see I. 19. 13 n.

5. **docte** : Maecenas is so addressed again *Ep.* I. 19. 1. — **sermones** : *i.e.* the literature. For
the case cf. 9. 10. — **utriusque** :
the two which to a Roman contained all literature and learning,
Greek and Latin. The expression
appears to have been not uncommon, *e.g.* Plin. *N. H.* XII. 11.; cf.
Stat. *Silv.* V. *gemina lingua,* Plut.
Lucull. 1 ἤσκητο λέγειν ἱκανῶς ἑκα-
τέραν γλῶτταν.

6. **epulas** : the regular accompaniment of a sacrifice; cf. I. 36. 2.
— **album** : the prescribed color for
a victim to the gods above.

Libero caprum prope funeratus
  arboris ictu.

Hic dies, anno redeunte festus,
10 corticem adstrictum pice demovebit
  amphorae fumum bibere institutae
  consule Tullo.

Sume, Maecenas, cyathos amici
  sospitis centum, et vigiles lucernas
15 perfer in lucem ; procul omnis esto
  clamor et ira.

7. **Libero** : patron god (with Apollo) of poets ; cf. *Ep.* II. 2. 78 ; Juv. 7. 64. In II. 17. 28 Horace attributes his escape to Faunus.— **caprum** : cf. Verg. *G.* II. 380 *Baccho caper omnibus aris | caeditur*, for no other reason, he says, than because it eats the grape-vines.

9. **anno redeunte festus,** *a festival as the year comes round ;* cf. *S.* II. 2. 83 *sive diem festum rediens advexerit annus.* In both cases *annus* is strictly a part or season of the year, as in 23. 8, *Epod.* 2. 29.

10. **adstrictum pice** : showing that the wine had been carefully put up for long keeping. Cf. I. 20. 3 n.

11. **amphorae** : dative. — **fumum bibere** : to hasten the mellowing of the wine. The store room (*apotheca*) was purposely placed in a part of the house where the smoke could reach it. For the infinitive see Intr. 93.— **institutae,** *set.*

12. **Tullo** : probably L. Volcatius Tullus, consul B.C. 33 with Octavian, so that the wine would now be four years old. There was, however, another consul of this name in B.C. 66, who may be the

one referred to here. In that case the jar would be only a year older than the *pia testa* of 21. 1 *sqq.*

13. **sume** : cf. I. 27. 9. — **cyathos** : see I. 29. 8 n. — **amici** : a Greek form of expression, by which the cups are said to be his to whose health they are drunk ; cf. 19, 9 *sqq.* and Antiph. *ap.* Athen. X. 21 ἔγχει, παιδίον, | κυάθους θεῶν τε καὶ θεαινῶν μυρίους. The meaning here is somewhat modified, however, by **sospitis,** which shows that present safety is more prominent in the poet's mind than future welfare as a motive for drinking (cf. II. 7. 26 *sqq.*). We may translate : *for the preservation of your friend.* See Intr. 105 *a.*

14. **centum** : used vaguely, like μυρίους above, for a very large number ; cf. II. 14. 26.

15. **perfer,** *stay with ;* lit. 'endure to the end.' The real object is implied in **vigiles,** as if it were *vigilias sub lucernis perfer.* This the invalid Maecenas would not be disposed to do in any ordinary drinking party ; hence the assurance that follows, **procul** etc., though these words seem to imply that there are to be other guests present.

Mitte civilis super urbe curas :
occidit Daci Cotisonis agmen,
Medus infestus sibi luctuosis
20   dissidet armis,

servit Hispanae vetus hostis orae
Cantaber sera domitus catena,
iam Scythae laxo meditantur arcu
cedere campis.

25   Neglegens ne qua populus laboret,
parce privatus nimium cavere et
dona praesentis cape laetus horae ;
linque severa.

17. **super** : see I. 9. 5 n.

18. **occidit**: emphatic, as in I. 28. 7 and IV. 4. 70. — **Cotisonis agmen**: see introd. note, and I. 26. 4 n.

19. **Medus** : see I. 2. 22 n ; Intr. 127. — **sibi** : with **infestus**; but its force cannot help being felt with **luctuosis** also. Intr. 76. — **luctuosis** : cf. 6. 8, where it is also used in reference to civil strife.

20. **dissidet** : used absolutely; cf. *dissideat miles*, Tac. *Ann.* I. 46. 1.

21. **servit** : cf. *occidit*, 17 n, and for the meaning, II. 2. 12. — **Hispanae orae** : the mountainous district along the bay of Biscay. For **orae** cf. I. 12. 55, 26. 4. The genitive with *hostis* in this relation is rare.

22. **sera** : because he was **vetus hostis**. Livy remarks (XXVIII. 12. 12) that of all the continental provinces of the Romans, Spain was the first in which they gained a footing, the last to be completely subdued, and that not till his own day. — **domitus** : referring perhaps to their reduction by

Statilius Taurus B.C. 29; see II. 6. 2 n.

23. **Scythae** : the marauding raids of these tribes had been checked by the operations of Crassus, but not yet entirely suppressed (cf. II. 9. 23 *sq.*) ; and this is all that Horace asserts (**meditantur cedere**). — **laxo**, *unstrung*.

24. **cedere** : Intr. 94 *f.* — **campis** : those south of the Danube which were exposed to their raids.

25. **neglegens**, etc. : after stating these good reasons, Horace returns to the exhortation begun in 17. **neglegens, privatus,** and **laetus** are all a part of the exhortation, the first two repeating the idea of *mitte civilis curas*, 17. — **ne** : after the idea of fear or anxiety implied in **neglegens** (here = *securus*) ; cf. *terruit ne*, I. 2. 5 n.

26. **privatus** : *i.e.* for the moment. Cf. *S.* II. 1. 71 *sqq.* — **nimium cavere,** *borrow trouble*. **cavere** is used absolutely as in *S.* II. 7. 68 ; for the mood, see Intr. 94 *k.*

27. **dona**, etc. : cf. I. 9. 13 *sqq.*, 11. 8, II. 16. 25 *sqq.*, III. 29. 41 *sqq.*

IX.

Donec gratus eram tibi
　　nec quisquam potior bracchia candidae
cervici iuvenis dabat,
　　Persarum vigui rege beatior.

5　Donec non alia magis
　　arsisti neque erat Lydia post Chloen,
multi Lydia nominis,
　　Romana vigui clarior Ilia.

Me nunc Thressa Chloe regit,
10　　dulcis docta modos et citharae sciens,

IX. A lyrical idyl, portraying with exquisite skill a lovers' quarrel and reconciliation. The brief dialogue tells the whole story. Lydia's lover has wounded her by too marked attentions to Chloe, and her resentment has sent him off in a passion. Both are sorry and proud. He makes the first overtures towards a reconciliation in terms of tender regret, mixed with reproach; she replies in the same strain, with no sign of yielding. He then tries to break her down by a show of indifference, but she answers him with equal defiance. Finally he virtually confesses his fault and offers to make amends, and she, while asserting her woman's privilege of the last word in the quarrel, consents and owns that she loves him after all. This is the only ode of Horace in dialogue form. — Metre, 171.

1. **eram** : cf. *parabat*, I. 37. 8 n.
2. **potior**, *favored rival.*
3. **dabat** : the simple form for the compound (*circumdabat*) is poetical ; cf. Intr. 129.
4. **Persarum rege** : see II. 2 17 n.

5. **donec,** etc. : in this and in the second pair of strophes Horace observes the rule of amoebean verse which requires that the second speaker shall match the verses of the first, and, if possible, produce something better and stronger. Cf. Verg. *Ecll.* 3 and 7.— **aliā** : cf. *virgine*, II. 4. 8 ; Intr. 72.
6. **arsisti** : the perfect, for variety, matching the imperfect of vs. 1, but with the same force. Roby 1667. — **post,** *second to.*
7. **multi Lydia nominis,** *a Lydia of great renown ;* her name was on everybody's lips as the fortunate object of his choice ; cf. **clarior.** This verse belongs with the preceding, the name being repeated as in I. 13. 1, 2.
8. **Romana** : as the mother of the Roman race. She was a Trojan woman according to the tradition which Horace follows; see 3. 32 n.
9. **Thressa Chloe**: for this designation and that in 14, cf. I. 27. 10 *sq.* The names are chosen for their pleasing sound.
10. **modos** : for the case cf. *sermones.* 8. 5.

pro qua non metuam mori,
       si parcent animae fata superstiti.
Me torret face mutua
       Thurini Calais filius Ornyti,
15   pro quo bis patiar mori,
       si parcent puero fata superstiti.
Quid si prisca redit Venus,
       diductosque iugo cogit aeneo,
si flava excutitur Chloe,
20   reiectaeque patet ianua Lydiae?
Quamquam sidere pulchrior
       ille est, tu levior cortice et improbo
iracundior Hadria,
       tecum vivere amem, tecum obeam libens.

X.

Extremum Tanain si biberes, Lyce,
saevo nupta viro, me tamen asperas

11. **mori** : Intr. 94 *l.*

12. **animae**, *my love.*— **super-stiti**, *and let her live ;* proleptic.

15. **mori** : Intr. 94 *a.*

16. **puero** : see I. 9. 16 n.— **su-perstiti** : cf. vs. 12 n.

17. **prisca** : poetical for *pristina.*
— **redit** : for the present in this and the following verses, see Intr. 78.

18. **iugo aeneo** : cf. I. 33. 11 n.

19. **flava** : see I. 5. 3 n.— **excu-titur** : *sc.* from her control of me (*regit*, 9); cf. Verg. *A.* V. 679 *excus-saque pectore Iuno est.*

20. **Lydiae** : dative, as **reiec-tae** shows. **ianua patet** is not altogether metaphorical; see 15. 9 n.

21. **sidere pulchrior**: cf. 19. 26 *puro similem Vespero; Il.* VI. 401 ἀλίγκιον ἀστέρι καλῷ (of Asty-anax).

22. **levior** : *i.e.* less steadfast, more fickle. — **improbo**, *horrid.*

23. **iracundior Hadria** : cf. I. 33. 15.

24. **vivere** : Intr. 94 *c.*

X. A serenade, of the kind called παρακλαυσίθυρον, in which the lover pleads before the barred door of his mistress' house (cf. I. 25. 7 *sq.*). In accordance with Horace's usual practice in verses of this kind the names are Greek, but the setting is Roman. Lyce is of Etruscan origin, and the mistress of a wealthy mansion.

porrectum ante foris obicere incolis
 plorares Aquilonibus.

5 Audis quo strepitu ianua, quo nemus
 inter pulchra satum tecta remugiat
 ventis, et positas ut glaciet nivis
  puro numine Iuppiter?

Ingratam Veneri pone superbiam,
10 ne currente retro funis eat rota :
 non te Penelopen difficilem procis
  Tyrrhenus genuit parens.

Her infatuated lover plies her in turn with reproaches for her cruelty, with warning and sarcasm, with appeals to pity, and finally with the impotent threat that he will leave her for good.— Metre, 172.

1. **extremum,** *the far off;* cf. *ultima,* II. 18. 4 n.— **si biberes :** *i.e.* if you lived on its banks, among the Sarmatians, where 'peccare nefas, aut pretium est mori' (24. 24). For the form of expression, cf. II. 20. 20 n, IV. 15. 21.

2. **saevo viro :** in contrast with the actual fact (vs. 15).— **asperas,** *pitiless.*

3. **porrectum :** implying that he has waited long. — **obicere :** Intr. 94 *m ;* cf. Plaut. *Aul.* 308 *aquam hércle plorat, quóm lavat, profúndere* (of a miser).— **incolis,** *that are at home there.*

5. **nemus,** etc.: cf. *Ep.* I. 10. 22 *inter varias nutritur silva columnas.* In the wealthier Roman houses the second court (*peristylium*) was expanded into a garden, with space even for large trees.

7. **ventis:** causal ablative.— **ut :** see I. 9. 1 n ; Intr. 114. The question depends on the general idea

of perception in **audis,** the specific meaning of which is lost at this distance. Cf. I. 14. 3 n, II. 1. 21 n. — **glaciet,** etc.: *i.e.* the night is clear (**puro**) and so cold that the light coating of snow on the ground (**positas**), which had softened in the sunshine, is frozen hard.

8. **puro numine,** *in cloudless majesty;* cf. I. 34. 7 n.—**Iuppiter:** see I. 1. 25 n.

10. **ne,** etc.: *i.e.* your high flight in virtue is beyond your powers, and will end in a sudden and violent fall. The figure is that of a windlass, with which a man is raising a weight that proves too heavy, and the handle breaks or slips from his grasp.— **retro:** with **currente,** and then, by inference, with **eat.**

11. **non te :** cf. *non ego* I. 18. 11 n. — **difficilem :** cf. 7. 32.

12. **Tyrrhenus,** etc.: in contrast with the supposition in vs. 1. The Etruscans reached a high point of civilization, which was on the decline when the Romans came in contact with them, and had left traditions of luxury and effeminacy with their accompanying vices. See Momm. *Hist.* Bk. II. Ch. IV.

O quamvis neque te munera nec preces
nec tinctus viola pallor amantium
15   nec vir Pieria paelice saucius
    curvat, supplicibus tuis

parcas, nec rigida mollior aesculo
nec Mauris animum mitior anguibus :
non hoc semper erit liminis aut aquae
20   caelestis patiens latus.

XI.

Mercuri, nam te docilis magistro
movit Amphion lapides canendo,
tuque testudo, resonare septem
    callida nervis,

13. **quamvis** : Intr. 83.

14. **tinctus viola pallor** : cf. Verg. *E.* 2. 47 *pallentis violas.* The tint was a pale yellow (wan).

15. **vir saucius** : Intr. 105 *a.*— **Pieria** : cf. *Thressa*, 9. 9. — **paelice** : causal abl., as in I. 14. 5.— **saucius** : of love, as Verg. *A.* IV. 1.

16. **curvat** : a fresh word, for the 'faded metaphor' *flectit.* — **supplicibus,** *worshippers ; i.e.* if no personal consideration moves you, spare us in pure mercy (like a goddess). There is an undertone of irony in this and the next words.

17. **rigida** : continuing the figure in **curvat.**

18. **Mauris anguibus** : said to be particularly sa vage on account of the heat ; Sal. *Iug.* 89. 5. Cf. Lucan's descript on of the snakes of the Libyan desert, *B. C.* IX. 630 *sqq.* — **ahi um** : Intr. 44.

19. **non hc** , etc.: the comic effect of this final touch is obvious.

— **liminis** : cf. *Epod.* 11. 22. — **aquae caelestis** : cf. *Ep.* II. 1. 135. The reference to rain (cf. vs. 8) shows that he has in mind other occasions besides the present.

20. **latus** : cf. II. 7. 18 n.

XI. The theme of this ode is the beautiful story of Hypermnestra and Lynceus, which is presented in a setting that adds not a little to its charm. The poet begins as if with no definite theme in mind. He calls on his lyre, and on Mercury, who gave the lyre its magic power, to play a strain to which even Lyde shall listen, — Lyde, the shy young girl, playful as a colt and with as little thought of love. He appeals to the past achievements of the lyre, how, in the hands of Orpheus, it charmed the woods and streams and wild beasts, yes, even the monsters of the underworld, and Ixion and Tityos in their torment, and the Danaids, — let Lyde hear

5   nec loquax olim neque grata, nunc et
     divitum mensis et amica templis,
     dic modos Lyde quibus obstinatas
        adplicet auris,

     quae velut latis equa trima campis
10   ludit exsultim metuitque tangi,
     nuptiarum expers et adhuc protervo
        cruda marito.

the tale of the Danaids. Thus he comes upon his theme naturally, as it were, and without design. He shows his skill further in disposing of the disagreeable part of the story first, the crime and the subsequent punishment of the wicked sisters ; and against this dark background he paints the bright picture of the one who was found faithful. His taste is shown no less in leaving off at the point where the heroic girl is left to face death as the consequence of her devoted courage and womanly pity. Ovid has treated the same subject in the *Heroides* (14), following the lines laid down by Horace, so that the two poems afford an excellent opportunity of comparing the two poets, and the lyric with the elegiac treatment.—Metre, 174.

1. **Mercuri**: although his appeal is to the lyre, he invokes Mercury first, because the lyre is his handiwork (I. 10. 6 n), and without his inspiration it is a voiceless shell. — **nam**: introducing the reason for addressing the god,— a Homeric form of expression, *e.g. Odys.* I. 337; cf. Verg. *A.* I. 65 *Aeole, namque tibi, etc.* The reason is given, after Horace's manner, in the form of a particular example standing for the general fact.— **te magistro** : abl. absolute, but containing the main thought : it was thy teaching and his willingness to learn of thee that gave Amphion his (well-known) power. **docilis** is more than *doctus*, enforcing the idea of dependence.

2. **movit,** etc.: the stones were said to have moved into their places in the wall under the spell of his music; see *Ep.* II. 3. 394 *sqq.*

3. **resonare**: Intr. 101 *c.*

4. **nervis** : ablative.

5. **nec loquax neque grata,** *without voice or charm.* — **olim** : *i.e.* when a mere shell. — **et**: often placed at the end of the verse in Horace, but always, except here and IV. 13. 6, coalescing by elision with the preceding word.

6. **mensis** : the use of the lyre at banquets dates from Homeric times; cf. *e.g.* the story of the Phaeacians. — **amica**: cf. 4. 25 n and Intr. 119 *a.* — **templis** : *i.e.* in religious ceremonies ; cf. I. 36. 1 n. Porphyrio says : ' Fidicines hodieque Romae sacrificiis adhiberi videmus.'

7. **dic modos** : cf. I. 32. 3.

9. **trima** : the time prescribed for breaking in a colt was in its fourth year (Verg. *G.* III. 190).

10. **ludit,** etc.: see Intr. 123. — **exsultim,** *bounding over.* The word is found here only. — **tangi** : Intr. 94 *l.*

12. **cruda** : the same figure as in II.* 5. 10.

Tu potes tigris comitesque silvas
ducere et rivos celeris morari ;
15   cessit immanis tibi blandienti
        ianitor aulae

Cerberus, quamvis furiale centum
muniant angues caput eius atque
spiritus taeter saniesque manet
20   ore trilingui ;

quin et Ixion Tityosque voltu
risit invito ; stetit urna paulum
sicca, dum grato Danai puellas
        carmine mulces.

13. **tu** : the lyre. The poet is recalling the feats of Orpheus ; cf. I. 12. 7 *sqq.* — **comites,** *in thy train.* — **-que** : Intr. 119 *b.*

15. **cessit,** etc.: for the descent of Orpheus to the lower world in quest of Eurydice, see Ovid, *M.* X. 8 *sqq.*, Verg. *G.* IV. 457 *sqq.* — **immanis** : used of Cerberus also in Verg. *A.* VI. 418 *recubans immanis in antro.* Some join it here with **aulae** ; cf. *fera regia Ditis,* Ov. *M.* IV. 438. — **blandienti** : cf. I. 12. 11, 24. 13.

16. **ianitor aulae** : better taken as expressing a single idea ('palace-doorkeeper'), modified by **immanis.** For **aulae,** cf. II. 18. 31.

17. **Cerberus,** etc.: see I. 2. 7 n. The repulsive picture of the monster serves to enhance the impression of the power of music. But some critics have doubted whether Horace wrote the strophe, which certainly has a prosaic flavor. They object particularly to the unpoetical pronoun **eius,** which Vergil nowhere uses. Horace has it, however, IV. 8. 18, as well as

in the Satires, and it occurs two or three times in Ovid. — **quamvis** : Intr. 83.— **furiale,** *fury-like ;* cf. II. 13. 35 *sq.* — **centum** : see 8. 14 n.

18. **angues** : conceived as growing like hair about his neck ; cf. Verg. *A.* VI. 419 *horrere videns iam colla colubris.*

20. **ore trilingui** : cf. II. 19. 31 n.

21. **quin et** : cf. II. 13. 37 n.— **Ixion** : cf. Verg. *G.* IV. 484 *Ixionii cantu rota constitit orbis.*—**Tityos** : see 4. 77, II. 14. 8 n.

22. **risit** : Intr. 77.—**invito** : *i.e.* in spite of their torture. — **urna** : used collectively, — the one in which each carried water to the *dolium ;* Intr. 127.

25. **audiat Lyde,** etc.: Horace's readers were familiar with the myth of the Danaids, — how the Argive king accepted the overtures of his brother Aegyptus for a reconciliation, and married the latter's sons to his fifty daughters, but instructed the brides to murder their husbands on the wedding night,— and with the doom of the wicked

25 Audiat Lyde scelus atque notas
    virginum poenas et inane lymphae
    dolium fundo pereuntis imo,
        seraque fata

    quae manent culpas etiam sub Orco.
30 Impiae (nam quid potuere maius?),
    impiae sponsos potuere duro
        perdere ferro.

    Vna de multis face nuptiali
    digna periurum fuit in parentem
35 splendide mendax et in omne virgo
        nobilis aevum ;

damsels to pour water into a bot-
tomless cistern till they filled it ;
they were reminded of the story
whenever they went to the library
of the temple of Apollo on the
Palatine (I. 31), where the statues
of Danaus and his daughters lined
the portico, alternating with the
marble columns (Ov. *Tr.* III. 1.
61 *sq.*, Prop. III. 31. 3 *sq.*). Horace
could therefore pass lightly over
these outlines and use them as an
introduction to the golden deed
of the one interesting Danaid. —
notas : modifying **scelus** as well
as **poenas ;** Intr. 119 *a.*
26. **lymphae:** with **inane ;** Intr.
66 *c.* For the order of words here,
see Intr. 111.
27. **fundo :** instrumental abl.
(the way by which). — **pereuntis,**
going to waste.
28. **sera,** etc.: *i.e.* the doom
(punishment), long delayed, which
overtakes the guilty person at last,
even though he go free all his
life.
29. **sub :** cf. 5. 9. Orcus is the
person (not the place), as in II.
18. 30.

30. **impiae . . . impiae :** the
parenthetical clause supplies the
requisite pause to make the repetition more effective (Intr. 116 *g*);
cf. *surge,* 37 *sq. Pietas,* as a human obligation, commonly denotes
that of blood-relationship, but is
sometimes extended to marriage
and other obligations that were
regarded as having a sacred character. Cf. Ov. *M.* XIII. 301 *pia
coniunx.* So Hypermnestra, Ov.
Her. 14. 129, calls her punishment
pretium pietatis iniquum.
31. **potuere :** in a moral sense,
—*they had the heart ;* different
from its use in 30, where it denotes
simple possibility, — ' What wickedness *could* be greater ? ' — **duro,**
pitiless ; cf. the Homeric νηλέι
χαλκῷ.
33. **una,** *only one.*
35. **splendide mendax :** a fine
oxymoron. Cf. Tac. *H.* IV. 50
*servus egregio mendacio se Pisonem
esse respondit, ac statim obtruncatur;*
Soph. *Ant.* 74 ὅσια πανουργήσασα.
mendax implies that Danaus had
bound his daughters by a promise
or oath to commit the deed.

' Surge ' quae dixit iuveni marito,
' surge, ne longus tibi somnus, unde
non times, detur ; socerum et scelestas
40   falle sorores,

quae, velut nanctae vitulos leaenae,
singulos eheu lacerant.   Ego illis
mollior nec te feriam neque intra
     claustra tenebo :

45   me pater saevis oneret catenis,
quod viro clemens misero peperci ;
me vel extremos Numidarum in agros
     classe releget.

I pedes quo te rapiunt et aurae,
50   dum favet nox et Venus, i secundo
omine et nostri memorem sepulcro
     scalpe querellam.'

37. **quae,** *she.*

38. **surge :** *sc.* from sleep, suggesting the figurative expression for death that follows.—**longus:** as in II. 14. 19 and IV. 9. 27, for 'eternal.' In all of these cases *longus* gets its expressive force from the substantive (*labor, somnus, nox*), which denotes a familiar experience of limited duration.—**unde :** for *inde unde,* 'from a quarter from which.'

40. **falle,** *elude ;* cf. I. 10. 16 n, *Ep.* I. 5. 31. — **sorores :** sc. *tuas ;* cf. Ov. *Her.* 14. 123 *si qua piae, Lynceu, tibi cura sororis.* First cousins were called *fratres* and *sorores* (*patrueles*).

42. **singulos lacerant :** a confusion of the figure with the reality (Intr. 123), **singulos** referring to the men, **lacerant** to the lions. — **eheu :** in her account of the affair in Ov. *Her.* 14. 35, she is made to say, *circum me gemitus morientum*

audire videbar ; | *et tamen audibam, quodque verebar erat.*

43. **intra claustra :** *i.e.* where others would kill you.

44. **tenebo :** for *retinebo ;* Intr. 129.

45. **me:** Intr. 116 *b, g ;* not continuing the emphasis of **ego,** but contrasted with **te.**   The two sentences of this strophe are virtually concessive clauses added to the expression of her determination in 42–44: 'I will not compass your death, let my father do his worst to me.'

47. **extremos:** see 10. 1 n.

49. **pedes et aurae:** *i.e.* to the coast, and then across the sea ; cf. *Epod.* 16. 21 *sq.*

50. **Venus :** who, as inspirer of Hypermnestra's act, has given him the opportunity to escape.

51. **nostri,** *of me,* as in 27. 14 and Juv. 3. 318 ; cf. 28. 9 n. — **sepulcro :** Intr. 69.

XII.

Miserarum est neque amori dare ludum neque dulci
   mala vino lavere, aut exanimari metuentis
   patruae verbera linguae.

2 Tibi qualum Cythereae puer ales, tibi telas
   operosaeque Minervae studium aufert, Neobule,
   Liparaei nitor Hebri,

3 simul unctos Tiberinis umeros lavit in undis,
   eques ipso melior Bellerophonte, neque pugno
   neque segni pede victus ;

XII. This ode is a study in pure
Ionics, based apparently on an ode
of Alcaeus, beginning ἔμε δείλαν,
ἔμε πασᾶν κακοτάτων πεδέχοισαν
(*Fr.* 59). Alcaeus wrote a number of poems in this metre, but
Horace seems to have found the
task of naturalizing it in Latin
too difficult, or the effect unsatisfactory; at least, this is the only
example he has left us.   In form
it is a monologue, the complaint
of a love-sick girl, who frets against
the restraints under which she is
brought up, and sighs for the freedom of a young man. The names
are Greek, but the local coloring
is, as usual, wholly Roman. —
Metre, 168.

1. **ludum**, *free play;* cf. Plaut.
Bacch. 1083 *nimis nolo ei desidiae
dare ludum.* — **lavere**: *i.e.* wash
them away. For the form, see
II. 3. 18 n. — **aut**, *or else; or, if
they do;* cf. 24. 24; Tac. *Ann.*
III. 73. 1 *huc adrogantiae venerat,
ut sedem sibi atque exercitui pos-
tularet, aut bellum inexplicabile
minitaretur.* — **metuentis**: accusative; the force of the genitive
miserarum has faded, at this
distance, into a vague idea of

necessity, so that *eas* is felt to
be understood as the subject of
exanimari. — **patruae**: not necessarily of an actual uncle.   The
word *patruus*, like *noverca* (see
Epod. 5. 9 n), had become proverbial for severity untempered
by parental affection or sympathy;
cf. *S.* II. 3. 88 *ne sis patruus
mihi.* For the form, see Intr. 65.
— **verbera**, *the lashings.*

2. **tibi qualum (aufert)**, *steals
away your wool-basket.* The verb
here, though used figuratively, has
its literal (physical) meaning ; with
its other subject, **nitor Hebri**, it
is purely metaphorical. — **opero-
sae**: applied to Minerva (in contrast with Venus) as patroness
of the various handicrafts, particularly of spinning and weaving
(Ἀθηνᾶ Ἐργάνη). — **Minervae**:
objective gen.— **Neobule**: a name
borrowed from Archilochus, for
its pleasing sound and metrical
value ; cf. *Leuconoe,* I. 11. —
Liparaei Hebri: cf. I. 27. 10,
II. 4. 2, III. 9. 9, 14. The name
Hebrus is taken from the river
in Thrace; cf. 7. 23 n. — **nitor**: cf.
I. 19. 5.

3. **simul**: see I. 4. 17 n. —

4 catus idem per apertum fugientis agitato
   grege cervos iaculari et celer arto latitantem
   fruticeto excipere aprum.

XIII.

O fons Bandusiae, splendidior vitro,
dulci digne mero non sine floribus,
      cras donaberis haedo,
         cui frons turgida cornibus

unctos : for the exercise that preceded the bath. On this whole
passage see I. 8. 5 *sqq.*, III. 7. 25
sqq., with notes. — eques: a construction according to sense (as
if *Hebrus*, instead of nitor Hebri
had been the subject of the main
verb) justified by the intervention of the dependent clause with
Hebrus understood as its subject.
—Bellerophontē : from the form
Bellerophontes ; cf. 7. 15 n. —
segni: with both pugno and
pede; Intr. 119 *a.* The ablatives
are better taken as causal.
   4. fruticeto: Intr. 69. — excipere: *i.e.* to attack him when he is
driven out, and kill him before he
can escape. For the infinitives
see Intr. 101 *b* and *c.*

XIII. To the spring of Bandusia. Where the spring was which
Horace has immortalized under
this name, cannot be determined.
There is evidence, dating from the
beginning of the twelfth century,
of the existence of a 'fons Bandu-
sinus' near Venusia, and this tradition, in itself of no great value,—
for it was very common in the
middle ages for a classical name
to be attached to a place without
the least reference to truth, — re-

ceives some support from the name
itself, which, being probably a corruption of the Greek Πανδοσία,
is one we should expect to find
in the neighborhood of Venusia,
rather than in the Sabine district
where Horace had his farm. There
was on Horace's farm a spring
which we know he admired and
valued highly (cf. *S.* II. 6. 2, *Ep.*
I. 16, 12 *sqq.*), and which would fit
in all respects our poem ; but we
do not know that it was called
Bandusia or had any name at all.
Some have imagined that Horace,
on coming into possession of his
new home, revived there a name
familiar and dear to him in the
place of his birth. Fortunately
our ignorance need not mar our
enjoyment of the poem, which
would lose none of its exquisite
beauty if we were obliged to rele-
gate the spring entirely to the
realm of fancy. — Metre, 173.
   1. Bandusiae : apparently the
name of the place, not of the
nymph of the spring. — splendidior vitro, *brighter than crystal.*
Ovid applies the same phrase
to Galatea (*M.* XIII. 791). The
brightness, of course, implies the
transparency of the water, as of
the glass. Cf. *splendor aquai,*

5   primis et venerem et proelia destinat ;
    frustra : nam gelidos inficiet tibi
      rubro sanguine rivos,
        lascivi suboles gregis.

    Te flagrantis atrox hora Caniculae
10   nescit tangere, tu frigus amabile
      fessis vomere tauris
        praebes et pecori vago.

    Fies nobilium tu quoque fontium,
    me dicente cavis impositam ilicem
15   saxis unde loquaces
        lymphae desiliunt tuae.

Lucr. IV. 211.   For **vitro**, cf. I. 17. 20 n.

2. **mero** : poured into the water as a libation to the divinity of the spring.   That the poet will make these slighter offerings of wine and flowers, along with the greater sacrifice promised in the next verse, goes without saying.   The regular time for making such offerings was the festival of the Fontanalia (or Fontinalia), October 13. — **non sine** : cf. I. 23. 3 n. — **floribus** : cf. Varro *L. L.* VI. 22 (*Fontanalibus*) *et in fontes coronas iaciunt et puteos coronant.*   That they also sacrificed animals appears from the present passage and from the *Acta Fratr. Arv.* (A.D. 183), where a sacrifice of two wethers is recorded.   It is not necessary, however, to suppose that this ode was written on the eve of the Fontanalia.   Cf. Martial VI. 47.

5. **destinat,** *foretokens.*

6. **frustra : nam,** etc. : cf. 7. 21 n. — **gelidos, rubro :** see Intr. 122.

9. **te . . . tu**: cf. I. 10. 9 n ; Intr. 116 *g.* — **hora,** *season;* cf. Ep. II. 3. 302 *sub verni temporis horam.* The whole phrase means the furious heat of the dog-days; see I. 17. 17 n.

10. **tangere,** *come nigh.*   For the mood see Intr. 94 *o.* — **frigus,** etc. : *i.e.* during the mid-day rest.

12. **vago** : answering to **fessis vomere** ; the aimless movement of the grazing flock is contrasted with the steady-going ox at his work.

13. **nobilium,** *famous ; i.e.* such as Hippocrene, Castalia, Arethusa, etc.   The poet has kept his word. — **fontium** : Intr. 62.

14. **cavis,** etc. : with consummate skill Horace has painted the whole scene for us in these few finishing strokes. — **impositam,** *that stands upon;* cf. IV. 14. 12.

15. **loquaces** : with **desiliunt.** The fine effect of this passage is due in large measure to the succession of liquids and expressive vowel sounds; Intr. 131.

XIV.

Herculis ritu modo dictus, o plebs,
morte venalem petiisse laurum
Caesar Hispana repetit penatis
    victor ab ora.

5 Vnico gaudens mulier marito
prodeat, iustis operata sacris,
et soror clari ducis et decorae
    supplice vitta

XIV. Early in the year B.C. 24 Augustus returned to Rome after an absence of nearly three years in the West, where he had reduced the Cantabrians to temporary submission and settled the affairs of Gaul. During the Cantabrian campaign he had lain sick at Tarraco for many months, — a period of grave anxiety for all thoughtful and peace-loving Romans, in view of the disorders that would inevitably follow his death. There was no doubt genuine rejoicing among the great mass of the people over his recovery and safe return. As he had declined the honor of a triumph for success achieved largely by his lieutenants, a public thanksgiving (*supplicatio*) would naturally be decreed. In anticipation of such a thanksgiving Horace wrote the present ode. He pictures the outward manifestations of gratitude and rejoicing, in which the women may be expected to take a prominent part; and then proceeds with his own preparations for celebrating the day in a light-hearted strain, in which, however, we are not permitted to forget the significance of the occasion. — Metre, 174.

1. **Herculis ritu**, *like Hercules;*
referring both to the dangerous enterprise and the victorious return. — **modo** (with **dictus**): *i.e.* at the time of his illness. — **dictus**, *he who was said.* — **o plebs**, *O ye people.* The word had lost its earlier meaning of a political class, and signified, like *populus,* the mass of the citizens in distinction from their rulers; cf. II. 2. 18.

2. **venalem,** *whose price is.* — **petiisse,** *to have gone in quest of.*

3. **Hispana ora** : cf. 8. 21 n.

5. **unico gaudens,** *whose whole joy is in ;* cf. *unicis Sabinis,* II. 18. 14 n. *Vnicus,* from its use with *filius, filia,* etc., had come to connote a concentration of interest and affection on a single object, who is one's 'all.'— **mulier:** Livia. She was a woman of great ability and force of character, tempered with good sense and tact, which enabled her to keep the affection of her husband to the end. Her private life was above reproach (*sanctitate domus priscum ad morem,* Tac. *Ann.* V. 1. 5).

6. **prodeat** : on a day of thanksgiving, besides the institution of public sacrifices, the temples, which were closed to the laity on ordinary occasions, were thrown open and were thronged with crowds of

virginum matres iuvenumque nuper
10　　sospitum ; vos, o pueri et puellae
non virum expertae, male ominatis
parcite verbis.

Hic dies vere mihi festus atras
eximet curas : ego nec tumultum
15　　nec mori per vim metuam tenente
Caesare terras.

people of every age and class, who passed through the streets from shrine to shrine, crowned with wreaths and singing hymns. — **iustis,** *due ; i.e.* those prescribed by the ritual. — **operata :** *i.e.* at home, before setting out to take part in the public thanksgiving. — **sacris :** the other reading, *iustis divis* (*scilicet quod Caesari victoriam et reditum merenti dederint,* Porphyrio), would be more appropriate if **operata** referred to the public ceremonies of the day. But **operata,** which implies an actual sacrifice ('*operationes*' *enim sacrificia dixerunt,* Porph.), cannot well apply to the mere presence of Livia and the women at the public ceremonies, in which they would take no active part ; and if it could, it ought to be *operatura,* as Bentley pointed out.

7. **soror :** Octavia.

8. **supplice :** in distinction from the plain one worn ordinarily by free-born ladies. The 'thanksgiving fillet' would seem to have been a wreath of olive twined with a woolen ribbon. — **vitta :** abl. with **decorae,** as in II. 16. 6.

9. **virginum matres,** etc.: *i.e.* mothers with their sons and daughters (or daughters-in-law) about them, the former just home from the wars (**nuper sospitum**). Some join **nuper sospitum** with **vir-**

ginum also, but this is a strained interpretation and confuses the picture.

10. **vos :** the younger children, who would especially need this caution. This is indicated by the word **pueri** (in contrast with **iuvenes,** above) and more explicitly in the phrase attached to **puellae.** Cf. the very similar expression for 'boys and girls,' *Ep.* II. 1. 132 *castis cum pueris ignara puella mariti.*

11. **non virum expertae :** the MS. reading, *iam virum expertae,* would make the whole phrase a bungling and needless repetition of **virginum iuvenumque,** above. — **male ominatis,** etc. : equivalent to *favete linguis,* III. 1. 2 n. If the text is correct, the hiatus (Intr. 185) is due to the feeling that the two words belong together as a compound.

12. **parcite :** *abstain from ;* cf. *Epod.* 17. 6 *parce vocibus sacris.*

13. **vere mihi festus :** used predicatively : cf. 8. 9 n. — **atras curas :** those caused by the precarious state of Caesar's health. Cf. III. 1. 40 n.

14. **tumultum,** *insurrection ;* a war in the city or in Italy (cf. Cic. *Phil.* VIII. 2 *sqq.*). He is thinking of personal danger.

15. **mori :** Intr. 95. — **tenente :** *sc.* as ruler ; cf. 17. 8, *S.* I. 7. 18.

I, pete unguentum, puer, et coronas
et cadum Marsi memorem duelli,
Spartacum si qua potuit vagantem
20   fallere testa.

Dic et argutae properet Neaerae
murreum nodo cohibere crinem ;
si per invisum mora ianitorem
fiet, abito.

25   Lenit albescens animos capillus
litium et rixae cupidos protervae ;
non ego hoc ferrem calidus iuventa
consule Planco.

17. **unguentum, coronas, ca-
dum**: cf. II. 3. 13 n. — **puer**: see
I. 19. 14 n.

18. **Marsi duelli** : the Social
War, B.C. 90, 89. The Marsi were
among the bravest of the *socii ;*
cf. I. 2. 39 n. — **memorem** : *i.e.*
stored at that time. Cf. Juv. 5. 31
*calcatamque tenet bellis socialibus
uvam* (*dives*).

19. **Spartacum**: the Servile War
occurred B.C. 73–71. — **vagantem** :
i.e. marauding.

20. **fallere** : cf. 11. 40 n.

21. **argutae**, *sweet-voiced ;* cf.
argutae Thaliae, IV. 6. 25. — **properet** : Gr. 339. — **Neaerae** : a
music girl.

22. **murreum**, *chestnut ;* it is
defined by Porphyrio as (*color*)
medius inter flavum et nigrum. —
nodo cohibere : instead of a more
elaborate coiffure, which would
keep him waiting ; cf. II. 11. 23 n.

23. **ianitorem** : the *ostiarius* of
the house where Neaera lodged.

24. **abito**: the second form of the
imperative (2d person), referring
to a point of future time removed
by an interval from the present.

25. **albescens**: Horace was only
forty-one, but his hair turned gray
early (Intr. 29).

27. **non ego**: cf. I. 18. 11 n.—
ferrem : Gr. 308 *a.* — **calidus iuventa** : in contrast with the actual
fact implied in **albescens**, etc.

28. **consule Planco**: the year
was that of Philippi. The reminiscence, like those of vss. 18 and
19, is not without design. To his
playful reminder of the unpleasant
experiences of civil war and insurrection, from which the rule of
Augustus had afforded a happy
escape, Horace adds an intimation
of his own change from a hot partisan to a lover of peace and quiet.

XV. Horace here portrays the
same type of character that he
attacks with more severity in I. 25,
IV. 13, and some of the Epodes,
— that of the woman of faded
beauty who still tries to play the
part of a young girl. — Metre, 171.

1. **pauperis** : a reason why she
should stay at home and work; cf.
vs. 13.

2. **fige** : more forcible than *pone*

XV.

Vxor pauperis Ibyci,
    tandem nequitiae fige modum tuae
famosisque laboribus ;
    maturo propior desine funeri
5   inter ludere virgines
        et stellis nebulam spargere candidis.
Non, si quid Pholoen satis,
    et te, Chlori, decet : filia rectius
expugnat iuvenum domos,
10   pulso Thyias uti concita tympano.
illam cogit amor Nothi
    lascivae similem ludere capreae :
te lanae prope nobilem
        tonsae Luceriam, non citharae decent
15   nec flos purpureus rosae
        nec poti vetulam faece tenus cadi.

(I. 16. 2), implying (with **tandem**) permanency : 'put an end to it once for all.'

3. laboribus : sarcastic ; 'everybody knows (**famosis**) that at your years such capers are hard work.'

4. maturo, *the full time of ;* it could not be called untimely if it should occur in the near future.— **propior,** *getting near (as you are).*

5. inter ludere : Intr. 115 *c.* For this use of **ludere,** cf. II. 12. 19 n.

6. stellis, etc. : her presence is like a shadow on the bright company.

7. non, si : cf. II. 10. 17 n.— **Pholoen** (sc. *decet*) : her daughter. —**satis,** *well.*

9. expugnat : not a mere figure of speech ; cf. Sen. *N. Q.* IV. *Praef.* 6 *dicebat adulationibus nos non claudere ostium, sed aperire,*

et quidem sic ut amicae opponi solet, quae si impulit, grata est, si effregit, gratior.

10. pulso, *by the beating of ;* Intr. 105 *a.* — **Thyias :** see II. 19. 9 n. — **tympano :** see I. 18. 13 n.

12. lascivae, etc. : scornful characterization of the mother's conduct.— **similem :** the adjective for the adverb, as in I. 23. 1.

13. prope tonsae Luceriam : Intr. 115 *b.* Apulian wool was the best in the Roman market (Plin. *N. H.* VIII. 190). As it was this that gave the town its distinction (**nobilem**) the epithet suggests the excellence of the wool.

14. citharae, etc. : the description is that of a music girl at a banquet.

16. poti : passive. — **vetulam :** reserved for this place to point and

XVI.

Inclusam Danaen turris aenea
robustaeque fores et vigilum canum
tristes excubiae munierant satis
nocturnis ab adulteris,

5   si non Acrisium, virginis abditae
custodem pavidum, Iuppiter et Venus
risissent : fore enim tutum iter et patens
converso in pretium deo.

Aurum per medios ire satellites

emphasize the incongruity between her age and the scene which these words suggest.

XVI. Reflections on the power and the impotence of riches. Gold is a mighty weapon : it can bring to nought the counsels of kings ; it can break through walls of rock ; it can destroy princely houses, take cities, subvert thrones ; but it cannot confer happiness. Wealth brings trouble and danger, and it cannot keep pace with growing desire ; contentment is better than great possessions. Heaven can vouchsafe no richer boon than moderate means with a contented spirit. The ode is addressed to Maecenas, and is very similar in sentiment to II. 2 and 16, and III. 1. — Metre, 172.

1. **Danaen** : Horace, with mild irony, treats the highly poetical myth of Jupiter descending to Danae in a golden shower as the testimony of mythology to the power of gold. — **aenea**: cf. 3. 65 n.

2. **robustae**, *oaken ;* cf. I. 3. 9.

3. **tristes**, *grim.* — **munierant**: see Intr. 82. The indicative expresses what had been the fact

until the occurrence of the event indicated in the protasis ; the precautions had been sufficient (and would have continued to be) if the power of gold had not been brought to bear against them. Cf. Tac. *Ann.* IV. 9. 1 (of the speech of Tiberius to the senate on the death of his son) *magno ea fletu ei mox precationibus faustis audita ; ac, si modum orationi posuisset, misericordia sui gloriaque animos audientium impleverat.*

4. **adulteris** : cf. I. 33. 9 n.

6. **pavidum**: Acrisius had been told by an oracle that his daughter's son would slay him.

7. **fore enim**, etc.: the construction shows that the thought is quoted, and the context shows it is that of the two divinities.

8. **pretium**, *a bribe.* — **deo**: dative.

9. **per medios**: *i.e.* not secretly, by outwitting them, but right under their eyes ; it paralyzes and disarms them. This idea of the power of gold is kept up in the metaphors that follow (**perrumpere, concidit, diffidit, subruit**). — **ire** : Intr. 94 *c.* — **satellites**, *royal guards.*

10　　et perrumpere amat saxa potentius
　　　ictu fulmineo ; concidit auguris
　　　　　Argivi domus, ob lucrum

　　　demersa exitio ; diffidit urbium
　　　portas vir Macedo et subruit aemulos
15　　reges muneribus ; munera navium
　　　　　saevos inlaqueant duces.

　　　Crescentem sequitur cura pecuniam
　　　maiorumque fames ; iure perhorrui

10. **saxa** : *i.e.* those of the wall of a city or stronghold, as in *Ep.* II. 3. 395.

11. **ictu** : Intr. 75.— **concidit** ... **diffidit** : Intr. 116 *b*, *c* ; cf. I. 28. 7.— **auguris Argivi** : Amphiaraus, the prophet-hero of Argos, brother-in-law of king Adrastus. When the latter was organizing the expedition of the 'Seven against Thebes,' Amphiaraus, who foresaw its disastrous end and his own death, was betrayed into the necessity of joining it by his wife Eriphȳle, who had been bribed by Polynices with the golden necklace of Harmonia. The consequences were the death of Amphiaraus, the murder of Eriphyle in revenge by their son Alcmaeon, and the madness of the latter under his mother's curse.

13. **diffīdit**, *clove asunder*.

14. **vir Macedo** : Philip, the father of Alexander. His success in accomplishing his purposes by bribery was proverbial, so that the mention of his name is unnecessary ; cf. Cic. *ad Att.* I. 16. 12 *Philippus omnia castella expugnari posse dicebat in quae modo asellus onustus auro posset ascendere.* A Delphic oracle was quoted, advising him to fight 'with silver spears': and it was said ὅτι τὰς

πόλεις αἱρεῖ τῶν Ἑλλήνων οὐ Φίλιππος, ἀλλὰ τὸ Φιλίππου χρυσίον. (Plut. *Aem. Paul.* 12).— **subruit,** *undermined.*

15. **muneribus; munera**: Intr. 116 *e.* — **navium duces** : these words would recall to Horace's readers a conspicuous example of their own time, Menodorus, the freedman admiral of Sextus Pompeius, who deserted to Octavian, then back to Pompey, and finally to Octavian again.

16. **saevos,** *stern ; i.e.* for all their sternness.

17. **crescentem,** etc.: the preceding reflections on the power of wealth convey no suggestion of its desirability as a possession ; on the contrary, its wonderful power is always a power for evil, and the suggestion of danger to the possessor is not far removed ; just as in these days we might speak with admiration of electricity as a mighty force, which, however, we should shrink from handling. This underlying thought now comes to the surface.— **cura** : here simply the worry of managing great wealth.

18. **maiorum**: neuter.—**fames**: cf. *Ep.* I. 18. 23 *argenti sitis importuna famesque,* Verg. *A.* III. 57 *auri sacra fames ;* and, for the

late conspicuum tollere verticem,

20   Maecenas, equitum decus.

Quanto quisque sibi plura negaverit,
ab dis plura feret. Nil cupientium
nudus castra peto et transfuga divitum
partis linquere gestio,

25   contemptae dominus splendidior rei,
quam si quicquid arat impiger Apulus
occultare meis dicerer horreis,
magnas inter opes inops.

---

thought, II. 2. 13 *sqq.;* Juv. 14. 139
*crescit amor nummi quantum ipsa
pecunia crevit.*

19. **late conspicuum**: proleptic. The wise man will shrink
from the dangerous prominence
which great wealth gives.— **tollere**: Intr. 94 *l.* — **verticem**: an
appropriate word with **tollere**; cf.
I. 1. 36, 18. 15.

20. **equitum**: Maecenas is himself a shining example of the wisdom of moderation ; Intr. 21.

21. **quanto**, etc.: in this para-
doxical sentence **plura** gets its
meaning in each case from the
context ; in the first clause it
means those things which we have
in mind when we speak of ' denying ourselves,' that is, in general,
luxuries ; in the second clause it
means the gifts of the gods, that
is, those enjoyments and satisfac-
tions that come to us, not of our
own seeking, but as the fruits of a
well-trained mind and character.
In particular, Horace means that
self-denial develops a contented
spirit, which is the only condition
of happiness, and his teaching
here, as in II. 2. 17 *sqq.*, falls in
with that of the Stoics ; see Cic.
Paradoxa 6.

22. **nil cupientium**, *of the contented.* The figure of the two
camps is not intended to conform
in all respects to Horace's actual
circumstances, but to express vividly his strong conviction of the
superiority of contentment over
riches. The figure is, as often,
confused with the reality ; see
Intr. 123.

23. **nudus peto**, *I leave all and
set out for ; i.e.* I surrender all that
I possess, in exchange for the
more precious treasure of contentment. — **transfuga**, etc.: *i.e.* I am
(like) a soldier in the camp of the
rich whose heart is in the other
camp, so that he holds cheap the
luxuries about him.

25. **contemptae**, *insignificant*
(*sc.* in the eyes of the wealthy); cf.
Cic. *Parad.* 6. 47 *meam pecuniam
contemnis, et recte ; est enim ad
volgi opinionem mediocris, ad tuam
nulla, ad meam modica.* — **splendidior**: *sc.* in the eyes of the wise;
cf. II. 2. 21 *sqq.*

26. **quicquid**, etc.: cf. I. 1. 10 n.
— **arāt**: here used for the whole
work of production by the farmer;
cf. the use of *trahunt*, II. 18. 8 n.
For the prosody, see Intr. 179.—
impiger Apulus : cf. *pernicis*

Purae rivus aquae silvaque iugerum
30   paucorum et segetis certa fides meae
fulgentem imperio fertilis Africae
     fallit sorte beatior.

Quamquam nec Calabrae mella ferunt apes,
nec Laestrygonia Bacchus in amphora
35   languescit mihi, nec pinguia Gallicis
     crescunt vellera pascuis,

Apuli, Epod. 2. 42. The soil of the Apulian lowlands was excellent for tillage as well as for pasture (Strabo, VI. 284).

27. **occultare**: a fresh word, for the more usual *condere* (cf. I. 1. 9). — **meis**: emphatic; Intr. 116 *b*.

28. **magnas,** etc., *being (really)*, etc.; expressing the actual fact in contrast with what people say **(dicerer)**.

29. **rivus aquae silvaque**: cf. Horace's description of his farm, *Ep.* I. 16. 5 *sqq.*; also I. 22. 9 *sqq.*, *Ep.* I. 14. 1 *sqq.*

30. **segetis certa fides**: in contrast with *fundus mendax*, III. 1. 30 n, and *spem mentita seges, Ep.* I. 7. 87. **segetis** is possessive genitive; cf. Cic. *ad Fam.* XVI. 17. 1 *ager etiam fidelis dici potest.* The poet, 'desiderans quod satis est,' can always count on his crops yielding enough for his needs; it is only the man who is intent on growing rich that is worried by the uncertainties of farming.

31. **fulgentem imperio**: the man holding for the time the splendid position of proconsul. The proconsulships of Asia and Africa were the highest positions of dignity and power attainable by a Roman citizen; they were assigned by lot each year to the two senior consulars. Others take the words

as an extravagant expression for great landed possessions in Africa; but the examples cited in support of this view (vs. 41, below, and II. 2. 9 *sqq.*) refer to regal power. Horace has already used the great landowners for comparison (vss. 26 *sq.*); he now uses exalted station and outward splendor, as he does in II. 2. 17. The epithet **fertilis** contributes to the picture, suggesting the great resources of the province, which give it its importance and prominence.

32. **fallit sorte beatior**: literally 'being happier in lot (than he), escapes his notice,' *i.e. is a happier lot than his, though he does not suspect it.* The construction is formed after the Greek idiom (λανθάνει ὀλβιώτερον ὄν, the Latin language, however, providing no equivalent for ὄν).

33. **quamquam**, etc.: with these typical forms of wealth cf. I. 31. 5 *sqq., Epod.* 1. 25 *sqq.;* Intr. 117 *a.* — **Calabrae apes**: cf. II. 6. 14.

34. **Laestrygonia**: *i.e.* Formian; see 17. 1 n, and cf. *Sabina*, I. 9. 7 n. For the wine, see I. 20. 10 n. — **Bacchus**: Intr. 130.

35. **languescit**, *is mellowing;* cf. *languidiora vina*, 21. 8. — **Gallicis**: *i.e.* of Cisalpine Gaul, where white wool of a fine quality was grown (Plin. *N. H.* VIII. 190).

36. **pascuis**: Intr. 69.

importuna tamen pauperies abest,
nec, si plura velim, tu dare deneges.
Contracto melius parva cupidine
40   vectigalia porrigam
quam si Mygdoniis regnum Alyattei
campis continuem.   Multa petentibus
desunt multa; bene est cui deus obtulit
parca quod satis est manu.

37. **importuna,** *pinching.*
38. **nec si,** etc.: cf. *Epod.* i. 31.
— **dare:** Intr. 94 *k.*
39. **contracto,** etc.: cf. II. 2.
9 *sqq.* — **melius porrigam** : suggested by **si plura velim.** The sense is : If I *should* find my income too small for my expenses, a better way to enlarge it will be to cut down my desires till they come within it ; the other way, seeking for more, never brings satisfaction ; desire is never satisfied by feeding it.   Horace is here preaching on a Stoic text ; cf. Cic. *Parad.* 6. 49 *O di immortales! non intellegunt homines quam magnum vectigal sit parsimonia.* — **cupidine:** see II. 16. 15 n.
40. **vectigalia,** *income;* properly, public revenues, but sometimes used of private income, especially for purposes of comparison, as here and *S.* II. 2. 100 ; cf. also Cic. *l.c.*
41. **Mygdoniis:** *i.e.* Phrygian ; see II. 12. 22 n. — **Alyattei:** king of Lydia, father of Croesus. For the form, cf. *Vlixei,* I. 6. 7 n.
42. **campis :** dative ; Intr. 56. — **continuem,** *unite; sc.* under my sway, so as to enjoy the entire revenues of both countries.   The word is often used of buying up large tracts of land, *e.g.* Liv. XXXIV. 4. 9 *quid legem Liciniam excitavit de quingentis iugeribus*

nisi ingens cupido agros continuandi? — **multa petentibus,** etc.: the converse of *quanto quisque . . . feret,* 21 *sq.*
43. **bene est** (sc. *ei*), *blessed is the man.*

XVII.   To L. Aelius Lamia, in regard to whom see I. 26, introd. note.   The ode, it would seem, is addressed to him simply as a compliment, the substance of it being a light sketch in the spirit of I. 9, very likely a study from the Greek, which it would be idle to attempt to connect with Lamia's personality.   The scene is laid in the country, near the seashore. 'A great storm is brewing ; you must stay indoors to-morrow, and your servants can do no work.   Make ready to enjoy with them the holiday thus provided for you.' — Metre, 176.
1. **ab Lamo :** equivalent to *Lamo orte,* the idea of descent being implied in **nobilis.** Lamus was the mythical founder of the city of the Laestrygones (Λάμου αἰπὺ πτολίεθρον | Τηλέπυλον Λαιστρυγονίην, *Odys.* X. 81), which was identified with Formiae: cf. Cic. *ad Att.* II. 13. 2 *si vero in hanc* Τηλέπυλον *veneris* Λαιστρυγονίην, *Formias dico.*   That the Lamiae, one of the oldest and wealthiest families of Formiae, should place

XVII.

Aeli vetusto nobilis ab Lamo,
(quando et priores hinc Lamias ferunt
    denominatos et nepotum
        per memores genus omne fastos,

5   auctore ab illo ducis originem
    qui Formiarum moenia dicitur
        princeps et innantem Maricae
            litoribus tenuisse Lirim

this name at the head of their pedigree, was inevitable. At this time they had little political distinction to boast of, and were therefore all the more likely to make much of the antiquity of their family. The father of our Lamia, when he went into politics as a supporter of Cicero, was still only a knight, though a distinguished one ; in B.C. 44 Cicero supported him for the praetorship, with what success is unknown. (See Cic. *ad Fam.* XI. 16. 1, 17. 1.) His son, Horace's friend, was the first of the family who held the consulship, but that was at least twenty-five years after the date of this ode. We may therefore take this allusion to his pedigree as serious (not humorous, as some take it), and attribute it to the same motive as in the case of Maecenas (I. 1. 1, III. 29. 1, *S.* I. 6. 1, etc.), who likewise was without political distinction. A century later, when the Lamiae had become *nobiles* by the attainment of high curule office, we find them named as types of high nobility (Juv. 4. 154, 6. 385), a further evidence of the antiquity of their ancestry, as their *nobilitas* was even then not over three generations old.

2. **quando,** etc.; the four verses beginning here are with some reason suspected of being interpolated. If they are genuine, the whole genealogical dissertation, **quando — late tyrannus,** is parenthetical, and consists of a protasis, **quando — fastos,** introducing (and giving the reason of) a main statement, **auctore — tyrannus.** **—priores :** *i.e.* the earliest of the name; 'earlier' than the great body of descendants (**genus omne**) whose names are in the records. —**hinc,** *after him ;* cf. *unde,* I. 12. 17 n.

4. **fastos :** here used of family records.

5. **auctore :** sc. *generis;* cf. I. 2. 36. It is in apposition with **illo,** which is used substantively. — **ducis :** if *ducit* is read, **genus** is its subject, and the *whole* parenthetical clause depends on **quando.**

7. **innantem,** *that floods ;* referring to the marshes and inlets which prevail on that part of the coast. — **Maricae,** *Marica's.* She was an old Italian divinity, variously identified with Aphrodite and Circe, whose grove was at the mouth of the Liris, ten miles from Formiae.

8. **tenuisse :** cf. 14. 15 n.

late tyrannus,) cras foliis nemus
10   multis et alga litus inutili
        demissa tempestas ab Euro
            sternet, aquae nisi fallit augur

annosa cornix ; dum potes, aridum
    compone lignum ; cras genium mero
15   curabis et porco bimenstri
            cum famulis operum solutis.

9. **late tyrannus**: the Homeric εὑρὺ κρείων; cf. *late regem*, Verg. *A.* I. 21. For the construction see Mdv. 301 *c*. Obs. 2. — **nemus**: *i.e.* the ground under the trees. For this construction with *sterno*, cf. IV. 14. 32, where, as here, the simple verb is used for *consterno* (Intr. 129).

10. **inutili**; its worthlessness was proverbial ; cf. *vilior alga, S.* II. 5. 8, Verg. *E.* 7. 42.

11. **Euro**: cf. *Epod.* 16. 54.

12. **aquae augur**: after the Greek ὑετόμαντις (cf. Euphorion, *Fr.* 65 ὑετόμαντις ὅτε κρώξειε κορώνη). Vergil describes its action when 'calling rain,' *G.* I. 388 *tum cornix plena pluviam vocat improba voce | et sola in sicca secum spatiatur harena.* Cf. 27. 10, Lucr. V. 1083. — **fallit** : used absolutely, as in *Epod.* 16. 45 *numquam fallentis olivae.*

13. **annosa** : it was supposed to live to an extraordinary age, — through nine generations of men, according to Hesiod (Plut. *Moral.* 415 C); cf. IV. 13. 25. — **dum potes** : *i.e.* today, before the storm wets it.

14. **compone**, *get in a store.* — **genium** : a man's *genius* was conceived to be an attendant spirit, divine but not immortal, insepara-

bly associated with his life in all its phases of enjoyment or depression, 'naturae deus humanae, mortalis in unum | quodque caput, voltu mutabilis, albus et ater' (*Ep.* II. 2. 187) ; and on its varying moods depended his happiness or unhappiness. The conception was not unlike that of the soul in the parable of the rich man, Luke 12. 16 *sqq.* ('I will say to my soul, Soul, thou hast much goods laid up for many years ; take thine ease, eat, drink, and be merry.') Hence, to deny one's self reasonable comforts was to 'cheat one's genius' (Ter. *Ph.* 44) ; and to take a holiday or otherwise give one's self up to enjoyment was *piare* (*Ep.* II. 1. 144) or *placare* (*Ep.* II. 3. 210) *genium*, or, more commonly, *indulgere genio.* Horace here substitutes *curare*, a word often used for bodily comfort (*curare corpus, curare cutem*, etc.). — **mero** : cf. Pers. 2. 3 *funde merum genio; Ep.* II. 1. 144 ; Tib. II. 2. 8.

15. **curabis** : Intr. 90.—**porco** : an offering to the Lares (cf. 23. 4, *S.* II. 3. 164), whose worship was associated with every act of family life. The flesh of the victim would furnish forth the simple feast ; see I. 36. 2 n.

16. **operum** : Intr. 67.

XVIII.

Faune, nympharum fugientum amator,
per meos finis et aprica rura
lenis incedas, abeasque parvis
    aequus alumnis,

5 si tener pleno cadit haedus anno,
larga nec desunt Veneris sodali
vina craterae, vetus ara multo
    fumat odore.

Ludit herboso pecus omne campo,

XVIII. A hymn to Faunus. The first half is a prayer for the favor of the god, which has been merited by constant and liberal offerings. In the second half his benign influence is set forth in a description of his festival on the 5th of December. This appears to have been a festival peculiar to the country, for in Rome his great day was the *Lupercalia*, on the 15th of February. For the attributes of Faunus, see I. 17. 2 n. — Metre, 174.

1. **nympharum**, etc. : this is a characteristic that belongs strictly to Pan and the Satyrs ; cf. Stat. *Silv.* II. 2. 100 *sqq.*, Mart. IX. 61. 13.

3. **lenis**, *in mercy.* — **incedas** : the mere presence of the god was believed to carry with it some influence, blessing or blight, according to his mood ; cf. I. 17. 5 *sqq.* — **abeasque aequus**, *and carry away a kindly feeling ; i.e.* may the god be pleased with all he sees, to the very end, and go away with a desire to bless.

4. **alumnis**, *younglings* of the herd and flock, as in 23. 7.

5. **si**, etc. : a modest form of statement common in prayers, introducing the ground on which the appeal is based ; cf. *S.* II. 6. 6 *sqq.*, and see note on *poscit*, I. 31. 1. — **tener haedus** : one of the *parvi alumni ;* cf. I. 4. 12. — **pleno anno** : *i.e.* at the close of it, on the recurrence of the festival in December. — **cadit** : as a victim ; cf. Verg. *A.* I. 334.

6. **Veneris sodali** : an epithet of the mixing-bowl not found elsewhere. It merely expresses the familiar association of 'love and wine.'

7. **craterae** : dative. When the bowl was filled, a libation would be made to the god first ; but the main use of the wine, as of the kid, was to contribute to a spirited celebration of the god's day. — **vetus** : suggesting the antiquity of the festival. Notice the asyndeton, which is continued through the rest of the ode. — **multo odore** : for *multo ture* (cf. I. 30. 3) ; so *colores* for flowers, Prop. I. 2. 9 *aspice quos summittat humus formosa colores.*

9. **ludit**, etc. : the appeal to the god has merged insensibly into a description of the festival, which

10   cum tibi nonae redeunt Decembres ;
      festus in pratis vacat otioso
          cum bove pagus ;

      inter audacis lupus errat agnos,
      spargit agrestis tibi silva frondis,
15   gaudet invisam pepulisse fossor
          ter pede terram.

now continues, bridging over the change in grammatical construction. The scene is a grassy meadow, — green even in December in the Italian climate, — where the whole countryside is gathered about the old altar. The sacrifice is followed, as usual, by feasting, after which the people stroll about the fields and woods, or amuse themselves with dancing and other merrymaking. Cattle and flocks peacefully grazing form the border of the picture. — **campo**: Intr. 69.

10. **tibi**, *thy;* dative of reference. — **redeunt** : cf. 8. 9 n.

11. **festus vacat**, *is making holiday.* — **otioso**, *freed from toil.* Both man and beast are enjoying a day of rest.

12. **pagus** : a few MSS. have *pardus*, a substitution evidently due to some lively monk, who remembered Isaiah 11. 6 *habitabit lupus cum agno et pardus cum haedo accubabit.*

13. **inter** : Intr. 115 *b*. — **audacis** : *i.e.* they are not afraid of him, for they feel to-day the presence of Faunus, who was also *Lupercus* (interpreted as *'qui lupum arcet'*); and he is cowed by the same presence.

14. **spargit**, etc. : cf. *Epod.* 11. 5

December silvis honorem (*=frondis*) *decutit.* The point here is that the woods of themselves strew the ground with leaves in honor of the god, referring to the common practice of strewing the ground with boughs on festal or solemn occasions ; cf. Verg. *E.* 5. 40 *spargite humum foliis* (in honor of Daphnis). — **agrestis**: *i.e.* natural, artless.

15. **invisam** : because of the incessant hard work he is condemned to spend upon it. — **pepulisse** : Intr. 94 *d*, 81 *a*. For the expression cf. I. 37. 2 *pulsanda tellus*, I. 4. 7 *terram quatiunt pede*, IV. 1. 28. — **fossor** : the lowest grade of farm-laborer, the typical clown (Cat. 22. 10, Pers. 5. 122). He was employed especially in working the soil in orchards and vineyards ; cf. Verg. *G.* II. 264. On large estates he was usually a slave in fetters (cf. Ov. *Tr.* IV. 1. 5 *hoc est cur cantet vinctus quoque compede fossor,* | *indocili numero cum grave mollit opus*) ; but in our present picture we must imagine him a free laborer for hire, a *farm-hand*, or perhaps the *pauper colonus* himself (cf. I. 1. 11 n, 35. 5).

16. **ter** : *i.e.* in a dance with triple beat (*tripudium*) ; cf. IV. 1. 28.

XIX.

Quantum distet ab Inacho
    Codrus, pro patria non timidus mori,
narras et genus Aeaci
    et pugnata sacro bella sub Ilio :
5   quo Chium pretio cadum
    mercemur, quis aquam temperet ignibus,
quo praebente domum et quota
    Paelignis caream frigoribus, taces.

XIX. This ode portrays, in a lively dramatic form which reminds of I. 27, a symposium. There are two distinct scenes, one occupying the first eight verses, and the other the remainder of the poem. How these are to be combined, Horace has by no means made clear. Perhaps the most probable explanation is this : On a sunny winter afternoon a company of literary friends sit together in some garden or elsewhere out of doors, and one of their number has been discoursing at great length on subjects which the poet begins to think are very ancient history. The sun is sinking low, the air grows chill, the cold evening is coming on. Suddenly the poet 'takes the floor,' and interrupts the learned discourse with a demand that the company consider a question of much nearer concern, — where, when, and how they can prepare to spend a merry evening. Then, as if carried away by his imagination, but really with the purpose of carrying his hearers with him, he plays the *magister bibendi* before them, with spirited dramatic action, as if the symposium had already begun, — a performance for which the serious and quiet picture in the opening verses supplies a fit-

ting background. There is a similar anticipation of a scene of revelry in II. 7. 21 *sqq.*; cf. also III. 14. 17 *sqq.* The whole bears the impress of a Greek origin, and the only Roman name in the poem is to be explained, so far as we can see, as merely a passing compliment. — Metre, 171.

1. **quantum distet** : *i.e.* in time. — **Inacho** : see II. 3. 21 n.

2. **Codrus** : the last king of Athens ; said to have deliberately sacrificed his life in battle, like the Roman Decii, to ensure victory to his countrymen (Cic. *Tusc.* I. 116). — **mori** : Intr. 101 *a*.

3. **genus Aeaci** : Telamon and Peleus and their descendants, Ajax, Teucer, Achilles, Neoptolemus, etc.

4. **pugnata bella** : so also *Ep.* I. 16. 25. — **sacro Ilio** : after the Homeric "Ἴλιος ἱρή (*e.g. Il.* IV. 46). For the gender, see I. 10. 14 n.

5. **quo**, etc. : the contemplated symposium is one towards which each guest contributes his share. — **Chium cadum** : cf. *Sabina diota,* I. 9. 7 n ; III. 16. 34. The Chian was a choice Greek wine.

6. **aquam** : to mix with the wine.

7. **quo praebente**, etc. : *i.e.* at whose house and when ? — **quota** : sc. *hora ;* cf. *S.* II. 6. 44.

8. **Paelignis** : *i.e.* such as pre-

Da lunae propere novae,
10   da noctis mediae, da, puer, auguris
Murenae.   Tribus aut novem
       miscentur cyathis pocula commodis.
Qui Musas amat imparis,
       ternos ter cyathos attonitus petet
15   vates ; tris prohibet supra
       rixarum metuens tangere Gratia
nudis iuncta sororibus.

vails in that mountainous region ; cf. *Sithonia nive,* 26. 10.

9. **da,** *fill up.* The object to be supplied is *cyathos* (*vini*), which the cup-bearer was to pour into the guests' goblets. Cf. *sume cyathos,* 8. 13, addressed to the guest. The genitives that follow depend on this *cyathos* understood ; see 8. 13 n. — **lunae novae,** etc.: three general toasts to begin the evening with, Horace having in mind no doubt the Greek practice of beginning a drinking bout with three libations. From the first we may infer that the time of the supposed revel was the new moon, or perhaps the first day of the month, which in Greek continued to be called νου-μηνία (= *nova luna*) after the lunar month had been abandoned ; **noctis mediae** implies that that hour was to be included in their programme ; **auguris Murenae** is best explained as a toast in honor of Murena's accession to the college of augurs. Whether this was the Licinius Murena of II. 10 is uncertain. We do not know that Licinius Murena was ever augur, but he may have been ; and we know of no other Murena who was a friend of Horace.

10. **da:** Intr. 116 *h.* — **puer:** see I. 19. 14 n ; but we may perhaps imagine an actual boy here ; cf. I. 29. 7 n.

11. **tribus aut novem cyathis:** expressing, not the quantity of wine in the cups, but the *proportion* of wine in the mixture. The Romans were in the habit of reckoning fractions by twelfths (*unciae*), and the cyathus, which as a measure was one twelfth of a sextarius, served as the *uncia* in mixing wine. *Tres cyathi,* then, meant $\frac{3}{12}$ wine ($+ \frac{9}{12}$ water); and *novem cyathi* $= \frac{9}{12}$ wine ($+ \frac{3}{12}$ water). — **aut:** the *magister* offers a choice between these alternatives only.

12. **commodis,** *at your pleasure;* proleptic, and having the force of an adverb with *miscentur.* For the meaning cf. IV. 8. 1.

13. **qui,** etc.: the bard himself, who seeks a strong inspiration, will name the number of the Muses as his choice, that is, he will take the stronger mixture ; but he who fears the effect of too great exhilaration will choose the number of the gentle Graces (see 21. 22 n).— **imparis :** in reference to their number, nine.

14. **attonitus,** *rapt.* — **petet,** *will call for.*

15. **tris supra :** Intr. 115 *b.*

16. **rixarum metuens :** cf. *patiens pulveris,* I. 8. 4 n ; III. 24. 22.

Insanire iuvat : cur Berecyntiae
cessant flamina tibiae ?
20   Cur pendet tacita fistula cum lyra ?
Parcentis ego dexteras
odi : sparge rosas ; audiat invidus
dementem strepitum Lycus
et vicina seni non habilis Lyco.
25 Spissa te nitidum coma,
puro te similem, Telephe, Vespero
tempestiva petit Rhode ;
me lentus Glycerae torret amor meae.

— **Gratia iuncta sororibus** : *i.e.*
the three Graces (in their traditional
posture); cf. *Gratia cum Nymphis
geminisque sororibus*, IV. 7. 5 n.

18. **insanire iuvat** : cf. *dulce
mihi furere*, II. 7. 28. — **Berecyntiae** : see I. 18. 13 n.

19. **tibiae** : see I. 1. 32 n. The
Phrygian pipes were distinguished
by the fact that one of the pair
had a curved end which gave it a
deeper tone ; cf. Cat. 63. 22 *tibicen
ubi canit Phryx curvo grave cala-
mo.* Hence it was sometimes called
a horn, as in I. 18. 13 ; cf. Ov. *F.*
IV. 181 *inflexo Berecyntia tibia
cornu.* See Howard, *Harv. Studies,*
IV. p. 35.

20. **pendet** : *sc.* on the wall. —
fistula : see I. 17. 10 n.

21. **dexteras**, *a hand.*

22. **sparge**: emphatic, implying
a generous supply of the flowers,
which in winter were more costly
than usual. — **invidus**, *with envy;*
proleptic.

23. **dementem**: cf. *dementis
ruinas*, I. 37. 7. Intr. 124. — **Lycus** : the old fellow who lives near
by with a young wife (apparently)
who does not care for him, is

introduced as a foil to set off the
hilarity of the revelers, and at the
same time leads to the suggestion
of the *amica*, whose presence completes the poet's picture.

24. **vicina**, *our fair neighbor.*—
non habilis : *i.e.* too young, — or
rather, he is too old for her.

25. **spissa**: as far as possible
from baldness. — **te ... te** : corresponding to **Lycus ... Lyco.**
— **nitidum**, *who look so spruce ;*
here of the general effect of the
person's make-up, as in II. 12. 19
and *S.* II. 1. 64 (not, as in I. 4. 9
and *nitentis capillos*, II. 7. 7, with
special reference to the oil put on
the hair).

26. **puro** : *i.e.* shining through
a clear atmosphere ; cf. *pura luna*,
II. 5. 19 ; III. 10. 8. For the comparison, cf. 9. 21.— **Telephe** : one
of the guests, addressed by name,
as in I. 27. 10, to give a touch of
personal interest to the scene.

27. **tempestiva**, *who IS suitable;*
in contrast with **non habilis**, 24,
and, as there, with more reference
to the man than to the woman.

28. **lentus torret** : see I. 13
8 n.

XX.

Non vides quanto moveas periclo,
Pyrrhe, Gaetulae catulos leaenae?
Dura post paulo fugies inaudax
    proelia raptor,

5   cum per obstantis iuvenum catervas
ibit insignem repetens Nearchum:
grande certamen, tibi praeda cedat,
    maior an illa.

Interim, dum tu celeres sagittas
10   promis, haec dentis acuit timendos,

XX. The subject of this ode is the attempt of a youth, who is called Pyrrhus, to win away the handsome boy Nearchus from the (unnamed) girl who claims him as her lover. The treatment is highly figurative, so much so that the reader needs to guard against losing sight of the actual story in the graphic metaphors. Pyrrhus is likened to the bold hunter who is preparing to carry off the lion's whelps; the girl to the she-lion who watches over them. Then, with a sudden shifting of the scene, the poet pictures the beautiful boy, complacently watching the impending contest. The Greek origin of the composition is apparent. — Metre, 174.

1. **moveas**, *disturb.*

2. **Gaetulae** : cf. I. 23. 10 n.

3. **post paulo** : the usual order, *paulo post* is avoided on account of its prosaic rhythm; so in the corresponding place in the hexameter, *Sat.* I. 2. 120, *Ep.* I. 6. 43. *Post paulo*, however, occurs also in prose. — **inaudax raptor** : the contrast (Intr. 116 a), amounts to an oxymoron : a robber and

afraid! **inaudax** is not found elsewhere.

5. **iuvenum catervas** : these stand, in the metaphor, for the hunter's attendants, — the lioness will not be daunted by them ; but the metaphor is for the moment put out of sight by the introduction of the boy in his proper person (**Nearchum**): the *iuvenes* are Pyrrhus' companions ; the girl will rush boldly among them to recover the boy. The figure and the reality are here blended (Intr. 123), and after vs. 10 the figure is dropped entirely.

6. **insignem,** *peerless;* lit. 'conspicuous' (among all the rest) ; there is none like him.

7. **grande certamen**: in apposition with the action expressed or implied in the preceding verses, in which all the elements of a contest are set before us. Cf. *opus*, II. 1. 6 n.— **tibi praeda cedat,** *whether the prey* (Nearchus) *shall fall to you* (*i.e.* as the prize of victory); cf. Verg. *A.* XII. 183 *cesserit Ausonio si fors victoria Turno.*

8. **maior** : *i.e.* victorious.— **illa:** sc. *sit.*

arbiter pugnae posuisse nudo
   sub pede palmam
fertur et leni recreare vento
   sparsum odoratis umerum capillis,
15 qualis aut Nireus fuit aut aquosa
   raptus ab Ida.

XXI.

O nata mecum consule Manlio,

11. posuisse, *has placed;* present perfect.—**nudo**: simply a stroke to make the picture more graphic.

13. fertur, *I am told;* cf. 5. 41 n.
—**leni recreare,** etc.: as he stands there, the breeze blows his long locks about his bare shoulders.

15. qualis, *as fair as.*— **Nireus**: Νιρεύς, ὃς κάλλιστος ἀνὴρ ὑπὸ Ἴλιον ἦλθεν | τῶν ἄλλων Δαναῶν μετ' ἀμύμονα Πηλείωνα, *Il.* II. 673. Cf. *Epod.* 15. 22.— **aquosa**: *i.e.* rich in springs (πολυπίδακος Ἴδης, *Il.* XIV. 157).

16. raptus: Ganymede, son of Laomedon, ὃς δὴ κάλλιστος γένετο θνητῶν ἀνθρώπων (*Il.* XX. 233), carried off by the eagle of Jove to become cup-bearer to the gods. For this use of the participle, see Intr. 103.

XXI. M. Valerius Messaka Corvinus, in whose honor this ode is written, had studied with Horace at Athens and fought with him at Philippi. He afterwards served with distinction under the triumvirs, — under Antony, as long as he could do so with self-respect, and then under Octavian, on whose side he fought at Actium. He was consul in the year of that battle, and afterwards earned a triumph (B.C. 27) by his successes

against the Aquitanians. From this time on he abstained as much as possible from participation in public affairs, and devoted himself especially to practice in the courts, where his eloquence, which, when he was still very young, had won Cicero's commendation (*ad Brut.* I. 15. 1, B.C. 43), gave him great eminence (*S.* I. 10. 29). He was distinguished also by wealth and high social position, and by a nobility of character which shone through his presence and address (*quodammodo praeferens in dicendo nobilitatem suam,* Quint. X. I. 113). He was devoted to literature, and gathered about him a circle of writers, the most famous of whom was Tibullus. The subject of the ode is the praise of wine. The poet stands before the *amphorae* in the *apotheca,* selecting one to be opened on the occasion of a visit from Messala, and gives utterance to his reflections on the potencies for good or ill with which the jar has stood charged this many a year. — Metre, 176.

1. nata mecum: *i.e.* filled and stored the year I was born.—**consule Manlio**: L. Manlius Torquatus, cos. B.C. 65. Cf. *Epod.* 13. 6 *tu vina Torquato move consule pressa meo.*

seu tu querellas sive geris iocos
seu rixam et insanos amores
seu facilem, pia testa, somnum,

5   quocumque lectum nomine Massicum
servas, moveri digna bono die,
descende, Corvino iubente
promere languidiora vina.

Non ille, quamquam Socraticis madet
10   sermonibus, te negleget horridus:
narratur et prisci Catonis
saepe mero caluisse virtus.

Tu lene tormentum ingenio admoves

2. **tu ... geris**: Intr. 120.—
querellas, *sighs*. It means dole-
ful utterance of any sort, in op-
position to the gayety expressed
by **iocos.**—**geris**: *i.e.* potentially,
to be brought to pass when the
jar is opened.

3. **rixam et insanos amores**:
cf. I. 13. 9 *sqq*., 17. 25 *sqq*.

4. **facilem**: cf. II. 11. 8 n; III.
1. 20 *sqq*.—**pia,** *faithful;* as con-
scientiously keeping its charge.—
testa: cf. I. 20. 2, III. 14. 20.

5. **quocumque nomine,** *on
whatever account* (*i.e.* for whatever
end); breaking off the unfinished
list with a single comprehensive
phrase, which we should introduce
by 'in short'; cf. I. 28. 15 n.—
lectum Massicum, *Massic vintage.* **lectum,** referring properly
to the grapes ('gathered') is here
used for the whole process of producing wine; cf. *arat,* 16. 26 n.
For **Massicum,** see I. 1. 19 n.

6. **moveri**: *sc.* from its place
in the *apotheca;* cf. *Epod.* 13. 6.
For the inf., see Intr. 101 *e.*—
bono die: the choicest wines were
reserved for choice occasions (cf.

I. 37. 5 n). The compliment to
Corvinus is obvious.

7. **descende**: from the store-
room, in the upper part of the
house; see 8. 11 n.

8. **promere**: depending on **iubente.**—**languidiora**: a quality
acquired by long keeping; cf.
languescit, 16. 35 n. The wine
here would be perhaps forty years
old.

9. **non ille**: cf. *non ego,* I. 18.
11 n.—**madet,** *is steeped; i.e.* is a
philosopher through and through.

10. **negleget horridus,** *be so
rude as to slight.*

11. **et,** *even.*—**prisci Catonis
virtus,** *excellent old Cato;* see
Intr. 126 *b,* and cf. Juv. 4. 81 *venit
et Crispi iucunda senectus* ('cheerful old Crispus'). Horace is
speaking of the elder Cato ('the
Censor'); cf. *priscis Catonibus,
Ep.* II. 2. 117. Cicero also represents him as fond of *modica convivia* (*de Sen.* 44 *sqq.*).

13. **tu**: see I. 10. 9 n.—**tormentum,** *spur* (literally, 'rack');
it stimulates the mind to give out
its thoughts, as the rack draws

plerumque duro ; tu sapientium
15   curas et arcanum iocoso
            consilium retegis Lyaeo ;

tu spem reducis mentibus anxiis
virisque et addis cornua pauperi,
    post te neque iratos trementi
20   regum apices neque militum arma.

Te Liber et, si laeta aderit, Venus
segnesque nodum solvere Gratiae
    vivaeque producent lucernae
        dum rediens fugat astra Phoebus.

confession from the criminal. Cf. *Ep.* II. 3. 434 *reges dicuntur multis urgere culullis | et torquere mero quem perspexisse laborant.*

14. **plerumque duro** : *i.e.* not susceptible to ordinary influences; cf. Silius XI. 285 *Bacchi munera duram | laxarunt mentem.* For **plerumque**, cf. I. 34. 6 n.— **sapientium** : limiting **curas** only.

15. **curas,** *grave thoughts.*

16. **iocoso Lyaeo,** *with the merry 'Releaser';* *i.e.* with wine, amid merriment. See I. 7. 22 n. There is nothing inconsistent in saying the wine-jar does these things 'with wine': the jar is personified.

18. **viris** : object of **addis,** for the position of which see Intr. 119 *a.* — **cornua** : the emblem of confidence and independence, like our 'holding up one's head'; cf. Ov. *Am.* III. 11. 3, 6 *scilicet adserui iam me, fugique catenas, | . . . venerunt capiti cornua sera meo,* and *A. A.* I. 239 *tum pauper cornua sumit* (an imitation of the present passage).

19. **post te** : cf. *post vina,* I. 18. 5 ; III. 7. 6. — **iratos apices** : Intr. 124. — **trementi** : transitive ; Intr. 51 *a.*

20. **apices** : see I. 34. 14 n.

21. **te** : *i.e.* thy ministrations ; very much as in vs. 19. — **Liber**: here the god himself ; the favoring divinities whom the *cadus* serves will bless its work.

22. **nodum** : formed by the twining of their arms round one another ; cf. 19. 17. — **solvere** : Intr. 101 *b.* — **Gratiae**: they stand for the charm of social converse, sparkling with wit, but ruled by courtesy, with nothing excessive or unseemly to mar its perfect enjoyment. Cf. 19. 16.

23. **vivae** : cf. *vigiles,* 8. 14. — **producent**: cf. *S.* I. 5. 70 *prorsus iucunde cenam producimus illam.* — **lucernae** : the personality of the divinities is, after all, half merged in the things they typify, — wine, love, gracious intercourse, — to which the lights are added as a fourth influence in prolonging the enjoyment.

XXII.

Montium custos nemorumque virgo,
quae laborantis utero puellas
ter vocata audis adimisque leto,
    diva triformis,

5   imminens villae tua pinus esto,
quam per exactos ego laetus annos
verris obliquum meditantis ictum
    sanguine donem.

XXII. A dedicatory poem, in which Horace consecrates the towering pine that stands by his country house to Diana, and vows an annual sacrifice. The invocation to the goddess has much in common with Catullus' hymn (*c.* 34), especially with these verses (9–16):

> Montium domina ut fores
> silvarumque virentium
> saltuumque reconditorum
> amniumque sonantum.
> Tu Lucina dolentibus
> Iuno dicta puerperis,
> tu potens Trivia et notho es
> dicta lumine Luna.

— Metre, 174.

1. **custos**: so Neptune is *sacri custos Tarenti*, I. 28. 29; cf. Suet. *Dom.* 5 *novam excitavit aedem in Capitolio Custodi Iovi.*—**nemorum** (sc. *custos*): cf. I. 21. 5 *sqq.* In *C.S.* I she is *silvarum potens;* in Verg. *A.* XI. 557, *nemorum cultrix.* According to Servius (on *Georg.* III. 332) 'omnis quercus Iovi est consecrata, et omnis lucus Dianae.'

2. **quae laborantis**, etc.: cf. *C. S.* 13 *sqq.* Diana, in this capacity, was sometimes identified with Iuno Lucina; cf. Cat. *l.l.;* Cic. *N. D.* II. 68.—**puellas**: *i.e.* young women, at their first childbirth.

3. **ter**: see I. 28. 36 n.—**vocata**: cf. Ter. *Ad.* 487.—**adimis**

leto: the opposite of *dare leto;* see 7. 17 n.

4. **triformis**: properly an epithet of Hecate, with whom Diana, owing to their many common attributes, was more or less confused; cf. Verg. *A.* IV. 511 *tergeminamque Hecaten, tria virginis ora Dianae.* The significance of the triple figure of Hecate has been variously explained in ancient and modern times; see Preller-Robert,*Gr. Myth.* I. 324.

5. **imminens villae**: a large tree, therefore, as we might suppose. — **tua**: predicate.

6. **quam donem**, *one on which I may bestow;* descriptive relative clause, defining the purport of **tua esto.** — **per exactos annos**, *on the completion of each year; i.e.* at each anniversary of the dedication. Cf. *pleno anno,* 18. 5 n, and, for the distributive force of **per,** II. 3. 6 n.—**laetus**: corresponding to the *lubens* of votive inscriptions; cf. Allen's *Early Remnants,* 69 n, 70, 111. 3, 113.

7. **obliquum ictum**: a reminiscence of the wild-boar hunt in the Odyssey, where the boar wounds Ulysses, λικριφὶς ἀίξας (XIX. 451); so Ovid *M.* VIII. 344 *obliquo latrantes dissipat ictu.*—**meditantis,**

XXIII.

Caelo supinas si tuleris manus
nascente luna, rustica Phidyle,
  si ture placaris et horna
    fruge Laris avidaque porca,

5 nec pestilentem sentiet Africum
fecunda vitis nec sterilem seges
  robiginem aut dulces alumni
    pomifero grave tempus anno.

practicing. The description, as in 1 3. 4 *sq.* and IV. 2. 57 *sqq.*, is a substitute for a more prosaic statement of the age of the victim,—a young boar whose tusks are just growing.

8. **donem**: the tree, by its dedication, becomes a sanctuary of the goddess, and, as such, the offering may be said to be bestowed upon it.

XXIII. A pure life and devout spirit needs no costly sacrifice to win the favor of heaven. To set forth this truth the poet represents himself as talking with a country woman,—a farmer's wife,—whose pious soul is troubled at the meagreness of the offerings which her narrow means allow her to make, and comforting her with the assurance that her prayers will be answered. — Metre, 176.

1. **caelo**: Intr. 53. — **supinas**: *i.e.* with the palms upward. This was the attitude assumed in prayer to the gods above; cf. Verg. *A.* III. 176; Liv. XXVI. 9. 7 (*matronae*) *nixae genibus, supinas manus ad caelum ac deos tendentes, orantesque.* — **si . . . si**: Intr. 116 *h.*

2. **nascente luna**: *i.e.* at the new moon. The offering was usually made, however, at least in the city, at the beginning of the

calendar month ; cf. Prop. V. 3. 53 *raris adsueta kalendis | vix aperit clausos una puella Lares.* See 19. 9 n. — **Phidyle** : Φειδύλη ('thrifty'; cf. φείδομαι) ; the name is apparently chosen to suit the character.

3. **ture** : cf. Tib. I. 3. 34 *reddere menstrua tura Lari.*—**horna fruge**: a bunch or wreath of the new grain. Cf. Tib. I. 10. 20 *stabat in exigua ligneus aede deus. | Hic placatus erat seu quis libaverat uvam | seu dederat sanctae spicea serta comae.* For **horna** (a poetical word) cf. *horna vina, Epod,* 2. 47.

4. **porca**: *cf.* 17. 15 n, *S.* II. 3. 165.

5. **nec**, etc.: for the position of the subjects in this strophe, see Intr. 116 *b.* — **pestilentem Africum**: the Sirocco ; see II. 14. 15, 16 nn.

6. **fecunda**, *full-clustered.* — **sterilem**: Intr. 125.

7. **robiginem**: the seriousness of this evil to the Italian farmer may be inferred from the fact that Robigo (or Robigus) was worshipped as a god, and a day (*Robigalia*, April 25) set apart for a formal service of propitiation ; see Ovid *Fast.* IV. 901 *sqq.* — **alumni**: see 18. 4 n.

8. **pomifero anno**: *i.e.* autumn;

Nam quae nivali pascitur Algido
10   devota quercus inter et ilices
aut crescit Albanis in herbis
victima pontificum securis
cervice tinguet : te nihil attinet
temptare multa caede bidentium
15   parvos coronantem marino
rore deos fragilique myrto.

cf. *annus hibernus, Epod.* 2. 29, and
see 8. 9 n. — **grave,** *oppressive,
sickly;* cf. Liv. III. 6. 2 *grave tempus et forte annus pestilens erat
urbi agrisque, nec hominibus magis
quam pecori;* see also II. 14. 15 n ;
S. II. 6. 18 *sq.,* Juv. 4. 56 *letifero
autumno.*

   9. **nivali Algido** : cf. *gelido
Algido,* I. 21. 6 n. Here and on
the Alban mount the college of
pontiffs possessed pastures, in
which victims were raised for the
great public sacrifices. For the
case of **Algido,** see Intr. 69.

   10. **devota . . . victima** : Intr.
120. — **inter** : Intr. 115 *b.*

   13. **tinguet:** Intr. 79.—**te nihil
attinet,** *you have no occasion, it is
not for you.*

   14. **temptare,** *to beset.*—**bidentium**: a technical word for animals
full-grown for sacrifice (about two
years old). They were so named
from the two prominent incisors
which displace the two front milk
teeth on the lower jaw of the
sheep at about that age (Hyginus
ap. Gell. XVI. 6. 14 ; Serv. on *Aen.*
IV. 57).

   15. **parvos:** the position brings
out the incongruity of *multa caedes*
with the small effigies which she
decks with her simple garlands.
The Lares were small figures of
wood or bronze, or of more precious metal if the means of the

family permitted ; cf. Tib. I. 10.
20 (quoted above) ; Petron. 29
Lares argentei ; Juv. 8. 110. The
typical form was that of a youth
in a sleeveless tunic, girded high
(*succinctus,* Pers. V. 31), holding a
drinking-horn aloft in his right
hand and a bowl in his left. See
Baumeister, pp. 77, 811. Their altar was the hearth, on (or beside)
which they stood ; cf. *Epod.* 2.
66 n, and Plaut. *Aul.* 1 *sqq.* —
coronantem, *whom you crown.*
This service was enjoined oftener
than once a month ; cf. Cato *de
Agr.* 143. 2 (*vilica*) *kalendis idibus
nonis, festus dies cum erit, coronam
in focum indat, per eosdemque dies
Lari familiari pro copia supplicet;*
Plaut. *Aul.* 23 *huic filia unast;
ea mihi cotidie | aut ture aut vino
aut aliqui semper supplicat; | dat
mihi coronas;* Juv. 9. 137 *o parvi
nostrique Lares, quos ture minuto |
aut farre et tenui soleo exorare
corona.* — **marino rore:** in this
order in Plin. XI. 38 and Col. IX.
4. 6. It is an aromatic shrub
(rosemary), which was used in
worship by people who could not
afford incense.

   16. **deos:** object of both **temptare** and **coronantem** ; Intr. 76.
— **fragili,** *brittle ;* referring to
the twigs used in the garland. —
myrto : see I. 4. 9 n, and **cf.**
I. 38. 5.

Immunis aram si tetigit manus,
non sumptuosa blandior hostia,
mollivit aversos Penatis
20   farre pio et saliente mica.

17. **immunis,** *guiltless, blameless.* In this sense it is not found elsewhere, except with a genitive, as *immunes caedis manus,* Ov. *Her.* 14. 8. Many editors, therefore, reject this interpretation and render the word 'bringing no gift,' citing IV. 12. 23 and *Ep.* I. 14. 33. But in neither of these places does *immunis* mean simply 'bringing no gift': in IV. 12. 23 it means 'exempt from the obligation to contribute' (ἀσύμβολος); in *Ep.* I. 14. 33, 'without being required to make presents.' In both cases it has its fundamental meaning, '*qui vacat a muneribus quae alii praestare debent*' (Forcellini). From this meaning Orelli deduced its use here : the hand that comes to the altar '*immunis,*' comes, not from any obligation to make an offering in atonement for sin, but purely as an expression of gratitude and piety, or to deprecate some undeserved calamity; **immunis** is then *immunis piaculi,* rather than *immunis sceleris.* At any rate, the meaning 'guiltless' appears to be required (as well as suggested) by the context. Innocence in the worshipper is the point on which the whole sentence turns. Under the other interpretation it is, no doubt, possible to get in this essential idea of innocence by restricting the application of the strophe to Phidyle, instead of taking it as the enunciation of a general truth ; but this gives it only a subordinate place : the main thought is then 'bringing no gift' (for **immunis** is the emphatic word). And this, as a description of Phidyle, is in conflict both with vss. 3, 4, and with the last verse ; for the *mola salsa* was regarded as an offering ; cf. Plin. N. H. *Praef.* 11 *dis lacte rustici multaeque gentes et mola tantum salsa litant qui non habent tura.* But the language of the strophe is obscure, and its meaning much disputed.

18. **sumptuosa hostia:** instrumental abl. with the comparative, as in *altior ruinis,* 5. 40. The verse is commonly understood in a parenthetical and conditional sense, — 'it would gain nothing in persuasiveness by a costly offering.' But perhaps it is less harsh to take it as more direct, — 'without the aid of a costly victim to make it more persuasive.' This, of course, is only possible if we take **immunis** as 'guiltless.'

19. **mollivit :** Intr. 80. — **aversos,** *unwilling;* not 'hostile' (*adversos*), still less 'offended' (*iratos*), but needing to be melted to pity ; cf. *Epod.* 10. 18. — **Penatis :** here not distinguished from the Lares ; cf. Ov. *Tr.* I. 3. 43 *illa etiam ante Lares passis adstrata capillis* | *contigit extinctos ore tremente focos,* | *multaque in adversos effudit verba Penates.*

20. **farre,** etc.: a poetical paraphrase for *mola salsa* (cf. *fruges salsae,* Verg. *A.* II. 133), the mixture of crushed spelt and salt which was used in connection with all sacrifices ; here it accompanies simple prayer. The ablatives are instrumental.—**saliente :** *i.e.* when thrown on the fire.

XXIV.

Intactis opulentior
    thesauris Arabum et divitis Indiae
caementis licet occupes
    Tyrrhenum omne tuis et mare Apulicum,
5   si figit adamantinos
    summis verticibus dira Necessitas
clavos, non animum metu,
    non mortis laqueis expedies caput.

XXIV. In this ode Horace in-
veighs against the vice and corruption of the age with more than
his wonted vigor. The root of
the evil is the insatiable greed for
wealth, which is deterred by no
danger and scruples at no crime.
Here is a chance for immortal
fame ! Who will seize it by
mastering unbridled license, and
putting it under the control of
law ? In place of futile complaints
let us have punishment. But even
laws will avail little against the evil,
unless supported by a thorough-
going reform in public sentiment.
The ode is referred with some
probability to the year 28 B.C. for
the same reason that the sixth ode
is assigned to that year (see introd.
note to 6); but it may well have
been earlier. It comes nearer than
most of the odes of its class to
the spirit of the sixteenth Epode.
— Metre, 171.

1. **intactis,** etc.: the first sentence (vss. 1–8) consists of a concessive clause with **licet** (vss. 1–4),
depending on a conditional sentence (vss. 5–8). — **intactis :** *i.e.*
not yet reached by Roman conquest and plundered, as, for example, those of the rich provinces
of Asia had been.

2. **thesauris Arabum**: cf. *Arabum gazis,* I. 29. 1. For the abl.,
see Intr. 75. — **divitis Indiae :**
from very early times a thriving
trade had been carried on between
India and western Asia. The
articles that found their way to
Rome were for the most part of a
very costly sort,— especially ivory,
precious stones, silks, and fine
cotton goods, — which naturally
gave rise to a popular impression
of great wealth in the land from
which they came.

3. **caementis**: see 1. 33 *sqq.* nn.

4. **Tyrrhenum,** etc.: *i.e.* though
you line the whole coast of Italy
with your seaside villas. — **Āpūli-
cum:** see Crit. App.

5. **figīt :** Intr. 179.

6. **summis verticibus :** *i.e.*
those of your palaces. The rich
man in his luxurious mansions is
as helpless in the face of his doom
as the poorest beggar in his hut.
The same thought is put in another way in II. 18. 18 *sqq.* and
29 *sqq. ;* but there, as here, the
figure is suggested by the building
operations of the rich man himself.
verticibus is probably ablative
(Intr. 69). — **Necessitas :** cf. I.
35. 17 n.

7. **clavos :** the driving of the

Campestres melius Scythae,

10   quorum plaustra vagas rite trahunt domos,

vivunt et rigidi Getae,

immetata quibus iugera liberas

fruges et Cererem ferunt,

nec cultura placet longior annua,

15   defunctumque laboribus

aequali recreat sorte vicarius.

Illic matre carentibus

privignis mulier temperat innocens,

nail signifies unalterable doom (see I. 35. 18 n), here the doom of death, from which he can find no escape in his palaces, any more than in the speed of horses or triremes (1. 38 *sqq.*).

8. **mortis laqueis**: cf. *OT. Psalms* 18. 5.

9. **campestres**, *of the steppes;* put first to bring this feature of nomad life, which is expanded in the next verse, into clearer contrast with the palace-building Romans. For the epithet, cf. *profugi Scythae*, I. 35. 9; IV. 14. 42.

10. **quorum**: better taken with **domos**. — **vagas**, *from place to place;* proleptic. — **rite**, *such is their custom ; i.e.* it is not exceptional, but the regular thing among them.

11. **rigidi**, *rigorous ;* cf. *Ep.* I. 1. 17; II. 1. 25 *rigidis Sabinis.* — **Getae** : they occupied the plains between the Transylvanian Alps and the Danube (Wallachia).

12. **immetata** : not divided up for individual ownership. — **liberas** : *i.e.* common to all.

13. **Cererem** : Intr. 1 30.

14. **annua** : ablative. Horace here ascribes to the Getae the custom which Caesar records of the Suevi, *B. G.* IV. 1. In contrast with the avarice of Roman land-

owners, these simple communities raise only as much produce each year as is needed for their own sustenance, and the work of tillage can be done by a limited number of persons, whose places are taken (**vicarius**) at the end of the year by another squad on the same terms.

15. **defunctum laboribus**: cf. *functum laboribus*, II. 18. 38.

16. **aequali sorte** : abl. of manner.

17. **illic**, etc.: here begins the exposition of the thought in *melius vivunt* (9, 11): simple habits of life are conducive to virtuous living. Like Tacitus in the *Germania*, Horace invests his barbarians with something of the halo of a golden age, to emphasize the contrast with the vices of Rome. The whole force of the comparison, as in 6. 17 *sqq.*, is directed against the women, their husbands and sons being reserved for treatment later in the ode. — **matre carentibus**, *motherless* (*orbis*); a favorite form of paraphrase with Horace ; cf. 26. 10 n, I. 28. 1 n.

18. **temperat**, *treats with forbearance ;* cf. Cic. *Verr.* II. 2. 4 *superatis hostibus temperavit.* For the proverbial severity of a *no-*

nec dotata regit virum

20   coniunx, nec nitido fidit adultero ;

dos est magna parentium

virtus et metuens alterius viri

certo foedere castitas,

et peccare nefas aut pretium est mori.

25   O quisquis volet impias

caedis et rabiem tollere civicam,

si quaeret pater urbium

subscribi statuis, indomitam audeat

verca, see note on *patruae*, 12. 1.—
innocens, *keeping herself blameless ;* a part of the predicate.

19. **nec dotata**, etc., *no wife
with great dowry*, etc. ; *i.e.* there
exists no such phenomenon at all
among them. — **regit virum** : cf.
Plaut. *Men.* 766 *ita istaec solént
quae virós subservíre | sibi postulánt
dote frétae, feróces ; Aul.* 532 *sqq. ;*
Martial. VIII. 12. If a marriage
was dissolved at the instance of
the husband, he was obliged to
surrender the dowry, or the greater
part of it, — a rule that gave to
wealthy married women a large
measure of independence.

20. **nitido** : cf. 19. 25 n and *S.*
II. 1. 64. — **fidit** : *i.e.* for aid and
comfort against her husband. With
this verb **dotata** is not understood
as part of the subject ; rather
fidit adultero is parallel to **dotata
regit.**

21. **magna** : with **dos**. — **parentium virtus** : as a guaranty of
pure blood and a wholesome moral
training.

22. **metuens**, *that shrinks from ;*
cf. 19. 16 n, and *metuit tangi*,
11. 10. It stands in contrast
with *fidit*, above, as **dos**, etc.,
with *dotata.* — **alterius** : see 5.
34 n.

23. **certo foedere** : a loosely
attached descriptive ablative, char-
acterizing the *castitas* as an obligation mutually binding and never
violated.

24. **nefas** : sc. *est*, parallel with
est in vs. 21, *illic* being understood
with both. — **aut** : see 12. 1 n. It
follows the idea of prohibition in
nefas. — **pretium** : cf. Juv. 13.
105 *ille crucem sceleris pretium
tulit, hic diadema.*

25. **quisquis volet ... si quaeret** : not different in sense from
si quis volet ... et quaeret. If any
one wishes to secure immortal
fame by putting away civil strife
and bloodshed from the state, let
him strike at the root of the evil
in the rampant licentiousness of
the times. — **impias** : see II. 1.
30 n.

26. **civicam** : see II. 1. 1 n.

27. **si quaeret**, etc.: *i.e.* if he
seeks to have his name inscribed
on the pedestals of statues in numerous cities, with the title 'Pater
Vrbis' or the like. *Pater* was a
common term of honor for a public benefactor, as *pater patriae*,
pater senatus, etc. (see II. 1. 50 n) ;
and possibly Horace intended the
word in this general sense here,
so that **urbium** should be taken

refrenare licentiam,

30   clarus post genitis, — quatenus, heu nefas !

virtutem incolumem odimus,

        sublatam ex oculis quaerimus invidi.

Quid tristes querimoniae,

        si non supplicio culpa reciditur,

35   quid leges sine moribus

        vanae proficiunt, si neque fervidis

pars inclusa caloribus

        mundi nec Boreae finitimum latus

with **statuis**; but cf. Stat. *Silv.* III. 4. 48 *pater inclitus urbis* (of Domitian) ; CIL. III. 2907 PARENS · COLONIAE, XI. 3083 PATR · PATRIAE · ET · MUNICIP (both of Augustus).

28. **subscribi**: Intr. 94 *c.*

29. **refrenare licentiam** : cf. IV. 15. 9 *sqq.*

30. **clarus**: sc. *futurus* (*and he will be*). — **post genitis** : a paraphrase for *posteris* not found elsewhere. — **quatenus**, *in as much as* (so also *S.* I. 1. 64); an archaic use of the word (Festus, p. 258) revived by the Augustan poets, from whom it was received into later prose (*e.g.* Vell. II. 68. 4 ; Tac. *Ann.* III. 16. 5). It here introduces the reason of **post genitis** : the true benefactors of their race are not appreciated in their lifetime ; cf. *Ep.* II. 1. 5–14. — **heu nefas** : cf. IV. 6. 17.

31. **incolumem**, *in the living.*

32. **quaerimus**: for *requirimus* (Intr. 129), in the sense of *desideramus, we mourn.* — **invidi** : this belongs with both verbs: the spirit which stones the prophets and that which builds their tombs are one and the same. The glory of the dead is used to disparage the living. Cf. *Ep.* II. 1. 88 *sq.*

33. **quid**, etc.: the reformer's work must be unpopular, because no gentle measures will do ; he must attack the evil with pains and penalties. — **tristes**, *dismal.*

34. **reciditur** : cf. *S.* I. 3. 122 *et magnis parva* (sc. *delicta*) *mineris | falce recisurum simili te.* The metaphor of pruning, keeping back (re-) luxuriant growth, is appropriate here ; cf. *refrenare*, above.

35. **sine moribus vanae,** *which are*, etc. These words express the general truth exemplified in the clauses that follow. In English we should be more likely to state it in a separate sentence: ' Laws with no moral sentiment behind them are futile ; what good do they do (for example) if the passion for wealth has so completely taken the place of right principles in a man's mind that no hardship or peril can deter him from the pursuit of his object ? ' With **leges sine moribus,** cf. IV. 5. 22 *mos et lex ;* Tac. *Ger.* 19 *plus ibi boni mores valent quam alibi bonae leges.*

37. **pars**: as in 3. 55.—**inclusa,** *intrenched ;* in the same sense as *domibus negata,* I. 22. 22.

38. **latus** : sc. *mundi ;* cf. I. 22. 19.

           durataeque solo nives
40   mercatorem abigunt, horrida callidi
      vincunt aequora navitae,
           magnum pauperies opprobrium iubet
      quidvis et facere et pati,
           virtutisque viam deserit arduae ?
45   Vel nos in Capitolium,
           quo clamor vocat et turba faventium,
      vel nos in mare proximum
           gemmas et lapides aurum et inutile,

39. **duratae,** *frozen hard, never melting.* — **solo** : Intr. 69.

40. **mercatorem** : a favorite type with Horace of restless activity : cf. I. 1. 16, *S.* I. 1. 6, *Ep.* I. 1. 45. — **horrida callidi** : Intr. 116 *a*. For the asyndeton in this sentence, cf. 18. 9 *sqq.*

42. **magnum opprobrium,** *as a great,* etc.; cf. *S.* II. 3. 91 *sq.* — **pauperies**: see I. 1. 18 n.—**iubet,** etc. : cf. *Ep.* I. 1. 46 *per mare pauperiem fugiens, per saxa, per ignis.*

43. **quidvis** : any and everything, without distinction (of right or wrong); cf. *omne,* 3. 52 n. — **et facere et pati** : cf. Livy II. 12. 9 *et facere et pati fortia Romanum est.*

44. **virtutis viam** : *i.e.* the path which Virtue prescribes, and which leads to her, as in Hes. *Op.* 289 τῆς δ' ἀρετῆς ἱδρῶτα θεοὶ προπάροιθεν ἔθηκαν | ἀθάνατοι· μακρὸς δὲ καὶ ὄρθιος οἶμος ἐς αὐτήν. — **deserit** : *deserere,* which Bentley wished to read, would be more strictly consistent ; but the personification of **pauperies** with **iubet** is no more than a figure of speech ; here it becomes vivid, and **pauperies,** before a mere abstraction, is in-

vested with the qualities and actions of the *pauper.* The same thing occurs in *paupertas impulit audax ut versus facerem, Ep.* II. 2. 51. Cf. also *indulgens sibi hydrops,* II. 2. 13 n, and *virtus temptat iter,* III. 2. 21. — **arduae** : Intr. 124.

45. In an access of poetic fervor, which may remind us of *Epode* 16, Horace calls for a general sacrifice of the costly luxuries which are the source of so much evil : no change of heart is genuine which does not engender a contempt for these things. — **in Capitolium** : *i.e.* as an offering to Jove ; see 30. 8 n. The reader will supply the missing verb for himself before reaching **mittamus,** so that the adaptation of the latter to the second proposition does no violence to the sense.

46. **clamor et turba** : *i.e.* a shouting crowd ; Intr. 126 *a.*—**vocat** : *i.e.* such a reception awaits us. Horace imagines a procession of rich citizens marching to the Capitol, each carrying his valuables, with applauding throngs lining the way, as in a triumph.

48. **gemmas et lapides** : it is not clear that these stood for distinct classes of precious stones ;

summi materiem mali,

50   mittamus, scelerum si bene paenitet.
Eradenda cupidinis
    pravi sunt elementa et tenerae nimis
mentes asperioribus
    formandae studiis.   Nescit equo rudis

55 haerere ingenuus puer
    venarique timet, ludere doctior,
seu Graeco iubeas trocho,
    seu malis vetita legibus alea,

we know, for example, that pearls were called by both names. The mention of the two is simply for greater fullness of expression, — *jewels and precious stones.*—aurum et : Intr. 114.— inutile, *good for nothing ;* with something more than a merely negative force.

49. materiem : cf. Sal. *Cat.* 10 *primo pecuniae, deinde imperi cupido crevit ; ea quasi materies omnium malorum fuere,* where *quasi* shows that Sallust was still conscious of the metaphor in *materies* (the 'stuff' of which these evils are made).

50. bene : *i.e.* sincerely.

51. eradenda, etc. : coming down to a more practical view of the problem, Horace urges that contempt for luxury be inculcated by a healthier moral and physical training of youth ; cf. 2. 1 *sqq.*, 6. 37 *sqq.*

52. elementa, *the germs.* — tenerae nimis : *i.e.* those which are now *over-indulged* must (instead) be moulded, etc.

54. studiis, *training.* — equo : Intr. 71.— rudis : reinforcing nescit and opposed to doctior: ' Put him in the saddle, he is awkward and doesn't know how to keep his seat; tell him to play, he will show

his proficiency, whether it be with, etc.'

55. haerere : Intr. 94 *o.* — ingenuus : it might be excusable in a slave or freedman.

56. venari: Intr. 94 *l.*—ludere: Intr. 101 *c.*

57. seu . . . seu: for the use of these conjunctions, see I. 4. 12 n. — Graeco, for the contrast between the traditional Roman forms of exercise, such as hunting and riding (*Romanis sollemne viris opus, Ep.* I. 18. 49), which were valued as good training for a soldier (hence called *militia*), and the athletic sports imported from Greece, cf. *S.* II. 2. 9 *sqq.* The *trochus* is named with the *pila* and *discus, Ep.* II. 3. 379 *sq.*, among the '*arma*' of the Campus (see I. 8. 10 n). — iubeas, malis : sc. *eum ludere.* For the construction of the ablatives, cf. *S.* I. 5. 49 *pilā ludere.*

58. vetita legibus: Cicero mentions a condemnation for gambling in his time (*Phil.* 2. 56) and elsewhere classes *aleatores* with '*omnes impuri impudicique*' (*in Cat.* 2. 23); but in Horace's day the law was obviously much neglected. Ovid speaks of treatises written to teach the game (*Tr.* II. 471 *sqq.*).

cum periura patris fides
60   consortem socium fallat et hospites,
indignoque pecuniam
        heredi properet.   Scilicet improbae
crescunt divitiae : tamen
        curtae nescio quid semper abest rei.

XXV.

Quo me, Bacche, rapis tui
        plenum ?   Quae nemora aut quos agor in specus
velox mente nova ?   Quibus
        antris egregii Caesaris audiar

59. **cum fallat, properet** : the *cum*-clause here defines the character of the situation by an added picture ; see Hale's *Cum-Constructions*, p. 191. In English we should rather begin a new sentence, *Meanwhile, etc.* — **periura fides** : see I. 5. 5 n.

60. **consortem socium,** *his partner.* In mercantile language *sors* is capital.—**hospites** : cf. *perfidus hospitam*, I. 15. 2 n.

61. **pecuniam properet** : cf. *deproperare coronas*, II. 7. 24 n.

62. **scilicet,** *yes ;* introducing the poet's reflections on the picture he has just drawn : Wealth goes right on growing, in spite of morality and honor and everything else (**improbae**), but it is forever doomed to fail to satisfy its possessor ; 'semper avarus eget' (*Ep.* I. 2. 56). — **improbae,** *graceless.*

64. **curtae** : proleptic, expressing the aspect which the property (**rei**) presents to its covetous owner.

XXV. This short ode is a tribute to Augustus, whose glory is heralded none the less effectively because it is mentioned only incidentally, as it were, in a poem which purports to be merely the prelude to a greater work. The ode is cast in dithyrambic form : the poet represents himself as hurried away by the irresistible power of Bacchus to the wilds, haunted of nymph and maenad, where, under the joyous inspiration of the god himself, he shall rise to the level of his lofty theme. Whether the ode was called forth by some particular occasion does not appear.— Metre, 171.

1. **tui plenum** : cf. *pleno Bacchi pectore*, II. 19. 6.

2. **agor in** : Intr. 119 *a.*

3. **velox mente nova** : he feels like a changed being, moved by swift impulses. These are characteristic of orgiastic possession ; cf. Cat. 63. 19 *mora tarda mente cedat*, and the whole picture there portrayed.

4. **antris** : dative (Intr. 54),— ' What caves shall hear me ? ' He is not thinking of an audience in the caves.— **egregii** : see I. 6. 11 n. — **audiar** : future ; a question of fact, like *quo rapis, etc.*, above.

5   aeternum meditans decus
        stellis inserere et consilio Iovis?
Dicam insigne, recens, adhuc
        indictum ore alio.   Non secus in iugis
exsomnis stupet Euhias,
10   Hebrum prospiciens et nive candidam
Thracen ac pede barbaro
        lustratam Rhodopen, ut mihi devio
ripas et vacuum nemus
        mirari libet.   O Naiadum potens
15 Baccharumque valentium
        proceras manibus vertere fraxinos,

5. **aeternum**: proleptic.—**meditans**, *essaying in song*.   The
word is used not only of silent
composition, but of bursts of song,
as **audiar** shows (cf. Verg. *E.* 6.
82 *omnia quae Phoebo quondam
meditante beatus | audiit Eurotas*);
yet enough of the idea of contemplation is still present to attach
an infinitive to, and **inserere** is
rather complementary (Intr. 94 *f*)
than infinitive of purpose.

6. **stellis inserere**, etc.: *i.e.* to
extol to heaven.   For **stellis**, cf.
arcis attigit igneas, 3. 10 n.

7. **dicam**: the subject of my song
will be, etc.; see I. 6. 5 n.—**insigne**:
cf. I. 12. 39 *insigni camena*.—
recens, *fresh;* not hackneyed.

8. **indictum**, etc. : cf. *Ep.* I.
19. 32 *non alio dictum prius ore.*
— **non secus**, etc. : the picture is
that of a Thracian bacchante who
has come upon a height (**iugis**)
where a view of the whole valley of
the Hebrus, with Rhodope beyond,
bursts upon her, and stands gazing
in rapture at the beautiful scene.

9. **exsomnis** : because in the
full flush of her frenzy ; every

nerve is alive.   Sleep comes with
the reaction from this excitement
(cf. Cat. 63. 35 *sq.*).

11. **pede barbaro lustratam** :
i.e. inhabited by a foreign people ;
she has strayed far away into a
strange land.

12. **ut**: with **non secus**, instead
of the usual *ac*, which would be
harsh after **ac** in vs. 11; cf. Plaut.
Aul. 22 *pariter moratum ut páter
avosque huiús fuit;* Plin. *Ep.* I. 20. 1
*cui nihil aeque in causis agendis
ut brevitas placet.*

13. **ripas**: used absolutely, as in
I. 23 and IV. 2. 31.— **vacuum**,
untenanted; repeating the idea
implied in **devio**.   Intr. 119 *a*.

14. **mirari** : see I. 4. 19 n. —
Naiadum potens : cf. II. 19. 3.

15. **valentium**, etc.: the allusion
is to the destruction of Pentheus
by the bacchantes, who tore up
by the roots the tree on which he
sat (Eurip. *Bacch.* 1109).   It is
mentioned to recall the super-
human power which the inspiration of Bacchus confers.

16. **vertere**: for *evertere;* Intr.
129.   For the mood, see Intr. 94 *n*

nil parvum aut humili modo,
  nil mortale loquar.   Dulce periculum est,
O Lenaee, sequi deum
20   cingentem viridi tempora pampino.

XXVI.

Vixi puellis nuper idoneus
et militavi non sine gloria :
  nunc arma defunctumque bello
  barbiton hic paries habebit,
5   laevum marinae qui Veneris latus
custodit.   Hic, hic ponite lucida

17. **nil**, etc.: my song shall be
elevated both in matter and manner. — **parvum** : cf. 3. 72.
18. **mortale**: *i.e.* of mere human
inspiration. — **dulce**, *fascinating*.
— **periculum** : because the near
presence of the god is overpowering. The same mingling of joy
and fear is expressed II. 29. 5 *sqq.*
19. **Lenaee**: supposed to mean
'god of the wine-press' (ληνός). —
deum, *a god*.
20. **cingentem**, etc.: repeated
in the suspected verse, IV. 8. 33,
with the necessary change of **cingentem** to *ornatus*. Here, however, it is more natural to take
cingentem with the subject of
sequi, understood, — the poet.

XXVI. Our poet will have no
more of love. He has acquitted
himself in that field not without
glory ; now he will hang up his
arms in Venus' shrine, for he has
no longer any taste for her service.
Only at the very end he lets a little
word escape him which betrays
the humorous aspect of the situation : it is Chloe's hard heart that

is at the bottom of it all. — Metre,
176.
1. **vixi**: the perfect definite, implying 'it is all over now.'— **puellis idoneus** : *i.e.* capable of making himself agreeable to them. —
nuper, *till lately.*
2. **militavi** : the figure is a common one ; cf. IV. 1. 2; Ov. *Am.* I.
9. 1 *militat omnis amans et habet
sua castra Cupido.*
4. **hic paries**, etc. : *i.e.* the side
of the shrine on the right (as
you looked at it) of the image of
the goddess. It was customary
to dedicate implements or other
tokens of completed service ; cf.
Ep. I. 1. 4 *Veranius* (a gladiator)
armis | *Herculis ad postem fixis ;
S.* I. 5. 65, where a former slave is
asked *donasset iamne catenam* | *ex
voto Laribus.*
5. **laevum**: there appears to be
no special significance in the choice
of this side. — **marinae** : as being
sea-born and exercising power over
the sea ; cf. I. 3. 1 n; IV. 11. 15.
6. **hic, hic**: Intr. 116 *d.* — **ponite** : addressed to the slaves who
carry the articles referred to ; cf.

       funalia et vectis et arcus
       oppositis foribus minacis.

     O quae beatam diva tenes Cyprum et
10   Memphin carentem Sithonia nive,
       regina, sublimi flagello
       tange Chloen semel arrogantem.

                    XXVII.

          Impios parrae recinentis omen

I. 19. 14. — **lucida**: expressing not
their present condition, but their
essential property.

  7. **funalia**: used for going about
at night, since the streets were
not lighted. See Juv. 3. 282 *sqq.*
— **vectis** : to pry open doors where
admittance was refused : cf. Ter.
Eun. 773 *primum aedis expugnabo.
. . . In medium huc agmen cum
vecti, Donax!* — **arcus** : unless
this is the name of some imple-
ment for forcing doors, the text
is probably corrupt. If we could
imagine the lover going about
armed with bow and arrows on
such an expedition, it would still
be difficult to see why he should
threaten barred doors with them.

  8. **foribus** : Intr. 58 *a.*

  9. **quae tenes Cyprum** : cf. I.
3. 1, 30. 2, and for this use of
teneo, III. 4. 62 n. — **beatam**: Cyprus was an island of great and
varied resources ; cf. I. 1. 13 n.

  10. **Memphin**: Herodotus (II.
112) mentions a sanctuary ξείνης
Ἀφροδίτης there.—**carentem**, etc.:
a poetical paraphrase for 'where
it never snows' ; cf. *matre carentibus*, 24. 17 n. — **Sithonia** : see I.
18. 9 n, and cf. Verg. *E.* 10. 66 ;
Intr. 117.

  11. **regina**: cf. I. 30. 1.—**sublimi**, *uplifted.*

  12. **semel**, *just once* ; cf. I. 24.
16 n.

XXVII. The story of Europa.
The myth is treated on a plan
similar to that of the eleventh
ode. As a setting for his picture
Horace has here, as there, constructed a situation : his imaginary
friend Galatea is about to set out
on a journey to the East ; he reluctantly bids her farewell, with a
prayer for good omens and friendly words of warning against the
treachery of the sea, through all
of which runs an undercurrent of
unspoken protest at her incurring
such risk ; he thinks of her on the
sea at night, with nothing but the
waves about her and the stars
overhead, and this recalls the lonely ride of Europa on the back of
the bull. In dealing with the subject, as in the case of Hypermnestra, he disposes of the familiar
features of the story briefly (vss.
25–32, 73–76), or by allusion, and
selects for lyrical treatment a
single scene, — the remorse and
despair of Europa when she is left
alone on the shore of Crete. —
Metre, 174.

  1. **impios** : emphatic. The sense
is, 'May all bad omens be spent
in confounding the wicked : I will

ducat et praegnans canis aut ab agro
rava decurrens lupa Lanuvino
     fetaque volpes ;

5   rumpat et serpens iter institutum,
si per obliquum similis sagittae
terruit mannos : ego cui timebo
     providus auspex,

antequam stantis repetat paludes
10   imbrium divina avis imminentum,

guard her whose safety I have at
heart by calling up a good sign to
anticipate and counteract whatever
there may be of evil import.' With
the idea, which we have here and
in vss. 21 *sqq.*, of diverting (rather
than averting) ill by directing its
force elsewhere, cf. the prayers in
I. 28. 25 *sqq.* and *Epod.* 5. 53 *sqq.*
— parrae : this bird is mentioned
also by Plautus (*Asin.* 260) as an
ominous fowl, and by Festus (p.
197) as classed with both *oscines*
and *alites* (see vs. 11 n) ; but it has
not been identified. For this reason the precise meaning of reci-
nentis cannot be determined, but it
probably expresses a droning repetition of the note ; cf. *Ep.* I. 1. 55.

2. ducat, *attend . . . on their
way.* — agro Lanuvino : Lanuvi-
um was situated on a height, to
the right of the Appian Way,
beyond Aricia. Horace has in
mind a journey to Greece or Asia,
by the Appian Way to Brundisium
and thence by sea ; cf. vss. 19 *sq.*
The uncertainties of so long a
journey would invest such omens
as are here mentioned with unspeakable terror in the mind of
the average Roman, who was a
very superstitious person.

3. rava : cf. *Epod.* 16. 33 *ravos
leones.*

5. rumpat (sc. *impiis*) : not
simply ' interrupt' by frightening
the horses, but *break off*, as institutum shows. The superstitious
traveller would feel it necessary
to go back and begin the journey anew, after due expiatory
offerings.

6. per obliquum : modifying
the idea of darting implied in similis sagittae, though grammatically attached to terruit.

7. mannos, *ponies ;* the Celtic
name of a Gallic breed of horses,
small in size, fashionable for driving ; cf. *Epod.* 4. 14, *Ep.* I. 7.
77. — ego : the emphasis falls
on this word because the person
contrasted with impios is not
definitely expressed, but appears
only as one in whom the poet is
interested ; as if we should say
' May all evil signs go to plague
the wicked ; for *my* friends I will
pray, etc.' — cui : suggesting its
antecedent in the same case. The
future timebo makes the reference
indefinite ; but of course he means
Galatea.

9. stantis, *stagnant.*

10. divina, *prophetic ;* with the
objective genitive, as *Ep.* II. 3.
218 *divina futuri ;* Intr. 66 *b.* —
avis : the crow (*cornix*) ; cf. 17.
12 n.

oscinem corvum prece suscitabo
solis ab ortu.

Sis licet felix, ubicumque mavis,
et memor nostri, Galatea, vivas,
15   teque nec laevus vetet ire picus
nec vaga cornix.

Sed vides quanto trepidet tumultu
pronus Orion?   Ego quid sit ater

11. **oscinem**: an augural term, used of birds whose notes were observed in divination, in distinction from those called *alites* (cf. 3. 61) or *praepetes* (Verg. *A.* III. 361), whose flight was regarded as significant. All the birds mentioned in this ode, together with the owl (*noctua*) are mentioned by Festus (*l. l.*) as belonging to the first class ; the vulture and the eagle are examples of the second (cf. Liv. I. 7. 1 ; Tac. *Ann.* II. 17. 2).

12. **solis ab ortu**: a favorable quarter ; see below, vs. 15 n.

13. **sis licet**, etc.: after this general introduction, he addresses Galatea directly with parting words of good will and friendly warning. — **sis**: optative subjunctive, to which **licet** is joined paratactically to intimate that he interposes no objection (as 'providus auspex') to her going. For this use of **licet**, cf. Plaut. *Rud.* 139 *meá quidem hercle caúsa salvos sís licet ;* Ovid *M.* III. 405 *sic amet ipse licet, sic non potiatur amato.* It is akin to *per me licet.*

14. **memor nostri**: apparently a formula of parting ; cf. Juv. 3. 318, *vale nostri memor.* For *nostri*, cf. 28. 9 n.

15. **laevus**, *ill-boding.* There is a confusion in the use of this word, owing to the fact that whereas

from its application to the left hand there naturally grew up about it the meaning of 'awkward, untoward, unlucky,' — the opposite of *dexter* (cf. *dextro tempore*, *S.* II. 1. 18, with *tempore laevo*, *S.* II. 4. 4), — in Roman augury it came to have just the opposite meaning, because, as the *auspex* sat facing south, the east, which was the favorable quarter (see above, vs. 12 n) was on his left. The same is true of *sinister.* The Roman poets constantly use both words in the sense of 'inauspicious,' either following the common as opposed to technical usage or, perhaps, under the influence of their Greek models ; for in Greek divination δεξιὸς ὄρνις was a lucky sign, and ἀριστερὸς unlucky.

16. **cornix**: see vs. 10 n, and cf. Verg. *E.* 9. 14 *nisi me | ante sinistra cava monuisset ab ilice cornix.*

17. **trepidet**: to the poet's vivid imagination, the constellation itself seems to tremble with the excitement of the storm which it brings.

18. **pronus Orion**: equivalent to *devexus Orion*, I. 28. 21 n. — — **ater**: *i.e.* in the darkness of the storm (cf. II. 16. 2 n), but with the implication which attaches to the word ; see I. 28. 13 n.

Hadriae novi sinus et quid albus
20   peccet Iapyx.

Hostium uxores puerique caecos
sentiant motus orientis Austri et
aequoris nigri fremitum et trementis
        verbere ripas.

25   Sic et Europe niveum doloso
credidit tauro latus et scatentem
beluis pontum mediasque fraudes
        palluit audax.

Nuper in pratis studiosa florum et
30   debitae Nymphis opifex coronae,
nocte sublustri nihil astra praeter
        vidit et undas.

19. **Hadriae sinus** : called *Io-nius sinus, Epod.* 10. 19. — **novi** : Horace had probably crossed it on his way to Greece (Intr. 7).— **albus** : cf. *candidi Favonii,* 7. 1, *albus Notus,* I. 7. 15, and see Intr. 125. It stands here in contrast with **ater** ; Intr. 116 *c*.

20. **peccet,** *plays tricks ;* he is fair, but not to be trusted. — **Ia-pyx** : see I. 3. 4 n.

21. **hostium** : cf. Verg. *G.* III. 513 *di meliora piis erroremque hostibus illum!* and see vs. 1 n, above. — **uxores puerique** : those who are dear to the enemy, not one (Galatea) who is dear to us.— **caecos motus** : *i.e.* squalls, coming without warning ; cf. *caeca fata,* II. 13. 16.

22. **sentiant** : cf. II. 7. 9 *Philippos et celerem fugam | sensi.*— **orientis** : unusual for *surgentis, e.g.* Verg. *A.* III. 481 *surgentis Austros.*

23. **aequoris,** etc. : observe the resonance of these verses, due

mainly to the persistent *r*-sounds ; Intr. 131.— **nigri:** cf. *ater,* vs. 18 n.

24. **verbere** : *sc.* of the surf.— **ripas** : see I. 2. 14 n.

25. **sic** : *i.e.* with the same readiness that you show to venture upon the sea. Horace represents Europa as having *voluntarily* taken her ride through the water ; see vs. 42 n.— **et,** *too.* — **Europe** : the story is told by Ovid, *M.* II. 836 *sqq., Fast.* V. 605 *sqq.* — **doloso credidit** : cf. *perfidis se credidit,* 5. 33 ; Intr. 116 *a*.

26. **latus** : cf. II. 7. 18. — **scatentem beluis** : cf. I. 3. 18 n.

27. **medias,** *all about her ;* she had come *in medias fraudes.* — **fraudes,** *dangers ;* lit. 'pitfalls.' For the accusatives, see Intr. 51 *a*.

28. **palluit audax,** *braved with blanched cheek.* The oxymoron is the result of the substitution for some colorless word like *vidit* (cf. I. 3. 19) of one that paints the danger on her face.

29. **nuper** : emphatic, in con-

Quae simul centum tetigit potentem
oppidis Creten, ' Pater, — o relictum
35   filiae nomen, pietasque' dixit
     ' victa furore !

Vnde quo veni ?   Levis una mors est
virginum culpae.   Vigilansne ploro
turpe commissum, an vitiis carentem
40   ludit imago

vana, quae porta fugiens eburna
somnium ducit ?   Meliusne fluctus

trast with her present situation
(nocte sublustri, etc.); cf. *plerumque* I. 34. 7.

30. debitae : *i.e.* vowed.

31. praeter : Intr. 115 *b*.

33. quae simul, etc. : Horace
follows a form of the myth, according to which the bull disappears,
on landing in Crete, and Europa
is left alone awhile till Jupiter
returns in his proper shape to
claim her as his bride.   It is here
that, with the reaction from the
excitement of the ride, remorse
sets in. — simul : see I. 4. 17 n.—
centum oppidis : after the Homeric Κρήτην ἑκατόμπολιν (*Il.* II.
649) ; cf. *Epod.* 9. 29.

34. pater: the word which comes
first to her lips in her distress
instantly reminds her that she has
recklessly thrown away a father's
love and protection, and she
breaks off with bitter self-reproach,
o relictum, etc.   For the nominatives in exclamation, nomen pietasque, cf. Cic. *Phil.* 14. 31 (quoted
2. 13 n) and *Ep.* II. 3. 301.   The
accusative is usual.

35. filiae : defining genitive ;
Gr. 214 *f.*

36. furore, *mad folly.*

37. unde quo : not in reference

to place, but contrasting her present situation with that of yesterday. — una mors : cf. Prop. V. 4.
17 *et satis una malae potuit mors
esse puellae, | quae voluit flammas
fallere, Vesta, tuas ?*

38. virginum, *a maiden's ;* the
plural (used generically) makes it
less direct, and so more natural.
She feels now, in her defenseless
situation, the full force and consequence of having broken through
the restraints of filial duty and
maidenly reserve, under the impulse of a temporary fascination
(furore, 36). — culpae : dative ;
for the meaning, see 6. 17 n.— vigilans : emphatic ; she cannot
believe her senses ; it must be all
a dream.

40. ludit imago : cf. Verg. *A.*
I. 407 *quid natum totiens crudelis
tu quoque falsis | ludis imaginibus?*

41. porta eburna : cf. Verg. *A.*
VI. 893 *sunt geminae somni portae,
quarum altera fertur | cornea, qua
veris facilis datur exitus umbris, |
altera candenti perfecta nitens elephanto, | sed falsa ad caelum mittunt insomnia manes* (an imitation
of *Odys.* XIX. 562 *sqq.*).

42. meliusne, etc. : a taunt at
herself and her foolish choice in

ire per longos fuit, an recentis
    carpere flores ?

45 Si quis infamem mihi nunc iuvencum
    dedat iratae, lacerare ferro et
    frangere enitar modo multum amati
      cornua monstri.

Impudens liqui patrios penatis,
50 impudens Orcum moror.   O deorum
    si quis haec audis, utinam inter errem
      nuda leones !

Antequam turpis macies decentis
    occupet malas teneraeque sucus

leaving the unexciting but safe amusements of childhood for a dangerous pleasure. — **fluctus longos** : cf. *longus pontus*, 3. 37.

45. nunc: emphatic; in contrast with the time when she wreathed his horns with flowers.

46. lacerare : with **cornua**, as vs. 71 shows.

47. enitar, *I'd try with all my might;* an expression of rage, tempered by consciousness of physical weakness. — **modo** : cf. 14. 1. — **multum** : Intr. 49.

49. impudens, etc.: in the swift fluctuations of her feelings, rage is succeeded by shame, mingled with fear of what may happen to her, — starvation, slavery, — and a desire, gradually shaping itself into a purpose, to end her life. It is as shameful for her now to live as it was to leave her home. Oh, if the lions would devour her ! Yes, that would be better than starving slowly and losing all her beauty. But why wait to starve ? The thought of her absent father spurs her to action. ' Let your own hand do it, ere you, a king's daughter, become

the concubine of a foreign lord and the hated slave of his wife.'

50. Orcum moror, *I put off death* (lit., 'keep him waiting'); *i.e.* I ought to die, but shamelessly hold back.

51. si quis: here equivalent to *quisquis;* cf. *Ep.* I. 18. 57. — **inter** : Intr. 115 *c.* — **errem** : *i.e.* come upon them by chance ; she has not yet reached the thought of taking her own life.

52. nuda, *defenseless.*

53. antequam, etc.: this is not mere vanity, but the outcropping of a deep-seated feeling of the ancients, based on the belief that one entered the underworld in the form in which he left life ; see the descriptions in *Aeneid* VI., and cf. Stat. *Silv.* II. 1. 154 (on the death of a favorite boy) *gratum est, Fata, tamen quod non mors lenta iacentis | exedit puerile decus, manesque subi-vit | integer et nullo temeratus corpora damno, | qualis erat.*—**turpis**, *unsightly ;* cf. *turpes luctus*, II. 20. 22 n.—**decentis** : cf. I. 4. 6 n.

54. tenerae praedae : a paraphrase for *mihi*, with the added suggestion of youthfulness (**tene-**

55   defluat praedae, speciosa quaero
           pascere tigris.

     Vilis Europe, pater urget absens,
     quid mori cessas ?   Potes hac ab orno
     pendulum zona bene te secuta
60   laedere collum ;

     sive te rupes et acuta leto
     saxa delectant, age te procellae
     crede veloci, nisi erile mavis
           carpere pensum

65   regius sanguis, dominaeque tradi
     barbarae paelex.'   Aderat querenti
     perfidum ridens Venus et remisso
           filius arcu ;

rae). — sucus defluat: cf. Ter.
Eun. 318 Ch. *Color vérus, corpus
sólidum et suci plénum.* Pa. *Anni?*
Ch. *Anni? Sédecim.* We express
it otherwise : ' the bloom fades,'
or the like.

55. speciosa, (*still*) *fair to see* ;
not a strong word, like *pulcher*,
but merely deprecating the ugli-
ness of emaciation.

56. pascere : Intr. 94 *c.*

57. vilis, etc.: the thought of
her father spurs her resolution.
The words are not a quotation of
what she imagines he would say,
but she knows well what his stern
sentence would be, and under its
influence urges herself on to put
an end to her shame. — vilis: and
hence, as a princess, unfit to live.

59. bene te secuta, *which,
luckily, you have brought with you.*
The bitter irony of these words is
enhanced by the double meaning
given to them by the significance
of the girdle as the emblem of
maidenhood.

60. laedere, *bruise ;* used, in
the same spirit of bitter mockery,
for the harsher *elidere.* As her
resolution assumes fixed shape
(' deliberata morte ferocior ') she
can jest with death ; cf. te delec-
tant and te crede, below.

61. sive : Intr. 119 *d.* — leto :
dative with acuta ; Intr. 58 *c.*

62. saxa : those at the bottom
of the cliffs (rupes). — procellae,
the gale (that blows over the cliffs).

63. erile : apportioned by a
mistress (*era*), *a slave's.*

64. carpere pensum : here of
spinning an assigned portion of
wool ; cf. the picture in Prop. IV.
6. 15 *tristis erat domus, et tristes sua
pensa ministrae* | *carpebant, medio
nebat et ipsa loco ;* Cat. 64. 310.

65. tradi: *i.e.* to be put at her
mercy ; cf. II. 4. 11 n.

66. paelex: and hence the especial object of her cruelty.

67. perfidum : see Intr. 48. —
remisso, *unstrung ;* his work was
done.

mox, ubi lusit satis, 'Abstineto'
70   dixit 'irarum calidaeque rixae,
cum tibi invisus laceranda reddet
cornua taurus.

Vxor invicti Iovis esse nescis.
Mitte singultus, bene ferre magnam
75   disce fortunam : tua sectus orbis
nomina ducet.'

XXVIII.

Festo quid potius die
Neptuni faciam ?   Prome reconditum,

69. **lusit** : sc. *Venus.* — **absti-neto** : the second form of the imperative, here referring to a designated point of future time (**cum reddet**).

70. **irarum, rixae** : Intr. 67.

71. **invisus laceranda**, etc.: in mocking allusion to vss. 45 *sqq.*

73. **uxor esse** : for *te uxorem esse ;* Intr. 99 *b.* — **invicti** : suggesting, perhaps, the necessity of submission.

74. **mitte** : Intr. 129.

75. **sectus orbis**, *a hemisphere.* Horace follows those geographers who divided the world into two parts, Europe and Asia ; cf. Varro *L. L.* V. 31 *ut omnis natura in caelum et terram divisa est, sic caeli regionibus terra in Asiam et Europam ;* Plin. *N. H.* III. 5 (*Europam*) *plerique merito non tertiam portionem fecere, verum aequam, in duas partes . . . universo orbe diviso.*

76. **nomina**: Intr. 128.—**ducet,** *will take ;* lit. 'will draw' (*sc.* from you, implied in **tua**); cf. *S.* II. 1. 66 *duxit ab oppressa meritum Carthagine nomen.*

XXVIII. An ode for Neptune's day. This festival, the *Neptunalia,* occurred on the twenty-third of July, and was celebrated by the people in the open air, picnic fashion, on the banks of the Tiber or the seashore, with arbors (*um-brae*) to shelter them from the midsummer sun. Such, however, is not the celebration contemplated in the ode. It is past noon, and the poet, feeling in the mood for a carouse, bethinks himself that it is a holiday. 'Why not, then ? Come, Lyde, bring down a jar of that fine old Caecuban, and we will celebrate the day together.' Horace speaks, apparently, in the person of a country poet, and the thrifty Lyde keeps his house. We cannot define the picture more exactly, and it is not probable that Horace did so. — Metre, 171.

1. **potius** : *sc.* than that which has occurred to me. The answer to the question is implied in the order which he gives ; cf. II. 3. 9–16.

2. **reconditum,** *hoarded ;* cf. *repostum Caecubum, Epod.* 9. 1 n. For the force of **re-**, cf. I. 10. 17 n.

Lyde, strenua Caecubum,
    munitaeque adhibe vim sapientiae.
5 Inclinare meridiem
    sentis et, veluti stet volucris dies,
parcis deripere horreo
    cessantem Bibuli consulis amphoram.
Nos cantabimus invicem
10   Neptunum et viridis Nereidum comas ;
tu curva recines lyra
    Latonam et celeris spicula Cynthiae ;

3. **strenua**: best taken, in an
adverbial sense, with **prome.** —
Caecubum: see I. 20. 9 n, 37. 5 n.

4. **munitae,** (*your*) *well-en-
trenched; i.e.* which you steadily
maintain, against all temptations
and distractions. — **adhibe vim,**
give a shock to. The meaning is
' Be frivolous for once'; cf. *dulce
est desipere in loco,* IV. 12. 28.

5. **inclinare meridiem**: as the
whole vault of heaven was supposed to revolve with the sun
('vertitur interea caelum,' Verg.
A. II. 250 ; cf. Lucr. V. 510), it
was natural to think of it as erect
or vertical when the sun is overhead, and to speak of the day
(the bright hemisphere) or mid-
day declining, as well as the sun
itself ; cf. Juv. 3. 316 *sol inclinat ;*
Tac. *Ann.* XII. 39. 2 *inclinabat dies.*

6. **stet,** *stood still.* — **et** : used
here to connect contrasted state-
ments (= *et tamen*); cf. Juv. 13. 91
hic putat esse deos et peierat.

7. **deripere,** *to bring down in
haste ;* the de- as in *Epod.* 5. 46
lunamque caelo deripit ; cf. *descende,* 21. 7 n. For the infinitive,
see Intr. 94 *k.* — **horreo:** here for
the *apotheca vinaria ;* see 8. 11 n,
and, for the case, Intr. 70.

8. **cessantem**: simply reinforc-

ing the idea already expressed in
parcis deripere. — **Bibuli** : M.
Calpurnius Bibulus, consul with
Julius Caesar, B.C. 59. See II. 3.
8 n, and cf. III. 21. 1.

9. **nos,** *I.* Horace uses the
plural of the personal pronoun in
this sense only where the speaker
(usually himself) is placed in direct
contrast with some other person
or persons, as here and I. 6. 5 and
17, *Epod.* 1. 5, *S.* I. 4. 41, 6. 18,
Ep. I. 15. 25, 17. 5 ; or in such
personal relation as is implied in
the phrases *nostri memor* (III. 11.
51, 27. 14), *meminit nostri* (*Ep.* I.
3. 12), *studio nostri* (*Ep.* I. 13. 4),
noris nos (*S.* I. 9. 7). — **invicem** :
in reference to the subjects, not
the singers.

10. **viridis** : the colors of the
sea are attributed to the divinities
that dwell there; cf. *caerula mater*
(Thetis), *Epod.* 13. 16 ; Ov. *M.*
XIII. 960 *hanc ego* (Glaucus) *tum
primum viridem ferrugine bar-
bam |* . . . *et caerula bracchia vidi.*

11. **curva lyra** : cf. I. 10. 6. —
recines, *shall sing in response.*
There is a specimen of this sort of
amoebean song in Verg. *E.* 3. 60 *sqq.*
For the future, see Intr. 90.

12. **Latonam,** etc.: notice the
parallelism to vs. 10 ; in each case

summo carmine quae Cnidon
  fulgentisque tenet Cycladas, et Paphum
15 iunctis visit oloribus ;
  dicetur merita Nox quoque nenia.

XXIX.

Tyrrhena regum progenies, tibi
non ante verso lene merum cado
  cum flore, Maecenas, rosarum et
  pressa tuis balanus capillis

one object of the verb is a divinity,
the other some attribute of a divinity (comas, spicula). Cf. I.
21. 5–8 and 9–12. — Cynthiae :
see I. 21. 2 n.

13. summo, *at the close of ;* so
Juv. 1. 5 *summi libri.* Cf. *Ep.* I.
1. 1 *summa dicende camena.* —
quae, etc.: see I. 30. 1, III. 26. 9.
The verb to be supplied (*cantabi-
tur* or the like) is readily suggested
by carmine and the preceding
verbs.

14. fulgentis . see I. 14. 19 n.
—tenet: cf. 4. 62 n. — Cycladas :
Naxos in particular was devoted to
the worship of Aphrodite. There
is evidence also of her worship in
Delos and Ceos, and it was, no
doubt, widespread among all the
islands in the range of Phoenician
commerce.

15. iunctis oloribus : cf. IV.
1. 10, and, for the construction,
Martis equis, 3. 16 n. — visit : see
I. 4. 8 n.

16. dicetur : see I. 6. 5 n. —
Nox : implying, like 19. 10, that
the symposium is to be prolonged
into the night. — nenia : here not
a dirge, as in II. 1. 38, but a song
of slow measure, sung low, a good-
night song.

XXIX. The last place in the
collection before the epilogue,
which the poet reserves for himself and his muse alone, is given
to Maecenas, — an arrangement
which Horace afterwards repeated
in the first book of the Epistles.
An invitation to his patron to
visit him in the country, presumably on his Sabine farm, is made
the occasion of a discourse on
Horace's favorite maxim, 'Carpe
diem.' 'Here, in the middle of
the dog days, you are cooping yourself up in the hot city, worried
with cares of state and harrassing
your soul over Scythians and
Chinese. There may be too much
of this. A wise providence has
hidden the future from us. Only
the past is securely ours ; the
present is for us to control and
use ; all else is beyond our power.
Fortune is fickle : welcome what
she brings, but let not our happiness wait on her favor.' The
ode purports to have been written
in July, and the allusions to the
responsibilities of Maecenas point
to B.C. 26 or 25, the two sum-
mers which Augustus spent in the
West (see intr. note to Ode 14), as
the probable date. — Metre, 176.

5   iamdudum apud me est : eripe te morae,
      ne semper udum Tibur et Aefulae
        declive contempleris arvum et
          Telegoni iuga parricidae.

      Fastidiosam desere copiam et
10   molem propinquam nubibus arduis;
        omitte mirari beatae
          fumum et opes strepitumque Romae.

1. **Tyrrhena**, etc.: see I. 1. 1 n.

2. **verso,** *broached;* lit. 'tipped,' in pouring the wine into the *cratera.* Cf. *S.* II. 8. 39. As the *cadus* contained about five gallons, it would ordinarily hold out for more than one occasion.— **lene**: coupled with *generosum, Ep.* I. 1 5. 18 *sqq.;* cf. *languidiora vina,* 21. 8 n.

3. **flore**, etc.: see II. 3. 13 n.

4. **pressa tuis capillis** : cf. II. 7. 20, and, for a burlesque on this sort of compliment, see Juv. 4. 68. — **balanus** : properly the nut, called 'ben nut' (*myrobalanus,* Plin. *N. H.* XII. 100), growing in Arabia and Egypt ; here the fragrant oil pressed from the nut.

5. **iamdudum**, etc.: *i.e.* I have long been waiting for you; this then is a second and more urgent invitation. — **morae,** *procrastination*, which holds him, as it were, captive.

6. **ne semper contempleris,** *so as not to go on gazing forever at; i.e.* only looking at these beautiful places in the distance, and never coming to them. See vs. 10 n.— **udum Tibur** : so Ovid *F.* IV. 71 *moenia Tiburis udi ;* cf. I. 7. 13 *sq.* — **Aefulae** : an old Latin hilltown (cf. **declive**) probably between Praeneste and Tibur. It was garrisoned on the approach of Hannibal by the *Via Latina* in B.C. 211 (Liv. XXVI. 9. 9).

8. **Telegoni** : son of Ulysses and Circe. Sent by the latter in search of his father, he came to Ithaca, where he was obliged to plunder the country for provisions. He was set upon by Ulysses and Telemachus ; and in the contest that ensued unwittingly slew his father (Hygin. *Fab.* 127). — **iuga** : those of Tusculum, of which Telegonus was the reputed founder; cf. *Epod.* 1. 29 n.

9. **fastidiosam,** *cloying;* Intr. 125.

10. **molem,** *massive structure, pile ;* cf. II. 15. 2. The splendid mansion which Maecenas built in his park on the Esquiline (see *S.* I. 8. 7 n) was furnished with a lofty tower, afterwards known as *turris Maecenatiana,* from which Nero is said to have watched the great fire (Suet. *Nero* 38). This 'alta domus' (*Epod.* 9. 3) commanded a view of the whole city and of the neighboring country as far as the Tusculan and Sabine hills (cf. vss. 6 *sqq.*).

11. **mirari** : cf. 25. 14, and see I. 4. 19 n ; for the mood, Intr. 94 *j.* —**beatae**: see I. 4. 14 n, III. 26. 9.

12. **fumum,** etc. : a graphic composite picture, combining the striking features of the scene, — the splendid houses and temples (evidences of wealth) looming up in the smoky atmosphere, with

Plerumque gratae divitibus vices,
mundaeque parvo sub lare pauperum
15   cenae sine aulaeis et ostro
sollicitam explicuere frontem.

Iam clarus occultum Andromedae pater
ostendit ignem, iam Procyon furit
et stella vesani Leonis,
20   sole dies referente siccos;

the ceaseless roar of the distant
streets. — **opes**, *splendor*. — **strepitum** : cf. *Ep*. II. 2. 79 *inter
strepitus nocturnos atque diurnos*
(sc. *urbis*).

13. **gratae** (sc. *sunt*), etc.: cf. Lucr.
III. 1057 *haud ita vitam agerent
ut nunc plerumque videmus | quid
sibi quisque velit nescire et quaerere
semper | commutare locum, quasi
onus deponere possit; | exit saepe
foras magnis ex aedibus ille, | esse
domi quem pertaesumst, subitoque
revertit | . . . currit agens mannos
ad villam praecipitanter*, etc. —
vices, *change*. The thought in
this verse is simply of the *fastidiosa
copia*, of change for the sake of
change ; it grows out of what he
has been saying. But close to this
lies the thought of the cares that
go with riches, and this brings him
to the second point in his plea
and the main theme of the ode,—
the cares, not of riches (**divitibus**
belongs to **gratae** only, and not
to **explicuere frontem**), but those
of which Maecenas permits himself to be the victim.

14. **mundae**, *of simple elegance*.
Horace himself defines this word
(*S*. II. 2. 65) as the happy mean
between pretentious show and
slovenliness. Cf. *Ep*. II. 2. 199
*pauperies immunda domus procul
absit*. — **sub** : see I. 5. 3 n. — **lare** :
cf. I. 12. 44 n ; we may render it

here by *roof*, which conveys for us
the same idea of home shelter. —
pauperum : *a poor man's ;* cf.
virginum, 27. 38 n. For the meaning, see I. 1. 18 n.

15. **aulaeis**: a canopy suspended
over the *triclinium* in fashionable houses, ostensibly to catch
the dust from the ceiling ; see
S. II. 8. 54, Verg. *A*. I. 697. —
ostro : in the *aulaea* and in the
upholstery of the couches.

16. **explicuere** : Intr. 80.

17. **iam**, etc. : this description
of the dog days, — a time for rest,
— paves the way to his protest
against Maecenas' persistent devotion to public business. The
constellations used to mark the
hot season are Cassiopea, represented by Cepheus (on earth an
Ethiopian king, husband of Cassiopea and father of Andromeda),
rising July 9 ; **Procyon** ('quod
sidus apud Romanos non habet
nomen,' Plin. *N. H.* XVIII. 268),
rising July 15, eleven days before
the Dog Star (see I. 17. 17 n); and
the Lion, whose brightest star,
which we call Regulus ('regia in
pectore leonis stella,' Plin. *N. H.*
XVIII. 271), rises July 30, according
to Pliny. — **clarus** : with **ostendit**;
cf. *strenua*, 28. 3 n. — **occultum** :
sc. *antea ;* cf. *quietos*, vs. 40.

18. **furit, vesani**: cf. *Ep*. I. 10. 16
rabiem Canis et momenta Leonis,

iam pastor umbras cum grege languido
rivumque fessus quaerit et horridi
  dumeta Silvani, caretque
    ripa vagis taciturna ventis :

25 tu civitatem quis deceat status
curas et urbi sollicitus times
  quid Seres et regnata Cyro
    Bactra parent Tanaisque discors.

Prudens futuri temporis exitum
30 caliginosa nocte premit deus,
  ridetque si mortalis ultra
    fas trepidat. Quod adest memento

componere aequus : cetera fluminis

cum semel accepit solem furibundus acutum.

19. **stella** : probably not used loosely for 'constellation' (as in Verg. *G.* I. 222), but for the conspicuous star Regulus (see vs. 17 n).

20. **siccos**, *of drouth.*

21. **iam** : referring to the time of year, when the scene he paints may be witnessed any day.

22. **rivum** : cf. II. 5. 6 *iuvencae ... fluviis gravem solantis aestum.* — **fessus**, *wearily;* cf. *clarus,* 17 n. — **horridi** : an attribute borrowed from the **dumeta** which he inhabits.

23. **Silvani** : see *Epod.* 2. 22 n.

24. **taciturna** : a part of the predicate ; it is silent because there is no motion in the air.

25. **tu civitatem** : cf. II. 9. 9. The reference is perhaps to the recent settlement of the government, B.C. 27, many details of which had no doubt still to be worked out.

26. **urbi** : with **times**.

27. **Seres** : cf. I. 12. 56 n. There is a touch of irony in the mention

of these remote peoples; the city cannot be in imminent peril.— **regnata Cyro** : a part of his empire ; cf. II. 2. 17 n. For the construction, cf. *regnata Phalantho,* II. 6. 11, and see Intr. 51 *e,* 55.

28. **Bactra** : the remotest dependency of Parthia. — **Tanais** : *i.e.* the Scythians; cf. IV. 15. 24. The river stands for the country through which it flows ; cf. II. 9. 21 *Medumque flumen gentibus additum victis ;* II. 20. 20 n. — **discors** : another reason for feeling secure at Rome.

29. **prudens deus** : cf. I. 3. 21 n. — **temporis** : Intr. 76.

30. **nocte premit** : cf. I. 4. 16.

31. **ultra fas** : cf. *scire nefas,* I. 11. 1.

32. **trepidat** : see II. 11. 4 n. — **memento** : see I. 7. 17 n.

33. **componere aequus** : both words, in contrast with **trepidat**, express coolness and deliberation. — **cetera** : *i.e.* the future, for the past does not here come into consideration.

> ritu feruntur, nunc medio alveo
> 35   cum pace delabentis Etruscum
>   in mare, nunc lapides adesos
>
> stirpisque raptas et pecus et domos
> volventis una, non sine montium
>   clamore vicinaeque silvae,
> 40   cum fera diluvies quietos
>
> inritat amnis.   Ille potens sui
> laetusque deget, cui licet in diem
>   dixisse 'Vixi ; cras vel atra
>   nube polum pater occupato,

34. ritu : as in 14. 1 ; cf. *S.*
II. 3. 268 *tempestatis prope ritu
mobilia.* — **medio alveo :** rivers
capable of producing such floods
as are described in the next
strophe are often, especially in
mountainous countries, at other
times quiet brooks, gliding along
the middle of a broad channel.
Cf. IV. 7. 3.

35. cum pace, *peaceably* (not
'peacefully'), expressing the disposition of the stream ; cf. **inritat,**
41.   The same personification appears in **clamore** and **fera dilu-
vies.**—Etruscum: Intr.117*a*,176*b*.

36. adesos : from long lying in
the channel.

37. raptas : with all three substantives.

38. una, *along.*

41. potens sui, *independent,*
not subject to any other control ;
with especial reference, however,
to the control of the passions.
The man who is always taking
thought for the morrow is the
slave of desire and hence of fear ;
'nam qui cupiet, metuet quoque ;
porro | qui metuens vivet, liber
mihi non erit umquam' (*Ep.* I. 16.
65).

42. in diem, *day by day ;* cf. *S.*
II. 6. 47.   *Quotidie* would be less
suitable, because the idea is of
one day added each time to the
series of days.

43. dixisse : Intr. 81 *b.* — **vixi :**
in a pregnant sense. The man
who can say, at the close of each
day, 'I have lived' is one who has
got out of that day's life the satisfaction and enjoyment it could
yield, in contrast with the man
who neglects these in his anxiety
to provide the means to 'live' in
the future.   Cf. Martial II. 90. 3
*vivere quod propero pauper nec
inutilis annis,* | *da veniam : prope-
rat vivere nemo satis ;* | *differat hoc
patrios optat qui vincere census ;*
I. 15. 11 *non est, crede mihi, sapi-
entis dicere 'vivam' ; sera nimis
vita est crastina ; vive hodie.* The
view of life here inculcated is the
same as in I. 9. 13 *sqq.*

44. pater : cf. I. 2. 2 n. — **occupato :** the longer form of the
imperative (3d pers.) is here used
with concessive force.

45. sole : here for sunshine, as
Verg. *A.* IX. 461 *iam sole infuso*
(of the dawn) ; cf. its use for 'day,'
IV. 2. 46. — **puro :** see 10. 8 n. —

45   vel sole puro : non tamen inritum
      quodcumque retro est efficiet, neque
        diffinget infectumque reddet
          quod fugiens semel hora vexit.'

      Fortuna, saevo laeta negotio et
50   ludum insolentem ludere pertinax,
        transmutat incertos honores,
          nunc mihi, nunc alii benigna.

      Laudo manentem : si celeris quatit
      pennas, resigno quae dedit et mea

inritum, diffinget, infectum : the
distinction may be illustrated in
this way : a deed of gift (for example) may be rendered *void* (**inritum**) before going into effect, by
a subsequent deed, superseding it,
or it may be modified by *recasting*
(**diffinget**), or it may be destroyed
and put out of existence (**infectum**) ; but if the gift has been
received *and enjoyed*, then no
power can do any of these things.
So it is with the 'dona praesentis
horae' (8. 27).

46. **retro** : *i.e.* past ; with the
same thought of a *current* of
events as in **hora vexit**.

47. **diffinget** : cf. I. 35. 39.

48. **semel** : cf. I. 24. 16 n, *C. S.*
26. — **vexit** : sc. *secum ;* cf. Verg.
G. I. 461 *quid vesper serus vehat.*
There is nothing in **fugiens**
(*fleeting*, that which comes but
does not stay ; cf. 30. 5) to require us to take **vexit** in the sense
of *avexit*. It is simply the experience, the enjoyment of 'the passing hour.'

50. **ludum** : as war is the *ludus*
of Mars, I. 2. 37 ; cf. II. 1. 3. For
ludum ludere, see Intr. 45 *a*. —
insolentem, *heartless ;* see I. 5.
8 n. — **ludere** : Intr. 101 *b.*

51. **transmutat honores** : cf. I.
34. 14 *sqq.*

54. **pennas** : a regular attribute
of Fortuna ; cf. I. 34. 15 n. — **resigno**, *I surrender.* In this sense
the word is found in classical
literature only here and *Ep.* I. 7.
34, but it must have been common
in ordinary speech, as is evidenced
by the corresponding use of its
modern derivatives. It was a
commercial word, having no reference to the breaking of seals (as
it has in *Ep.* I. 7. 9 *testamenta
resignat*), but probably derived
from the use of *signare* instead of
scribere (cf. Paul. *ex* Fest. 284),
for making an entry in the account
book ; *resignare* would then be to
make an entry *opposite* (on the
credit side), balancing the former
and thus cancelling the claim for
which it stood ; just as *rescribere*
was used in the sense of *repay, e.g.*
S. II. 3. 76, Ter. *Ph.* 922 *argentum
rursum iube rescribi.* In fact Festus says : '*resignare*' *antiqui pro
'*rescribere*' ponebant ut adhuc
'subsignare' dicimus pro 'subscri-
bere*' (p. 281). — **mea**, *my own*
(Intr. 116 *b*) ; in contrast with the
uncertain tenure of all other so
called possessions.

55   virtute me involvo probamque
          pauperiem sine dote quaero.
      Non est meum, si mugiat Africis
      malus procellis, ad miseras preces
      decurrere et votis pacisci,
60   ne Cypriae Tyriaeque merces
      addant avaro divitias mari :
      tunc me biremis praesidio scaphae
      tutum per Aegaeos tumultus
      aura feret geminusque Pollux.

55. me involvo : as with a cloak, — his one remaining possession. The metaphor is borrowed from Plato, in whose ideal state αἱ γυναῖκες ἀρετὴν ἀντὶ ἱματίων ἀμφιέσονται (*Rep.* V. 457 A).

56. quaero : *sc.* as a bride, as is shown by **sine dote**, following **probam**, by which **pauperies** was at once personified.

57. meum, *my way;* a colloquial expression ; cf. Plaut. *Trin.* 631 *néque meumst neque fácere didici;* ib. 123 CA. *Quid féci ?* ME. *Quod homo néquam.* CA. *Non istíc meumst ?* — **mugiat Africis,** etc.: cf. I. 14. 5.

59. votis pacisci : a cynical, but not untruthful designation of the transaction ; see I. 31. 1 n.

60. Cypriae Tyriaeque : Intr. 117 *a.*

61. avaro : cf. *avidum mare,* I. 28. 18.

62. tunc, *in such a case.* — **biremis** : here not 'bireme,' but *two-oared,* merely indicating, however, the size of the boat, — small enough to be rowed with two oars (*duorum scalmorum navicula,* Cic. *de Or.* I. 174). — **scaphae** : the boat carried or towed by a ship, like our life-boat or dory ; cf.

Petron. 101 *quomodo possumus egredi navi ? . . . quin potius . . . per funem lapsi descendimus in scapham ?* It could be rigged with a sail, as here (**aura feret**). The meaning in these two strophes is the same as in the preceding : the ship and its rich freight are the gifts of Fortune ; if the heavy-laden vessel is about to founder in the storm of adversity, he will not moan over his loss, but will take to the life-boat and cheerfully sail away : the essentials of happiness make a light and safe cargo.

63. Aegaeos tumultus : cf. II. 16. 2.

64. aura, etc. : *i.e.* the breeze (in contrast to **Africis procellis**) granted by the twin divinities, — the recompense of a more genuine piety. — **geminus Pollux** : for Castor and Pollux ; so Ov. *A. A.* I. 746 *geminus Castor,* probably in the same sense. It was common to use one name for both, 'quia ambo licenter et Polluces et Castores vocantur' (Serv. on Verg. *G.* III. 89). Their temple at Rome was commonly known as *aedes Castoris* (Suet. *Iul.* 10) or *Castorum* (Plin. *N. H.* X. 121). For their protection of mariners, see I. 3. 2 n.

XXX.

Exegi monumentum aere perennius
regalique situ pyramidum altius,
quod non imber edax, non Aquilo impotens
possit diruere aut innumerabilis

XXX. This ode was written as an epilogue, as I. 1 is the prologue, of the three books (see introd. note to I. 1). Each poem is carefully adapted in spirit and tone to the place it occupies. When Horace sat down to arrange his odes for publication, he was already well assured of his success as a lyric poet by the approbation of the limited but competent circle of readers who were acquainted with his work ; and as the goodly collection grew under his hand, he might well feel a pardonable pride in his achievement. It meant for him, what his earlier successes might not have meant, lasting fame. He had completed the first considerable body of lyric poetry ever published in Latin ; its place was assured, as its quality was unique, in the literature of Rome, — the literature of the eternal city, the metropolis of the world. It is not surprising that the closing poem is a song of triumph ; and if it is characterized by a candor which our modern poets do not permit themselves, we must make allowance for difference of time and custom. That it did not offend the taste of Horace's countrymen, we may infer from the fact that he was imitated by other poets (cf. Propert. IV. 1. 35 and 57 *sqq.;* Ovid *Am.* I. 15. 41 *sq.*, *M.* XV. 871 *sqq.;* Phaedr. IV. *Epil.* 5 *sq.*; Martial VIII. 3. 5 *sqq.*); and, knowing Horace, we may feel sure he

had Greek precedent to fall back upon, if need be, as well as the example of Ennius in the well known epitaph (see II. 20. 21 n). — Metre, 169.

1. **exegi,** *I have completed ;* so Ovid *M.* XV. 871 *iamque opus exegi, quod nec Iovis ira nec ignis | nec poterit ferrum nec edax abolere vetustas.* — **monumentum :** Horace's work was literally a *monumentum* in the wider sense of that word (cf. *moneo*), but he here calls it figuratively a *monument,* in our narrower sense, for the purpose of comparison. — **aere :** a common material for memorials, especially statues and inscribed tablets.

2. **regali :** *i.e.* magnificent ; cf. II. 15. 1 n. — **situ pyramidum :** for 'the crumbling pyramids' (cf. Intr. 126 *b*), an intimation, like **edax** and **impotens** below, of the destructive forces to which material monuments are subject. Translate, '*the crumbling magnificence of,*' etc., or the like. For this use of *situs* cf. Mart. VIII. 3. 5 *et cum rupta situ Messalae saxa iacebunt, | altaque cum Licini marmora pulvis erunt, | me tamen ora legent.* — **altius :** the highest of them, the great pyramid of Ghizeh, was about 480 feet,— higher than any other monument known to the Romans.

3. **quod,** *one that ;* descriptive relative clause. — **impotens :** cf. I. 37. 10 n, *Epod.* 16. 62. For the

5   annorum series et fuga temporum.
       Non omnis moriar, multaque pars mei
       vitabit Libitinam ; usque ego postera
       crescam laude recens ; dum Capitolium
       scandet cum tacita virgine pontifex,
10   dicar, qua violens obstrepit Aufidus

conjunctions in this clause, cf. II.
9. I n.

5. **fuga** : cf. *fugaces anni*, II.
14. I ; *fugiens hora*, III. 29. 48.

6. **non omnis**, etc.: cf. Ov. *Am.*
I. 15. 41 *ergo etiam cum me supre-
mus adederit ignis, | vivam, pars-
que mei multa superstes erit.*—
-**que** : cf. I. 27. 16 n.

7. **Libitinam** : *i.e.* the funeral
pyre and the tomb ; cf. *S.* II. 6.
19. By an edict of Servius Tullius
a fee was to be paid, on the occasion of every death, at the temple of Venus Libitina, and there
also the requisite implements for
the funeral were to be obtained.
Hence Libitina became synony-
mous with death, as *Ep.* II. 1. 49,
but usually with more suggestion
of the funeral rites than of death
in the abstract ; so that this clause
is not a mere repetition of **non
omnis moriar.**—**usque** : lit. 'on
and on,' denoting an indefinite
series of repetitions ; cf. *Ep.* I. 10.
24 ; Cat. 5. 9. It modifies **cre-
scam** (and hence the whole clause),
but with nearer reference to **pos-
tera**, which does not mean 'of
posterity,' but simply 'later.' The
'later praise' will be in every case
greater than that which preceded
it.

8. **recens**, *ever fresh.* — **dum
Capitolium**, etc. : cf. 3. 42. The
one thing unchangeable beyond all
else to a Roman was his religious
institutions, the head and centre
of which was the worship of Jove,

with Juno and Minerva, in their
ancient temple on the Tarpeian
hill (**Capitolium**). With this
Horace joins, in the graphic sketch
which he uses to express his
meaning, the priestesses of Vesta,
whose worship was equally significant of perpetuity; cf. 5. 11 *sq.* What
procession is referred to we do not
definitely know; but it must have
been a stated — perhaps monthly
— observance, sufficiently designated to Horace's readers by the
features he mentions.

9. **virgine, pontifex** : these are
taken by some to mean the chief
Vestal (*Virgo Maxima*) and the
Pontifex Maximus ; but more
probably they are used collectively
(Intr. 127) for the Vestal virgins
and the pontifices. The former
marched in reverent silence (**tacita**), amid the hymns and chants
which must have formed part of
the ceremony. This clause is best
taken with what follows, as the
preceding statement is already
provided with the notion of perpetuity in **usque.** Horace couches
his prophecy in three utterances
which are progressive in point of
definiteness : the first is vague,—
'I shall not wholly die'; the second explains this, — 'my fame will
survive and increase from age to
age'; and finally he names the
achievement for which men will
praise him (**dicar — deduxisse
modos**).

10. **dicar**, etc.: in accordance

et qua pauper aquae Daunus agrestium
regnavit populorum ex humili potens,
princeps Aeolium carmen ad Italos

with the Latin preference for the
personal construction (cf. *videor
mihi* and the like), for 'It will be
said that I.' We may translate, *I
shall be named as one who.* — **qua**,
etc.: best taken with **dicar**, and
expressing the pride with which
his birth-place will cherish his
fame ; but his motive in inserting
this reference is much the same as
in IV. 9. 2 *longe sonantem natus
ad Aufidum*, and S. II. 1. 34. It
grows, like the mention of other
personal characteristics in *Ep.* I.
20. 20 *sqq.*, out of the poet's desire
to be to his readers something
more than a mere name. — **violens** : it is a mountain torrent in
the part where Horace knew it
best ; cf. IV. 14. 25–28, S. I. 1. 58.
— **obstrepit** : here used absolutely, but without losing the force
of ob-, — 'fills one's ears with its
roar' ; cf. Liv. XXI. 56. 9 *nihil
sensere, obstrepente pluvia*.'

11. **pauper aquae** : cf. *Epod.*
3. 16 *siticulosae Apuliae*. For the
genitive see Intr. 66 *c*. — **Daunus** :
see I. 22. 14 n. — **agrestium** : even
in Horace's time Apulia was still
a farming and grazing country,
with comparatively few towns ; cf.
16. 26 n.

12. **populorum**, *tribes*. The
genitive is commonly explained as
an imitation of the Greek genitive
after ἄρχω, βασιλεύω, and the like.
But as no instance of this construction in Latin is cited until
about two centuries after Horace
wrote, and then only in a few
provincial writers, who have the
genitive with *dominor*, and as no
such violent departure from the
Latin idiom is found elsewhere in

Horace, it may be questioned
whether this ready explanation is
open to us. For **populorum potens,** on the other hand, we have a
perfect parallel in 25. 14 *Naiadum
potens;* and for the position of
regnavit, in that of *musa,* II. 12.
13, of *te,* IV. 1. 19, of *equitavit,* IV.
4. 43, and many similar examples.
— **ex humili potens** : this has
been taken in agreement with the
subject of **dicar**, as Horace speaks
of *potentes vates,* IV. 8. 26, and
contrasts, on occasion, his lowly
birth with his subsequent eminence
(II. 20. 5, *Ep.* I. 20. 20) ; but to
use the term *potens* of himself,
would have been, as Bentley rightly
held, an unnecessarily offensive
assumption. It is moreover out
of place if applied to Horace, and
disturbs the course of thought,
which is centred on the one distinction which Horace felt to be
forever his, — that of being the
first to master the problem of
Latin lyric verse. Grammatically
also it goes more naturally with
Daunus, who did, in fact, according to the legend, rise from the
condition of a refugee from Illyr-
icum to be king of his adopted
country (Festus, p. 69). For the
construction, cf. Cic. *de Part. Or.*
57 *nihil est tam miserabile quam
ex beato miser*. The whole clause
then may be rendered : *where poor
in water Daunus reigned, o'er rustic
tribes a lord from low estate*, or
the like.

13. **princeps** : a little more
than *primus ;* he was not merely
first, but a leader, a pioneer. —
Aeolium carmen : cf. I. 1. 34,
35 nn, II. 13. 24, IV. 3. 12. — **Ita-**

deduxisse modos.   Sume superbiam
15   quaesitam meritis et mihi Delphica
lauro cinge volens, Melpomene, comam.

los : here for 'Latin'; cf. *Italiae
ruinis*, 5. 39, *res Italas* (= *res Ro-
manas*) *Ep.* II. 1. 2. Since Roman
citizenship had been extended to
all Italians, as the Latin language
spread throughout the peninsula,
the more comprehensive term
came naturally to be used in place
of the narrower one.

14. **deduxisse,** *composed;* cf. *S.*
II. 1. 4 *mille die versus deduci
posse;* Ov. *M.* I. 4, *perpetuum dedu-
cite carmen.* The figure is from
spinning; cf. *Ep.* II. 1. 225 *tenui
deducta poemata filo.* — **modos,**
rhythm; the inherent musical quality of the language, its structure
in reference to the various elements of rhythm, in much of which
it differed from the Greek. To
succeed in writing lyric poetry,
he had to make it conform to
these conditions. — **sume super-**

biam : cf. *pone superbiam,* 10. 9.
The muse is addressed as the
divinity who has given him the
power to achieve success (cf. IV.
3. 17 *sqq.*), and who therefore may
be called upon both to take pride
in his achievement and to crown
him with the laurel of victory.
The self-gratulation of the poem
is skilfully softened by this recognition in the closing verses of
dependence on an inspiration not
the poet's own.

15. **quaesitam meritis,** *well
earned.* — **Delphica :** cf. IV. 2. 9
laurea Apollinari. — **volens,** *gra-
ciously;* a set formula in prayers,
usually with *propitius;* cf. *C. S.*
49 n ; Liv. I. 16. 3 *precibus expo-
scunt uti volens propitius suam
semper sospitet progeniem.*

16. **Melpomene :** see I. 12. 2 n,
IV. 3. 1.

LIBER QVARTVS

I.

Intermissa, Venus, diu
    rursus bella moves ?   Parce precor, precor.
Non sum qualis eram bonae
    sub regno Cinarae.   Desine, dulcium
5   mater saeva Cupidinum,
    circa lustra decem flectere mollibus

For the facts relating to the composition and publication of the fourth book of the Odes, and the significance of its lack of a dedication, see Intr. 31, 32.

I. As if to show that he is still young at heart, as befits the lyric poet, Horace opens the new volume with an ode on love at fifty, and himself poses for the picture, as usual. He protests that he has no longer either fitness or inclination for the merry service of Venus, but the stealthy tear and the tongue-tied silence betray the unexpected passion. To offset the picture by a contrast, he pays a passing tribute to the gifts and accomplishments of his young friend Paullus Fabius Maximus. — Metre, 171.

1. **intermissa:** with **bella.** The word comes naturally to the front in a sentence the real purport of which is that the poet after a silence of many years has resumed his lyre ; for the proper province of the lyre is the emotions, and above all others love ; cf. I. 6. 10 and 17 *sqq.*, II. 1. 37 *sqq.*

2. **bella :** for the figure, cf. vs. 16 and III. 26. 2 *sq.* — **moves :** cf. I. 15. 10 n ; Verg. *G.* I. 509 *hinc movet Euphrates, illinc Germania bellum.* — **parce :** cf. II. 19. 7 *sq.* — **precor :** Intr. 116 *d.*

4. **regno,** *sway ;* cf. *regit,* III. 9. 9. — **Cinarae :** alluded to elsewhere in terms which show that she was a real person, and that this was probably her real name. She was presumably a freedwoman, and had the characteristic faults of her class and condition of life, but she had a good heart and a genuine attachment for the poet ; cf. *Ep.* I. 14. 33 *quem scis immunem (empty-handed) Cinarae placuisse rapaci.* She was now dead (cf. 13. 22 *sq.*), and there is a touch of tenderness in Horace's allusion to her (**bonae**). See Intr. 30.

5. **mater,** etc. : a reminiscence of I. 19 ; but the phrase is expanded by the insertion of the epithet **dulcium**, in designed contrast with **saeva**, expressing the 'bitter-sweet' of love.

6. **circa lustra decem :** for the omission of the pronoun (*me*) cf.

iam durum imperiis ; abi
> quo blandae iuvenum te revocant preces.

Tempestivius in domum
10   Paulli purpureis ales oloribus

comissabere Maximi,
> si torrere iecur quaeris idoneum.

Namque et nobilis et decens
> et pro sollicitis non tacitus reis

15   et centum puer artium
> late signa feret militiae tuae,

Ov. *M*. I. 20 (*pugnabant*) | *mollia cum duris, sine pondere* (sc. *corporibus*) *habentia pondus.* Horace was fifty in B.C. 15. For lustra, cf. II. 4. 23 *sq.*—flectere: see II. 19. 17 n, and cf. III. 7. 25, *Ep.* II. 3. 163. The present is here conative, as durum shows.

7. imperiis : better taken as dative with durum, which, in contrast with mollibus, expresses a species of incapacity (*hardened, unresponsive*) ; see Intr. 58 *c*, and cf. Cic. *Arch.* 19 *durior ad haec studia,* and *S.* I. 4. 8 *durus componere versus,* where *durus* denotes another kind of incapacity (Intr. 101 *c*).

8. revocant : the prefix implies that they may rightfully claim her presence ; cf. *repetantur,* I. 9. 20 n.

9. tempestivius : in reference to the age of Paullus ; cf. III. 19. 27 n.

10. Paulli Maximi : cos. B.C. 11, and hence probably about twenty years younger than Horace (*i.e.* approaching thirty at this time), and of about the same age as Ovid, who was his intimate friend (*Pont.* I. 2, II. 3). He belonged to one of the noblest families in Rome, and enjoyed the close confidence of Augustus, whose cousin he had married. His death in A.D. 14 preceded that of the emperor by a few months (*Tac. Ann.* I. 5. 2).— purpureis : the hue of divine beauty; cf. III. 3. 12 n.— ales, *on the wings of,* but referring to her chariot drawn by swans ; cf. III. 28. 15, and for the ablative oloribus, cf. *Martis equis,* III. 3. 16 n.

11. comissabere, *carry thy revels.*

12. torrere : see Intr. 94 *c.*— iecur : cf. I. 13. 4 n.

13. et . . . et . . . : notice the cumulative force of the fivefold repetition, and cf. vs. 29 n.— decens : cf. I. 4. 6 n.

14. pro sollicitis, etc. : cf. II. 1. 13; Ov. *Pont.* I. 2. 118 (*vox tua*), | *auxilio trepidis quae solet esse reis.*— non tacitus : for the litotes, cf. I. 12. 21, IV. 9. 31.

15. centum : cf. II. 14. 26.— puer, *a lad ;* see I. 9. 16 n.— artium, *accomplishments.*

16. signa, etc.: cf. *bella,* vs. 2 n. The grouping of words in this verse is at variance with Horace's usual manner, which would give us *late militiae* ‖ *signa feret tuae* (cf. vss. 10, 12, 14, 22, 28, 30, 32,

et quandoque potentior
       largi muneribus riserit aemuli,
Albanos prope te lacus
20   ponet marmoream sub trabe citrea.
Illic plurima naribus
       duces tura, lyraque et Berecyntia
delectabere tibia
       mixtis carminibus non sine fistula ;
25   illic bis pueri die
       numen cum teneris virginibus tuum

34, 40 ; Intr. 113) ; and that is
perhaps what he really wrote.

17. **quandoque**, *whenever*, but
looking forward to only one occurrence, as in 2. 34. — **potentior** :
sc. by the force of personal
charm.

18. **largi**, *lavish*.— **muneribus** :
better taken with **potentior** ; see
Intr. 75. — **riserit** : *sc.* in triumph.

19. **Albanos lacus** : the principal ones were Albanus and Nemorensis (Nemi), both near the
Appian road. It is not known
that Fabius had a country-seat in
the neighborhood, and the ceremonial proposed is on a scale
hardly in keeping with the idea of
a private chapel. The poet appears
to have in mind a public shrine,
a new centre of the worship of
Venus.

20. **ponet**, *set up ;* see 8. 8 n.
— **marmoream**, *in marble ;* cf.
S. II. 3. 183 *aeneus ut stes.* —
trabe : used collectively (= *trabibus*, III. 2. 28 ; Intr. 127), and
meaning the inside finish of the
roof. — **citrea**, *of African cedar.*
This tree grew to a great size on
the slopes of Mt. Atlas, and was
highly prized for its durability and
the beauty of its veining and

color. The Romans used it especially for the circular tops of
dining tables (*orbes*), some of
which were handed down through
generations and brought enormous
prices ; see Plin. *N. H.* XIII. 91
sqq. It was known to the Greeks
(θύον or θύα) from early times, and
is mentioned by Theophrastus
(Plin. *N. H.* XIII. 101) as the
material of the timber work of
ancient temples.

21. **plurima**, *abundance of.*

22. **tura** : cf. I. 19. 14, 30. 3. —
lyra, tibia : instrumental ablative
with **delectabere**. — **Berecyntia** :
i.e. Phrygian ; see I. 18. 13 n, III.
19. 19 n.

24. **mixtis carminibus**(*strains*) :
abl. abs. expressing manner ; *i.e.*
by a concert of those instruments,
with the *fistula*, as in III. 19. 18 *sqq.*
The recurrence of the final **ā** is
perhaps intended to make the
description more realistic. — **non
sine** : see I. 23. 3 n. — **fistula** :
see I. 17. 10 n.

25. **illic** : Intr. 116 *h.* — **bis die** :
morning and evening. — **pueri
cum virginibus** : for the employ-
ment of choirs of children in religious ceremonies, cf. I. 21 and
intr. note to *C. S.* (p. 331).

laudantes pede candido
        in morem Salium ter quatient humum.
    Me nec femina nec puer
30   iam nec spes animi credula mutui
    nec certare iuvat mero
        nec vincire novis tempora floribus.
    Sed cur heu, Ligurine, cur
        manat rara meas lacrima per genas?
35   Cur facunda parum decoro
        inter verba cadit lingua silentio?
    Nocturnis ego somniis
        iam captum teneo, iam volucrem sequor
    te per gramina Martii
40   campi, te per aquas, dure, volubilis.

27. **laudantes** : a hymn is to
accompany the dance. — **candido** : more graphic than *nudo*.

28. **morem Salium** : see I. 36.
12 n. — **ter** : see III. 18. 16 n. —
quatient humum : cf. I. 4. 7,
37. 2.

29. **nec . . . nec**, etc. : corresponding to the fivefold repetition
of *et*, vs. 13 n.

30. **animi mutui** : *i.e.* that my
love would be returned; cf. III.
9. 13 *face mutua*. For animi, cf.
I. 16. 28 n. For **credula mutui**,
cf. *credulus aurea*, I. 5. 9 n.

31. **certare, vincire** : complementary infinitives joined with
substantives as subjects of iuvat;
cf. *ames dici*, I. 2. 50 n. — **mero** :
i.e. in a drinking contest; cf. I. 36.
13 *sq.*

32. **novis** : *i.e.* those of spring.
— **floribus** : cf. I. 4. 9 n, 5. 1 n.

33. **sed cur**, etc. : with this unexpected break-down of his renun-

ciation of love, cf. III. 26. 11 *sq.*—
Ligurine : the same name as in
the tenth ode.

34. **rara** : *i.e.* a single one, that
is on his cheek before he knows
it; the same idea as in I. 13. 6.
The opposite is *plurima lacrima*,
Ep. I. 17. 59.

35. **cur**, etc. : cf. I. 8. 3 *sqq.;*
Intr. 116 *f.*— **facunda** : with lingua. — **parum**: with **decoro**. For
the metre of this verse, see Intr.
171.

36. **cadit lingua** : cf. Cat. 51. 7
nam simul te, Lesbia, adspexi, . . .
lingua sed torpet (after Sappho
Fr. 2 ὡς γὰρ εὔιδον βροχέως σε,
φώνας | οὐδὲν ἔτ' εἴκει · | ἀλλὰ καμ
μέν γλῶσσα ἔαγε).

38. **iam . . . iam** = *nunc . . .
nunc.*

40. **aquas** : *sc.* of the Tiber; cf.
III. 7. 26 *sqq.* — **volubilis** : cf. *Ep.*
I. 2. 43 (*amnis*) *labitur et labetur
in omne volubilis aevum.*

II.

Pindarum quisquis studet aemulari,
Iulle, ceratis ope Daedalea

II. In B.C. 16 the disturbed condition of the whole German frontier reached a crisis in the humiliating defeat of M. Lollius, the emperor's legate on the Rhine, in his effort to repel an incursion of the Sygambri and other German tribes, who had actually crossed the river and invaded Gaul. Augustus proceeded at once to the province, taking with him his stepson Tiberius; and although the Germans withdrew on the news of his approach, and gave hostages for their future good behaviour, he was occupied for three years in settling the affairs of the western provinces, and did not return to Rome until July 4, B.C. 13. It was during this interval (in B.C. 15) that he planned and carried out, through his two step-sons, the brilliant campaign against the restless Alpine tribes which is celebrated in Odes 4 and 14. The present ode was written during his absence, and most probably in the winter of B.C. 16–15; for it contains no mention of the Alpine victories, beside which the overawing of the Sygambri and their allies was an insignificant achievement. The occasion appears to have been a suggestion from Jullus Antonius that Horace should celebrate the exploits of Augustus, — not particularly those just reported, — in Pindaric odes. The poet replies with a fine eulogy of Pindar, and a warning: 'The man who ventures on such a flight is foredoomed to suffer a great fall. My gift is of a very different and much humbler sort. Yet we shall sing our song of Caesar, — you, with your more sonorous lyre, and I, too, if I shall compose anything worth the while, — when we join with the people in rejoicing and thanksgiving over his triumphant return.'

Jullus Antonius was a son of the triumvir Antonius and Fulvia, born B.C. 44. He was brought up by his stepmother, Octavia, and married her daughter Marcella; and he was treated with equal generosity by Augustus, who raised him to the highest offices of state, — the consulship in B.C. 10. He requited these benefits with the basest betrayal of confidence, and was put to death in B.C. 2 for adultery with the emperor's daughter Julia. He was evidently a man of literary tastes, and is said to have written an epic, *Diomedea*, in twelve books, and some works in prose. — Metre, 174.

1. **Pindarum**: a poem such as Horace was invited to write would have been in the manner of Pindar, the great lyric poet of Thebes (B.C. 522–448) and the classical model for odes of personal victory and triumph. — **aemulari**, *to emulate*, *i.e.* to compose successfully in his style, but with no idea of rivalry.

2. **Iulle**: an old *cognomen* of the Julian *gens*, used as a *praenomen*; cf. *Paullus (Fabius) Maximus*, I. 10. Like *Paullus* it was sometimes written with a single *l*. It was the name of the mythical ancestor of the family, from which

nititur pennis, vitreo daturus
    nomina ponto.

5   Monte decurrens velut amnis, imbres
    quem super notas aluere ripas,
    fervet immensusque ruit profundo
        Pindarus ore,

    laurea donandus Apollinari,
10 seu per audacis nova dithyrambos
    verba devolvit numerisque fertur
        lege solutis,

their gentile name *Iulius* is formed, as *vilicus* from *villa*, *milia* from *mille*, etc. (Lachm. on Lucr. I. 313). Vergil, it appears, set the fashion of writing it as a trisyllable, with one *l*. — ceratis, *wax-jointed.* — ope Daedalea, *by the hand of a Daedalus* (the adjective here having its proper general force, unlike *Herculeus* I. 3. 36) ; *i.e.* such as Daedalus made for his son Icarus, with the result that the boy fell into the sea which thenceforth bore his name.

3. nititur, *soars;* cf. Verg. *A.* IV. 252 *paribus nitens Cyllenius alis.* — vitreo, *crystal;* cf. Verg. *A.* VII. 760 *vitrea te Fucinus unda,* | *te liquidi flevere lacus,* and see III. 13. 1 n, I. 17. 20 n.— daturus : Intr. 104 *b.*

4. nomina : cf. III. 27. 76 n.

5. monte : Intr. 70. — velut, quem : Intr. 114.— amnis : the comparison is a common one ; cf. *S.* I. 10. 62 *rapido ferventius amni ingenium ;* Cic. *Acad.* II. 119 *veniet flumen orationis aureum fundens Aristoteles.*

6. notas : cf. I. 2. 10.

7. fervet immensusque ruit, *rushes along with measureless, seething flood.* For the confusion

of the poet with the river in the comparison, see Intr. 123. — profundo ore, *deep-mouthed, i.e.* gifted with deep and rich utterance, the 'beatissima rerum verborumque copia' which Quintilian (X. I. 61) ascribes to him. For the expression cf. Ov. *Pont.* IV. 16. 5 *magni Rabirius oris ; S.* I. 4. 43 *os magna sonaturum* (a requisite endowment of a genuine poet). os has nothing to do with the mouth of the river, where the phenomenon described in vs. 7 is seldom witnessed.

9. laurea Apollinari : cf. III. 30. 15.— donandus : the adjective use of the gerundive, expressing fitness or desert, is exceptionally frequent in this book ; cf. *audiendum* 45, *laudande* 47, *loquenda* 4. 68,. *socianda* 9. 4, *dicenda* 9. 21, etc.

10. seu, etc. : a series of hypothetical clauses with donandus as their common apodosis (cf. *moriture, seu,* etc., II. 3. 4 n), conveying the general meaning that Pindar was successful in whatever kind of poetry he undertook. — nova : *i.e.* newly coined, referring particularly to new compounds.— dithyrambos: originally a species

seu deos regesve canit, deorum

sanguinem, per quos cecidere iusta

15   morte Centauri, cecidit tremendae

flamma Chimaerae,

sive quos Elea domum reducit

palma caelestis pugilemve equumve

dicit et centum potiore signis

20   munere donat,

flebili sponsae iuvenemve raptum

plorat et viris animumque moresque

of choral song which grew up in connection with the worship of Dionysus and partook of the wild and tumultuous character of its origin. In its artistic form, which it owed to Arion (600 B.C.), it still retained, as the impassioned expression of strong enthusiasm, its earlier characteristics of unusual freedom of language (**audacis**) and disregard of strict metrical symmetry (**numeris lege solutis**).

11. verba devolvit . . . fertur : the figure of the river is still kept up.

13. deos canit : in his Hymns and Paeans. — **reges :** *i.e.* heroes (**deorum sanguinem**), as in *S.* I. 10. 42. The examples given are Theseus and Perithous (cf. I. 18.8), and Bellerophon. The reference is to Pindar's Encomia.

15. cecidit : Intr. 116 *g.*

16. flamma Chimaerae : for 'the fiery Chimaera'; Intr. 126 *b.*

17. sive quos, etc.: *i.e.* in his Odes of Victory (Ἐπινίκια), still extant, in honor of those who won prizes at the great national games (Olympian, Pythian, Nemean, Isthmian). The Olympian festival (**Elea**) is put forward to represent **all** four, as boxing and racing

(vs. 18) stand for the various contests provided on each occasion (Intr. 117).

18. palma : see I. 1. 5 n. — **caelestis** (predicative acc. with **quos**): cf. *evehit ad deos*, I. 1. 6 n. — **pugilemve equumve :** in partitive apposition with **quos.** Cf. 3. 4, and (with this whole passage) *Ep.* II. 3. 83 *musa dedit fidibus divos puerosque deorum | et pugilem victorem et equum certamine primum . . . referre.* The steed is mentioned instead of his master, — here (with **quos**) at some sacrifice of logical connection, — as the real winner of the race.

19. dicit : see I. 6. 5 n. — **signis,** *statues.*

20. munere, *a boon ;* cf. Ode 8, in which this thought is developed at length.

21. flebili sponsae, etc.: in his Eulogies (Θρῆνοι). This completes Horace's partial review of Pindar's work in lyric poetry. — **flebili :** here in an active sense ; cf. I. 24. 9 and see II. 14. 6 n. — **-ve :** Intr. 114.—**raptum :** more forcible than *ereptum;* Intr. 129.

22. For the elision of **-que** at the end of this and the next verse, see Intr. 174 *b.*

aureos educit in astra nigroque
        invidet Orco.

25   Multa Dircaeum levat aura cycnum,
     tendit, Antoni, quotiens in altos
     nubium tractus : ego apis Matinae
          more modoque

     grata carpentis thyma per laborem
30   plurimum circa nemus uvidique
     Tiburis ripas operosa parvus
          carmina fingo.

23. **aureos**: proleptic, like *aeternum*, III. 25. 5. For the meaning, see I. 5. 9 n. — **educit**, etc.: *i.e.* exalts them in men's estimation and makes them immortal. — **in astra** : cf. *stellis inserere*, III. 25. 6 n. — **nigro** : cf. I. 24. 18 n.

24. **invidet** (*i.e.* rescues from) **Orco** : cf. 8. 28 *sq.*

25. Reverting to the subject of the opening verses and the figure of the first strophe, Horace concludes this introductory portion of the ode with a contrast between the strong poetic impulse which sustained Pindar in his lofty flight and his own humbler gift of artistic workmanship. — **multa aura**, *a full, strong breeze.* — **Dircaeum** : *i.e.* Theban, from the famous spring and brook Dirce, near the city. — **cycnum** : a stock metaphor, especially in Alexandrine literature ; see II. 20, intr. note. For the prosody, cf. 3. 20 n.

27. **apis**, etc.: a frequent simile; cf. *Ep.* I. 3. 21, 19. 44 ; Plat. *Io* 534 A λέγουσι γὰρ πρὸς ἡμᾶς οἱ ποιηταί, ὅτι ... τὰ μέλη ἡμῖν φέρουσιν ὥσπερ αἱ μέλιτται ; Arist. *Birds* 749. — **Matinae**: *i.e.* of my native Apulia ; cf. I. 28. 3 n.

28. **more modoque** : one of

those (often alliterative) phrases, common in all languages, in which two words, presenting slightly different aspects of the same thing, readily coalesce to form a fuller expression of a single idea ; cf. ' might and main,' ' hearth and home,' ' safe and sound,' etc.; Intr. 131.

29. **per laborem**: more expressive than *labore*, per (= ' in the course of ') suggesting prolonged toil ; cf. the phrases *per otium*, *per ludum et iocum*, *per iram* (*aliquid facere*).

30. **plurimum** : with **laborem**. — **circa nemus**, etc. : Horace's own favorite haunts ; but the details still apply to the bee ; the comparison and its subject are purposely blended (Intr. 123).

31. **Tiburis**: limiting both **nemus** and **ripas** ; Intr. 119 *a*. — **ripas** : *sc.* of the Anio and the brooks implied in **uvidi** ; cf. I. 7. 14, III. 29. 6, IV. 3. 10. For this absolute use of *ripa*, cf. III. 25. 13. — **operosa parvus**: still keeping before our minds the ' little toiler ' to whom he is comparing himself.

33. **concines** : standing first, with the emphasis of assurance (cf. I. 6. 1 n), to correct the im-

Concines maiore poeta plectro
Caesarem, quandoque trahet ferocis
35   per sacrum clivum merita decorus
      fronde Sygambros ;

quo nihil maius meliusve terris
fata donavere bonique divi
nec dabunt, quamvis redeant in aurum
40   tempora priscum.

pression given by the preceding strophes, that the praises of Augustus would not be sung. There is no antithesis between Horace and Antonius as to which should be the singer, — that would require *tu* to be expressed. There is a contrast between their methods of work, but it is subordinate to the main thought, which is contained in the two emphatic words, **concines** and **Caesarem** (Intr. 116 *b*); see intr. note. — **maiore plectro** (descriptive abl.; cf. II. 1. 40 n) : as we might speak of a painter 'wielding a larger brush,' in contrast to a miniature painter. It means, therefore, not a greater poet, but one who works with a freer and bolder stroke, neglecting nicety of finish, — a description that might well apply to Antonius, whose training was in epic. For the *plectrum*, see I. 26. 11 n.

34. quandoque : see 1. 17 n. — **trahet** : in contrast with **ferocis** (Intr. 116 *a*); an appropriate verb, as implying their unwillingness to go (cf. *Ep.* II. 1. 191); but in fact the prisoners preceded the victor's car ; see I. 12. 54 n.

35. per, *down ;* cf. *Epod.* 7. 8 n. — **sacrum clivum** : that part of the Sacra Via from the elevation on which the arch of Titus stands down to the Forum. The name occurs only here and Mart. I. 70. 5.

36. fronde : the laurel wreath worn by the *triumphator*. — **Sygambros** : a German tribe, dwelling on the south of the Lippe. Their warlike spirit (cf. **ferocis**, 34 ; *caede gaudentes*, 14. 51) gave them the lead among their countrymen at this time, and their feat of routing a Roman army invested them in Roman eyes with exaggerated importance. They were subsequently removed to the left bank of the Rhine, and furnished auxiliaries to the Roman armies.

37. nihil : cf. *nil*, I. 12. 17 n ; *Ep.* II. 1. 17 *nil oriturum alias, nil ortum tale fatentes* (*sc.* as Augustus).—**maius meliusve** : Intr. 131. Cf. Cic. *Acad.* I. 7 *nec ullum . . . maius aut melius a dis datum munus homini.*

38. boni, *kind ;* cf. 5. 1.

39. nec dabunt : in such phrases the same verb is usually repeated, as II. 13. 20 *rapuit rapietque*, *Ep.* I. 2. 43 *labitur et labetur*, *C. S.* 2 *colendi semper et culti*, *Ep.* II. 1. 17 (above), etc.; but the variation here is softened by the separation of the words. — **quamvis**, etc.: *i.e.* though the golden age (*tempus aureum*, *Epod.* 16. 64, 65 n) should return.—**redeant**: *i.e.* change back into ; cf. Ov. *M.* XIV. 766 (*deus*) *in iuvenem rediit*.

40. tempora, *the world ;* literally 'the generations,' as in *Ep.*

Concines laetosque dies et urbis
publicum ludum super impetrato
fortis Augusti reditu forumque
    litibus orbum.

45 Tum meae, si quid loquar audiendum,
vocis accedet bona pars, et 'O sol
pulcher, o laudande !' canam, recepto
    Caesare felix.

Teque dum procedis, 'Io Triumphe !'
50 non semel dicemus 'Io Triumphe !'
civitas omnis, dabimusque divis
    tura benignis.

II. 1. 130.— priscum : cf. *Epod.* 2. 2 n.

41. concines : Intr. 116 *h.* — laetos dies : a variation on *festos dies.*

42. ludum : for the more usual *ludos.* — super : with the abl. (see I. 9. 5 n), expressing the subject of rejoicing, as in III. 8. 17 *super urbe curas,* the subject of anxiety. — impetrato, *vouchsafed to our prayers ;* cf. vs. 54 n.

43. fortis : cf. *S.* II. 1. 16.— forum litibus orbum : the third paraphrase in this strophe for a technical term (*iustitium*). For litibus, see Intr. 66 *c,* N. It is clear that when this ode was written, the return of Augustus in the near future, though no definite time had been set (cf. *quandoque,* vs. 34), was confidently anticipated, so that the manner of his reception was talked over by those in authority. His return was delayed long beyond their or his own expectation, as appears from 5. 3 *sq.,* and his entry into the city was then made, by his own choice, unannounced and by night ; the

triumph which Horace and his friends anticipated never came off. The *publicus ludus,* however, took place.

45. loquar : less common than *dico* for poetical utterance, but cf. 15. 1.—audiendum : cf. *donandus,* vs. 9 n, and *laudande,* vs. 47.

46. bona pars, *a liberal measure.* — sol : *i.e.* day, the sun of each new day being, for poetical purposes, another sun ; cf. *C. S.* 10, *Epod.* 2. 41 n.

47. recepto Caesare : see Intr. 105.

49. teque . . . dicemus, *and on thy name . . . shall we call.* The cry of the soldiers and people, as the triumphant pageant advanced, io triumphe, was regarded as a shout of greeting to the personified Triumphus, triumphe being vocative ; cf. *Epod.* 9. 21 *Io Triumphe, tu moraris aureos* | *currus et intactas boves ?* | *Io Triumphe, nec Iugurthino parem* | *bello reportasti ducem,* etc.

50. non semel : *i.e.* again and again (litotes).

51. civitas : in apposition with

> Te decem tauri totidemque vaccae,
> me tener solvet vitulus, relicta
> 55 matre qui largis iuvenescit herbis
> in mea vota,
>
> fronte curvatos imitatus ignis
> tertium lunae referentis ortum,
> qua notam duxit niveus videri,
> 60 cetera fulvus.

the subject of **dicemus**; cf. *aetas*, I. 35. 35.

52. **tura**: cf. 1. 22 n. Incense was burned on temporary altars on the streets as the procession passed.

53. **te**: emphatic, in anticipation of the comparison to be drawn between the two sacrifices. Each must make an offering according to his substance. Cf. II. 17. 30 *sqq*.

54. **solvet**: *sc*. from the obligation of our vows, which the granting of our prayers has made binding. — **relicta matre**: *i.e.* weaned. The detailed description which follows is in Horace's favorite manner; see I. 2. 7 n. It serves here to heighten the contrast between the rich Antonius, who can send victims by the score to the altar, and the owner of a modest farm, who knows well every creature in his small herd, and to whom the sacrifice is therefore more of a personal matter; and it furnishes the ode, at the same time, with a pleasing close, drawing the reader's mind away from the stirring picture just described, to rest, in parting, on a quiet rural scene. Cf. the close of III. 5.

55. **iuvenescit**: bear in mind that *iuventus* is not precisely 'youth,' in our sense, but the prime of life.

56. **in**: *i.e.* with them in view, for their fulfilment.

57. **curvatos**: *i.e.* crescent. — **ignis**: cf. I. 12. 47.

58. **tertium referentis ortum**: *i.e.* on the third evening after the new moon. Cf. III. 29. 20, and see note on *reducit*, II. 10. 15.

59. **qua** (*i.e. in fronte*): qualifying **niveus**, which, to correspond with **fulvus**, is put as a characteristic of the animal, and not merely of the spot. — **duxit**, *has got, has taken on;* cf. Ov. *M*. III. 484 *ut variis solet uva racemis | ducere purpureum nondum matura colorem.* — **niveus videri**: Intr. 102.

60. **cetera**: Intr. 44.

III.

Quem tu, Melpomene, semel
   nascentem placido lumine videris,
illum non labor Isthmius
   clarabit pugilem, non equus impiger
5 curru ducet Achaico
   victorem, neque res bellica Deliis

III. The steady growth of Horace's reputation, culminating in
the official recognition of his eminence in his appointment to write
the Secular Hymn in B.C. 17, had
the usual effect of success in
silencing to a considerable degree
the small critics, of whose attacks
he complains occasionally in his
earlier writings. He could now
speak without either vanity or
false modesty of the attainment of
what in presenting to the public
his first collection of odes he had
held up as the summit of his aspiration. He speaks of it in the
present poem in a spirit rather of
gratitude than of boasting. His
muse is here, at least, no mere
creature of fancy or literary con-
vention; she is to him 'a power,
not himself,' but above him and
working in him; and to her he
renders all the praise for what he
has done. There is a reminiscence
of I. 1 in the contrast between the
meditative life of the poet, seeking
his inspiration in the seclusion of
grove and stream, and the exciting pursuit of the great prizes of
physical prowess, athletic victory
for the Greek, triumph in war for
the Roman. — Metre, 171.

1. Melpomene: cf. III. 30. 16,
I. 12. 2 n. — semel: cf. I. 24. 16 n,
C. S. 26.

2. nascentem, etc.: an idea

borrowed originally perhaps from
the Chaldean astrologers (see note
on *adspicit*, II. 17. 17), but Horace
found it in his Greek poets; cf.
Hes. *Theog.* 81 ὅντινα τιμήσωσι Διὸς
κοῦραι μεγάλοιο (*i.e.* the Muses) |
γεινόμενον τ᾽ ἐσίδωσι διοτρε-
φέων βασιλήων, | τῷ μὲν ἐπὶ γλώσσῃ
γλυκερὴν χείουσιν ἐέρσην, | τοῦ δ᾽
ἔπε᾽ ἐκ στόματος ῥεῖ μείλιχα.

3. labor: for the Greek πόνος,
κάματος, often applied by Pindar
to these struggles. — Isthmius:
cf. *Olympico*, I. 1. 3 n; *Elea*, IV.
2. 17 n; Intr. 117.

4. pugilem, equus: see 2. 18 n.

5. ducet, *draw; sc.* in the race.
—Achaico: *i.e.* Greek (in contrast with the Roman type of triumph next presented).

6. victorem, *to victory;* proleptic, like pugilem. — res bellica: a paraphrase for *bellum* (like
res ludicra, Ep. II. 1. 180, for the
drama), but more comprehensive,
— the business of war with all its
vicissitudes, *the fortunes of war.*—
Deliis: *i.e.* of laurel, so called as
sacred to Apollo; cf. *Delphica
lauro*, III. 30. 15; *laurea Apollinari*, IV. 2. 9. For the practice,
cf. Ov. *Tr.* IV. 2. 51 *tempora
Phoebea lauro cingetur*, '*Io'que* |
*miles 'Io' magna voce 'Triumphe'
canet.*

8. quod regum, etc.: in accordance with the Roman traditional

> ornatum foliis ducem,
> > quod regum tumidas contuderit minas,
> ostendet Capitolio ;
> 10   sed quae Tibur aquae fertile praefluunt
> et spissae nemorum comae
> > fingent Aeolio carmine nobilem.
>
> Romae, principis urbium,
> > dignatur suboles inter amabilis
> 15 vatum ponere me choros,
> > et iam dente minus mordeor invido.
>
> O testudinis aureae
> > dulcem quae strepitum, Pieri, temperas,
> o mutis quoque piscibus
> 20   donatura cycni, si libeat, sonum,

idea that their mission was to extend the blessings of peace and good government ; cf. *C. S.* 51 n. — **contuderit**, *crushed to earth ;* carrying out the figure in **tumidas.** — **minas** : cf. II. 12. 11 *ductaque per vias | regum colla minacium.*

9. **Capitolio** : Intr. 69. The triumphal pageant culminated in a sacrifice to Jupiter by the *triumphator* on the Capitol.

10. **sed quae Tibur,** etc.: cf. I. 1. 29 n. The environs of Tibur are put as a type of beautiful natural scenery in general (Intr. 117), but serve at the same time to prepare us for the transition to Horace's own case (cf. 2. 30 *sq.*). — **aquae** : cf. I. 7. 13 *sq.* — **praefluunt** : for the more common *praeterfluunt*, as in 14. 26.

11. **comae** : cf. I. 21. 5 n.

12. **Aeolio carmine** : see III. 30. 13 n.

13. The enunciation of the foregoing general truth has paved the way for Horace's own experience, which illustrates it. — **Romae** : the city is personified. — **principis,** *queen ;* cf. *Ep.* I. 7. 44 *regia Roma.*

14. **dignatur ponere me,** *deems me worthy a place.* — **suboles,** *the children, i.e.* the Roman nation. — **inter vatum choros** : cf. I. 1. 35 n.

16. **iam minus,** *less and less.* — **dente invido** : Intr. 124 ; cf. Cic. *Balb.* 57 *more hominum invident, . . . non illo inimico, sed hoc malo dente carpunt; Epod.* 6. 15 n.

17. **testudinis** : cf. I. 10. 6 n. — **aureae** : cf. I. 5. 9 n; *aureo plectro,* II. 13. 26 n ; Pind. *Pyth.* I. 1 χρυσέα φόρμιγξ, 'Απόλλωνος καὶ ἰοπλοκάμων σύνδικον Μοισᾶν κτέανον.

18. **Pieri** : see note on *Haemo,* I. 12. 6. — **temperas,** *dost modulate.*

19. **quoque,** *even,* as in *Ep.* II. 2. 36 ; an uncommon use of the word.

20. **donatura** : Intr. 104 *e.* — **cycni** : with the penult short ; in 2. 25 it is long.

totum muneris hoc tui est,
    quod monstror digito praetereuntium
  Romanae fidicen lyrae ;
    quod spiro et placeo, si placeo, tuum est.

IV.

Qualem ministrum fulminis alitem,

21. **muneris :** cf. 2. 20 n; 10. 1.
— **tui est :** to be read *tuist ;* see
I. 3. 37 n.

22. **monstror,** etc.: a sort of
public recognition often alluded
to by Greek and Roman writers,
in itself of ambiguous significance
(cf. Ov. *Am.* III. 6. 77) and need-
ing the specification of vs. 23 ; cf.
Lucian, *Herod.* 2 εἴ πού γε φανείη
μόνον, ἐδείκνυτο ἂν τῷ δακτύλῳ,
Οὗτος ἐκεῖνος Ἡρόδοτός ἐστιν . . . ὁ
τὰς νίκας ἡμῶν ὑμνήσας.

23. **Romanae fidicen lyrae,**
as minstrel, etc.; cf. *Ep.* I. 19. 32
hunc (sc. *Alcaeum*) *ego Latinus
volgavi fidicen.* The title contains the same meaning as *Aeolium
carmen ad Italos deduxisse modos,*
III. 30. 13 ; the claim there made
is now publicly recognized.

24. **quod spiro,** etc.: *i.e.* my
inspiration (*spiritus,* II. 16. 38, IV.
6. 29) and such success as I win.
The clause is the subject of **est.**
— **tuum est** (see vs. 21 n): *i.e.* is
thy achievement, not mine ; the
praise belongs to thee.

IV. In the spring of B.C. 15,
while Augustus was in Gaul (see
intr. note to Ode 2), Drusus, the
younger of his step-sons, then
twenty-three years old, led an
army up the Adige and defeated
the united forces of the Raetians
and Vindelicians near Tridentum
(Trent). The professed object of
the expedition was to put a stop
to the predatory raids of the
mountain tribes into the Po valley.
To complete the work, Drusus
crossed the Brenner pass and attacked the Breuni and Genauni in
the valley of the Inn, while his
brother Tiberius invaded the
country from the west, coming
from Gaul by way of the Rhine
and Lake Constance. By this
combined movement, the Romans
crushed out all resistance. They
scoured the valleys of eastern
Switzerland and the Tyrol, driving the mountaineers from their
strongholds, and doing the work
of subjugation so thoroughly, that
this whole mountain region (the
Raetian Alps), with the country of
the Vindelicians, extending northward to the Danube, was added
to the empire (as the province of
Raetia) by this single campaign.

The celebration of this brilliant
exploit, the glory of which the
emperor shared with the young
conquerors, was a kind of task
for which Horace had often de-
clared his unfitness (*e.g.* in *S.* II.
1. 12 *sqq.*, and, only recently, in Ode
2); and he undertook it, Suetonius
says, in deference to the express
wish of Augustus. The present
ode is concerned only with the
first victory of Drusus, in the Tri-
dentine Alps ; and we must suppose that Horace wrote it soon

cui rex deorum regnum in avis vagas
permisit expertus fidelem
Iuppiter in Ganymede flavo,

5   olim iuventas et patrius vigor
nido laborum propulit inscium,
vernique iam nimbis remotis
insolitos docuere nisus

after that event, before the news of the equally brilliant and much more important successes of the two brothers later in the season had reached Rome. These form the subject of Ode 14, written subsequently. Following the example of Pindar, Horace devotes the smaller part of his ode to the exploit it celebrates, and takes his main theme from the heroic age of Rome. Nothing could have been invented more suitable to his purpose than the dramatic episode of the fight on the Metaurus (B.C. 207), in which the most conspicuous part was played by a Nero, and the other chief actor was a Livius. The transition from the praises of Drusus to the glorification of his ancestors is skilfully effected by an analysis of his excellence, in which the honors are evenly divided between heredity and good home training, for the latter of which he was indebted to Augustus. — Metre, 176.

1–16. The subject of the ode is introduced by an elaborate simile in two parts, the first designed to picture to us the impetuous valor of the young hero, the other the terror his appearance inspired in the enemy.

1. ministrum fulminis : appositional attribute (κεραυνοφόρος) of alitem (Intr. 126 c). So in Ovid *M.* XII. 560 the eagle is *volucris quae*

fulmina curvis ferre solet pedibus, and in Verg. *A.* V. 255, *Iovis armiger*.

2. rex . . . regnum . . . : notice the antithesis : the king of heaven has made his servant a king. — regnum permisit : cf. *S.* I. 3. 123. — in : cf. III. 1. 5 n.

3. expertus (sc. *eum*) fidelem, *having proved his loyalty ;* cf. *comitem abnegat,* I. 35. 22 n.

4. in, *in the case of.* — Ganymede : see III. 20. 16 n. — flavo, *fair-haired* (ξανθός) ; see note on *Pyrrha* I. 5. 3.

5. olim, *one day.* Originally an adverbial form of *olle* (*ille*), meaning 'at that time' (*i.e.* not at this time), *olim* came to be applied in a vague way to any action not present, whether past ('once,' 'once upon a time'), — its commoner use, — or future, as *S.* II. 5. 27 *si res certabitur olim* ('sometime,' 'ever') ; and hence, by an easy step, to an action cited as the type of a class and which may therefore occur at any time, either with the present tense, as *S.* I. 1. 25 *pueris olim dant crustula blandi doctores* ('sometimes'), or with the 'gnomic' perfect, as here. Cf. the use of *ille* itself with such a perfect, Verg. *A.* XI. 809.

6. nido : Intr. 70. — laborum, *toil and struggle ;* cf. 3. 3 n ; for the case, Intr. 66 *b.* — propulit, etc. : Intr. 80.

7. verni : *i.e.* soft, gentle. Hor-

venti paventem, mox in ovilia
10   demisit hostem vividus impetus,
        nunc in reluctantis dracones
            egit amor dapis atque pugnae ;

    qualemve laetis caprea pascuis
        intenta fulvae matris ab ubere
15   iam lacte depulsum leonem
            dente novo peritura vidit :

ace's ornithology is at fault here, as the young eagles are not sufficiently grown to fly till late summer or autumn. — iam ... mox ... nunc : marking three stages in the growth of the eaglet's strength and courage, — his first timid ventures in flying, his attack upon an unresisting prey, and finally his entering with zest into a fight with a dangerous foe.—nimbis, *storm-clouds* (of winter).

11. dracones, *snakes*. The Greek name is perhaps a reminiscence of the description in *Il.* XII. 200 *sqq.* (cf. Verg. *A.* XI. 751 *sqq.*).

13. qualemve : while the case shows that Drusus is compared to the lion, the design of this comparison is to bring out the other side of the picture, and therefore the roe is made more prominent. The student should use his ingenuity to render accurately these shades of meaning in good English. — laetis, *glad, i.e.* luxuriant ; the word in this connection had almost ceased to be metaphorical ('*laetas segetes' etiam rustici dicunt* Cic. de *Or.* III. 155). — pascuis intenta : the point to be brought out is the helpless surprise of the victim.

14. fulvae : a common epithet of the lion, as Verg. *A.* II. 722, IV. 159, VIII. 552, etc. — matris ab ubere, etc.: a difficult passage,

and not improbably corrupt, as iam seems hardly in keeping with the point of the comparison, which would rather require *vix* or *nuper.* Some editors have taken refuge in an interpretation which refers fulvae matris ab ubere (depending on a verbal idea contained in pascuis intenta, which is held to imply the direction of the attention *away from* something else) to the roe and lacte depulsum to the lion. But, to say nothing of the feebleness of applying the same description to the two contrasted animals, it is not probable that Horace gratuitously weakened his comparison by representing the enemies of Drusus as inexperienced and *naturally* timid. Some have taken ubere as an adjective, and this would be appropriate enough, as implying that the lion, though young, was richly nurtured by a vigorous mother ; but as *ab ubere depulsus*, as well as (*a*) *lacte depulsus*, is a technical phrase (*e.g.* Verg. *G.* III. 187, *E.* 7. 15), this explanation appears to be excluded. If the text is correct, we shall have to take lacte depulsum as used to express a single idea (*weaned*), to which matris ab ubere is attached to give an additional detail to the picture.

16. peritura : Intr. 104 *b.* With vidit it has something of the same

videre Raetis bella sub Alpibus
Drusum gerentem Vindelici (quibus
mos unde deductus per omne
20   tempus Amazonia securi

force as Vergil's *sensit medios de-*
lapsus in hostem (*A.* II. 377), *i.e.*
the roe becomes aware of the lion's
presence and of its own doom
at the same moment ; cf. also
Ov. *M.* IX. 545 *superata fateri*
cogor.

17. **videre** : the epanastrophe
in the absence of *talem*, marks
the beginning of the apodosis.—
— **Raetis** : for *Raeticis* (Intr. 65).
The epithet is sufficient, in Horace's
suggestive manner, to indicate the
participation of the Raetians in
the conflict. The Vindelici were
evidently more prominent in people's minds at Rome, probably
because they were more aggressive, having advanced beyond their
own borders, and were a new
enemy, while the strongholds and
the raids of the Raetians were a
familiar story.— **bella** : Intr. 128.

18. **Drusum** : younger son of
Ti. Claudius Nero and Livia, but
born after his mother's marriage
to Augustus. Of singularly winning nature, he was a favorite
with Augustus and with the people,
who hoped he would be the emperor's successor. But he died in
his thirtieth year (B.C. 9), from the
effects of a fall from his horse,
while engaged in his third campaign in Germany. He was the
father of the equally popular Germanicus and of the emperor Clau-
dius.— **quibus**, *their ;* cf. *tibi*, III.
18. 10 n. The interrogative is
unde, and the gist of the question
is contained, as often, in the dependent word (**deductus**), — *whence*
the custom was derived which arms,

etc.; cf. *S.* I. 6. 12 *Valeri, unde Tar-*
quinius pulsus fugit. This ill-timed
digression could be removed from
the text without detriment to the
metre, and one would gladly blot
it out as unworthy of Horace's
taste, were it not even more difficult to believe it the work of a
forger. If Horace wrote it, we
may suppose his object was, in
introducing the battle-axe of the
Vindelici, to make use of the
anticipated astonishment of the
reader at finding this Amazonian
weapon in the hands of Alpine
barbarians, to give his narrative
something of the rush of the un-
stemmed torrent of Pindaric utterance which he describes in Ode 2,
— as if the course of thought
were: 'whose right hand wields the
Amazonian battle-axe, — Where,
you will exclaim, did they get that
custom, after a thousand years?
But I cannot stop for the question
now; I must hurry on; there are
some things it is not given us to
know in this world.' Unfortunately
the last expression has the appearance of sarcasm, as if Horace had
interrupted his fine tribute to the
prince and the emperor to ridicule
some antiquarian who had attempted to solve the question ;
and some have supposed he was
guilty even of this breach of good
manners.

19. **per omne tempus**: *i.e.* from
the remotest antiquity to the present day ; modifying **deductus**.

20. **securi** : for the shape of it
see Baumeister *Denkmäler* I. pp.
60, 63.

dextras obarmet, quaerere distuli,
nec scire fas est omnia), sed diu
  lateque victrices catervae
    consiliis iuvenis revictae

25   sensere quid mens rite, quid indoles
  nutrita faustis sub penetralibus
    posset, quid Augusti paternus
      in pueros animus Nerones.

Fortes creantur fortibus et bonis ;
30   est in iuvencis, est in equis patrum
    virtus, neque imbellem feroces
      progenerant aquilae columbam :

21. **obarmet** : found only here
in Latin literature of the classical
period. The prefix has the same
force as in *obsero, obduro*, etc. —
quaerere : Intr. 94 *j*.

22. **nec scire**, etc.: *i.e.* there
are some things Heaven does not
intend us to know ; cf. III. 29. 29
sqq. — **sed** : resuming the narrative
after the digression. — **diu lateque
victrices** : probably referring to
a raid which preceded the battle
with Drusus.

24. **consiliis**, *strategy.* — **revic-
tae**, *beaten in their turn*, re- expressing the reversal of the tide
of victory.

25. **sensere** : emphatic (Intr.
116 *b*) ; they learned by *experience*
(in their own persons) ; cf. II. 7.
10. — **quid posset** : Intr. 47. This
and the two following strophes
are the poet's tribute of praise to
Augustus for his contribution to
the result achieved, before pro-
ceeding to his main theme, in
which Augustus has no part. —
mens . . . indoles, *mind . . . character.* — **rite nutrita**: for the order
see Intr. 120. The words **rite**,

faustis, and **penetralibus**, with
their religious associations, lend a
suggestion of sacredness to the
home life to which they refer.

26. **sub penetralibus** : cf. *sub
lare*, III. 29. 14 n.

27. **paternus in pueros animus**: cf. II. 2. 6 n.

28. **Nerones** : Drusus and his
elder brother Tiberius (Claudius
Nero), afterwards emperor. As
their father died soon after the di-
vorce of their mother and her marriage to Octavian (B.C. 38), they were
brought up in the house of the
latter. For **pueros**, see I. 9. 16 n.

29. **fortes**, etc.: this strophe is
to a certain degree concessive :
heredity is all-essential, but training is no less so. Hence the emphasis on **est** (Intr. 116 *g*), —*there
is* (undoubtedly). — **fortibus et
bonis** (ablative) : a frequent formula of commendation ; cf. *Ep.
I. 9. 13 scribe tui gregis hunc et
fortem crede bonumque ; Cic. Fam.
V. 19. 1 quod omnes fortes ac boni
viri facere debent.*

31. **virtus**, *excellence.* — **imbel-
lem feroces** : Intr. 116 *a*.

doctrina sed vim promovet insitam,
rectique cultus pectora roborant ;
35   utcumque defecere mores,
indecorant bene nata culpae.

Quid debeas, o Roma, Neronibus,
testis Metaurum flumen et Hasdrubal
devictus et pulcher fugatis
40   ille dies Latio tenebris,
qui primus alma risit adorea,

33. doctrina sed : Intr. 114.
For the emphatic positions of the
important words in this strophe,
see Intr. 116 *b*. For the sentiment
cf. Cic. *Arch.* 15 *ego idem contendo,
cum ad naturam eximiam atque
inlustrem accesserit ratio quaedam
conformatioque doctrinae, tum illud
nescio quid praeclarum ac singu-
lare solere exsistere ; Tusc.* II. 13.

34. recti : adjective ; cf. *Ep.* II.
2. 122 *sano cultu.* — **cultus pectora :** plurals of repeated occurrence. For **pectora** (the moral
nature), cf. I. 3. 9 n.

35. utcumque, *the moment ;* see
I. 17. 10 n. — **defecere mores,**
discipline breaks down.

36. bene nata, *a noble nature.*
For this use of the neuter plural,
cf. I. 34. 12 n.

37. Here Horace reaches his
main theme, the glorious ancestry
of Drusus. In the twelfth year of
the second Punic war, when Hannibal was at Canusium, awaiting
the arrival of his brother Hasdrubal, who had crossed the Alps
with a large army, the consul
Claudius Nero, who faced Hannibal in Apulia, intercepted a
despatch which put him in possession of Hasdrubal's plans. By a
rapid and secret march, with 7000
picked men, he joined his colleague Livius at Sena Gallica, and
the two consuls with their united
forces met and destroyed Hasdrubal's army at the river Metaurus.
Nero then hastily returned to his
own camp. The whole episode,
which was the turning point of
the war and of Hannibal's career,
occupied scarcely a fortnight, and
the first news which Hannibal
received of Nero's absence and
his own disaster came in the
ghastly form of his brother's head,
which the brutal Roman tossed
over the lines. Horace had perhaps recently read the account of
this episode in Livy's twenty-
seventh book (ch. 43 *sqq.*), which
was published about this time. —
quid debeas : depending on **testis** (sc. *est*).

38. Metaurum flumen : Intr.
65. — **Hasdrubal devictus :** Intr.
105 *a*.

39. pulcher dies : cf. *sol pulcher*, 2. 46.—**fugatis tenebris :** abl.
(Intr. 105 *a*), the cause of **pulcher.**

41. adorea, *victory* (more strictly, ' military glory ') ; an old word
(cf. Plaut. *Amph.* 193) apparently
revived by Horace and frequently
used by later writers. Originally
an adjective from *ador* (spelt), how
it came to have this meaning is
uncertain.

dirus per urbis Afer ut Italas
ceu flamma per taedas vel Eurus
per Siculas equitavit undas.

45   Post hoc secundis usque laboribus
Romana pubes crevit, et impio
vastata Poenorum tumultu
fana deos habuere rectos,

dixitque tandem perfidus Hannibal :
50   ' Cervi, luporum praeda rapacium,
sectamur ultro quos opimus
fallere et effugere est triumphus.

42. **dirus Afer** : cf. III. 6. 36.
— **per** : *i.e.* from one to another.
— **ut**, *since* (temporal); cf. *Epod.*
7. 19; *S.* II. 2. 128; Cic. *Brut.* 19
ut illos de re publica libros edidisti,
nihil a te sane postea accepimus.
For the position, see Intr. 114.

43. **ceu** : found here only in
Horace. — **flamma** : sc. *it* (zeugma). **Eurus**, however, is thought
as ' riding' over the sea in Eurip.
Phoen. 209 περιρρύτων ὑπὲρ ἀκαρ-
πίστων πεδίων Σικελίας Ζεφύρου
πνοαῖς ἱππεύσαντος, a passage
which Horace may have had in
mind here.

45. **usque**, *more and more;* cf.
III. 30. 7 n. — **laboribus**: cf. 3. 3 n.

46. **pubes**: cf. III. 5. 18, *Epod.*
16. 7. — **crevit**, *waxed stronger.*

47. **tumultu**, *riot. Tumultus,*
in a military sense, denoted a war
within or upon the Roman borders
(Cic. *Phil.* 8. 2 *sq.*), such as the
Social and Servile wars. The Hannibalic war took this form, and
the word is accordingly applied to
it in disparagement.

48. **rectos**, *upright, erect.*

49. **dixitque tandem**, etc.: this
speech, if we make due allowance
for poetical embellishment, does

not misrepresent the effect of the
disaster on Hannibal; cf. Liv.
XXVII. 51. 12 *Hannibal, tanto si-*
mul publico familiarique ictus luctu,
agnoscere se fortunam Carthaginis
fertur dixisse.— **perfidus**: a stock
epithet, born of unreasoning prejudice and hatred ; cf. Livy's portrait
of Hannibal, XXI. 4. 9, *inhumana*
crudelitas, perfidia plus quam Pu-
nica, nihil veri, nihil sancti, nullus
deum metus, nullum ius iurandum,
nulla religio.

50. **cervi** : Intr. 123. — **praeda**:
i.e. naturally, usually; cf. *negata,*
III. 2. 22 n.

51. **ultro**, *actually. Vltro*, which
commonly characterizes an action
as gratuitous or voluntary (going
beyond what the situation calls for
or permits), is often applied to
conduct which reverses the natural
relation of two parties, as when an
assailant demands redress of his
victim, an evil-liver denounces
vice, or the like, or when, as here,
the weak attacks the strong. —
opimus triumphus : after the
analogy of *spolia opima.*

52. **fallere** : cf. I. 10. 16, III.
11. 40 n. — **effugere est trium-**
phus : oxymoron.

Gens quae cremato fortis ab Ilio
iactata Tuscis aequoribus sacra
55   natosque maturosque patres
pertulit Ausonias ad urbis,

duris ut ilex tonsa bipennibus
nigrae feraci frondis in Algido,
per damna, per caedis, ab ipso
60   ducit opes animumque ferro.

Non hydra secto corpore firmior
vinci dolentem crevit in Herculem,
monstrumve submisere Colchi
maius Echioniaeve Thebae.

53. **gens quae,** etc. : Horace
had read the Aeneid when he
wrote this strophe; cf. III. 3. 40 n.
— **cremato ab,** *from the ashes of,*
i.e. from utter ruin. With this
idea **fortis** is contrasted by its
position.

54. **iactata,** etc. (with **gens**) :
i.e. through the utmost hardships.
— **sacra** : *i.e.* the images of the
gods and their belongings, — the
effigies sacrae divom Phrygiaeque
penates (Verg. *A.* III. 148).

56. **pertulit:** the prefix expresses
perseverance to the end; cf. *perfi-*
ciunt, vs. 73, and *persequitur,* III.
2. 14 n.

57. **duris ut,** etc. : Intr. 114,
123.

58. **nigrae frondis** : that of the
ilex itself (Intr. 124) ; cf. Verg.
E. 6. 54 *ilice sub nigra.* For
the case, see Intr. 66 *a.*—**Algido**:
see I. 21. 6 n, III. 23. 9 *sq.* ; Intr.
117.

59. **per** : *i.e.* in the course of,
right through it all ; cf. 2. 29 n.

60. **ducit,** *draws.*

61. **non** : with **firmior** and
maius.—**hydra** : this simile Hor-

ace might have found in Livy, but
in the mouth of Pyrrhus instead
of Hannibal ; see Flor. *Epit.* I. 18.
19 *cum Pyrrhus 'video me' inquit*
' plane procreatum Herculis semine,
cui quasi ab angue Lernaeo tot caesa
hostium capita quasi de sanguine
suo renascuntur.' The comparison more probably originated with
Pyrrhus' minister, Cineas (Plut.
Pyrrh. 19).

62. **vinci dolentem:** Intr. 94 *m.*

63. **monstrum,** *wonder.* The
allusion is to the crops of armed
men that sprang from the dragon's
teeth sown by Jason (**Colchi**) and
Cadmus (**Thebae**), — vastly more
formidable than the dragon itself.
So the Roman legions seemed to
spring from the very soil. — **sub-**
misere : cf. Lucr. I. 7 *tellus sub-*
mittit flores. — **Colchi** : cf. *Afro*
III. 3. 47 n.

64. **Echioniae:** Echion was one
of the five survivors of the fight
which Cadmus precipitated among
the earth-born warriors. He married Agave, daughter of Cadmus,
and became the father of Pentheus.

.65   Merses profundo, pulchrior evenit ;
       luctere, multa proruet integrum
          cum laude victorem geretque
             proelia coniugibus loquenda.

       Carthagini iam non ego nuntios
70   mittam superbos ; occidit, occidit
          spes omnis et fortuna nostri
             nominis Hasdrubale interempto.'

       Nil Claudiae non perficient manus,
       quas et benigno numine Iuppiter
75   defendit et curae sagaces
             expediunt per acuta belli.

---

65. **merses**: sc. *eam*, the *gens* of vs. 53, but under the figure of a marvelous being (**monstrum**) as in the preceding strophe. There is perhaps an allusion in this verse to the first Punic war, which was largely a naval contest. For the mood of **merses** and **luctere**, see Intr. 87. They here do service as conditional clauses. — **profundo**: Intr. 69. — **evenit** : here used in the very rare literal sense ; cf. *pereuntis*, III. 11. 27.

66. **proruet . . . geret**: the future, expressing what *will prove* true (in every case), when the trial is made, is here coupled with a present (**evenit**) of general statement. — **integrum**, *unscathed* (*sc.* in the previous contest).

67. **laude**, *credit, éclat ;* cf. *S.* I. 10. 49; *Cat.* 64. 112 *inde pedem sospes multa cum laude reflexit.* — **victorem**: *i.e.* the antagonist who has just overthrown him. Cf. Hannibal's comment on the Romans under Marcellus, Liv. XXVII. 14. I, *seu vicit, ferociter instat victis ;*

seu victus est, instaurat cum victoribus certamen.

68. **coniugibus loquenda**: *i.e.* memorable, the theme of many a fireside talk. For the gerundive, see 2. 9 n.

69. **Carthagini** : Intr. 53. — **iam non**, *no more.*

70. **occidit** : Intr. 116 *d.*

72. **Hasdrubale interempto** : there is a climax of pathos in these closing words, in which the depressing sense of personal bereavement, which underlies the despair pictured in the preceding verses, comes to the surface.

73–76. The ode closes with a brief epilogue, summing up the merits of the Claudii, which have been illustrated in the ancient and the modern instance given.

75. **curae sagaces** : their own wisdom, in contrast with the divine protection just spoken of.

76. **expediunt** : cf. Verg. *A.* II. 632 *flammam inter et hostes expedior.* — **acuta**, *crises.* — **belli** : Intr. 64.

V.

Divis orte bonis, optume Romulae
custos gentis, abes iam nimium diu ;
maturum reditum pollicitus patrum
    sancto concilio, redi.

5 Lucem redde tuae, dux bone, patriae ;
instar veris enim voltus ubi tuus
adfulsit populo, gratior it dies
    et soles melius nitent.

Vt mater iuvenem, quem Notus invido

V. The occasion of this ode was the unexpectedly prolonged absence of the emperor in the western provinces in B.C. 16–13 (see intr. note to Ode 2). The avowed, and no doubt the main object of his western journey was the settlement of the affairs of that part of the empire ; but it was whispered in the capital that the real cause of his departure was the hostility of those whom he had offended by his measures of reform. Possibly it was the poet's sense of the injustice of these people that stirred him to the exceptional warmth which characterizes this ode. But however that may be, the malcontents were a small body; the great majority of the citizens recognized their indebtedness to Augustus as the restorer of peace and security and the champion of good morals, and their dependence on his single life for the continuance of these blessings. The feeling of gratitude and devotion to which Horace here gives expression was one that was widespread and growing.— Metre, 172.

1. divis bonis : abl. abs. of attendant circumstances,—'when the gods were in kindly mood' (*sc.* towards mankind); equivalent to ' whose birth was blest of Heaven,' or the like. Cf. *S.* I. 5. 97 *Gnatia* (a town where water was scarce) *Lymphis* (= *Nymphis*) *iratis exstructa.* — **Romulae** : Intr. 65.

2. **custos** : cf. 15. 17 *custode rerum Caesare.*

4. **sancto,** *august;* cf. Enn. *Ann.* 298 M. *indu foro lato sanctoque senatu;* Verg. *A.* I. 426.

5. **lucem** : sc. *tuam* ('the light of thy countenance'), as the next verse shows. — **tuae,** *thy own ;* Intr. 116 *c.* — **dux bone** : see vs. 37 n.

6. **instar** : commonly used of size or quantity, rarely, as here, of quality.

7. **it dies :** cf. II. 14. 5 *quotquot eunt dies.*

8. **soles :** *i.e.* the sun of each successive day; cf. 2. 46 n.

9. **Notus, Carpathii :** Intr. 117; I. 3. 14, 7. 15 n. — **invido** : reflecting the mother's feeling; the obstructing winds seem to her to blow from pure spite.

10   flatu Carpathii trans maris aequora
       cunctantem spatio longius annuo
           dulci distinet a domo,

      votis ominibusque et precibus vocat,
      curvo nec faciem litore demovet,

15   sic desideriis icta fidelibus
           quaerit patria Caesarem.

      Tutus bos etenim rura perambulat,
      nutrit rura Ceres almaque Faustitas,
      pacatum volitant per mare navitae,

20   culpari metuit fides,

11. spatio longius annuo : his business has detained him beyond the close of navigation in November, so that he has to stay all winter; cf. III. 7. 1 *sqq.*

13. votis, etc.: cf. Liv. *Praef.* 13 *cum bonis potius ominibus votisque et precationibus deorum dearumque . . . libentius inciperemus.*—**vocat:** expressing literally the action of the mother as she stands gazing at the shore, but used with the preceding instrumental ablatives in the wider sense of seeking to bring him back, by making vows for his safety, by looking for favorable omens, and by prayers.

14. curvo : a standing epithet of the shore, as *Epod.* 10. 21, Verg. *A.* III. 223, Ov. *M.* XI. 352, etc.

15. desideriis : plural of repeated occurrence. — **icta,** *smitten.*

16. quaerit : for *requirit;* cf. III. 24. 32 and see Intr. 129.

17. tutus bos, etc.: the emphasis, enhanced by asyndeton, is on **tutus** (cf. I. 17. 5 *impune tutum per nemus,* etc.), **nutrit,** and **pacatum ;** Intr. 116 *b.* — **etenim :** introducing the reason why the country cannot bear to have Augustus long absent, — namely, the bless-

ings which his presence and care confer. — **perambulat :** *i.e.* in grazing.

18. rura : the repetition (after the emphatic **nutrit**) is without emphasis; it serves merely to continue the discourse (Intr. 116 *h*) and to keep the reader's mind on the country, the improvement of which was an important consideration in the emperor's policy. **rura** is here used for *arva,* as in *Epod.* 2. 3, and in a comprehensive sense, to include both the land and the crops (implied in **Ceres**) that grow on it. — **alma :** a standing epithet of a goddess; cf. 15. 31 *almae Veneris,* I. 2. 42 *almae Maiae,* Verg. *G.* I. 7 *alma Ceres,* etc. — **Faustitas :** a personification that does not occur elsewhere in literature, but was probably not invented by Horace. It is (with **alma**) the same as *Fausta Felicitas* (Fertility), a divinity to whom annual offerings were made on the Capitol.

19. pacatum : by the suppression of piracy, with special reference to Sextus Pompey; see *Epod.* 4. 19 n, and cf. *Mon. Anc.* 5. 1 *mare pacavi a praedonibus;* Suet. *Aug.* 98 *forte Puteolanum sinum*

nullis polluitur casta domus stupris,
mos et lex maculosum edomuit nefas,
laudantur simili prole puerperae,
culpam poena premit comes.

25   Quis Parthum paveat, quis gelidum Scythen,
quis Germania quos horrida parturit
fetus, incolumi Caesare?   Quis ferae
bellum curet Hiberiae?

Condit quisque diem collibus in suis

praetervehenti vectores nautaeque de navi Alexandrina . . . fausta omina et eximias laudes congesserant, 'per illum se vivere, per illum navigare, libertate atque fortunis per illum frui.'—**volitant,** *flit to and fro;* implying a light and rapid movement, unhindered by fear. The figure has reference quite as much to the oars as to the sails; cf. Cat. 4. 4 *sive palmulis opus foret volare sive linteo,* and, conversely, Verg. *A.* I. 301 *remigio alarum.*

20. **culpari metuit:** *i.e.* shrinks from even the suspicion of unfair dealing. For metuit, cf. II. 2. 7, and see Intr. 94 *l.*

21. **casta:** proleptic.

22. **mos et lex:** *i.e.* law, with a healthy moral sentiment in the community to support it; cf. III. 24. 35 n. The allusion is to the *lex Iulia de adulteriis,* passed by Augustus B.C. 18.—**edomuit:** the prefix denotes thoroughness; cf. I. 5. 8 n.

23. **simili prole:** instrumental ablative. For the meaning of **simili,** cf. Cat. 61. 217 *sit suo similis patri | Manlio et facile omnibus | noscitetur ab insciis | et pudicitiam suae | matris indicet ore.*

24. **premit comes:** as in *S.* II. 7. 115 (*Cura*) *comes atra premit*

sequiturque fugacem; cf. III. 2. 31 *sq.*

25. **Parthum:** see 15. 6 n.—**Scythen:** cf. 14. 42, III. 8. 23 n.

26. **Germania quos,** etc.: see intr. note to Ode 2.—**parturit:** cf. I. 7. 16 n.

27. **fetus,** *spawn.* The whole description represents them as something not quite human, the monstrous brood of an uncouth mother-land.

28. **bellum Hiberiae:** Horace has in mind particularly the stubborn struggle of the Cantabrians for their independence; cf. II. 6. 2 n.

29. **condit,** *brings to a close, i.e.* spends the whole (quietly, without interruption): cf. Verg. *G.* I. 458 *at si, cum referetque diem condetque relatum, | lucidus orbis erit; E.* 9. 51 *saepe ego longos | cantando puerum memini me condere soles.*—**collibus:** more graphic than *agris* (Intr. 117); the poet selects vine-dressing, as one of the lighter occupations of the farmer, for his picture of contented country life; cf. *Epod.* 2. 9 *sqq.* — **suis:** emphatic (Intr. 116 *b*). Secure possession of property was one of the blessings of the reign of Augustus (Vell. II. 89. 4), and a country population of small farmers who

30   et vitem viduas ducit ad arbores ;
      hinc ad vina redit laetus et alteris
            te mensis adhibet deum ;

      te multa prece, te prosequitur mero
      defuso pateris, et Laribus tuum
35   miscet numen, uti Graecia Castoris
            et magni memor Herculis.

owned the land they tilled was
always regarded by wise statesmen
as the most solid foundation of
Roman power.

30. **viduas,** *unwedded;* a common meaning of the word. For
the figure, see note on *caelebs,* II.
15. 4.—**ducit:** here apparently for
maritat (cf. *Epod.* 2. 10), though
the subject of *duco* in this sense is
regularly the bridegroom.

31. **redit:** sc. *domum.*—**alteris
mensis:** for *mensa secunda,* when
the guests sat over their wine.
The poet skips the more substantial (and prosaic) part of the evening meal.

32. **adhibet,** *invites;* cf. Verg.
A. V. 62 *adhibete Penates epulis.*
The allusion, which is expanded
in the following strophe, is to the
libations made to Augustus—they
were even enjoined by the Senate
(Dio LI. 19. 7)—at public and private banquets. To that extent,
as an invisible presence at the
feast, he was put on a par with
the gods (**deum**), particularly with
the Lares, for whom a portion of
the meal was always set aside. Cf.
Ov. *F.* II. 633 *et libate dapes ut,
grati pignus honoris,* | *nutriat in-
cinctos missa patella Lares;* | *iam-
que ubi suadebit placidos nox umida
somnos,* | *larga precaturi sumite
vina manu,* | *et 'Bene vos, bene te,
patriae pater, optime Caesar'* | *dicite
suffuso ter bona verba mero.*

33. **te prosequitur,** *thy name
he hails.* The verb retains its
proper sense of 'accompanies' (*sc.*
the thought of thee, the mention
of thy name).—**prece,** *with blessings;* cf. vs. 37. For the number,
see I. 2. 26 n.

34. **defuso,** *with the pouring
out of;* Intr. 105 *a.*—**Laribus :**
dative; Intr. 56.

35. **uti Graecia,** etc.: cf. *Ep.*
II. 1. 1–17, where Horace points
out that the Romans paid to Augustus in his lifetime the honors
which Greece rendered her benefactors only after their death.—
Castoris : sc. *numen,* whereas
Herculis is in closer relation with
memor; the result in the reader's
mind is a dependence of the two
proper names ἀπὸ κοινοῦ on both
numen and **memor**; Intr. 76,
120.

37. **o utinam :** cf. I. 35. 38;
Intr. 185. This prayer for long
life to Augustus is conceived in
the same spirit as that of I. 2.
45 *sqq.,* the essence of it being
that his country's happiness is
bound up with his life. Similar
is the fine tribute of *Ep.* I. 16. 25
sqq.—**dux bone :** repeated from
vs. 5. The word **dux** conveys a
much warmer expression of personal allegiance than the formal
princeps; cf. Walt Whitman's *My
Captain.*—**ferias :** *i.e.* peace, regarded as an interval of repose

'Longas o utinam, dux bone, ferias
praestes Hesperiae !' dicimus integro
sicci mane die, dicimus uvidi,
40   cum sol Oceano subest.

VI.

Dive, quem proles Niobea magnae

and enjoyment between the wars
which preceded and those which
must (it is implied) follow this
happy age.

38. **integro die,** *when the day
is whole, i.e.* when the whole day
is before us.

39. **sicci**: cf. I. 18. 3, *Ep.* I. 19.
9.—**dicimus**: Intr. 116 *h.*—**uvidi**:
cf. II. 19. 18, *S.* II. 6. 70 *seu quis
capit acria fortis | pocula, seu mo-
dicis uvescit laetius.*

VI. Horace's authorship of the
hymn sung at the secular festival
of B.C. 17 was deemed by the
authorities worthy of mention on
the pillars of marble and bronze
erected to commemorate the occasion (see intr. note to *C. S.*),
and the interesting line, CARMEN
COMPOSVIT·Q·HORATIVS·FLACCVS,
is among the fragments of the inscription recently discovered. But
Horace chose also to record his
distinction in his own way, in a
'*monumentum aere perennius.*' It
takes the form of a prelude to the
hymn. Invoking the aid of the
two divinities to whom the hymn
is mainly addressed, and chiefly the
minstrel Apollo, he calls upon the
lads and maidens of the chorus to
heed well his instructions, remind-
ing the maidens in particular of
the satisfaction they will have all
their lives long in recalling their

part in the memorable pageant,
and closes with the seemingly incidental mention of his own name.
— Metre, 174.

1. **dive**: Apollo. The invocation, interrupted by the long digression on Achilles, which re-
counts the invaluable service of
the god to Rome, is resumed in
vs. 25, and the actual prayer is
contained in vs. 27. The verses
extolling the prowess of Apollo
and those relating to Diana (33 *sq.*,
38–40) look like 'chips from the
workshop' in which the Secular
Hymn was constructed. — **quem
vindicem,** *whose vengeance;* Intr.
105 *a.*—**proles Niobea**: seven sons
and seven daughters, slain by the
arrows of Apollo and Diana to pun-
ish their mother Niobe for sneering
at Latona as the mother of only
two children (*Il.* XXIV. 602 *sqq.*,
Ov. *M.* VI. 155 *sqq.*). The story is
the subject of a famous sculptured
group now preserved in Florence
(see Baumeister, III. pp. 1673 ff.).
A similar (probably not the same)
group, regarded as the work of
either Scopas or Praxiteles (Plin.
N. H. XXXVI. 28), existed in Rome
in Horace's time, in a temple of
Apollo built by C. Sosius. — **magnae**: *i.e.* boastful; so in Greek
μεγάλη γλῶσσα (Soph. *Antig.* 127),
ἔπος μέγα (Theogn. 159), etc.; cf.
Ovid *M.* VI. 150 *nec tamen ad-*

vindicem linguae Tityosque raptor
   sensit et Troiae prope victor altae
      Phthius Achilles,

5   ceteris maior, tibi miles impar,
   filius quamvis Thetidis marinae
   Dardanas turris quateret tremenda
      cuspide pugnax,

   (ille, mordaci velut icta ferro
10 pinus aut impulsa cupressus Euro,
   procidit late posuitque collum in
      pulvere Teucro ;

monita est (Niobe) verbis minoribus uti.

2. **raptor**: indicating the crime (see III. 4. 77 n) that drew down Apollo's vengeance on him, and so taking the place of **magnae linguae** with **sensit.**

3. **sensit**: cf. 4. 25 n.— **prope victor**: according to the prophecy put into the mouth of the dying Hector (*Il.* XXII. 359) Achilles was slain by Paris, with the aid of Apollo, in the very gate of the city : ἤματι τῷ ὅτε κέν σε Πάρις καὶ Φοῖβος Ἀπόλλων | ἐσθλὸν ἐόντ' ὀλέσωσιν ἐνὶ Σκαιῇσι πύλῃσιν.— **altae,** *towering ;* the Homeric Ἴλιος αἰπεινή (*Il.* XIII. 773); cf. also I. 16. 18 n.

4. **Phthius**: from Phthia, in the southern part of Thessaly, the land of the Myrmidons (*Il.* II. 683).

5. For the positions of the two pairs of contrasted words, cf. II. 10. 13 ; Intr. 116 *c.*

6. **filius Thetidis**: in apposition with the subject, enforcing the concession, — 'although he *was* the son of Thetis and,' etc.

7. **Dardanas**: Intr. 65.—**turris**

quateret: a hyperbole like *Lernam tremefecerit arcu* (*Hercules*), Verg. *A.* VI. 803. For the mood, see Intr. 83.—**tremenda cuspide**: modifying both **quateret** and **pugnax** (Intr. 76); for the latter, cf. Liv. XXII. 37. 8 *pugnaces missili telo gentes;* Intr. 73. The spear of Achilles is described in *Il.* XVI. 141 as βριθὺ μέγα στιβαρόν· τὸ μὲν οὐ δύνατ' ἄλλος Ἀχαιῶν | πάλλειν, ἀλλά μιν οἶος ἐπίστατο πῆλαι Ἀχιλλεύς.

9–24. These strophes are parenthetical, and are introduced to enforce the indebtedness of the Romans to Apollo by a graphic picture of the ruthless fury with which Achilles would have exterminated the whole Trojan race, had the god not cut short his career and joined with Venus in entreating Jove to spare a remnant of the doomed people.— **ille . . . ille** : both emphatic (Intr. 116 *b*), but in different ways : the first is *even he* (mighty as he was); the second, *he* would not (as others did).

11. **procidit late** : see Intr. 123. Cf., however, *Odys.* XXIV.

ille non inclusus equo Minervae
  sacra mentito male feriatos
15 Troas et laetam Priami choreis
    falleret aulam,

sed palam captis gravis, heu nefas heu,
  nescios fari pueros Achivis
  ureret flammis, etiam latentem
20   matris in alvo,

ni tuis victus Venerisque gratae
  vocibus divum pater adnuisset
  rebus Aeneae potiore ductos
    alite muros ;)

39 σὺ δ' (Ἀχιλλεῦ) ἐν στροφάλιγγι
κονίης (pulvere) κεῖσο μέγας μεγα-
λωστί, and, for the whole comparison, Cat. 64. 105 *sqq.*

12. **Teucro**: Intr. 65. This
name of the Trojans is unknown
to Homer, but was familiar to the
Romans, when this ode was written, from the Aeneid.

13. **Minervae**: gen. with sacra,
as *Iunonis sacra, S.* I. 3. 11.

14. **sacra**: for the plural, cf.
Cat. 63. 9 *typanum, tubam Cy-
belles, tua, mater, initia;* Intr.
128. — **mentito**: see Intr. 51 *e*,
and cf. Mart. III. 43. 1 *mentiris
iuvenem tinctis, Laetine, capillis.*—
male feriatos, *keeping untimely
holiday.* For the whole story, see
Verg. *A.* II.

16. **falleret**, *steal upon,* come
upon them unawares; cf. I. 10.
16, III. 11. 40. The impf. subj. is
that of softened assertion in past
time, with a vaguely implied apodosis, 'if he had lived,' 'if he had
been present,' or the like. This
construction is naturally continued
in **ureret ni pater adnuisset**,
which is *urat ni pater adnuerit*

transferred to past time. Cf. *S.*
I. 3. 5 *si peteret, non quicquam
proficeret; si collibuisset, citaret;*
Gr. 311 *a*, 307 *f.*

17. **palam captis**: in contrast
with the secrecy implied in **mentito** and **falleret**. It contains a
distinct assertion : *he would have
captured them in open fight, and,*
etc.—**gravis,** *with merciless hand.*
— **heu . . . heu**: a sigh of horror
at the enormity to be described;
cf. I. 15. 9.—**nefas** : exclamatory,
as in III. 24. 30.

18. **nescios fari**: a paraphrase
for *infantes,* and a reminiscence
of the Homeric νήπια τέκνα; see
Intr. 101 *c.*

19. **latentem** : more graphic
than the plural, on the principle
of Intr. 117.

21. **ni** : not found elsewhere in
the Odes.

22. **divum pater** : cf. I. 2. 2,
12. 13 *sqq.*—**adnuisset**: Intr. 51 *f.*

23. **potiore alite** : cf. *mala avi,*
I. 15. 5 n.—**ductos,** *built;* a natural word for construction that
proceeds in a line; cf. *ducere fos-
sam, vallum,* etc.

25   doctor argutae fidicen Thaliae,
      Phoebe, qui Xantho lavis amne crinis,
      Dauniae defende decus Camenae,
          levis Agyieu.

      Spiritum Phoebus mihi, Phoebus artem
30   carminis nomenque dedit poetae.
      Virginum primae puerique claris
          patribus orti,

      Deliae tutela deae, fugacis
      lyncas et cervos cohibentis arcu,

25. **doctor**, etc.: after propiti-
ating the god by recounting his
beneficent deeds, the poet now
addresses him in the character
(*Apollo Musagetes*) in which he
wishes him to respond to the
present appeal. The meaning of
the strophe (even if we cannot
accept the reading *Argivae* for
argutae) is: Inspirer of the Greek
lyrists, support now the Daunian
poet. — **argutae**: see III. 14. 21,
and cf. *Odys.* XXIV. 62 μοῦσα
λίγεια. — **fidicen**: serving as an
attributive to **doctor**; Intr. 126 *c*.
— **Thaliae**: Intr. 117; see also
note on *Clio*, I. 12. 2.

26. **Xantho**: in Lycia. — **lavis
crinis**: cf. III. 4. 61 n.

27. **Dauniae**: for 'Italian,' as
in II. 1. 34 (Intr. 117 *b*); but the
word is chosen with special reference to Horace himself; see I.
22. 14 n, and cf. III. 30. 10 *sqq.* —
Camenae: see I. 12. 39 n.

28. **lēvis**: *i.e.* beardless, youthful; see I. 21. 2 n, II. 11. 6 n. —
Agyieu: an epithet of Apollo as
guardian of the streets (ἀγυιαί).

29. From his prayer to the god
the poet now turns to address the
chorus, and begins, as in II. 19. 9,
by declaring his commission.—**spi-**

ritum: see II. 16. 38 n. — **artem**:
i.e. technical knowledge and skill,
contrasted in the chiastic order with
spiritum. The main emphasis, however, is on **Phoebus**. Intr. 116 *c*,*g*.

30. **carminis**: limiting **artem**
only. — **poetae**: Gr. 214 *f.* The
word occurs here only in the Odes.
Horace's favorite word is *vates;*
cf. vs. 44, 3. 15, I. 1. 35, II. 6. 24, etc.

31. **virginum primae**, etc.: see
intr. note to *C. S.* (p. 331).

33. **Deliae deae**: Diana (Artemis) was regarded by the Greeks
as the special protectress of chaste
youth and maidenhood (Preller-
Robert, *Gr. Myth.* I. 320); cf.
Cat. 34. 1 *Dianae sumus in fide |
puellae et pueri integri.* This gives
the poet an opportunity to bring
in the goddess, who could have no
place in the preceding invocation,
and he dwells on some of her
attributes, in this and the next
strophe, so that she may not be left
with a bare mention alongside of
the elaborate praises of her brother.
— **tutela**: here in a passive sense,
— *wards;* cf. II. 17. 23, where it
is active. — **fugacis cohibentis**,
who stays . . . in their flight.

34. **lyncas et cervos**: perhaps
suggested by Diana's words in

35 Lesbium servate pedem meique
        pollicis ictum,

rite Latonae puerum canentes,
rite crescentem face Noctilucam,
prosperam frugum celeremque pronos
40   volvere mensis.

Nupta iam dices ' Ego dis amicum,
saeculo festas referente luces,
reddidi carmen docilis modorum
        vatis Horati.'

Callim. *Hymn. in Dian.* 16 ὁππότε
μηκέτι λύγκας | μήτ' ἐλάφους
βάλλοιμι.

35. Lesbium pedem : *i.e.* the
Sapphic metre; cf. *Lesboum barbiton,* I. 1. 34 n.

36. pollicis ictum : *sc.* on the
lyre. Horace represents himself
as training the chorus (χοροδιδά-
σκαλος); but this is to be taken, as
Porphyrio understood it ('suaviter
hoc dicitur, quasi ipse lyram per-
cutiat'), as a poetic fiction. In
view of Horace's disposition and
of the silence of the inscription,
we cannot suppose that he actually
directed the performance.

37. rite, etc. : *i.e.* singing the
Secular Hymn, the main theme of
which is briefly given in this strophe.
rite has reference to ceremonial
form. — **Latonae puerum :** cf. I.
21. 3 n.

38. crescentem, *expanding;*
the participle had not hardened
into an adjective denoting shape,
like our 'crescent'; cf. 2. 57. —
face : so Cicero calls the sun
Phoebi fax in the poem on his
consulship (*Div.* I. 18). — **Noctilucam :** an epithet of Luna, who
appears to have had, under this
name, a temple on the Palatine

which was illuminated at night
(Varro *L.L.* V. 68).

39. prosperam frugum : Intr.
66 *a.* — **celerem volvere :** Intr.
101 *b.* Cf. Cat. 34. 17 *tu cursu,
dea, menstruo | metiens iter an-
nuum | rustica agricolae bonis |
tecta frugibus exples.*

41. iam (with **nupta**): *i.e.* even
after marriage (many years hence).
This appeal is addressed to the
girls only, in whose lives such participation in a public function must
be a rare and memorable occurrence. — **dices :** the chorus of girls
is addressed in the singular, after
the practice of the Greek drama ;
but the words suggested would of
course be spoken by each girl for
herself.— **amicum :** cf. I. 26. 1 n.

42. saeculo : see intr. note to
C. S. (p. 328).—**referente :** cf. III.
29. 20, II. 10. 15 n.— **luces :** *i.e.
dies;* cf. 11. 19, 15. 25. The festival
lasted three days.

43. reddidi, *rendered;* cf. 11.34
*condisce modos, amanda voce quos
reddas.* Like the English word,
reddo conveys the idea of giving
out what has been put into one
(cf. I. 3. 7 n). So, also, *chorda
sonum reddit, Ep.* II. 3. 348. —
docilis modorum : Intr. 66 *b.*

VII.

Diffugere nives, redeunt iam gramina campis
    arboribusque comae ;
mutat terra vices et decrescentia ripas
    flumina praetereunt ;
5 Gratia cum Nymphis geminisque sororibus audet
    ducere nuda choros.
Immortalia ne speres, monet annus et almum
    quae rapit hora diem :

VII. The ingredients which go
to make up this ode are the same
as those of I. 4, — the coming of
spring, the uncertainty of life and
sureness of death, the wisdom of
enjoying while we may. The materials, however, are here managed
somewhat differently and with a
freer hand.   The rapid renewal of
the seasons is made to remind us
that the years are passing swiftly
away, with no renewal for us ; and
the studied symmetry of the earlier
ode, in which these two motives
are nicely balanced on the lesson
they inculcate, is abandoned for a
more natural sequence of thought.
Torquatus, for whom the ode was
written, was an advocate of some
distinction, and was on terms of
familiar acquaintance with the
poet, as appears from *Ep.* I. 5,
which is addressed to him. —
Metre, 163.

1. campis, arboribus: Intr. 53.
2. comae: cf. I. 21. 5 n, IV. 3.
11.

3. mutat terra vices: summing up what has been partially
expressed in the first couplet.
terra is the face of the earth, and
is further limited, by flumina following, to the dry land. mutat is
intransitive, as often in Livy, with

vices as cognate object; cf. Verg.
G. I. 418 *ubi tempestas et caeli mo-
bilis umor | mutavere vices.*   For
the meaning of vices, cf. I. 4. 1,
III. 29. 13. — decrescentia: after
the winter floods, due to melting
snows on the mountains (cf. 12. 3
sq.).

4. praetereunt, *flow by* (instead
of *over*).

5. Gratia cum geminis soro-
ribus: *i.e.* the three Graces (Aglaia,
Euphrosyne, Thalia ; Hes. *Theog.*
909) ; cf. III. 19. 16 n. For the
scene cf. I. 4. 6, where Venus, instead of the Graces, leads the
dance.

7. immortalia, *immortality ;* cf.
ima, I. 34. 12 n. — ne speres, monet: cf. I. 18. 7, 8 nn. — annus,
etc. : *i.e.* (1) the swift panorama of
the seasons (set forth in detail in
vss. 9–12), which the revolving year
keeps ever before our eyes, and
(2) the rapid flight of time as we
experience it in our daily concerns.
— almum: as the time of life-
giving sunshine ; cf. *alme Sol,
C. S.* 9.

8. rapit hora: cf. III. 29. 48
quod fugiens semel hora vexit. It
is the passage, not of the years, but
of the hours, that brings home to
us the rapid flight of time.

frigora mitescunt Zephyris, ver proterit aestas,
10   interitura simul

pomifer autumnus fruges effuderit, et mox
        bruma recurrit iners.

Damna tamen celeres reparant caelestia lunae :
        nos ubi decidimus

15   quo pater Aeneas, quo Tullus dives et Ancus,
        pulvis et umbra sumus.

Quis scit an adiciant hodiernae crastina summae
        tempora di superi ?

Cuncta manus avidas fugient heredis, amico
20   quae dederis animo.

9. **Zephyris :** see note on *Favoni*, I. 4. 1.— **proterit,** *tramples
down ;* of the devastating effect of
the scorching heat on the bloom
of spring ; cf. Ov. *M.* II. 791 (*Invidia*) *quacumque ingreditur, flo-
rentia proterit arva | exuritque
herbas.*

10. **interitura :** Intr. 104 *b.*

11. **pomifer :** cf. III. 23. 8 n,
Epod. 2. 17. As in the latter passage, autumn is personified. — **effuderit :** as from a horn of plenty ;
cf. I. 17. 14 *sqq.*

12. **iners :** in contrast with nature's activity in other seasons.

13. **damna caelestia :** *i.e.* those
of the seasons, as just described,
having their origin in the air and
sky (*caelum*), in contrast with us
men of earth. — **celeres lunae :**
i.e. the rapid succession of the
months (cf. *soles*, 5. 8 n). The
moon, however, is put as a representative of the whole celestial
system (Intr. 117). Cf. *Cat.* 5. 4
*soles occidere et redire possunt: |
nobis cum semel occidit brevis
lux, | nox est perpetua una dor-
mienda.*

14. **decidimus :** cf. *Ep.* II. 1. 36
*scriptor abhinc annos centum qui
decidit.*

15. **quo pater Aeneas,** etc. :
sc. *deciderunt.* Cf. *Ep.* I. 6. 27 *ire
tamen restat Numa quo devenit et
Ancus ;* Lucr. III. 1025 *lumina sis
oculis etiam bonus Ancus reliquit*
(quoted from Ennius). — **pater :**
cf. I. 2. 50 n, Verg. *A.* II. 2, etc. —
Tullus dives : cf. Liv. I. 31. 1 *cum
in magna gloria magnisque opibus
regnum Tulli ac tota res Romana
esset.*

16. **pulvis :** in the tomb ; **umbra :** in the underworld.

17. **quis scit,** etc. : cf. I. 9. 13
sqq., Ep. I. 4. 12 *sqq.* — **hodiernae
summae** (sc. *temporum ;* see I. 4.
15 n): the sum that has accumulated thus far.

19. **cuncta,** etc. : cf. II. 3. 20,
14. 25 *sqq.* and *Ep.* I. 5. 13 (also
addressed to Torquatus). This
attitude towards the heir is emi-
nently natural in a childless old
fellow like Horace. — **amico dederis animo :** suggested no doubt
by such expressions as *Il.* IX. 705
τεταρπόμενοι φίλον ἦτορ | σίτου καὶ

Cum semel occideris et de te splendida Minos
    fecerit arbitria,
non, Torquate, genus, non te facundia, non te
   ' restituet pietas.

25 Infernis neque enim tenebris Diana pudicum
    liberat Hippolytum,
nec Lethaea valet Theseus abrumpere caro
    vincula Pirithoo.

οἴνοιο. But the habit of thought which marks off the emotions and appetites as a distinct portion of our nature (cf. *aeger animi*, etc.) easily takes the further step of attributing to the *animus* a quasi-separate existence and personality; cf. Plaut. *Trin.* 305 *quí homo cum animo inde áb ineunte aetáte depugnát suo,* | *... si ánimus hominem pépulit, actumst, ánimo servit, nón sibi ;* | *sín ipse animum pépulit, vivit, víctor victorúm cluet.* The conception of this personality, as we have it here, however, as a sort of *numen,* to be kept contented and in good humor with us (amico), is more commonly expressed by *genius* (see III. 17. 14 n).

  21. semel: cf. I. 24. 16 n.— splendida, *stately;* Intr. 124. The splendor is that of his court.— Minos: cf. I. 28. 9; Verg. *A.* VI. 432 *sqq.*

  23. genus : Torquatus belonged to the Manlian gens, among the oldest of the Roman noble houses. — facundia : there is an appropriateness in confronting the orator with the judgment-seat of Minos as a type of the inexorable doom of death. Notice that in the varying metrical accent on nón ... non té ... nón te, the stress here falls on te.

  24. pietas : cf. II. 14. 2.

  25–28. Birth, eloquence, piety

must fail where a goddess' love and a hero's strength have been baffled.

  26. Hippolytum : son of Theseus, beloved of Diana, and the victim of the fury of his stepmother, Phaedra, whose advances he had repulsed. Horace follows Euripides (*Hippol.* 1436 *sqq.*), and does not accept the Roman form of the myth (cf. Verg. *A.* VII. 761 *sqq.* and Ov. *M.* XV. 533 *sqq.*), according to which Hippolytus was restored to life and was the divinity worshipped in the grove of Diana at Aricia under the name of Virbius.

  27. abrumpere : Intr. 94 *n.*

  28. Pirithoo : see III. 4. 80 n.

VIII. In this ode, written for C. Marcius Censorinus (consul B.C. 8), a man of amiable disposition and literary tastes, Horace takes as his theme the value of poetry as a vehicle of enduring fame, and not only, as in III. 30, asserts its superiority over material monuments, but claims for it the power to confer actual immortality, and even divinity. The ode appears to have been sent as a present to Censorinus, perhaps at the season of the Saturnalia, — a circumstance that gives occasion for a preliminary comparison between poems and material works of art, as gifts to a friend. — Metre, 169.

VIII.

Donarem pateras grataque commodus,
Censorine, meis aera sodalibus,
donarem tripodas, praemia fortium
Graiorum, neque tu pessima munerum
5   ferres, divite me scilicet artium
quas aut Parrhasius protulit aut Scopas,
hic saxo, liquidis ille coloribus
sollers nunc hominem ponere, nunc deum.
Sed non haec mihi vis, non tibi talium

1. **pateras** : see I. 19. 15 n. —
commodus : with **donarem**, as
in *Ep.* II. 1. 227 (*ut nos*) *commodus
ultro arcessas*, and its opposite in
Ep. I. 18. 75 (*ne te*) *incommodus
angat*. Here, from its close connection with **grata**, it has the
meaning of 'anticipating their
tastes.'

2. **aera** : the same kind of a
plural as our equivalent, *bronzes*
(Intr. 128), but referring here particularly to the bronze vessels
(λέβητες) which, like bowls and
tripods, were often given as prizes
(**praemia**) in the Greek national
games. The three are mentioned
together in Pind. *Isth.* 1. 18 ἐν τ'
ἀέθλοισι θίγον πλείστων ἀγώνων καὶ
τριπόδεσσιν ἐκόσμησαν δόμον καὶ
λεβήτεσσιν φιάλαισί τε χρυσοῦ
(cf. *Il.* XXIII. 259, 264, 267, 270).
Specimens of these 'antiques,' often elaborately wrought, had been
brought to Rome in great numbers,
and were highly prized.

3. **donarem** : Intr. 116 *h.* —
fortium, *gallant;* as winners in
the games.

5. **ferres** : for *auferres* (cf. Intr.
129), as often with *pretium, palmam,*
etc.; cf. vs. 22, III. 16. 22 ; *Ep.* I.

17. 43 *tacentes plus poscente ferent.*
—**divite me** : expressing the condition of **donarem**, and introduced
by **scilicet**, *I mean, of course.* —
artium : used concretely, *works of
art ;* cf. *Ep.* I. 6. 17 ; Intr. 66 *c.*

6. **Parrhasius** : of Ephesus, a
famous painter at Athens in the
time of Socrates. He was a contemporary and rival of Zeuxis, according to the well-known story of
the painting of the grapes and the
curtain.— **protulit**, *created;* cf. *Ep.*
II. 3. 58, 130; Tib. I. 10. 1 *quis fuit
horrendos primus qui protulit en-
ses?* — **Scopas** : of Paros, the most
eminent sculptor of his time (first
half of 4th century B.C.). Many
of his works were in Rome in
Horace's day; cf. note on *proles
Niobea,* 6. 1.

7. **liquidis** : suggesting by contrast the hardness of the stone.

8. **ponere** : apparently a technical word for representing an object,
either in sculpture or painting : cf.
I. 20, *Ep.* II. 3. 34.   For the mood,
see Intr. 101 *c.*

9. **non haec mihi vis**, *this is
not in my power* (*i.e.* to make such
presents).   For this use of **vis**
cf. *Epod.* 5. 94.

10   res est aut animus deliciarum egens :
      gaudes carminibus ; carmina possumus
      donare et pretium dicere muneri.
      Non incisa notis marmora publicis,
      per quae spiritus et vita redit bonis
15   post mortem ducibus, non celeres fugae
      reiectaeque retrorsum Hannibalis minae,
      non incendia Carthaginis impiae

10. **res, animus :** the meaning is that to make such presents to a man of means like Censorinus, even if Horace had the power to do it, would be merely giving him what he already had or could easily get, and did not really care for ; whereas a poem, which Horace could give, was something he liked and could not buy. **res** is for *res familiaris*, as *Ep.* I. 1. 80, II. 1. 106, and often. — **deliciarum,** *bric-a-brac.* For the case, see Intr. 66 *c*.

11. For the arrangement of words in this verse, in which each of the three ideas expressed is in contrast with something that precedes, see Intr. 116 *b* and *e*.

12. **pretium dicere :** for the usual *pretium statuere, pretium ponere*, etc., and taking, like these, a dative of the thing assessed (**muneri**) ; cf. *S.* II. 3. 23 *callidus huic signo* (sc. *pretium*) *ponebam milia centum.*

13. Horace here begins his *pretii dictio*, which continues to the end of the ode. — **incisa :** with instrumental abl., as in Liv. VI. 29. 9 *tabula his ferme incisa litteris* (Gr. 225 *d*), instead of *incisae marmoribus notae*, or the more common prose construction, *in marmoribus;* but Horace is comparing with poetry, not the inscriptions, but the statues with their inscriptions. — **notis :** *i.e.* letters ; cf. Ov. *Tr.* III.

3. 71 *quosque legat versus oculo properante viator | grandibus in tituli marmore caede notis.* — **marmora :** *i.e.* statues, as the relative clause shows. — **publicis :** set up by authority of the state (*i.e.* by order of the senate).

14. **spiritus et vita :** the same thing under two aspects (notice the number of **redit**) ; cf. 9. 10 *sq.* and 2. 28 n. For the thought, cf. Verg. *A.* VI. 847 *excudent alii spirantia mollius aera, ... vivos ducent de marmore voltus.*

15. **ducibus :** Intr. 53. — **non celeres fugae,** etc.: *i.e.* the dramatic close of Hannibal's enterprise and (if we accept vs. 17) the burning of the great city which had well-nigh conquered Rome, were events so impressive and of such momentous import, that they would of themselves, without any written record, carry the name of Africanus down through the ages; but these brilliant memories cannot equal the glory conferred by poetry. — **fugae :** from the field of Zama (B.C. 202). For the number, see Intr. 128.

16. **reiectae minae :** *i.e.* the reduction of Carthage to the attitude of submission to which he had threatened to reduce Rome; cf. 3. 8.

17. For the grounds for believing this verse and other parts of

eius, qui domita nomen ab Africa
lucratus rediit, clarius indicant
20 laudes quam Calabrae Pierides ; neque
si chartae sileant quod bene feceris,
mercedem tuleris. Quid foret Iliae
Mavortisque puer, si taciturnitas
obstaret meritis invida Romuli ?
25 Ereptum Stygiis fluctibus Aeacum
virtus et favor et lingua potentium

the ode spurious, see Crit. App.
— impiae : see note on *perfidus*,
4. 49.

18. eius : cf. III. 11. 17 n. —
qui domita nomen, etc.: cf. *S.*
II. 1. 66 *qui duxit ab oppressa
meritum Carthagine nomen.* ab
Africa modifies ἀπὸ κοινοῦ both
nomen lucratus and rediit; Intr.
76.

19. lucratus, *enriched by, richer
by ;* an allusion perhaps to the
indignant reply of Scipio to those
who impugned his honesty in the
management of his brother's Asiatic campaign, — that his surname
was the only profit he brought
home from Africa; ' *nam cum
Africam totam potestati vestrae
subiecerim, nihil ex ea quod meum
diceretur praeter cognomen rettuli* '
(Val. Max. III. 7. 1 d).

20. Calabrae Pierides : *i.e.* the
poetry of Ennius, a native of
Rudiae, in Calabria, whose historical epic, *Annales*, included the
second Punic war. He was, moreover, a close friend and admirer
of Scipio, and wrote one or more
separate poems in his honor. For
Pierides, see note on *Haemo*, I.
12. 6.

21. chartae, *books, literature.*
The word had come to be used
for literary works, as in 9. 31, or

even for definite portions of such
works, as Cat. 1. 6 *omne aevum
tribus explicare chartis (i.e.* in three
volumes). — sileant : used transitively, as in 9. 31.

22. tuleris : the future perfect
(Gr. 281 Rem.) carries the reader
forward to the final result of the
whole transaction : you will not
have done a good deed without having received your just reward for it.
— Iliae Mavortisque puer: cf. 6.
37, I. 12. 25, and see I. 2. 17 n.
Mavors is an old name of Mars,
preserved in the ritual and adopted
by the earlier poets.

23. taciturnitas invida : cf. 9.
33 *lividas obliviones.* We need
not think here of envious detractors, but only of the spite with
which we readily endow whatever
stands between us and what we
regard as our just due. Cf. 5. 9 n.

25. Aeacum : see II. 13. 22 n.
He was celebrated in particular
by Pindar (*Isth.* 8. 23, etc.).

26. virtus, *the genius ;* properly
their excellence (*sc.* as poets); cf.
Ep. II. 3. 370 *actor causarum mediocris abest virtute diserti Messalae.*
Some editors, however, understand
by virtus the merit of Aeacus
himself. — potentium : as having
power to grant or withhold immortality.

vatum divitibus consecrat insulis.
Dignum laude virum Musa vetat mori ;
caelo Musa beat.   Sic Iovis interest
30   optatis epulis impiger Hercules,
clarum Tyndaridae sidus ab infimis
quassas eripiunt aequoribus ratis,
ornatus viridi tempora pampino
Liber vota bonos ducit ad exitus.

27. **divitibus insulis:** see *Epod.*
16. 42 n; for the case, Intr. 69. —
consecrat, *hallows, i.e.* makes immortal; cf. *sacrare,* I. 26. 11 n.
For the number, see Intr. 77.

29. **caelo beat**: *i.e.* deifies, —
a step beyond the mere conferring
of immortality (as in the case of
Aeacus) expressed by vs. 28. —
sic: *i.e.* through the power of
poetry. The claim appears to involve a confusion between a purely
subjective immortality in the memory and worship of mankind, —
immortality of fame, — and a real,
objective existence and activity
after death (cf. Tac. *A.* IV. 38. 5
*optimos quippe mortalium altissima
cupere: sic Herculem et Liberum
apud Graecos, Quirinum apud nos
deum numero additos ;* . . . *cetera
principibus statim adesse: unum in-
satiabiliter parandum, prosperam
sui memoriam*); but it is not necessarily a denial of the latter.
Granted that Romulus, Hercules,
and the rest have been translated
to heaven, they still cannot dis-
pense with the aid of the poets,
who have made their glory known
to men; for without this they
would not be worshipped, and so,
in effect, would not be gods at all,
but, like the rest of the dead, mere
'pulvis et umbra.' Cf. Ov. *Pont.*
IV. 8. 55 *di quoque carminibus, si
fas est dicere, fiunt,* | *tantaque*

maiestas ore canentis eget. — **interest epulis,** etc.: in each of the
three cases a particular privilege
or function is put for the general
fact that they are gods; Intr. 117 *a.*

30. **optatis:** as the object of
his ambition; cf. *Ep.* II. 3. 412
optatam cursu contingere metam.

31. **clarum sidus:** in apposition
with **Tyndaridae**; cf. I. 3. 2 n. —
ab infimis aequoribus, *from* (going to) *the bottom of the sea.*

32. **quassas ratis**: cf. I. 1. 17.

33. **viridi tempora pampino**:
repeated from III. 25. 20.

34. **vota,** etc.: so Vergil expresses the deification of Daphnis,
E. 5. 79 *ut Baccho Cererique, tibi
sic vota quotannis* | *agricolae faci-
ent ; damnabis* (= *bonos duces ad
exitus*) *tu quoque votis.*

IX. M. Lollius (cos. B.C. 21), to
whom this ode is addressed, was
a trusted lieutenant of the emperor,
who employed him on various important missions. He organized,
as first propraetor, the province of
Galatia, and in B.C. 18 was made
governor of Belgian Gaul, where,
two years later, he suffered a humiliating defeat at the hands of
the Sygambri (see intr. note to
Ode 2).   This reverse, however,
in no wise lowered him in the
esteem of his friends, — among
whom we must reckon Horace, —

IX.

Ne forte credas interitura quae
longe sonantem natus ad Aufidum
non ante volgatas per artis
verba loquor socianda chordis :

5   non, si priores Maeonius tenet
sedes Homerus, Pindaricae latent

nor of Augustus himself, who many years later (B.C. 1) gave him the most important of the imperial provinces, Syria, together with the confidential post of companion and adviser to his grandson, Gaius Caesar, who was sent at that time on a mission to Armenia. But the conduct of Lollius in the East, according to common report, was either a complete reversal of his previous career, or else, as Velleius charges (II. 97), his true character was at last unmasked; he was accused, it was said, of receiving bribes right and left from the potentates who had favors to ask of the young Caesar; and his sudden death, shortly after this came out, was attributed to suicide. He was succeeded by C. Censorinus, to whom the preceding ode is addressed.

It is singular that Horace should have placed on record, in one of his finest odes, his zealous testimony to the strict integrity of a man who died with such a reputation. But the evidence against Lollius is not free from doubt; Velleius, the chief witness, was a servile adherent of Tiberius, who was a personal enemy of Lollius. At any rate we may accept Horace's tribute, not only as the estimate in which Lollius was held when the ode was written, — probably

not long after the disaster of B.C. 16, to which vs. 36 appears to allude, — but as good evidence that up to that time his conduct had deserved the praise so lavishly bestowed. — Metre, 176.

1. **ne credas**: expressing the purpose of introducing the examples in the second and following strophes; cf. II. 4. 1 n.

2. **longe sonantem**: cf. 14. 25 *sqq.*, III. 30. 10 ; Intr. 3. — **natus ad Aufidum**: *i.e.* a mere provincial; see also III. 30. 10 n.

3. **non ante volgatas**: a more moderate statement of his claim than in III. 30. 13 *sq.;* cf. Intr. 26.

4. **verba socianda chordis :** a paraphrase for 'lyric poetry.' — **loquor**: of poetical utterance, as in III. 25. 18, IV. 2. 45, etc.

5. **non si**: see II. 10. 17 n. The argument which begins here and extends through vs. 28 is very similar to that of Ode 8, with this difference, however, that Horace is here concerned to maintain the power of *lyric* poetry to confer permanent fame, and therefore begins by showing that lyric, though it yields precedence in dignity to epos, is no less enduring (vss. 5–12). — **Maeonius**: cf. I. 6. 2 n.

6. **Pindaricae (camenae)**: see 2. 1–25 nn. — **(non) latent**, *is not lost to sight.*

Ceaeque et Alcaei minaces
     Stesichorique graves camenae,

nec, si quid olim lusit Anacreon,
10   delevit aetas ; spirat adhuc amor
     vivuntque commissi calores
          Aeoliae fidibus puellae.

Non sola comptos arsit adulteri
     crinis et aurum vestibus inlitum
15   mirata regalisque cultus
          et comites Helene Lacaena,

7. **Ceae :** see II. 1. 38 n.—
Alcaei : see Intr. 26.—**minaces :**
alluding to his invectives against
the tyrants of Lesbos ; see I. 32.
5 n, and cf. II. 13. 30 *sqq.*

8. **Stesichori :** a poet of Hi-
mera, in Sicily, contemporary with
Alcaeus and Sappho, distinguished
especially for perfecting the choral
ode. His subjects were chiefly
the heroic myths usually treated
in epic poetry (hence **graves**) ;
Quintilian (X. 1. 62) describes him
as *maxima bella et clarissimos ca-
nentem duces et epici carminis
onera lyra sustinentem ; reddit
enim personis in agendo simul lo-
quendoque debitam dignitatem.* See
also *Epod.* 17. 42 n.—**camenae :**
here of Greek poetry, as (conversely) *Pierides,* 8. 20, of Italian.
Cf. *Graiae camenae,* II. 16. 38 n.

9. **nec si,** etc.: *i.e.* and not only
lyrics on serious themes (such as
those just mentioned), but even
those written in lighter strain survive.—**olim,** *in his day ;* see 4.
5 n.—**lusit :** cf. I. 32. 1 n ; Cat.
50. 4 *scribens versiculos uterque
nostrum | ludebat numero modo
hoc modo illoc, | reddens mutua
per iocum atque vinum.* It is used
here, as often, of love poetry ; cf.

Ov. *Am.* III. 1. 27 *quod tenerae
cantent lusit tua musa puellae ;*
Cat. 68. 17.—**Anacreon :** born
in the island of Teos (cf. *Epod.*
14. 10), but a resident of various
Greek cities in succession ; for a
time at the brilliant court of Poly-
crates, tyrant of Samos (B.C. 533–
522), afterwards at Athens with
Hipparchus. He was a courtier
and man of pleasure, and a poet of
love and gayety. (The collection
of lyrics that bear his name are
imitations, of a much later date.)

10. **spirat vivuntque ; amor
. . . calores :** each pair expresses
one thing under two aspects ; cf.
spiritus et vita, 8. 14 n. For the
use of the verbs, see Intr. 121.

11. **commissi fidibus** (with
both **amor** and **calores**): cf. *S.*
II. 1. 30 *ille (Lucilius) velut fidis
arcana sodalibus olim | credebat li-
bris . . . quo fit ut omnis | votiva
pateat veluti descripta tabella | vita
senis ;* so the warm passion of
Sappho still lives and breathes
before us in her poems.

12. **Aeoliae puellae** (genitive,
limiting **fidibus**): see Intr. 26 and
II. 13. 24 *sq.*

13–28. The argument here is
for poetry in general, although

primusve Teucer tela Cydonio
    direxit arcu ; non semel Ilios
        vexata ; non pugnavit ingens
20   Idomeneus Sthenelusve solus
    dicenda Musis proelia ; non ferox
    Hector vel acer Deiphobus gravis
        excepit ictus pro pudicis
            coniugibus puerisque primus.

25 Vixere fortes ante Agamemnona

the examples are drawn from epic
only (Homer). The verses should
be read with careful observance of
the emphasis, which is helped by
rhythmical position (non sóla 13,
primúsve 17, nón semel 18, só-
lus 20, prímus 24, múlti and
ómnes 26) and anaphora (non);
see Intr. 116 *b* and *f*.

13. comptos crinis: apparently
the object ἀπὸ κοινοῦ of both arsit
(Intr. 72) and mirata; but the
former is gradually lost sight of
as the sentence proceeds, and does
not apply at all to comites. For
this characterization of Paris, cf.
I. 15. 14.

14. inlitum : lit. 'smeared on,'
implying extravagant and showy
embroidery, in oriental style (*pic-
turatas auri subtegmine vestis*, Verg.
A. III. 483).

15. mirata, *fascinated by;* cf.
I. 4. 19 n, *Epod.* 3. 10, *Ep.* I. 6. 1.
— cultus, *state.*

16. Helene Lacaena: cf. Verg.
A. II. 601 *Tyndaridis Lacaenae*, I.
650 *Argivae Helenae*. The addition
of the epithet is after the epic
manner; cf. Vergil's *Troius Aeneas*,
Sidonia Dido, etc.

17. Teucer: see I. 7. 21 n. He
figures in the Iliad as the best
bowman among the Greeks (*Il.*
XIII. 313).—Cydonio: *i.e.* Cretan;

see I. 15. 17 n. Cydonia was a town
on the northern coast of Crete.

18. Ilios, *a Troy; i.e.* the siege
(vexata) of Troy was not the only
great siege that ever took place.
For the form, see I. 10. 14 n.

20. Idomeneus : leader of the
Cretans in the Trojan war. —
Sthenelus : see I. 15. 24 n.

21. dicenda Musis proelia :
cf. 4. 68 n. For proelia, as the
object of pugnavit, see Intr. 51 *b*.
— non ferox, etc.: two instances
from the side of the defenders of
the city.

22. vel : rarely used in subordi-
nation to a negative, as here, though
-*ve* is common. — Deiphobus :
brother of Hector, and one of the
bravest of the Trojans. For his
subsequent fate, see Verg. *A.* VI.
494 *sqq.*

25. vixere : standing first with
the same emphasis that *fuere* would
have in this position, — an emphasis corresponding to that of the
preceding negatives. The series
of particular negations is here cut
short, and the fact implied in all
of them, — that there have been
in the world's history many Helens,
many Teucers, many Troys, — is
summed up in a general affirmative
statement, which serves to introduce the application of the whole

multi ; sed omnes inlacrimabiles
    urgentur ignotique longa
        nocte, carent quia vate sacro.

Paulum sepultae distat inertiae
30 celata virtus.   Non ego te meis
        chartis inornatum silebo
            totve tuos patiar labores

    impune, Lolli, carpere lividas
    obliviones.   Est animus tibi
35   rerumque prudens et secundis
            temporibus dubiisque rectus,

matter to the question in hand, the value of the poet. — **ante Agamemnona**: *i.e.* before the Trojan war, in which all these heroes distinguished themselves.

26. **inlacrimabiles**: not simply 'unwept,' but *beyond the reach of tears*, or the like; see II. 14. 6 n, and cf. *flebilis*, I. 24. 9.

27. **urgentur nocte**: cf. I. 24. 5 *Quintilium perpetuus sopor urget;* I. 4. 16 *iam te premet nox.*

28. **quia**: Intr. 114. — **sacro**: because inspired (cf. 3. 24, 6. 29), and singled out for the service of the Muses (III. 1. 3), and enjoying their favor and protection (III. 4. 21 *sqq.*).

29. **paulum**, etc.: the moral of the whole discourse, forming the transition to the tribute to Lollius: The sluggard dies, and his frailties are buried with him and forgotten; the hero is in no better case if his merits are not made known to men. — **inertiae, virtus**: abstract for concrete, as in III. 2. 17, 21; 4. 67; *Ep.* II. 1. 88.   For the case of **inertiae**, see Intr. 57.

30. **non ego te**: cf. I. 18. 11 n.

31. **chartis silebo**: cf. 8. 21 n. — **inornatum**: proleptic.

32. **labores**: *i.e.* arduous exertions; cf. 4. 6.   The word falls short of expressing achievement, and is appropriate in the defense of a man whose merits are under the cloud of temporary defeat (see intr. note).

33. **impune,** *unhindered.* — **carpere,** *to prey upon.*   The word aptly expresses the wearing and disintegrating effect of time. — **lividas obliviones**: cf. 8. 23 n ; Intr. 128.

34. **animus,** *a soul.*

35. **rerum prudens**: of the wisdom of experience (the opposite of *rerum inscitia, Ep.* I. 3. 33), in contrast with native gifts; cf. Verg. *G.* I. 416 *ingenium aut rerum prudentia.*

36. **dubiis,** *critical;* a variation on *adversis;* cf. II. 10. 13, Tac. *Ann.* I. 64. 6 *secundarum ambiguarumque rerum sciens.* — **rectus,** *steadfast;* properly 'erect' (cf. the literal use in 4. 48), 'not losing its balance.'

37. **vindex**, etc. : *i.e.* at once a champion and an example of strict integrity.   This is the one idea which Horace dwells upon through this and the next strophe, — the strength of Lollius' charac-

> vindex avarae fraudis et abstinens
> ducentis ad se cuncta pecuniae,
> consulque non unius anni,
> 40   sed quotiens bonus atque fidus
>
> iudex honestum praetulit utili,
> reiecit alto dona nocentium
> voltu, per obstantis catervas
> explicuit sua victor arma.
>
> 45   Non possidentem multa vocaveris
> recte beatum ; rectius occupat
> nomen beati, qui deorum
> muneribus sapienter uti

ter, which not only loathes venality and punishes it in others, but can itself resist temptation. For the use of **vindex, consul, iudex** with **animus**, cf. Verg. *A.* IX. 205 *animus lucis contemptor ;* Liv. I. 56. 8 *liberator ille populi Romani animus* (of Brutus). — **avarae :** *i.e.* prompted by greed. — **abstinens pecuniae :** see Intr. 66 *c.*

38. **ducentis :** *sc.* by its fascination. — **cuncta,** *all the world*, with the usual reservation in favor of a 'saving remnant.'

39. **consul,** etc.: in a purely figurative sense: incorruptible character has an intrinsic strength that exalts it above common men at all times when its power is displayed (**quotiens,** etc) ; its eminence is not temporary and accidental, like that of a politician raised to office for a few months. Cf. III. 2. 17 n, where the same figure is employed. It was suggested, no doubt, by the ideal sage of the Stoics, who unites in himself all perfections.

41. **iudex,** *as a judge.* — **honestum utili,** *virtue to expediency.* —

praetulit: in the manner indicated in the next clause.

42. **reiecit :** for the asyndeton here and in the next verse, cf. 5. 17–24, 8. 29–33, III. 18. 9–16. — **dona,** *bribes.*

43. **catervas :** sc. *nocentium,* who are compared to a swarm of foes through whom a brave warrior has to force his way to escape capture or the loss of his arms.

44. **explicuit :** *i.e.* has brought safely (out of the entanglement), has shaken them off, with his weapons intact. Cf. *expediunt,* 4. 76.

45. **non possidentem,** etc.: the poet's approval of the principles he has ascribed to his friend, not only as right, but as the true foundation of happiness. Cf. *Ep.* I. 16. 20 *neve putes alium sapiente bonoque beatum.* — **possidentem :** Intr. 103. — **vocaveris :** cf. *scripserit,* I. 6. 14 n. The subject is indefinite.

46. **recte beatum, rectius beati :** Intr. 116 *g.* — **rectius occupat,** *takes with a better claim.*

47. **beati :** defining gen., the regular construction in such phrases ; cf. *nomen poetae,* 6. 30 n.

duramque callet pauperiem pati
50   peiusque leto flagitium timet,
non ille pro caris amicis
aut patria timidus perire.

X.

O crudelis adhuc et Veneris muneribus potens,
insperata tuae cum veniet pluma superbiae
et quae nunc umeris involitant deciderint comae,
nunc et qui color est puniceae flore prior rosae

49. **pauperiem pati**: cf. I. 1.
18 n. For the inf., see Intr. 94 *o*.

50. **peius**: colloquial for *magis*,
with expressions of fear and aversion ; cf. *Ep.* I. 17. 30 *cane peius
et angui vitabit chlamydem ;* Cic.
Fam. VII. 2. 3 *oderam multo peius
hunc quam illum ipsum Clodium.*
So *male = valde*, as Ter. *Heaut.*
531 *timui male ;* Plaut. *Rud.* 920
*nimis id genus odi ego male mala-
cum.* With a verb expressing
favorable feeling, *deterius* is used
with weakening effect (= *minus*)
in *S.* I. 10. 89 *si placeant spe deterius nostra* (cf. I. 9. 24 n).

51. **non ille**: the pronoun serves
to bring the subject into renewed
prominence and single him out
from the mass of mankind ; cf.
neque tu, I. 9. 16 n ; Verg. *A.* I. 3.

52. **timidus perire**: Intr. 101 *a*.

X. The graver themes which
preponderate in this book are here
interrupted by four odes in lighter
strain, dealing with love and social
enjoyment. The first of them is
constructed in the same form as
I. 11, and, like that ode, is a warning: ' Beauty fades. Be not too
disdainful, proud boy, of the admirers who now court your favor:

the time will quickly come when
you will sigh in vain for the homage which you now hold so lightly.'
Horace found his theme already
treated in his Greek models; cf.
Anth. Pal. XII. 35, 186. For
the passionate admiration of the
Greeks for youthful beauty, cf.
Cat. 63. 64 *sqq.* — Metre, 170.

1. **Veneris muneribus**: cf. *Il.*
III. 54 τά τε δῶρ Ἀφροδίτης, ἥ τε
κόμη τό τε εἶδος; I. 18. 7 *munera
Liberi.*

2. **insperata**: *i.e.* before you
have begun to think of it; to be
taken with **veniet. — tuae superbiae**: poetical for *tibi superbo;*
see Intr. 126 *b*, and, for the case,
Intr. 53. — **pluma**, *down*, precisely
as we use the word ; but it is not
found elsewhere in this sense.

3. **umeris involitant**: cf. III.
20. 14, and, for the custom of boys
wearing their hair long, like girls,
II. 5. 21 *sqq.* — **deciderint**: *i.e.*
when shorn. The occasion was
attended with some formality ; cf.
Juv. III. 186 *crinem hic deponit
amati ; plena domus libis.*

4. **nunc**: Intr. 114.— **color**: *i.e.*
the cheeks (cf. **in faciem verterit**).
— **puniceae**, *red, red*; cf. III. 15.
15, where *purpureus* is used. The

5 mutatus, Ligurine, in faciem verterit hispidam,
   dices ' Heu,' quotiens te speculo videris alterum,
  ' quae mens est hodie, cur eadem non puero fuit,
   vel cur his animis incolumes non redeunt genae ? '

XI.

Est mihi nonum superantis annum
plenus Albani cadus ; est in horto,
Phylli, nectendis apium coronis ;
      est hederae vis

5   multa, qua crinis religata fulges ;
     ridet argento domus ; ara castis

latter was a darker (cf. II. 5. 12 n),
puniceus a clearer red (scarlet).

5. **Ligurine** : cf. 1. 33.—**verterit** : intransitive.

6. **speculo** : instrumental abl.
The *speculum* was commonly of
bronze or silver ; see Baumeister,
III. pp. 1691 *sqq.* — **alterum** : *i.e.*
changed beyond recognition. Cf.
III. 5. 34 n.

7. **puero** : sc. *mihi.*

8. **animis** : Intr. 53.

XI. An ode in honor of Maecenas' birthday. The poet represents himself, in the midst of
preparations for a festival, wel-
coming his fair neighbor Phyllis,
and explaining to her the nature
of the celebration which he has
invited her to share. The scene,
which is similar to that of III. 28,
is in the country. We need not
trouble ourselves to locate it more
definitely. The ode is chiefly interesting for its quiet testimony to
Horace's continued affection for
his old friend Maecenas, who is
mentioned here only in this book
(see Intr. 32). — Metre, 174.

2. **Albani** : accounted one of
the three or four best wines known
to the Romans ; cf. *S.* II. 8. 16.

3. **nectendis coronis** : dative
of purpose or service (cf. Intr. 59),
a construction surviving in prose
chiefly in legal phrases (Gr. 299 *b*);
cf. Liv. IV. 43. 10 *non ducem scri-
bendo exercitui esse.* — **apium** : cf.
I. 36. 16, II. 7. 24.

4. **vis multa,** *a plentiful supply.*
Vis, in this apparently colloquial
use, is often found in Cicero, as
Verr. II. 4. 103 *magna vis eboris ;
Tusc.* V. 91.

5. **qua** : with **fulges** only. —
crinis religata : cf. II. 11. 24 ;
Intr. 42.—**fulges** : a stronger word
than *nites,* I. 5. 13 ; so we speak
of 'brilliant' or 'dazzling' beauty.
It is probably from *fulgeo,* but
may be future, from an old form
fulgo, which Vergil has, *A.* VI.
826.

6. **ridet** : *i.e.* is bright and cheerful. The plate has been cleaned
and polished for the occasion ; cf.
Juv. 14. 59 *hospite venturo cessabit
nemo tuorum ;* | *'Verre pavimentum,
nitidas ostende columnas,* | . . . *hic*

vincta verbenis avet immolato
   spargier agno ;

cuncta festinat manus, huc et illuc
10   cursitant mixtae pueris puellae ;
sordidum flammae trepidant rotantes
   vertice fumum.

Vt tamen noris quibus advoceris
   gaudiis, Idus tibi sunt agendae,
15   qui dies mensem Veneris marinae
   findit Aprilem,

leve argentum, vasa aspera tergeat alter'; Ep. I. 5. 7 *iamdudum splendet focus et tibi munda supellex ;* ib. 23 *ne non et cantharus et lanx ostendat tibi te. Rideo* in this sense was a favorite word with Lucretius, as I. 8 *rident aequora ponti;* III. 22 (*divum sedes*) *large diffuso lumine rident.* Catullus uses it even of odors, 64. 284 *domus iucundo risit odore.* — **ara vincta verbenis**: cf. I. 19. 13, 14 nn.

7. **immolato agno** = *immolatione (caede) agni* (Intr. 105 *a*); cf. Verg. *A.* IV. 21 *sparsos fraterna caede Penates.*

8. **spargier**: archaic pres. inf., found here only in the lyric poems, but eight times in the Satires and Epistles.

9. **manus**: *i.e. familia.*

10. **pueris**: see I. 19. 14 n; for the case, Intr. 56. — **puellae**: *i.e. ancillae,* as its connection with **pueris** shows. It is very seldom used in this sense.

11. **sordidum,** *sooty.* — **trepidant**: cf. III. 27. 17 n. Even the fire on the hearth seems to share in the general flutter of eager expectation pictured above in **avet, festinat, cursitant.** — **rotantes vertice,** *whirling round.*

13. **ut noris**: the purpose of the following explanation, **Idus,** etc.; cf. 9. 1 n ; *Ep.* I. 12. 25 *ne tamen ignores quo sit Romana loco res, Cantaber,* etc.; *S.* II. 1. 80. — **advoceris**: here in the sense of *adhiberis,* and with the same construction; cf. 5. 32 *te mensis adhibet.*

15. **mensem Veneris**: there were various explanations of this. Horace has in mind the one according to which *Aprilis,* like Ἀφροδίτη, derived its name from ἀφρός, *sea-foam,* being the month in which the goddess rose out of the sea (hence **marinae**; see III. 26. 5 n). The month was no doubt sacred to her because of her activity at that season of the year; see I. 4. 5 n, and cf. Ov. *F.* IV. 1 *sqq.*

16. **findit**: according to the supposed derivation of *Idus* from *iduare,* an old word of Etruscan origin, meaning 'to divide' (Macrob. *Sat.* I. 15. 17).

17. **sollemnis**: the same as *festus* in III. 8. 9.—**sanctior**: the difference between *sollemnis dies* and *sanctus dies* is much the same as between 'holiday' and 'holy day.' Cf. Tib. IV. 5. 1 *qui mihi te,*

iure sollemnis mihi sanctiorque
paene natali proprio, quod ex hac
luce Maecenas meus adfluentis
20   ordinat annos.

Telephum, quem tu petis, occupavit
non tuae sortis iuvenem puella
dives et lasciva, tenetque grata
    compede vinctum.

25 Terret ambustus Phaethon avaras
spes, et exemplum grave praebet ales
Pegasus terrenum equitem gravatus
    Bellerophontem,

Cerinthe, dies dedit, hic mihi sanctus | atque inter festos semper habendus erit.

18. **paene**: cf. *prope*, 14. 20 n.

19. **luce**: cf. 6. 42 n. — **adfluentis**, *gathering;* lit. 'flowing to' him. The word contains no suggestion of old age or decline, like our 'advancing' years, but rather of an increased store of what the years bring; see II. 5. 14 n.

20. **ordinat**, *reckons.* The literal meaning is, that he makes out the series of his years with the Ides of April for the starting point (**ex hac luce**) of each, and not *e.g.* the Kalends of January, as it would be in the case of the calendar year.

21. **Telephum**: the same name is used in I. 13. 1 and III. 19. 26. — **petis**: as in I. 33. 13, III. 19. 27, and often. — **occupavit**: with its usual sense of anticipation: 'has got possession of him before you.'

22. **non tuae sortis**: *i.e.* above your station in life.

23. **dives**: so that you cannot hope to compete with her. The warning carries with it the soothing intimation that her failure to win casts no reflection on her personal attractions ; the contest was unequal from the outset. Observe the chiastic arrangement of the attributes of **iuvenem** and **puella**. — **tenet grata compede**: cf. I. 33. 14.

25. **terret**: for the position, cf. *monet*, I. 18. 8. — **ambustus Phaethon**: Intr. 105 *a.*

26. **grave**: there is only mock seriousness, of course, in the present application of it. — **ales**: cf. I. 2. 42, III. 12. 2.

27. **terrenum**: hence unfit to consort with a creature of the air (**ales**), and teaching by his fate the lesson **ut disparem vites**, as well as the sin of unlawful ambition (**ultra quam licet sperare nefas**). It was said that Bellerophon, after his victory over the Chimaera (cf. I. 27. 24), attempted to fly to heaven on Pegasus, with the result here indicated. — **gravatus**: Intr. 51 *a.*

28. **Bellerophontem**: see III. 7. 15 n.

semper ut te digna sequare et ultra
30   quam licet sperare nefas putando
disparem vites.   Age iam, meorum
finis amorum,

(non enim posthac alia calebo
femina,) condisce modos, amanda
35   voce quos reddas ; minuentur atrae
carmine curae.

XII.

Iam veris comites, quae mare temperant,
impellunt animae lintea Thraciae ;
iam nec prata rigent nec fluvii strepunt
hiberna nive turgidi.

29. **ut sequare**, etc.: depending
loosely on the notion of instruction
contained in **exemplum**; cf. Ter.
Heaut. 51 *exémplum statuite in me,
ut adulescéntuli | vobis placere stú-
deant potius quám sibi*, and the use
of an indirect question with *exem-
plar proposuit, Ep.* I. 2. 17.—**digna**:
cf. *ima summis*, I. 34. 12 n.

30. **putando**: approaching the
use of the present participle ; Gr.
301 (footnote).

31. **age iam**, etc. : the conclusion of the plea : 'Better content
yourself, then, with me ; and come,
let us enjoy the day together.'

32. **finis**: cf. Prop. I. 12. 19 *mi
neque amare aliam neque ab hac
desistere fas est; | Cynthia prima
fuit, Cynthia finis erit.* — **amorum**: cf. I. 27. 17 n.

33. **alia calebo**: cf. *quo calet*,
I. 4. 19 n; Intr. 72.

34. **condisce**: *i.e.* 'let me teach
you.'

35. **reddas**: see 6. 43 n.—**atrae
curae**: cf. III. 1. 40 n, 14. 13.

XII. We have in this ode the
same elements as in I. 4 and IV. 7.
It opens with a picture of spring.
The increasing warmth brings
thirst, and on this the poet hinges
an invitation to his friend to join
him in a carouse, to which each
shall contribute an equitable share.
The reminder of the shortness of
life, so prominent in the two odes
named, is brought in here also, but
only as a momentary thought (vs.
26). Of the friend addressed,
Vergilius, we know with certainty
nothing beyond what the lines re-
veal. That it was the author of
the Aeneid is not impossible, if
we suppose that Horace published
some years after Vergil's death a
poem which he had written in his
lifetime, and that two allusions
(vss. 15 and 25) which appear to
contradict what we know of Vergil
had their explanations in circumstances unknown to us; but it is
highly improbable. The Vergilius
of this ode we may conjecture was

5   Nidum ponit, Ityn flebiliter gemens,
    infelix avis et Cecropiae domus
    aeternum opprobrium, quod male barbaras
      regum est ulta libidines.

    Dicunt in tenero gramine pinguium
10   custodes ovium carmina fistula

a younger friend of Horace, who was trying to better his fortunes by attaching himself to one and another of the great men of the day, or possibly a man who was brought into close relations with noble patrons by his professional work. In one manuscript he is called *medicus Neronum*, which is worthless as testimony, but contains a suggestion. (The 13th poem of Catullus, in which a similar invitation is given, may well be read with this ode, by way of comparing the two poets.) — Metre, 172.

1. **veris comites** : cf. 7. 9, I. 4. 1 n, *Ep.* I. 7. 13. For **comites**, cf. I. 25. 19 *hiemis sodali, Euro.* — **temperant**, *calm*.

2. **impellunt lintea**: *i.e.* navigation is already open ; cf. I. 4. 2.— **Thraciae** : a literary epithet, as applied to the *Zephyri*, of Homeric origin ; cf. *Il.* IX. 5 Βορέης καὶ Ζέφυρος, τώ τε Θρήκηθεν ἄητον. It is more commonly applied to Boreas (Aquilo); cf. I. 25. 11 n, *Epod.* 13. 3.

3. **prata**: cf. I. 4. 4.—**nec fluvii**, etc.: cf. 7. 3 *sq.*

5. **Ityn** : son of the Thracian king Tereus and Procne, daughter of Pandion, king of Athens. His mother killed him, and served up his flesh to his own father in revenge (**male ulta**) for the outrage the latter had committed on her sister Philomela. When Tereus discovered the crime, and pursued the two sisters, all three were changed into birds. (See Ov. *M.*

VI. 424 *sqq.*) There is a confusion of names in the myth. According to the form adopted by Roman writers, Procne was turned into a swallow, and Philomela into a nightingale (*e.g.* Verg. *G.* IV. 15, Ov. *F.* II. 853 *sqq.*). For the case of **Ityn,** see Intr. 51 *a.* — **flebiliter gemens** : properly descriptive of the nightingale's plaintive note, and it is possible that Horace so intends it, following the other form of the myth and the example of the Greek poets, in whom the nightingale is associated with the spring (cf. *Odys.* XIX. 518; Sappho *Fr.* 19 ἦρος ἄγγελος, ἱμερόφωνος ἀηδών); but the swallow was proverbially, among both Greeks and Romans, the sign of spring, and is probably intended by **avis infelix** here. Cf. *Ep.* I. 7. 12 *te, dulcis amice, reviset* | *cum Zephyris et hirundine prima.*

6. **Cecropiae domus** : the Attic dynasty of which Cecrops was the founder.

7. **male**: in reference not to the act of vengeance, but to the manner of it. — **barbaras** : Intr. 124.

8. **regum** : the plural generalizes, and defines the conduct of Tereus as characteristic of his class, so that it is substantially equivalent to *regias ;* cf. *virginum,* III. 27. 38 n.

9. **dicunt carmina**: cf. *C. S.* 8, and see I. 6. 5 n.

10. **fistula** : see I. 17. 10 n; and for the case, I. 17. 18 n.

delectantque deum cui pecus et nigri
        colles Arcadiae placent.

Adduxere sitim tempora, Vergili ;
        sed pressum Calibus ducere Liberum
15   si gestis, iuvenum nobilium cliens,
        nardo vina merebere.

Nardi parvus onyx eliciet cadum,
        qui nunc Sulpiciis accubat horreis,
        spes donare novas largus amaraque
20   curarum eluere efficax.

11. **deum** : *i.e.* Faunus, here, as in I. 17. 1 *sqq.*, identified with Pan. — **nigri colles**: cf. *nigris Erymanthi silvis*, I. 21. 7 n.

14. **pressum Calibus**: cf. I. 20. 9 n. — **ducere** : cf. I. 17. 22 n. — **Liberum** : Intr. 130.

15. **iuvenum nobilium** : the word **iuvenum** appears to indicate definite persons, but we have no means of knowing who they were. — **cliens** : *i.e.* accustomed to be invited to their tables, where he was not required to contribute anything, — the same thought that is expressed in vs. 24.

16. **nardo** : see II. 11. 16 n. — **vina** : Intr. 128. The plural here obviously refers to a single jar. — **merebere** : equivalent to a mild command ; cf. Intr. 90.

17. **nardi** : Intr. 116 *h.* — **parvus** : the nard was very costly ; cf. *N. T.* Mark 14. 3 *sqq.* — **onyx** : usually denoting, when masculine, a box to hold ointment, originally one made of alabaster (cf. Plin. *N. H.* XXXVI. 60 *hunc aliqui lapidem (onychem) 'alabastriten' vocant, quem cavant et ad vasa unguentaria, quoniam optime servare incorrupta dicatur*), but later an ointment box of any material. —

eliciet : a personification of the *cadus* similar to that of III. 21. 1 *sqq.*

18. **Sulpiciis** : cf. Intr. 65 ; but this was the regular usage in the case of gentile and other personal names that were originally adjectives; cf. *Claudiae manus*, 4. 73; *lex Cornelia, Iulius (mensis), Colonia Agrippina, historia Augusta*, etc. The *horrea Sulpicia* stood at the foot of the Aventine, where the hill borders on the river, among numerous other buildings of the kind, which gave to the district the name of 'the Warehouses' (*Horrea*). It was built by the Galba family (hence also called *Galbiana*), and existed in Porphyrio's day (4th century or earlier), 'vino et oleo et similibus aliis referta.' The poet's wine is stored there. — **accubat**, *reclines*, the *cadus* having no base ; see Baumeister III. *fig.* 2335.

19. **spes donare**: cf. III. 21. 17. For the infinitive, see Intr. 101 *b.* — **amara curarum** : Intr. 64.

20. **eluere** : cf. III. 12. 1 *mala vino lavere*. For the mood, see Intr. 101 *b.*

21. **properas** : here expressing not haste in coming, but haste

Ad quae si properas gaudia, cum tua
velox merce veni ; non ego te meis
immunem meditor tinguere poculis,
    plena dives ut in domo.

25 Verum pone moras et studium lucri,
nigrorumque memor, dum licet, ignium
misce stultitiam consiliis brevem :
    dulce est desipere in loco.

XIII.

Audivere, Lyce, di mea vota, di
audivere, Lyce : fis anus ; et tamen
vis formosa videri,
    ludisque et bibis impudens

(eagerness) to come; cf. *S.* I. 9. 40
et propero (I am in a hurry to go)
quo scis. — **gaudia :** cf. 11. 14.

22. **merce :** *i.e.* the nard.

23. **immunem,** *scot-free, i.e.*
without paying your contribution;
in Greek, ἀσύμβολον, which Terence
has in Phor. 339 *asymbolum venire*
(sc. *ad cenam*). — **tinguere :** colloquial, like *siccus* and *uvidus* (5. 39),
irriguus (*S.* II. 1. 9).

24. **plena domo :** cf. II. 12. 24.

25. **verum,** *but really* (breaking
off the banter); the word occurs
here only in the lyric poems. —
moras : the plural (Intr. 128), of
delay persisted in for one reason
after another. — **studium lucri :**
see intr. note.

26. **nigrorum :** see I. 24. 18 n.

27. **consiliis,** *with your wisdom.*
Cf. III. 28. 4, and for the case,
see Intr. 56.

28. **dulce est desipere:** a Greek
idea; cf. Sen. *Dial.* IX. 17. 10 *sive
Graeco poetae credimus, 'aliquando*

et insanire iucundum est'; Menan-
der IV. 196 M. οὐ πανταχοῦ τὸ
φρόνιμον ἁρμόττει παρόν, καὶ συμ-
μανῆναι δ᾽ ἔνια δεῖ. — **in loco :** cf.
Ep. I. 7. 57 *et properare loco et
cessare;* Ter. *Ad.* 216 *pecúniam
in locó neglegere máximum inter-
dúmst lucrum.*

XIII. The Lyce who figures in
this ode as a fading beauty may
very well have been the same in
the poet's fancy as the Lyce of
III. 10, where her coldness and
arrogance were well suited to call
out the imprecations on her lover's
part, the fulfillment of which he
here recognizes with malicious
glee. The subject is the same as
that of III. 15 and I. 25. — Metre,
173.

1. **audivere,** etc.: the repetition
(Intr. 116 *g*) is that of taunting
exultation. — **vota :** cf. II. 8. 6 n.

4. **ludis :** cf. III. 15. 5, II. 12.
19 n.

5   et cantu tremulo pota Cupidinem
    lentum sollicitas.   Ille virentis et
        doctae psallere Chiae
            pulchris excubat in genis ;

    importunus enim transvolat aridas
10   quercus et refugit te quia luridi
        dentes, te quia rugae
            turpant et capitis nives ;

    nec Coae referunt iam tibi purpurae
    nec cari lapides tempora quae semel
15   notis condita fastis
            inclusit volucris dies.

5. **tremulo**: the effect of wine on a voice made unsteady by age.

6. **lentum,** *torpid, unresponsive;* different from *lentus amor,* III. 19. 28.   The same difference exists between *S.* I. 9. 64 *vellere coepi et pressare manu lentissima bracchia* and *Epod.* 15. 6 *lentis adhaerens bracchiis.* — **virentis**: cf. I. 9. 17.

7. **psallere**: Intr. 101 *c.*—**Chiae**: a name like *Delia, Lesbia,* etc.   It occurs in several inscriptions as a freedwoman's name.

8. **excubat,** *keeps watch ; i.e.* lurks there, ready to attack those who come within bowshot.

9. **importunus,** *the unmannerly boy.* — **aridas** : in contrast with *virentis,* 6; cf. I. 25. 17, 19.

10. **quercus** : a type of long life. — **te quia ... te quia** : the ἀπὸ κοινοῦ construction (Intr. 76) is helped out by the anaphora, **te** in vs. 10 being felt to be the object of **refugit,** while in vs. 11, where its repetition with **quia** serves to continue the dependent clause with another subject (Intr. 116 *h*), it is felt to be a part of that clause and the object of **turpant.**

12. **capitis nives** : cf. Lowell's 'Singer with the crown of snow.' The metaphor, so familiar to us, appears not to occur in classical literature before Horace (though Catullus, according to some texts, wrote *niveo vertice,* 64. 309).   Quintilian (VIII. 6. 17) condemns it as harsh and founded on too remote a likeness, coupling in his censure this passage with a verse of the poet Furius which Horace himself ridicules, *S.* II. 5. 41.

13. **Coae** : the silk stuffs manufactured in the island of Cos were notorious for their fine, semitransparent texture, which made them a favorite material with the class of which Lyce is a type.

15. **notis condita fastis inclusit** : Intr. 76.   The meaning is that she cannot get back her past years or disguise the fact that they are past, because they are, as it were, securely stored away and locked up in the calendar, where they are known to all men.   For the part attributed to the **volucris dies** in the flight of time, cf. *rapit hora diem,* 7. 8 n.

Quo fugit venus, heu, quove color, decens
quo motus ?   Quid habes illius, illius,
  quae spirabat amores,
20   quae me surpuerat mihi,

felix post Cinaram notaque et artium
gratarum facies ?   Sed Cinarae brevis
  annos fata dederunt,
    servatura diu parem

25 cornicis vetulae temporibus Lycen,
possent ut iuvenes visere fervidi
  multo non sine risu
    dilapsam in cineres facem.

18. **illius, illius**: Intr. 116 *d*.
The genitive is partitive, limiting
quid.

19. **spirabat amores**: Intr. 51
d (2) ; cf. Prop. I. 3. 7 (of the
sleeping Cynthia) *visa mihi mol-
lem spirare quietem*.

20. **surpuerat**: colloquial syncopation of *surripuerat;* cf. *sur-
pite*, *S.* II. 3. 283, and see Intr.
183. For the thought, cf. Cat. 51.
3 *qui sedens adversus identidem
te | spectat et audit | dulce riden-
tem, misero quod omnis eripit
sensus mihi.*

21. **felix post**, *favored above all
but.* For **post**, cf. III. 9. 6 n. —
Cinaram: see I. 4 n. — **nota**: she
was one of the noted beauties of
the day. — **artium gratarum**, *of
winning graces;* descriptive genitive. Some, however, make **et** =
etiam, and join the genitive with
nota, as in II. 2. 6.

22. **facies**: here not the face,
but her whole appearance, — a

vision, a figure; cf. Ter. *Eun.* 296
*o fáciem pulcram ! déleo omnis de-
hinc ex animo múlieres.*

24. **servatura**: Intr. 104 *a*. —
parem: proleptic, — *to equal, to
attain.*

25. **vetulae**, *poor old;* colloquial (cf. vs. 20 n) and disparaging ; cf. the more dignified *annosa
cornix*, III. 17. 13 n. —**temporibus**, *the years* (we require in English a definite measure of time to
form such a plural).

26. **possent ut**, etc., *to give . . .
a chance to behold.* The point of
the sarcasm is that Lyce is a
woman who will subject her fading charms to the ridicule of the
iuvenes fervidi,—hence the fates
have selected *her* as the instrument of their purpose.

28. **dilapsam in cineres**, *crum-
bled to ashes.* **in** expresses the
result of the change, as in *portus
curvatus in arcum* (Verg. *A.* III.
533) and the like.

XIV.

Quae cura patrum quaeve Quiritium
plenis honorum muneribus tuas,
    Auguste, virtutes in aevum
        per titulos memoresque fastos

5 aeternet, o qua sol habitabilis
inlustrat oras maxime principum?
    Quem legis expertes Latinae
        Vindelici didicere nuper

quid Marte posses.   Milite nam tuo
10 Drusus Genaunos, implacidum genus,
    Breunosque velocis et arcis
        Alpibus impositas tremendis

XIV. For the subject and occasion of this ode, see intr. note
to Ode 4. Tiberius, who was barely alluded to in that ode, naturally receives the larger share of
attention here, but the achievements of both brothers are treated
as merely incidental to the praises
of Augustus. His transcendent
merits are extolled in the opening
strophes, and, after disposing of
its proper subject, the poem re-
solves itself into a song of praise to
the great ruler before whose power
all nations bow. — Metre, 176.

1. patrum ... -ve Quiritium:
a paraphrase for the formal *senatus populusque Romanus.*

2. plenis, *adequate.*—honorum:
defining *muneribus ;* cf. I. 28. 3.

3. in aevum: cf. III. 11. 35 *in
omne aevum.* Here the idea of
omne is supplied by aeternet.

4. per titulos: *i.e.* by statues,
altars, trophies (see vs. 10 n), and
other monuments inscribed with
his achievements.—memores fastos: cf. III. 17. 4.

5. o qua, etc.: cf. Ter. *Phor.*
853 *o ómnium quantúmst qui ví-
vont hómo hominum ornatissume.*
— qua sol, etc.: *i.e.* in the whole
habitable world.

6. principum: see I. 2. 50 n;
but as there was no other *princeps*
in this sense, the word must be
used here vaguely for rulers in
general, under whatever title.

7. quem didicere quid posses: such anticipation, in the
main clause, of the subject of a
dependent question occurs in Horace only here and in vs. 17 *spectandus . . . quantis*, etc. It is
frequent in comedy, as Ter. *Eun.*
657 *ego illum nescio qui fuerit* (cf.
'I know thee who thou art').—
legis expertes Latinae: *i.e.* not
yet subjugated.

9. quid posses: cf. *quid posset*,
4. 25; Intr. 47. — Marte: cf. III.
5. 24, 34; Intr. 130. — milite tuo :
referring to the operations of *both*
brothers (vss. 10–16).

10. Genaunos . . . Breunos-
que: it is not clear whether Hor-

deiecit acer plus vice simplici ;
maior Neronum mox grave proelium
15   commisit immanisque Raetos
auspiciis pepulit secundis,

spectandus in certamine Martio,
devota morti pectora liberae
quantis fatigaret ruinis,
20   indomitas prope qualis undas

ace regarded these two tribes of
the Inn valley as a part of the
Vindelician nation, which included
at least four tribes (Plin. *N. H.*
III. 136), or as their allies, naming
the Vindelici in vs. 8 and 4. 18, as
he does the Sygambri in vs. 51
and 2. 36, because of their controlling influence in the confederacy.
The inscription on a trophy erected
a few miles from Nice to commemorate Augustus' conquest of
the Alpine tribes (CIL. V. 7817 ;
Plin. *l. l.*) is equally ambiguous. —
implacidum genus, *a merciless
breed;* cf. *immanis,* 15 n. *Impla-
cidus* occurs here first in extant
Latin literature.

11. **velocis,** *agile; i.e.* in their
warfare. — **arcis,** etc.: cf. *Ep.* II.
1. 252.

13. **deiecit,** *hurled down;* applying equally well to the barbarians (cf. *Ep.* II. 2. 30) and their
stronghold (cf. Verg. *A.* XII. 655
deiecturum arcis).—**plus vice simplici:** *i.e.* making them suffer
greater loss than they had inflicted.
For **vice,** cf. I. 28. 32 n. The ablative is modal, **plus** being used as
a simple adverb without influence
on the case, as often in prose.

14. **maior Neronum:** see 4.
28 n. His name, *Tĭbĕrĭus,* is excluded by its prosody. He was at
this time in his twenty-seventh
year. — **proelium:** according to

Dio (LIV. 22. 4) he fought several
pitched battles.

15. **immanis :** Strabo (IV. 6. 8)
describes the cruelty of the Alpine
barbarians towards the prisoners
captured in their raids as similar
to that attributed to Achilles in
6. 18–20.

17. **spectandus,** etc.: the passive of the personal construction
exemplified in vs. 7, where see
note. For the use of the gerundive, cf. *donandus,* 2. 9 n. For the
neglect of caesura in this verse,
see Intr. 155.

18. **devota :** Intr. 103. — **pectora :** cf. 4. 34 n. — **liberae,** *a freeman's* (cf. III. 5. 22): they were
determined to die rather than surrender ; a difficult foe, therefore,
to conquer.

19. **quantis:** Intr. 114.—**ruinis:**
cf. Liv. V. 43. 3 *strage et ruina
fudere Gallos.* The plural expresses
repeated occurrence, — *crushing
blows,* or the like. Horace here
and in the following comparison
has in mind the Roman pursuit
of the barbarians into their native
valleys.

20. **indomitas:** parallel to *devota morti liberae,* 18 n. — **prope**
(with **qualis**) = 'I had almost
said.' It adds to the effect of the
description, as a mark of the narrator's carefulness of statement.
Cf. 5. 18, *S.* II. 3. 268.

exercet Auster Pleiadum choro
   scindente nubis, impiger hostium
      vexare turmas et frementem
         mittere equum medios per ignis.

25 Sic tauriformis volvitur Aufidus,
   qui regna Dauni praefluit Apuli,
      cum saevit horrendamque cultis
         diluviem meditatur agris,

   ut barbarorum Claudius agmina
30 ferrata vasto diruit impetu,
      primosque et extremos metendo
         stravit humum, sine clade victor,

21. **Auster:** cf. III. 3. 4 *sq.* —
Pleiadum choro : cf. Prop. IV.
5. 36 *Pleiadum spisso cur coit igne
chorus.* They were harbingers of
storm as they approached their
setting in November ; cf. Prop.
III. 16. 51 *non haec* (*fulmina*)
*Pleiades faciunt neque aquosus
Orion.*

22. **scindente nubis :** the picture is of a black night with driving clouds, through the rifts of
which the stars are now and then
visible. — **impiger vexare :** Intr.
101 *b.*

24. **medios per ignis :** a stock
phrase for extreme peril ; cf. *S.* II.
3. 56 *sq., Ep.* I. 1. 46 *per mare pauperiem fugiens, per saxa, per ignis.*
It seems inapt here, however, and
possibly is used literally, in allusion to a definite incident known
to Horace and his readers, but
not to us, — a fight in a burning
village, perhaps.

25. **sic . . . ut :** a rare inversion (in an affirmative sentence)
of the usual form of comparison,
giving up the main clause to the
illustration, and remitting the sub-

ject illustrated to the relative
clause ; cf. Mart. IV. 13. 3 (of a
wedding) *tam bene rara suo mis-
centur cinnama nardo,* | *Massica
Theseis tam bene vina favis.* —
tauriformis : such compounds are
extremely rare in Horace. A river
god was sometimes represented in
the form of a bull with human
face (see Baumeister, I. *fig.* 604,
II. *figg.* 1136 *sq.*), suggested by the
rush and roar of the stream. Cf.
Verg. *G.* IV. 371 *gemina auratus
taurino cornua voltu Eridanus.* —
Aufidus : cf. III. 30. 10 n; Intr. 3.

26. **regna Dauni :** see I. 22.
14 n. — **praefluit :** see 3. 10 n.

29. **Claudius :** *i.e.* Tiberius ; cf.
vs. 14 n ; *Ep.* I. 3. 2. — **agmina
ferrata,** *mailed ranks.* The fact
is not mentioned elsewhere, but
Tacitus (*Ann.* III. 43. 3) mentions
Gallic troops, thirty-five years later,
'*quibus more gentico continuum
ferri tegimen; cruppellarios vocant.*'

30. **diruit :** as if they were a
fortress or a wall ; cf. Tacitus' account of the *cruppellarii* in battle
(*Ann.* III. 46. 6): *paulum morae
attulere ferrati, restantibus laminis*

te copias, te consilium et tuos
praebente divos.　Nam tibi, quo die
35　portus Alexandrea supplex
et vacuam patefecit aulam,

Fortuna lustro prospera tertio
belli secundos reddidit exitus,
laudemque et optatum peractis
40　imperiis decus adrogavit.

Te Cantaber non ante domabilis
Medusque et Indus, te profugus Scythes

adversum pila et gladios; sed miles correptis securibus, ut si murum perrumperet, caedere tegmina et corpora.

31. **metendo**: cf. Verg. *A.* X. 513 *proxima quaeque metit gladio.* For this use of the gerund, cf. 11. 30 n.

32. **stravit humum**: *sc.* with them; cf. III. 17. 9 n. — **sine clade victor**: so also Velleius (I. 95): *Raetos Vindelicosque . . . maiore cum periculo quam damno Romani exercitus, plurimo cum eorum sanguine perdomuerunt.*

33. **te, te, tuos**, etc.: see I. 10. 9 n. — **tuos divos**: *i.e.* the favor of the gods towards Augustus, as revealed in the auspices, was communicated to Tiberius and Drusus, who were simply his *legati;* see I. 7. 27 n.

34. **nam**: referring to **tuos divos**, and introducing the evidence of divine favor. — **quo die**: the 1st of August. The capitulation of Alexandria on that day in B.C. 30 was the end of the civil war, and the senate subsequently (B.C. 8) commemorated the event by changing the former name of the month, *Sextilis,* to *Augustus,* in honor of the emperor.

35. **portus**: there were three of them.

36. **vacuam**: having been deserted by Cleopatra, who had shut herself up in her mausoleum.

37. **lustro tertio**: *i.e.* at the expiration of fifteen years (from that day).　We need not suppose that the coincidence of date was exact, but it must have been near enough to be striking.

38. **reddidit,** *granted* (as something due, something striven for and earned); cf. Cat. 76. 26 *o di, reddite mi hoc pro pietate mea.*

39. **optatum**: cf. 8. 30 n. — **peractis imperiis**: *i.e.* on the deeds done in pursuance of thy orders.

40. **adrogavit,** *bestowed;* cf. *Ep.* II. 1. 35 *scire velim chartis pretium quotus adroget annus.*

41. **Cantaber**: see II. 6. 2 n.

42. **Medus**: see I. 2. 22 n, and IV. 15. 6 n. — **Indus, Scythes**: cf. *C. S.* 55, Suet. *Aug.* 21; *Mon. Anc.* 5. 50 *ad me ex India regum legationes saepe missae sunt, numquam antea visae apud quemquam Romanorum ducem; nostram amicitiam petierunt per legatos Bastarnae Scythaeque.* — **profugus**: cf. I. 35. 9 n.

miratur, o tutela praesens
    Italiae dominaeque Romae ;
45 te fontium qui celat origines
    Nilusque et Hister, te rapidus Tigris,
    te beluosus qui remotis
        obstrepit Oceanus Britannis,
    te non paventis funera Galliae
50 duraeque tellus audit Hiberiae,
    te caede gaudentes Sygambri
        compositis venerantur armis.

43. **tutela**: here in an active sense; cf. 6. 33 n. — **praesens**: cf. III. 5. 2, I. 35. 2 n.

44. **dominae**, *imperial;* cf. 3. 13.

45. **qui celat origines Nilus**: *i.e.* the Nile to its very source, standing for both the Egyptians and the Ethiopians. The source of the Nile was to the ancients much like what the north pole is to us; cf. Lucan X. 189 (Caesar speaks) *nihil est quod noscere malim | quam fluvii causas per saecula tanta latentis | ignotumque caput; spes sit mihi certa videndi | Niliacos fontes, bellum civile relinquam;* 268 *quae tibi noscendi Nilum, Romane, cupido est | et Phariis Persisque fuit Macetumque tyrannis,* etc.

46. **Hister**: standing for the Dacians ; see I. 26. 4 n.—**rapidus**: the name *Tigris* was said to mean 'arrow' (Varro *L. L.* V. 100).— **Tigris**: standing for the Armenians. For this use of the rivers to designate the peoples who dwell on their banks, cf. *Tanais*, III. 29. 28 n, and see II. 20. 20 n.

47. **beluosus**: not found elsewhere in classical Latin ; cf. I. 3. 18, III. 27. 26. The ocean, however, was peopled, by common report, with creatures of monstrous

form, not seen in Mediterranean waters : cf. Tac. *Ann.* II. 24. 6 (of Germanicus' soldiers, driven out into the North Sea in a storm) *ut quisque ex longinquo revenerat, miracula narrabant, . . . inauditas volucres, monstra maris, ambiguas hominum et beluarum formas, visa sive ex metu credita.*

48. **obstrepit Britannis**: cf. II. 18. 20 n.—**Oceanus** : standing, in this context, for the Britons, some of whose chiefs had sent envoys to Augustus to seek the alliance and protection of Rome (Strabo IV. 5. 3).

49. **non paventis funera**: Intr. 51 *a.* This well-known characteristic of the Gauls (cf. Lucan I. 459 *quos ille timorum maximus haud urguet, leti metus*) was attributed to the teachings of the Druids ; cf. Caes. *B. G.* VI. 14. 5 *imprimis hoc volunt persuadere, non interire animas, . . . atque hoc maxime ad virtutem excitari putant, metu mortis neglecto.* — **funera** : Intr. 128. — **Galliae** : like **Hiberiae**, gen. with **tellus** ; Intr. 65, 119 *a.*

50. **audit**, *heeds.*

51. **caede gaudentes**, *bloodthirsty;* cf. *ferocis*, 2. 34. — **Sygambri** : see intr. note to Ode 2.

XV.

Phoebus volentem proelia me loqui
victas et urbis increpuit lyra,
   ne parva Tyrrhenum per aequor
     vela darem.   Tua, Caesar, aetas

XV. This ode, in honor of Augustus, which fittingly closes the volume, is a companion-piece to Ode 14 (just as the similar tribute in Ode 5 was coupled with the praises of Drusus in Ode 4); and as early as the fourth century it was an open question whether the two were not written by Horace as one ode. Porphyrio held that they were, and they so appear in a few of our codices. But although both odes are devoted to the praises of Augustus, the subject is here treated in a different aspect. In Ode 14 Augustus is the invincible champion of Roman safety and supremacy against all nations; here he is the bulwark of peace and prosperity at home, the restorer of good morals and of good old customs, and of that old-time discipline which made Rome great. The ode was probably written not long after the return of Augustus from Gaul in B.C. 13. — Metre, 176.

1. **Phoebus,** etc.: the fancy was suggested to Horace, perhaps, by Verg. *E*. 6. 3 *cum canerem reges et proelia, Cynthius aurem | vellit et admonuit.*—**volentem,** etc.: cf. *Ep*. II. 1. 250 (written about the same time) *nec sermones ego mallem | repentis per humum quam res componere gestas | . . . si quantum cuperem possem quoque,* where, however, he is protesting his unfitness to write epic poetry; here, as in Ode 2, he has in mind lyric treatment (**loqui lyra**) of warlike

themes; cf. I. 6. 5 *sqq*., II. 1. 37 *sqq*.— **proelia**: Intr. 116 *b*. — **loqui**: cf. 2. 45 n.

2. **increpuit ne,** *cried out at me, not to.* Porphyrio explains this correctly: *non 'lyra increpuit,' sed 'volentem me proelia lyra loqui,' id est, lyrico carmine.* Most modern editors take **lyra** with **increpuit,** quoting Ov. *A. A.* II. 493 *haec ego cum canerem, subito manifestus Apollo | movit inauratae pollice fila lyrae.* But there the striking of the lyre is simply to attract the poet's attention to what the god is about to say, and there is no suggestion of 'rebuking with the lyre.' The only reason for this explanation of the text is the position of **increpuit**; but cf. vs. 15, *porrecta;* II. 6. 11 *regnata petam Laconi rura Phalantho;* IV. 1. 19 *Albanos prope te lacus ponet; Epod.* 6. 16 *inultus ut flebo puer.*

3. **parva**: of lyric, in comparison with more stately verse; cf. III. 3. 72, IV. 2. 31, *Ep*. II. 1. 257 *parvum carmen.*— **Tyrrhenum**: Intr. 117 *a.*

4. **vela darem**: a metaphor often used of poetical enterprise; cf. Prop. IV. 9. 3 *quid me scribendi tam vastum mittis in aequor? | non sunt apta meae grandia vela rati;* Verg. *G*. II. 41; Ov. *Tr*. II. 329. —**tua aetas**: put forward, in contrast with the forbidden **proelia,** etc., as a theme affording abundant scope for his lyre, in the varied blessings which he proceeds to recount.

5   fruges et agris rettulit uberes
et signa nostro restituit Iovi
derepta Parthorum superbis
postibus et vacuum duellis
Ianum Quirini clausit et ordinem
10   rectum evaganti frena licentiae
iniecit emovitque culpas
et veteres revocavit artis,

5. **fruges agris rettulit**: *sc.*
after the decay of agriculture due
to the civil wars. — **et . . . et . . .**
etc.: the polysyndeton, continuing
the enumeration without pause
through three strophes, gives the
impression of a throng of benefits pressing for utterance.   This
is succeeded through two more
strophes (vss. 17–24) by an enumeration of averted evils, which
are brought out with individual dis-
tinctness by the anaphora of **non**
(Intr. 116 *f*). Cf. 1. 13 and 29 nn.
6. **signa**: those captured from
Crassus at Carrhae (see III. 5. 5 n)
and Antony (III. 6. 9 n).   In B.C.
20 Augustus, then in the East,
organized an expedition against
the Parthians, and King Phraates,
who was just then in too much
trouble at home to fight the Romans, purchased a peace by sur-
rendering, among other things, the
famous standards.   This demon-
stration of the power of Rome,
without the shedding of a drop of
blood, Horace naturally includes
in his enumeration of the triumphs
of peace.—**nostro,** *our own;* Intr.
116 *b*.—**Iovi**: cf. III. 5. 12 n.   It
appears from this passage that
the standards were first deposited
in the Capitol, and they remained
there during Horace's lifetime.
They were afterwards transferred
to the temple of Mars Ultor (*Mon.*

Anc. 5. 40), but this temple was not
dedicated till B.C. 2.
7. **derepta**: hardly accurate, as
denoting eagerness or indignation
in the act, but well expressing the
feelings of the Romans.
8. **postibus**: *sc.* of their temples ; cf. *Ep.* I. 18. 57 *sub duce* (*i.e.*
Augusto) *qui templis Parthorum*
signa refigit.—**duellis**: Intr. 66 *c*, N.
9. **Ianum Quirini**: the famous
temple of Janus, a short distance
from the northern corner of the
Forum.   Horace purposely varies
from the official and prosaic designation, *Ianus Quirinus*, which
he evidently understood to mean
'Gateway of Quirinus' (Intr. 65);
cf. Ov. *M.* XIV. 836 *colle Quirini*
(= *Quirinali*).   Tradition ascribed
to Numa both the temple itself
and the injunction to close it only
in time of peace (Liv. I. 19. 2).—
clausit: for the first time in more
than 200 years.   It was closed
three times under Augustus (*Mon.*
Anc. 2. 42), — B.C. 29, 25, and a
third date, not definitely known,
but later than the composition of
this ode. — **ordinem evaganti**:
Intr. 51 *f*. The figure is military.
10. **frena licentiae iniecit**: cf.
III. 24. 29.
12. **artis,** *virtues*, as the context
shows ; cf. III. 3. 9 n.
13. **nomen**: cf. III. 3. 45. —
Italae: cf. II. 13. 18, III. 30. 13 n.

per quas Latinum nomen et Italae
crevere vires famaque et imperi
15   porrecta maiestas ad ortus
solis ab Hesperio cubili.

Custode rerum Caesare non furor
civilis aut vis exiget otium,
non ira, quae procudit ensis
20   et miseras inimicat urbis.

Non qui profundum Danuvium bibunt
edicta rumpent Iulia, non Getae,
non Seres infidive Persae,
non Tanain prope flumen orti.

14. **imperi**: for the position, see Intr. 119 a.

15. **porrecta**: sc. *est*. With maiestas it means 'made widely known and felt.' — **ortus solis**: poetical for *orientem* (*solem*). The plural is that of repeated occurrence (Intr. 128), *i.e.* not the places (regions of the East) where the sun rises, but the part of the earth (the East) where it rises day by day; cf. 5. 8 n. With the whole phrase, cf. Sall. *Cat.* 36. 4 *cum ad occasus ab ortu solis omnia domita armis parerent.*

17. **custode**, etc.: cf. 5. 2, III. 14. 15 *sq.* — **furor civilis**, *political madness* (= *civium ardor prava iubentium*, III. 3. 2); distinct from **ira**, below; cf. I. 37. 12, III. 27. 36.

18. **exiget**: used in this literal sense, with rare exceptions, only of persons (cf. II. 13. 31), and therefore in keeping with the half personification which runs through the whole sentence.

19. **ira, quae**, etc.: cf. I. 16. 18 *sqq.*

20. **miseras**: proleptic. — **ini-** micat: called by Porphyrio a *fictum verbum*, *i.e.* coined by Horace.

21. **qui Danuvium bibunt**: cf. II. 20. 20 n. The frontier of the empire was firmly established on the Danube by Augustus before he died, and remained so for centuries; but at this time the conquest of the tribes on the south bank was only half accomplished, and their submission had not lost, to Horace's readers, the impressiveness of novelty.

22. **edicta Iulia**: a general expression for the orders issued by Augustus and the terms imposed by him. — **rumpent**: the future is in keeping with the fact, stated above: the nations named will be reduced to obedience and made to keep the peace. — **Getae**: see III. 24. 11 n.

23. **Seres**: cf. I. 12. 56 n. — **infidi**: cf. *Ep.* II. 1. 112 *Parthis mendacior*, and see note on *perfidus*, 4. 49. — **Persae**: see I. 2. 22 n.

24. **Tanain prope orti**: cf. vs. 21 n, and see III. 29. 28 n.

25   Nosque et profestis lucibus et sacris
       inter iocosi munera Liberi,
          cum prole matronisque nostris
          rite deos prius adprecati,

       virtute functos more patrum duces
30   Lydis remixto carmine tibiis
          Troiamque et Anchisen et almae
          progeniem Veneris canemus.

25. **nos** : in contrast with the foreigners. The close of the ode is similar to that of Ode 5. — **et profestis et sacris** : *i.e.* every day alike. The picture is of cheerful every-day life, not merely of occasional enjoyment on holidays (cf. vs. 27 n). — **lucibus** : cf. 6. 42 n, 11. 19.

26. **iocosi** : cf. III. 21. 15 n. — **munera Liberi** : cf. 10. 1 n.

27. **cum prole**, etc.: *i.e.* each in his own family circle.

28. **adprecati** : a rare word, found only here in classical Latin.

29. **virtute functos**, *whose good work is done.* For the form of expression, see note on *functum laboribus*, II. 18. 38. — **more patrum** : with **canemus.** The custom was recorded by the elder Cato ; cf. Cic. *Tusc.* IV. 3 *in Originibus dixit Cato morem apud maiores hunc epularum fuisse, ut deinceps qui accubarent canerent ad tibiam clarorum virorum laudes atque virtutes.*

30. **Lydis** : said by Donatus (on Ter. *Ad., Praef.*) to have been suited to grave themes.—**remixto**:

another rare word, used also *Ep.* II. 3. 151, but not found elsewhere before Seneca. The **re-** lends to the action a suggestion of iteration or persistence, as in *respergo.* — **tibiis** : here ablative, the instrument being secondary to the song.

31. **-que** : introducing a distinct topic (cf. *famaque* 14, *nosque* 25), — the Julian line, which stands preëminent among the great throng of Roman worthies, and is a subject that takes us back to Troy and the divine founders of the Roman race. — **Anchisen et progeniem Veneris** : *i.e.* Anchises and Venus and their offspring, — different from *C. S.* 50 *Anchisae Venerisque sanguis* (*i.e.* Augustus). The theme of song is to be the whole Julian house ; but the interest, of course, centres in the one great figure who represented the house to Horace and his readers. The compliment to Augustus is indirect, but no less obvious than if he had been mentioned by name ; cf. *Iulium sidus*, I. 12. 47 n. — **almae** : cf. Lucr. I. 2 *alma Venus*, and see 5. 18 n.

CARMEN SAECVLARE.

In the summer of B.C. 17 Augustus instituted a remark-able festival, — one that, in the words of the herald who proclaimed the coming event, no living man had ever seen or would ever see again. The Quindecimviri, who had charge of the Sibylline Books, had produced an oracle which called for the celebration of the *ludi saeculares*.

The origin of this long forgotten festival was obscure. It appears to have grown out of the *ludi Terentini*, a religious observance associated with the oldest traditions of the Valerian family, and with a place in the Campus Martius called Terentum (or Tarentum), where there were hot springs and other evidences of volcanic influence. It was on the banks of the river, at the great bend below the Ponte San Angelo. The healing properties of these springs were said to have been first revealed to Valesius the Sabine, who commemorated his gratitude for the miraculous healing of his three children by the institution of sacrifices, with other ceremonies and entertainments, on three suc-cessive nights, at the ancient subterranean altar of Dis and Proserpina, which under the guidance of an oracle he had discovered on this spot. (See Val. Max. II. 4. 7.)

Tradition ascribed the first celebration of the *ludi Teren-tini* as a public institution to the consul Valerius Poplicola, in the first year of the Commonwealth, and mentioned sub-sequent celebrations by other Valerii. The first celebration known to history occurred about the middle of the third century B.C. It was instituted under instructions from the Sibylline Books, which had been consulted in consequence of certain alarming portents; and the oracle gave further directions that the celebration should be renewed every hundred years (Varro *ap*. Censor. 17. 7). It was at this time, then, according to Varro, that the *ludi Terentini* became *ludi saeculares*.

A *saeculum* was the longest span of human life. It was an idea borrowed from the Etruscans, in whose system, we are told, the life of a city or a state was measured in *saecula*, as a man's life is measured in years. The first *saeculum* was the life of that one of the children born at the time of founding the city who survived all his fellows; the second *saeculum* began at his death, and was measured in the same way; and so on. This system, which of course never existed except in theory, left the length of the *saeculum* a variable quantity, and when the Romans came to fix it arbitrarily, there was a conflict of views and of practice. Varro's notion of a *saeculum* was 100 years (*L. L.* VI. 11); and according to Livy (*Perioch*. XLIX) a celebration of the *ludi Terentini* at the beginning of the third Punic war occurred a hundred years after the last preceding celebration. The Quindecimviri under Augustus, on the other hand, found in their Sibylline oracle (vs. 2), — which, whatever its origin, was composed apparently as early as the Social war, — 110 years as the length of the *saeculum* (cf. *C. S.* 21). As the accounts of celebrations in the past were imperfect and contradictory, it is evident that there was room for wide divergence of opinion as to the proper year for celebrating the jubilee. The Quindecimviri found or constructed in their records a series of four dates, at intervals of 110 years, at which the festival had been, or ought to have been, observed; and the celebration of B.C. 17

was set down as the fifth. The emperor Claudius, taking
100 years as his *saeculum* and the foundation of the city as
his starting-point, celebrated the festival in A.D. 47 (A.V.C.
800); so that some people who witnessed the pageant
under Augustus did live to see it again, after all. Domitian
chose the year 88 ; for what reason, is not clear. The ninth
centennial of the city was celebrated by Antoninus Pius.
Subsequent celebrations are recorded for A.D. 204 (2 × 110
years from B.C. 17), 247 (A.V.C. 1000), 259, and 298.

Vergil's fourth eclogue shows that certainly as early as
B.C. 40, when the poem was written, and probably much
earlier, a Sibylline oracle was current, which foretold the
near approach of a regeneration of the world and the advent
of a new Golden Age. It was perhaps this prophecy and
the expectations and aspirations roused by it that suggested
to Augustus and his advisers the policy of signalizing his
reign as a new era of peace and happiness by celebrating
the *ludi saeculares* with a magificence that would at once
please and impress the people. The main outlines of the
celebration were prescribed by the oracle, which has been
preserved (Zosimus II. 5), and the details were worked out
by Ateius Capito, the most learned expert of the time in
pontifical law. Everything was done to make the occasion
memorable, and a lasting record was provided by the erection of two columns, one of marble and one of bronze,
inscribed with a full account of the celebration. These
monuments, which must have stood many centuries, were
finally destroyed and their material turned to other uses ;
but in 1890 some fragments of the marble column were
exhumed in the neighborhood of Terentum, and a considerable portion of the inscription was thus recovered.* It

---

* The inscription was edited, with a commentary, by Mommsen in
the *Monumenti Antichi della Reale Accademia dei Lincei*, Vol. I., p. 618
(1891). The article has also been printed separately.

originally consisted of 168 lines, and contained full particulars of all the preparations for the festival and of the
celebration itself, including the text of decrees, formulas of
prayer, and minute details of the ritual.

The celebration was preceded by a '*distributio suffimen-
torum*' and a '*frugum acceptio.*' For three days (May 26–28)
citizens who presented themselves, with their wives and
children, at certain designated places on the Capitoline and
Palatine, were supplied by the magistrates with pitch-pine,
sulphur, and bitumen (*suffimenta*) for purposes of purification. During the following three days the magistrates
received from the citizens offerings of wheat, barley, and
beans (*fruges*), which were used in part to remunerate the
musicians and actors in the scenic performances. The celebration proper began in the night before June 1, and was
continued without interruption through three nights and
three days. The addition of the three days, in which the
gods of heaven were joined in the honors of the festival,
was a signal departure from the old *ludi Terentini*, which
were devoted wholly to the gods of the underworld. The
ceremonies were all conducted by Augustus in person,
partly with the assistance of Agrippa. They took place by
night 'in campo ad Tiberim,' *i.e.* at Terentum ; by day, at
the appropriate temples.

The sacrifices of the first night were whole burnt offerings
(*hostiae prodigivae*), nine she-lambs and nine she-goats,
to the Fates (*Moerae;* cf. *C. S.* 25 *sqq.*). On the second
night the Ilithyiae (cf. *C. S.* 13 *sqq.*) were propitiated with
oblations of consecrated cakes ; and on the third a pregnant sow was sacrificed to Mother Earth (*Terra mater;*
cf. *C. S.* 29 *sqq.*). The sacrifices of the first night were
followed by scenic entertainments, which were given, as in
the days of Plautus, on a temporary stage, with no seats
provided for the audience (IN SCAENA QVOI THEATRVM

ADIECTVM NON FVIT, NVLLIS POSITIS SEDILIBVS). These
'*ludi Latini scaenici*' were kept up without interruption
through the three nights and days, but after the first night
they were given IN THEATRO LIGNEO QVOD ERAT CONSTI-
TVTVM SECVNDVM TIBERIM. The *ludi scaenici* of the third
day were followed by *ludi circenses* in a temporary circus
near the same place, and the people were further entertained by a series of scenic performances and other shows
not prescribed by the oracle (*ludi honorarii*), which lasted
seven days after the close of the festival proper (June 4–11).
The religious ceremonies of the first night were supple-
mented by *sellisternia* in honor of Juno and Diana (*i.e.*
Lucinae duae, according to Mommsen), conducted by 110
matrons ; and these were repeated on the following days.

On the first *day* of the festival (June 1) Augustus and
Agrippa each sacrificed a white bull to Jupiter, and on the
second day each a white cow to Juno Regina, on the
Capitol ; and after the latter sacrifice and its accompanying
prayers, Augustus (probably) led the 110 matrons in a
special prayer to Juno. On the third day the chief ceremonies were on the Palatine at the temple of Apollo
(cf. I. 31, intr. note), where Augustus and Agrippa made an
offering of consecrated cakes to Apollo and Diana. 'And
on the completion of the sacrifice,' the inscription goes on,
'27 boys who had been summoned for this service, sons of
fathers and mothers still living (*patrimi et matrimi*), and
as many girls, sang a hymn ; and in the same way on
the Capitol. The hymn was composed by Q. Horatius
Flaccus.'

It is clear from these words that Horace's hymn was first
sung on the Palatine, and that it was also sung on the
Capitol. Mommsen supposes that it was sung in solemn
procession from the Palatine to the Capitol and back, the
middle strophes, where the sacrifice of white cattle by

Augustus (vs. 49) evidently refers to the offerings of the first and second days, being sung on the Capitol itself. There was in all probability a procession, but the inscription does not connect the hymn with it in any way. In the hymn, not only Jupiter and Juno are invoked, but all the divinities who were honored in the whole festival; and Jupiter is appealed to, not in the middle strophes alone, but in the closing verses, where the chorus confidently claims the favor of 'Jove and all the gods.' There seems to be no good reason to depart from the plain meaning of the words of the inscription, that the ceremonies of the Palatine in their main features, including the singing of the hymn, were repeated on the Capitol; for the words EODEMQUE MODO IN CAPITOLIO do not appear to refer to the hymn alone. The explanation is perhaps to be found in the fact that the ceremonies of this third day were evidently the crowning event of the whole festival; and that while Augustus was desirous of exalting his patron god Apollo to the position of patron god of Rome, he may not, or his religious advisers may not, have felt at liberty to exclude the old gods of the Roman state from the honors of the day.

Horace adopted for his hymn the Sapphic strophe (Intr. 174). A striking feature of the poem is the very large proportion of feminine caesuras. It was rendered, we must assume, with instrumental accompaniment, and was made, for those who heard it, a beautiful and impressive performance. The number of the chorus, 27 of each sex, was prescribed by the ritual, as we may infer from Liv. XXVII. 37. 7 and XXXI. 12. 9, where choirs of 27 maidens are mentioned as singing hymns especially composed for ceremonies of propitiation. In every case, however, the number is stated not as 'twenty-seven,' but as 'thrice nine,' which probably had some religious significance connected with the number three, but may have been used as a sub-division for musical purposes. The division of the chorus into two main groups (boys and girls) was prescribed by the oracle (χωρὶς δὲ κόραι χορὸν αὐταὶ ἔχοιεν | καὶ χωρὶς παίδων ἄρσην στάχυς, vs. 20). The distribution of the various parts of the hymn between the two half-choirs, or among smaller groups, was probably a complicated matter ; at any rate, it cannot now be determined. The only indications in the hymn itself are in the ninth strophe (vss. 33-36), which was apparently divided between the two half-choirs, and in the first two and the last, which were probably sung by the full choir. Beyond this neither poem nor inscription gives any light.

Phoebe silvarumque potens Diana,
lucidum caeli decus, o colendi
semper et culti, date quae precamur
    tempore sacro,

5   quo Sibyllini monuere versus

1. **Phoebe, Diana**: although the hymn belongs in a sense to the whole festival and invokes in turn all the gods who were worshipped in the various ceremonies, it was first sung at the rites in honor of Apollo and Diana, before their temple on the Palatine, and these two deities are given a correspond-ing preëminence in it. This ar-rangement was determined by the policy of Augustus to raise the Palatine Apollo to the position of especial guardian of the Ro-man state. — **silvarum potens**: cf. *nemorum* (*custos*), III. 22. 1 n, and for this use of *potens*, I. 3. 1 n. — **Dïana**: cf. vs. 70, and see Intr. 178.

2. **decus**: referring to both di-vinities (as Sol and Luna ; cf. vss. 9, 36).—**colendi et culti**: *i.e.* who shall be worshipped in the future, as in the past; a comprehensive phrase, perhaps borrowed from the ritual, like our 'As it was in the beginning, is now, and ever shall be.' For the tenses, cf. *tulit et feret, Ep.* I. 7. 21 (Intr. 80).

5. **quo**: with **dicere**, vs. 8. — **versus**: they were Greek hexam-eters. The old Sibylline books, which King Tarquin was said to have purchased of the Sibyl, were burnt up in the fire which destroyed the Capitol in B.C. 83, but a new collection of oracles had since been gathered from various sources.

virgines lectas puerosque castos
dis quibus septem placuere colles
dicere carmen.

Alme Sol, curru nitido diem qui
10   promis et celas, aliusque et idem
nasceris, possis nihil urbe Roma
visere maius.

Rite maturos aperire partus
lenis, Ilithyia, tuere matres,
15   sive tu Lucina probas vocari
seu Genitalis.

6. **lectas, castos**: both attributes belong to the whole chorus;
Intr. 121. For **lectas**, cf. IV. 6.
31, and see introd. note.

7. **dis**: referring to the gods in
general. — **placuere** : used here,
as in III. 4. 24, like the perfect of
an inceptive verb; Rome has won
(and now enjoys, is established in)
their favor.

8. **dicere carmen**: cf. *dic melos*,
III. 4. 1 n.

9. **alme** : cf. *almum diem* IV.
7. 7 n.—**Sol** : so also in the oracle,
vs. 16 Φοῖβος Ἀπόλλων, | ὅστε καὶ
Ἥλιος κικλήσκεται.—**diem celas**:
i.e. by taking the day with him, as
it were, when he 'hides' his chariot
(under the earth); a poetical expression of the fact that night, as
well as day, is due to the sun; cf.
III. 6. 44.

10. **alius et idem** : *i.e.* through
all change forever the same. It
introduces the following prayer,
as if he had said ' In thy everlast-
ing course mayest thou,' etc.

12. **visere**: cf. I. 37. 25, II. 15. 3.

13. **aperire**: see Intr. 101 *a*, 102.

14. **lenis** : a part of the prayer.
— **Ilithyia** : goddess of the labor
of childbirth. In Homer she is

sometimes one (*Odys.* XIX. 188),
usually more in number, as *Il.*
XI. 270, where the Εἰλείθυιαι are
daughters of Hera. See Preller-
Robert, *Gr. Myth.* I. 511. In the
ceremonies of the second night
the offerings were made DEIS
[I]LITHYIS, but the prayer began
ILITHYIA VTI TIBI, etc.; so that
they do not appear to have been
regarded as distinct divinities, but
as one; as a 'diva triformis,' perhaps, but not distinctly identified
with Diana. Here, however, this
identity (cf. III. 22. 2 *sq*.) is silently
assumed, furnishing, as it does,
an excellent justification of the
prominence which the policy of
Augustus required to be given to
Diana.

15. **sive tu**, etc. = *vel Lucina,
si tu Lucina probas vocari, vel*,
etc.; cf. I. 2. 33 n. It was supposed to be pleasing to the gods
to be addressed by many titles,
and the choice of names was also
a pious precaution against giving
offense to a divinity, especially one
whose personality was so elusive
as in this case. Cf. Cat. 34. 21
*sis quocumque tibi placet | sancta
nomine*, and Callim. *Hymn. in*

Diva, producas subolem patrumque
prosperes decreta super iugandis
feminis prolisque novae feraci
    lege marita,

20

certus undenos deciens per annos
orbis ut cantus referatque ludos,
ter die claro totiensque grata
    nocte frequentis.

25   Vosque veraces cecinisse, Parcae,

Dian. 7, where Artemis prays Zeus for πολυωνυμίη. — **Lucina**: see III. 22. 2 n. — **vocari**: Intr. 94 *a*.

16. **Genitalis**: not found elsewhere as a title of this goddess; perhaps intended as the Latin equivalent of Γενετυλλίς, which was an epithet of Aphrodite, and was also used in the plural, like Εἰλείθυιαι, to denote attendant divinities who presided over childbirth (Preller-Robert I. 377, with n. 4).

17. **producas**, *rear;* cf. II. 13. 3. For the mood, see Intr. 87. — **patrum decreta**, etc.: the measure referred to was really a law (*lex Iulia de maritandis ordinibus*), passed by the votes of the *comitia*, with the approval of the senate, which was very reluctantly given; but it was the policy of Augustus to govern through the senate, which became, from now on, the law-making body of the empire, although the *comitia* continued to be held some years longer. The law was passed in B.C. 18. It discouraged celibacy by penalties, and encouraged marriage and the raising of children by relaxing somewhat the strictness of the conditions of legal marriage and by conferring on fathers of three or more children certain privileges

and immunities. See Merivale, Ch. XXXIII.

18. **super**: see I. 9. 5 n. Its use with the gerundive is very rare.

19. **prolis**: Intr. 66 *a*.

20. **marita**: see Intr. 65, and cf. Prop. V. 11. 33 *facibus maritis*.

21. **certus**, etc.: the two emphatic words of the strophe are the first and last (Intr. 116 *b*), the rest being a poetical paraphrase for the *saeculum* and the festival (see intr. note). The goddess is implored to propagate the race, that the repetition of the jubilee, age after age, may be assured (**certus**), and that each festival may be celebrated by great throngs of citizens. — **per**: *i.e.* extending through; the prepositional phrase here taking the place of a defining genitive (Madv. 298. 2).

22. **orbis**, *cycle.*— **ut**: Intr. 114. — **referatque**: Intr. 119 *b*.

25. **cecinisse**: see I. 15. 4 n, and, for the construction, Intr. 102. — **Parcae**: the Μοῖραι of the oracle and the inscription, who were worshipped on the first night. They were usually represented as three aged sisters, forever spinning the thread of destiny; see Cat. 64. 305 *sqq.* Originally goddesses of childbirth, their functions had special reference, on the one hand, to

quod semel dictum est stabilisque rerum
　　terminus servet, bona iam peractis
　　　　iungite fata.

Fertilis frugum pecorisque Tellus
30　spicea donet Cererem corona ;
　　nutriant fetus et aquae salubres
　　　　et Iovis aurae.

Condito mitis placidusque telo
　　supplices audi pueros, Apollo ;
35　siderum regina bicornis audi,
　　　　Luna, puellas.

the individual (see II. 3. 15 n);
but in a wider sense they were
regarded as developing the general course of human events in
accordance with the righteous decrees of an omnipotent power. Cf.
Hes. *Theog.* 904, where they are
the daughters of Zeus and Themis.

26. **quod semel dictum est:**
a paraphrase for *fatum ;* cf. III. 3.
58 n. It refers to the whole course
of Roman destiny, past and to
come. For **semel,** see I. 24. 16 n.
—**stabilisque:** for *quodque stabi-
lis* (cf. I. 1. 5 n), in which *quod*
(unlike the first **quod**) is the object
of its verb. — **rerum terminus:**
a figurative expression for immutable destiny; cf. Verg. *A.* IV.
614 *et sic fata Iovis poscunt, hic
terminus haeret.*

27. **servet:** optative subjunctive, hardly consistent with **semel
dictum est;** but the inconsistency
is no greater than we usually fall
into when we grapple with the
problem of free will and fate. It
anticipates the prayer that follows
(**bona,** etc.), which is also superfluous, if we insist on strict logical
consistency.

29. **fertilis frugum pecoris-**

que: a part of the prayer. For
the genitives, see Intr. 66 *a.* With
pecoris, *fecundus* would be more
usual, but cf. *S.* II. 4. 31 *mare
fertile testae,* Liv. V. 34. 2 (*Gallia*)
frugum hominumque fertilis. —
Tellus : worshipped as *Terra
Mater* on the third night.

30. **spicea,** etc.: a prayer for
abundant harvests. The figure is
based on the practice of making
an offering of first fruits to Ceres
in the shape of a wreath of ripe
ears of grain ; cf. Tib. I. 1. 15
*flava Ceres, tibi sit nostro de rure
corona | spicea, quae templi pendeat
ante foris ;* II. 1. 4 *spicis tempora
cinge, Ceres.*

31. **fetus:** of the *fruges* only,
continuing the thought of vs. 30.
—**salubres, Iovis:** Intr. 121. For
Iovis, see I. 1. 25 n.

33–36. After invoking in turn
the powers to whom the nocturnal
rites of the festival were dedicated,
the chorus closes this part of the
hymn with an interlude, addressed
to Apollo and Diana, which, however, is not disconnected in thought
with the preceding : Apollo spares
man and beast from pestilence (cf.
I. 21. 13 *sqq.*), Diana (as Luna)

Roma si vestrum est opus Iliaeque
litus Etruscum tenuere turmae,
iussa pars mutare laris et urbem
40   sospite cursu,

cui per ardentem sine fraude Troiam
castus Aeneas patriae superstes
liberum munivit iter, daturus
        plura relictis,

45   di, probos mores docili iuventae,
di, senectuti placidae quietem,
Romulae genti date remque prolemque
        et decus omne ;

gives increase to the crops (cf. IV.
6. 38 *sqq.*).

33. **condito telo**: see II. 10. 18
n. This is the attitude in which
he was represented in the Palatine
temple; see Baumeister p. 99.

35. **siderum regina**: cf. I. 12.
47 *sq.*, *Epod.* 15. 1 *sq.* — **bicornis**:
in reference to the two points of
the crescent; cf. IV. 2. 57 *sqq.*

37. **Roma**, etc.: here begins an
invocation to the great gods of
the Roman state, the gods of the
Capitol, and more particularly Jupiter and Juno, who were honored
on the first and second days of
the festival (see vss. 49 *sq.*). — **si**:
cf. III. 18. 5 n. Here the appeal is
to the interest of the gods in their
own handiwork. — **Iliae**: Intr. 65.

38. **litus Etruscum**: here for
the coast generally about the
mouth of the Tiber. — **tenuere**,
gained; cf. Liv. I. 37. 4 *montes
Sabini petebant, et pauci tenuere.*

39. **iussa pars**: *i.e.* if they were
a remnant under divine protection
(**sospite**) and guidance. In this
dependent clause, and especially
in iussa (Intr. 116 *b*), lies the gist

of the whole condition, which is
concerned, not with the well-known
fact of the migration of the Trojans to Italy, but with its explanation. — **laris**, *their homes.*

40. **cursu**: with **mutare**.

41. **sine fraude**: cf. II. 19. 20 n.

42. **castus**: in contrast with the
wickedness of the rest, which had
brought down the wrath of the
gods upon them; cf. III. 3. 18 *sqq.*
It is equivalent to Vergil's constant epithet, *pius.* — **patriae**: dative; cf. *mihi, Epod.* 5. 101.

43. **daturus**: Intr. 104 *b.*

44. **plura relictis**: *i.e.* a greater
city than Troy.

45. **probos mores**, etc.: in keeping with the policy of Augustus,
which this jubilee was meant to
emphasize, the blessings of peace
are made most prominent in this
prayer. — **docili, placidae**: both
proleptic and a part of the prayer;
intimating a fit state of mind on
the part of the citizens as a requisite condition of receiving the
blessing.

47. **Romulae**: Intr. 65.—**rem**,
wealth.—**prolemque**: Intr. 174 *b.*

quaeque vos bobus veneratur albis
50   clarus Anchisae Venerisque sanguis,
impetret, bellante prior, iacentem
lenis in hostem.

Iam mari terraque manus potentis
Medus Albanasque timet securis,
55   iam Scythae responsa petunt, superbi
nuper, et Indi.

49. **quae veneratur:** for this use of *veneror* with the construction of a verb of asking, cf. *S.* II. 6. 8 *si veneror stultus nihil horum.* — **bobus albis:** the sacrifices of the first and second days, as the inscription records. The tenor of the prayer to each of the two deities was in the main as follows: *Iuppiter optime maxime* (or *Iuno regina*) . . . *te quaeso precorque uti imperium maiestatemque populi Romani Quiritium duelli domique auxis, utique semper Latinum nomen tuearis, incolumitatem sempiternam victoriam valetudinem populo Romano Quiritibus tribuas, faveasque populo Romano Quiritibus legionibusque populi Romani Quiritium, remque publicam populi Romani Quiritium salvam serves, uti sis volens propitius populo Romano Quiritibus XVrum collegio mihi domo familiae.*

50. **sanguis:** *i.e.* descendant; cf. II. 20. 6, III. 27. 65, IV. 2. 14. This paraphrase for Augustus, instead of the use of his name, is more in keeping with the proprieties of the occasion, and also served, like **Romulae genti,** to keep up the main thought of the whole sentence, — the connection between Rome's present and future and her divinely ordered beginnings.

51. **bellante prior,** etc. : cf.

Vergil's famous *parcere subiectis et debellare superbos* (*A.* VI. 853). The thought is here the same : *tu regere imperio populos, Romane, memento, . . . pacique imponere morem.* Victory is the stepping-stone to peace and order (see vs. 45 n). This is set forth more fully in the next two strophes : in the first, victory ; in the second, the advent of peace and her attendant blessings.

53. **iam,** etc.: from this point on the chorus abandons the attitude of supplication to the gods and assumes that of confidence in their favor; cf. *Ep.* II. 1. 134 *poscit opem chorus et praesentia numina sentit.*

54. **Medus, Scythae, Indi:** cf. IV. 14. 42 n.—**Albanas:** for 'Roman,' with the same suggestion as above (see vs. 50 n).

55. **responsa petunt:** a phrase implying recognized superiority in the power appealed to, being applied commonly to the consultation of an oracle or to an embassy coming to the senate with a definite request or a question to be settled.

57. **Fides,** etc.: most, if not all, of these personified abstractions were deified and worshipped by the Romans. For **Fides,** see I. 35. 22 n. Augustus erected an altar to **Pax** on the Campus Mar-

Iam Fides et Pax et Honor Pudorque
priscus et neglecta redire Virtus
audet, adparetque beata pleno
60   Copia cornu.

Augur et fulgente decorus arcu
Phoebus acceptusque novem Camenis,
qui salutari levat arte fessos
    corporis artus,

65 si Palatinas videt aequus aras,
remque Romanam Latiumque felix
alterum in lustrum meliusque semper
    prorogat aevum ;

tius, and instituted stated sacrifices. **Honos** (*Good Repute*) had a
temple in connection with **Virtus**
(*Manly Worth*). For **Pudor priscus**, cf. I. 24. 6 and 7 n. For **Copia**,
cf. *Ep.* I. 12. 28 *aurea fruges* | *Ita-
liae pleno defundit Copia cornu*,
and I. 17. 14 n.

59. **audet**: Intr. 77.
61. **augur Phoebus**: cf. I. 2.
32.—**et** : Intr. 114.— **fulgente** :
in Homer his bow is silver (as *Il.*
I. 37, 49); in the other poets sometimes golden (*e.g.* Pind. *Ol.* 14. 10).
Here the bow is simply ornamental
(cf. **decorus** and vs. 33 n); Apollo
is relied upon as the prophet-god
who foresees the happy future, and
who promotes it as patron of arts
and letters and as god of healing.
These are his chief functions, for
which the poet finds a place here;
they could not well be brought in
at the outset (vs. 9), in the form
which the invocation there took.

62. **acceptus Camenis** : cf. II.
10. 18. For **Camenis**, see I. 12.
39 n.

63. **qui**, etc.: cf. I. 21. 13 *sqq.*,
and see Preller-Robert, *Gr. Myth.*

I. 277.—**fessos**, *enfeebled* (*sc.* by
sickness); a poetical use of the
word adopted by later prose writers ; cf. Cat. 64. 188 *non tamen
ante mihi languescent lumina mor-
te*, | *nec prius a fesso secedent cor-
pore sensus*, etc.; Tac. *Ann.* II. 71.
1 *fesso corpore, ubi finis* (*i.e.* mors)
aderat.

64. **corporis artus**, *our frame ;*
cf. Lucr. III. 128 *est igitur calor
ac ventus vitalis in ipso* | *cor-
pore, qui nobis moribundos deserit
artus.*

65. **si**: the conditional form implies no doubt of the truth of the
proposition, but puts it, with full
confidence, as the basis of the
conviction expressed in the conclusion ; cf. vs. 37, and III. 18.
5 n. — **aequus** : cf. I. 2. 47 n. —
aras : Intr. 128.

66. **remque**, etc.: a reminiscence, perhaps, of Enn. *Ann.* 477
M. *audire est operae pretium, pro-
cedere recte* | *qui rem Romanam
Latiumque augescere voltis.*—**felix** :
proleptic, with **Latium**.

67. **alterum** : see III. 5. 34 n.
The idea is 'from *lustrum* to *lu-*

quaeque Aventinum tenet Algidumque
70   quindecim Diana preces virorum
curat et votis puerorum amicas
adplicat auris.

Haec Iovem sentire deosque cunctos
spem bonam certamque domum reporto,
75   doctus et Phoebi chorus et Dianae
dicere laudes.

strum.' The word is chosen probably with reference to the successive periods of five years for which
Augustus received the *imperium.*
— **semper**: see note on *usque,*
III. 30. 7.

69. **Aventinum**: the seat of
the chief temple of Diana in Rome,
built originally, under Servius Tullius, as a common shrine of all the
Latin communities. — **tenet**: cf.
III. 4. 62 n. — **Algidum** : see I.
21. 6 n.

70. **quindecim virorum** : a
board, originally of two members
(*IIviri sacris faciundis*), charged
with the safe-keeping and interpretation of the Sibylline books,
and with the conduct of certain
religious ceremonies. The number
was increased to ten, then to fifteen, with corresponding change
of name. At this time, however,
there were actually 21 members,
with Agrippa as *magister conlegi.*
No prayers offered by them on
this occasion are mentioned, but
they took a leading part in all the
ceremonies, and prescribed the
forms of prayer. — **Diana** : cf. vs.
1 n.

71. **votis adplicat auris**: cf.
S. I. 1. 22 *votis ut praebeat au-
rem.* — **puerorum,** *children ;* cf.
Ep. I. 7. 7 *pueris pater et mater-
cula pallet.* In old Latin the singular also was used of either sex ;
cf. Naev. *Bell. Pun.* 30 M. *Cereris
puer, Proserpina.*

72. **curat, adplicat**: emphatic;
Intr. 116 *b.*

73. **haec sentire** (depending on
spem), *that this is the mind of ;*
referring to what has been said in
the last three strophes. Apollo
and Diana, who have assumed as
their special charge the welfare of
Rome, have done so with the full
consent and good will of all the
gods.

74. **reporto** : the chorus speaks
in the singular number, as in the
Greek drama ; cf. *dices,* IV. 6. 41 n.

75. **doctus,** etc.: cf. IV. 6. 43.
Phoebi et Dianae : with **laudes.**

76. **dicere** : see I. 6. 5 n.

Q. HORATI FLACCI

EPODON

LIBER

I.

Ibis Liburnis inter alta navium,
amice, propugnacula,

For a general account of the Epodes and the significance of the name, see Intr. 18–20.

I. This epode, which serves as a virtual dedication of the collection to Maecenas, is characterized by a much warmer expression of feeling than any of the other dedicatory poems, belonging as it does to a period when the poet's place in his patron's regard was assured, but the impulse of affection and gratitude had not yet lost its freshness. The occasion was the proposed departure of Maecenas, in the spring of B.C. 31, for the seat of war. Octavian, before setting out for the campaign of Actium, summoned all the most influential senators and knights to join him at Brundisium; and Maecenas naturally went with the rest. In this poem Horace begs to be allowed to go to the war with him, pleading the unhappiness and anxiety he would suffer if separated from his friend, while deprecating the suspicion of any selfish motive. Maecenas, it seems most probable, did not actually cross the sea, but returned to take charge of Rome and Italy during the absence of his chief (Dio LI. 3. 5, Vell. II. 88. 2), — though some scholars, in spite of these authorities, hold that he was present at the battle; and some think, mainly on supposed evidence in Epode 9, that Horace was with him. But the indications of that poem are very slight, and have little weight against the absence of any positive testimony and the silence of Horace himself. — Metre, 1 59.

1. **ibis**: the emphasis may be compared with that of *C.* I. 7. 26, II. 17. 10, *Ep.* II. 2. 39. In these instances, however, the emphasis is that of assurance; here it is that of reluctant conviction: 'You are really going!' The tone is half interrogative. Cf. Tibullus' appeal to Messala under the same circumstances: *Ibitis Aegaeas sine me, Messala, per undas*, I. 3. 1. — **Liburnis**: see *C.* I. 37. 30 n. The abl. is instrumental, though we render it with *in;* cf. Liv. XXVIII. 9. 10 *quadrigis urbem ineuntem.* — **alta**: in contrast with the light Liburnian biremes; suggesting the peril Maecenas will incur.

2. **propugnacula,** *battlements.*

paratus omne Caesaris periculum
   subire, Maecenas, tuo.
5 Quid nos, quibus te vita si superstite
    iucunda, si contra, gravis?
utrumne iussi persequemur otium,
   non dulce, ni tecum simul,
an hunc laborem, mente laturi decet
10   qua ferre non mollis viros?
Feremus, et te vel per Alpium iuga
  inhospitalem et Caucasum,

The ships of Antonius were not only of enormous size, but were furnished with towers (*turritis puppibus*, Verg. *A.* VIII. 693), so that their bulwarks looked like the walls of a fortress (Florus II. 21. 5)

4. subire tuo (sc. *periculo*): a choice paraphrase for 'to share,' corresponding with the expression in vs. 15 for sharing toil.

5. si: sc. *vivitur;* cf. vs. 8 n. The unusual insertion of *si* with the abl. abs. is explained by the fact that **te** (observe its position) is in thought the subject of two abl. abs. constructions, expressing alternative events. Expressed fully, his meaning is: *quibus vita si te superstite vivitur, iucunda; si mortuo, gravis*, or in more condensed form, *quibus te vita — si superstite, iucunda; si mortuo, gravis*. This natural conception of the thought is fixed by the euphemistic substitution of **si contra** (in which si is indispensable) for *si mortuo*. — **superstite**: here simply in the sense of continuing to live, unlike *C.* II. 17. 7, III. 9. 12, 16.

7. utrumne: the enclitic *-ne*, though frequently attached to an emphatic word after *utrum*, is not

found attached to *utrum* itself in any writer before Horace, who uses it here and twice elsewhere, *S.* II. 3. 251, 6. 73. Cf. also *uterne*, *S.* II. 2. 107; *quantane, S.* II. 3. 317; *quone*, ibid. 295. None of these forms occur in the Odes. *Vtrumne* is used by later prose writers. See Hand *Turs.* IV. p. 80. — **iussi**, *obediently.* Maecenas, then, it seems, had once refused Horace's request to be allowed to go. — **persequemur**, *consign myself to.* Cf. Cic. *de Off.* III. 1. *a re publica forensibusque negotiis prohibiti, otium persequimur.*

8. ni: sc. *persequimur* or the like. Cf. vs. 5 n.

9. laborem takes its construction from **otium** 7, but by a slight zeugma, on account of the different character of the object, the verbal notion suggested to the mind is not that of *persequor*, but rather of *suscipio, fero*, or the like, and first takes definite shape in **laturi**; hence the answer, **feremus 11.** — **mente laturi**, etc.: *i.e. ea mente* (*eum*) *laturi, qua decet*, etc.

10. non mollis: cf. *non amicos*, 11. 21, *non auspicatos, C.* III. 6. 10.

12. inhospitalem Caucasum: cf. *C.* I. 22. 6.

> vel Occidentis usque ad ultimum sinum
>   forti sequemur pectore.
>
> 15 Roges tuum labore quid iuvem meo,
>   imbellis ac firmus parum?
>
> Comes minore sum futurus in metu,
>   qui maior absentis habet,
>
> ut adsidens implumibus pullis avis
> 20   serpentium adlapsus timet
>
> magis relictis, non, ut adsit, auxili
>   latura plus praesentibus.
>
> Libenter hoc et omne militabitur
>   bellum in tuae spem gratiae,
>
> 25 non ut iuvencis inligata pluribus
>   aratra nitantur meis

13. **sinum**, *nook;* suggesting remoteness, — places off the line of ordinary travel and traffic. Cf. Verg. *G.* II. 122 *India, extremi sinus orbis.*

15. **roges**: for *si roges;* Gr. 310 *b.* — **tuum . . . meo**: parallel with *Caesaris . . . tuo*, vss. 3 *sq.;* but *labore* (not *laborem*) is required here by the metre, and standing before the hepthemimeral caesura gives a balance to the verse like that of 2. 19.

16. **firmus parum**: referring to his health and strength.

18. **maior habet**, *takes stronger possession of.*

19. **adsidens**, *brooding*. Its meaning is determined by the dative **pullis**, which, however, is not so closely connected with it, — since the bird is supposed to be absent from the nest, — as with **timet**, *fears for*. See Intr. 76.

21. **relictis**, *when she has left them.* — **non latura**, *though she would not afford.* For the conditional force of the fut. part., see

Intr. 104 *d.* — **ut adsit**, *even if she were there.* Gr. 266 *c.*

22. **praesentibus**: added (after **adsit**) for contrast with **relictis**. The Latin is fond of expressing both sides of a mutual relation; cf. Plaut. *Most.* 1075 *adsum praesens praesenti tibi;* Verg. *A.* IV. 83 *illum absens absentem auditque videtque;* Sat. II. 6. 81. But the repetition is not strictly tautological. Here the meaning is: ' without any thought that if she were there, they would find safety in her presence.'

23. **militabitur bellum**: cf. *pugnata bella, C.* III. 19. 4, and see Intr. 51 *b.*

25. **non ut**, etc.: *i.e.* not with an eye to the increase of my possessions (**pluribus** and **meis** contain the main ideas; Intr. 116*b*) in farm-lands or pastures, or the acquisition of splendid villas.

26. **nitantur**: the straining of the oxen, here poetically transferred to the plough, suggests a rich, heavy soil.

    pecusve Calabris ante sidus fervidum
        Lucana mutet pascuis,
    neque ut superni villa candens Tusculi
30   Circaea tangat moenia.
    Satis superque me benignitas tua
        ditavit ; haud paravero
    quod aut avarus ut Chremes terra premam,
        discinctus aut perdam nepos.

                              II.

        Beatus ille qui procul negotiis,
            ut prisca gens mortalium,

27. **pecusve,** etc. : sc. *mihi,*
suggested by **meis** 26.— **Cala-
bris,** etc.: cf. *C.* I. 31. 5 n.
  28. **mutet**: for the cases, see
Intr. 74.
  29. **superni**: the lofty situation
of Tusculum, commanding a mag-
nificent view over the Campagna,
together with the beauty of the
surrounding scenery and its near-
ness to the capital (15 miles distant), made it a favorite resort
for wealthy Romans, whose villas
covered the slope below the town
(in the neighborhood of the present Frascati), as those of their
successors do now. Besides Cicero's famous *Tusculanum,* Lucul-
lus, Hortensius, Cato, and Julius
Caesar had villas in the neighborhood.   Some of these country
houses were probably of marble,
and their brilliant whiteness (**can-
dens**), against the darker background of the hills or even of the
walls of the town itself (**tangat
moenia**), made them conspicuous
for miles around.
  30. **Circaea** : as having been
founded, according to tradition,

by Telegonus, the son of Circe.
Cf. *C.* III. 29. 8 n.
  31. **satis superque**: cf. 17. 19;
and, for the sentiment, *C.* II. 18. 12.
— **benignitas** : cf. *benignius, C.* I.
9. 6 n., and *malignus,* I. 28. 23 n.
  32. **paravero**: fut. perf., because
he is thinking of what he would
do with riches *after* they had been
acquired.   The indicative is emphatic: not 'I would not' (*haud
paraverim*), but 'I shall not.'
  33. **Chremes** : presumably a
typical miser in some well-known
comedy, not now extant. There is a
Chremes in four of Terence's plays,
but he is in no case a miser.
  34. **nepos** : like **avarus** in the
preceding verse, in apposition with
the subject of the verb.   In many
MSS. an *ut* is inserted before **nepos,** as in 2. 5 before *miles.*

  II. The banker's dream of the
delights of country life.   The
humorous surprise to which the
reader is treated at the end of this
really charming picture is thoroughly characteristic of Horace,
who gives us some of his most

paterna rura bobus exercet suis,
　　solutus omni faenore,
5　neque excitatur classico miles truci,
　　neque horret iratum mare,
　forumque vitat et superba civium
　　potentiorum limina.
　Ergo aut adulta vitium propagine
10　　altas maritat populos,
　aut in reducta valle mugientium
　　prospectat errantis greges,
　inutilisve falce ramos amputans
　　feliciores inserit,

poetic passages while protesting
that he has no gift for the higher
flights of poetry (*e.g. C.* II. 1, III.
3, *S.* II. 1. 12 *sqq.*). For a genuine
account of Horace's enjoyment of
country life, see *S.* II. 6. — Metre,
1 59.

2. **prisca gens:** the Golden Age.

3. **paterna:** see *C.* I. 1. 11 n.
The ideal farmer is owner of the
farm he tills, but unspoiled by ambition or avarice.

4. **faenore,** *money-lending.*

5. **neque excitatur,** etc.: cf.
Verg. *G.* II. 539 *necdum etiam
audierant inflari classica.* The
farmer's quiet life is contrasted
with the excitement of war, the
dangers of the sea (vs. 6), and the
worries and annoyances of the city
(vss. 7 *sq.*), as in *S.* I. 1. 4 *sqq.* Cf.
Verg. *G.* II. 501 *sq.* and the whole
passage (vss. 495–540). — **miles:**
cf. *nepos,* 1. 34 n.

7. **forum:** *i.e.* lawsuits and other
legal business, in which one might
be involved as suitor or defend-
ant, advocate, bondsman, etc., and
money transactions. — **superba,**
etc.: *i.e.* the humiliation of paying
court to the great, alluding par-

ticularly to the morning call (*salutatio*).

9. **ergo,** *and so; i.e.* with his
mind free from such cares and
annoyances. — **adulta:** after three
years' growth in the *seminarium.*

10. **maritat:** cf. *platanus caelebs,
C.* II. 15. 4 n, IV. 5. 30. The figure
appears to have passed early into
current speech ; cf. Cato, *R. R.* 32
arbores facito ut bene maritae sint.
— **populos** : these, with the elm,
were regarded as the most suitable, on account of the thinness
of their foliage. Their branches
were trimmed to form a series of
stages (*tabulata,* Verg. *G.* II. 361),
over which the vine was trained.

11. **in reducta valle:** cf. *C.* I.
17. 17. It is to be taken with
errantis.—**mugientium:** cf. Verg.
G. I. 272 *balantum* (sheep); III.
541 *natantum* (fishes).

13. **ramos:** *sc.* of fruit-trees.

14. **feliciores,** *more fruitful,*
its original meaning (cf. *fē-cundus,
fē-tus, fē-mina*). 'Felices arbores
Cato dixit quae fructum ferunt,
infelices quae non ferunt ' (Fest.
ap. Paul. p. 92). — **inserit:** *i.e.*
grafts; cf. *insitiva,* vs. 19 n.

15   aut pressa puris mella condit amphoris,
      aut tondet infirmas ovis ;
  vel, cum decorum mitibus pomis caput
      autumnus agris extulit,
  ut gaudet insitiva decerpens pira,
20   certantem et uvam purpurae,
  qua muneretur te, Priape, et te, pater
      Silvane, tutor finium.

  Libet iacere modo sub antiqua ilice,
      modo in tenaci gramine ;
25 labuntur altis interim ripis aquae,
      queruntur in silvis aves,

15. **pressa**: *sc.* from the comb.
Verg. *G.* IV. 140 *spumantia cogere
pressis | mella favis.* — **amphoris**:
Intr. 69.

16. **infirmas**: a standing epithet; cf. Ov. *Ib.* 43 *pecore infirmo.*

17. **decorum,** *graced.* Autumn
is personified ; cf. *C.* IV. 7. 11. —
mitibus: *i.e.* ripe ; cf. *immitis
uvae, C.* II. 5. 10.

18. **agris**: Intr. 69. — **extulit,**
has lifted up.

19. **ut gaudet,** *how happy he
is.* For the participle **decerpens,**
which here approaches the meaning of the infinitive with *gaudeo*
(Intr. 94 *d*), cf. *Ep.* II. 2. 106 *ri-
dentur mala qui componunt car-
mina, verum | gaudent scribentes.* —
insitiva: cf. vs. 14. The better
varieties can be propagated only
by grafting.

20. **et**: Intr. 114. — **purpurae**:
see *C.* II. 5. 12 n, and, for the case,
Intr. 57.

21. **qua**: relating to **pira** as
well as **uvam** (Gr. 198 *a*). — **Priape**: a genius of fertility, whose
statue, commonly of wood, was
set up in gardens and orchards,
'half god and half scarecrow.' See

S. I. 8. 2 n. — **pater**: cf. *C.* I. 2.
50 n.

22. **Silvane**: a very old Italian
divinity, whose attributes bear the
stamp of a time when the farmer
was a pioneer, and the forest
covered a large part of the land.
The 'god of the woods' was felt
to be very near to his life in all
its interests, was the protector of
his home, of his fields and flocks
(*arvorum pecorisque deo,* Verg. *A.*
VIII. 601; cf. *Ep.* II. 1. 143), and
of his borders (**custos finium**).
His statue was common in groves
and gardens.   See Preller-Jordan,
Röm. Myth. I. 392.

23. **iacere,** etc.: cf. *C.* I. 1. 21,
Verg. *E.* 1. 1.

24. **tenaci**: *i.e.* growing thick
and luxuriant, with matted roots,
in contrast with the sparse grass
of a light soil, which can be easily
pulled up.

25. **altis**: the scene is in summer or autumn, when the water in
the streams is low. — **interim**: as
he lies there. — **ripis**: cf. *C.* I. 2. 19
n ; here *by* or *between* their banks,
as in Lucr. II. 362 *summis labentia
ripis.*

frondesque lymphis obstrepunt manantibus,
    somnos quod invitet levis.
At cum tonantis annus hibernus Iovis
30   imbris nivisque comparat,
aut trudit acris hinc et hinc multa cane
    apros in obstantis plagas,
aut amite levi rara tendit retia,
    turdis edacibus dolos,
35   pavidumque leporem et advenam laqueo gruem
    iucunda captat praemia.
Quis non malarum quas amor curas habet
    haec inter obliviscitur?
Quod si pudica mulier in partem iuvet
40   domum atque dulcis liberos,

26. **queruntur**, *warble;* cf. Ov. *Am.* III. 1. 4 *et latere ex omni dulce queruntur aves.*

27. **frondesque**, etc.: *i.e.* the rustling of the leaves mingles with the plashing of the water. Cf. Prop. V. 4. 4 *multaque nativis obstrepit arbor aquis.* If the MSS. reading, *fontesque*, be retained, **lymphis** is instrumental abl., and **obstrepunt** is used absolutely (as in *C.* III. 30. 10) in the sense of striking upon the ear. In either case **obstrepunt** has as direct object a cognate acc., understood as the antecedent of **quod**, *a sound that.*

28. **levis**: cf. *C.* II. 16. 15.

29. **tonantis**: here not merely a stock epithet (cf. *C.* III. 5. 1), but helping to indicate the character of the season. — **annus**, *time* (of year); cf. *C.* III. 23. 8 n, and *frigidus annus*, Verg. *A.* VI. 311. — **Iovis**: see *C.* I. 1. 25 n, *C. S.* 32.

31. **trudit**: of close pursuit. Cf. the metaphorical use, *C.* II. 18. 15, *Ep.* I. 5. 17. — **hinc et hinc**,

on *every side;* cf. 5. 97. It is a poetical variation (but adopted in later prose) of *hinc* (*et*) *illinc;* cf. *C.* IV. 11. 9 *huc et illuc.* — **multa cane** : Intr. 127.

32. **plagas** : cf. *C.* I. 1. 28 n.

33. **amite** : according to Porphyrio, this name was given in his day to *furculae quibus retia in venatione vel in aucupio suspenduntur;* but the epithet **lēvi** seems to show that Horace had here in mind the poles (Intr. 127) of the clap-net. See Rich, *Dict. s. v.* — **rara**, *wide-meshed* (as compared with fishing-nets).

34. **turdis** : Intr. 59. Cf. Mart. III. 58. 26 *sed tendit avidis rete subdolum turdis.*

35. **pavidum, laqueo** : Intr. 135. — **advenam** : *i.e.* migratory.

37. **malarum quas . . . curas** : Intr. 118.

39. **quod si**: the apodosis begins at vs. 49. — **in partem** : strictly, equivalent to *partim* (cf. *in universum*, etc.); but the expression

Sabina qualis aut perusta solibus
          pernicis uxor Apuli,
sacrum vetustis exstruat lignis focum
          lassi sub adventum viri,
45   claudensque textis cratibus laetum pecus
          distenta siccet ubera,
et horna dulci vina promens dolio
          dapes inemptas adparet :
non me Lucrina iuverint conchylia
50   magisve rhombus aut scari,
si quos Eois intonata fluctibus
          hiems ad hoc vertat mare ;

is a condensed one for 'shares his
lot in caring for,' etc.

41. **Sabina** : cf. *C.* III. 6. 38 n;
Stat. *Silv.* V. 1. 122 *sqq.*, where this
description is imitated.—**perusta,**
tanned.— **solibus**: the plural expresses the repetition of the exposure, as in Lucr. V. 251 *perusta solibus adsiduis;* cf. *C.* IV. 5. 8 n.

42. **pernicis Apuli** : cf. *C.* III.
16. 26.

43. **sacrum,** etc.: preparations
to welcome her husband home to
his evening repast, — pleasing details of the picture of housewifely
devotion. The clauses stand in a
sort of apposition with **in partem
iuvet ;** hence the asyndeton. — **sacrum**: *sc.* to the Lares ; cf. *C.* III.
23. 15 n.—**vetustis,** *well seasoned.*

44. **sub** : cf. *C.* III. 7. 30 n.

45. **textis cratibus** : *i.e.* in a
fold made of these. — **laetum,**
lusty; so Verg. *G.* II. 144 *armenta
laeta.* Cf. *C.* IV. 4. 13 n.

47. **dulci** : Intr. 124.— **dolio** :
the vessel in which the new wine
was fermented, before bottling,
which the country people commonly did not wait for (cf. **horna**).

48. **inemptas**: *i.e.* costing nothing. Cf. Verg. *G.* 133 ; Mart.
IV. 66. 5 *saltus aprum, campus
leporem tibi misit inemptum.*

49. **Lucrina conchylia**: probably oysters, rather than the *Lucrina peloris* (*S.* II. 4. 32), a large
bivalve, which, at a later period at
least, was regarded as much inferior
to the Lucrine oyster. Cf. Mart.
VI. 11. 5 *tu Lucrina voras, me
pascit aquosa peloris;* III. 60. 3 *sq.*
— **iuverint magis** : Intr. 120.

50. **scari** : called by Ennius
(*Heduphagetica* 7) *cerebrum Iovis
paene supremi.*

51. **si quos** : sc. *scaros.* The
scar was found chiefly in the eastern part of the Mediterranean, but
was also caught in the neighborhood of Sicily, and in larger numbers after a storm, by which it was
thought the fish were driven to
those seas.—**intonata,** *thundering
down upon.* Cf. vs. 29 ; Intr. 51 *f.*

53. **Afra avis,** *the guinea-fowl,*
imported from Numidia ; a new
delicacy in Horace's day (Varro
R. R. III. 9. 18).

54. **attagen**: a species of grouse,

non Afra avis descendat in ventrem meum,
  non attagen Ionicus
55 iucundior quam lecta de pinguissimis
  oliva ramis arborum,
aut herba lapathi prata amantis et gravi
  malvae salubres corpori,
vel agna festis caesa Terminalibus,
60 vel haedus ereptus lupo.
Has inter epulas ut iuvat pastas ovis
  videre properantis domum,
videre fessos vomerem inversum boves
  collo trahentis languido,
65 positosque vernas, ditis examen domus,
  circum renidentis Laris.

brought from Asia Minor (Ioni-cus), 'quondam existimatus inter raras aves' (Plin. *N. H.* X. 133).

55. **pinguissimis** : Intr. 124.

57. **herba lapathi** : used in the *promulsis* of the more elaborate city dinner; cf. *S.* II. 4 . 29. — **gravi** : from torpid digestion.

58. **malvae** : cf. *C.* I. 31. 15. — **salubres corpori**: cf. Mart. X. 48.7.

59. **vel agna**, etc.: the farmer's ordinary diet was vegetables with salt meat; and fresh meat was a rare treat, indulged in only on oc-casions of public or private festiv-ity (cf. *S.* II. 2. 116 *sqq.*), unless of-fered by some unexpected chance, as here (vs. 60).—**Terminalibus** : the festival of Terminus, on the 23d of February. The victim sacrificed was either a lamb or a suckling pig. See Ov.*F.* II.655 *sqq.*

60. **haedus**, etc.: cf. Mart. X. 48. 14 *haedus inhumani raptus ab ore lupi.* The wolf was supposed to have good taste in selecting his victim ; cf. Plutarch, *Symp.* II. 9

τὰ λυκόβρωτα πρόβατα λέγεται τὸ κρέας γλυκύτατον παρέχειν.

61. **has inter**, etc.: the descrip-tion closes with a picture of the rest and simple enjoyment of the evening hour. Cf. the opening lines of Gray's Elegy.

63. **videre** : Intr. 116 *h.*

65. **positosque vernas**, *the home-born slaves* (in contrast with the costly imported slaves of wealthy houses) *seated* (on stools or on the ground) around the hearth (*focus Larium, quo familia convenit,* Plin. *N.H.* XXVIII. 267) in the atrium (*C.* I. 9. 5 n). Cf. *S.* II. 6. 66 *sq.* These slaves were seldom sold, if the master could afford to keep them, and, like the 'man-servants and maid-servants' of patriarchal times, formed a con-spicuous part of the wealth of a rich household. Cf. Tib. II. 1. 23 *turbaque vernarum, saturi bona signa coloni.* For the prosody of positos, see Intr. 135.

66. **renidentis**: an added touch

Haec ubi locutus faenerator Alfius,
    iam iam futurus rusticus,
omnem redegit Idibus pecuniam ;
70   quaerit Kalendis ponere.

III.

Parentis olim si quis impia manu
    senile guttur fregerit,

to the cheerfulness of the scene. The wooden figures of the Lares (see *C.* III. 23. 15 n), blackened with smoke, were cleansed from time to time, especially on any festive occasion, and rubbed with oil and wax to make them shine in the firelight. Cf. Juv. 12. 87 *graciles ubi parva coronas | accipiunt fragili simulacra nitentia cera.*

67. locutus : sc. *est.* — Alfius : a well-known *faenerator* of this name, probably of Cicero's time, is mentioned by Columella, I. 7. 2. The device of introducing a familiar character of a past generation as the type of a class is one Horace often adopted in his Satires.

68. iam iam futurus : cf. Tac. *Ann.* I. 47. 5 *ut iam iamque iturus, legit comites, conquisivit impedimenta, adornavit naves.*

69. redegit : the creditor could call in his loans at will, on giving his debtors due notice. Settlements were generally made on the Kalends, Nones, or Ides. Cf. *S.* I. 3. 87.

70. quaerit, etc.: the full force of the surprise is reserved for the very last verse, and is enhanced by the dry way in which this brief concluding item of the story is given, without comment. Notice the tense of quaerit, which brings the story close to us : it was only last week that Alfius called in his

money ; he will invest it again next week, if he can. — ponere : cf. *Ep.* II. 3. 421 *positis in faenore nummis.* For the mood, see Intr. 94 *c.*

III. A humorous diatribe against garlic, to which the poet attributes some acute sufferings that followed a dinner with Maecenas. The garlic, it would seem, was among the ingredients of a dish of herbs, such as the one of which Cicero once partook at an augural banquet ('nam dum volunt isti lauti terra nata . . . in honorem adducere, fungos, helvellas, herbas omnis ita condiunt ut nihil possit esse suavius,' *ad Fam.* VII. 26. 2) with similar results. Horace treats it as a practical joke on the part of Maecenas. — Metre, I 59.

1. olim, *ever.* Cf. *C.* IV. 4. 5 n.

2. guttur fregerit : see *C.* II. 13. 6 n.

3. edit : pres. subj.; an old form retained in colloquial use ; cf. *S.* II. 8. 90 ; Plaut. *Trin.* 339 *dé mendico mále meretur qui éi dat quod edit áut bibat.* — cicutis : the poison given to condemned criminals at Athens, made famous by the case of Socrates. Horace proposes garlic as a more efficient substitute. The plural of *cicuta* occurs also in *Ep.* II. 2. 53. — nocentius, *more poisonous ;* cf. *her-*

edit cicutis alium nocentius.
  O dura messorum ilia !
5 Quid hoc veneni saevit in praecordiis?
  Num viperinus his cruor
  incoctus herbis me fefellit, an malas
  Canidia tractavit dapes?
  Vt Argonautas praeter omnis candidum
10   Medea mirata est ducem,
  ignota tauris inligaturum iuga
  perunxit hoc Iasonem ;
  hoc delibutis ulta donis paelicem
  serpente fugit alite.
15 Nec tantus umquam siderum insedit vapor
  siticulosae Apuliae,

bas *nocentis,* S. I. 8. 22, with *Epod.*
5. 21 *sq.*

4. **o dura,** etc.: cf. Verg. *E.* 2.
10 *Thestylis et rapido fessis messo-
ribus aestu | alia serpullumque
herbas contundit olentis.*

5. **veneni :** Intr. 63.

6. **viperinus cruor :** see *C.* I.
8. 9 n.

7. **fefellit :** cf. *C.* III. 16. 32 n.
—**malas,** *baneful ;* cf. *S.* II. 1. 56
mala cicuta ; Verg. *A.* II. 471 *co-
luber mala gramina pastus.*

8. **Canidia :** see intr. note to
Epode 5.—**tractavit :** cf. *C.* II. 13.
10.

9. **ut Argonautas,** etc.: from
the mention of Canidia his mind
passes naturally to the queen of
sorceresses, and he asserts with
humorous assurance that this stuff
which he has eaten is no other
than the powerful drug which
Medea used to protect Jason and
destroy Glauce. — **ut :** temporal.
— **praeter omnis :** with **mirata
est.**—**candidum:** see *C.* I. 18. 11 n.

10. **mirata est :** cf. *C.* IV. 9.
15 n.

11. **tauris :** the fire-breathing
oxen which Jason was required to
yoke, to plough the land for sow-
ing the dragon's teeth. For the
case, see Intr. 76.

13. **hoc :** Intr. 116 *g.* The main
statement is in the participle **delibutis ;** cf. *ulta,* 5. 63, *deductus, C.*
IV. 4. 19. — **donis :** a robe and
crown, which burst into flames and
burned the wearer to death.—**paelicem :** Glauce (Creusa), daughter
of the Corinthian king Creon,
whom Jason was about to marry,
abandoning Medea. See 5. 61 *sqq.*

14. **serpente :** *i.e.* in a chariot
drawn by them. Cf. *C.* III. 3. 16
Martis equis Acheronta fugit. For
the singular, see Intr. 127.

15. **siderum:** see 16. 61, *C.* III.
29. 17 *sqq.*—**vapor,** *heat ;* cf. Lucr.
I. 663 *ignis uti lumen iacit atque
vaporem.*

16. **siticulosae :** cf. 2. 41 *sq., C.*
III. 30. 11, *S.* I. 5. 77 *sqq.,* 88 *sq.*

nec munus umeris efficacis Herculis
    inarsit aestuosius.
At si quid umquam tale concupiveris,
20   iocose Maecenas, precor
manum puella savio opponat tuo,
    extrema et in sponda cubet.

IV.

Lupis et agnis quanta sortito obtigit,
    tecum mihi discordia est,

17. **munus :** the robe which
the centaur Nessus, when mortally
wounded by the poisoned arrow
of Hercules, gave to Deianira,
who sent the fatal gift to her
husband on hearing of his love
for Iole (Ov. *M.* IX. 101 *sqq.*);
cf. 17. 31 *sq.*

18. inarsit (with **umeris**), *seared.*

19. **at :** in imitation of imprecations, where it expresses strong
emotion, as Ter. *And.* 666 *at tíbi
di dignum fáctis exitiúm duint,*
Cat. 3. 13 *at vobis male sit, malae
tenebrae | Orci.* Verg. *A.* II. 535.
— concupiveris, *crave.*

IV. The proscriptions and con-
fiscations of the civil wars, which
brought ruin to so many families,
brought sudden wealth to others,
and the rich upstart was a familiar
figure in the society of the day.
The vulgar striving of this per-
sonage for social recognition and
political distinction call out more
than once the expression of Horace's scorn, and in *S.* I. 6 he sets
forth at length his view of the
matter, illustrating it by a frank
discussion of his own case. The
present epode is an attack on one
of these parvenus, the bitterness

of which, in strong contrast with
the good-natured tone of the satire, leaves little doubt that the
poet is here not merely dealing
with a social type, but assailing a
real person, and probably one who
had crossed his own path. But
we are not informed who the person was. The inscription in some
MSS., 'ad Sextum Menam, Pompei
libertum' (see *C.* III. 16. 15 n) is
based on a highly improbable
guess; and there is not much
more to be said for the inscription
in other (and even in some of the
same) MSS., which names one Ve-
dius Rufus (perhaps the man described by Cicero, *ad Att.* VI. 1.
25) as the object of the attack. It
is to be observed that what excites
the poet's 'liberrima indignatio' is
not the servile origin of the man,
but his arrogant presumption in
pushing himself into notoriety and
usurping, in virtue of his ill-gotten
wealth, the distinctions which belong to merit. — Metre, 159.

1. lupis et agnis : immemorial
types of irreconcilable hostility;
cf. *Il.* XXII. 263. Ovid makes a
similar use of them, *Ib.* 43 *pax
erit haec nobis, donec mihi vita
manebit, | cum pecore infirmo* (cf.

Hibericis peruste funibus latus
et crura dura compede.

5 Licet superbus ambules pecunia,
fortuna non mutat genus.

Videsne, Sacram metiente te viam
cum bis trium ulnarum toga,

ut ora vertat huc et huc euntium

10 liberrima indignatio?

'Sectus flagellis hic triumviralibus
praeconis ad fastidium

2. 16 n) *quae solet esse lupis.* —
sortito: *i.e.* by nature; properly
an impersonal abl. abs. (Gr. 255 c).
For this use of the word, referring
to the original allotment in the
constitution of nature, cf. *S.* II.
6. 93 *terrestria quando | mortalis
animas vivunt sortita.*

3. **Hibericis:** *i.e.* made of Spanish *spartum*, a rush of exceedingly
tough fibre, of which ropes, as
well as coarse articles of clothing,
were made.—**peruste,** *tanned.* Cf.
Ep. I. 16. 47 *loris non ureris.* —
funibus: used for flogging slaves.
—**latus,** *hide;* see *C.* II. 7. 18 n.

4. **crura:** also taken with **peruste** (*galled*); cf. *Ep.* I. 10. 43.
For the two accusatives, see Intr.
43 — **compede:** worn only by
the lowest class of slaves in the
country, but by them even while
they were at work.

5. **ambules,** *walk abroad;* cf.
S. I. 4. 66

6. **fortuna:** *i.e.* wealth.

7. **Sacram viam:** the favorite
promenade of Rome. Cf. 7. 8 n,
S. I 9. 1. — **metiente te,** *as you
stride along;* cf. Plaut. *Pseud.* 1049
*quin hinc metimur grádibus mili-
táriis?*

8. **cum:** *i.e* wearing. Cf. Cic.
Brut. 56 *cum . . . sacrificium pu-*

blicum cum laena faceret. — **bis
trium ulnarum:** *sc.* in breadth.
The *ulna* was about half a yard.
The effect would be conspicuous
in the ample folds which fell from
the shoulders, draped with elaborate care; cf. *S.* II. 3. 183 *latus
ut in Circo spatiere.*

9. **ora vertat:** *i.e.* they flush
with indignation. Cf. *S.* II. 8. 35
vertere pallor tum parochi faciem.
— **huc et huc,** *up and down;* to
be taken with **euntium.** Cf. *hinc
et hinc,* 2. 31 n. In prose, *huc (et)
illuc* is used.

10. **liberrima,** *outspoken* (in the
words that follow). Cf. *liber amicus, S.* I. 4. 132; *multa cum libertate notabant,* ib. 5.

11. **sectus:** a vivid variation
on the usual *caesus;* cf. Tib. I. 9.
22 *verbere terga seca;* Juv. 10. 316.
— **triumviralibus:** *i.e.* by order
of the *triumviri capitales,* police
commissioners charged with the
execution of criminals and the
preservation of order. In exercising the latter function they had
power to inflict summary punishment on slaves and other low
characters.

12. **praeconis:** who stood by
while the flogging was administered, and proclaimed the offense.

arat Falerni mille fundi iugera
et Appiam mannis terit
15 sedilibusque magnus in primis eques
Othone contempto sedet.
Quid attinet tot ora navium gravi
rostrata duci pondere
contra latrones atque servilem manum,
20   hoc, hoc tribuno militum?'

13. **arat:** *i.e.* has under cultivation, owns. — **Falerni:** the *ager Falernus* was a rich wine-growing district on the Campanian side of Mt. Massicus. — **fundi,** *farm-land.*

14. **Appiam:** sc. *viam.*—**mannis,** *ponies,* fashionable for driving. The reference may be, however, to his journeys to his estates in Campania. Cf. *C.* III. 27. 7 n. — **terit:** cf. Mart. XI. 13. 1 *quisquis Flaminiam teris viator.*

15. **sedilibus primis:** the fourteen rows of seats in the theatre immediately behind the orchestra, which was occupied by the senators. These front rows, under a law passèd by L. Roscius Otho, tribune of the plebs, B.C. 67, were reserved for the equestrian order. — **magnus:** ironical; cf. *S.* I. 6. 72 *magni | quo pueri magnis e centurionibus orti.*

16. **contempto:** the law in his case defeats its own object, which was to exclude just such persons as he from the seats in question.

17. **ora rostrata,** *beaked fronts,* a fanciful expression for the usual term *rostra.* — **navium:** used generically; cf. *virginum, C.* III. 27. 38 n. — **gravi pondere,** *ponderous.* The freshness of these allusions gives the impression that the construction of the ships referred to was in progress or recently completed when the epode was written.

This would assign it to the year 37 or 36, when Octavian, after his disastrous defeat by Sextus Pompeius in 38, was engaged in building a new fleet of larger and stouter vessels.

19. **latrones,** etc.: the pirates and runaway slaves in the service of Sextus. Of the latter class Augustus asserts that he captured and returned to their masters about thirty thousand (*Mon. Anc.* 5. 1).

20. **hoc, hoc:** Intr. 116 *d.*— **tribuno militum:** cf. the case of Tillius, *S.* I. 6. 24 *sqq.*, and also 45 *sqq.*, where Horace admits the justice of the objection in his own case.

V. The clairvoyants and mediums of the present day had their counterpart in the professors of necromancy and magic who plied their trade with abundance of patronage and profit among a people so superstitious as the Romans. In this epode Horace exposes the practices of these persons in their worst form, where absurdity was carried to the point of crime. Four old hags, who have enticed a boy away from his home, suddenly seize him and drag him into their house, where he is to be subjected to a lingering death, buried in the ground up to his chin, with food

V.

'At o deorum quicquid in caelo regit
terras et humanum genus,
quid iste fert tumultus, et quid omnium
voltus in unum me truces?

in sight, that they may make a philter out of his marrow and liver. That children actually were made away with in the manner described, or at least that this was firmly believed, is shown by an epitaph (CIL. VI. 19747) on a boy, Iucundus, who had been so stolen: IN QVARTVM · SVRGENS · COMPRENSVS · DEPRIMOR · ANNVM | CVM POSSEM · MATRI · DVLCIS · ET · ESSE PATRI | ERIPVIT · ME · SAGA · MANVS CRVDELIS · VBIQVE | CVM · MANET IN · TERRIS · ET · NOCIT · ARTE SVA | VOS · VESTROS · NATOS · CONCVSTODITE PARENTES | NI · DOLOR · IN TOTO · PECTORE · FIXSVS · EAT. The leader of the unlovely quartet is Canidia, whom Horace has made a conspicuous figure in his earlier writings. Her real name, the scholiasts profess to know, was Gratidia, her birthplace Naples, and her trade the manufacture of perfumes. Tradition further asserts that Horace had been her lover, that the bitter lampoons which he has left us in this and the seventeenth epode were the outcome of a lover's quarrel, and that these are none other than the *celeres iambi* which he recants in *C.* I. 16. All this is highly improbable, and may be safely dismissed as an ill-contrived hypothesis to connect together the *data* of the poems. The earliest published poem in which Canidia is mentioned is perhaps *S.* I. 8, where her magic performances are ridiculed, but without a trace of bitterness. Equally devoid of personal feeling are the verses (*S.* II. 1. 48, 8. 95, *Epod.* 3. 8) where Horace makes a passing allusion to her as a poisoner. If she was a real person,—which seems, on the whole, probable,—we may safely assume that she was an *unguentaria;* as such she would be resorted to by the ignorant and superstitious for love potions and other nostrums known to the quackery of the day, and, unless her reputation belied her, she was also ready, like her famous successor, Locusta, to concoct more harmful drugs. She was a notorious character, whom Horace felt at liberty to use as a type of her class, in holding up their practices to ridicule.—Metre, 159.

1. **at**: expressing sudden emotion; cf. its use in imprecations (see 3. 19 n). The words are those of the boy, who has been seized by the women and dragged into the atrium of the house. — **deorum quicquid**: cf. Liv. XXIII. 9. 3 *iurantes per quicquid deorum est; S.* I. 6. 1 *Lydorum quicquid.* — **in caelo**: simply used to round out the phrase, like 'all the fish in the sea,' etc. A distinction between the gods of heaven and those of the underworld is not to be thought of in the mind of the frightened boy.

3. **fert**, *means;* lit. 'brings,' *i.e.* what will it lead to?— **quid**: sc. *ferunt.*

4. **voltus in me truces**: cf. *acer . . . voltus in hostem, C.* I. 2. 39.

5   Per liberos te, si vocata partubus
          Lucina veris adfuit,
      per hoc inane purpurae decus precor,
          per improbaturum haec Iovem,
      quid ut noverca me intueris aut uti
10   petita ferro belua ? '
      Vt haec trementi questus ore constitit
          insignibus raptis puer,
      impube corpus quale posset impia
          mollire Thracum pectora,
15   Canidia, brevibus implicata viperis
          crinis et incomptum caput,
      iubet sepulcris caprificos erutas,
          iubet cupressos funebris

5. **te**: Canidia.—**si vocata**, etc.:
see 17. 50 n. The allusion in both
places assumes that the poet's
readers are familiar with the
story.

6. **Lucina**: cf. *C. S.* 15, *C.* III.
22. 2 n.—**veris**: the poet's own
malice breaks through the fiction
in this insinuation, which is quite
out of character in the mouth of
the child.

7. **inane**: as not having secured
him the respect which it ought.—
purpurae decus: the purple border of his toga, which was a mark
at once of tender years and of
gentle breeding.

8. **improbaturum**: a mild term,
but sufficient when applied to the
deity, whose mere *displeasure* is
to be dreaded.

9. **ut noverca**: cf. Sen. *Contr.*
IV. 6 *hic tuus est ; quid alterum
novercalibus oculis intueris ?* and
see note on *patruae*, *C.* III. 12. 1.

12. **insignibus**: his *praetexta*
and the *bulla* or locket which he

wore on his breast, suspended
from his neck.

13. **impube corpus**: in apposition with **puer**. Even if the
ordinary symbols of youth and
innocence had failed to affect
them, the sight of his tender body
might have touched the heart of a
savage.

15. **brevibus**, etc.: Canidia's
make-up is that of a fury, which she
is called in *S.* I. 8. 45. Cf. Lucan's
description of Erichtho, VI. 654 *sqq.*

16. **crinis, caput**: Intr. 42.

17. **sepulcris**: Intr. 70.—**caprificos**: the wild fig-tree grew on
walls and tombs, and, sending its
roots into their cracks and joints,
sometimes split them apart, — a
type of the destructive forces which
mock the elaborate efforts of man
to immortalize his memory. Cf.
Mart. X. 2. 9 *marmora Messalae
findit caprificus;* Juv. 10. 144 *sq.*
Here it is chosen from its association with the tomb and death.

18. **cupressos**: also associated

et uncta turpis ova ranae sanguine

20   plumamque nocturnae strigis

herbasque quas Iolcos atque Hiberia

mittit venenorum ferax,

et ossa ab ore rapta ieiunae canis

flammis aduri Colchicis.

25   At expedita Sagana, per totam domum

spargens Avernalis aquas,

horret capillis ut marinus asperis

echinus aut currens aper.

with the tomb, but here branches used at some funeral (*funebris*) are meant. See *C.* II. 14. 23 n.

19. **ūncta**, *smeared.* Cf. *C.* II. 1. 5. — **ranae**: sc. *rubetae*, a poisonous frog; cf. Plin. *N.H.* VIII. 110 *ranae rubetae, quarum et in terra et in humore vita, plurimis refertae medicaminibus deponere ea cotidie ac resumere pastu dicuntur, venena tantum semper sibi reservantes.* Cf. Juv. 1. 69.

20. **strigis**: limiting both **ova** and **plumam**. The *strix* was a bugbear of the nursery, described as a screeching, owl-like bird which carried off unguarded babies from their cradles (Ov. *F.* VI. 131 *sqq.*). Pliny was unable to identify it (*N.H.* XI. 232), and it was probably nothing but a mythical distortion of the sceeech-owl itself, which from its appearance and habits was naturally regarded as a bird of ill omen (*funebris et maxime abominatus, . . . noctis monstrum . . . ; itaque in urbibus aut omnino in luce visus dirum ostentum est*, Plin. *N.H.* X. 34).

21. **Iolcos**: cf. vs. 45 and *C.* I. 27. 21 n. — **Hiberia**: under the Caucasus range, adjacent to Colchis.

22. **venenorum** : Intr. 66 *a*.

23. **ieiunae**: in order to impart to the potion the craving of baffled appetite.

24. **Colchicis**: *i.e.* kindled with certain forms and spells which were supposed to give them magic potency; cf. *C.* II. 13. 8 n. With this whole witch's outfit, cf. Prop. IV. 6. 27 *illum turgentis ranae portenta rubetae | et lecta exsectis anguibus ossa trahunt | et strigis inventae per busta iacentia plumae | cinctaque funesto lanea vitta toro.*

25. **expedita**: *i.e.* with her skirt tucked up (cf. *succincta, S.* I. 8. 23) so as not to impede her brisk movements. — **Sagăna**: Canidia's companion in *S.* I. 8, where it is implied that there were two sisters of this name.

26. **spargens**, etc.: the usual form of purification (*lustratio*) in sacrifices to the gods below, funeral rites, etc.; cf.Verg. *A.* IV. 635, VI. 229 *sq.* — **Avernalis**: cf. Verg. *A.* IV. 512. Lake Avernus was supposed to be connected with the underworld.

28. **currens**: not added in reference to **capillis asperis**, — as if his bristles were erect only when he runs, — but as part of the picture which Sagana rushing about the house suggests.

Abacta nulla Veia conscientia

30   ligonibus duris humum

exhauriebat ingemens laboribus,

       quo posset infossus puer

longo die bis terque mutatae dapis

       inemori spectaculo,

35   cum promineret ore quantum exstant aqua

       suspensa mento corpora,

exsecta uti medulla et aridum iecur

       amoris esset poculum,

interminato cum semel fixae cibo

40   intabuissent pupulae.

---

29. Veia: the third witch, who
digs in the *impluvium* the hole in
which the boy is to be buried.

30. ligonibus: Intr. 128. — **duris:** the epithet hints at the labor-
iousness of her task, the hardness
of the tool implying a difficult substance to dig into, as the earth in
the *impluvium* was. Cf. **ingemens
laboribus,** below.

31. exhauriebat: properly used
of removing the earth after digging
it loose with the hoe (Caes. *B. G.*
V. 42. 3 *gladiis caespites circum-
cidere, manibus sagulisque terram
exhaurire cogebantur*); here it
stands for both operations. — **ingemens:** cf. Verg. *G.* I. 45 *de-
presso incipiat iam tum mihi tau-
rus aratro | ingemere*.

32. quo: adverb (lit. ' into
which ') with **infossus;** cf. Caes.
B.G. VII. 73. 9 (*taleae) in terram
infodiebantur*.

33. longo: *sc.* to the boy, in his
torture. — **bis terque,** *again and
again;* cf. *Ep.* II. 3. 440 *bis terque
expertum frustra*. — **mutatae:** to
tempt his appetite by variety.

34. inemori, *pine to death at;*

found only here. The prefix has
the same force as in *ingemere,* 31
indormire, S. I. 1. 71, etc., and the
simpler form *immori, Ep.* I. 7. 85.
Cf. also *intabuissent,* 40 n. The
poor boy's passionate craving for
food was to be conveyed, through
his vital parts, into the philter, and
endow the latter with the power of
exciting insatiable desire.

36. suspensa mento: a fanciful
paraphrase for *natantia.*

37. exsecta, aridum: see Intr.
121. — **medulla:** the innermost
part of the body and the hardest
to reach; cf. its figurative use, *Ep.*
I. 10, 28, Cat. 64. 93 *imis exarsit
tota medullis,* etc.; hence imagined
to be the most potent medium of
magic influence. — **iecur:** the seat
of the passions; cf. I. 13. 4.

39. semel: with **cum,** and applying to the whole clause. —
fixae, *fastened upon.* — **cibo:** dative with both **fixae** (Intr. 56) and
intabuissent (cf. Sen. *de Cons.
ad Polyb.* 5. 2 *quid iuvat dolori
intabescere?*); Intr. 76.

41. defuisse: implying more
than *afuisse,* — that she belonged

Non defuisse masculae libidinis
    Ariminensem Foliam
et otiosa credidit Neapolis
    et omne vicinum oppidum,
45   quae sidera excantata voce Thessala
        lunamque caelo deripit.
Hic inresectum saeva dente livido
    Canidia rodens pollicem
quid dixit aut quid tacuit? 'O rebus meis
50   non infideles arbitrae,

in the company, and would have been missed if absent. — **libidinis**: Intr. 61.

42. Foliam: apparently a notorious character at Naples. There is no little art in the way she is introduced: by basing her presence only on hearsay, and attempting no details of her part in the orgy, the poet gives the impression that the evidence as to the others was explicit and trustworthy.

43. otiosa: and hence gossipy (*otium serendis rumoribus natum*, Curt. VIII. 9. 1); a characteristic, according to the Roman standard, of the Greeks (*gens lingua magis strenua quam factis*, Livy VIII. 22. 8). Cf. *NT. Acts*, 17. 21: 'Now all the Athenians and the strangers sojourning there spent their time in nothing else but either to tell or to hear some new thing.' Naples in particular was proverbial for its idle life; cf. Ovid *M.* XV. 711 *in otia natam Parthenopen.* The shores of the bay, too (**omne vicinum oppidum**), were lined with villas, the resort of people of leisure, and no doubt hotbeds of gossip.

45. sidera: cf. 17. 4. *sq.*, and Tib. I. 2. 43 *hanc (sagam) ego de caelo ducentem sidera vidi.* — **Thes-**

sala: *i.e.* magic; cf. *Colchicis* 24 n, and see *C.* I. 27. 21 n.

46. lunam: cf. 17. 78, and Verg. *E.* 8. 69 *carmina vel caelo possunt deducere lunam.*—**deripit**: present of customary action, not historical.

47. hic, *then;* but it refers not so much to the time as to the circumstances and surroundings of the act,—the stage of preparation described in what precedes. Cf. Verg. *A.* I. 728 *hic regina gravem gemmis auroque poposcit | implevitque mero pateram.* — **inresectum**: cf. *S.* I. 8. 26 *scalpere terram unguibus . . . coeperunt.* For the prefix re- cf. *C.* III. 24. 34 n.

48. rodens: in her violent agitation.

49. tacuit: *i.e.* 'thought,' since *tacere* with an object means to refrain from saying *what one knows or thinks.* The words that follow are to be regarded as partly spoken or muttered, and partly expressing the thoughts which passed through her mind, but were not spoken aloud. — **rebus meis**, *my cause, my fortunes* (cf. *C.* IV. 6. 23), in contrast with **hostilis domos** 53; dat. after **adeste** (cf. *tuis rebus adero*, Cic. *ad Fam.* VI. 14. 3), with which **arbitrae** is joined as predicate nominative.

50. non infideles: *i.e.* true to

Nox et Diana, quae silentium regis,
    arcana cum fiunt sacra,
nunc, nunc adeste, nunc in hostilis domos
    iram atque numen vertite.⌐

55 Formidolosis dum latent silvis ferae
    dulci sopore languidae,
senem, quod omnes rideant, adulterum
    latrent Suburanae canes,
nardo peructum quale non perfectius

60   meae laborarint manus.

the obligation of secrecy which her
trust imposed upon them. — **arbitrae**: equivalent, under the circumstances, to *consciae*. See next
note.

51. **Nox et Diana**: cf. Ov. *M.*
VII. 192 (of Medea) '*Nox*,' *ait
arcanis fidissima*, . . . | *tuque tri-
ceps Hecate, quae coepti conscia
nostris | adiutrixque venis cantus-
que artisque magorum*, and see *C.*
III. 22. 4 n.— **silentium**: essential
for magic rites.

53. **nunc, nunc**: Intr. 116 *d.*—
hostilis: not those of her rivals
(which would require *inimicas*),
but those of 'the enemy' in general— a common clause in ancient
prayers. Cf. *C.* III. 27. 21 n.

54. **iram atque numen**, *your
all-powerful wrath*. Intr. 126 *a.*

55–60. Though she has already
made preparations for concocting
a more potent drug, she is not
without hope that an ointment
previously applied, though thus
far ineffective, may still do its
work.

57. **senem**: named Varus in
vs. 73, an old fop. There is no
evidence to show whether Horace
had a real person in mind.— **quod
omnes rideant**, *amid general
laughter*. The laughter is at the

foppery of the old man; cf. Plaut.
Cas. 222 *sénectan aetate únguenta-
tus pér vias, ignáve, incedis?*

58. **latrent**: transitive as in *Ep.*
I. 2. 66 ; Intr. 51 *c* (2). She hopes
to hear the barking of the dogs as
an indication of his approach; cf.
Verg. *E.* 8. 107.— **Suburanae**:
i.e. those of the neighborhood.
The Subura, the slums of Rome,
was in the hollow, east of the fo-
rums, between the Esquiline and
the Quirinal and Viminal hills.
It was the most densely settled
and the busiest and noisiest (*cla-
mosa* Mart. XII. 18. 2) part of the
city, full of small shops, eating-
houses, and low resorts. Cf. Pers.
5. 32 *sq.* Here was the house of
Canidia.

59. **nardo**: see *C.* II. 11. 16 n.—
quale non: *quo non* would be
more usual. With **quale** the other
term of the comparison (*tale*) is
understood: 'of a sort, of which
. . . none more perfect (than this)';
cf. *S.* I. 5. 41 (*Varius Vergiliusque*)
*animae qualis neque candidiores
terra tulit.*

61. **quid accidit**: as the stillness remains unbroken, she tries
to think what unforeseen circumstance has counteracted her drugs.
— **minus**: here equivalent to *pa-*

Quid accidit? Cur dira barbarae minus
    venena Medeae valent,
quibus superbam fugit ulta paelicem,
    magni Creontis filiam,
65 cum palla, tabo munus imbutum, novam
    incendio nuptam abstulit?
Atqui nec herba nec latens in asperis
    radix fefellit me locis.
Indormit unctis omnium cubilibus
70   oblivione paelicum?
A, a, solutus ambulat veneficae
    scientioris carmine.
Non usitatis, Vare, potionibus,
    o multa fleturum caput,

rum, expressing simply failure to come up to her expectations; cf. Cic. *Div.* I. 24 *at non numquam ea quae praedicta sunt minus eveniunt;* Plaut. *Cas.* 918 *monebo, si qui meministi minus.*

62. **Medeae :** *i.e.* identical in their composition with those Medea used on the occasion referred to. Cf. Tib. I. 2. 51 (of a *saga*): *sola tenere malas Medeae dicitur herbas.*

63. **quibus :** with **ulta** which here contains the main statement, like *delibutis,* 3. 13. — **superbam :** as a triumphant rival.— **paelicem :** cf. 3. 13 n.

65. **tabo imbutum,** *plague-tainted ; tabum* here in the sense of *tabes,* as in Ov. *M.* XV. 627 *pallidaque exsangui squalebant corpora tabo.*

66. **abstulit :** cf. *C.* II. 16. 29, *S.* I. 9. 31.

67. **nec fefellit :** *i.e.* I have found and gathered every one (of those required by Medea's recipe).

69. **indormit,** etc.: as there are still no signs of his approach, she casts about for the cause of her failure. Her first thought is that her spells have proved ineffective : 'Can it be that he is going to sleep over (and in spite of) the magic drugs with which I have anointed his bed?' For **indormit,** cf. *inemori,* 34 n.

71. **a, a :** Intr. 185. Her second thought flashes upon her as the true explanation, — 'Some rival has done this!'—and at once puts her in a fury that spurs her on to redoubled efforts. — **solutus :** cf. *C.* I. 27. 21.—**ambulat :** cf. 4. 5 n.

72. **carmine,** *spell ;* cf. 17. 4 n.

73. **non usitatis :** cf. *C.* II. 20. 1. The meaning is : I will brew a potion of no ordinary power, that will bring you swiftly back to me.

74. **multa fleturum,** *doomed to shed many a tear;* cf. *flebit, S.* II. 1. 46, and see Intr. 45 *b,* 104 *b.*— **caput:** cf. *C.* I. 24. 2.

75   ad me recurres, nec vocata mens tua
          Marsis redibit vocibus :
      maius parabo, maius infundam tibi
          fastidienti poculum,
      priusque caelum sidet inferius mari,
80   tellure porrecta super,
      quam non amore sic meo flagres uti
          bitumen atris ignibus.'
      Sub haec puer iam non, ut ante, mollibus
          lenire verbis impias,
85   sed dubius unde rumperet silentium,
          misit Thyesteas preces :

75. **nec vocata,** etc.: *i.e.* and the
incantations which will draw your
heart back to me will not be of the
Marsic sort.   Others, following
Porphyrio, interpret thus: 'And
your heart (when I once get control of it) will not return (to those
who now control it) at the call of
Marsic spells.' But the contrast of
the emphatic **Marsis** (Intr. 116 *b*)
with **maius** 77 makes the former
more probable.   For **mens** in this
sense, cf. *C.* I. 13. 5 n.

76. **Marsis vocibus:** here used
disparagingly for the simple spells
of the Italian countryside.   The
Marsi were especially noted for
snake-charming and magic cures
(Gell. XVI. 11. 1); cf. 17. 29 n.

77. **maius :** *i.e.* in quality, more
powerful. — **infundam,** *adminis-
ter ;* stronger than *dabo ;* cf. Cic.
Phil. 11. 13 *at hic nuper sororis
filio infudit venenum, non dedit.*

79. **inferius :** for the prosody
see Intr. 135.

81. **uti bitumen,** etc.: a comparison drawn from her own occu-
pations.   Cf. Verg. *E.* 8. 82.

82. **atris :** here used of the ac-

tual color of the flames, and not
like *nigris, C.* IV. 12. 26.

83. **sub haec,** *hereupon ;* cf. *S.*
II. 8. 43, and see *C.* III. 7. 30 n.

84. **lenire :** Intr. 91.

85. **dubius,** etc.: *i.e.* with varied
emotions pressing for utterance.
— **unde,** etc.: *i.e.* what he should
say first, **unde** being used as with a
'word of beginning,' which **rumperet silentium** is in effect ; cf.
Cornif. *ad Herenn.* I. 14 *inde inci-
piemus narrare, unde necesse erit.*

86. **Thyesteas preces :** familiar to Romans from the *Thyestes*
of Ennius.   Cf. Cic. *in Pis.* 43
*Thyestea est ista exsecratio poetae
volgi animos, non sapientium moventis.*   The curse is quoted *l.l.*
and *Tusc.* I. 107. Varius also,
and, subsequently, Seneca, wrote
a *Thyestes.*   For **preces** in this
sense, cf. *S.* II. 6. 30; Caes. *B. G.*
VI. 31. 5 *omnibus precibus detesta-
tus Ambiorigem.*   For an actual
instance of such dying imprecations, see Tac. *Ann.* VI. 24. 3.

87. **venena,** etc.: an obscure
and undoubtedly corrupt passage
for which no satisfactory expla-

'Venena magnum fas nefasque non valent
    convertere humanam vicem
Diris agam vos ; dira detestatio
90   nulla expiatur victima.

Quin ubi perire iussus exspiravero,
    nocturnus occurram furor,
petamque voltus umbra curvis unguibus,
    quae vis deorum est manium,
95   et inquietis adsidens praecordiis
    pavore somnos auferam.

Vos turba vicatim hinc et hinc saxis petens
    contundet obscaenas anus ;
post insepulta membra different lupi
100   et Esquilinae alites;

nation or emendation has been suggested. See Crit. App. The general meaning appears to be this : Sorcery (**venena**) has no power to reverse, after the manner of men (**humanam vicem**), the great law of righteousness and sin ; *i.e.* your drugs may influence mortal minds, as you claim ; if you incur the sin of taking my innocent life, they cannot save you from the vengeance of heaven, which will give effect to my dying imprecations ; and when these have been pronounced, repentance will come too late (**nulla expiatur victima**). For **fas nefasque convertere**, cf. Verg. *G.* I. 505 *fas versum atque nefas ;* Ov. *M.* VI. 585 *fasque nefasque* | *confusura ruit ;* for **humanam vicem**, *Sardanapali vicem in meo lectulo mori,* Cic. *ad Att.* X. 8. 7, is quoted. For the infin. **convertere**, see Intr. 94*n.*

89. **diris,** *curses,* as in Tac. *l. l.* **dira detestatio** is a more solemn expression for the same thing.

90. **nulla,** etc.: such was the current belief. Cf. *C.* I. 28. 34; Plin. *N.H.* XXVIII. 19 *defigi quidem diris precationibus nemo non metuit.*

92. **furor :** here used as a masculine form for *furia, an avenging spirit.*

93. **umbra :** cf. Verg. *A.* IV. 386 *omnibus umbra locis adero ; dabis, improbe, poenas.*

94. **quae vis :** *i.e.* the power to return to earth and torment their murderers ; cf. Val. Flacc. III. 384 *sqq.*—**deorum manium :** the (sanctified) spirits of the righteous. Cf. Liv. III. 58. 11 *manesque Verginiae . . . per tot domos ad petendas poenas vagati, nullo relicto sonte, tandem quieverunt.*

95. **inquietis :** proleptic.—**adsidens :** as a nightmare.

97. **hinc et hinc :** cf. 2. 31 n.

98. **obscaenas,** *uncanny, gruesome ;* the cause of the popular aversion ; cf. Verg. *G.* I. 470.

99. **post :** adverb.

100. **Esquilinae :** those that

neque hoc parentes, heu mihi superstites,
    effugerit spectaculum.'

VI.

Quid immerentis hospites vexas canis
    ignavus adversum lupos?
Quin huc inanis, si potes, vertis minas
    et me remorsurum petis?

haunted the hill when it was the Potters' Field of Rome. Cf. *S.* I. 8. 8 *sqq.* For the hiatus, see Intr. 185.

101. **neque hoc effugerit** (fut. pf.) : *i.e.* and it will not pass by without their having seen it. — **heu mihi superstites** : the boy forgets for the moment his own horrible situation in pity for the unhappy lot of his parents, doomed to suffer an affliction from which in the regular course of nature they should be spared. The double pathos of this reversal of the order of nature impressed the ancients, whose vague and cheerless notions of future life afforded them no consolation for bereavement or untimely death, with a force which we cannot well appreciate. With admirable art the poet breaks off at this point, having carried us, along with the tender thoughts of the boy, past the repulsive scene about to be enacted, and leaving us with the picture of the bereaved parents consoled by the punishment of the murderers of their child. He illustrates here in narrative the precepts which he gives for the stage, *Ep.* II. 3. 182 *sqq.*

VI. A challenge, addressed to a scurrilous poet, who is taunted with prudently confining his abuse

to those who were powerless to respond. The person addressed is unknown to us. The character attributed to him corresponds with the account given by Tacitus (*Ann.* I. 72. 4.) of Cassius Severus, who was banished by Augustus under the law of treason, — the first instance in which that law was applied to restrict liberty of speech. Cassius, however, belonged to a younger generation than Horace, and the inscription '*ad Cassium Severum,*' found in some manuscripts, can be no more than a guess. Equally conjectural is the inscription *ad Mevium* (cf. Epode 10), and the suggestions of Bibaculus, Anser, and others have no evidence to rest on. — Metre, 159.

1. **hospites,** *passers by, wayfarers;* frequently used in this sense (like *viator, e.g.* Mart. XI. 13. 1) in epitaphs in which the reader is directly addressed. Cf. Allen's *Remnants of Early Latin,* 137, 138. — **canis** : *i.e.* one set to watch the flocks; cf. vs. 6.

3. **inanis** : *i.e.* all bark and no bite. — **si potes,** *if you dare;* cf. *C.* III. 11. 31 n.

4. **remorsurum** : Intr. 104 *c.*

5. **Molossus aut Lacon** : without *canis ;* cf. our 'Newfoundland,' ' Skye,' etc. These superior breeds are mentioned together by Vergil, *G.* III. 405. The Molos-

5   Nam qualis aut Molossus aut fulvus Lacon,
      amica vis pastoribus,
   agam per altas aure sublata nivis
      quaecumque praecedet fera.
   Tu cum timenda voce complesti nemus,
10   proiectum odoraris cibum.
   Cave, cave : namque in malos asperrimus
      parata tollo cornua,
   qualis Lycambae spretus infido gener
      aut acer hostis Bupalo, —
15 an, si quis atro dente me petiverit,
      inultus ut flebo puer?

sian as house-dog occurs *S.* II.
6. 114.

6. **vis**: cf. Lucr. VI. 1222 *fida
canum vis ;* Verg. *A.* IV. 132 *odora
canum vis.*

7. **sublata** : *i.e., arrecta.*

9. **complesti** : Intr. 183.

10. **proiectum,** *flung to you,*
with a suggestion of contempt in
the action, *proicere* meaning usually ' to throw away.' The ordinary
word in this connection is *obicere.*
But see Crit. App. — **odoraris
cibum :** *i.e.* you are ready to be
bribed to hold your tongue; you
are seeking blackmail.

11. **cave, cave** : Intr. 116 *d.*

12. **parata** : Intr. 124. — **tollo
cornua :** a metaphorical expression, not inconsistent with what
precedes, because the figure of the
two dogs has been abandoned, and
Horace begins in vs. 11. to speak
in his own person. Cf. *S.* I. 4. 34.

13. **Lycambae :** attacked with
such bitterness by the poet Archilochus, to whom he had first
promised and then refused (**infido**)
his daughter Neobule, that both
father and daughter were driven
to suicide. Cf. *Ep.* I. 19. 25, 30

sq. The dative depends on the
general notion of hostile attack,
derived from *tollo cornua* 12. —
spretus : Intr. 103. — **gener,** *as
a son-in-law.*

14. **hostis :** the poet Hipponax.
His resentment against Bupalus
was roused by a joke of the latter,
who, with another sculptor, named
Athenis, had made a likeness of
the poet's features, which are said
to have been uncommonly homely,
and exhibited it for the entertainment of their friends (Plin. *N. H.*
XXXVI. 12):

15. **an,** etc. : with this conclusion, cf. 17. 76 *sqq.* — **atro dente :**
i.e. with malicious abuse. *Ater*
seems to be used as in *versibus
atris, Ep.* I. 19. 30 ; cf. the similar
use of *niger, S.* I. 4. 85, 91, 100.
The tooth is figuratively the weapon of envy and malice ; cf. *C.* IV.
3. 16; Ov. *Tr.* IV. 10. 123 *nec . . .
livor iniquo | ullum de nostris dente
momordit opus ;* Mart. V. 28. 7
(*homo malignus*) *robiginosis cuncta
dentibus rodit.*

16. **flebo :** the order is com-
parable to that of *S.* II. 1. 60
dives, inops, Romae, seu fors ita

VII.

Quo, quo scelesti ruitis ? aut cur dexteris
    aptantur enses conditi ?
Parumne campis atque Neptuno super
    fusum est Latini sanguinis, —
5   non ut superbas invidae Carthaginis
    Romanus arcis ureret,
intactus aut Britannus ut descenderet
    Sacra catenatus via,

iusserit exsul, | *quisquis erit vitae*
scribam color, where as here the
hyperbaton gives the impression
of strong feeling that cannot wait
for orderly utterance.

VII. On the threatened renewal
of civil war.   The occasion cannot
be determined with certainty, but
it was probably the outbreak of
hostilities between the triumvirs
and Sextus Pompeius in the spring
of B.C. 38, owing to their failure
to carry out the stipulations of the
treaty made at Misenum the preceding August.   The treaty had
been hailed with delight by the
people, as affording them a prospect of peace at last, after a dozen
years of civil dissension and bloodshed ; and the rude shattering of
their hopes within a twelvemonth
might well awaken the gloomy
feeling which Horace expresses, —
that the curse of fraternal strife
had been fastened upon the nation
by the crime with which its career
had begun.   A poem in this spirit
could hardly have come from
Horace at a later date.   It is cast
in dramatic form, the poet throwing himself in front of the combatants, as it were, to make his
appeal. — Metre, 159.

1. **quo, quo** : Intr. 116 *d.* —
scelesti : cf. *C.* I. 2. 29, 35. 33
sqq., II. 1. 5. — **ruitis** : cf. *C.* I. 3.
26. — **cur dexteris**, etc. : *i.e.* why
do you grasp the hilt of your
sheathed swords ?

2. **conditi** : *sc.* in the scabbard.
Cf. '*put up* your sword.'

3. **campis** : Intr. 69. — **Neptuno** : Intr. 130. — **super** : Intr.
115 *b*.   For the meaning cf. *C.* I. 9.
5 n.

5. **non ut** : added as if the fact
implied in the preceding question
had been stated affirmatively, —
' blood enough has been shed, and
not (as of old) to destroy a powerful rival, nor to win new conquests,
but, etc.' — **invidae** : cf. Sal. *Cat.*
10. 1 *Carthago aemula imperi Romani.* — **Carthaginis**, *a Carthage.*

6. **arcis** : Intr. 128.

7. **intactus** : cf. *C.* III. 24. 1 n.
The epithet is here substantially,
though not literally, accurate, as the
raids of Julius Caesar into Britain
had made no permanent impression, and the Romans had no foot-
hold in the island. With this allusion cf. *C.* III. 5. 3, and see intr.
note to *C.* I. 35.

8. **Sacra via** : the street leading from the Velia, with a gentle
descent (**descenderet**) to the Fo-

sed ut secundum vota Parthorum sua
10   urbs haec periret dextera.

neque hic lupis mos nec fuit leonibus,
      numquam nisi in dispar feris.

Furorne caecus an rapit vis acrior
      an culpa?   Responsum date !

15   Tacent, et albus ora pallor inficit,
      mentesque perculsae stupent.

Sic est : acerba fata Romanos agunt
      scelusque fraternae necis,

ut immerentis fluxit in terram Remi
20   sacer nepotibus cruor.

rum ; a favorite promenade of Rome at this time (cf. 4. 7, *S.* I. 9. 1) and the most brilliant portion of the route of the triumphal procession, which passed from the Campus Martius through the Velabrum and the Circus Maximus, along the foot of the Palatine to the Velia, and thence down the *Sacra via* (cf. *C.* IV. 2. 35 n), and through the Forum to the foot of the *clivus Capitolinus.* — **catenatus** : *i.e.* as a prisoner before the triumphal car.

9. secundum, etc. : cf. *C.* II. 1. 31 n ; *Il.* I. 255 ἦ κεν γηθήσει Πρίαμος Πριάμοιό τε παῖδες | ἄλλοι τε Τρῶες μέγα κεν κεχαροίατο θυμῷ, | εἰ σφῶιν τάδε πάντα πυθοίατο μαρναμένοιιν. The feeling is the complement of that referred to in 5. 53, *C.* III. 17. 1 n.—**Parthorum:** the successors of Carthage as the most powerful rival of Rome. — **sua**: emphatic; Intr. 116 *c.* For the thought, cf. 16. 2.

11. hic mos : *i.e.* seeking to destroy their own kind. For the arrangement of words in this verse,

see Intr. 120 ; for the tense of **fuit**, Intr. 80.

12. dispar : used substantively for *dispar animal* or the like. — **feris**: here in its adjective use.

13. an rapit : Intr. 119 *a.* — **vis acrior** : *sc.* than your own strength ; some irresistible force (meaning that of fate). Cf. *maturior vis*, *C.* II. 17. 6, where, as here, *vis* is used vaguely of a force above human control.

14. culpa, *guilt* (of fratricide ; cf. *C.* I. 35. 33.), which pursues you like a curse, and goads you on to new wickedness.

15. tacent, etc. : he pauses a moment for a reply, and then turns, as it were, to the bystanders. — **albus,** *ghastly ;* cf. 10. 16 n.

16. perculsae, *with dismay ; sc.* at the thought that they are swept on by some mighty force.

17. acerba fata : the *vis acrior* of vs. 13, as **scelus,** etc. repeats *culpa,* 14. — **agunt** : cf. 5. 89 *diris agam vos.*

19. ut : cf. *C.* IV. 4. 42 n.

20. sacer, *a curse to.* Cf. 16. 9.

VIII.

Rogare longo putidam te saeculo
　　viris quid enervet meas,
cum sit tibi dens ater et rugis vetus
　　frontem senectus exaret,
5　hietque turpis inter aridas natis
　　podex velut crudae bovis !
Sed incitat me pectus et mammae putres,
　　equina quales ubera,
venterque mollis et femur tumentibus
10　　exile suris additum.
Esto beata, funus atque imagines
　　ducant triumphales tuum,
nec sit marita quae rotundioribus
　　onusta bacis ambulet.

VIII. An affected taste for literature combined with gross sensu-
ality is the subject satirized, with
a degree of coarseness to which
Horace rarely descends, in this
epode. The person attacked is
represented as a woman of wealth
and noble family, and the portrait
appears to have been drawn from
life.— Metre, 159.

1. **rogare te** : the inf. expresses
indignation (Intr. 92), the ground
of which is given in **putidam**, etc.
— **longo saeculo** : hyperbole for
longa aetate.

3. **dens** : used collectively; Intr.
127.— **ater** : cf. *C.* II. 8. 3.—
vetus, *extreme*.

7. **sed**, etc.: ironical.

11. **esto**, *you may be*, concessive. The apodosis begins in vs.
17.— **beata**, *rich.* — **atque** : Intr.
114. Its position makes **funus**,
another and a somewhat brutal

suggestion of her age (cf. *C.* III.
15. 4), more prominent. — **imagines** : the masks which, worn by
dummies dressed in the costume
of the ancestors they represented,
preceded (**ducant**) the bier in the
funeral procession.

12. **triumphales** : *i.e.* of ancestors who had triumphed. This
would be indicated by the insignia
worn with the mask, and would be
a mark of the highest nobility.

13. **nec** : Intr. 89 N.— **marita** :
for *matrona.* Cf. Ov. *F.* II. 139
hic castas duce se iubet esse maritas.
— **rotundioribus** : *i.e.* more perfect in shape; cf. Plin. *N. H.* IX.
112 *dos omnis* (sc. *unionibus*) *in
candore, magnitudine, orbe, levore,
pondere.*

14. **bacis**, *pearls.* — **ambulet** :
cf. 4. 5 n.

15. **quid quod** : continuing the
concessive sentence in another

15   Quid quod libelli Stoici inter sericos
        iacere pulvillos amant?
     Inlitterati num minus nervi rigent?
        minusve languet fascinum,
     quod ut superbo provoces ab inguine,
20   ore adlaborandum est tibi?

IX.

     Quando repostum Caecubum ad festas dapes
        victore laetus Caesare
     tecum sub alta (sic Iovi gratum) domo,
        beate Maecenas, bibam,
5   sonante mixtum tibiis carmen lyra,
        hac Dorium, illis barbarum,
     ut nuper, actus cum freto Neptunius
        dux fugit ustis navibus,

---

form. Cf. *C.* II. 18. 23 n. — **seri-cos**, *silken;* cf. *punico*, 9. 27 n.

16. **iacere amant:** *i.e.* are always lying there; Intr. 94 *c.*

IX. To Maecenas, on the arrival at Rome of the first tidings of victory from Actium. The poet calls on his patron (who, according to the best evidence, was in Rome at this time; see intr. note to Epode 1) to institute a thanksgiving banquet for the great victory, as he had done a few years before, on the defeat of Sextus Pompeius. Meantime he pursues his own reflections on the contest and its glorious issue, and bids his slave bring larger cups and wine, which 'antehac nefas depromere,' but in which they may now wash away their anxieties for Caesar's fortunes. The epode was written in September, B.C. 31, nearly a year before *C.* I. 37, which celebrates the death of Cleopatra.— Metre, 1 59.

1. **repostum:** Intr. 183.—**Cae-cubum:** see *C.* I. 20. 9 n, 37. 5.—**dapes:** cf. *C.* II. 7. 17 n.

2. **victore Caesare:** Intr. 105*a.*

3. **alta:** see *C.* III. 29. 10 n.— **Iovi:** see *C.* II. 7. 17 n.

4. **beate:** cf. *C.* I. 4. 14 n.

5. **tibiis:** cf. *lituo, C.* I. 1. 23 n. — **carmen**, *melody.* See Intr. 51 *c.*

6. **hac,** etc.: a construction according to the sense, as if the preceding words had been *carmen sonantibus mixtim tibiis lyraque*, or the like. — **Dorium:** spirited, but serious, adapted to warlike themes; **barbarum:** *i.e.* Phrygian (cf. *C.* III. 19. 18, IV. 1. 22, Cat. 63, 22), a more lively style, suited to revels and orgies (cf. Cat. 64. 264).

7. **nuper:** in B.C. 36, after the

minatus urbi vincla quae detraxerat

10   servis amicus perfidis.

Romanus eheu (posteri negabitis)
    emancipatus feminae

fert vallum et arma, miles et spadonibus
    servire rugosis potest,

15   interque signa turpe militaria
    sol adspicit conopium.

Ad hoc frementis verterunt bis mille equos
    Galli canentes Caesarem,

hostiliumque navium portu latent

20   puppes sinistrorsum citae.

battle of Naulochus. — **actus** : cf.
C. III. 7. 5. — **freto** : sc. *Siculo.*
For the case see Intr. 70. — **Nep-
tunius dux** : Sextus Pompeius ; a
mocking recognition of his claim
to be the son of Neptune.

9. **vincla** : Intr. 183.

10. **servis** : cf. 4. 19 n. For the
case, Intr. 76. — **perfidis** : as having run away from their masters,
and now fighting against them.

11. **Romanus**, *a son of Rome ;*
referring to the soldiers of Antonius ; see Intr. 127. — **posteri
negabitis** : cf. *credite posteri, C.*
II. 19. 2 n.

12. **emancipatus**, *in bondage to.*

13. **fert**, etc. : *i.e.* marches in
the ranks, serves as a soldier ;
enhancing the humiliation of his
subjection to a woman. [In the
same way **miles**, in the next clause,
is contrasted with **spadonibus**.
Cf. *C.* III. 5. 9. — **et** : Intr. 114.

14. **potest** : cf. *C.* III. 11. 31 n.

15. **turpe** (with **conopium**), *a
disgraceful sight.*

16. **sol adspicit** : implying a
sense of shame that the Roman
soldiery should be seen in the

light of day in such effeminate
company. — **conopium** : cf. Prop.
IV. 11. 45 *foedaque Tarpeio cono-
pia tendere saxo* (*ausa*). The scorn
concentrated upon this foreign
word is pointed not only at the
foreign abomination itself, but at
the outrage to Roman tradition
and sentiment in allowing a woman
to exercise authority in camp; cf.
Tac. *Ann.* III. 33. 2 *haud enim
frustra placitum olim ne feminae in
socios aut gentes externas traheren-
tur; inesse mulierum comitatui quae
... Romanum agmen ad similitudi-
nem barbari incessus convertant.*

17. **verterunt** : Intr. 178.

18. **Galli** : Galatians, under the
younger Deiotarus, who deserted
to Octavian before the battle. —
canentes Caesarem : cf. Verg.
A. VII. 698 *ibant aequati numero,
regemque canebant.*

19. **hostiliumque**, etc. : an obscure passage, not explained by
any account of the battle that has
come down to us. It seems clear,
however, that Horace is speaking
of a defection in the naval forces
of Antonius, corresponding to that

Io Triumphe, tu moraris aureos
    currus et intactas boves?
Io Triumphe, nec Iugurthino parem
    bello reportasti ducem,
25 neque Africanum, cui super Carthaginem
    virtus sepulcrum condidit.
Terra marique victus hostis punico
    lugubre mutavit sagum;

just referred to in his land army; and we may suppose that the first account that reached Rome not only reported such a defection, but described the manœuvre by which it was accomplished. What this manœuvre was we cannot determine. **sinistrorsum** is very likely a nautical term; and with **citae** means ' with a swift movement to port.' By this movement, it would seem, the ships were reported to have abandoned the fleet and taken refuge in the harbor from which they had sailed out to battle.

21. **io Triumphe**: cf. *C*. IV. 2. 49 n. — **tu moraris**: equivalent to an exhortation to make haste; cf. the colloquial use of *cessare*, as Ter. *And*. 343 *cessas adloqui? C*. III. 27. 58. — **aureos currus**, *the gilded car*, in which Caesar shall ride to the Capitol. Intr. 128.

22. **intactas** (sc. *iugo*) : an essential requirement in sacrificial animals. — **boves**: with the sacrifice of which on the Capitol the ceremonies of the triumph closed.

23. **nec Iugurthino**, etc. : *i.e.* a greater than Marius is awaiting his triumph,—a greater than Africanus (Minor). The mention of the Jugurthine war, rather than the repulse of the Germanic invasion by Marius in B.C. 102 and 101, a far greater achievement, may have been due to the recent

appearance of Sallust's *Iugurtha*. — **parem** : sc. *huic quem nunc reportaturus es*.

24. **reportasti**: more commonly used of the spoils of war, of glory, or even of the triumph itself (Plin. *N. H. Praef.* 30) ; sometimes, as here, of the triumphant general ; cf. Cic. *post Red.* 28 *non reducti sumus in patriam*, . . . *sed equis insignibus et curru aurato reportati*.

25. **neque Africanum**: sc. *huic parem reportasti*. — **super** : in a figurative sense. Cf. *C*. III. 5. 39 *o magna Carthago, probrosis | altior Italiae ruinis !*

26. **sepulcrum** : here (with **virtus condidit**) thought of as the monument rather than as the place of burial.

27. **hostis** : Antonius. — **punico**: used like *Tyrius* (*e.g. S*. II. 4. 84 *Tyrias vestis*) for *purple. Puniceus* is the commoner form in this sense; cf. *C*. IV. 10. 4 n. A purple or white cloak was usually worn by a general going into battle. Cf. Val. Max. I. 6. 11. (of Crassus at Carrhae) *pullum* (the color of mourning) *ei traditum est paludamentum, cum in proelium exeuntibus album aut purpureum dari soleat*. For the case see Intr. 74.

28. **lugubre,** *sombre;* the change was like putting on mourning. — **sagum** : a plain soldier's mantle in place of the general's cloak

aut ille centum nobilem Cretam urbibus,

30   ventis iturus non suis,

exercitatas aut petit Syrtis Noto,

aut fertur incerto mari.

Capaciores adfer huc, puer, scyphos

et Chia vina aut Lesbia,

35   vel quod fluentem nauseam coerceat

metire nobis Caecubum.

Curam metumque Caesaris rerum iuvat

dulci Lyaeo solvere.

(more properly called *paludamen-tum*); see vs. 27 n. This change of dress Horace probably assumes as a matter of course; he could hardly have received any authentic report to that effect. The same was told of Pompey after Pharsalus (Caes. *B. C.* III. 96. 3) : *equum nactus detractis insignibus imperatoriis decumana porta se ex castris eiecit*).

29. ille . . . petit: Intr. 120.— centum, etc. : cf. *C.* III. 27. 33 n. — nobilem, *famous.* Cf. *C.* I. 8. 12, 12. 27.

30. iturus : Intr. 104 *b.*— non suis : *i.e. adversis.*

31. exercitatas : cf. *C.* IV. 14. 20 *undas exercet Auster.*— Syrtis : see *C.* I. 22. 5 n ; II. 6. 3 n.

32. incerto: *i.e.* where his course is uncertain ; Intr. 124.

33. puer : see *C.* I. 19. 14 n. — scyphos : see *C.* I. 27. 1 n.

34. Chia . . . Lesbia : sweet and mild Greek wines, likely to be drunk in excess, with the result mentioned (no doubt with less offense to Roman taste than to ours) in the next verse. The effect was counteracted by drinking the harsher Italian wines along with the Greek (see *S.* II. 8. 15), and sometimes the two were

mixed (*S.* I. 10. 24).— aut, *or* (else); one of the two.

36. metire : *sc.* with *cyathi.* See *C.* III. 19. 11 n.

37. curam solvere : cf. *curis expeditis*, I. 22. 11 n. — rerum : objective genitive ; cf. Verg. *A.* II. 413 *ereptae virginis ira.*

38. Lyaeo : cf. *C.* III. 21. 16 n. —solvere : Intr. 94 *c.*

X. Bavius and Mevius, two poets of the old school, made themselves so offensive by their criticism and detraction to the literary circle to which Horace belonged, that their names have become inseparably associated with those of their betters whom they decried, and have thus escaped the oblivion which speedily overtook their works. The milder tempered Vergil confines his expression of dislike to a single verse, *E.* 3. 90 *qui Bavium non odit amet tua carmina, Mevi.* Horace, in this epode, makes a voyage of Mevius to Greece the occasion of a vituperative personal attack, in which he gives free rein to his hatred and contempt, and which acquires additional force by contrast with the good wishes usually spoken on such an occasion.— Metre, 159.

X.

Mala soluta navis exit alite,
　　ferens olentem Mevium :
ut horridis utrumque verberes latus,
　　Auster, memento fluctibus ;
5　niger rudentis Eurus inverso mari
　　fractosque remos differat ;
insurgat Aquilo, quantus altis montibus
　　frangit trementis ilices,
nec sidus atra nocte amicum adpareat,
10　qua tristis Orion cadit,
quietiore nec feratur aequore
　　quam Graia victorum manus,
cum Pallas usto vertit iram ab Ilio
　　in impiam Aiacis ratem.
15　O quantus instat navitis sudor tuis
　　tibique pallor luteus

1. **mala alite** : cf. *mala avi*, C. I. 15. 5 n; to be taken with **soluta**, for which cf. *C*. III. 2. 29.

3. **ut verberes** : optative subj. (Gr. 267 *b*), **memento** being parenthetical.—**latus** : *sc.* of the ship.

4. **Auster**, etc. : all the winds unfavorable to a voyage to Greece are called upon to concentrate their fury on the ill-fated ship.

5. **niger**: cf. *C*. I. 5. 7 n.—**Eurus**: cf. *C*. I. 28. 2 5.—**inverso mari** : cf. Verg. *A*. I. 84 *incubuere mari, totumque a sedibus imis | una Eurusque Notusque ruunt* (*upheave*).

6. **differat**: cf. 5. 99.

7. **quantus**, *as powerful as when.* — **montibus** : Intr. 69.

10. **tristis** : cf. *C*. I. 3. 14.— **Orion**: see *C*. I. 28. 21 n ; Intr. 178. — **cadit**: cf. *C*. III. 1. 27 n.

12. **Graia victorum manus** : cf. Cat. 31. 13 *Lydiae lacus undae*. The shifting of the attribute is similar to that of Intr. 124.

13. **cum Pallas**, etc. : for the story see *Odys*. IV. 499 *sqq*., Verg. *A*. I. 39 *sqq*. — **Ilio** : see *C*. I. 10. 14 n.

14. **impiam** : Intr. 124. Ajax had dragged Cassandra from the altar of Pallas ; cf. Verg. *A*. II. 403 *sqq*.

15. **quantus instat**, etc.: cf. *C*. I. 15. 9.

16. **lūteus**: expressing the greenish yellow hue of paleness in dark complexions, such as are common in southern Europe ; cf. Tib. I. 8. 52 *nimius luto corpora tingit amor ;* Cat. 64. 100 *magis fulgore expalluit auri; C*. III. 10. 14 n.

et illa non virilis eiulatio
　　preces et aversum ad Iovem,
　Ionius udo cum remugiens sinus
20　　　Noto carinam ruperit.
Opima quod si praeda curvo litore
　　porrecta mergos iuverit,
libidinosus immolabitur caper
　　et agna Tempestatibus.

XI.

Petti, nihil me sicut antea iuvat
　　scribere versiculos amore percussum gravi,

17. **illa** : insinuating that it was habitual with him. — **non virilis** : cf. Cic. *Tusc.* II. 55 *ingemescere non numquam viro concessum est, idque raro ; eiulatus ne mulieri quidem.*

18. **et** : cf. Intr. 114. — **aversum** : cf. *C.* III. 23. 19 n.

19. **Iŏnius sinus** : the same as *Hadriae sinus, C.* III. 27. 19. The adjective should not be confused with *Iŏnicus,* 2. 54, *C.* III. 6. 21. — **udo** : *i.e.* rainy.

20. **Noto** : ablative with **remugiens**; cf. *ventis, C.* III. 10. 7.

21. **opima praeda,** *a rich treat.* — **quod si** : introducing the conclusion as in *C.* I. 1. 35. Intr. 114. The savage bitterness of this closing malediction is not softened, but rather enhanced by a cynical observance of the proprieties of language in abstaining from any direct mention of death and suppressing the real subject of the sentence, — either *tu* (if *iuveris* had been used) or *corpus tuum,* which is implied, however, in **porrecta** (cf. *C.* III. 10. 3).

22. **mergos** : among the most voracious of birds, but Horace is wrong in thinking they eat carrion.

23. **immolabitur** : even the usual thank-offering for a friend's safe return from sea is to have its counterpart on the luckless end of this voyage.

24. **agna Tempestatibus** : cf. Verg. *A.* V. 772.

XI. The poet professes to have lost all interest in writing verses, being once more a victim of love, after a long respite. Of Pettius, to whom the piece is addressed, we know no more than what here appears, — that he was the friend to whom Horace confided his feelings in his last love-affair, the description of which occupies the greater part of the poem. The names Inachia and Lyciscus are of course fictitious. — Metre, 165.

1. **nihil** : Intr. 47.

2. **versiculos** : the diminutive conveys mild disparagement. — **amore** : not consciously personified in this verse, though the thought takes that turn in the next (qui me, etc.) ; hence the simple

amore qui me praeter omnis expetit
    mollibus in pueris aut in puellis urere.
5 Hic tertius December, ex quo destiti
    Inachia furere, silvis honorem decutit.
Heu me, per urbem (nam pudet tanti mali)
    fabula quanta fui ! Conviviorum et paenitet,
  in quis amantem languor et silentium
10   arguit et latere petitus imo spiritus !
   'Contrane lucrum nil valere candidum
    pauperis ingenium!' querebar adplorans tibi,
  simul calentis inverecundus deus
    fervidiore mero arcana promorat loco.
15 'Quod si meis inaestuet praecordiis
    libera bilis, ut haec ingrata ventis dividat

ablative. — **gravi** : an attribute
in accordance with the conception
of love implied in **percussum**,
with which it may well be rendered adverbially, *sorely smitten.*

3. **amore**: for this use of anaphora, cf. *arva*, 16. 42 n; *aere*, ib. 65.

4. **in** : cf. *C.* I. 17. 19 n.—**urere**:
Intr. 94 *h.*

5. **hic tertius**, etc., *this December, which is smiting*, etc., *is the
third since*, etc.—**December**: used
in the same way *Ep.* I. 20. 27.

6. **Inachiā** : Intr. 72. — **honorem**, *their glory, i.e.* their foliage;
cf. *C.* I. 17. 16; Verg. *G.* II. 404 *frigidus et silvis Aquilo decussit honorem.*

7. **nam**, etc.: excusing the exclamation **heu me**.

8. **fabula**, *food for gossip ;* cf.
Ep. I. 13. 9, and the use of *risus*,
S. II. 2. 107 *o magnus posthac inimicis risus.* — **quanta**, **et** : Intr.
114.— **paenitet**, *I dislike ;* historical present.

9. **quīs** : see *C.* I. 26. 3 n. —
amantem (sc. *me*) **arguit** : cf. *C.*

I. 13. 7; *Ep.* I. 19. 6 *laudibus ar-
guitur vini vinosus Homerus.* —
languor, *listlessness.*

11. **contrane**, etc., *to think that,
etc.* For the construction, see
Intr. 92. — **candidum** : cf. *S.* I.
5. 41.

12. **adplorans** : accompanying
(ad-) my lament with tears.

13. **simul** : see *C.* I. 4. 17 n. —
inverecundus : cf. *verecundum
Bacchum, C.* I. 27. 3 n. Here the
epithet indicates the actual effect
of the wine, breaking down the
restraints of modesty.

14. **mero** : abl. with **calentis**.—
arcana : sc. *mea ;* **calentis** agrees
with the implied possessive genitive, as in *mea ipsius* and similar phrases. — **promorat** : Intr.
86, 183. — **loco** : from their place,
i.e. the place where they are kept
(as secrets),—his own knowledge.

15. **quod si**, etc.: continuing
the quotation of his words to
Pettius on former occasions.

16. **libera bilis** ; cf. *liberrima*

fomenta volnus nil malum levantia,
    desinet imparibus certare submotus pudor.'
Vbi haec severus te palam laudaveram,
20   iussus abire domum ferebar incerto pede
ad non amicos heu mihi postis et heu
    limina dura, quibus lumbos et infregi latus.
Nunc gloriantis quamlibet mulierculam
    vincere mollitia amor Lycisci me tenet ;
25   unde expedire non amicorum queant
libera consilia nec contumeliae graves,
    sed alius ardor aut puellae candidae
        aut teretis pueri longam renodantis comam.

---

indignatio, 4. 10 n. For **bilis,** cf. *C.* I. 13. 4 n. — **ut :** expressing result : if my wrath could burn so hotly as to burst forth and scatter to the winds the 'poultices' with which I now vainly try to nurse my sore, etc. — **ingrata,** *thankless, unprofitable.* Cf. Lucr. III. 937 *commoda perfluxere atque ingrata interiere.* — **ventis :** cf. *C.* I. 26. 2 *tradam ventis.*

17. **fomenta :** *i.e.* the *querellae* (cf. *querebar,* 12) with which he tried to console himself and keep alive his hopes.

18. **desinet submotus pudor :** poetical for *desinam submoto pudore* (Intr. 105 *a*). **pudor** is the false pride which keeps him from giving up the contest. — **imparibus :** cf. vs. 11 *sq.,* and see Intr. 57.

19. **haec laudaveram,** *had uttered these praiseworthy sentiments;* lit., had commended this course (as the one I should pursue). For the construction, cf. *promorat,* vs. 14, and see Intr. 86. — **severus :** in contrast with his subsequent conduct. — **te palam :** for *coram te ;* cf. Ov. *Trist.* V. 10. 39 *meque*

palam de me tuto mala saepe loquuntur.

20. **iussus :** *sc.* by Pettius, urging him to carry out his sensible resolution. — **ferebar :** observe the tense. — **incerto,** *irresolute.* Intr. 124. Cf. Tib. II. 6. 14.

21. **non amicos :** cf. I. 10 n. **heu . . . heu :** to be taken, not with **non amicos** and **dura,** but with the whole sentence, a sigh over the collapse of his brave purpose. — **postis :** for the door itself, where he was not admitted.

22. **dura :** in a literal sense, explained by the words that follow ; cf. *C.* III. 10. 2 *sqq.* — **infregi :** Intr. 119 *a.*

24. **vincere :** Intr. 94 *d.*

25. **expedire :** cf. *C.* I. 27. 24.

26. **libera,** *frank.* Cf. vs. 16. —**contumeliae :** *sc.* of Lyciscus.

27. **puellae :** objective genitive with **ardor** (= *amor*); cf. the use of *ardere* with the accusative, Intr. 72.

28. **teretis :** cf. *C.* II. 4. 21 n. — **renodantis :** equivalent to *nodo solventis,* **re-** having the same force as in *refigere, recludere,* etc.;

XII.

Quid tibi vis, mulier nigris dignissima barris?
  Munera cur mihi quidve tabellas
mittis, nec firmo iuveni neque naris obesae?
  Namque sagacius unus odoror,
5   polypus an gravis hirsutis cubet hircus in alis,
  quam canis acer ubi lateat sus.
Qui sudor vietis et quam malus undique membris
  crescit odor, cum pene soluto
indomitam properat rabiem sedare, neque illi
10 iam manet umida creta colorque
stercore fucatus crocodili, iamque subando
  tenta cubilia tectaque rumpit!

cf. Val. *Flacc.* V. 380 (*Dianam*)
renodatam pharetris. For the
practice of boys wearing their hair
long, cf. *C.* II. 5. 23 *sq.*, III. 20. 14,
IV. 10. 3. The knot was presum-
ably for convenience on undress
occasions, or to make the hair
wavy when it was let down.

XII. A coarse lampoon on a
woman whose advances had become repulsive. — Metre, 162.

2. **tabellas,** *notes.*

3. **naris obesae:** *i.e.* with a dull
sense of smell; in contrast with
sagacius, 4.

4. **unus:** common with the
superlative, but seldom used, as
here, to add force to the comparative; cf. Verg. *A.* I. 15 *quam Iuno
fertur terris magis omnibus unam |
posthabita coluisse Samo.*

5. **pōlypus:** an offensive tumor
that grew in the nose; hence we
must supply from **cubet in alis**
some such general idea as *adsit.*
In the quantity of the **o,** Horace
here and *S.* I. 3. 40 follows the
Doric form πώλυπος. — **gravis,**
reeking. — **cubet hircus :** an extravagant figure, but based on a
common colloquial use of the
word *hircus* in this sense.

7. **qui :** exclamatory. The poet
here drops the form of address
and turns to the reader. — **vietis :**
Intr. 181. For the position of
vietis and **membris,** see Intr.
120.

10. **umida:** *sc.* with perspiration.
— **creta :** *i.e.* a cosmetic made of
it.

11. **stercore crocodili:** cf. Plin.
N. H. XXVIII. 108 (of the smaller
species of crocodile) *in terra tantum odoratissimisque floribus vivit;
ob id intestina eius diligenter ex-
quiruntur, iucundo nidore farta;
'crocodileam' vocant;* . . . *inlita
quoque ex oleo cyprino molestias in
facie enascentis tollit, ex aqua vero
morbos omnis quorum natura ser-
pit in facie, nitoremque reddit.*
color, then, is rouge made from
crocodilea.

12. **tecta,** *the canopy.*

Vel mea cum saevis agitat fastidia verbis:
  ‘ Inachia langues minus ac me ;
15 Inachiam ter nocte potes, mihi semper ad unum
    mollis opus.   Pereat male quae te
Lesbia quaerenti taurum monstravit inertem,
  cum mihi Cous adesset Amyntas,
cuius in indomito constantior inguine nervus
20   quam nova collibus arbor inhaeret.
Muricibus Tyriis iteratae vellera lanae
  cui properabantur ? Tibi nempe,
ne foret aequalis inter conviva, magis quem
  diligeret mulier sua quam te.
25 O ego non felix, quam tu fugis ut pavet acris
  agna lupos capreaeque leones.’

13. **vel cum** : the ellipsis after **vel** is to be supplied from the general sense of the preceding sentence,— *quam odiosa est* or the like.

14. **Inachiā**: Intr. 72.—**minus ac** : cf. 15. 5 *artius atque*. This use of *atque* or *ac* for *quam* after a comparative occurs repeatedly in the Satires, in these two places in the Epodes, in the later poems not at all.

17. **Lesbia**: an *ancilla* or *lena*. For the order, see Intr. 118.

18. **Cous Amyntas** : a made-up name, like *Cnidius Gyges*, *C.* II. 5. 20, *Thressa Chloe*, III. 9. 9, etc.

20. **nova**: *i.e.* young.

21. **iteratae**: cf. *bis Afro murice tinctae*, *C.* II. 16. 35 n.

22. **cui** : Intr. 114. Here the pronoun itself gains emphasis (Intr. 116 *b*). — **properabantur** : transitive as in *C.* III. 24. 62.

23. **ne foret**, etc. : *i.e.* that this might be inferred from the fact that he had received such a costly present from her.— **magis quem.** the construction is **quem magis diligeret mulier sua** (= *amica*) **quam te** *tua deligeret*.

25. **o ego** : Intr. 185. For the case, cf. *C.* III. 27. 34 n. — **pavet**: Intr. 51 *a*.

26. **agna lupos**: cf. 4. 1 n. — **capreae leones**: cf. *C.* IV. 4. 13 *sqq*.

XIII. A light piece, constructed of the same materials as *C.* I. 9, and probably, like that ode, a study from the Greek. A stormy day, keeping the poet and his friends indoors, gives them at once the inclination and excuse for ‘ taking a portion from the solid day ’ to enjoy a jar of old wine together. Horace’s usual maxims on the enjoyment of life are here illustrated by a story of Chiron and Achilles, as in *C.* I. 7 by that of Teucer.— Metre, 164.

1. **contraxit** : *i.e.* has drawn it closer about the earth; referring to the heavy storm clouds, in con-

XIII.

Horrida tempestas caelum contraxit, et imbres
  nivesque deducunt Iovem ; nunc mare, nunc siluae
Threicio Aquilone sonant : rapiamus, amici,
  occasionem de die, dumque virent genua
5 et decet, obducta solvatur fronte senectus.
  Tu vina Torquato move consule pressa meo.
Cetera mitte loqui ; deus haec fortasse benigna
  reducet in sedem vice.   Nunc et Achaemenio

trast with the open expanse of
the clear sky.

2. **deducunt Iovem**: the descent of Jupiter (see I. 1. 25 n) to
Earth in showers was an old conception of primitive physical spec-
ulation, and became a commonplace in later Greek and in Latin
literature. Cf. Verg. *E.* 7. 60 *Iuppiter et laeto descendet plurimus
imbri; G.* II. 325 *tum pater omni-
potens fecundis imbribus aether |
coniugis in gremium laetae descen-
dit.* — siluae : Intr. 182.

3. **Threicio Aquilone**: cf. *Thracio vento,* I. 25. 11 n, and see Intr.
185.— amici : see note on vs. 6.

4. **de die** : the meaning simply
is, that the day brings with it this
opportunity, and will carry it away
out of our reach if we do not
promptly lay hands on it; cf. *C.*
III. 8. 27. — **dum virent genua**:
i.e. while our physical powers are
in full vigor; a part (where the
weakness of age is conspicuous)
standing for the whole body; Intr.
117 *b.*

5. **decet**: cf. *C.* III. 15. 8.—**obducta**, *clouded.*—**solvatur fronte**:
cf. *curis expeditis,* I. 22. 11 n. —
senectus : here for the qualities
commonly associated with that
time of life ; cf. Cic. *C. M.* 65

*morosi et anxii et iracundi et diffi-
ciles senes.* For the contrast with
virent, cf. *C.* I. 9. 17 *sqq.*

6. **tu** : the poet here turns to
one of the company, and investing
him with the office of master of
ceremonies, addresses him in this
representative capacity through
the rest of the ode, as in *C.* I. 9.
The abruptness of the address,
without any name, is a little awkward, and has led some editors to
suspect *amici*, vs. 3 (see Crit. App.),
or to explain it as *nos amici* (nom.),
meaning the poet and a single companion. — **Torquato** : see *C.* III.
21. 1 n. — **move** : cf. (*testa*) *moveri
digna bono die,* ibid. 6.—**pressa**:
cf. *C.* IV. 12. 14.— **meo**: *i.e.* in the
year of the poet's birth.

7. **cetera**: cf. *C.* I. 9. 9 n. Here,
however, it appears from what follows that Horace had something
definite in mind, — perhaps the
unsatisfactory state of political
affairs. — **mitte**, *forbear.* — **loqui**:
Intr. 94 *j.* — **deus**, *Heaven;* see
C. I. 3. 21 n.—**benigna vice**, *with
generous reparation;* cf. *C.* IV. 14.
13 *plus vice simplici.* The allusion
is probably to the losses which
Horace and his friends had suffered in the civil war.

8. **sedem** (sc. *suam*): *i.e.* their

perfundi nardo iuvat et fide Cyllenea
10   levare diris pectora sollicitudinibus,
nobilis ut grandi cecinit centaurus alumno:
'Invicte, mortalis dea nate puer Thetide,
te manet Assaraci tellus, quam frigida parvi
findunt Scamandri flumina lubricus et Simois,
15 unde tibi reditum certo subtemine Parcae
rupere, nec mater domum caerula te revehet.
Illic omne malum vino cantuque levato,
deformis aegrimoniae dulcibus adloquiis.'

proper place or condition. Cf. the wish of Augustus, in Suet. *Aug.* 28 : *ita mihi salvam ac sospitem rem publicam sistere in sua sede liceat . . . ut optimi status auctor dicar.*—**Achaemenio**: see *C.* III. 1. 44 n.

9. **nardo** : see *C.* II. 3. 13 n.— **Cyllenea**: as having been invented by Mercury (cf. *C.* I. 10. 6), who was born on Mt. Cyllene in Arcadia. For the metre, see Intr. 132.

10. **levare**, etc.: cf. *C.* IV. 11. 35 *minuentur atrae carmine curae.*— **diris**, *ill-boding.*

11. **grandi**, *tall;* cf. Juv. 7. 210 *metuens virgae iam grandis Achilles.* — **cecinit**: implying an oracular character in his utterance. Cf. *C.* I. 15. 4 n. — **centaurus** : Chiron. — **alumno** : Achilles.

12. **invicte** : used substantively, as in Verg. *A.* VI. 365 *eripe me his, invicte, malis.* — **mortalis dea** : Intr. 116 *a*.

13. **Assaraci** : king of Troy, brother of Ganymede, great-grand-father of Aeneas. — **parvi** : probably more accurate than the Homeric μέγας πόταμος (*Il.* XX. 73).

14. **findunt**, *cleave;* poetical for ' flow through.' — **flumina**, *streams.* For the plural (a remi-

niscence perhaps of the Homeric ῥέεθρα), see Intr. 128. — **lubricus**: *i.e.* flowing with a smooth, swift current. — **et** : Intr. 114.

15. **unde** : used attributively with **reditum** ; cf. *unde periculum*, *C.* II. 12. 7 n. — **certo subtemine** : *i.e.* by an immutable decree ; cf. *C. S.* 25 n, Verg. *A.* X. 814 *sq.*, Gray, *The Bard*, 48 *sqq.* The ablative is better taken as instrumental.

16. **rupere** : cf. 16. 35 *reditus abscindere.* — **nec mater**, etc. : cf. Tib. I. 7. 1 *Parcae fatalia nentes | stamina, non ulli dissoluenda deo.* — **caerula** : as a sea-goddess ; cf. Ov. *Her.* 9. 14 *Nereus caerulus*, and see *C.* III. 28. 10 n.

17. **illic**, etc. : the envoys sent by Agamemnon find him engaged with the lyre, *Il.* IX. 186. — **levato** : cf. *abstineto*, III. 27. 69 n ; the time is implied in illic.

18. **deformis** : Intr. 125. — **adloquiis**, *solace ;* in apposition with **vino cantuque**.

XIV. In reply to Maecenas's urgent expostulation at the poet's indolence and delay in completing some poetry (apparently the book of Epodes), Horace protests that he is in love and can't help him-

XIV.

Mollis inertia cur tantam diffuderit imis
　　oblivionem sensibus,
pocula Lethaeos ut si ducentia somnos
　　arente fauce traxerim,
5　candide Maecenas, occidis saepe rogando:
　　deus, deus nam me vetat
inceptos, olim promissum carmen, iambos
　　ad umbilicum adducere.

self, quotes the example of Anacreon, and turns upon his patron
with an *argumentum ad hominem* :
' You are in love yourself, and you
may thank your stars your plight
is not so bad as mine.' The tone
of familiarity with which he addresses Maecenas is very noticeable. — Metre, 160.

1. **mollis inertia,** etc.: indirect
question, containing the gist of
Maecenas's　reproaches. — **cur** :
Intr. 114. — **imis** : *i.e.* to their very
centre ; it pervades them through
and through.

2. **sensibus** : dative, as with
divido (*e.g.* 11. 16), *distribuo*, etc.

3. **Lethaeos somnos** : the
sleep of utter forgetfulness. Cf.
Verg. *A.* VI. 714 *Lethaei ad flu-
minis undam | securos latices et
longa oblivia potant.* — **ut si**, etc. :
illustrating, not so much the degree
of forgetfulness, as the completeness (**imis sensibus**) with which
it has possessed him. — **ducentia** :
cf. *Ep.* I. 2. 31 *ad strepitum citharae cessatum ducere somnum ;*
Ovid *M.* II. 735 (of Mercury's
wand) *qua somnos ducit et arcet.*
— **somnos** : Intr. 128.

4. **arente fauce** : *i.e.* eagerly
and copiously; cf. Ov. *M.* XV.
330 *parum moderato gutture traxit.*

5. **candide** : referring to Maecenas's character in general (cf.
candidum ingenium, 11. 11), though
called out by his frank reproof
on this occasion, as *iocose Maecenas*, 3. 20; cf. *Ep.* I. 4. 1 *Albi,
nostrorum sermonum candide iudex*, I. 6. 67 *si quid novisti rectius
istis, candidus imperti.* — **occidis** :
an extravagance of colloquial language ; cf. Plaut. *Pseud.* 931 *occidis
me quom istuc rogitas; C.* II. 17. 1 n.

6. **deus, deus** : made emphatic
(Intr. 116 *d*, 114) because it sums
up his whole plea : 'a superior
power controls me and I am not
responsible.' The god is of course
Love.

7. **inceptos**, etc. : for the order,
cf. *Ep.* II. 1. 234 *acceptos regale
nomisma Philippos*, Verg. *E.* 2. 3
*inter densas umbrosa cacumina
fagos.* Intr. 109. — **olim promissum** : *i.e.* for which the public has
long been waiting ; cf. *Ep.* II. 3. 45
promissi carminis auctor. — **carmen** : apparently used here not
of a single poem, but generically
(*verse*), like *nomisma*, quoted above.
— **iambos** : probably the whole
collection of epodes, which Horace
designates by this name *Ep.* 1. 19.
23, II. 2. 59 ; see Intr. 18.

8. **ad umbilicum adducere,**

Non aliter Samio dicunt arsisse Bathyllo
10   Anacreonta Teium,
qui persaepe cava testudine flevit amorem
non elaboratum ad pedem.
Vreris ipse miser ; quod si non pulchrior ignis
accendit obsessam Ilion,
15   gaude sorte tua : me libertina nec uno
contenta Phryne macerat.

to bring to the end of the scroll, i.e.
to finish. The *umbilici* of a Roman book were the ends (often
ornamented) of the stick or reed
on which the long strip of papyrus
was rolled, and there is some reason to believe the name was also
applied to the stick itself. In
reading, the scroll was held hori-
zontally, the left hand gradually
rolling up the part already read,
while the part in the right was
gradually unrolled. The pages
followed one another laterally from
left to right, the last being next to
the stick.

9. **non aliter :** more commonly
used in returning to the main
theme *after* an illustration, as Verg.
A. I. 399, Ov. *M.* VIII. 473, etc.;
cf. *C.* IV. 15. 25 n. — **Bathyllo :**
a favorite boy. For the case see
Intr. 72.

11. **testudine :** see *C.* I. 10. 6 n.
— **flevit amorem :** *i.e.* gave expression to it in woful chants.
The corresponding word for light
and cheerful strains is *ludere,* as
si quid olim lusit Anacreon, C. IV.
9. 9 n ; cf. *C.* I. 32. 1 n. For the
construction see Intr. 51 *a.*

12. **non elaboratum :** this criticism is not very well understood,
as none of Anacreon's verses on
Bathyllus are preserved. But apparently it is intended to enforce
Horace's plea by pointing out that

Anacreon, in similar circumstances,
could not bring his mind to the
proper tension for composing polished verses. For the litotes, cf.
1. 10 n.

13. **ureris :** cf. *C.* I. 19. 5. —
ipse : no need for me to tell *you*
how it is. — **quod si :** here, as in
C. III. 1. 41, introducing a supposition assumed to be true, like *si
quidem.* — **ignis,** *flame* (cf. *C.* I.
27. 20 n), with a play on the double
meaning of the word: if the 'flame'
that warms you is as beautiful as
the one (Helen) that fired Ilion,
etc. The scholiasts profess to
know that the 'flame' referred to
was Terentia, who subsequently
became Maecenas's wife; see *C.* II.
12 intr. note.

15. **nec :** adding to **libertina**
another characteristic, that carries
the disparagement still farther, —
and not . . . either.

16. **macerat :** see *C.* I. 13. 8 n.
He comes back at the end to the
idea (**mollis**) with which he began.

XV. In the character of a
slighted lover, Horace heaps angry reproaches on the faithless
Neaera, recalls her ardent vows of
eternal devotion, tells her she will
find he is man enough to resent
her perfidy, and turns away with a
parting shaft over the shoulders of
his unknown rival, whom he warns

XV.

Nox erat et caelo fulgebat luna sereno
    inter minora sidera,
cum tu, magnorum numen laesura deorum,
    in verba iurabas mea,
5 artius atque hedera procera adstringitur ilex
    lentis adhaerens bracchiis,
dum pecori lupus et nautis infestus Orion
    turbaret hibernum mare
intonsosque agitaret Apollinis aura capillos,
10 fore hunc amorem mutuum.
O dolitura mea multum virtute Neaera !
    nam si quid in Flacco viri est,

of her treachery, which must inevitably bring upon him a like fate, and then the man over whom he is now enjoying his short-lived triumph will have his turn to laugh. The subject is similar to that of *C.* I. 5, but there is a marked contrast in the tone of the two poems. The greater vehemence of the epode is no doubt due to the fact that Horace was not only younger but was dealing with a fresh experience. — Metre, 160.

2. **inter**, etc.: cf. *C.* I. 12. 47.

3. **laesura** : Intr. 104 *c.*

4. **in verba mea** : *i.e.* repeating after me the oath as I dictated it. The expression, originally applied to the *sacramentum*, or military oath administered by the consul to his soldiers, came to be used for an oath of allegiance in general (cf. Tac. *Ann.* I. 7. 3 *consules primi in verba Tiberii Caesaris iuravere*), or figuratively of other kinds of devotion, as *Ep.* I. 1. 14.

5. **artius**, etc.: cf. *C.* I. 36. 20.— **atque** : see 12. 14 n.

7. **dum pecori lupus :** left without a verb by a change of the sentence from the form in which it was first conceived, *dum pecori lupus et nautis Orion infestus esset;* into this the description of Orion as *turbator hiberni maris,* coming in as an after-thought, was, instead of being simply added, incorporated in such a way as to supersede *esset.* For the comparison, see 4. 1 n.— **Orion** : see *C.* I. 28. 21 n and Intr. 178.

9. **intonsos,** etc.: another paraphrase for 'forever,' for the god's long locks were the mark of his eternal youth ; see *C.* I. 21. 2 n.

10. **hunc** : *i.e.* 'my.' — **mutuum**, *returned,* as in *animi mutui, C.* IV. 1. 30.

11. **dolitura :** Intr. 104 *b.* — **virtute**, *spirit ;* see *C.* III. 2. 17 n. The consciousness of the fundamental meaning of the word appears in *si quid viri,* 12.

12. **Flacco :** there is a touch of self-respect in the use of the name. Cf. *Teucro,* I. 7. 27 n.

non feret adsiduas potiori te dare noctis,
    et quaeret iratus parem ;
15 nec semel offensi cedet constantia formae,
    si certus intrarit dolor.
Et tu, quicumque es felicior atque meo nunc
    superbus incedis malo,
sis pecore et multa dives tellure licebit
20   tibique Pactolus fluat,
nec te Pythagorae fallant arcana renati,
    formaque vincas Nirea,
heu heu, translatos alio maerebis amores ;
    ast ego vicissim risero.

13. **potiori**: see *C.* III. 9. 2 n.
14. **et** : see note on *-que*, *C.* I.
27. 16. — **parem**: *i.e.* one who will
reciprocate his feelings.
15. **offensi** : sc. *Flacci*, limiting
constantia; cf. *calentis*, 11. 13, 14 n.
— **formae**, *to beauty.* Cf. Ov. *Am.*
III. 11. 37 *nequitiam fugio, fugien-
tem forma reducit.*
16. **certus**, *confirmed.* This
verse betrays his weakness in spite
of his brave words : the door to a
reconciliation is not yet absolutely
closed ; cf. 11. 15 *sqq.*
17. **et tu . . . felicior**, etc. : cf.
Tib. I. 2. 87; 5. 69 *at tu, qui potior
nunc es, mea fata timeto.*
18. **superbus incedis malo** :
cf. 4. 5.
19. **sis pecore**, etc. : no wealth,
no wisdom, no beauty can save
you from the inevitable result of
her caprice. — **sis licebit**: con-
formed to the time of **maerebis**,
23.
20. **tibi fluat** : *i.e.* you enjoy
the benefit of it ; cf. *tibi tollit, C.*
II. 16. 34. — **Pactolus** : in Lydia,
famous for the gold found in its
sands.

21. **nec te fallant** : *i.e.* you
have the capacity to comprehend
them. — **arcana**, *the mysteries, i.e.*
his abstruse philosophical specula-
tions. — **renati** : see *C.* I. 28. 10 n.
22. **Nirea** : see *C.* III. 20 15. n.
23. **heu heu** : here expressing
scornful pity.
24. **ast** : a quaint form, in colloquial use as late as Cicero, who
sometimes used it in his letters
(*e.g. ad Att.* I. 16. 17). It was
much affected by Vergil, but
Horace used it only in his earliest
writings (here and twice in the
first book of the Satires). — **rise-
ro** : expressing stronger assurance
than the simple future; cf. Ter.
Heaut. 85 *crede inquam mihi :
aut consolando aut consiliis aut re
iuvero.*

XVI. This epode, the best of
Horace's political poems, is probably the earliest also. It belongs
to the first years after his return
from Philippi, before his introduction to Maecenas, — the period of
sollicitum taedium (*C.* I. 14. 17),
when he was still the mourner for

XVI.

Altera iam teritur bellis civilibus aetas,
  suis et ipsa Roma viribus ruit.
Quam neque finitimi valuerunt perdere Marsi
  minacis aut Etrusca Porsenae manus,
5 aemula nec virtus Capuae nec Spartacus acer
  novisque rebus infidelis Allobrox,

a lost cause, and could see no hope for his country in any of the contending factions, and no prospect but the wasting away of her strength in civil strife that could end only in her falling a prey to some foreign invader. The verses are full of a genuine feeling which we miss in the odes that deal with matters of state; they glow with youthful enthusiasm and a patriotic fervor which has not yet yielded to the seductive charm of personal friendship or been cooled into political wisdom. In form, as well as in poetic sentiment, the epode is among the most perfect pieces that Horace has left us. — Metre, 161 ; see also 184.

1. **altera,** *a second;* looking back to the times of Marius and Sulla. — **teritur,** *is wasting away.* — **aetas,** *generation.*

2. **suis ipsa :** in prose, *suis ipsius.*

3. **quam,** *her whom.* In his list of the dangerous enemies whom Rome had withstood, Horace follows the order of distance rather than of time. — **neque,** etc.: notice the variety in the use of conjunctions.—**perdere :** Intr. 94 *n.* — **Marsi :** see *C.* III. 14. 18 n, I. 2. 39 n.

4. **aut :** Intr. 114.— **Etrusca,** etc. : cf. 10. 12 n. — **Porsenae :** king of Clusium, who took up the

cause of the banished Tarquins, forced the city to surrender, and imposed terms of peace, which did not, however, include the restoration of the kings. Cf. Tac. *Hist.* III. 72 (referring to the burning of the Capitol in A.D. 69 in much the same spirit in which Horace writes here) *nullo externo hoste, propitiis si per mores nostros liceret deis, sedem Iovis optimi Maximi, . . . quam non Porsenna dedita urbe neque Galli capta temerare potuissent, furore principum exscindi.*

5. **Capuae :** cf. Cic. *Leg. Agr.* 2. 87 *quo in oppido maiores nostri nullam omnino rem publicam esse voluerunt ; qui tres solum urbes in terris omnibus, Karthaginem, Corinthum, Capuam, statuerunt posse imperii gravitatem ac nomen sustinere.* This jealousy of the Romans was aroused by the conduct of the Capuans after the battle of Cannae, when they joined Hannibal and openly aspired (**aemula**) to supplant Rome in the hegemony of Italy. — **Spartacus :** see *C.* III. 14. 19 n.

6. **novis rebus,** *in times of treason;* referring to the Catilinarian conspiracy, when the Allobrogian envoys were tampered with by the conspirators, but thought it for their own interest to betray them. The tribe itself, however, which occupied the district between the

nec fera caerulea domuit Germania pube
    parentibusque abominatus Hannibal,
impia perdemus devoti sanguinis aetas,
10   ferisque rursus occupabitur solum.
Barbarus heu cineres insistet victor et urbem
    eques sonante verberabit ungula,
quaeque carent ventis et solibus ossa Quirini
    (nefas videre) dissipabit insolens.

Rhone and the Isère, soon after
revolted, and was reduced by C.
Pomptinus, B.C. 54. Cf. Cic. *in Cat.*
3. 4 *sqq.*, Sal. *Cat.* 40 *sqq.* Their
treachery at such a critical time
seems to have exaggerated their
importance in the eyes of the
Romans, as in the case of Capua.

7. **caerulea,** *blue-eyed,* a noted
characteristic of the German ; cf.
Juv. 13. 164 *caerula quis stupuit
Germani lumina ?* Tac. *Ger.* 4
(*omnibus*) *truces et caerulei oculi,
rutilae comae, magna corpora.* —
Germania : referring to the great
invasion of the Cimbri and Teu-
tones, who were defeated and
destroyed, the latter at Aquae
Sextiae in B.C. 102, the former at
Vercellae in 101, by Marius, —
probably the greatest peril to
which Rome had been exposed
since the destruction of the city
by the Gauls.

8. **parentibus abominatus :**
cf. *matribus detestata, C.* I. 1. 24.
Intr. 54.

9. **impia aetas :** in apposition
with the subject of **perdemus.**
Cf. *C.* I. 35. 34. — **devoti sanguinis,** *with a curse in our blood.* Cf.
7. 20.

10. **feris :** Intr. 55. — **rursus :**
as in the times before Romulus.
How this is to be brought about
is indicated in the next two couplets.

11. **barbarus :** such as the
Parthian (I. 12. 53), the Dacian
(III. 6. 14), the German, etc. —
cineres: *sc.* of the burned city.
— **insistet,** *will set his foot upon ;* with acc. as in Ter. *Eun.*
294 *quam insistam viam, incertus
sum.*

12. **eques** (with **barbarus**), *on
horse.* — **sonante :** in fancy the
poet hears the clatter of the hoofs
breaking the stillness of the deserted street.

13. **carent,** *are sheltered from ;*
in contrast with the profanation to
which they are to be exposed. —
solibus : cf. 2. 41 n, *C.* IV. 2. 46 n.
—**ossa Quirini:** according to
Varro, as quoted by Porphyrio,
Romulus was buried behind the
Rostra ; it would appear that the
story of his apotheosis (Liv. I. 16)
was by no means generally accepted at this time.

14. **nefas** (sc. *est*) **videre:** cf.
scire nefas, I. 11. 1 ; the act of
desecration is a sin so abominable
that one would turn away or cover
his eyes to avoid the pollution of
even beholding it.   For the omission of *est,* cf. *C.* I. 11. 1, 37. 5,
III. 24. 24; Verg. *A.* VIII. 173 *quae
differre nefas.* — **insolens:** cf. *C.*
I. 16. 21.

15. **forte :** here equivalent to
forsitan, the clause being virtually
a condition, *si forte quaeritis,* etc.

15 Forte quid expediat communiter aut melior pars
        malis carere quaeritis laboribus.
    Nulla sit hac potior sententia: Phocaeorum
        velut profugit exsecrata civitas
    agros atque laris patrios habitandaque fana
20   apris reliquit et rapacibus lupis,
    ire pedes quocumque ferent, quocumque per undas
        Notus vocabit aut protervus Africus.
    Sic placet, an melius quis habet suadere? Secunda
        ratem occupare quid moramur alite?

— **quid expediat**, *what it is best
to do.* — **communiter**: equivalent
to *omnes.* — **pars** (sc. *vestrum*):
in apposition with the subject of
quaeritis; cf. *aetas*, vs. 9 n.
16. **carere**, *to be rid of.* Best
taken as infinitive of purpose
(Intr. 93); cf. Verg. *E.* 4. 54 *quantum sat erit tua dicere facta;* Lucr.
III. 1030 *iter dedit legionibus ire
per altum.* If we read *quod expediat* (see Crit. App.), **carere**
is complementary infinitive with
quaeritis; Intr. 94 *c.*
17. **sit**, ... *perhaps ... is;* po-
tential subjunctive. — **sententia**:
the technical term for a proposition brought forward in a deliberative body. The poet in fancy
addresses his countrymen of kindred spirit (**melior pars**) sitting
in council. The actual proposition
begins with **ire**, 21, which is in
apposition with **hac** (sc. *sententia*).
— **Phocaeorum**: the inhabitants
of Phocaea, a powerful Athenian
colony in Ionia, itself the mother
city of Massilia and other important colonies in the West. According to Herodotus (I. 164 *sq.*), they
left their city in a body to escape
subjection to the Persians, and
sailed away to Aleria, in Corsica.
A part of them, however, subse-

quently returned. For the metre,
see Intr. 132.
18. **velut**: Intr. 114. — **profū-
git**: here transitive; a poetical
usage in Horace's time. — **exse-
crata**: used absolutely, — having
sworn (with imprecations) *sc.* that
they would not return; *under a
curse.* 'They pronounced powerful curses on any of their number
who should desert the enterprise;
and, in addition to this, they
dropped into the sea a lump of
iron, and swore never to return to
Phocaea till this iron should re-
appear' (Herod. *l. l.*).
19. **patrios**: suggesting, like
fana, the most hallowed associations. — **habitanda**, etc.: a typical
picture of utter desolation; cf. vs.
10 and *C.* III. 3. 40.
21. **pedes**, etc.: *i.e.* by land, in
contrast with **per undas**; cf. *C.*
III. 11, 49 n.
22. **vocabit**, *shall invite us.*
Cf. Cat. 4. 19 *laeva sive dextera
| vocaret aura.* — **protervus**: cf.
C. I. 26. 2, and *praecipitem Africum*, I. 3. 12 n.
23. **sic placet**, *is such your
pleasure?* keeping up the figure of
a deliberative assembly. — **suadere**: Intr. 94 *n.* — **secunda alite**:
cf. 10. 1 n.

25 Sed iuremus in haec : ' Simul imis saxa renarint
        vadis levata, ne redire sit nefas ;
    neu conversa domum pigeat dare lintea quando
        Padus Matina laverit cacumina,
    in mare seu celsus procurrerit Appenninus,
30   novaque monstra iunxerit libidine
    mirus amor, iuvet ut tigris subsidere cervis
        adulteretur et columba miluo,
    credula nec ravos timeant armenta leones,
        ametque salsa levis hircus aequora.'
35 Haec et quae poterunt reditus abscindere dulcis
        eamus omnis exsecrata civitas,
    aut pars indocili melior grege ; mollis et exspes
        inominata perprimat cubilia.

25. **in haec** (sc. *verba*): cf. 15.4 n.
— **saxa**: for the mass of iron in the
oath of the Phocaeans, which Horace evidently had in mind, as **renarint** shows. Setting out with this,
the poet proposes a series of impossible contingencies to bind them
more firmly to their hard resolve.
For other examples of the use of
this favorite figure (σχῆμα ἀδυνάτου),
cf. *C.* I. 29. 10 *sqq.*, 33. 7 *sq.*; *Il.* I.
234 *sqq.*; Verg. *E.* I. 59 *sqq.*, 8. 27 *sqq.*
    26. **vadis**: Intr. 70.
    28. **Matina**: see *C.* I. 28. 3 n.
    29. **procurrerit**: cf. Ov. *F.* IV.
419 *terra tribus scopulis vastum
procurrit in aequor.* The Apennines are an interior range. The
figure is the converse of the preceding. For the metre, see Intr. 132.
    30. **monstra**, *unnatural crea-
tures ;* proleptic: the **mirus amor**
turns them into **monstra**.
    31. **tigris**, etc.: the picture of
these monstrous unions is heightened by the reversal of the natures
of the animals : the tiger becomes

submissive, the deer bold. The
dove, moreover, was a type of con-
jugal fidelity ; cf. Prop. III. 7. 27
*exemplo iunctae tibi sint in amore
columbae ;* Plin. *N. H.* X. 104.
    32. **et**: Intr. 114. — **miluo**: da-
tive. Intr. 56.
    33. **credula**, *confiding, trustful;*
proleptic. — **ravos** : cf. III. 27. 3.
    34. **lēvis** : like a sea animal ;
proleptic.
    35. **haec**: cognate object of **ex-
secrata.** — **quae**, *whatever else;* cf.
quisquis, C. II. 1. 25 n ; I. 19. 12. —
reditus: see *C.* III. 5. 52 n ; Intr. 128.
    36. **exsecrata civitas**: repeated
from 18. For the construction of
civitas, cf. *aetas*, 9 n.
    37. **pars melior**: cf. vs. 15. —
indocili grege : the kind of people who are too dull or too deep
in their ruts to take new ideas ;
with too little energy (**mollis**) for
action and enterprise, and too
little spirit to hope (**exspes**).
    38. **inominata**, *ill-starred;* found
here only.

Vos, quibus est virtus, muliebrem tollite luctum,
40   Etrusca praeter et volate litora.

Nos manet Oceanus circumvagus ; arva beata
        petamus, arva divites et insulas,

reddit ubi Cererem tellus inarata quotannis
        et imputata floret usque vinea,

45 germinat et numquam fallentis termes olivae
        suamque pulla ficus ornat arborem,

39. **muliebrem** : in contrast (Intr. 116 *a*) with **virtus**, for which see 15. 11 n. — **tollite**: cf. *C.* I. 27. 2 n.

40. **Etrusca**, etc. : the usual route of voyagers to the West. — **praeter**: Intr. 115 *b*. — **et** : Intr. 114.

41. **nos** : the change of person (cf. *vos*, 39) implies that his appeal has been successful ; they are now with him, and he turns from exhortation to consolation, pointing to the greater recompense in store for those who make the sacrifice he demands. — **circumvagus** : a word probably of Horace's own coining, expressing the ever-changing movements of the sea, and a happy variation on the Homeric ἀψόρροος, which Ovid (*M.* I. 30) more literally renders *circumfluus*, an epithet properly applicable to a river, which the ocean was in Homeric geography (cf. *Il.* XX. 7). That the ocean, however, surrounded the habitable lands was also taught by Roman geographers ; see Plin. *N. H.* II. 166 *sq.*

42. **arva** : repeated to form the connection with **divites insulas**, etc. ; cf. *aere*, 65; *amore* 11. 3 ; Intr. 116 *h*. The epithet **beata** is not repeated, and is unnecessary in such close connection with **divites insulas**, with which **arva**

is joined in hendiadys. — **et** : Intr. 114. — **insulas** : the 'Isles of the Blest' (μακάρων νῆσοι) of Hesiod (*Op.* 170 *sqq.*), — the Elysian plain of Homer (*Odys.* IV. 563 *sqq.*) — were the mythical abode, situated in the ocean towards the setting sun, of departed heroes. Later mythology transferred Elysium to the underworld, while the 'Insulae Fortunatae' came to be recognized in ancient geography and were placed off the coast of Africa, on the basis of reports of traders, who claimed to have seen islands in those seas (probably the Madeiras); see Plin. *N. H.* IV. 119, VI. 202. It is said that Sertorius at one time thought of abandoning the contest with the aristocracy and setting sail with his followers in search of the 'Happy Isles' (Plutarch, *Sert.* 8) ; and it is not unlikely that the same scheme actually suggested itself to Horace and his friends after Philippi.

43. **Cererem** : Intr. 130.

45. **numquam fallentis** : cf. *fundus mendax*, *C.* III. 1. 30. It implies exemption from care, as **inarata** and **imputata**, above, from toil.

46. **suam**: emphatic (Intr. 116 *b*); the finer varieties of the fig, as of the pear (cf. 2. 19 n) can be propagated only by grafting. Cf. Verg. *G.* II. 81 *sq.* (of the grafted tree)

mella cava manant ex ilice, montibus altis
    levis crepante lympha desilit pede.
Illic iniussae veniunt ad mulctra capellae,
50   refertque tenta grex amicus ubera,
nec vespertinus circum gemit ursus ovile,
    neque intumescit alta viperis humus ;
61 nulla nocent pecori contagia, nullius astri
    gregem aestuosa torret impotentia.
53 Pluraque felices mirabimur, ut neque largis
    aquosus Eurus arva radat imbribus,

exsilit ad caelum ramis felicibus arbos | *miraturque novas frondes et non sua poma.* — pulla : *i.e.* fully ripe.

47. mella, etc.: for the skilful construction of this and the next verse see Intr. 131. — montibus : Intr. 70.

48. levis, etc.: the beauty of this verse, which has caught up some of the music of the brook itself, was remarked by Porphyrio. It is not, however, a merely ornamental addition to the description. A natural supply of water for man and beast in contrast with a parched country like Apulia, or with the artificial supply of the city, is a necessary part of the picture ; cf. *Ep.* I. 10. 20 *sq.* — pede : a bold extension of the metaphor in desilit. Cf. Lucr. V. 272 *qua via secta semel liquido pede labitur unda.*

49. illic, etc.: the flocks and herds need no keeper to drive them or to guard them from danger. Cf. *C.* I. 17. 5 *sqq.*

50. refert, *brings home.*—tenta = *distenta,* 2. 46 ; Intr. 129. — amicus : corresponding to iniussae, 49.

51. vespertinus : with adverbial force ; cf. *Ep.* I. 6. 20 *navus mane*

forum, vespertinus pete tectum. — circum gemit : Intr. 115 *c.*

52. intumescit : the action of the vipers is attributed to the ground, as where we say 'the place was swarming with ants' or the like. — alta : proleptic, with intumescit.

61, 62. This couplet is found in all the MSS. after vs. 60, where it is obviously out of place and interrupts the course of thought, which (from vs. 57 to the close of the poem) is of the immunity of the Happy Isles from corrupting human and moral influences.   It must have stood originally somewhere before vs. 57, and has been misplaced in copying (see Crit. App.).

61. nullius : Intr. 116 *b.*—astri : such as those mentioned, *C.* III. 29. 17 *sqq.*

62. aestuosa impotentia, *furious heat,* causing pestilence. Cf. Virg. *G.* III. 478 *sqq.* For impotentia, cf. *impotens, C.* I. 37. 10 n, III. 30. 3 ; and for this application of it, III. 29. 18 *sq.*

53. ut, *how,* after mirabimur, as in *C.* III. 4. 17 after *mirum foret.* — neque, etc. : the climate is temperate, free from extremes of storm and drouth.

54. aquosus : cf. *udo Noto,* 10.

55 pinguia nec siccis urantur semina glaebis,
    utrumque rege temperante caelitum.
Non huc Argoo contendit remige pinus,
    neque impudica Colchis intulit pedem ;
non huc Sidonii torserunt cornua nautae,
60 laboriosa nec cohors Ulixei :
63 Iuppiter illa piae secrevit litora genti,
    ut inquinavit aere tempus aureum ;
65 aere, dehinc ferro duravit saecula, quorum
    piis secunda vate me datur fuga.

19 n, *pluvias Hyadas*, Verg. *A*. III. 516 ; Intr. 125.— **Eurus**: cf. *C*. III. 17. 11.— **radat**: *i.e.* floods them and washes away the crops.

55. **siccis**: proleptic.—**glaebis**: Intr. 69.

56. **utrumque**: *i.e.* both excess of rain and drouth.— **rege**: Jupiter ; see *C*. I. 1. 25 n.

57. **non huc**, etc.: no man, not even the boldest navigator, has ever trodden the shores of this paradise; it has remained uncontaminated by the degeneracy which (largely through the corrupting influence of commerce) has spread over the rest of the world,— a bit of the Golden Age, set apart by Jove for his elect.— **Argoo**: cf. *Etrusca*, 4, and see 10. 12 n. — **remige**: used collectively (Intr. 127) and impersonally, like a body of troops, in the instrumental ablative (Madv. 254 Obs. 3). — **pinus**: for the ship; cf. *C*. I. 14. 11 *Pontica pinus* ; Cat. 64. 1 *Peliaco quondam prognatae vertice pinus | dicuntur liquidas Neptuni nasse per undas*.

58. **Colchis**: Medea.

59. **Sidonii**: for the Phoenician traders in general. Intr. 117 *b*.—

torserunt cornua: *i.e.* directed their course; a paraphrase for the commonplace *vela dare*. The action expressed is that of swinging the yards into position.

60. **laboriosa**: the epithet belonging properly to Ulysses (πολύτλας, πολυτλήμων), is here transferred to his men. Cf. 17. 16, and see Intr. 124.

63. **piae genti**, *for a righteous people*, meaning the nation which the poet and his companions should found ; cf. *piis*, 66.

64. **inquinavit**, *alloyed*.

65. **aere**: with **duravit** ; for the anaphora, cf. *arva* 42 n. — **quorum**, *from which ;* objective genitive. The present is then with Horace, as with Hesiod, the age of iron. In Hesiod, however (*Op*. 109 *sqq*.), the iron age is the fifth, there being a silver age between the gold and the bronze, and a fourth,—the age of the heroes, not named after any metal, — preceding that of iron. The legend appears in various forms in other poets ; see Mayor on Juv. 13. 30.

66. **vate me**, *according to my prophecy*.

XVII.

Iam iam efficaci do manus scientiae,
supplex et oro regna per Proserpinae,
per et Dianae non movenda numina,
per atque libros carminum valentium
5   refixa caelo devocare sidera,
Canidia, parce vocibus tandem sacris
citumque retro solve, solve turbinem.

XVII. Horace's muse fairly runs riot in this burlesque, in which he makes his final attack on Canidia. He represents himself as one of her victims, reduced to submission at last by her powerful art ; and in his humble recantation and piteous appeal for mercy, as well as in Canidia's stern reply, he manages to reiterate, with telling irony, all his old charges against her. Our poet tempted fate in thus giving loose rein to his fancy; for this poem, sifted through learned brains, has come out a confession that he had been a veritable lover of the witch. See intr. note to Epode 5. — Metre, 158.

1. iam iam : Intr. 116 *d.* — do manus, *surrender,* as a vanquished soldier who throws down his arms and holds out his hands to be bound.

2. et, et, atque : Intr. 114. — per : Intr. 115 *a.*

3. Dianae : see 5. 51 n. She is here more distinctly identified with Hecate ; cf. *S.* I. 8. 33. — non movenda : equivalent, according to Porphyrio, who is followed by modern editors, to *non lacessenda,* 'not to be provoked' (cf. III. 20. 1) ; but there is reason to think that Horace uses the phrase in the sense of *inexorable,* a standing

attribute of the powers of the lower world; cf. *C.* II. 3. 24, 14. 6, 18. 34 *sqq.,* etc. This use of *moveo* is common in such connection ; cf. vs. 8, *C.* I. 21. 16, Verg. *G.* IV. 505 *quo fletu manis, quae numina voce moveret ?* — numina : Intr. 128.

4. libros : conjuring books, containing instructions and magic formulas. — carminum : cf. 5. 72 n.

5. refixa : proleptic, — *dislodge and.* Cf. Verg. *A.* V. 527 *caelo ceu saepe refixa | transcurrunt crinemque volantia sidera ducunt.* — devocare : Intr. 94 *n.*

6. parce : cf. III. 14. 12 n. — vocibus sacris : a respectful expression, in accordance with the claims of sorcery, for the gibberish that accompanied the whirling of the *turbo ;* see Lucian (quoted below).

7. citum : best taken as a participle (proleptic) with retro, *whirl backward and untwist ;* cf. 9. 20. — solve, solve (Intr. 116 *d*) : in reference to the binding constraint which the whirling of the *turbo* was supposed to exert on the heart of the person sought to be influenced. Cf. Prop. IV. 6. 26 *staminea rhombi ducitur ille rota;* Ov. *Am.* I. 8. 7. — turbinem : the Latin name for the magic rhomb ($\rho \acute{o} \mu \beta o s$), which was not, it seems, a real wheel

Movit nepotem Telephus Nereium,
in quem superbus ordinarat agmina
10　Mysorum et in quem tela acuta torserat.
Luxere matres Iliae addictum feris
alitibus atque canibus homicidam Hectorem,
postquam relictis moenibus rex procidit
heu pervicacis ad pedes Achillei.
15　Saetosa duris exuere pellibus
laboriosi remiges Ulixei

but a small lozenge-shaped board (hence the name) attached by one end to a cord and whirled round to make a loud buzzing sound. It is so defined by Hesychius : ξυλή-ριον, οὖ ἐξῆπται σχοινίον, καὶ ἐν ταῖς τελεταῖς δινεῖται ἵνα ῥοιζῇ. The use of it to charm back a lover is described by Lucian, *Dial. Meretr.* 4. 5. εἶτα (ἡ γραῦς) ἐκ τοῦ κόλπου προκομίσασα ῥόμβον ἐπιστρέφει, ἐπῳ-δήν τινα λέγουσα ἐπιτρόχῳ τῇ γλώτ-τῃ, βαρβαρικὰ καὶ φρικώδη ὀνόματα. It is used in mystic rites among uncivilized peoples at the present day, and in Greece was no doubt a survival from ancestral barba-rism. See Andrew Lang's *Custom and Myth*, pp. 29 *sqq.*

8. **nepotem** : Achilles, whose mother Thetis was the daughter of Nereus. — **Telephus** : king of Mysia and son-in-law of Priam. He resisted the Greeks in their invasion of the Troad, and was wounded by Achilles. Having been told by an oracle that he could be healed only by the rust of the spear which had made the wound, he was obliged to throw himself on the compassion of his enemy.

11. **luxere**, etc.: *i.e.* Achilles was moved by pity to grant even his bitterest enemy honorable burial. *Lugere* is the term for

formal mourning; cf. Liv. II. 7. 4 *matronae annum ut parentem eum luxerunt.* The reference is to the affecting scene in the *Iliad*, XXIV. 719 *sqq.*, on Priam's return from the Greek camp with Hector's body. — **Iliae** : Intr. 65. — **addic-tum**, etc.: by Achilles, as a consola-tion to Patroclus ; cf. *Il.* XXIII. 179 χαῖρέ μοι, ὦ Πάτροκλε, καὶ εἰν Ἀΐδαο δόμοισιν, . . . Ἕκτορα δ' οὔ τι | δώσω Πριαμίδην πυρὶ δαπτέμεν, ἀλλὰ κύνεσσιν.

12. **homicidam** : cf. Ἕκτορος ἀνδροφόνοιο, *Il.* XXIV. 724, and Andromache's proud words, *ib.* 737 *sqq.*

14. **heu** : the pathos lies in the humiliation of the powerful mon-arch, who placed himself at the mercy of his enemy (**relictis moenibus**) ; cf. *Ilio relicto, C.* I. 10. 14 n) and threw himself at his feet. — **pervicacis** : implying that the appeal might well have seemed hopeless. — **Achillei**: see *C.* I. 6. 7 n.

15. **saetosa** : when they were changed into swine. The story is told *Odys.* X. 135 *sqq.* — **pellibus**: ablative ; see Gr. 225 *d.*

16. **laboriosi**, *much afflicted ;* better taken here (in spite of 16. 60) with **Vlixei**, being the Latin equivalent of the Homeric πολύ-τλας, πολυτλήμων.

volente Circa membra ; tunc mens et sonus
relapsus atque notus in voltus honor.
Dedi satis superque poenarum tibi,
20   amata nautis multum et institoribus.
Fugit iuventas et verecundus color,
reliquit ossa pelle amicta lurida,
tuis capillus albus est odoribus ;
nullum a labore me reclinat otium,
25   urget diem nox et dies noctem, neque est
levare tenta spiritu praecordia.
Ergo negatum vincor ut credam miser,
Sabella pectus increpare carmina
caputque Marsa dissilire nenia.
30   Quid amplius vis ? O mare et terra, ardeo

17. **sonus**: *i.e.* voice.

18. **honor**, *grace*, in contrast with the brutish form from which they emerged ; cf. 11. 6, *C.* II. 11. 9.

20. **amata**, etc. : a mock compliment, in which the poet's irony for the first time breaks through its disguise. — **multum** : Intr. 49. — **institoribus**: see *C.* III. 6. 30 n.

21. **fūgit**: see Intr. 77 ; both **iuventas** and **color** here combine to form one idea, — the sensitive complexion of healthy youth.

22. **reliquit**, *has left behind*. — **ossa**, etc. : cf. our 'nothing but skin and bones,' and Plaut. *Capt.* 135 *ossa atque pellis sum miser macritudine*.

23. **albus**, *bleached*. — **odoribus**: *i.e.* magic ointments ; cf. 5. 59.

24. **a labore reclinat** : cf. the opposite expression, *in aliquid incumbere*. — **labore**, *distress* — **otium** : cf. *C.* II. 16. 1 n.

25. **urget**, etc. : cf. *truditur dies die*, *C.* II. 18. 15. — **neque**, *but . . . not*. — **est levare** : Intr. 94 *n*.

26. **tenta spiritu**, *heaving*. — **praecordia** : here used for the lungs ; translate *breast*.

27. **negatum** (sc. *a me*): Intr. 103. The clauses in the next two verses are in apposition with it.

28. **Sabella** : cf. *S.* I. 9. 29 *sqq.* The Sabines, like the Marsi and Paeligni (vs. 60), were noted for their practice of magic. — **pectus**: cf. *C.* I. 3. 10 n. — **increpare**, *do assail*.

29. **Marsa** : cf. 5. 76 n. — **dissilire**, *splits* (with pain). This effect was believed to be produced, in a literal sense, on snakes; cf. Verg. *E.* 8. 71, Lucil. 512 *Marsus colubras disrumpit cantu.*—**nenia**: *i.e.* an incantation. The name suggests a slow crooning chant ; cf. *C.* III. 28. 16 n.

30. **o mare et terra**: a common exclamation in every-day life, either in distress or in joy. Cf. Ter. *Ad.* 790 *o caélum, o terra, o mária Neptuni!* Plaut. *Trin.* 1070 *mare terra caélum, di vostrám fidem!*

quantum neque atro delibutus Hercules
Nessi cruore nec Sicana fervida
virens in Aetna flamma: tu, donec cinis
iniuriosis aridus ventis ferar,
35   cales venenis officina Colchicis.
Quae finis aut quod me manet stipendium?
Effare! Iussas cum fide poenas luam,
paratus expiare seu poposceris
centum iuvencis, sive mendaci lyra
40   voles, sonare 'Tu pudica, tu proba
perambulabis astra sidus aureum.'
[Infamis Helenae Castor offensus vicem
fraterque magni Castoris, victi prece

---

31. **atro**: cf. *C.* I. 37. 27 n.

32. **Nessi cruore**: see 3. 17 n. —**Sicana**: better taken with **flamma**; **fervidā**, with **Aetnā**.

33. **virens**, *that burns un-dimmed.* — **cinis**, *cinder*.

34. **iniuriosis**, *ruthless;* cf. *C.* I. 35. 13 n. — **ventis**: dative, the winds being personified; Intr. 55.

35. **cales**, *are hot;* cf. *calet uno scribendi studio, Ep.* II. 1. 108. Here a humorous turn is given to the figure by the extravagance of **officina**, *a very laboratory.* Cf. Plaut. *Truc.* 586 *tun . . . quae sis stabulum flagiti?*—**Colchicis**: see *C.* II. 13. 8 n.

36. **quae finis**: see *C.* II. 18. 30 n. — **me manet**: *i.e.* will be exacted of me, as your vanquished enemy.

37. **poenas luam**, *will do penance.*

38. **seu**, etc.: for the construction, cf. I. 4. 12 n.

39. **centum iuvencis**: a hecatomb. — **mendaci**: another touch of irony, lurking in the intentional ambiguity of the epithet, which can be applied to what follows, as

well as to what he has previously said of her in his verse.

40. **sonare**: cf. *C.* II. 13. 26 n. — **tu pudica**, etc.: cf. Cat. 42. 24.

41. **perambulabis**, *you will stroll among;* a word in humorous contrast with the dignity of the splendid destiny promised; cf. *C.* IV. 5. 17. — **aureum**: cf. Verg. *A.* II. 488 *aurea sidera.*

42. **infamis**, etc.: the poet appeals once more to precedent, the famous case of Stesichorus (see *C.* IV. 9. 8 n), who, having become suddenly blind, was made aware that it was a penalty, inflicted (according to the version which Horace follows) by Castor and Pollux, for the aspersions (in his Ἰλίου πέρσις) on the character of their sister Helen; whereupon he promptly recanted (*Fr.* 44): Οὐκ ἔστ᾽ ἔτυμος λόγος οὗτος· | οὐδ᾽ ἔβας ἐν νηυσὶν ἐυσσέλμοις, | οὐδ᾽ ἵκεο πέργαμα Τροίας· and his sight was restored. — **Helenae vicem**: cf. Plaut. *Most.* 1145 *ut tú meam timeás vicem;* Liv. XXXIV. 32. 6 *ne nostram vicem irascaris.*

adempta vati reddidere lumina:

45   et tu (potes nam) solve me dementia,
o nec paternis obsoleta sordibus,
nec in sepulcris pauperum prudens anus
novendialis dissipare pulveres!
Tibi hospitale pectus et purae manus,

50   tuusque venter Pactumeius, et tuo
cruore rubros obstetrix pannos lavit,
utcumque fortis exsilis puerpera.
Quid obseratis auribus fundis preces?
Non saxa nudis surdiora navitis

55   Neptunus alto tundit hibernus salo.
Inultus ut tu riseris Cotyttia

44. **vati**: Intr. 76.

45. **potes nam**: a form of appeal, at once flattering and persuasive, often inserted in prayers; cf. *C.* III. 11. 1 *sq.*, *S.* II. 3. 283, 284, *Odys.* V. 25. For the position of **nam**, see Intr. 114.

46. **o nec**, etc.: in imitation of Stesichorus he boldly proclaims false what all the world knows to be true, and true what all know to be false. — **paternis**, etc.: *i.e.* a low-born creature, brought up in squalid poverty. Cf. *C.* II. 10. 6 n.

47. **sepulcris pauperum**: *e.g.* on the Esquiline, where she is represented as performing her magic rites in *S.* I. 8. The bodies of the poor were often buried (not burnt), and would usually be unprotected; cf. *S.* I. 8. 8 *sq.*

48. **novendialis**: *i.e.* just buried, the last rites at the tomb being completed on the ninth day after death. — **dissipare**: Intr. 101 *c.* — **pulveres**: Intr. 128.

49. **hospitale**, etc.: probably referring to the story told in Epode 5.

50. **tuus . . . tuo**: Intr. 116 *g.* — **venter**, *own child;* cf. Liv. I. 34. 3. — **Pactumeius**: apparently a child Canidia tried to palm off on her lover as her own.

51. **lāvit**: see *C.* II. 3. 18 n.

52. **fortis exsilis**: another mock compliment, implying that the whole performance was a sham. Cf. 5. 5 *sq.*

53–81. Canidia's reply.

54. **non saxa**, etc.: *i.e.* they are not more deaf, when Neptune, etc. — **nudis**: *i.e.* stripped of all they possessed, implying that they have been shipwrecked. — **surdiora**: cf. *C.* III. 7. 21.

55. **Neptunus**: cf. *Ep.* I. 11. 10, where, as here, the personality of the god is not entirely merged in his element (Intr. 130), as it is, *e.g.* in 7. 3. — **hibernus**: cf. 2. 29; Stat. *Theb.* III. 26 *fragor hiberni subitus Iovis.*

56. **inultus ut tu**, etc., *What, let you go unwhipped for having divulged and ridiculed;* Gr. 332 *c.* — **Cotyttia**: properly the grossly sensual orgies of the Thracian

volgata, sacrum liberi Cupidinis,
et Esquilini pontifex venefici
impune ut urbem nomine impleris meo?

60 Quid proderit ditasse Paelignas anus
velociusve miscuisse toxicum?
Sed tardiora fata te votis manent:
ingrata misero vita ducenda est in hoc,
novis ut usque suppetas doloribus.

65 Optat quietem Pelopis infidi pater,
egens benignae Tantalus semper dapis,
optat Prometheus obligatus aliti,

goddess Cotytto, which had been introduced into Athens and so became known at Rome, though they had not become prevalent there at this time. Canidia is represented as pursuing her questionable practices under this high-sounding but unsavory name. Where Horace had exposed these orgies does not appear; there can be no allusion to any of his extant poems.

58. Esquilini: *i.e.* such as is practiced there; cf. *venenis Colchicis*, 35. — **pontifex:** the meaning is obscure; either she taunts him with being an adept in sorcery himself, or with assuming authority over a matter in which he had no right to meddle; cf. *curiosus*, 77. The latter is substantially the explanation of Porphyrio.

59. ut urbem, etc.: referring to *S.* I. 8.

60. quid proderit, etc.: *i.e.* what was the use of my learning sorcery, at great expense, and surpassing my teachers in skill, if I fail to apply it at a time like this, when you have so wronged and insulted me? — **Paelignas:** see vs. 28 n.

61. velocius: *i.e.* in its effects. We speak of a 'slow poison,' 'a rapid fever,' 'galloping consumption.'

62. sed tardiora, etc., *but* (no *velox toxicum* is in store for you) *a more lingering*, etc. — **fata:** cf. *C.* III. 11. 28 ; Intr. 128. — **votis** (sc. *tuis*): cf. 70 *sqq.;* Intr. 75.

63. in hoc (acc.) : directing attention emphatically to her savage purpose in prolonging his life ; cf. *ad hoc, S.* II. 1. 36.

64. novis: *i.e.* new kinds of. Cf. *C.* II. 15. 20. — **ut usque suppetas,** *that you may be always on hand as a subject for.*

65. optat quietem: cf. *otium rogat, C.* II. 16. 1, and note the different form of anaphora (Intr. 116 *g*) in the two places. — **infidi:** as having cheated his charioteer, Myrtilus, by whose aid he had won Hippodamia, out of his promised reward, and thrown him into the sea ; cf. *periuri Pelopis,* Cat. 64. 346. — **pater:** see *C.* I. 28. 7 n.

66. benignae, *generous;* spread in profusion before him. Cf. *benignius C.* I. 9. 6 n. — **dapis:** Intr. 66 *c.*

67. obligatus: in a literal sense,

optat supremo conlocare*Sisyphus
in monte saxum : sed vetant leges Iovis.

70   Voles modo altis desilire turribus,
modo ense pectus Norico recludere,
frustraque vincla gutturi nectes tuo
fastidiosa tristis aegrimonia.
Vectabor umeris tunc ego inimicis eques,

75   meaeque terra cedet insolentiae.
An quae movere cereas imagines,
ut ipse nosti curiosus, et polo
deripere lunam vocibus possim meis,
possim crematos excitare mortuos

80   desiderique temperare pocula,
plorem artis in te nil agentis exitus ?

bound upon (so as to be exposed to).

68. **supremo** : poetical for *summo.* Cf. *clamore supremos | implerunt montis,* Verg. *G.* IV. 460. — **Sisyphus** : see *C.* II. 14. 20 n.

70. **turribus** : Intr. 70.

71. **ense Norico** : cf. *C.* I. 16. 9 n. — **pectus recludere** : cf. Verg. *A.* X. 601 *pectus mucrone recludit;* Juv. 4. 110 *iugulos aperire.*

72. **vincla,** *a rope.* Intr. 128, 183. — **gutturi nectes** : cf. *C.* I. 29. 5; *Ep.* I. 19. 31 *nec sponsae laqueum nectit.*

73. **fastidiosa** : in an active sense, as in *C.* III. 29. 9.

74. **vectabor,** etc. : she will finally compel him to acknowledge her mastery in the most humiliating manner. Cf. the scene in Plaut. *Asin.* 698 *sqq.* — inimicis, *of my foe,* i.e. the poet ; Intr. 124.

75. **meae insolentiae** : in prose, *mihi insolenti ;* cf. *tuae superbiae,* *C.* IV. 10. 2 n. — **cedet** : *i.e.* will

give way under my feet (as I rise into the air).

76. **an,** etc.: cf. 6. 15 *sq.* — **movere,** *make move* (as if they were alive). — **cereas imagines** : cf. *S.* I. 8. 30 *sqq.,* Verg. *E.* 8. 80 *sq.*

77. **ut ipse,** etc. : alluding to his account in *S.* I. 8. In this charge of eavesdropping he puts into her own mouth an unconscious indirect confession of the accuracy of his report.

78. **deripere lunam** : cf. vs. 5 and 5. 46 n. — **vocibus** : cf. vs. 6 n.

79. **possim** : Intr. 116 *h.* — **excitare** (*to call up*) **mortuos** : cf. *S.* I. 8. 29, 41.

80. **desideri pocula** : cf. *amoris poculum,* 5. 38, and the description of one there given. — **temperare,** *brew ;* cf. *C.* I. 20. 11 n.

81. **te** : better taken as ablative, *in your case,* in contrast with all others. — **nil agentis** : proleptic : (*proving*) *ineffective.* — **exitus**: here (with **plorem**) virtually equivalent to ' failure.'

CRITICAL APPENDIX.

———◦◦———

FOR a copious *apparatus criticus* of the poems, students are referred to the Orelli-Hirschfelder edition and to the *Editio Minor* of Keller and Holder, with Keller's *Epilegomena*. For the convenience of those to whom these works are not readily accessible a selection of the more important and interesting variants from the text of this edition is here given. Sources are indicated as follows :

> M⁰ denotes the unanimous testimony of the MSS.
> M, clear preponderance of manuscript testimony.
> M, good manuscript support.
> m, slight   "   "
> B, the four Blandinian MSS.
> Bᵛ, the *Blandinius vetustissimus*.
> (Where B or Bᵛ is added, M⁰, M, etc. refer to *existing* manuscripts only.)

In addition to the MS. tradition of the poems themselves, reference is sometimes made to evidence found in the *commentary* of Porphyrio (Porph.), or in other Latin grammarians and commentators (gr.).

In citing these various authorities discrepancies of spelling are disregarded.

Conjectures are usually credited to their authors.

THE ODES.

BOOK I.

I. 35 inseris M *inseres* M
II. 39 **Marsi Tanaquil Faber** *Mauri* M⁰
III. 19 turbidum M B *turgidum* M   37 ardui M B *arduum* M
IV. 8 visit M *urit* M.
VI. 2 alite M⁰ *aliti* Passerat   7 duplicis M *duplices* M B gr.
VII. 2 Epheson M gr. *Ephesum* M   5 urbem M *arcis* m   9 dicet M *dicit* M   17 perpetuos M *perpetuo* M

VIII. 2 **properes** M *properas* m gr. 6, 7 **equitat, temperat** m *equitet, temperet* M

XII. 2 **sumis** M *sumes* M Bᵛ 3 **recinet** (or *retinet*) M Bᵛ *recinit* M 31 **quod** M *quia* M B 41 **intonsis** Quint. IX. 3. 18 *incomptis* Mº 57 **latum** M *laetum* M

XIII. 2 **cerea** Mº *lactea* gr. 6 **manet** M *manent* M

XV. 20 **crinis** M Bᵛ *cultus* M 22 **gentis** M *genti* M Bᵛ 24 **te** M Bᵛ *et* M 36 **Iliacas** Mº *Pergameas* edition of 1500 *Dardanias, barbaricas* (see note)

XVI. 8 **sic** M *si* m Bentley

XVII. 9 **haediliae** M *haedilia* M *haeduleae* Bentley (but see Bücheler's explanation in note) 14 **hic** m *hinc* M

XVIII. 5 **crepat** M Bᵛ *increpat* m

XIX. 2 **iubet** M *iubent* M **Semeles** m *Semelae* M 12 **attinent** M *attinet* m

XX. 5 **care** M *clare* m 10 **tu** Mº *tum* Porph. on *S.* II. 2. 48 **bibes** M *bibis* m

XXI. 5 **coma** M *comam* M B

XXII. 11 **expeditis** M B *expeditus* m

XXIII. 1 **vitas** m *vitat* M gr. **inuleo** M B *hin(n)uleo* m 5 **vepris** . . . **ad ventum** Bentley et al. *veris adventus* Mº

XXV. 20 **Euro** Ald. ed. of 1501 *Hebro* Mº

XXVI. 9 **Pimplei** N. Heinsius *Piplea* Mº

XXVIII. 3 **litus** M *latum* M 15 **nox** M *mors* M 31 **fors et** (or *forset*) M B *forsit* m *forsan* M

XXXI. 9 **Calena** Mº *Calenam* (Porph.?) Bentley 10 **et** M *ut* M

XXXII. 1 **poscimur** M gr. *poscimus* M gr. 15 **mihi cumque** Mº *medicumque* Lachmann *metuumque* E. Rosenberg.

XXXV. 17 **saeva** M *serva* M B

Book II.

II. 5 **vivet** M *vivit* m 7 **aget** M *agit* M Porph.

III. 18 **lavit** M *lavat* M 28 **exsilium** M *exitium* M

V. 13 **currit** M *curret* M

VI. 18 **amicus** Mº *amictus* N. Heinsius 19 **fertili** M *fertilis* m gr.

X. 18 **cithara** M *citharae* M

XI. 23 **in comptum** M *incomptum* M 24 **comam** M *comas* M *comae* M (*in comptum . . . comae* M *in comptum . . . comas* m *incomptum . . . comam* M *incomptum . . . comas* M)

XII. 25 **cum** M *dum* M 28 **occupet** M *occupat* m

XIII. 16 timet M⁰ *timetve* Lachmann   23 discriptas M *descriptas* M *discretas* M   38 laborem M Porph. *laborum* M B

XVII. 14 Gyas Lambinus *gigas* M⁰

XVIII. 8 clientae M *clientiae* M *clientes* M

XX. 3 terris M *terra* M   13 notior M *ocior* M *tutior* Bentley.

Book III.

I. 39 triremi et m *triremi* M

II. 27 volgarit M *volgavit* M

III. 12 bibet M *bibit* M   34 discere M *ducere* M

IV. 9 Apulo M⁰ *avio* O. Keller   10 nutricis M *altricis* M   limen Apuliae M Porph. *limina Pulliae* M   For *Pulliae* (which Kiessling and Hertz, following a hint in Porphyrio, retain as the name of Horace's nurse) various conjectures have been proposed: *sedulae* (Bentl.), *villulae, pergulae, patriae, Dauniae*, etc.   38 abdidit M *addidit* M *reddidit* m   43 turbam M *turmam* M   47 turmas M B *turbas* M (43, 47 turbam ... turmas M *turbam ... turbas* M *turmam ... turbas* M)   69 Gyas Lambinus *gigas* M⁰ (cf. II. 17. 14)   78 reliquit M *relinquit* M

V. 15 trahenti Canter *trahentis* M⁰   17 periret M⁰ *perirent* Glareanus *perires* Lachmann   37 inscius M *aptius* m *anxius* Jani   51 propinquos M *amicos* M

VI. 10 non auspicatos M *inauspicatos* M   22 artibus M *artubus* M Porph.   27 impermissa M *intermissa* M

VII. 4 fide m *fidei* M   15 Bellerophontae M *Bellerophonti* m   20 movet M *monet* M

VIII. 5 sermones M gr. *sermonis* M   27 cape M *rape* M

IX. 5 alia M *aliam* m   21 quamquam M *quamvis* M

X. 6 satum M Bᵛ *situm* M   18 aniṛ.um M *animo* M

XI. 52 scalpe M B *sculpe* m

XII. 4 arto M Bᵛ *alto* M

XIV. 6 sacris M *divis* M Porph.   7 clari M *cari* M   11 non Bentley *iam* M⁰   male ominatis M Bᵛ *male nominatis* M *male inominatis* Bentley

XV. 2 fige M *pone* M   16 vetulam M *vetula* M

XVII. 4 fastos M *fastus* M   5 ducis M⁰ *ducit* D. Heinsius

XVIII. 12 pagus M *pardus* M

XIX. 1 distet M *distat* M   27 Rhode M *Chloe* M

XX. 3 paulo M B *paulum* M   8 illa Peerlkamp *illi* M⁰

XXI. 5 nomine M *numine* M   10 negleget M *neglegit* M

XXIII. 19 mollivit M *mollibit* M

XXIV. 4 Tyrrhenum Mᵒ   Apulicum M *Ponticum* M *Punicum* m
publicum M Bᵛ (*terrenum . . . publicum* Lachmann)   60 hospites M B
hospitem M

XXV. 6 consilio M *concilio* M

XXVII. 5 rumpat M *rumpit* M   15 vetet M B *vetat* m   48 mon-
stri M *tauri* M   55 defluat M *defluit* M   71 reddet M *reddit* M

XXIX. 2 verso M *versum* M   34 alveo M *aequore* M

BOOK IV.

I. 9 domum M *domo* M   18 largi M *largis* M   20 citrea M Bᵛ
Cypria M   22, 23 lyra, Berecyntia, tibia m Bᵛ *lyrae, Berecyntiae,
tibiae* M

II. 2 Iulle M *Iule* M   (The former is found as *praenomen* of this
Antonius CIL. 12010; see Mommsen in *Hermes* XXIV. 155)   7 fervet M *fervit* M   33, 41 concines Mᵒ *concinet* Lachmann   49 teque
dum procedis M Bᵛ *tuque* m *procedit* m

IV. 7 verni M *vernis* M   17 Raetis N. Heinsius, Bentley, m
Raeti M   18 Vindelici M *et Vindelici* m   36 indecorant M Porph.
dedecorant M   65 merses M *mersus* M   evenit M *exiet* m   66 proruet M *proruit* m   73 perficient M *perficiunt* Bᵛ m

VI. 21 victus Mᵒ *flexus* Bᵛ   25 argutae M *Argivae* m

VII. 15 pater M Bᵛ   *pius* M   Tullus dives M *dives Tullus* M
17 quis scit M *qui scit* m *qui scis* m   summae M *vitae* M Bᵛ

VIII. 1 commodus M *commodis* M   12 muneri M B *muneris* m
15 celeres fugae M *celeris fuga* M

The text of this ode is suspected for several reasons: (1) It is the
only ode in which the number of verses is not a multiple of four (see
Intr. 157). (2) Verse 17 is open to suspicion, (a) because caesura is
neglected; (b) because Carthage was not burned by the Scipio who
defeated Hannibal and whose praises were sung by Ennius, but by the
younger Africanus (Scipio Aemilianus), many years after Ennius' death.
The first of the two objections to vs. 17 is not conclusive; for Horace
sometimes neglects caesura, though nowhere else in Asclepiad verse.
The historical difficulty is more serious; for although it is possible to
understand the words in a sense consistent with the historical fact (see
note on vs. 15), their more obvious and natural meaning would expose
Horace to the imputation of gross ignorance. There is no sufficient
ground for rejecting any other verse, and no just ground for suspicion
except in the case of vs. 33, which is a repetition, with only a necessary

change in the first word, of III. 25. 20.   The attempt has been made, however, to bring the ode into conformity with Meineke's canon in various ways.   Vss. 17 and 33 are bracketed by Kiessling; 17 and 28 by Nauck ; 15 *non*–19 *rediit*, 28, and 33 by Meineke, etc.

  IX. 31 silebo M *sileri* M   52 perire M B V *peribit* M

  X. 5 Ligurine m *Ligurinum* M   6 speculo M *in speculo* M

  XIII. 14 cari M *clari* M

  XIV. 4 fastos M *fastus* M (cf. III. 17. 4)   28 meditatur M Porph. gr. *minitatur* M B   35 Alexandrea M *Alexandria* m   49 paventis M *paventes* M

  XV. 15 ortus M *ortum* m   18 exiget M Porph. *exigit* m *eximet* M

CARMEN SAECVLARE.

  5 quo m *quos* M *quod* M B   26 dictum est M *dictum* M   27 servet M B *servat* m   46 senectuti M *senectutis* M   51 impetret M B *imperet* M   57 Honor M *Honos* M   65 aras M B *arcis* M   68 prorogat M *proroget* M   71, 72 curat, adplicat M B *curet, adplicet* m

THE EPODES.

  I. 5 si M *sit* Aldine ed. of 1478   10 qua M *quem* M   15 labore Glareanus *laborem* M o   21 ut adsit M Porph. *ut sit* M *uti sit* m   26 meis M *mea* m   28 pascuis M B *pascua* M   34 nepos M *ut nepos* M

  II. 18 agris M *arvis* M   25 ripis M *rivis* M B   27 frondesque Markland *fontesque* M o   65 positosque M *postosque* m

  IV. 8 trium C. Barth *ter* M o

  V. 1 regit M B *regis* M   3 et M B *aut* M   15 implicata M *inligata* M Porph.   18 cupressos M *cupressus* M   21 atque M *aut* M   28 currens M o *Laurens* N. Heinsius   37 exsecta M B *exsucta* m   55 formidolosis M B *formidolosae* M   dum M *cum* M   60 laborarint M B V *laborarunt* M   63 superbam M B *superba* M   65 imbutum M *infectum* M   87 magnum M o Porph. *magica* Bentley *maga non* M. Haupt *maga num* . . ., *num valent* C. W. Nauck   88 convertere humanam vicem M o *non vertere humanas vices* Bentley *convertere humana vice* Madvig *convertere humana invicem* O. Keller

VI. 2 **adversum** M *adversus* M   3, 4 **vertis, petis** M *verte, pete* M BV   10 **proiectum** M *porrectum* m (a XV. century MSS. in the Harvard library)

VII. 12 **numquam** Aldine ed. of 1490 *umquam* M⁰   13 **caecus** M *caecos* m   15 **albus ora pallor** M *ora pallor albus* M

IX. 1 **repostum** M *repositum* M   17 **ad hoc** Bentley *ad hunc* (or *adhunc*) M *adhuc* m *at huc* m *at hinc* Cuningham   25 **Africanum** M *Africano* M *Africani* Madvig

X. 19, 20 **sinus Noto** M *sinu Notus* M B   22 **iuverit** M *iuveris* m

XI. 2 **percussum** M gr. *perculsum* M   9 **languor** M *et languor* m

XIII. 3 **amici** M *amice* Bentley *amico* Kiessling

XV. 15 **offensi** Gogavius, Bentley *offensae* M

XVI. 14 **videre** M *videri* M B   15 **quid** M *quod* m *forte* (*quod expediat!*) Rutgers   33 **ravos** M B *flavos* M *saevos* m   51 **ovile** M *ovili* M B   61, 62 after 60 M⁰, and by some editors so retained ; by others variously placed, after 48, 50, 52, or 56   61 **astri** M *Austri* M   65 **aere** M *aerea* M

XVII. 5 **refixa** M *defixa* M   11 **luxere** M *unxere* M B   17 **Circa** M *Circe* M   18 **relapsus** M *relatus* M   33 **virens** M *urens* m *furens* m   36 **quae** M *qui* m   40 **sonare** M *sonari* m   42 **vicem** m *vice* M   57 **sacrum** M *sacra* M   60 **proderit** M *proderat* M   64 **doloribus** M *laboribus* M   67 **aliti** M B *alite* M   72 **nectes** M *innectes** M   80 **pocula** M *poculum* M   81 **exitus** M *exitum* M